GAAS GUIDE

A Comprehensive Restatement of Standards for Auditing, Attestation, Compilation, and Review

MARK S. BEASLEY, PH.D., CPA
JOSEPH V. CARCELLO, PH.D., CPA

CCH

a Wolters Kluwer business

This publication is designed to provide accurate and authoritative information in regard to the subject matter covered. It is sold with the understanding that the publisher is not engaged in rendering legal, accounting, or other professional services. If legal advice or other professional assistance is required, the services of a competent professional person should be sought.

—From a *Declaration of Principles* jointly adopted by a Committee of the American Bar Association and a Committee of Publishers and Associations

ISBN: 978-0-8080-2947-2
ISSN: 1088-9159

© 2012 CCH. All Rights Reserved.
4025 W. Peterson Ave.
Chicago, IL 60646-6085
800 248 3248
CCHGroup.com

Portions of this work were published in a previous edition.

Printed in the United States of America

SUSTAINABLE FORESTRY INITIATIVE

Certified Sourcing
www.sfiprogram.org
SFI-01028

GAAS Guide

by Mark S. Beasley and Joseph V. Carcello

Highlights

CCH's *GAAS Guide* highlights professional standards, including recent pronouncements, for CPAs involved in audit, attestation, compilation, and review engagements. The 2013 *GAAS Guide* includes detailed analyses of critical components of the complete listing of Statements on Auditing Standards (SASs), Statements on Standards for Attestation Engagements, and Statements on Standards for Accounting and Review Services, along with numerous practitioner aids that can easily be incorporated into any CPA firm's practice.

2013 Edition

The 2013 Edition of CCH's *GAAS Guide* has been updated to reflect the latest available professional standards. Most importantly, it has been updated to reflect changes in auditing standards and the related Codification of Statements on Auditing Standards resulting from the Auditing Standards Board's Clarity and Convergence Project. This edition includes coverage of SAS-122 (essentially all AU-C sections) (Clarification and Recodification), issued in October 2011, SAS-123 (AU-C 200, AU-C 230, AU-C 260, AU-C 705, AU-C 720, AU-C 915, and AU-C 935) (Omnibus Statement on Auditing Standards — 2011), issued in October 2011, SAS-124 (AU-C 910) (Financial Statements Prepared in Accordance with a Financial Reporting Framework Generally Accepted in Another Country), issued in October 2011, and SAS-125 (AU-C 905) (Alert that Restricts the Use of the Auditor's Written Communication), issued in December 2011.

SAS-122 is particularly noteworthy as it represents the culmination of the ASB's efforts to clarify the auditing standards and to largely converge its standards with the standards of the International Auditing and Assurance Standards Board. As such, SAS-122 supersedes most of the existing auditing standards and recodifies the clarified and converged standards in one place (essentially similar to the design of SAS-1 many years ago). In addition, as part of its efforts, the ASB has issued these new standards using a new codification numbering sequence. That numbering system recodifies the former "AU" section numbers as designated by SAS Nos. 1–121 by using a new "AU-C" numbering. AU-C section numbers are the same as the equivalent ISA numbers for clarified SASs that are based on equivalent ISAs. AU-C section numbers for clarified SASs with no equivalent ISAs have been assigned new numbers. The AU-C section number is a temporary identifier to avoid confusion with references to existing "AU" sections in AICPA Professional Standards, which remain effective through 2013. The "AU-C" identifier will revert to "AU" in 2014, by which time SAS-122 becomes fully effective for all engagements. We adopt this new numbering sequence in this year's *Guide*. We believe that the 2013 edition of the *GAAS Guide* is among the first commercially available products that covers the ASB's clarified, converged, and recodified auditing standards.

The 2013 Edition of the *GAAS Guide* incorporates these new requirements throughout the affected auditing standards and includes coverage of the following:

- Statements on Auditing Standards Nos. 122 through 125

- Statements on Standards for Attestation Engagements Nos. 1 through 17, including all issued interpretations

- Statements on Standards for Accounting and Review Services Nos. 1 through 20, including all issued interpretations

The extensive coverage of these AICPA standards is particularly relevant to CPAs who serve nonpublic entity clients. The above standards represent those applicable to nonpublic company engagements. The guidance contained in this edition is also relevant to CPAs who serve public company clients. Although the Public Company Accounting Oversight Board (PCAOB) is responsible for establishing professional standards applicable to audits of public companies, the guidance contained in this edition is also directly relevant to CPAs serving public companies because the PCAOB's Interim Auditing Standards continue to embrace many of the provisions in the AICPA's professional standards.

The 2013 *GAAS Guide* contains an appendix to help CPAs understand the key provisions of changes affecting the auditing profession resulting from the passage of the Sarbanes-Oxley Act of 2002 (SOX):

- *Appendix A: The Sarbanes-Oxley Act of 2002* This appendix provides an excellent one-source overview of the key provisions of SOX. CPAs wanting a quick, reader-friendly summary of SOX's provisions will find this appendix helpful.

To help CPAs recognize important unique considerations for audits of public companies, this edition includes summaries of issues having implications for audits of public companies. These summaries, labeled "Public Company Implication," are incorporated throughout the coverage of the AICPA's AU-Cs. CPAs who audit public companies will find that these summaries help them identify key differences between audits of public and nonpublic companies.

Owing to the attention focused on corporate scandals involving allegations of fraudulent financial reporting, the need for auditors to detect material misstatements due to fraud is critical. To help sensitize CPAs to issues affecting auditor responsibility for fraud, this edition contains "Fraud Pointers," which integrate fraud issues related to a particular professional standard's requirement. This should aid CPAs in considering fraud risks throughout the entire audit engagement.

To keep CPAs abreast of potential changes affecting the AICPA Professional Standards and other developments affecting auditing practice, this edition contains overviews of outstanding exposure drafts. Throughout the book, highlights labeled "Important Notice for 2013" explain key elements of potential changes, including proposed redrafts of existing professional standards and other regulatory changes, alerting CPAs to issues that may affect their engagements.

Sample letters, reports, and checklists on the free companion CD-ROM can be printed and customized to meet your auditing needs.

Automate your CCH Engagement Guides with ProSystem *fx* Engagement

By integrating your CCH *Engagement Guides* with ProSystem *fx* Engagement, you can achieve a fully paperless audit workflow. ProSystem *fx* Engagement, a member of the CCH ProSystem *fx* Office suite, enables firms to increase convenience and efficiency by automating workpaper preparation, management, and workflow within a state-of-the-art paperless engagement system. ProSystem *fx* and CCH are pleased to offer this high-quality combination of software and content to the accounting community. To sample ProSystem *fx* Engagement, please call 1-800-PFX-9998, or visit the ProSystem *fx* web site at CCHGroup.com/ProSystem.

CCH Learning Center

CCH's goal is to provide you with the clearest, most concise, and up-to-date accounting and auditing information to help further your professional development, as well as a convenient method to help you satisfy your continuing professional education requirements. The CCH Learning Center* offers a complete line of self-study courses covering complex and constantly evolving accounting and auditing issues. We are continually adding new courses to the library to help you stay current on all the latest developments. The CCH Learning Center courses are available 24 hours a day, seven days a week. You'll get immediate exam results and certification. To view our complete accounting and auditing course catalog, go to: **http:/CCHGroup.LearningCenter.**

Accounting Research Manager®

Accounting Research Manager® is the most comprehensive, up-to-date, and objective online database of financial reporting literature. It includes all authoritative and proposed accounting, auditing, and SEC literature, plus independent, expert-written interpretive guidance. And, in addition to our standard accounting and SEC libraries, you can enjoy the full spectrum of financial reporting with our Audit library.

The Audit library covers auditing standards, attestation engagement standards, accounting and review services standards, audit risk alerts, and other vital auditing-related guidance. You'll also have online access to our best-selling

---

*CCH is registered with the National Association of State Boards of Accountancy (NASBA) as a sponsor of continuing professional education on the National Registry of CPE Sponsors. Participating State boards of accountancy have final authority on the acceptance of individual courses for CPE credit. Complaints regarding registered sponsors may be addressed to NASBA, 150 Fourth Avenue North, Suite 700, Nashville, TN 37219-2417. Telephone: 615-880-4200.

* CCH is registered with the National Association of State Boards of Accountancy (NASBA) as a Quality Assurance Service (QAS) sponsor of continuing professional education. Participating state boards of accountancy have final authority on the acceptance of individual courses for CPE credit. Complaints regarding QAS program sponsors may be addressed to National Registry of CPE Sponsors, 150 Fourth Avenue North, Suite 700, Nashville, TN 37219-2417. Telephone: 615-880-4200.

GAAS Practice Manual, Knowledge-Based Audits™ of Commercial Entities, Knowledge-Based Audits™ of Employee Benefit Plans, Knowledge-Based Audits™ of Financial Institutions, Knowledge-Based Compilations and Reviews, CPA's Guide to Effective Engagement Letters, CPA's Guide to Management Letter Comments, and be kept up-to-date on the latest authoritative literature via the *GAAS Update Service.*

With **Accounting Research Manager®**, you maximize the efficiency of your research time, while enhancing your results. Learn more about our content and our experts by visiting us at **http:/www.accountingresearchmanager.com.**

7/12

Our Peer Review Policy

Thank you for purchasing the 2013 *GAAS Guide*. Each year we bring you the best engagement guides available, with accompanying electronic audit documents and practice aids. To confirm the technical accuracy and quality control of our materials, CCH, a Wolters Kluwer business, voluntarily submitted to a peer review of our publishing system and our publications (see the Peer Review Statement on the following page).

In addition to peer review, our publications undergo strict technical and content reviews by qualified practitioners. This ensures that our books, audit documents, and practice aids meet "real world" standards and applicability.

Our publications are reviewed every step of the way—from conception to production—to ensure that we bring you the finest guides on the market.

Updated annually, peer reviewed, technically accurate, convenient, and practical—the 2013 *GAAS Guide* shows our commitment to creating books and audit documentation you can trust.

Peer Review Statement

Caldwell, Becker, Dervin, Petrick & Co., L.L.P.
CERTIFIED PUBLIC ACCOUNTANTS

Quality Control Materials Review Report

November 12, 2009

Executive Board
CCH, a Wolters Kluwer business
and the National Peer Review Committee

We have reviewed the system of quality control for the development and maintenance of GAAS Practice Manual (2010 Edition) (hereafter referred to as *materials*) of CCH, a Wolters Kluwer business (the organization) and the resultant materials in effect at October 31, 2009. Our quality control materials peer review was conducted in accordance with the Standards for Performing and Reporting on Peer Reviews established by the Peer Review Board of the American Institute of Certified Public Accountants. The organization is responsible for designing a system of quality control and complying with it to provide users of the materials with reasonable assurance that the materials are reliable aids to assist them in conforming with those professional standards that the materials purport to encompass. Our responsibility is to express an opinion on the design of the system and the organization's compliance with that system based on our review. The nature, objectives, scope, limitations of, and the procedures performed in a Quality Control Materials Review are described in the standards at www.aicpa.org/prsummary.

In our opinion, the system of quality control for the development and maintenance of the quality control materials of CCH, a Wolters Kluwer business was suitably designed and was being complied with during the year ended October 31, 2009, to provide users of the materials with reasonable assurance that the materials are reliable aids to assist them in conforming with those professional standards the materials purport to encompass. Also, in our opinion, the quality control materials referred to above are reliable aids at October 31, 2009. Organizations can receive a rating of *pass*, *pass with deficiency(ies)*, or *fail*. CCH, a Wolters Kluwer business has received a peer review rating of *pass*.

CALDWELL, BECKER, DERVIN, PETRICK & CO., LLP.
CALDWELL, BECKER, DERVIN, PETRICK & CO., L.L.P.

20750 Ventura Boulevard, Suite 140 • Woodland Hills, CA 91364
(818) 704-1040 • FAX (818) 704-5536

Contents

Preface

CCH's 2013 *GAAS Guide* describes the engagement standards, practices, and procedures in use today, including Statements on Auditing Standards (SASs) and their Interpretations, Statements on Standards for Attestation Engagements (SSAEs) and their Interpretations, and Statements on Standards on Accounting and Review Services (SSARS) and their Interpretations.

The 2013 Edition of the *GAAS Guide* has been updated to reflect the latest available professional standards. Most importantly, it has been updated to reflect changes in auditing standards and the related Codification of Statements on Auditing Standards resulting from the Auditing Standards Board's (ASB) Clarity and Convergence Project. This edition includes coverage of SAS-122 (essentially all of the AU-C sections) (Clarification and Recodification), issued in October 2011, SAS-123 (AU-200, AU-C 230, AU-C 260, AU-C 705, AU-C 720, AU-915, and AU-C 935) (Omnibus Statement on Auditing Standards — 2011), issued in October 2011, SAS-124 (AU-C 910) (Financial Statements Prepared in Accordance with a Financial Reporting Framework Generally Accepted in Another Country), issued in October 2011, and SAS-125 (AU-C 905) (Alert that Restricts the Use of the Auditor's Written Communication), issued in December 2011.

SAS-122 is particularly noteworthy as it represents the culmination of the ASB's efforts to clarify the auditing standards and to largely converge its standards with the standards of the International Auditing and Assurance Standards Board (IAASB). As such, SAS-122 supersedes most of the existing auditing standards and recodifies the clarified and converged standards in one place (essentially similar to the design of SAS-1 many years ago). In addition, as part of its efforts, the ASB has issued these new standards using a new codification numbering sequence, which we adopt in this year's *Guide*. That numbering system recodifies the former "AU" section numbers as designated by SAS Nos. 1–121 by using a new "AU-C" numbering. AU-C section numbers are the same as the equivalent ISA numbers for clarified SASs that are based on equivalent ISAs. AU-C section numbers for clarified SASs with no equivalent ISAs have been assigned new numbers. The AU-C section number is a temporary identifier to avoid confusion with references to existing "AU" sections in AICPA Professional Standards, which remain effective through 2013. The "AU-C" identifier will revert to "AU" in 2014, by which time SAS-122 becomes fully effective for all engagements. We believe that the 2013 edition of the *GAAS Guide* is among the first commercially available products that covers the ASB's clarified, converged, and recodified auditing standards.

The *GAAS Guide* incorporates these new requirements throughout the affected auditing standards and includes coverage of AICPA pronouncements up through the following standards:

- SAS-121 (AU-C 905) (Alert that Restricts the Use of the Auditor's Written Communication)

- SSAE-17 (AT 301) (Reporting on Compiled Prospective Financial Statements When the Practitioner's Independence Is Impaired)

- SSARS-20 (Revised Applicability of Statements on Standards for Accounting and Review Services)

All the exhibit materials in the book appear on the accompanying CD-ROM. All the sample letters, reports, and checklists found in this guide can be printed and customized to meet all your auditing, attestation, compilation, and review engagement needs.

Each section is organized using a consistent structure that is simple and insightful. The opening of each section begins with a list of "Authoritative Pronouncements" that identifies the specific professional standards pertinent to that section. That list is followed by an "Overview" that highlights key provisions of the relevant section, followed by "Definitions," then by "Requirements" that identify the essential professional responsibilities that must be satisfied in each part of your engagement. Next, under the label "Analysis and Application of Procedures," you will find a concise discussion of how each specific requirement should be applied. Finally, many of the sections contain "Practitioner Aids" to help you apply the promulgated standards to your specific engagements.

A continuing feature of the 2013 Edition is the inclusion throughout most sections of additional insights to help you identify unique issues related to your implementation of the professional standards requirements, including suggestions to help you better plan and execute your engagements. This highlighted guidance is summarized as one of the following:

- Engagement Strategy

- Fraud Pointer

- Important Notice for 2013

- Observation

- Planning Aid Reminder

- Public Company Implication

These highlights are easy to find and can help you understand many of the important subtleties contained in the professional standards guidance.

The AICPA's Auditing Standards Board issues auditing standards applicable to the audits of nonpublic companies. The 2013 *GAAS Guide* contains up-to-date AICPA professional standard guidance applicable to those engagements.

The Public Company Accounting Oversight Board (PCAOB), which was created by the Sarbanes-Oxley Act of 2002 (SOX), announced that the PCAOB "will establish auditing and other professional standards for registered public accounting firms." The PCAOB adopted all existing Statements on Auditing Standards (SASs) in effect as of April 16, 2003 (up through SAS-101) as its Interim Auditing Standards. As a result, much of the guidance contained in this 2013 Edition is relevant to auditors of public companies. The 2013 Edition contains Public Company Implications, which highlight issues that are unique for audits of public companies.

To help CPAs understand the impact of the Sarbanes-Oxley Act of 2002, we have included an appendix that highlights key provisions of the act:

- *Appendix A: The Sarbanes Oxley Act of 2002* This appendix provides an excellent one-source overview of the key provisions of SOX. CPAs wanting a quick and reader-friendly summary of SOX's provisions will find this appendix helpful.

The PCAOB has issued its own auditing standards that apply to audits of financial statements of public companies. As the 2013 Edition of the *GAAS Guide* went to press the PCAOB had issued 15 PCAOB Auditing Standards (one of which has been superseded). Although the PCAOB Auditing Standards continue to embrace SAS-1 through SAS-101 as the PCAOB's "Interim Auditing Standards," auditors of public companies should continue to monitor the standards-setting activities of the PCAOB.

This 2013 Edition continues to provide what has always been the most important feature of the *GAAS Guide*—readability. The utmost care has been exercised to avoid the difficult language and organization of many of the original pronouncements. Essential material is placed at your fingertips for quick integration into your practice. There is no more need to wonder exactly what a standard means or how it is to be used in a real engagement.

Acknowledgments

Thanks are due to Vincent J. Love, CPA, of New York, NY, for his thoughtful, thorough review of the 2013 edition.

Mark S. Beasley
Raleigh, North Carolina

Joseph V. Carcello
Knoxville, Tennessee

About the Authors

Mark S. Beasley is the Deloitte Professor of Enterprise Risk Management and Professor of Accounting in the Department of Accounting at North Carolina State University, in Raleigh, N.C., where he teaches auditing courses in the undergraduate and masters programs. He recently completed seven years' service as a member of the COSO Board. Dr. Beasley received a BS in accounting from Auburn University and a Ph.D. from Michigan State University. He is a Certified Public Accountant (CPA) in North Carolina and has worked in public accounting, where he was an Audit Manager with Ernst & Young. Dr. Beasley also worked as a Technical Manager with the AICPA's Auditing Standards Division, in New York City. He is a member of the American Institute of Certified Public Accountants, the American Accounting Association, the Institute of Internal Auditors, and ISACA. Dr. Beasley also serves as Director of North Carolina State University's Enterprise Risk Management Initiative, which provides thought leadership on enterprise risk management and its integration with strategy planning and governance.

Dr. Beasley actively conducts research related to financial statement fraud, corporate governance, and auditor quality. His work has been published in journals such as the *Journal of Accounting Research, Contemporary Accounting Research, Auditing: A Journal of Practice & Theory, Accounting Horizons, Journal of the American Taxation Association, Journal of Accountancy*, and *The CPA Journal*, among numerous others. He served on COSO's Enterprise Risk Management project Advisory Council and the AICPA's Antifraud Programs and Controls Task Force. He has previously served on Auditing Standards Board task forces, including the SAS No. 99 Fraud Task Force. Dr. Beasley is the co-author of several continuing education courses, an auditing textbook, and an auditing casebook.

Joseph V. Carcello is the Ernst & Young and Business Alumni Professor in the Department of Accounting and Information Management and the Director of Research of the Corporate Governance Center at the University of Tennessee, in Knoxville, Tenn., where he teaches auditing and financial accounting courses in the undergraduate and MAcc. programs. Dr. Carcello received a BS in accounting from SUNY at Plattsburgh, a MAcc from the University of Georgia, and a Ph.D. from Georgia State University. He is a Certified Public Accountant (CPA), a Certified Internal Auditor (CIA), and a Certified Management Accountant (CMA). Dr. Carcello worked in public accounting, where he was an Audit Senior with Ernst & Young. He is a member of the American Institute of Certified Public Accountants, the American Accounting Association, the American Bar Association (associate), the Association of Certified Fraud Examiners, the Financial Executives International, the Institute of Internal Auditors, and the Institute of Management Accountants.

Dr. Carcello has taught continuing professional education courses for two of the Big 4 accounting firms, AICPA, Institute of Internal Auditors, The Institute of

Management Accountants, the Tennessee and Florida Societies of CPAs, local and regional accounting firms, and he has provided consulting services on revenue recognition to the software industry. He has also served as an expert witness for the Securities and Exchange Commission and testified before the U.S. Treasury Advisory Committee on the Auditing Profession. Dr. Carcello is a member of the PCAOB's Investor Advisory Group and Standing Advisory Group, and he previously served as a member of COSO's Small Business Control Guidance Advisory Group Task Force.

Dr. Carcello actively conducts research related to corporate governance (particularly audit committee performance), fraudulent financial reporting, and going-concern reporting. His work has been published in journals such as *The Accounting Review, Journal of Accounting Research, Contemporary Accounting Research, Auditing: A Journal of Practice & Theory, Accounting Horizons, Journal of Accounting and Public Policy*, and *Journal of Accountancy*, among numerous others. Dr. Carcello is the co-author of CCH's *GAAP Guide, Volume I* and a financial accounting textbook.

AU-C Preface
Preface to the Codification of Statements on Auditing Standards: Principles Underlying an Audit Conducted in Accordance with Generally Accepted Auditing Standards

AU-C Preface

CODIFICATION OF STATEMENTS ON AUDITING STANDARDS

The preface contains the principles underlying an audit conducted in accordance with generally accepted auditing standards. The principles provide a framework to help explain an audit and understand it; however, but these principles are not requirements and do not carry any authority.

Purpose of an Audit

An audit's purpose is to increase the degree of confidence users can place in an entity's financial statements. The auditor achieves this purpose by expressing an opinion on "whether the financial statements are prepared, in all material respects, in accordance with the applicable financial reporting framework."

Responsibilities

The auditor is responsible for:

- Having appropriate competence and capabilities to perform the audit.
- Complying with relevant ethical requirements, including independence and due care requirements.
- Maintaining professional skepticism and exercising professional judgment throughout the planning and performance of the audit.

Performance

The auditor obtains reasonable assurance about whether the financial statements as a whole are free from material misstatement, whether due to fraud or error, in order to express an opinion.

Reasonable assurance is a high, but not absolute, level of assurance that is attained by:

- Adequately planning the work and properly supervising any assistants.
- Determining the appropriate materiality level(s).
- Obtaining a sufficient understanding of the entity and its environment, including its internal control, to identify and assess the risks of material misstatement whether due to error or fraud.
- Obtaining sufficient appropriate audit evidence about the existence of material misstatements by designing and implementing appropriate responses to assessed risks.

Absolute assurance is unable to be obtained due to inherent limitations arising from the nature of financial reporting, the nature of audit procedures, and the need for audits to be conducted within a reasonable period of time at a reasonable cost.

Reporting

The auditor must either express in his or her written report an opinion regarding the financial statements taken as a whole or state that an opinion cannot be expressed.

AU-C 200
General Principles and Responsibilities

SECTION 200

OVERALL OBJECTIVES OF THE INDEPENDENT AUDITOR AND THE CONDUCT OF AN AUDIT IN ACCORDANCE WITH GENERALLY ACCEPTED AUDITING STANDARDS

Authoritative Pronouncements

SAS-122 — Statements on Auditing Standards: Clarification and Recodification

SAS-123 — Omnibus Statement on Auditing Standards — 2011

Overview

This section describes the auditor's overall objectives; the nature and scope of an audit designed to enable the auditor to meet those objectives; the scope, authority, and structure of GAAS; and requirements establishing the auditor's general audit responsibilities, including the obligation to comply with GAAS.

One overall objective of the auditor is to obtain reasonable assurance about whether the financial statements as a whole are free from material misstatement, whether due to fraud or error. This enables the auditor to express an opinion on whether the financial statements are presented fairly in all material respects in accordance with an applicable financial reporting framework. Reasonable assurance is obtained when sufficient appropriate audit evidence has been obtained to reduce the audit risk to an acceptably low level. The auditor cannot provide absolute assurance, because of inherent limitations resulting in most audit evidence being persuasive rather than conclusive.

PLANNING AID REMINDER: If reasonable assurance cannot be obtained and a qualified audit opinion is insufficient, GAAS requires the auditor disclaim an opinion or withdraw from the engagement if doing so is not prohibited by law or regulation.

The auditor is to express an opinion, or disclaim an opinion, when he or she is associated with financial information. An auditor is associated with financial information when he or she has performed sufficient audit procedures to be able to report in compliance with GAAS.

Another overall objective of the auditor is to report on the financial statements and communicate as required by GAAS in accordance with his or her findings. An audit conducted in accordance with GAAS and the relevant ethical requirements allows the auditor to form an audit opinion. The form of opinion expressed depends on the applicable financial reporting framework, laws, and regulations. In some circumstances the auditor may provide an opinion on specific matters other than the financial statements, such as on the effectiveness of internal control, in which case, additional work would be required to provide such an opinion. The audit opinion does not provide assurance about the entity's future viability or management's efficiency or effectiveness in conducting the entity's affairs.

An audit is conducted to provide users with additional confidence in the financial statements. In planning and performing an audit, the auditor is required to identify and assess risks of material misstatement, whether due to fraud or error, based on an understanding of the entity and its environment, including its internal control; obtain sufficient appropriate audit evidence about whether material misstatements exist by designing and implementing appropriate responses to the assessed risks; and form an opinion on the financial statements, or conclude that an opinion cannot be formed, based on an evaluation of the audit evidence obtained.

Materiality is applied in planning and performing an audit and in evaluating the effects of identified misstatements on the audit and uncorrected misstatements on the financial statements. Misstatements are generally considered material if they could reasonably be expected to influence the economic decisions of users relying on the financial statements. The auditor's judgment of materiality may be affected by his or her perception of users' financial information needs and the size and nature of a misstatement. Auditors are responsible for detecting misstatements that are material at the opinion level, which is generally the financial statements as a whole or, for governmental entities, each reporting unit.

An entity's financial statements are prepared and presented by management with oversight from those charged with governance. While GAAS does not impose responsibilities on management or those charged with governance, an audit conducted in accordance with GAAS presumes that both parties have fundamental responsibilities that are not relieved by the conduct of an audit.

Definitions

Applicable financial reporting framework	The financial reporting framework adopted by management and those charged with governance (as applicable) for preparing and presenting financial statements that is acceptable given the nature of the entity and the objective of the financial statements, or that is required by law or regulation.
Audit evidence	Information used by the auditor to arrive at the conclusions on which the auditor's opinion is based. This includes information in the accounting records underlying the financial statements and other information. Sufficiency is a measure of the quantity of audit evidence; appropriateness is a measure of the quality of audit evidence.
Audit risk	Risk that the auditor expresses an inappropriate audit opinion when the financial statements are materially misstated, which is a function of the risks of material misstatement and detection risk.
Auditor	The person or persons conducting the audit, typically the engagement partner, other engagement team members, the firm, or their governmental equivalents.

Detection risk	Risk that the procedures performed by the auditor to reduce audit risk to an acceptably low level will not detect an existing misstatement that could be material, either individually or when aggregated with other misstatements.
Financial reporting framework	A set of criteria used to determine measurement, recognition, presentation, and disclosure of all material items appearing in the financial statements. Examples include accounting principles generally accepted in the United States (GAAP), International Financial Reporting Standards (IFRS) issued by the International Accounting Standards Board, and special-purpose frameworks.
	A fair presentation framework requires compliance with framework requirements and acknowledges that to achieve fair presentation of the financial statements, management may need to provide disclosures beyond those specifically required in the framework, or, in rare circumstances, to depart from a framework requirement. If a financial reporting framework requires compliance with framework requirements but does not make either of the preceding acknowledgements, it is not a fair presentation framework.
Financial statements	A structured representation of historical financial information intended to communicate an entity's economic resources or obligations at a point in time or changes therein for a period of time in accordance with a financial reporting framework. Related notes are included, which typically summarize significant accounting policies and other explanatory information. The term "financial statements" may refer to a single financial statement or a complete set.
Historical financial information	Information expressed in financial terms in relation to a particular entity, derived primarily from that entity's accounting system, about past economic events, conditions, or circumstances.
Interpretive publications	GAAS auditing interpretations and exhibits, auditing guidance in AICPA Audit and Accounting Guides, and AICPA Auditing Statements of Position.
Management	The person(s) with executive responsibility for the conduct of the entity's operations, which may include some or all of those charged with governance.
Misstatement	A difference between the amount, classification, presentation, or disclosure of a reported financial statement item and that which is required for the item to be in accordance with the applicable financial reporting framework. If expressing an opinion regarding the fair presentation of the financial statements in all material respects, misstatements include adjustments of items that the auditor judges necessary for such fair presentation. Misstatements may be due to fraud or error.
Other auditing publications	Publications other than interpretive publications, including auditing articles in professional journals and the AICPA's *CPA Letter*; continuing professional education programs and other instruction materials, textbooks, guidebooks, audit programs, and checklists; and other auditing publications from the AICPA, state CPA societies, other organizations, and individuals.

Premise, relating to the responsibilities of management and those charged with governance (as appropriate) on which an audit is conducted *or* premise	Management and those charged with governance (as appropriate) have the following responsibilities that are fundamental to conducting an audit in accordance with GAAS: (1) To prepare and present (fairly present in the case of a fair presentation framework such as GAAS) the financial statements in accordance with the applicable financial reporting framework, including designing, implementing, and maintaining internal control relevant to the preparation and presentation of financial statements free from material misstatement; and (2) To provide the auditor with access to all information relevant to financial statement preparation and fair presentation of which management and those charged with governance (as appropriate) are aware, additional information the auditor may request from management and those charged with governance for the purpose of the audit, and unrestricted access to persons within the entity from whom the auditor needs to obtain audit evidence.
Professional judgment	The application of relevant training, knowledge, and experience, within the context provided by auditing, accounting, and ethical standards, in making informed decisions about the appropriate courses of action in the circumstances of the audit engagement.
Professional skepticism	An attitude that includes a questioning mind, being alert to conditions that may indicate possible misstatement due to fraud or error, and a critical assessment of audit evidence.
Reasonable assurance	In the context of financial statement audits, a high, but not absolute, level of assurance.
Risk of material misstatement	Risk that the financial statements are materially misstated prior to the audit, which at the assertion level is the risk that a misstatement could occur in an assertion about a class of transaction, account balance, or disclosure that could be material, either individually or when aggregated with other misstatements.
	There are two components of the risk of material misstatement. Inherent risk is the risk before considering any related controls. Control risk is the risk that a material misstatement will not be prevented, or detected and corrected, on a timely basis by the entity's internal control.
Those charged with governance	The person(s) or organization(s) responsible for overseeing the strategic direction of the entity and the obligations related to the accountability of the entity, which includes overseeing the financial reporting process. Those charged with governance may include management personnel.

Requirements

The auditor is presumptively required to adhere to the following guidance when conducting an audit in accordance with GAAS:

1. Comply with relevant ethical requirements relating to financial statement audit engagements.

2. Plan and perform an audit with professional skepticism.

3. Exercise professional judgment in planning and performing an audit.

4. To obtain reasonable assurance, obtain sufficient appropriate audit evidence to reduce audit risk to an acceptably low level, allowing reasonable conclusions to be drawn on which to base an audit opinion.

5. Comply with all AU-C sections relevant to the audit. AU-C sections are relevant when the section is in effect and the circumstances addressed by the AU-C exist.

6. Have an understanding of the entire text of an AU-C section, including its application and explanatory material, in order to understand its objectives and properly apply its requirements.

7. Do not represent compliance with GAAS in the audit report unless the requirements of AU-C 200 and all other AU-C sections relevant to the audit have been complied with.

8. To achieve the auditor's overall objectives, when planning and performing the audit use the objectives stated in relevant AU-C sections and consider the interrelationships among GAAS to (1) determine whether any audit procedures additional to those required by individual AU-C sections are necessary to pursue the objectives stated in each AU-C section and (2) to evaluate whether sufficient appropriate audit evidence has been obtained.

9. Comply with each requirement of an AU-C section unless the entire AU-C section is not relevant to the audit, the requirement is not relevant because it is conditional and the condition does not exist, or, in rare circumstances, it is necessary to depart from a presumptively mandatory requirement.

10. The degree of responsibility imposed on auditors by professional requirements depends on the type of requirement.

    a. For an unconditional requirement, indicated by the word *must* in GAAS, the auditor must comply with the requirement in all cases where it is relevant.

    b. For a presumptively mandatory requirement, indicated by the word *should* in GAAS, the auditor must comply with the requirement in all cases where it is relevant except in rare circumstances when the auditor judges it necessary to depart from such requirement.

11. The need to depart from a presumptively mandatory requirement is expected to occur only when the requirement is for a specific procedure to be performed that would be ineffective in achieving the requirement's intent in the circumstances. In these situations, alternative audit procedures should be performed to achieve the intent of that requirement.

12. Consider interpretive publications applicable to the audit.

13. If auditing guidance from another auditing publication is applied, use professional judgment to assess the relevance and appropriateness of that guidance to the circumstances of the audit.

14. If an objective in a relevant AU-C section cannot be achieved, evaluate whether that prevents the auditor from achieving his or her overall objectives, thereby requiring the auditor to modify the audit opinion or withdraw from the engagement in accordance with GAAS. Failure to achieve an objective represents a significant finding or issue requiring documentation.

Financial Statement Preparation

Although the auditor expresses an opinion on the client's financial statements, the responsibility for the financial statements rests with management. Nonetheless, the auditor can make suggestions to the client about the form and content of the financial statements or may draft the financial statements based on information the client provides.

PUBLIC COMPANY IMPLICATION: Section 302 of the Sarbanes-Oxley Act of 2002 (SOX) requires the CEO and CFO of public companies to prepare a written statement that certifies the appropriateness of the annual and quarterly financial statements and disclosures, including certification that based on their knowledge those financial statements and disclosures fairly present, in all material respects, the operations and financial condition of the issuer. Thus, in an audit of a public company's financial statements, the auditor would not be responsible for drafting the financial statements based on information provided by the client. Rather, management is responsible for preparing the financial statements. although similar public certifications by the senior officers of private companies are not required, representations similar to those required by Section 303 are often included in the management representation letter signer by the senior officers of private companies.

Management is responsible for identifying the applicable financial reporting framework for the entity's financial statements and making judgments regarding reasonable accounting estimates and appropriate accounting policies in the context of that framework when preparing the financial statements. The applicable financial reporting framework may encompass financial accounting standards established by an authorized or recognized standards-setting organization and legislative or regulatory requirements. Other sources that may encompass or provide direction on the application of financial reporting frameworks include the legal and ethical environment, published accounting interpretations and views on emerging accounting issues, widely recognized general and industry practices, and accounting literature. If a conflict exists between information from different sources, the source with the highest authority prevails.

PLANNING AID REMINDER: The responsibilities of management and those charged with governance are very important to the conduct of an audit, so the auditor is required to obtain the agreement of the client regarding those responsibilities prior to accepting an audit engagement.

The form and content of the financial statements are determined by the financial reporting framework used. There are general purpose and special purpose financial statements, prepared to meet the financial information needs of a wide range of users or those of specific users, respectively. There are fair presentation frameworks, such as GAAP or IFRS, and regulatory or contractual-based frameworks. The financial reporting framework also determines what constitutes a complete set of financial statements. Many frameworks are intended to provide information about an entity's financial position, financial performance, and cash flows. For these frameworks, a complete set of financial statements might include a balance sheet, income statement, statement of changes in equity, cash flow statement, and related notes. For other frameworks, a single financial statement and its related notes may constitute a complete set of financial statements.

Ethical Requirements

The auditor is subject to the ethical requirements prescribed by the AICPA Code of Professional Conduct, to more restrictive rules of state boards of accountancy and applicable regulatory agencies, and, in the case of audits of governmental entities, to *Government Auditing Standards*. The AICPA Code of Professional Conduct establishes the fundamental principles of professional ethics, which include responsibilities, the public interest, integrity, the scope and nature of services, objectivity and independence, and due care.

OBSERVATION: Many state boards of accountancy require CPAs licensed in their state to comply with the AICPA Code of Professional Conduct and other AICPA authoritative standards even if those CPAs are not members of the AICPA.

OBSERVATION: Statement on Quality Control Standards No. 8 (A Firm's System of Quality Control) details firm responsibilities for establishing policies and procedures to obtain reasonable assurance that the firm and its personnel comply with relevant ethical requirements, including those pertaining to independence. AU-C 220 allows that the engagement team can rely on the firm's quality control system in meeting quality control responsibilities for an audit engagement unless the engagement partner determines it is inappropriate to do so.

The auditor must be independent of the entity in order to perform a GAAS audit unless (1) GAAS provides differently or (2) the auditor is required by law or regulation to accept the engagement and report on the financial statements. Unless one of these exceptions applies, the auditor is precluded from issuing a report under GAAS if he or she lacks independence.

The need for independence in both fact and appearance is a result of the auditor's responsibility to users of the financial statements. Because the users of financial statements have no way of verifying the fairness of the financial statements, they must rely on the work of an independent auditor. If it is suspected that the auditor is not independent, then the integrity and fairness of the financial statements are questionable and the auditor's assurance is of little value to the reader. The auditor is also required to use due care, meaning he or she should have the appropriate competence and capabilities to perform the audit and issue an appropriate auditor's report. Rule 101 of the AICPA Code of Professional Conduct is applicable to professional services provided by a CPA that require independence.

PUBLIC COMPANY IMPLICATIONS: If the client is a public entity, regulations established by the Securities and Exchange Commission and the Public Company Accounting Oversight Board (PCAOB) must be considered. SOX authorizes the PCAOB to issue independence and ethics standards applicable to audits of public company financial statements. Additionally, SOX explicitly includes provisions related to the performance of nonaudit services, audit partner rotation, and auditor acceptance of employment at the client. In April 2003, the PCAOB adopted the provisions of the AICPA's Code of Professional Conduct on integrity and objectivity (Rule 102) as its "Interim Ethics Standards." The PCAOB also designated Rule 101 of the Code of Professional Conduct and the related interpretations and ethical rulings plus Standards Nos. 1, 2, and 3, and Interpretations 99-1, 00-1, and 00-2 of the Independence Standards Board (ISB) as its "Interim Independence Standards." ISB Standard No. 1 and Interpretations 00-1 and 00-2 have been superseded by PCAOB Rule 3526.

PCAOB Rule 3526 requires the registered public accounting firm to make certain disclosures to the client's audit committee regarding independence both before it accepts an initial engagement and no less frequently than yearly thereafter. Before accepting an initial engagement, the registered firm must (1) communicate in writing to the audit committee all relationships between the firm and the potential client and individuals in financial reporting oversight roles at the potential client that may potentially affect the firm's independence and (2) discuss with the audit committee the potential independence effects of these relationships. These communications must be updated at least annually. And, at least annually, the registered firm must communicate to the audit committee in writing that the firm is independent. The registered firm must document these communications.

PCAOB Rule 3520 requires registered public accounting firms to be independent of their clients. Under Rule 3521 a registered public accounting firm is not independent if it performs any service for a client during the audit or professional engagement period for a contingent fee or commission. Under Rule 3522 a registered public accounting firm is not independent if it performs tax services during the audit or professional engagement period that involve the marketing, planning, or opining in favor of the tax treatment of a transaction if the transaction is confidential (i.e., the taxpayer cannot disclose the transaction) or involves an aggressive tax position as defined by the PCAOB. The audit period is the period covered by the financial statements being audited or reviewed. The professional engagement period begins on the earlier of when the initial engagement letter is signed or the audit, review, or attest procedures begin, and it ends when the registered firm or the client notifies the SEC that there is no longer a client relationship. In addition, under Rule 3523 a registered public accounting firm is generally not independent if it provides tax services to a client person in a financial reporting oversight role or a family member of such a person during the professional engagement period. A person in a financial reporting oversight role has the ability to influence the contents of the financial statements or those who prepare the financial statements (e.g., board members, CEO, president, CFO, COO, general counsel, chief accounting officer, controller, director of internal audit, director of financial reporting, treasurer). However, if a board member is in a financial reporting oversight role solely because he or she is a member of the board, the registered firm is not prohibited from providing tax services to the board member. Finally, if a registered public accounting firm seeks to perform allowable tax services or allowable nonaudit services related to internal control over financial reporting for a client, the registered firm, as required by the Sarbanes-Oxley Act, must obtain pre-approval from the audit committee to perform the service. In either instance, the registered firm must (1) describe in writing to the audit committee the scope of the service and the potential effect of the service on the firm's independence and (2) document the substance of its discussion with the audit committee (Rule 3524 and Rule 3525). Additionally, in the case of allowable tax services, the registered firm must disclose (1) the fee structure for the arrangement, (2) the existence of any side letter or other amendment or agreement related to the service, and (3) whether the registered firm has any referral agreement, referral fee, or fee-sharing arrangement with a third party related to the service (Rule 3524).

PCAOB Rule 3502 prohibits an individual at a registered public accounting firm from knowingly or recklessly taking an action, or failing to take a required action, where the individual's behavior is likely to lead to the registered firm's violation of the Sarbanes-Oxley Act, PCAOB rules and standards, SEC rules, or provisions of the securities laws.

Professional Skepticism

Every task performed by a professional person is approached with a mental attitude. In an audit engagement, that mental attitude is described as professional skepticism. The auditor's use of professional skepticism is important for reducing the risks of overlooking unusual circumstances, over-generalizing audit conclusions, or using inappropriate assumptions to determine the nature, timing, and extent and evaluate the results of audit procedures. Professional skepticism involves being alert to contradictory audit evidence, information that causes the reliability of documents or responses to inquiries to be questioned, conditions that may indicate fraud, and circumstances suggesting the need for additional audit procedures beyond those required by GAAS.

FRAUD POINTER: A research monograph issued by the AICPA in 2000 entitled "Fraud Related SEC Enforcement Actions against Auditors: 1987-1997" examined fraud-related SEC enforcement actions in which auditors were cited by the SEC for alleged audit deficiencies. Two of the 10 most frequently cited audit deficiencies noted by the SEC against auditors related to the lack of due professional care and the lack of appropriate professional skepticism. In some cases, auditors merely accepted management assertions at face value or ignored known management integrity issues.

Professional skepticism does not suggest that the auditor assumes the client's management is dishonest or that everything management says is incorrect.

> **FRAUD POINTER:** AU-C 240 emphasizes the importance of exercising professional skepticism when assessing the risk of material misstatements in the financial statements due to fraud. First, the auditor should approach the engagement with a questioning mind-set that recognizes that fraud is possible in any entity, regardless of the auditor's prior experience with the entity and the auditor's views about management integrity. Second, the auditor should critically evaluate evidence obtained throughout the performance of audit procedures by always questioning whether the evidence obtained suggests that fraud might be present. The auditor should not let his or her beliefs about management's integrity allow him or her to accept less than persuasive evidence.

While the auditor is required to consider the reliability of information to be used as audit evidence, he or she may assume records and documents are genuine unless there is reason to believe otherwise. If there is doubt about a record or document's authenticity, the auditor must investigate further and determine what additional audit procedures are needed to resolve the matter.

Professional Judgment

Exercising professional judgment throughout the audit is important, especially regarding matters such as:

- Materiality and audit risk
- The nature, timing, and extent of audit procedures used to meet GAAS requirements and gather audit evidence
- Evaluating if sufficient appropriate audit evidence has been obtained and GAAS and overall objectives have been achieved
- Evaluating management's judgments in applying the applicable financial reporting framework
- Drawing conclusions based on the audit evidence obtained

Professional judgment does not provide justification for decisions not otherwise supported by the facts and circumstances of the engagement or by sufficient appropriate audit evidence. When matters are particularly difficult or contentious, the auditor may consult with engagement team members or others to assist in making informed and reasonable judgments. Significant professional judgments made in reaching conclusions on significant audit matters should be documented such that an experienced auditor with no previous connection to the audit is able to understand those judgments. Professional judgments can be evaluated based on whether a judgment reflects competent and appropriate application of auditing standards and accounting principles given the facts and circumstances known to the auditor up to the date of his or her report.

Sufficient Appropriate Audit Evidence

Obtaining and evaluating audit evidence comprises most of the auditor's work in forming an audit opinion. Audit evidence is cumulative in nature and is primarily obtained from audit procedures performed during the audit, but it may also be obtained from previous audits if the auditor has evaluated the effect any changes since that audit or from a firm's quality control procedures for client acceptance and continuance. Audit evidence may be information that supports or contradicts management assertions and, in some cases, the absence of information may constitute audit evidence such as when management refuses to provide a requested representation.

The auditor uses professional judgment in determining whether sufficient appropriate audit evidence has been obtained. Sufficiency and appropriateness of audit evidence are interrelated. Sufficiency is a measure of the quantity of audit evidence and the quantity needed generally increases as the auditor's assessment of the risks of material misstatement increases and as the quality of audit evidence decreases. However, increased quantity may not be able to compensate for poor-quality audit evidence. Appropriateness is a measure of the quality, or relevance and reliability, of audit evidence. The reliability of audit evidence is affected by its source, its nature, and the circumstances under which it is obtained.

Audit Risk

The assessment of audit risk is a matter of professional judgment based on audit procedures to obtain information about that risk and other evidence obtained throughout the audit. Audit risk is a function of the risks of material misstatement and detection risk.

Risks of material misstatement

Risks of material misstatement exist at two levels:

1. *Overall financial statement level* Risks relating pervasively to the financial statements as a whole that may affect several assertions.

2. *Assertion level* Risks relating to particular classes of transactions, account balances, and disclosures that are assessed to determine the nature, timing, and extent of further audit procedures necessary to obtain sufficient appropriate audit evidence.

There are two components of risks of material misstatement, inherent risk and control risk, which exist independently of the audit. Inherent risks may vary among assertions due to factors such as complex calculations, estimates subject to significant uncertainty, or circumstances of the entity and its environment. Control risk is a function of the effectiveness of management's design, implementation, and maintenance of internal control relevant to financial reporting. Control risk may be reduced by effective internal controls but can never be eliminated due to inherent limitations such as the potential for human error, collusion, or management override of controls. The auditor may assess inherent and control risk either separately or on a combined basis, and may make this assessment using either quantitative or qualitative measures of risk.

Detection risk

Detection risk is the other component affecting audit risk and it relates to the nature, timing, and extent of audit procedures. For a given level of audit risk, there is an inverse relationship between the acceptable level of detection risk and the assessed risks of material misstatement at the assertion level. For example, the greater the risk level, the lower the detection risk that the auditor can accept. Lower detection risk means that the audit evidence needs to be more persuasive. Detection risk is a function of an audit procedure's effectiveness and its application by the auditor. Adequate planning, proper assignment of engagement team personnel, use of professional skepticism, and supervision and review of audit work performed increase the effectiveness of an audit procedure and its application and decrease the chance that an auditor might select an inappropriate audit procedure, misapply an appropriate audit procedure, or misinterpret audit results. Due to the inherent limitations of an audit, detection risk can be reduced but not eliminated.

Inherent limitations of an audit

The inherent limitations of an audit prevent the auditor from obtaining absolute assurance that the financial statements are free from material misstatement; therefore, there is a risk that some material misstatements of the financial statements may not be detected. Discovery of such a material misstatement does not necessarily indicate a failure to conduct an audit in accordance with GAAS. Whether the auditor has performed an audit in accordance with GAAS is determined by the audit procedures performed in the circumstances, the sufficiency and appropriateness of the audit evidence obtained, and the suitability of the auditor's report based on a evaluation of the evidence given the auditor's overall objectives.

PLANNING AID REMINDER: Inherent limitations and matters of difficulty, time, or cost do not provide a valid basis for the auditor to omit an audit procedure for which there is no alternative or to be satisfied with evidence that is less than persuasive.

The principal inherent limitations of an audit arise from:

- The nature of financial reporting
- The nature of audit procedures
- The need for the audit to be conducted in a reasonable period of time at a reasonable cost

The nature of financial reporting is such that for many financial statement items there is a degree of uncertainty and management must make judgments, which results in financial statements having an inherent level of variability. This is often the case with accounting estimates and, while the variability cannot be eliminated, the auditor should consider the reasonableness of estimates as well as the qualitative aspects of the entity's accounting practices including indicators of bias in management's judgments.

The nature of audit procedures is such that there are practical and legal limitations on the auditor's ability to obtain audit evidence. When performing audit procedures, the auditor cannot be certain that information is complete, because management or others may not provide all the relevant information intentionally or unintentionally or fraud may exist, causing the auditor to believe invalid audit evidence is valid. Also, since an audit is not an official investigation of wrongdoing, the auditor does not have specific legal powers such as the power of search that would be necessary for such an investigation.

The need for the audit to be conducted in a reasonable period of time at a reasonable cost means that it may be impracticable to address all information that may exist or pursue every matter exhaustively, because there is a balance that needs to be struck between the reliability of information and its cost. The auditor should plan the audit so it will be performed effectively, undertake greater audit effort in areas most expected to contain risks of material misstatement, and use testing and other means to examine populations for misstatements. The auditor is required to have a basis for the identification and assessment of risks of material misstatement at the financial statement and assertion levels by performing risk assessment procedures and related activities and to use testing and other means of examining populations to provide a reasonable basis for drawing conclusions about the population.

OBSERVATION: Other AU-C sections identify specific audit procedures to use to reduce the effect of inherent limitations due to certain assertions or subject matters such as fraud (AU-C 240), related-party relationships and transactions (AU-C 550), noncompliance with laws and regulations (AU-C 250), and events or conditions that may affect an entity's ability to continue as a going concern (AU-C 570).

Nature and Content of GAAS

The AICPA Code of Professional Conduct requires an auditor comply with Statements on Auditing Standards (SASs) issued by the Auditing Standards Board. GAAS provides the auditor with guidance regarding his or her overall objectives and general responsibilities. For some engagements, the auditor may be required to comply with auditing requirements in addition to GAAS, such as *Government Auditing Standards*. In these circumstances, GAAS does not override laws or regulations that govern an audit, but an audit conducted to adhere to those laws and regulations may not comply with GAAS. The auditor may also conduct an audit in accordance with GAAS and PCAOB standards, International Standards on Auditing (ISAs), *Government Auditing Standards,* or the auditing standards of a specific country or jurisdiction, in which case the auditor may need to perform additional audit procedures to comply with those standards as well.

PUBLIC COMPANY IMPLICATION: SOX authorizes the PCAOB to issue auditing standards for audits of public company financial statements. In April 2003, the PCAOB adopted existing auditing standards previously issued by the Auditing Standards Board as the PCAOB's "Interim Auditing Standards." Thus, GAAS promulgated by the Auditing Standards Board as of April 16, 2003 constitute the "Interim Auditing Standards." Since then, the PCAOB has begun to issue PCAOB Auditing Standards that amend or supersede portions of the "Interim Auditing Standards."

AU-C sections clearly state the scope, effective date, and any specific limitation on that AU-C's applicability and, unless otherwise stated, may be applied before the effective date specified. An AU-C contains both professional requirements and related guidance in applying it. In fulfilling professional responsibilities, the auditor should consider the entire text of an AU-C.

PUBLIC COMPANY IMPLICATION: An auditor's professional requirements as specified in AU-C 200 are quite similar to an auditor's professional requirements in the audit of a public company, as specified by the PCAOB in Rule 3101 (Certain Terms Used in Auditing and Related Professional Practice Standards).

The related guidance in an AU-C is also referred to as application or explanatory material and is intended to be descriptive rather than imperative (i.e., it does not impose a performance obligation upon the auditor). For example, explanatory material may (1) further explain the meaning of a requirement or what it is intended to cover, (2) include particular audit procedures that may be appropriate, and (3) provide additional information that the auditor may find helpful in applying his or her professional judgment. The procedures or actions suggested by the explanatory material are denoted by the words *may, might,* or *could.*

The application and other explanatory material may include introductory material, definitions, appendixes, and additional considerations specific to audits of governmental and smaller, less complex entities. Introductory material may explain the AU-C section's purpose and scope, relationship to other AU-C sections, subject matter, context, and responsibilities of the auditor and others in relation to the AU-C's subject matter. Definitions provide the meanings attributed to certain terms for purposes of GAAS that will carry the same meaning throughout GAAS unless otherwise indicated but are not intended to override definitions established for other purposes. When an AU-C provides considerations specific to smaller, less complex entities, they typically refer to an entity with ownership and management concentrated in one or a small number of individuals that has simple transactions or recordkeeping, or few products, lines of business, internal controls, levels of management, or personnel.

Objectives in AU-C Sections

AU-C sections contain objectives that link the requirements of that AU-C section to the auditor's overall objectives, assisting the auditor in understanding what needs to be accomplished and how to accomplish it and in deciding whether more needs to be done to achieve the objectives given the circumstances of the audit. Objectives in AU-C sections are subject to inherent limitations and should be understood in the context of the auditor's overall objectives and as they relate to the objectives and requirements of other relevant AU-C sections.

While proper application of the requirements of relevant AU-Cs is expected to provide the auditor with sufficient basis for achieving his or her objectives, the auditor must determine the audit procedures that are necessary to fulfill GAAS requirements and achieve GAAS objectives. In some cases, this may mean the auditor needs to perform audit procedures in addition to those required by GAAS in order to meet the objectives specified in GAAS.

If the auditor concludes that sufficient appropriate audit evidence has not been obtained to achieve his or her overall objectives, the auditor may:

- Evaluate whether further relevant audit evidence has or will be obtained by complying with other AU-C sections

- Extend the work performed in applying one or more requirements

- Perform other procedures the auditor judges necessary in the circumstances

PLANNING AID REMINDER: If none of these procedures is practical or possible, sufficient appropriate audit evidence will not be obtained and the auditor will need to determine the effect on his or her report or on his or her ability to complete the engagement.

Complying with Relevant Requirements

An AU-C may specify that an auditor "should consider" a procedure. In this instance, there is a presumptive requirement that the auditor will consider the procedure. However, although an auditor essentially has to consider the procedure, he or she does not necessarily have to perform the procedure.

An auditor may, in rare circumstances, depart from a presumptively mandatory requirement. In these situations, the auditor must document why he or she departed from the requirement and how he or she accomplished the objective of the presumptively mandatory requirement through other procedures.

ENGAGEMENT STRATEGY: An engagement planning strategy is to start with the assumption that all AU-Cs apply, given that most are relevant in every audit. As planning proceeds, the auditor might identify exceptions that exist for unique situations. For example, the use of specialists, audits of service organizations, or the audit of fair values might not be applicable. Auditors may wish to identify a list of the most frequent exceptions, which could be used when planning all audit engagements, and assume that all other AU-Cs are applicable.

PUBLIC COMPANY IMPLICATION: PCAOB standards are very similar to AU-C 200 as it relates to the auditor's performance responsibility. The PCAOB's Rule 3101 (Certain Terms Used in Auditing and Related Professional Practice Standards) states that PCAOB standards create unconditional responsibilities, presumptively mandatory responsibilities, and responsibilities to consider. Unconditional responsibilities are denoted by the words *must, shall,* and *is required.* Presumptively mandatory responsibilities are denoted by the word *should.* Responsibilities to consider are denoted by the words *may, might, could,* and similar language.

Interpretive Publications

Interpretative publications are issued under the authority of the Auditing Standards Board. Guidelines established in interpretative publications are not auditing standards but, rather, provide specific direction on how auditing standards are to be observed in particular situations, especially for clients who operate in specialized industries.

Auditing Interpretations are discussed throughout this text. AICPA Audit and Accounting Guides, which are listed below, and AICPA Statements of Position (Auditing and Attestation) may be purchased from the AICPA:

- Airlines
- Analytical Procedures
- Assessing and Responding to Audit Risk in a Financial Statement Audit
- Audit Sampling
- Auditing Derivative Instruments, Hedging Activities, and Investments in Securities
- Auditing Revenue in Certain Industries
- Brokers and Dealers in Securities
- Casinos
- Compilation and Review Engagements
- Construction Contractors
- Depository and Lending Institutions: Banks and Savings Institutions, Credit Unions, Finance Companies, and Mortgage Companies
- Employee Benefit Plans
- Entities with Oil and Gas Producing Activities
- Government Auditing Standards and Circular A-133 Audits
- Health Care Entities
- Investment Companies
- Life and Health Insurance Entities
- Not-for-Profit Entities
- Property and Liability Insurance Entities
- Prospective Financial Information
- Service Organizations: Applying SSAE No. 16, Reporting on Controls at Service Organizations (SOC 1)
- State and Local Governments

Other Auditing Publications

An auditor is not "expected to be aware of the full body of other auditing publications," and such publications have no authoritative status. In determining whether an other auditing publication is relevant and appropriate, the auditor may presume publications published by the AICPA and reviewed by the AICPA Audit and Attest Standards Staff are appropriate. For other publications, the auditor may consider the degree to which the publication is recognized as being helpful in understanding and applying GAAS and the issuer or author is recognized as an authority in auditing matters.

PLANNING AID REMINDER: The auditor's responsibilities to follow professional requirements do not apply to Auditing Interpretations issued by the Auditing Standards Board or to any other interpretive guidance or other auditing publications. Therefore, the words *must* or *should* in an interpretive document do *not* represent unconditional or presumptively mandatory requirements, respectively.

Failure to Achieve an Objective

The auditor uses judgment to determine whether objectives have been achieved. Circumstances that may cause failure to achieve an objective include those preventing the auditor from complying with the relevant requirements of an AU-C section or that result in it not being practical or possible for the auditor to obtain the necessary audit evidence to achieve the objective. The auditor documents a failure to achieve an objective to provide evidence of the basis for his or her conclusions about achievement of his or her overall objectives and to assist in making that evaluation.

Practitioner's Aid

Professional skepticism is a key element to exercising due professional care in the conduct of an audit. The practitioner's aid presented in Exhibit AU-C 200-1 is based on the guidance provided in the AICPA's Practice Alert 98-2 (Professional Skepticism and Related Topics). Practice Alerts are based on existing auditing standards and are issued by the AICPA to help practitioners improve the efficiency and effectiveness of their audits.

EXHIBIT AU-C 200-1—PROFESSIONAL SKEPTICISM

Key Questions on Skepticism	Suggested Guidance Provided by Practice Alert 98-2
• What is professional skepticism?	Professional skepticism is an attitude that includes a questioning mind and working practices that encompass a critical assessment of audit evidence.
• Should professional skepticism be exercised throughout the audit?	Because audit evidence is gathered and evaluated throughout an engagement, professional skepticism must be exercised throughout the entire engagement.
• Does professional skepticism mean that statements made by management should never be accepted?	The auditor should strike a balance between disbelief and unquestioning acceptance. Generally there is a need to corroborate management's responses.
• What level of evidence should the auditor obtain in exercising professional skepticism?	Evidence should be persuasive rather than convincing.

Key Questions on Skepticism	Suggested Guidance Provided by Practice Alert 98-2
• Do representations by management provide persuasive evidence?	Representations by management, without further corroboration, rarely provide persuasive evidence.
• What are some audit areas that may demand particular scrutiny?	Management responses to questions resulting from the application of analytical procedures.
	Representations regarding recoverability of assets or deferred charges.
	Accruals (or lack thereof), particularly for unusual events or transactions.
	Substance of large and unusual (particularly period-end) transactions.
	Vague contract terms or conditions.
	Existence of nonstandard journal entries.
	Lack of copies of original documents.
	Presence of fraud or illegal acts.
• Which conditions related to nonstandard journal entries may suggest heightened skepticism with respect to a particular account balance?	Journal entries processed outside the normal course of business.
	Transactions that are complex or unusual in nature.
	Estimates and period-end adjustments.
	Journal entries indicative of potential problems with the accounting systems.
	Item has been prone to client error in the past.
	Item has not been reconciled on a timely basis or contains old reconciling items.
	Represents a particular risk specific to the client's industry.
	Represents account balances affecting the company's book value and liquidity (e.g., account balances that are used in determining loan covenant ratios).
• Does the use of photocopies or draft copies (rather than originals) have an effect on audit skepticism?	Yes; it may be more difficult to identify alterations on photocopied material, and draft copies might not include all relevant information. With the use of scanners, original documents can be altered in a way that makes detection especially difficult.
• When originals are not available, what alternative procedures are available to the auditor?	The auditor should consider whether the originals should be obtained and inspected.
• Should the auditor accept fax or e-mail confirmation responses?	The auditor should consider whether (1) to confirm the information over the telephone and/or (2) to request that the original confirmation be returned directly to the auditor.

SECTION 210

TERMS OF ENGAGEMENT

Authoritative Pronouncements

SAS-122—Statements on Auditing Standards: Clarification and Recodification

Overview

AU-C 210 provides the auditor with guidance regarding his or her responsibilities in agreeing on the terms of the audit engagement with management and those charged with governance (as appropriate). The auditor should only accept or continue an audit engagement when the basis upon which the audit is to be performed has been agreed upon by establishing the presence of the preconditions for an audit and confirming that the auditor and management and those charged with governance (as appropriate) share a common understanding of the terms of the audit engagement.

PLANNING AID REMINDER: AU-C 210 addresses audit preconditions that are within the entity's control, whereas AU-C 220 deals with the auditor's responsibilities that are within his or her control regarding the acceptance of an audit engagement.

Definitions

Preconditions for an audit	The use by management of an acceptable financial reporting framework in the preparation of the financial statements and the agreement of management and, when appropriate, those charged with governance to the premise on which an audit is conducted.
Recurring audit	An audit engagement for an existing audit client for whom the auditor performed the preceding audit.
Management	In AU-C 210, the term "management" should be read as "management and, when appropriate, those charged with governance" unless the context suggests otherwise.

Requirements

The auditor is presumptively required to perform the following procedures when agreeing to the terms of an audit engagement with management:

1. To determine whether the preconditions for an audit are present:

   a. Determine whether the financial reporting framework to be applied in the financial statement preparation is acceptable.

   b. Obtain management's agreement that it acknowledges and understands its responsibility (1) for preparing and fairly presenting the financial statements in accordance with the applicable financial reporting framework; (2) for designing, implementing, and maintaining internal control relevant to preparing and fairly presenting financial statements free from material misstatement due to fraud or error; and (3) to provide the auditor with access to all information management is aware of that is relevant to the financial statements' preparation and fair presentation, additional information the auditor may request from management for purposes of the audit, and unrestricted access to persons within the entity from whom the auditor needs to obtain audit evidence.

2. Do not accept an engagement if management or those charged with governance impose a scope limitation that the auditor believes will result in a disclaimer of opinion on the financial statements as a whole unless the audit is required by law or regulation, in which case, the auditor is permitted but not required to accept the engagement.

3. If the preconditions for an audit are not present, discuss the matter with management. Do not accept the engagement unless required by law or regulation if the financial reporting framework to be applied in preparing the financial statements is unacceptable or management's agreement of its acknowledgement and understanding of its responsibilities has not been obtained.

4. Agree upon the audit engagement terms with management.

5. Record agreed-upon terms of the audit engagement in an engagement letter or other suitable form of written agreement that includes:

   a. The financial statement audit's objective and scope

   b. The auditor's responsibilities

   c. Management's responsibilities

   d. A statement that because of the inherent limitations of an audit and those of internal control, there is some risk that some material misstatements may not be detected even though the audit is planned and performed properly in accordance with GAAS

   e. Identification of the applicable financial reporting framework for the financial statement presentation

   f. Reference to the expected form and content of any reports the auditor will issue and a statement that in some circumstances a report may differ from its expected form and content

6. Before accepting an initial audit or reaudit engagement, request the entity's permission to inquire of any predecessor auditor about matters that will assist in determining whether to accept the engagement and request the entity's authorization of the predecessor auditor to fully respond to the auditor's inquiries. If an entity refuses to authorize the predecessor auditor to respond in full or in part, inquire about the reasons and consider the implications in deciding whether to accept the engagement.

7. If the predecessor auditor provides no response or a limited response, consider the implications in deciding whether to accept the engagement. Evaluate a predecessor auditor's response before accepting the engagement.

8. On recurring audits, evaluate whether the terms of the audit engagement need to be revised. If the terms do not need revision, remind the entity of the engagement terms and document that reminder.

9. Do not agree to a change in the audit engagement terms when there is no reasonable justification for the change.

10. If prior to completing the audit engagement the auditor is requested to change the audit engagement to an engagement that provides a lower level of assurance, determine whether there is reasonable justification for the change.

11. If the audit engagement terms are changed, the auditor and management should agree on and record the new engagement terms in an engagement letter or other suitable written agreement.

12. If the auditor concludes there is no reasonable justification for the change in audit engagement terms and is not permitted by management to continue the original audit engagement, he or she should withdraw from the engagement when possible under law and regulation; communicate the circumstances to those charged with governance; and determine if any legal, contractual, or other obligation exists to report the circumstances to other parties, such as owners or regulators.

13. If law or regulation prescribes a specific layout, form, or wording of the auditor's report that differs significantly from GAAS requirements, evaluate whether users might misunderstand the auditor's report and, if so, whether the auditor would be permitted to reword the prescribed form to be in accordance with GAAS requirements or attach a separate report. Do not accept the engagement unless required by law or regulation if rewording the form or attaching a separate report would not be permitted or would not mitigate the risk of users misunderstanding the auditor's report. An audit conducted in accordance with such law or regulation does not comply with GAAS; so, the auditor should not make reference in his or her report to the audit having been conducted in accordance with GAAS.

Analysis and Application of Procedures

Preconditions for an audit

The auditor should determine whether the financial reporting framework to be applied to the financial statements is acceptable in determining whether the preconditions for an audit exist. An acceptable financial reporting framework provides the auditor with suitable criteria or benchmarks for auditing the financial statements by allowing reasonably consistent evaluation or measurement of a subject matter using professional judgment. The framework also provides the criteria for management to fairly present the entity's financial statements. Factors that may impact the auditor's determination of the acceptability of a financial reporting framework include the nature of the entity, the purpose and nature of the financial statements, and whether the financial reporting framework is prescribed by law or regulation.

Financial statements may be prepared in accordance with a financial reporting framework designed to meet the common financial information needs of a wide range of users. These general purpose financial reporting frameworks are established by bodies designated by the AICPA Council in Rule 203 of the AICPA Code of Professional Conduct to establish such principles and include the following:

- The Financial Accounting Standards Board's (FASB) *Accounting Standards Codification*, promulgated by FASB

- International Financial Reporting Standards, promulgated by the International Accounting Standards Board

- Statements of the Governmental Accounting Standards Board (GASB), promulgated by GASB

- Statements of Federal Financial Accounting Standards, promulgated by the Federal Accounting Standards Advisory Board

Financial statements may also be prepared in accordance with a special purpose framework, such as one prescribed by law or regulation, and the acceptability of special purpose financial statements is addressed in AU-C 800.

PLANNING AID REMINDER: If after accepting an audit engagement the applicable financial reporting framework is found to be unacceptable and use of the framework is not prescribed by law or regulation, management may decide to use another acceptable framework. If this occurs, the previously agreed-upon engagement terms will no longer be accurate and new terms should be agreed upon and recorded to reflect the framework change.

The auditor also needs to obtain management's agreement that it acknowledges and understands its responsibilities in establishing whether the preconditions for an audit exist. This agreement helps prevent misunderstandings about the respective responsibilities of management and the auditor. The auditor may want to make management aware that written representations of its fulfillment of certain responsibilities will be required by AU-C 580, other AU-C sections, and possibly in support of other audit evidence. If management will not acknowledge its responsibilities or agree with the expectation to provide written representations, the auditor will not be able to obtain sufficient appropriate audit evidence and the engagement should not be accepted unless required to do so by law or regulation. If required to accept the engagement, the auditor may need to explain to management the importance of these matters and their implications for the auditor's report.

ENGAGEMENT STRATEGY: As a precondition of the audit of special purpose financial statements, AU-C 800 requires the auditor to obtain management's agreement that it acknowledges and understands its responsibility to include all informative disclosures that are appropriate for the special purpose framework used.

Management is responsible for maintaining the internal control necessary for the preparation and fair presentation of the financial statements. Management determines what internal control is necessary by considering management's needs, the complexity of the business, the nature of the entity's risks, and relevant laws or regulations. Internal control only provides reasonable assurance about achieving the entity's financial reporting objectives due to its inherent limitations, and an audit does not act as a substitute for management's maintenance of the necessary internal control. Management's agreement about its responsibility for internal control does not imply that the auditor will find that the entity's internal control has achieved its purpose or is free of deficiencies.

The auditor should consider whether to accept an audit engagement when there is a scope limitation imposed by management. Some scope limitations do not preclude the auditor from accepting the engagement, such as restrictions imposed by management that the auditor believes will result in a qualified opinion or restrictions imposed by circumstances beyond management's control. If an entity is required by law or regulation to have an audit and management imposes a scope limitation the auditor expects will result in disclaiming an opinion on the financial statements as a whole, the auditor is neither precluded from nor required to accept the engagement.

Agreement on audit engagement terms

The auditor reaches an agreement on the terms of the audit engagement with management or those charged with governance of the entity. If the agreement on engagement terms is only with those charged with governance, the auditor is still required to obtain management's agreement that it acknowledges and understands its responsibilities. Agreeing on audit engagement terms before the audit begins helps to avoid misunderstandings, reducing the risk that the entity may rely inappropriately on the auditor to protect the entity against certain risks or to perform certain functions that are the entity's responsibility. The form and content of the audit engagement letter varies; information on the auditor's responsibilities may be based on the summary of those responsibilities contained in AU-C 200 (*Overall Objectives of the Independent Auditor and the Conduct of an Audit in Accordance with Generally Accepted Auditing Standards*) and the description of management's responsibilities is addressed in the requirements of AU-C 210.

The understanding between the auditor and the client may also include the following:

- Elaboration of the audit scope, including reference to the guidance to the auditor adheres to
- The form of any other communication of the audit engagement results
- Arrangements regarding audit planning and performance, including the audit team composition

- That at the conclusion of the engagement management will provide the auditor with a letter that confirms certain representations made during the audit

- Management's agreement to provide the auditor with draft financial statements and accompanying information in time to allow the auditor to complete the audit in the proposed timetable

- Management's agreement to inform the auditor of subsequent events it becomes aware of that may affect the financial statements

- The basis on which fees are computed and any billing arrangements

- A request for management to agree to the terms of the engagement and acknowledge receipt of the engagement letter

---

OBSERVATION: AU-C 265 requires the auditor of financial statements to communicate in writing to management and those charged with governance significant deficiencies and material weaknesses that were identified. Although an audit of financial statements is not designed to perform procedures to detect control deficiencies, AU-C 265 requires communication when the auditor identifies significant deficiencies and material weaknesses in internal control over financial reporting.

PUBLIC COMPANY IMPLICATION: The Sarbanes-Oxley Act of 2002 (SOX) requires all public companies to issue an internal control report that includes management's assessment of the effectiveness of internal controls. Furthermore, the auditor must attest to and issue a report on management's assessment of internal control for the large accelerated filer public companies. Thus, in the audit of accelerated filer public companies, the auditor must issue an opinion on the financial statements and an opinion on internal controls. The audit of financial statements and the audit of internal controls are meant to be integrated. For this reason, when obtaining an understanding with the client in the audit of a public company, the auditor must modify the discussion to reflect the unique responsibility for internal controls that is applicable to public companies.

Some other matters, such as the following, may also be included as part of the understanding with the client when relevant:

- Arrangements concerning involvement of specialists or internal auditors, if applicable

- Arrangements involving a predecessor auditor

- Any limitation or other arrangements regarding the liability of the auditor or the client, such as indemnification to the auditor for liability arising from known misrepresentations to the auditor by management (regulators may restrict or prohibit such liability limitation arrangements)

- Conditions under which access to the auditor's documentation may be granted to others

- Additional services to be provided relating to regulatory requirements

- Arrangements regarding other services to be provided in connection with the engagement

Exhibit AU-C 210-1 provides an example of an audit engagement letter demonstrating the incorporation of many of these matters.

Communications with the predecessor auditor

A successor auditor is required to communicate with the predecessor auditor before accepting an engagement; however, an auditor may make a proposal on an engagement before the communication has been made. More than one auditor may make a proposal on the same engagement. Under this circumstance, the predecessor auditor is not expected to respond to inquiries made by the auditor until (1) the client has selected a successor auditor and (2) the successor auditor has accepted the engagement subject to the consideration of the responses received from the predecessor auditor. The responsibility to initiate the communication, which can be either oral or written, rests with the successor auditor.

ENGAGEMENT STRATEGY: Rule 301 of the AICPA's Code of Professional Conduct prohibits an auditor from disclosing confidential information except when the client agrees to the disclosure. To reconcile the requirements of AU-C 210 with Rule 301, the successor auditor should ask the prospective client to grant permission to discuss the impending engagement with the predecessor auditor. The client should not place any restrictions on the exchange of information between the successor and predecessor auditors. If the successor auditor cannot obtain required information from the predecessor auditor because of client restrictions, the successor auditor should consider the reasons for the restrictions and take the circumstances into consideration when deciding whether to accept the client. Likewise, the auditor is required by Rule 301 to keep information obtained from the predecessor auditor confidential regardless of whether the engagement is accepted.

The predecessor auditor is expected to respond promptly and fully to the successor auditor's inquiries in accordance with the Code of Professional Conduct unless there are unusual circumstances such as pending, threatened, or potential ligation or disciplinary proceedings. Under these circumstances, the predecessor auditor may decide to not respond fully to the inquiries but should clearly state that the response is limited.

Inquiries directed by the successor auditor to the predecessor auditor may include matters such as the following:

- Information related to the integrity of management

- Disagreements between the predecessor auditor and the client concerning accounting principles, audit procedures, or other "similarly significant matters"

- Predecessor auditor's communications with management and those charged with governance concerning fraud, illegal acts by the client, and matters related to the client's internal control

- The predecessor auditor's understanding of the reason for the change in auditors

---

FRAUD POINTER: AU-C 240 notes that the auditor should consider other information obtained in an audit, such as procedures related to the acceptance and continuance of clients, when assessing the risks of material misstatements due to fraud. Information obtained from the predecessor auditor about management's integrity, disagreements between management and the predecessor auditor, and the reasons for the change in auditors can provide relevant insights to the successor auditor, particularly when combined with other information gathered by the successor auditor to assess fraud risks.

PLANNING AID REMINDER: When the most recent financial statements have been compiled or reviewed, a successor-predecessor auditor relationship does not exist; however, the auditor is not prohibited from following the guidance established by AU-C 510.

Recurring audits

When deciding if the terms of a recurring audit engagement need to be revised, the auditor may consider the following factors:

- Indications that the entity misunderstands the nature and scope of the audit
- Any revised or special terms of the audit engagement
- A change of senior management
- Significant changes in ownership or the nature or size of the entity's business
- Changes in the legal or regulatory requirements, the financial reporting framework adopted in preparing the financial statements, or other reporting requirements

If the terms of a recurring audit engagement do not need to be revised, the auditor reminds the entity of those terms via a written or oral reminder. If the reminder is oral, the auditor may document the reminder by including with whom the discussion took place, when, and the significant points discussed.

Accepting a Change in the Audit Engagement Terms

The auditor considers whether to agree to a change in audit engagement terms based on whether there is a reasonable justification for the change. Reasonable bases for requesting a change in terms include changing circumstances affecting the entity's requirements or misunderstandings about the nature of the service originally requested. Change requests may be unreasonable if the change relates to information that is incorrect, incomplete, or otherwise unsatisfactory; for example, if the auditor is requested to change an audit to a review engagement to avoid a qualified opinion or a disclaimer of opinion.

If the auditor concludes that there is a reasonable justification for changing an audit engagement to a review or other service, the report on the other service will not reference the original audit engagement or any procedures performed in the original audit engagement unless the revised engagement is an agreed-upon procedures engagement and reference to those procedures is a normal part of the report.

In circumstances where the auditor is conducting an audit in accordance with a law or regulation that prescribes an audit report that is not in compliance with GAAS, conducting the audit in accordance with GAAS may not be mentioned in the report. Regardless, the auditor is encouraged to apply GAAS to the extent practicable in the audit, including the AU-C sections addressing the auditor's report.

Practitioner's Aids

EXHIBIT AU-C 210-1—AUDIT ENGAGEMENT LETTER

To the [appropriate representative of those charged with governance] of Averroes Company:

[*The objective and scope of the audit*]

You have requested that we audit the financial statements of Averroes Company, which comprise the balance sheet as of December 31, 20X5, and the related statements of income, changes in stockholders' equity, and cash flows for the year then ended. We are pleased to confirm our acceptance and our understanding of this audit engagement by means of this letter. Our audit will be conducted with the objective of our expressing an opinion on the financial statements.

[*Auditor's responsibilities*]

We will conduct our audit in accordance with auditing standards generally accepted in the United States (GAAS). Those standards require that we plan and perform the audit to obtain reasonable assurance about whether the financial statements are free of material misstatement. An audit involves performing procedures to obtain audit evidence about the amounts and disclosures in the financial statements. The procedures selected depend on the auditor's judgment, including the assessment of the risks of material misstatement of the financial statements, whether due to fraud or error. An audit also includes evaluating the appropriateness of accounting policies used and the reasonableness of accounting estimates made by management, as well as evaluating the overall presentation of the financial statements.

Because of the inherent limitations of an audit, together with the inherent limitations of internal control, an unavoidable risk that some material misstatements may not be detected exists, even though the audit is properly planned and performed in accordance with GAAS.

In making our risk assessments, we consider internal control relevant to the entity's preparation and fair presentation of the financial statements in order to design audit procedures that are appropriate in the circumstances, but not for the purpose of expressing an opinion on the effectiveness of the entity's internal control. However, we will communicate to you in writing concerning any significant deficiencies and material weaknesses in internal control relevant to the audit of the financial statements that we have identified during the audit.

[*Management's responsibilities and identification of the applicable financial reporting framework*]

Our audit will be conducted on the basis that management and, where appropriate, those charged with governance acknowledge and understand that they have responsibility:

a. For the preparation and fair presentation of the financial statements in accordance with accounting principles generally accepted in the United States;

b. For the design, implementation, and maintenance of internal control relevant to the preparation and fair presentation of financial statements that are free from material misstatement, whether due to fraud or error; and

c. To provide us with:

   i. Access to all information of which management is aware that is relevant to the preparation and fair presentation of the financial statements such as records, documentation, and other matters;

   ii. Additional information that we may request from management for the purpose of the audit; and

   iii. Unrestricted access to persons within the entity from whom we determine it necessary to obtain audit evidence.

As part of our audit process, we will request from management and, where appropriate, those charged with governance, written confirmation concerning representations made to us in connection with the audit.

[*Other relevant information*]

[*Insert other information, such as fee arrangements, billings and other specific terms, as appropriate.*]

[Reporting]

[*Insert appropriate reference to the expected form and content of the auditor's report. Example follows:*]

We will issue a written report upon completion of our audit of Averroes Company's financial statements. Our report will be addressed to the board of directors of Averroes Company. We cannot provide assurance that an unqualified opinion will be expressed. Circumstances may arise in which it is necessary for us to modify our opinion, add an emphasis of matter or other matter paragraph(s), or withdraw from the engagement.

We will also issue a written report on [*Insert appropriate reference to other auditor's reports expected to be issued*] upon completion of our audit.

Please sign and return the attached copy of this letter to indicate your acknowledgement of, and agreement with, the arrangements for our audit of the financial statements including our respective responsibilities.

Averroes Company

Acknowledged and agreed on behalf of Averroes Company by

(signed)

Name and Title:

Date:

EXHIBIT AU-C 210-2—PROSPECTIVE CLIENT EVALUATION FORM

Exhibit AU-C 210-2 is a prospective client evaluation form that can be helpful in determining whether a client should be accepted. Once a client is accepted, the form can be used as an integral part of the planning of the accepted engagement.

Use this form to document the evaluation of a prospective client who has requested audited financial statements. The memo format is only a guide. The auditor should exercise professional judgment to determine how the form should by modified by adding, deleting, or revising captions to the memo format.

The evaluation process does not imply that our firm is vouching for the integrity or reliability of the prospective client.

Name of Prospective Client: _____

Date of Financial Statements: _____

1. Describe how contact was established with the prospective client.

_____

_____

_____

2. Provide a background of the principals that represent the client.

_____

_____

_____

3. Describe the nature of the products and/or services provided by the prospective client.

_____

_____

_____

4. Describe the services and dates of services provided by the predecessor CPA.

_____

_____

_____

5. Explain the reason(s) why the prospective client has decided to seek the services of another CPA.

_____

_____

_____

6. Summarize the explanation for the change of accountants as understood by the predecessor CPA. (If the predecessor CPA firm has not been contacted, provide the reason that contact was not made.)

_____

_____

_____

7. Summarize the history of the prospective client and other CPA firms (other than the predecessor CPA firm) that have provided service for the past 10 years.

_____

_____

_____

8. Explain why the client desires audited financial statements, and identify external parties who may rely on the statements.

_____

_____

_____

9. Describe any litigation that the client and its principals have been involved in during the past 5 years.

_____

_____

_____

10. Summarize information obtained from credit bureaus, etc., concerning the credit rating of the client and its principals.

_____

_____

_____

11. Other information: _____

_____

_____

Prepared By: _____

Date: _____

Client Accepted (Yes or No): _____

Acceptance Date: _____

Signature of CPA: _____

SECTION 220

QUALITY CONTROL FOR AN ENGAGEMENT CONDUCTED IN ACCORDANCE WITH GENERALLY ACCEPTED AUDITING STANDARDS

Authoritative Pronouncements

SAS-122—Statements on Auditing Standards: Clarification and Recodification

SQCS-8 — A Firm's System of Quality Control (Redrafted)

Overview

AU-C 220 provides auditors with guidance regarding their responsibilities for quality control procedures in audits of financial statements, engagement quality control reviews, and other engagements conducted in accordance with generally accepted auditing standards (GAAS).

OBSERVATION: AU-C 220 is applicable to auditors in government audit organizations who perform financial audits in accordance with GAAS.

According to Statement on Quality Control Standards (SQCS) No. 8, *A Firm's System of Quality Control,* an accounting firm should adopt a system of quality controls to provide reasonable assurance that the firm and its personnel comply with professional standards and applicable legal and regulatory requirements and the reports issued by the firm or engagement partners are appropriate in the circumstances. Quality control standards relate to the conduct of a firm's audit practice, and those quality control standards should be implemented for each audit to provide the auditor with reasonable assurance at the engagement level as well. The engagement team may rely on the firm's quality control system unless the engagement partner determines it is inappropriate to do so based on available information.

SQCS-7 notes that the firm's system of quality control should include policies and procedures addressing each of the following elements:

- Leadership responsibilities for quality within the firm (the "tone at the top")
- Relevant ethical requirements
- Acceptance and continuance of client relationships and specific engagements
- Human resources
- Engagement performance
- Monitoring

PUBLIC COMPANY IMPLICATION: PCAOB Auditing Standard (AS) No. 7, *Engagement Quality Review,* establishes quality review standards for audits of public companies. Unlike the concurring review requirement adopted by the PCAOB as part of its interim standards, which only pertained to firms that were members of the AICPA's SECPS, AS 7 applies to all firms registered with the PCAOB. In addition to applying to audits performed under PCAOB standards, the proposed standard would also apply to reviews. However, the procedures required to be performed by the engagement quality reviewer for a review of interim financial information would be more limited. For all such engagements, an engagement review would be required to be conducted before the report is issued. The engagement reviewer would be required to be a partner of the firm performing the engagement, another person in an equivalent position in the firm, or an individual outside the firm who is associated with a registered public accounting firm. The engagement reviewer would be required to have competence, independence, integrity, and objectivity. He or she would be required to have the level of competence needed to have an overall responsibility for a comparable engagement. To maintain objectivity, the engagement reviewer would not be permitted to make decisions for the engagement team, supervise the team, or assume responsibilities of the team. Certain review procedures are required on every audit engagement, and review procedures generally involve discussions with engagement personnel and review of documents. Review procedures must be performed with due professional care and professional skepticism. Required engagement quality review procedures are more limited when the service being reviewed is an interim review. In addition, the engagement quality reviewer would be required to review documentation in the areas that he or she reviewed. The engagement quality reviewer would be required to assess whether this documentation indicates that the engagement team responded appropriately to significant risks and whether the documentation supports conclusions reached by the engagement team. The engagement quality reviewer must adequately document his or her review procedures. Finally, the firm would not be permitted to issue its report (or communicate its conclusion to the client if no report was to be issued) until the engagement quality reviewer granted his or her concurring approval.

The AICPA Professional Issues Task Force published Practice Alert No. 01-1, *Common Peer Review Recommendations,* which identifies common peer review findings that are helpful to professionals as they consider critical and significant issues in planning and performing audits. The issues are grouped in the following categories: (1) implementation of new professional standards or pronouncements, (2) application of GAAP pertaining to equity transactions, (3) application of GAAP pertaining to revenue recognition considerations, (4) documentation of audit procedures and audit findings, and (5) miscellaneous findings. Practice Alerts can be downloaded from the AICPA website (http://www.aicpa.org).

Definitions

Engagement partner	The partner or other person in the firm who is responsible for the audit engagement, its performance, and the auditor's report issued by the firm and who has the appropriate authority from any required professional, legal, or regulatory bodies.
Engagement quality control review	A process designed to provide an objective evaluation before the report release date of the significant judgments made and conclusions reached by the engagement team in formulating the auditor's report. This process is only for those audit engagements for which the firm has determined an engagement quality control review is required.
Engagement quality control reviewer	A partner, staff member, suitably qualified external person, or a team of such people, none of whom are part of the engagement team, with sufficient and appropriate experience and authority to objectively evaluate the significant judgments made and the conclusions reached by the engagement team in formulating the auditor's report.
Engagement team	All partners or staff performing the engagement and any individuals, except for external specialists, engaged by the firm or a network firm who perform audit procedures on the engagement.
Firm	A form of organization permitted by law or regulation whose characteristics conform to resolutions of the Council of the AICPA and that practices public accounting.
Monitoring	An ongoing process of considering and evaluating the firm's system of quality control, including inspection or a periodic review of engagement documentation, reports, and clients' financial statements for a selection of completed engagements, designed to provide the firm with reasonable assurance that its system of quality control is designed appropriately and operating effectively.
Network firm	A firm or other entity that belongs to a network as defined below.
Network	An association of entities that includes at least one firm that cooperate for the purpose of enhancing the firms' ability to provide professional services and that share at least one of the following characteristics: (1) use of a common brand name; (2) common control among the firms through ownership, management, or some other means; (3) profits or costs, excluding the costs of operating the network; (4) costs of developing audit methodologies, manuals, and training; (5) common business strategy, including accountability for performance related to the strategy; (6) significant professional resources; and (7) required common quality control procedures.
Partner	Any individual with authority to bind the firm in the performance of a professional services engagement. This may include an employee who has not assumed the benefits and risks of ownership.
Personnel	Partners and staff.
Professional standards	Standards established by bodies that set auditing and attest standards applicable to the engagement being performed and relevant ethical requirements.

Relevant ethical requirements	Ethical requirements the engagement team and engagement quality control reviewer are subject to, consisting of the AICPA Code of Professional Conduct and the more restrictive rules of applicable state boards of accountancy and applicable regulatory agencies.
Staff	Professionals other than partners, including any specialists employed by the firm.
Suitably qualified external person	An individual outside the firm with the competence and capabilities to act as an engagement partner (for example, a partner of another firm).

Requirements

The auditor is presumptively required to perform the following procedures regarding quality control procedures for financial statement audits:

Engagement Partner Responsibilities

1. Take responsibility for the overall quality on each assigned audit engagement. Certain procedures may be delegated to engagement team members, their work may be used, and the firm's quality control system may be relied upon.

2. Observe and inquire as necessary throughout the audit for evidence of noncompliance with relevant ethical requirements by engagement team members.

3. If the engagement partner becomes aware that engagement team members have not complied with relevant ethical requirements, consult with others in the firm to determine the appropriate action.

4. Form a conclusion on compliance with independence requirements relevant to the audit engagement and, in doing so:

   a. Obtain relevant information from the firm and network firms (as applicable) to identify and evaluate circumstances and relationships that threaten independence

   b. Evaluate information on any identified breaches of the firm's independence policies and procedures to determine whether they threaten independence

   c. Take appropriate action to eliminate or reduce threats to independence to an acceptable level by applying safeguards or withdrawing from the engagement if appropriate and possible under law or regulation. Promptly report any inability to resolve the matter to the firm so the firm may take appropriate action.

5. Determine that appropriate procedures regarding client and audit engagement acceptance and continuance have been followed and that the conclusions reached are appropriate.

6. If the engagement partner obtains information that would have caused the firm to decline the audit engagement had the information been available, promptly communicate that information to the firm so the firm and engagement partner can take the necessary action.

7. Determine that the engagement team and any auditor's specialists have the appropriate competence and capabilities to (1) perform the audit engagement in accordance with professional standards and applicable legal and regulatory requirements and (2) enable an auditor's report to be issued that is appropriate in the circumstances.

8. Take responsibility for (1) the direction, supervision, and performance of the audit engagement in compliance with professional standards, applicable legal and regulatory requirements, and the firm's policies and procedures and (2) the auditor's report being appropriate in the circumstances.

9. Take responsibility for reviews being performed in accordance with the firm's review policies and procedures.

10. On or before the date of the auditor's report, review the audit documentation and talk with the engagement team to determine that sufficient appropriate audit evidence has been obtained to support the conclusions reached and for the auditor's report to be issued.

11. With regards to consultations:

   a. Take responsibility for the engagement team consulting as appropriate on difficult or contentious matters.

   b. Determine that the engagement team consulted appropriately during the engagement, both within the team and between the team and others inside or outside the firm.

   c. Determine that the party consulted agreed with the nature and scope of consultations and understood the conclusions resulting from the consultations.

   d. Determine that the conclusions resulting from consultations have been implemented.

12. For any audit engagements requiring an engagement quality control review:

   a. Determine that an engagement quality control reviewer has been appointed.

   b. Discuss significant findings or issues arising during the audit engagement or the engagement quality control review with the engagement quality control reviewer.

   c. Do not release the auditor's report until the completion of the engagement quality control review.

Engagement Quality Control Reviewer Responsibilities

13. Objectively evaluate the significant judgments made and conclusions reached by the engagement team in formulating the auditor's report. This evaluation should involve:

   a. Discussion of significant findings or issues with the engagement partner

   b. Review of the financial statements and the proposed auditor's report

   c. Review of selected audit documentation relating to the significant judgments made and conclusions reached by the engagement team

   d. Evaluation of the conclusions reached in formulating the auditor's report and consideration of whether the proposed auditor's report is appropriate

Differences of Opinion

14. If differences of opinion arise within the engagement team with those consulted or between the engagement partner and the engagement quality control reviewer where applicable, the firm's policies and procedures for resolving differences of opinion should be followed by the engagement team.

Monitoring

15. With regards to the monitoring process, the engagement partner should consider:

   a. The results of the firm's monitoring process based on the latest information the engagement partner received from the firm and other network firms (as applicable)

   b. Whether noted deficiencies in that information may affect the audit engagement

Documentation

16. The following audit documentation should be included:

   a. Issues identified regarding compliance with relevant ethical requirements and their resolution

   b. Conclusions on compliance with independence requirements relevant to the audit engagement and any relevant discussions with the firm supporting these conclusions

   c. Conclusions regarding client and audit engagement acceptance and continuance

   d. The nature, scope, and conclusions of consultations during the audit engagement

17. For an engagement quality control review, the engagement quality control reviewer should document:

   a. The performance of procedures required by the firm's policies on engagement quality control review

   b. The date that the engagement quality control review was completed

   c. That the reviewer is unaware of any unresolved matters that would cause the reviewer to believe that the significant judgments made and conclusions reached by the engagement team were inappropriate

Analysis and Application of Procedures

Engagement Partner Responsibilities

Audit quality responsibilities

By taking responsibility for the overall quality on an audit engagement, the engagement partner emphasizes that quality is essential to performing audit engagements and, more specifically, to:

- Performing work that complies with professional standards and legal and regulatory requirements

- Complying with applicable firm quality control policies and procedures

- Issuing auditor's reports appropriate to the circumstances

- The engagement team's ability to raise concerns without fear of reprisal

Relevant ethical requirements

In considering relevant ethical requirements, the engagement partner may look to the fundamental principles of professional ethics established by the AICPA Code of Professional Conduct: responsibilities, the public interest, integrity, objectivity and independence, and due care.

The engagement partner must form a conclusion regarding compliance with independence requirements relevant to the audit engagement. If threats to independence are identified that cannot be reduced to an acceptable level, appropriate action may involve eliminating the activity or interest that creates the threat or withdrawing from the engagement if possible under law or regulation.

Client and audit engagement acceptance and continuance

Information such as the following can assist the engagement partner in determining whether conclusions regarding client and audit engagement acceptance and continuance are appropriate:

- The integrity of the entity's principal owners, key management, and those charged with governance
- Whether the engagement team is competent and has the necessary capabilities, time, and resources to perform the audit engagement
- Whether the firm and engagement team can comply with relevant ethical requirements
- The implications of significant findings or issues arising during the current or previous audit engagement on relationship continuance

Engagement team assignment

The engagement partner may determine the capabilities and competence of the engagement team as a whole, by considering factors such as the team's:

- Understanding and practical experience with similar audit engagements
- Understanding of professional standards, legal and regulatory requirements, and the firm's quality control policies and procedures
- Technical expertise, including IT and other specialized areas of accounting and auditing
- Knowledge of the client's industry
- Ability to apply professional judgment

Engagement performance

The engagement partner takes responsibility for the direction, supervision, performance, and review of the audit engagement. To direct the engagement team, that engagement partner may inform the team of matters such as the following:

- Team member responsibilities, including the need to comply with relevant ethical requirements and to plan and perform the audit with professional skepticism
- Responsibilities of each partner involved in the audit engagement
- Objectives of the work to be performed
- Nature of the entity's business
- Risk-related issues
- Problems that may arise
- The detailed approach to performance of the engagement

Supervision of the engagement team may involve tracking audit engagement progress; considering the competence and capabilities of individual team members; identifying matters for consultation or consideration by qualified engagement team members; and addressing significant findings or issues arising during the audit engagement, considering their significance, and appropriately modifying the planned approach

Review responsibilities and procedures are determined based on the guidance in SQCS-8 that suitably experienced team members review the work of other team members and involve consideration of whether:

- Work was performed according to professional, legal, and regulatory requirements

- Significant findings or issues for further consideration were raised

- Appropriate consultations occurred and their conclusions were documented and implemented

- The nature, timing, and extent of work performed was appropriate, does not need to be revised, supports the conclusions reached, and was appropriately documented

- Evidence obtained is sufficient and appropriate to support the auditor's report

- Objectives of the engagement procedures were achieved

The engagement partner may review items relating to critical areas of judgment, significant risks, or other areas the partner considers important to ensure significant findings and issues are resolved on or before the date of the auditor's report. If an engagement partner takes over during an audit, in order to assume the necessary responsibilities, he or she may apply these review procedures to the work performed up to the date of change.

PLANNING AID REMINDER: The engagement partner may, but is not required to, review all audit documentation. The partner is required to document the extent and timing of the reviews.

Direction, supervision, and review of an engagement team member with specialized expertise may include agreeing to the nature, scope, and objectives of that member's work; the respective roles of that member and the rest of the team; the nature, timing, and extent of communication between that member and the rest of the team; and evaluating the adequacy, relevance, reasonableness, and consistency of that member's work and findings with other audit evidence.

Consultations

Engagement team members have a professional responsibility to bring difficult or contentious matters that may require consultation to the attention of the appropriate personnel. Consultations will be most effective when those consulted have the appropriate knowledge, authority, and experience and are given the relevant facts to enable them to provide informed advice. The engagement team may consult with those outside the firm if the firm lacks appropriate internal resources.

Engagement Quality Control Review

The engagement quality control review should be completed before the auditor's report is released; however, review documentation may be completed after the report release date as part of final audit file assembly. If the review is completed after the date of the auditor's report and identifies the need for additional procedures or evidence, the report date is changed to the date when those additional procedures are completed or the additional evidence is obtained.

The engagement partner, by remaining alert to changes in circumstances, can identify situations where an engagement quality control review becomes necessary during the course of the engagement. For some firms, none of the firm's audit engagements may meet the criteria that would require an engagement quality control review.

OBSERVATION: The engagement partner's responsibilities for the audit engagement and its performance are not reduced by the performance of an engagement quality control review.

An engagement quality control review's extent may vary depending on audit complexity and the risk of an inappropriate auditor's report and may include consideration of matters such as:

- Significant risks identified during the audit and responses to those risks, including fraud risk
- Judgments made, especially regarding materiality and significant risks
- The significance and handling of misstatements identified during the audit
- Matters to be communicated to management, those charged with governance, and regulatory bodies where applicable
- The engagement team's evaluation of the firm's independence for purposes of the audit
- Whether appropriate consultations took place on matters involving differences of opinion or other difficult or contentious matters and the conclusions of these consultations
- Whether audit documentation reviewed reflects the work performed related to significant judgments and supports the conclusions reached

Monitoring

When considering whether deficiencies in monitoring affect the audit engagement, the engagement partner may determine that measures the firm took to resolve the deficiency are sufficient in the context of the audit.

OBSERVATION: AU-C 220 points out that if a firm is found to have deficiencies in its system of quality control or violates specific policies or controls, it does not mean that a particular audit engagement was not performed in accordance with generally accepted auditing standards or that the auditor's report was not appropriate.

SECTION 230

AUDIT DOCUMENTATION

Authoritative Pronouncements

SAS-122—Statements on Auditing Standards: Clarification and Recodification

Overview

Audit documentation (working papers) should (1) support the auditor's representation that the engagement has been planned and performed in accordance with GAAS and applicable legal and regulatory requirements and (2) substantiate the type of audit report (such as an unqualified or qualified opinion) issued. However, the specific type, content, and extent of documentation is to some degree dependent upon the characteristics of the particular engagement and the audit methodology employed. The specific nature of the audit documentation is a matter of the auditor's professional judgment.

The auditor must prepare audit documentation for each engagement in sufficient detail for an experienced auditor with no previous involvement with the engagement to understand the following:

- The nature, timing, and extent of audit procedures performed

- The results of the audit tests performed and the evidence collected

- Conclusions drawn on significant matters and significant professional judgments made in reaching these conclusions

Definitions

Audit documentation	Record of audit procedure performed, relevant audit evidence obtained, and conclusions the auditor reached. Also called working papers or workpapers.
Audit file	One or more folders or other storage media, in physical or electronic form, containing the records that constitute the audit documentation for a specific engagement.
Documentation completion date	Date, no later than 60 days following the report release date, on which the auditor has assembled for retention a complete and final set of documentation in the audit file.
Experienced auditor	An individual (whether internal or external to the firm) who has practical audit experience and a reasonable understanding of audit processes, GAAS and applicable legal and regulatory requirements, the business environment in which the entity operates, and auditing and financial reporting issues relevant to the entity's industry. (Practical audit experience does not mean the auditor is required to have performed comparable audits.)
Report release date	Date the auditor grants the entity permission to use the auditor's report in connection with the financial statements.

Requirements

The auditor is required to perform the following procedures related to audit documentation:

Timely Preparation of Audit Documentation

1. Prepare audit documentation on a timely basis.

Documentation of Audit Procedures Performed and Audit Evidence Obtained

2. Prepare audit documentation sufficient to enable an experienced auditor with no previous connection to the audit to understand (a) the nature, timing, and extent of the audit procedures performed to comply with GAAS and applicable legal and regulatory requirements; (b) the results of audit procedures performed and the audit evidence obtained; and (c) conclusions reached on significant audit findings and significant professional judgments made in reaching those conclusions.

3. To document the nature, timing, and extent of audit procedures performed, record (a) the identifying characteristics of the specific items or matters tested, (b) who performed the audit work and the date work was completed, and (c) who reviewed the audit work and the date and extent of the review.

4. Include in the audit documentation abstracts or copies of significant contracts or agreements that were inspected during the audit.

5. Document discussions of significant findings with management, those charged with governance, and others. Include the nature of the findings discussed, and when and with whom the discussions occurred.

6. If information was identified that is inconsistent with the auditor's final conclusion regarding a significant finding, document how the inconsistency was addressed.

7. Document the justification for any departure from a relevant presumptively mandatory requirement. Also document how the alternative audit procedures performed were sufficient to achieve the intent of that requirement.

8. Additional documentation is required for matters arising after the date of the auditor's report. Document (a) the circumstances encountered; (b) new or additional audit procedures performed, audit evidence obtained, conclusions reached, and their effect on the audit report; and (c) when and by who changes to the audit documentation were made and reviewed.

Assembly and Retention of the Final Audit File

9. Document the report release date in the audit documentation.

10. Complete the administrative process of assembling the final audit file on a timely basis, no later than the documentation completion date (i.e., no later than 60 days following the report release date).

11. Do not discard any audit documentation after the documentation completion date before the end of the specified retention period, a minimum of five years from the report release date.

12. If audit documentation needs to be modified or added to after the documentation completion date, document the specific reasons for making the changes and when and by whom the changes were made and reviewed.

Analysis and Application of Procedures

Timely preparation of audit documentation

Timely preparation of audit documentation enhances audit quality and facilitates the effective review and evaluation of audit evidence obtained and conclusions reached before the auditor's report is finalized.

PLANNING AID REMINDER: The report release date is often the date the auditor delivers the audit report to the entity. However, when there are delays in releasing the report, the auditor may become aware of a fact that might have affected the audit report if it was known. AU-C 561 addresses the auditor's responsibilities in such circumstances.

Documentation of audit procedures performed and audit evidence obtained

Sufficiency of audit documentation for an experienced auditor

The form, content, and extent of audit documentation will vary, and the following factors should be considered:

- Size and complexity of the entity
- Identified risks of material misstatement
- Degree of professional judgment required to perform the procedures and evaluate the results
- Nature of audit procedures used
- Significance of the audit evidence obtained
- Nature and extent of identified exceptions
- Need to document a conclusion (or the basis for a conclusion) that is not evident from reviewing the documentation of the work performed
- Audit methodology and tools used

Audit documentation (which may be in hard-copy form, electronic form, or other medium) developed for an engagement should demonstrate that the three standards of fieldwork were satisfied. The documentation generally includes the following:

- Audit plans
- Analyses
- Issues memoranda
- Confirmation letters
- A representation letter
- Checklists
- Correspondence concerning and summaries of significant findings or issues
- Abstracts/copies of entity documents (including significant contracts or agreements that support the accounting for specific transactions)

The auditor is not required to include items such as superseded, incomplete, corrected, or duplicate documents in the audit documentation. The auditor also cannot rely on oral explanations to support the work performed or the conclusions reached, although oral explanations can supplement the audit documentation.

Compliance with AU-C 230 will generally result in sufficient, appropriate audit documentation; however, other AU-C sections contain specific documentation requirements applicable to particular circumstances (see Exhibit AU-C 230-1). Audit documentation serves to provide evidence that the audit complies with GAAS. However, the auditor is not required to document every matter considered during the audit. Furthermore, the auditor is not required to separately document compliance for matters for which the existing audit documentation demonstrates compliance; for example:

- An audit plan demonstrates the auditor has planned the audit
- A signed engagement letter demonstrates the auditor's agreement to the terms of the audit engagement with management or those charged with governance
- A qualified auditor's report demonstrates compliance with GAAS requirements to express a qualified opinion

There are various ways compliance with general audit requirements can be demonstrated. For example, professional skepticism may be documented by evidence of specific procedures performed to corroborate management's responses to the auditor's inquiries. Engagement partner responsibility for the direction, supervision, and performance of the audit in compliance with GAAS may be documented by the partner's involvement in team discussions about the susceptibility of the entity's financial statements to material misstatements.

Significant audit findings or issues encountered during an engagement should be documented. The following are examples of significant findings or issues:

- Significant matters related to the selection, application, and consistency of significant accounting practices, particularly related to accounting for complex or unusual transactions and the accounting for items dependent on estimates, uncertainties, and management assumptions
- Matters leading to significant risks
- The results of audit procedures suggesting that the financial statements could be materially misstated
- The results of audit procedures suggesting a need to revise the auditor's assessment of and response to the risks of material misstatement
- The application of required audit procedures was difficult
- Findings that could lead to a modification of the standard auditor's report

The form, content, and extent of audit documentation regarding significant findings will vary depending on the extent of professional judgment exercised. It is appropriate for the auditor to document professional judgments when the findings, issues, and judgments are significant, as in the following circumstances:

- When considering information or factors that should be considered and the consideration is significant
- When concluding as to the reasonableness of areas of subjective judgments
- When concluding as the a document's authenticity when conditions caused the auditor to believe the document may not be authentic

---

ENGAGEMENT STRATEGY: The auditor may find it helpful to prepare a completion memorandum, or summary of the significant issues or findings identified during the audit and how they were addressed. This summary can facilitate effective and efficient reviews and inspections of the audit documentation as well as help the auditor identify any AU-C section objectives not being achieved that could prevent him or her from achieving the overall objectives of the auditor.

In auditing smaller, less complex entities, audit documentation will generally be less extensive. However, documentation should still be sufficient for an experienced auditor to determine if a GAAS audit was performed, because the audit may be subject to external review.

Identification of items tested and of the preparer and reviewer

Documenting the identifying characteristics of items tested improves the auditor's ability to review and supervise work performed and to investigate exceptions and inconsistencies. For example, if 50 payroll transactions are tested as part of the tests of controls, the audit documentation must specifically identify which 50 items were tested possibly by listing the payroll check numbers. Likewise, if accounts are confirmed as part of the audit of receivables, the specific accounts confirmed must be documented.

PLANNING AID REMINDER: In some instances it is not necessary to specifically list each item tested. For example, if systematic sampling is used it is sufficient to identify the starting point and the sampling interval. However, the method of documentation must enable an experienced auditor to reconstruct which specific sample items were tested as part of the engagement.

The requirement for documenting who reviewed audit work and the date and extent of the review does not require each individual working paper to contain evidence of its review. What must be documented is what audit work was reviewed, who reviewed the work, and when it was reviewed.

Documentation of discussions of significant findings

Documentation of discussions of significant findings with management, those charged with governance, or other personnel within or external to the entity such as those providing professional advice, is not limited to auditor-prepared documentation. Documentation may include documents such as entity-prepared minutes of meetings if they provide an appropriate record of the discussion.

Documentation of inconsistencies

Documentation of information identified that is inconsistent with the auditor's final conclusion may include procedures performed and documentation of consultations or resolutions of differences in professional judgment among the engagement team or between the engagement team and others consulted.

ENGAGEMENT STRATEGY: Documentation as discussed in AU-C 230 is essential in supporting an auditor against claims of malpractice. Auditors should ensure that their audit procedures, results, and conclusions are well documented and carefully reviewed. Such steps are an important part of minimizing liability risk.

Documentation of departure from a relevant requirement

GAAS requires the auditor to comply with requirements that are relevant to the audit. Accordingly, the auditor is only required to document departure from relevant requirements. Requirements are not relevant in cases where (1) the AU-C section is not relevant or (2) the requirement is conditional and the condition does not exist.

Matters arising after the date of the auditor's report

Circumstances in which the auditor performs audit procedures or draws new conclusions after the date of his or her report are rare, but they do occur. Such circumstances include when the auditor becomes aware of facts that existed at the date of his or her report that might have caused the opinion in the report to be modified or the financial statements to be amended or when the auditor concludes necessary audit procedures were omitted.

Assembly and retention of the final audit file

Assembly of the audit file on a timely basis

While 60 days is the normal period of time auditors have to complete assembling the audit file, auditors may have fewer than 60 days to complete this process due to statutes, regulations, or the firm's quality control policies. Prior to the documentation completion date, the auditor may change the audit documentation to

- Complete the documentation and assembly of the audit evidence that was gathered prior to the date of the auditor's report
- Assemble the audit file (e.g., delete or discard superseded documentation and cross-reference working papers)
- Sign off on file completion checklists
- Add information to the file received after the date of the auditor's report (e.g., an original of a confirmation that was previously faxed)

ENGAGEMENT STRATEGY: The auditor is required to document auditor independence and staff training. The most efficient means of documenting these items may be centrally within the firm, although the firm can choose to include the documentation at the engagement level.

Retention of the audit file

Audit documentation should be retained for a period of time that is sufficient to meet the quality control policies of the CPA firm, and any applicable legal or regulatory requirements, which may in some instances specify retention periods longer than five years.

PUBLIC COMPANY IMPLICATIONS: The Sarbanes-Oxley Act of 2002 (SOX) required the PCAOB to adopt an auditing standard that requires auditors to prepare and maintain audit documentation for a period of at least seven years. The nature and extent of documentation retained must be in sufficient detail to support the auditor's conclusions. SOX makes the knowing and willful destruction of audit documentation within the seven-year period a criminal offense. The PCAOB's AS-3 (Audit Documentation) contains the audit documentation requirements applicable to audits of public companies. The PCAOB states that a failure to prepare adequate audit documentation is serious, and inadequate audit documentation in a high-risk area is a *very serious* (authors' emphasis) violation of PCAOB standards. The PCAOB also states that an oral explanation of audit procedures without written documentary evidence is insufficient. In addition, audit documentation should be prepared at the time the audit procedure is performed. Failure to maintain sufficient documentation leads to the presumption that the procedures were not applied, the evidence was not obtained, and the conclusions reached lacked adequate support. AU-C 230 bears many similarities to AS-3.

Audit documentation is the property of the auditor. The auditor may at his or her option make available to the client copies of the audit documentation as long as the effectiveness and integrity of the audit process is not compromised. In addition, governmental regulators may have a right to the audit documentation based on law, regulation, or the audit contract. When regulators request access to audit documentation, the auditor should consider the following guidance:

- Consider notifying the client that regulators have requested access to the audit documentation, and state that the auditor intends to comply with the request.

- Make arrangements (time, date, place, etc.) with the regulators concerning access to the audit documentation.

- Establish procedures that allow the auditor to maintain control over the audit documentation.

In addition to the above procedures, the auditor should consider sending a letter to the regulatory agency (probably requesting a signed acknowledgment of receipt of the letter) that explains the role of the auditor and the nature of the audit documentation. (Exhibit AU-C 230-2 is an example of such a letter.) The auditor should not agree to transfer the ownership of the audit documentation to the regulatory agency.

When a regulatory agency requests the auditor's audit documentation but there is no legal basis for the request (no applicable law, regulation, or audit contract requirement), the auditor should evaluate the purpose for the request.

That evaluation should include consultation with legal counsel. If the auditor agrees with the request, the auditor should obtain permission for access to the audit documentation from the client (preferably in writing). In some instances the client may request an inspection of the audit documentation before granting the regulatory agency access to it. If the auditor agrees to the client's request, the auditor should maintain control over the audit documentation.

Some regulatory agencies may hire a third party to inspect audit documentation. Under this circumstance, the auditor should follow the same procedures that would apply if the regulatory agency itself were inspecting the audit documentation. In addition, the auditor should obtain from the regulatory agency a statement (preferably in writing) that the third party is "acting on behalf of the regulator and agreement from the third party that he or she is subject to the same restriction on disclosure and use of audit documentation and the information contained therein as the regulator."

> **OBSERVATION:** The guidance in this section does not apply to requests from (1) the Internal Revenue Service, (2) peer review programs (and similar programs) established by the AICPA or state societies of CPAs, (3) proceedings arising from alleged violations of ethical standards, or (4) subpoenas.

Modification of addition of audit documentation after the document completion date

The auditor may find it necessary to modify or add audit documentation after the documentation completion date to clarify existing audit documentation in response to comments received during monitoring inspections. All new documentation created, including notes made on preexisting documents, should be dated and initialed.

Practitioner's Aids

Exhibit AU-C 230-1 is a checklist for audit documentation required by various AU-C sections.

EXHIBIT AU-C 230-1—AU-Cs THAT IDENTIFY SPECIFIC AUDIT DOCUMENTATION REQUIREMENTS

Reference	Nature of Documentation
AU-C 210, *Terms of Engagement* (paragraphs .10, .13, and .16)	The agreed-upon terms of the engagement should be documented in the engagement letter or other suitable written agreement.
	For recurring engagements when the auditor concludes the terms of the preceding engagement do not need to be revised, the auditor should remind management and the terms and the reminder should be documented.
	When there are changes to the terms of the engagement, the new terms should be documented in an engagement letter or other suitable form of written agreement.

Reference	Nature of Documentation
AU-C 220, *Quality Control for an Engagement Conducted in Accordance with Generally Accepted Auditing Standards* (paragraphs .25 and .26)	Issues and conclusions reached related to compliance with ethical and independence requirements and acceptance and continuance of client relationships. The engagement quality reviewer should document that procedures required for the quality review have been performed, the date the review was completed, and that the reviewer is not aware of any unresolved matters that would cause him or her to believe that the significant judgments that the engagement team made and the conclusions it reached were not appropriate.
AU-C 240, *Consideration of Fraud in a Financial Statement Audit* (paragraphs .43-.46).	Document the audit team brainstorming discussion on fraud (when it occurred, who participated, what was discussed, conclusions reached). Procedures performed to identify and assess the risks of material misstatement due to fraud. Risks identified and the auditor's response (both the overall responses and responses at the assertion level). If revenue recognition is not identified as a risk factor, the reasons why. Results of procedures related to management override of controls. Other conditions or analytical procedures that led the auditor to perform additional auditing procedures. Fraud-related communications to management, the audit committee, and others.
AU-C 250, *Consideration of Laws and Regulations in an Audit of Financial Statements* (paragraph .28)	Description of the identified or suspected noncompliance with laws and regulations and the results of discussion with management, and those charged with governance.
AU-C 260, *The Auditor's Communication with Those Charged with Governance* (paragraph .20)	Required communications to those charged with governance about matters involving the auditor's responsibilities, the planned scope and timing of the audit, and significant audit findings.
AU-C 265, *Communicating Internal Control Related Matters Identified in an Audit* (paragraphs .11-.16)	Communication of significant deficiencies and material weaknesses in internal control made to management and those charged with governance.
AU-C 300, *Planning an Audit* (paragraph .14)	Document the overall audit strategy, the audit plan, and any significant changes made during the audit engagement to the overall audit strategy or to the audit plan.
AU-C 315, *Understanding the Entity and Its Environment and Assessing the Risks of Material Misstatement* (paragraph .33)	Audit team discussion of the susceptibility of the client's financial statements to error or fraud (when the discussion occurred, who participated, subjects discussed, and planned audit responses).

Reference	Nature of Documentation
	The auditor's understanding of the entity's environment and its internal control (including sources of information and risk assessment procedures).
	The auditor's assessment of the risk of material misstatement at the financial statement level and the assertion level and the auditor's basis for these assessments.
	Risks identified and evaluation of related controls.
AU-C 320, *Audit Risk and Materiality in Conducting an Audit* (paragraph .14)	Materiality for financial statements as a whole.
	Materiality level(s) for particular classes of transactions, account balances. or disclosures.
	Performance materiality.
AU-C 330, *Performing Audit Procedures in Response to Assessed Risks and Evaluating the Audit Evidence Obtained* (paragraphs .30-.33)	Overall audit response to the assessed risk of misstatement at the financial statement level.
	Nature, timing, and extent of further audit procedures performed.
	Linkage of procedures to risks at the assertion level.
	Results of audit procedures.
	Decision regarding the operating effectiveness of controls obtained in a prior audit and their use in the current audit.
	Determination not to use external confirmation procedures for accounts receivable when the account balance is material.
	Demonstrate that the financial statements agree or reconcile with the underlying accounting records.
AU-C 450, *Evaluation of Misstatements Identified during the Audit* (paragraph .12)	Amount below which misstatements would be regarded as clearly trivial.
	All misstatements accumulated during the audit and whether they have been corrected.
	The auditor's conclusion about whether uncorrected misstatements are material, individually or in the aggregate, and the basis for that conclusion.
AU-C 501, *Audit Evidence— Specific Considerations for Selected Items* (paragraph .20)	Basis for determination to not seek direct communication with the entity's legal counsel.

Reference	Nature of Documentation
AU-C 520, *Analytical Procedures* (paragraph .08)	When substantive analytical procedures are performed, document (1) expectations where not evident from work performed, (2) results of comparing expectations to recorded amounts or ratios computed, and (3) additional procedures (and their results) arising from identifying unexpected results.
AU-C 540, *Auditing Accounting Estimates, Including Fair Value Accounting Estimates, and Related Disclosures* (paragraph .22)	For those accounting estimates leading to significant risks, the basis for the auditor's conclusions about the reasonableness of accounting estimates and their disclosure.
	Indicators of possible management bias, if any.
AU-C 550, *Related Parties* (paragraph .28)	Names of identified related parties and the nature of the related-party relationships.
AU-C 570, *Going Concern* (paragraph .18)	Document (1) circumstances that raised substantial doubt about the entity's ability to continue as a going concern, (2) elements of management's plans the auditor considered significant in overcoming adverse conditions, (3) procedures performed to evaluate management's plans, (4) audit conclusions, and (5) the effect of the matter on the financial statements and the audit report.
AU-C 915, *Reports on Application of Requirements of an Applicable Financial Reporting Framework* (paragraph .13)	The reporting accountant's rationale for not consulting with the continuing accountant.
AU-C 930, *Interim Financial Information* (paragraphs .42-.43).	Documentation in support of the review of interim financial information, including • Nature, timing, and extent of procedures performed and results. • Results of review procedures performed and evidence obtained. • Findings or issues that may indicate that the interim financial information is materially misstated, the auditor's actions to address these findings, and the basis for the final conclusions reached.
AU-C 935, *Compliance Audits* (paragraphs .39-.42)	Document certain oral communications to management and the audit committee or its equivalent.

Exhibit AU-C 230-2 is an example of a letter that may be sent to a regulatory agency in response to its request for access to the auditor's documentation.

EXHIBIT AU-C 230-2—LETTER FOR REGULATORY AGENCY THAT REQUESTS ACCESS TO AUDIT DOCUMENTATION

Your representatives have requested access to our audit documentation in connection with our audit of the December 31, 20X8 financial statements of [*name of client*]. It is our understanding that the purpose of your request is [*state purpose: for example*, "to facilitate your regulatory examination"].

Our audit of [*name of client*]'s December 31, 20X8 financial statements was conducted in accordance with auditing standards generally accepted in the United States of America, the objective of which is to form an opinion as to whether the financial statements, which are the responsibility and representations of management, present fairly, in all material respects, the financial position, results of operations, and cash flows in conformity with generally accepted accounting principles. Under generally accepted auditing standards, we have the responsibility, within the inherent limitations of the auditing process, to design our audit to provide reasonable assurance that errors and fraud that have a material effect on the financial statements will be detected, and to exercise due care in the conduct of our audit. The concept of selective testing of the data being audited, which involved judgment both as to the number of transactions to be audited and as to the areas to be tested, has been generally accepted as a valid and sufficient basis for an audit to express an opinion on financial statements. Thus, our audit, based on the concept of selective testing, is subject to the inherent risk that material errors or fraud, if they exist, would not be detected. In addition, an audit does not address the possibility that material errors or fraud may occur in the future. Also, our use of professional judgment and the assessment of materiality for the purpose of our audit means that matters may have existed that would have been assessed differently by you.

The audit documentation was prepared for the purpose of providing the principal support for our report on [*name of client*]'s December 31, 20X8, financial statements and to aid in the conduct and supervision of our audit. The audit documentation is the principal record of auditing procedures performed, evidence obtained, and conclusions reached in the engagement. The auditing procedures that were performed were limited to those we considered necessary under generally accepted auditing standards to enable us to formulate and express an opinion on the financial statements taken as a whole. Accordingly, we make no representation as to the sufficiency or appropriateness, for your purposes, of either the information contained in our audit documentation or our auditing procedures. In addition, any notations, comments, and individual conclusions appearing on any of the audit documents do not stand alone, and should not be read as an opinion on any individual amounts, accounts, balances, or transactions.

Our audit of [*name of client*]'s December 31, 20X8, financial statement was performed for the purpose stated above and has not been planned or conducted in contemplation of your [*state purpose: for example*, "regulatory examination"] or for the purpose of assessing [*name of client*]'s compliance with laws and regulations. Therefore, items of possible interest to you may not have been specifically addressed. Accordingly, our audit and the audit documentation prepared in connection therewith, should not supplant other inquiries and procedures that should be undertaken by the [*name of regulatory agency*] for the purpose of monitoring and regulating the financial affairs of the [*name of client*]. In addition, we have not audited any financial statements of [*name of client*] since [*date of audited balance sheet referred to in the first paragraph above*] nor have we performed any auditing procedures since [*date*], the date of our auditor's report, and significant events or circumstances may have occurred since that date.

The audit documentation constitutes and reflects work performed or evidence obtained by [*name of auditor*] in its capacity as independent auditor for [*name of client*]. The documents contain trade secrets and confidential commercial and financial information of our firm and [*name of client*] that is privileged and confidential, and we expressly reserve all rights with respect to disclosures to third parties. Accordingly, we request confidential treatment under the Freedom of Information Act or similar laws and regulations when requests are made for the audit documentation or information contained therein or any derived there from. We further request that written notice be given to our firm before distribution of the information in the audit documentation [*or copies thereof*] to others, including other governmental agencies, except when such distribution is required by law or regulations. [*If it is expected that copies will be requested, add the following:* Any copies of our audit documentation that we agree to provide you will be identified as "Confidential Treatment Requested by [*name of auditor, address, and telephone number*]."]

The above illustrative letter should be appropriately modified to reflect the circumstances of the engagement. Some of the modifications that may be needed include the following:

- When the audit has been conducted in accordance with GAAS and other established auditing procedures (such as generally accepted governmental auditing standards), the letter should be appropriately modified.

- When the audit was conducted in accordance with the Single Audit Act of 1984, and other federal audit requirements, the letter should be modified to explain the object of the audit.

- When the letter is sent to the regulatory agency at the request of management (rather than by law, regulation, or audit contract), the letter should state that "the management of X Company has authorized us to provide you access to our audit documentation in order to facilitate your regulatory examination."

- When the financial statements are based on regulatory accounting principles, the letter should be appropriately modified.

- When the regulatory agency has asked for photocopies of the audit documentation, the letter should state that "any photocopies of our audit documentation we agree to provide you will be identified as 'Confidential Treatment Request by [*name of auditor, address, telephone number*].'"

- When the audit engagement has not been completed, the letter should be modified to describe that fact and to put the regulatory agency on guard that the workpapers may change based on the performance of additional audit procedures (generally, the auditor should not agree to supply the regulatory agency with incomplete audit documentation).

SECTION 240

CONSIDERATION OF FRAUD IN A FINANCIAL STATEMENT AUDIT

Authoritative Pronouncements

SAS-122—Statements on Auditing Standards: Clarification and Recodification

Overview

AU-C 240 states that an auditor "is responsible for obtaining reasonable assurance that the financial statements as a whole are free from material misstatement, whether caused by fraud or error." Auditing standards note that the presence of intent distinguishes errors and fraud. Unintentional misstatements are errors, whereas intentional misstatements are due to fraud. AU-C 240 states that the auditor "is concerned with fraud that causes a material misstatement in the financial statements" and identifies the two relevant types of fraud, namely (1) misstatements arising from fraudulent financial reporting and (2) misstatements arising from misappropriations of assets.

The risk of the auditor not detecting a material misstatement due to fraud is higher than the risk of not detecting a material misstatement due to error. This is because there are often attempts to conceal fraud and there may be collusion, making detection even more difficult. Management fraud is also more difficult to detect than employee fraud because of management's ability to manipulate procedures or override controls. Therefore, while obtaining reasonable assurance throughout the audit, the auditor is responsible for maintaining an attitude of professional skepticism.

The auditor has three main objectives when considering fraud in a financial statement audit: (1) to identify and assess the risk of material misstatement of the financial statement due to fraud, (2) to obtain sufficient appropriate audit evidence about the assessed risks of material misstatement due to fraud, through designing and implementing appropriate responses, and (3) to respond appropriately to identified or suspected fraud. Due to the inherent limitations of an audit, an unavoidable risk exists that some material misstatements of the financial statements may not be detected, even though the audit is properly planned and performed in accordance with GAAS.

PUBLIC COMPANY IMPLICATION: In 2010 the PCAOB issued eight auditing standards (AS-8 through AS-15) related to the auditor's assessment of and response to risk. The standards bear many similarities to the eight risk-assessment standards adopted by the Auditing Standards Board in 2006. The PCAOB's standards emphasize the importance of considering fraud risk in a financial statement audit, and they require the auditor to integrate his or her assessment of fraud risk into his or her general risk-assessment procedures. In particular, a discussion of fraud risk is contained in AS-8, AS-9, AS-12, AS-13, and AS-14. AS-12 and AS-13 provide the most detailed discussion of the auditor's responsibility in assessing and responding to fraud risk. Although there are a number of differences between the PCAOB's and ASB's risk standards, the risk-assessment concepts contained in the PCAOB standards should be familiar to most auditors. As is currently the case, audit risk is the risk that the auditor will issue an inappropriate opinion on financial statements that are materially misstated. The auditor is to reduce audit risk to a low level through the application of audit procedures. As a result, the amount of audit effort devoted to particular accounts, classes of transactions, and disclosures should vary based on their respective risk.

While AU-C 240 outlines the auditor's responsibilities to detect material misstatements due to fraud, it is important to remember that the primary responsibility for the prevention and detection of fraud rests with those charged with governance of the entity and management. Those charged with governance should consider the potential for override of internal controls or other inappropriate influence over the financial reporting process. Management should place a strong emphasis on fraud prevention and exhibit a strong commitment to creating a culture of honesty and ethical behavior.

Definitions

Fraud	An intentional act by one or more individuals among management, those charged with governance, employees, or third parties involving the use of deception that results in a misstatement in financial statements that are the subject of an audit.
Fraud risk factors	Events or conditions that indicate an incentive or pressure to perpetrate fraud, provide an opportunity to commit fraud, or indicate attitudes or rationalizations to justify a fraudulent action.

Requirements

The auditor is presumptively required to perform the following procedures in considering the possibility that fraud related to financial statements exists in an audit engagement:

Professional Skepticism

1. Maintain an attitude of professional skepticism throughout the audit. Recognize the possibility that a material misstatement due to fraud could exist regardless of past experience of the honesty and integrity of management and those charged with governance.

2. Records and documents may be accepted as genuine unless there are conditions leading the auditor to believe a document may not be authentic or may have undisclosed modified terms, in which case the auditor should investigate further.

3. Investigate further inconsistent or otherwise unsatisfactory responses to inquiries of management, those charged with governance, or others.

Discussion among the Engagement Team

4. Key engagement team members, including the engagement partner, should exchange ideas and discuss how and where the entity's financial statements may be susceptible to material misstatement due to fraud, how management could perpetrate and conceal fraudulent financial reporting, and how entity assets could be misappropriated. Emphasis should be placed on known external and internal fraud risk factors affecting the entity, the risk of management override of controls, circumstances that might be indicative of earnings management or manipulation of other financial measures, the importance of maintaining professional skepticism throughout the audit, and how the auditor might respond to the susceptibility of the entity's financial statements to material misstatement due to fraud.

5. Communication about the risks of material misstatement due to fraud should continue among team members throughout the audit.

Risk Assessment Procedures and Related Activities

6. Inquire of management regarding its assessment of the risk that the financial statements may be materially misstated due to fraud; its process for identifying, responding to, and monitoring risks of fraud in the entity as well as any communication with those charged with governance regarding this process; and communication to employees regarding its views on business practices and ethical behavior.

7. Inquire of management and others within the entity as appropriate, including internal audit if it exists, to determine whether they have knowledge of any actual, suspected, or alleged fraud affecting the entity.

8. If there is an internal audit function, inquire whether it has performed any procedures to identify or detect fraud during the year, if management has responded satisfactorily to any findings of these procedures, and obtain its views about the risks of fraud.

9. Obtain an understanding of how those charged with governance exercise oversight of management's processes for identifying and responding to fraud risks and the internal control established to mitigate those risks (unless all of those charged with governance are involved with managing the entity).

10. Inquire of those charged with governance regarding their views about the risks of fraud and whether they have knowledge of any actual, suspected, or alleged fraud affecting the entity. These inquiries are made in part to corroborate management responses.

11. Evaluate analytical procedures performed as part of risk assessment procedures, including procedures relating to revenue accounts, to identify any unusual or unexpected relationships that indicate risks of material misstatement due to fraud.

12. Consider whether other information obtained indicates risks of material misstatement due to fraud.

13. Evaluate whether information obtained from the risk assessment procedures, including analytical procedures performed, and related activities performed indicate the presence of one or more fraud risk factors, because these may indicate risks of material misstatement due to fraud.

Identification and Assessment of Risks of Material Misstatement Due to Fraud

14. Identify and assess the risks of material misstatement due to fraud throughout the audit at the financial statement level, and at the assertion level for classes of transactions, account balances, and disclosures.

15. Presume that risks of fraud in revenue recognition exist and evaluate which revenue types, transactions, or assertions create these risks.

16. Treat assessed risks of material misstatement due to fraud as significant risks. Obtain an understanding of the entity's controls relevant to these risks and evaluate if the design and implementation of these controls mitigate fraud risks.

Responses to Assessed Risks of Material Misstatement Due to Fraud

17. Determine overall responses to address the assessed risks of material misstatement due to fraud at the financial statement level. In determining these responses, assign and supervise personnel considering their knowledge, skill, and abilities and the assessment of the risks of material misstatement due to fraud for the engagement; evaluate whether the entity's selection and application of accounting policies is indicative of fraudulent financial reporting; and incorporate an element of unpredictability in selecting the nature, timing, and extent of audit procedures.

18. Design and perform further audit procedures whose nature, timing, and extent are responsive to the assessed risks of material misstatement due to fraud at the assertion level.

19. Design and perform audit procedures responsive to the risks of management override of controls.

    a. Test the appropriateness of journal entries and adjustments by (1) obtaining an understanding of the entity's financial reporting process and controls as well as of control design and implementation; (2) inquiring about inappropriate or unusual activity of those involved in the financial reporting process; (3) considering fraud risk indicators, controls, the nature and complexity of accounts, and entries processed outside the normal course of business; (4) selecting entries and adjustments made at the end of a reporting period; and (5) considering the need to test entries and adjustments throughout the period.

    b. Review accounting estimates by evaluating whether management judgments in making estimates indicate a possible bias that may represent a risk of material misstatement due to fraud. If there is a possible bias, reevaluate accounting estimates taken as a whole and perform a retrospective review of management judgments related to significant and highly sensitive accounting estimates in the prior year's financial statements.

    c. Evaluate whether the business rationale of significant transactions outside the normal course of business or otherwise unusual transactions suggests the transactions may have been entered into to engage in fraud.

    d. Determine whether audit procedures other than those already identified need to be performed in order to respond to the identified risks of management override of controls.

Evaluation of Audit Evidence

20. Evaluate whether the results of audit procedures, including analytical procedures, indicate a previously unrecognized risk of material misstatement due to fraud. If not already performed, perform analytical procedures relating to revenue through the end of the reporting period to identify any unusual or unexpected relationships that indicate risks of material misstatement due to fraud at this time.

21. Evaluate whether identified misstatements are indicative of fraud. If misstatements do indicate fraud, evaluate the implications for other aspects of the audit, including the evaluation of materiality, management and employee integrity, and reliability of management representations.

22. If an identified misstatement may be the result of fraud and management is believed to be involved, reevaluate the assessment of the risks of material misstatement due to fraud and the impact on procedures that respond to these risks. Consider whether the circumstances indicate possible collusion involving management, employees, or third parties.

23. Evaluate the audit implications when the auditor concludes or is unable to conclude whether the financial statements are materially misstated as a result of fraud.

Auditor Unable to Continue the Engagement

24. If the ability to continue performing the audit due to a misstatement resulting from fraud or suspected fraud is questioned, determine the professional and legal responsibilities applicable, including any requirement to report to those who made the audit appointment or to regulatory authorities and consider whether withdrawal from the engagement is appropriate or legally permitted. If the auditor withdraws, discuss the withdrawal and its reasons with the appropriate level of management and those charged with governance and determine if a professional or legal requirement exists to report the withdrawal and its reasons to those who made the audit appointment or to regulatory authorities.

Communications to Management and Those Charged with Governance

25. Inform the appropriate level of management on a timely basis of any fraud identified and of information indicating fraud may exist.

26. Communicate with those charged with governance (unless all of those charged with governance are involved in managing the entity) on a timely basis regarding identified or suspected fraud involving management, employees with significant internal control roles, or others where the fraud results in a material misstatement in the financial statements.

27. Communicate with those charged with governance any other fraud-related matters that are relevant to their responsibilities in the auditor's judgment.

Communications to Regulatory and Enforcement Authorities

28. Determine whether the auditor has a responsibility to report the occurrence of or suspicion of fraud to a party outside the entity. There are some circumstances in which the auditor's legal responsibilities may override the duty of confidentiality to the client.

Documentation

29. Documentation of the understanding of the entity and its environment and the assessment of the risk of material misstatement should include significant decisions reached during the engagement team discussion regarding the susceptibility of the entity's financial statements to material misstatement due to fraud; how the discussion occurred, when it occurred, and who participated; and the identified and assessed risks of material misstatement due to fraud at the financial statement and assertion level.

30. Documentation of the responses to the assessed risks of material misstatement should include overall responses to the assessed risks of material

misstatement due to fraud at the financial statement level, the nature, timing, and extent of audit procedures, and the linkage of those procedures with the assessed risks of material misstatement due to fraud at the assertion level. This documentation should also include the results of audit procedures, including those addressing the risk of management override of controls.

31. Document communication about fraud made to management, those charged with governance, regulators, and others.

32. Document the reasons for a conclusion that the presumption of the existence of a risk of material misstatement due to fraud related to revenue recognition is not applicable to an engagement.

Analysis and Application of Procedures

Characteristics of Fraud

Fraudulent financial reporting

The intentional misstatement of information (through either commission or omission) in financial statements is referred to as "fraudulent financial reporting." Intent is often difficult to determine and the audit is not designed to determine intent, but to obtain reasonable assurance about whether the financial statements as a whole are free from material misstatement, whether due to fraud or error. Fraudulent financial reporting may be caused in an effort to manage earnings and often involves management override of controls. AU-C 240 lists the following as examples of fraudulent financial reporting:

- Intentional misapplications of accounting principles relating to amounts, classification, manner of presentation, or disclosure (e.g., disclosing a loss contingency based on the standards established by generally accepted accounting principles when, in fact, the contingency should be accrued).

- Manipulation, falsification, or alteration of the accounting records or supporting documents that financial statements are prepared from (e.g., the inclusion of false amounts in the accounts receivable subsidiary ledger).

- Misrepresentation in, or intentional omission from, the financial statements of events, transactions, or other significant information

---

IMPORTANT NOTICE FOR 2013: In 2007 the U.S. Department of the Treasury, at the behest of Treasury Secretary Henry Paulson, created the Advisory Committee on the Auditing Profession. The Advisory Committee, co-chaired by Arthur Levitt, a former SEC chairman, and Donald Nicolaisen, a former SEC chief accountant, was created to examine the sustainability of a strong and viable auditing profession, and its recommendations have the potential to affect auditing practice. The Advisory Committee made three recommendations that involve fraudulent financial reporting: (1) that the SEC and PCAOB clarify in the auditor's report the auditor's responsibility for detecting fraud, (2) that parties with an interest in fraud (e.g., academics, auditors, investors, public companies, regulators, and users) develop best practices with respect to fraud prevention and detection, and (3) that a center (under the auspices of the PCAOB) be created for auditing firms and others to share experiences, practices, data, and commission research regarding fraud prevention and detection.

Misappropriation of assets

Theft of assets that results in the misstatement of financial statements is referred to as "misappropriation of assets" (theft or defalcation). Misappropriation can result from a variety of deliberate actions, such as the unauthorized removal of inventory and the payment for assets that have never been received by the client. The auditor is required to plan and perform the audit to detect material misstatements due to misappropriation of assets.

OBSERVATION: In 2010 the Committee of Sponsoring Organizations of the Treadway Commission (COSO) issued a study titled "Fraudulent Financial Reporting 1998-2007: An Analysis of U.S. Public Companies" that examined about 350 cases of SEC enforcement actions against public companies alleging financial statement fraud. Of those cases, the majority involved fraudulent financial reporting. Only 14% of the cases involved misappropriations of assets. However, auditors of nonpublic entities might conclude that the risk of material misstatements due to misappropriations of assets is likely to be higher in nonpublic companies than in public companies.

Consideration of Fraud in Governmental and Not-for-Profit Audits

The auditor's responsibilities relating to fraud in an audit of a governmental or not-for-profit entity may be a result of additional legislation, regulation, and requirements. Thus, an auditor may have a responsibility to consider risks of fraud beyond considering risks of material misstatement of the financial statements for these entities.

Professional Skepticism

An important element in identifying fraudulent financial statements is the mindset of professional skepticism that the auditor brings to an engagement. An auditor should guard against becoming complacent in the collection and evaluation of audit evidence even when past experience with the client has provided no indication of dishonesty or deception on the part of management. Although fraud is not a purely random event, the auditor should always consider that fraud could occur in any audit engagement no matter what the circumstances.

PLANNING AID REMINDER: Common characteristics of litigation against auditors related to fraudulent financial statements include (1) accepting management's representations without obtaining corroborative evidence, (2) allowing management to influence the scope of audit procedures, and (3) ignoring conditions that suggest that there is an unreasonable degree of risk related to the engagement.

The auditor is not expected to be an authentication expert, but when conditions lead the auditor to believe a document may not be authentic or may have undisclosed modified terms, he or she should investigate further, possibly by confirming directly with a third party or using the work of a specialist to assess the document's authenticity.

Discussion among the Engagement Team

The extent of the discussion among the engagement team and how it occurs will vary across engagements and may depend on factors such as whether there should be multiple discussions in audits involving multiple locations, whether to include specialists assigned to the audit team in discussions, and whether to consult with others internal or external to the firm to acquire additional information, if appropriate.

The discussion may include a consideration of matters such as management's involvement in overseeing employees with access to cash or assets susceptible to misappropriation, unusual or unexplained changes in behavior or lifestyle of management or employees the audit team is aware of, types of circumstances that might indicate the possibility of fraud, how unpredictability will be incorporated into audit procedures, which audit procedures might be selected to respond to fraud risks, and any allegations of fraud the auditor is aware of.

ENGAGEMENT STRATEGY: The discussion or process may be performed prior to the execution of the other procedures listed in AU-C 240 (and discussed in the remainder of this Section) or as part of those procedures. In practice, the discussion for the potential for material misstatement of the financial statements due to fraud will generally be fluid and take a course dictated to some degree by the developments during the engagement. It is not particularly important when this procedure is performed but rather it is the professional attitude maintained by the auditor with respect to the procedure that is important. If the procedure is merely part of a checklist along with other audit procedures, it is unlikely that an effective audit will be performed. On the other hand, if the auditor believes that fraud could arise in any engagement and he or she remains sensitive to this possibility throughout the engagement, the chance of identifying material fraudulent financial statements will be enhanced.

FRAUD POINTER: If conducted with the appropriate mind-set, the brainstorming among audit team members about how and where they believe material misstatements due to fraud might occur and how management could perpetrate and conceal fraud can provide important insights to all audit team members about the presence of fraud risks. By setting aside prior beliefs about management's integrity, the brainstorming session can be an effective tool in reminding audit team members about the importance of maintaining an appropriate questioning mind-set that recognizes that fraud is possible in any engagement. The brainstorming session is meant to be a dialogue of information exchanged between all audit team members, not a one-way communication from the audit partner or manager to all other audit team members. Even though a sole practitioner has no team members, he or she should document his or her thoughts on these matters.

Risk Assessment Procedures and Related Activities

To assess the risk of material misstatement due to fraud, AU-C 240 requires, as part of an auditor's development of an understanding of the client's business and industry, that the following procedures be performed as the basis for identifying risks of material misstatement due to fraud:

- Make inquiries of appropriate personnel in order to identify their views on the risks of fraud and how those risks have been addressed.

- Consider unusual or unexpected relationships that have been identified during the performance of analytical procedures as part of the planning the engagement.

- Consider whether other information provides insight into the possible existence of fraud risk factors.

- Consider whether fraud risk factors exist.

FRAUD POINTER: AU-C 240 notes that the set of information to be gathered by the auditor to assess fraud risks should be comprehensive and should not be solely based on a completed fraud risk factor checklist. Auditors assess fraud risk factors and combine that information with information obtained through inquiries of others within the entity, from the performance of planning phase analytical procedures, and through the performance of other procedures. More complete sets of information from multiple sources are expected to increase the auditor's ability to identify circumstances where fraud risk is heightened.

Information gathered through inquiries

The auditor's inquiry of management regarding the nature, extent, and frequency of management's assessment of the risk of fraud and prevention and detection controls in place are relevant to the auditor's understanding of the entity's control environment. Management's failure to perform such an assessment may, in some circumstances, indicate management does not place much importance on internal control. In smaller, less complex entities management's assessment may focus on the risks of employee fraud or misappropriation of assets.

ENGAGEMENT STRATEGY: AU-C 580 requires that the client make certain written representations concerning fraud that relate to management's knowledge of fraud or suspected fraud affecting the entity that involve management, employees who have significant roles in internal control, or others where fraud could materially misstate financial statements. The representations also relate to management's knowledge of fraud or suspected fraud received from communications by others, such as employees, former employees, analysts, regulators, and short sellers, among others. As auditors make the required AU-C 240 inquiries, an effective engagement strategy is to consider making specific inquiries of the items to be explicitly addressed in the management representation letter. The auditor might find it helpful to state at the time of inquiry that he or she will be requesting written representations of management's responses at the end of fieldwork. That might lead to less confusion at the end of fieldwork, because the representation letter is signed by management.

The auditor may direct inquiries about the existence or suspicion of fraud to others within the entity to corroborate management responses or to provide information regarding possible management override of controls. Inquiries may be directed to operating personnel not directly involved in the financial reporting process, employees with different authority levels, employees involved in initiating, processing, or recording complex or unusual transactions or their supervisors, in-house legal counsel, the chief ethics officer or equivalent person, or those charged with dealing with fraud allegations. These inquiries are one way in which the auditor exercises professional skepticism of management responses.

FRAUD POINTER: Forensic experts note that the use of inquiry can be an effective tool in fraud investigation. People who might be reluctant to voluntarily share information about actual or possible fraud are often more likely to reveal that information if directly asked. As a result, auditors should take seriously the inquiries they make of those within an entity—the information obtained could be invaluable.

The auditor is also responsible for obtaining an understanding of the oversight exercised by those charged with governance over management's processes for identifying and responding to fraud risks and the internal control established to mitigate those risks. To obtain this understanding, the auditor may attend meetings where these discussions occur, read minutes from these meetings, or make inquiries of those charged with governance.

FRAUD POINTER: In January 2005, the AICPA's Antifraud Programs and Controls Task Force issued a document entitled "Management Override of Internal Controls: The Achilles' Heel of Fraud Prevention," which provides guidance to audit committees to help them address the ever-present fraud risk resulting from management override of internal control. The document notes that the audit committee, or the board when there is no audit committee, plays a vital role in overseeing the actions of management. For many organizations, the audit committee is in the best position to most likely prevent, deter, and detect fraud resulting from management override of controls. The document identifies specific actions an audit committee can take to address the risk of management override of internal controls. Auditors may find the document helpful in their discussions with audit committees about how the audit committee is addressing this ever-present risk of fraud.

Information gathered through analytical procedures

Analytical procedures performed during planning may help identify the risks of material misstatements due to fraud. The degree of reliance that can be placed on analytical procedures is dependent on the source, completeness, and reliability of the data; the level of the disaggregation; and the nature of the analysis. For example, analytical procedures performed during planning that indicate risks of material misstatement due to fraud may be performed at a high level and need to be combined with further audit evidence to identify risks of material misstatement due to fraud.

ENGAGEMENT STRATEGY: Analytical procedures relating to revenue that may identify unusual or unexpected relationships indicating risks of material misstatement due to fraud may include a comparison of sales volume based on recorded revenue with production capacity as an excess of sales volume over production capacity could indicate recording fictitious sales. Another analytical procedure that may be performed is a trend analysis of revenues and sales returns by month during and shortly after the reporting period to identify the existence of undisclosed side agreements allowing customers to return goods that would preclude revenue recognition. A trend analysis of sales by month compared with units shipped could identify a material misstatement of recorded revenues.

Information gathered through other procedures

Other information obtained through the performance of other procedures might provide insight into the possible existence of fraud risk. Specific information about risks of material misstatement due to fraud should be combined with other information, such as the following, that has come to the auditor's attention:

- Discussions among engagement personnel (as discussed earlier)
- Information considered when the engagement was accepted (if a new engagement) or continued
- Results from the review of interim financial statements

Information gathered through considering fraud risk factors

AU-C 240 describes fraud risk factors as "events or conditions that indicate an incentive or pressure to commit fraud or provide an opportunity to commit fraud." For example, a fraud risk factor exists if key management personnel's compensation is significantly dependent on operating results. The circumstance does not mean that fraud exists but rather that the likelihood of fraud is influenced by the circumstance and as the number of fraud risk factors increases the audit approach must reflect that environment.

FRAUD POINTER: Three conditions are present when fraud exists: (1) an incentive or pressure that motivates management or others to engage in fraud, (2) an opportunity for the individual to carry out the fraud, (3) the perpetrator has an attitude or set of ethical beliefs that allow him or her to justify committing an unethical or dishonest act. AU-C 240 organizes the examples of fraud risk factors along these three conditions of fraud. When auditors identify fraud risk factors across the three conditions, fraud risk is likely to be high. Likewise, the absence of one or all three of the conditions listed above does not suggest that the auditor should conclude that the possibility of fraudulent acts is nonexistent or very low. In fact, it is often difficult for an auditor to observe management's attitude or ability to rationalize a fraudulent act, because it involves management's state of mind.

In smaller, less complex entities some of these considerations may be less relevant. For example, there may not be a written code of conduct, but there may be a culture emphasizing integrity and ethical behavior. Failure to have certain controls can often be compensated by other conditions in the entity. However, management dominated by one individual can be a weakness because of the potential for management override of controls

Identification and Assessment of Risks of Material Misstatement Due to Fraud

Material misstatement due to fraudulent financial reporting of revenue recognition is ordinarily a presumed risk that varies across entities according to their particular circumstances, pressures, and incentives. However, this presumption of risk may be rebutted if the auditor concludes no risk of material misstatement due to fraud related to revenue recognition exists for a particular audit.

FRAUD POINTER: The Committee of Sponsoring Organizations of the Treadway Commission (COSO) issued a study in 2010 ("Fraudulent Financial Reporting: 1998-2007, An Analysis of U.S. Public Companies") that found that 61% of the fraudulent financial reporting enforcement actions by the SEC involved revenue recognition. SAS-99 states that "the auditor should ordinarily presume that there is a risk of material misstatement due to fraud relating to revenue recognition."

In obtaining an understanding of the design, implementation, and monitoring of the entity's controls relevant to fraud risks, the auditor may learn that management has chosen to accept certain risks rather than establish controls. This understanding can be useful to the auditor in identifying fraud risk factors that could affect the assessment of the risks that the financial statements may contain material misstatements due to fraud.

Responses to Assessed Risks of Material Misstatement Due to Fraud

After completion of the procedures described so far, the auditor is in a position to determine how to respond to identified risks of material misstatements due to fraud through the performance of audit procedures. AU-C 240 states that the auditor may respond by modifying the

1. Overall approach to the audit at the financial statement level
2. Nature, timing, and extent of procedures at the assertion level
3. Procedures related to possible management override of controls
4. Other audit procedures

Overall approach to the audit at the financial statement level

AU-C 240 states that the auditor's overall responses to address the assessment of risks of material misstatement generally reflect an increased level of professional skepticism.

Assignment and supervision of personnel is one overall response and, in some instances, it is appropriate for the auditor to assign personnel with special skills, such as information technology or even forensic experience, or for more experienced auditors to participate in the engagement. The intensity of the supervision of the engagement should reflect the assessed level of risk.

Unpredictability of audit procedures is another overall response that is important to help prevent individuals in the entity who are familiar with the normal audit procedures from being able to conceal fraudulent financial reporting. As the assessment of the risks of material misstatement due to fraud increases, the auditor should likewise increase the unpredictability of the audit approach. This strategy may range from changing the timing of audit procedures to varying the locations of procedures.

As the risk of fraud increases at the financial statement level, the auditor's concern with the appropriateness and quality of accounting principles selected and applied should increase. For example, the auditor should consider if management appears to be selecting and applying accounting principles that consistently have the same overall impact on the financial statements (e.g., consistently increase earnings before taxes).

Nature, timing, and extent of procedures at the assertion level

The specific nature (i.e., use procedures that generate more reliable evidence), timing (i.e., perform procedures at or near year-end), and extent (i.e., the size of the audit sample) of audit procedures are affected by the assessed of risks of material misstatement due to fraud at the assertion level.

Procedures related to possible management override of controls

AU-C 240 recognizes that management is in a unique position to engage in fraud by bypassing existing controls. Therefore, an auditor must always consider the risk of management override of controls.

Fraudulent financial reporting often involves recording inappropriate or unauthorized journal entries throughout the year or at period end or making adjustments to amounts reported in the financial statement that are not reflected in formal journal entries. Thus, the auditor should review journal entries and other adjustments to assess their appropriateness. When the auditor is selecting specific journal entries and other adjustments for testing (as well as the nature and timing of how those entries will be tested), there are several relevant factors:

- Fraud risk factors or other conditions that relate to specific classes of entries
- The quality of controls that relate to entries, including whether entries are processed manually or automated
- The financial reporting process and the client's evidential support (including electronic support) for entries
- Entries with unusual characteristics such as unique authorization sources, posting dates, dollar amounts, and accounts involved
- Entries that affect accounts that are characterized by their complexity, high degree of subjectivity because of estimates, past history of errors, or identification with risk factors suggesting possible material misstatement due to fraud

- Entries that are not considered part of the routine (sales, purchases, payroll, etc.) journal entries made during the period

---

PLANNING AID REMINDER: AU-C 240 points out that in planning which entries should be tested, the auditor should take into consideration that fraudulent entries are often made at the end of an accounting period.

The preparation of financial statements requires the inclusion of significant accounting estimates that are based on the judgment of management. Fraudulent financial reporting is often executed through the manipulation of accounting estimates. AU-C 540 (*Auditing Accounting Estimates, Including Fair Value Accounting Estimates, and Related Disclosures*) requires the auditor to perform a retrospective review as a risk assessment procedure, and the auditor may include any review of management's judgments and assumptions to look for biases that could represent a risk of material misstatement due to fraud as part of this review. The purpose of the review is to indicate the existence of any possible management bias, not to question the auditor's professional judgments made in the prior year based on available information.

ENGAGEMENT STRATEGY: Challenging estimates made by a client and supporting those challenges can be difficult; however, AU-C 240 requires that the auditor perform a retrospective review of estimates made in previous years by the client. If the client has exhibited consistent bias in the past, that history should be considered in assessing material misstatement due to fraud. As part of the engagement strategy, the auditor should have access to information obtained in prior years about significant estimates in order to evaluate the consistency of management's assumptions and judgments in the current year relative to prior years.

In considering management override of controls, the auditor also analyzes the business basis for significant unusual transactions. Business transactions should make sense given the fundamental characteristics of a client. Transactions that appear unusual to the auditor should be investigated in order to determine their rationale. This process should include the following procedures:

- Consider whether the transaction is overly complex.

- Determine whether the transaction has been discussed with the audit committee or board of directors.

- Consider whether the transaction is driven by its accounting implication rather than sound business strategy.

- Determine whether a transaction that involves unconsolidated related parties has been properly reviewed and approved by the audit committee or board of directors.

- Determine whether a transaction involves a (1) previously unidentified related party or (2) party that cannot fulfill its obligation without support from the client.

ENGAGEMENT STRATEGY: AU-C 240 points out that because management can override controls, it is unlikely that audit risk can be reduced to an appropriately low level by performing only tests of controls. As a result, substantive testing is likely to be part of the engagement strategy.

Evaluation of Audit Evidence

AU-C 240 emphasizes the critical evaluation of audit evidence related to the occurrence of possible fraud that is primarily qualitative, based on the auditor's judgment. This evaluation can provide additional insight into risks of material misstatement due to fraud and whether there is a need to perform additional audit procedures.

Evaluating the results of analytical procedures performed as part of substantive tests or in the overall review stage of the engagement

As required by AU-C 520 (*Analytical Procedures*), analytical procedures should be performed as part of the overall review of financial information and considered for possible performance as part of substantive procedures. The performance of these latter (non-planning stage) analytical procedures might identify fraud risks that had not previously come to the auditor's attention.

PLANNING AID REMINDER: AU-C 240 requires (as part of the overall review stage of the engagement) the auditor to apply substantive analytical procedures to revenue through the end of the period.

Professional judgment must be exercised to identify trends and relationships that appear to be unusual and therefore subject to further investigation; however, AU-C 240 points out that unusual relationships might come to the auditor's attention "because management or employees generally are unable to manipulate certain information to create seemingly normal or expected relationships." For example, the following unexpected relationships might be based on fraudulent activities:

- There are material differences between sales according to the accounting records and sales according to production reports because fictitious sales have been recorded by the management personnel who had access to the accounting records but not to production statistics.

- There are unusual relationships between the current year's inventory, accounts payable, sales, or costs of goods sold and those of the previous year because of inventory theft and the perpetrator was unable to adjust the affected accounts.

- There is an unusual relationship between net income and cash flows from operations because fictitious revenue was recorded through receivables and not cash.

FRAUD POINTER: AU-C 240 states that unusual and unexpected relationships involving year-end revenue and income should be particularly relevant to the auditor's concern with the possible existence of fraudulent financial statements. For example, the recognition of unusually large amounts of revenue from unusual transactions needs to be considered by the auditor.

FRAUD POINTER: The auditor should evaluate management's responses to inquiries (particularly inquiries related to substantive analytical procedures and analytical procedures performed as part of the overall review stage of the audit) to determine whether the responses are vague, implausible, or inconsistent with other evidence obtained. Management representations on significant issues should be supported by corroborating audit evidence.

Responding to misstatements that might relate to fraud

When a fraudulent act or possible fraudulent act is discovered and that act does not appear to have a material impact on the financial statements, the auditor should nonetheless consider the implications of the fraud, especially the person(s) involved in the act. For example, if the fraudulent act that has financial statement implications was conducted by a high-level management individual, the auditor should consider whether the circumstance calls into question the integrity of management and the reliability of previously obtained evidence. Also, if there are numerous misstatements, even if their cumulative effect is not material, this may be indicative of fraud risk because fraud is rarely an isolated occurrence.

PLANNING AID REMINDER: The identification of fraudulent acts has an effect on the auditor's determination of materiality because the level of materiality is a function of both quantitative and qualitative factors. That is, if fraudulent misstatements are identified during the engagement, the level of materiality for the engagement decreases.

Auditor Unable to Continue the Engagement

The auditor may question the ability to continue performing the audit under circumstances such as the following:

- The entity does not take action the auditor considers appropriate regarding fraud, even if the fraud is not material to the financial statements.
- The auditor's work indicates the financial statements have a significant risk of material and pervasive fraud.
- The auditor has significant concern about the competence or integrity of management or those charged with governance.

The auditor may find it appropriate to seek legal advice in considering whether to withdraw from an engagement and determining an appropriate course of action. Factors that could impact the auditor's decision to withdraw include the involvement of management or those charged with governance and the effects on the auditor from continuing to have an association with the entity. For example, concerns about management's integrity may arise on the day the auditor plans to sign the auditor report. Even at that point, the auditor may need to perform additional procedures or consider withdrawal. It is important to note that withdrawal may not be an option to auditors on some governmental and not-for-profit audits due to mandates, public interest considerations, contractual requirements, or law or regulation.

Communications to Management and Those Charged with Governance

When the auditor believes fraud might have occurred (whether consequential or inconsequential), the matter should be communicated to the appropriate level of management. In communications with those charged with governance, the auditor may communicate orally or in writing. AU-C 260 identifies factors to consider in making this determination, but the auditor may consider documenting all of these communications in writing given their sensitive nature.

ENGAGEMENT STRATEGY: The auditor and the audit committee should come to an understanding about the need for communication with the audit committee when lower-level employees are involved in fraudulent acts.

There are several examples of other fraud-related matters the auditor may wish to discuss with those charged with governance, including the auditor's evaluation of the entity's control environment, management actions that may be indicative of fraudulent financial reporting, and significant deficiencies or material weaknesses in controls to address risks of material misstatement due to fraud.

Communications to Regulatory and Enforcement Authorities

Generally, the auditor is not required to communicate the possible or actual existence of fraud to other parties due to the confidential relationship with the client; however, AU-C 316 points out that it might be necessary to communicate such information under the following circumstances:

- Communication might be required by statute, regulation, courts of law, or waived by agreement.

- There may be a statutory duty to report the occurrence of fraud to supervisory authorities.

- There may be a duty to report misstatements to authorities if management and those charged with governance fail to take corrective action.

RISK ASSESSMENT STRATEGY: The auditor should consider seeking legal counsel when determining whether a third party should be informed of possible fraud related to a client's financial statements.

Practitioner's Aid

Exhibit AU-C 240-1 discusses authoritative guidance that is helpful in the audit of revenue reported in a client's financial statements. Exhibit AU-C 240-1 summarizes an approach described in the AICPA's Audit Guide *Auditing Revenue in Certain Industries*. The Audit Guide (which is available for purchase from the AICPA) notes that based on SEC Accounting and Auditing Enforcement Releases from between January 1987 and 1997 "more than half of the frauds involved overstating revenues by recording them either fictitiously or prematurely."

EXHIBIT AU-C 240-1—GUIDANCE FOR AUDITING REVENUE IN CERTAIN INDUSTRIES

Revenue should be recognized when it has been earned or substantially earned. Generally this means that revenue is recorded when goods are delivered or services are performed. Management has the primary responsibility for the fair presentation of revenue and related accounts such as allowances for uncollectible accounts, sales returns, and provisions for customer rebates and refunds. The AICPA's Audit Guide *Auditing Revenue in Certain Industries* points out that factors such as the (1) tone at the top, (2) role of the audit committee, (3) effectiveness of the internal audit function, and (4) adoption of effective internal control have an impact on the proper reporting of revenue in the financial statements based on GAAP.

The recognition of revenue consistent with GAAP can involve the application of a variety of pronouncements, including the following:

- ASC 360-20 (Real Estate Sales)
- ASC 470-40 (Product Financing Arrangements)
- ASC 605 (Revenue Recognition)
- ASC 952 (Franchisors)
- ASC 985 (Software)

The Audit Guide identifies the following specific factors that might indicate that a client is not reporting revenues in accordance with GAAP:

- Side agreements
- Channel stuffing
- Related-party transactions and significant unusual transactions
- Nature of business and accounting for revenue
- Integrity of evidence

Side agreements

Arrangements whereby the normal terms of a sale are modified in order to encourage a particular customer to accept shipment of goods that it would generally not accept (or record as a purchase) constitute a side agreement. These arrangements are generally characterized as relieving "the customer of some of the risk and rewards of ownership." Side agreements often result in revenue being recorded when the recognition is not in accordance with GAAP. Since side agreements are an exception to the normal sales conditions and are known only to a few key management personnel, this circumstance presents a challenge to the auditor; however, the Audit Guide points out that being aware that such an agreement could exist is a starting point for discovering their actual existence.

> **FRAUD POINTER:** The existence of side agreements undisclosed by management to the auditor is a significant fraud risk factor and potentially calls into question the integrity of top management. Side agreements can be either written or oral. The auditor should usually inquire about the existence of side agreements during the confirmation process.

Channel stuffing

The Audit Guide defines the channel stuffing strategy as a "marketing practice that suppliers sometimes use to boost sales by inducing distributors to buy substantially more inventory than they can promptly resell." The client's objective is to record more sales in the current period than would typically be recorded if sales were simply driven by market conditions. The auditor should be alert to identifying irregular sales patterns and consider their effect on the current financial statements. For example, there may be a need to create or increase provisions for returned goods or special discounts related to side agreements.

Related-party transactions and significant unusual transactions

Related-party transactions can be the basis for the recording of fraudulent transactions. For example, a client might sell inventory or capital assets to a related-party at an inflated price. The Audit Guide points out that individual related-party transactions that are kept relatively small but executed frequently could nonetheless have a material impact on the financial statements.

Another transaction type that can result in the reporting of fraudulent information in the financial statements involves highly complex transactions whether or not they involve related parties.

Nature of business and accounting for revenue

Revenue is generally recognized when earned; however, the nature of the client's industry can increase the risk that fraudulent revenue recognition schemes are present. The Audit Guide reminds auditors to consider factors such as the following as they relate to the probability that a client could inappropriately recognize revenue:

- The manner by which the client recognizes revenue based on the nature of its industry
- A recent change in the manner by which a client recognizes revenue
- The existence of client sales and payment terms that differ from industry norms or the client's normal internal policies
- Shipment policies that provide a basis for the inappropriate recognition of revenue

> **PUBLIC COMPANY IMPLICATION:** The SEC staff has issued guidance specific to revenue recognition that is relevant to auditors of public companies. SAB-101 and SAB-104 summarize the SEC staff's views of the appropriate accounting for revenue recognition in financial statements. The guidance includes an analysis of the criteria that must be satisfied in order to recognize revenue. Auditors of public companies should consider the guidance in SAB-101 and SAB-104.

Integrity of evidence

The integrity of the evidence that supports the recognition of revenue is another risk factor that should be considered by the auditor. The Audit Guide lists the following as some of the conditions related to evidence that can suggest the improper recording of revenue:

- Responses from management with respect to revenue recognition are "inconsistent, vague, or implausible."
- Audit evidence to support revenue transactions is missing.
- Company personnel have signed bills of lading (rather than the common carrier).
- Shipping documents have been altered.

Indicators of improper revenue recognition

There is no comprehensive checklist to determine when conditions suggest that a client might be inappropriately recording revenue; however, the Audit Guide presents the following (categorized as (1) absence of an agreement, (2) lack of delivery, and (3) incomplete earnings process) as indicators that should raise the auditor's suspicions about fraudulent revenue transactions.

Absence of an agreement

- Sales are based on letters of intent rather than signed contracts or agreements.
- Goods are shipped before they are authorized by a customer.
- Sales are recorded at the date of shipment to a new customer even though the customer can return the goods with no obligation.
- Sales are recorded even though the customer has the right to cancel the sale.
- Sales are recorded even though certain terms of the agreement, such as a consignment sales arrangement, have not been satisfied.

Lack of delivery

- Sales are recorded before delivery occurs.
- Sales are based on transactions that were executed after the end of the accounting period.
- Sales are based on shipments to warehouses or other locations that have not been authorized by the customer.
- Sales are recorded but a critical component of the order has not been shipped.
- Sales are recorded based on the receipt of purchase orders.

Incomplete earnings process

- Sales are recorded but receipt of payment from the customer is based on other material conditions that must be satisfied by the client.
- Sales are recorded but goods are unassembled.

- Sales are recorded based on shipments to freight forwarders but the goods will be returned to the client for modifications as dictated by the customer.

- Sales are recorded even though the client is obliged to perform additional work (such as debugging a client application).

Audit Procedures

The Audit Guide lists the following as authoritative and nonauthoritative procedures that the auditor should consider in obtaining "reasonable assurance about whether the financial statements are free of material misstatement, whether caused by error or fraud":

- Determine an appropriate audit risk level.
- Develop a knowledge of the business.
- Consider internal control over revenue recognition.
- Consider fraud in the financial statements.
- Consider related-party transactions.
- Perform analytical procedures.
- Perform cutoff tests, vouch transactions, and perform other tests.
- Send appropriate confirmations.
- Evaluate accounting estimates related to revenue transactions.
- Observe inventory.
- Obtain appropriate management representations.
- Consider the adequacy of financial statement disclosures.
- Evaluate audit evidence.

Determine an appropriate audit risk level

The auditor's awareness of fraud risk factors, related-party transactions, and other questionable revenue recognition characteristics of a client can occur as part of accepting or continuing an engagement, as part of planning the engagement, and as part of developing an understanding of a client's business and environment, including its internal control, or during the performance of tests of controls and substantive procedures. For this reason, during the entire engagement the auditor may need to reevaluate the levels of inherent risk and control risk related to revenue recognition to determine the nature, timing, and extent of audit procedures appropriate for the audit of revenue and related accounts.

Develop knowledge of the business

The Audit Guide notes that an auditor should be aware of a variety of characteristics of a client's revenue recognition process, including the following:

- Products and services sold
- The effect of seasonal or cyclical trends on revenue
- Marketing and sales policies, both internal and industry-wide

- Policies with respect to pricing, returns, discount credit granting, and payment terms
- Personnel (particularly in the marketing and sales activities) who record sales, extend credit, and authorize shipments
- Compensation benefits that are related to sales volume
- Classes and categories of customers
- The client's role in "placing products with end users, and how the company manages, tracks and controls its inventory that is held by distributors"
- Accounting principles that are appropriate for the client's sales activities

The Audit Guide points out that making inquiries of appropriate management personnel can help to better understand high-audit-risk conditions such as unusual or complex revenue transactions and sales contracts with unusual or complex terms.

FRAUD POINTER: Making appropriate inquiries is only a starting point in determining whether the client has recognized revenue inappropriately. The auditor should attempt to corroborate representations obtained through inquiry using other audit procedures, such as obtaining written confirmation from an independent source.

The auditor should read sales contracts in order to understand the responsibilities accepted by the client and their implications for revenue recognition. The Audit Guide notes that reading sales contracts and sales correspondence might alert the auditor to the existence of side agreements.

When a client executes complex sales agreements or is involved in related-party transactions, care must be taken in the assignment of personnel to ensure that the training and experience of an auditor is sufficient for the demands of this phase of the engagement. In some instances it is appropriate to seek expert assistance from members of the firm who are not part of the engagement, and in some instances it is necessary to use the work of an outside specialist.

Consider internal control over revenue recognition

As with other significant components of a client's internal control, the auditor should develop an understanding of internal control over revenue transactions that satisfies the requirements established by AU-C 315 (*Understanding the Entity and Its Environment and Assessing the Risks of Material Misstatement*). Internal control related to revenue recognition should, among other things, include an understanding of (1) how nonstandard revenue contracts are approved, (2) the accounting implications for changing standard contracts, (3) the development of estimates related to revenue transactions, and (4) related-party transactions. Based on the auditor's understanding of internal control related to revenue recognition, an appropriate level of control risk should be assessed and in turn tests of controls should be performed. If the results from performing tests of controls suggest that internal control over revenue recognition is ineffective, the nature, timing, or extent of substantive procedures must be modified in order to provide more persuasive audit evidence.

Consider fraud in the financial statements

AU-C 240 requires that an auditor specifically assess the risk of material misstatement of the financial statements due to fraud and consider that assessment in designing the audit procedures to be performed. The Audit Guide points out that the auditor's assessment relative to financial statement fraud is dependent upon factors such as (1) professional skepticism and its effect on the nature, timing, and extent of audit procedures, (2) management's selection and application of accounting principles for revenue recognition, and (3) management's ability to circumvent internal control related to revenue recognition.

Consider related-party transactions

AU-C 550 (*Related Parties*) provides guidance for the planning and application of procedures for related-party transactions. The Audit Guide identifies the following as procedures that may be appropriate for substantive procedures for revenue recognition that involves a related party:

- Understand the purpose of the transaction.
- Examine documentation that supports the transaction.
- Determine whether the board of directors (or other appropriate personnel) has approved the transaction.
- Confirm the details of the transaction with external parties.
- When the transaction raises questions about its substance, refer to various sources of information to determine whether the transaction appears to be reasonable.
- When the transaction creates material uncollected balances or obligations, obtain information about the financial viability of the related party.

Perform analytical procedures

AU-C 520 (*Analytical Procedures*) provides guidance for the performance of analytical procedures in an audit engagement. The Audit Guide notes that the following analytical procedures "are particularly useful in identifying unusual fluctuations in the revenue cycle that warrant additional consideration":

- Compare monthly and quarterly sales to comparable periods for the current year and previous years and evaluate the amounts in the context of current industry conditions and current client strategies.
- Review sales recorded a few days before and a few days after the end of the year.
- Compare gross profit ratios to those for previous years and to budgeted amounts, and evaluate the amounts in the context of current industry conditions and current client strategies.
- Compare the amount of inventory in the distribution channel with the amounts for prior periods to consider whether there may be channel stuffing.

- Compare the trends of sales in the distributor channel and evaluate the amounts in the context of current industry conditions and current client strategies.

- Compare revenue deductions, such as discounts, to those of the previous year and budgeted amounts, and evaluate the amounts in the context of current industry conditions and current client strategies.

- Evaluate sales credits and returns after the end of the year with regard to the figures for similar periods of the previous year to determine whether there may have been contingent sales or other unusual sales arrangements.

- Evaluate the ratio of returns and allowances to sales.

- Compare the aged trial balance of receivables with those of previous years.

- Evaluate the amount of cash receipts collected after the end of the year to cash receipts activities during the year to determine whether receipts are unusually slow to materialize.

Perform cutoff tests, vouch transactions, and perform other tests

The auditor should perform appropriate cutoff tests, vouch transactions, and perform other audit procedures to determine whether sales and related transactions are recorded in the appropriate accounting period.

Send appropriate confirmations

AU-C 505 (*External Confirmations*) provides guidance for the use of confirmations in an audit engagement. The Audit Guide notes that the auditor should consider confirming the details of complicated or unusual sales transactions, including possible unfilled obligations on the part of the client.

PLANNING AID REMINDER: AU-C 240 states that there is generally a heightened risk of fraud involving revenue recognition. Therefore, the auditor should consider confirming the terms of material revenue transactions, including inquiring about the existence of side agreements. The auditor should be more likely to confirm the terms of revenue transactions if they are unusual or complex. In addition, AICPA Practice Alert 03-1 (Audit Confirmations) states that the auditor should be more likely to confirm transaction terms and the existence of side agreements if any of the following conditions exist: (1) significant sales or sales volume at or near the end of the reporting period, (2) use of nonstandard contracts or contract clauses, (3) use of letters of authorization instead of signed contracts or agreements, (4) altered dates on contracts or shipping documents, (5) contracts or agreements that are linked with each other or that happen concurrently (e.g., sales to and purchases from the same party), (6) lack of evidence that the customer has accepted the product, (7) presence of bill-and-hold transactions, (8) sales with extended payment terms or nonstandard installment receivables, (9) sales without involvement from the accounting/finance department or where the accounting/finance department does not monitor relationships with distributors/retailers, (10) unusual sales volume to distributors/retailers, (11) sales involving a commitment for future upgrades, especially if not involving software, (12) sales involving significant uncertainties or obligations for the seller, (13) sales to value-added resellers or distributors whose financial viability is questionable, (14) an abnormally large increase in a receivable from a customer, and (15) aggressive accounting policies and practices by the client.

Evaluate accounting estimates related to revenue transactions

AU-C 540 (*Auditing Accounting Estimates, Including Fair Value Accounting Estimates and Related Disclosures*) describes the auditor's responsibilities and the audit procedures with respect to estimates that are part of the client's financial statements. The Audit Guide notes that this general guidance should be applied to material accounts such as sales, sales returns, the allowance for doubtful accounts, and revenue recognized under the percentage-of-completion method used to account for long-term construction contracts.

Observe inventory

The Audit Guide reminds auditors that appropriate cutoff procedures for the observation of inventories at the end of the year have implications for the recognition of revenues in the proper accounting period. In addition, the Guide notes that if a client has numerous shipping facilities the auditor should (1) observe inventory counts at all locations on the same date or (2) observe only some of the locations on an unannounced basis. Also, if the client is in an industry where inventory obsolescence is an issue, the auditor should determine whether client personnel used to count the inventory have the expertise to identify obsolete inventory.

Obtain appropriate management representations

AU-C 580 (*Management Representations*) provides guidance in obtaining written representations from a client. The Audit Guide states that some of the items that should be considered for representation by the client are as follows:

- There has been no fraud that could have a material effect on the financial statements.

- Related-party transactions, including sales and amounts receivable from related parties, have been properly recorded and disclosed.

- All financial records and related data have been made available.

- Significant estimates and material concentrations that are required to be disclosed.

- The effects of any uncorrected financial statement misstatements aggregated by the auditor during the current engagement and pertaining to the latest period presented are immaterial, both individually and in the aggregate, to the financial statements taken as a whole. (A summary of such items should be included in or attached to the letter.)

If the client has been involved in unusual revenue transactions, the auditor should consider whether it is appropriate to ask for representation concerning the details of these transactions.

Consider the adequacy of financial statement disclosures

The financial statements should reflect disclosures "with regard to revenue recognition policies, information about major customers or significant concentrations of credit risk, related-party transactions, and the effect of significant revisions to estimates in percentage-of-completion contracts."

Evaluate audit evidence

The Audit Guide points out that "to the extent the auditor remains in substantial doubt about any assertion of material significance, he or she must refrain from forming an opinion until he or she has obtained sufficient appropriate audit evidence to remove such substantial doubt, or the auditor must express a qualified or disclaimer of opinion."

OBSERVATION: In addition to providing general guidance for the audit of revenue and related accounts, the Audit Guide provides specific guidance for the high-technology manufacturing industry.

SECTION 250

CONSIDERATION OF LAWS AND REGULATIONS IN AN AUDIT OF FINANCIAL STATEMENTS

Authoritative Pronouncements

SAS-122 Statements on Auditing Standards: Clarification and Recodification

Overview

The laws and regulations an entity is subject to constitute its legal and regulatory framework. The effect of laws and regulations on the financial statements of entities varies widely. Some laws and regulations have a direct effect on the determination of material amounts and disclosures in the financial statements, and for these laws and regulations the auditor must obtain sufficient appropriate audit evidence. Other laws and regulations do not have a direct effect on the entity's financial statements, but compliance may be fundamental to operating aspects of the business such that noncompliance may have a material effect on the financial statements. For these laws and regulations, the auditor is required to perform specified audit procedures that may identify instances of noncompliance with these laws and regulations. The auditor may also become aware of acts of noncompliance through other audit procedures during the audit, so it is important to maintain an attitude of professional skepticism throughout the audit.

PLANNING AID REMINDER: AU-C 250 establishes professional standards relating to the auditor's responsibility for considering laws and regulations in the course of the audit of the entity's financial statements. An auditor might accept other engagements that impose a different responsibility for detecting illegal acts. Such engagements include professional services subject to governmental auditing standards or special engagements designed to determine compliance with specific laws or regulations.

In general, the auditor lacks the expertise and is not responsible for identifying and evaluating all acts of noncompliance with laws and regulations. The auditor is responsible for "obtaining reasonable assurance that the financial statements, as a whole, are free from material misstatement, whether caused by fraud or error." Even if an audit is properly performed and planned in accordance with GAAS, there is a risk that material misstatements may not be detected. There are several inherent limitations that may prevent the auditor from detecting material misstatements resulting from noncompliance with laws and regulations: (1) many laws and regulations primarily relate to the operating aspects of an entity and may not affect the financial statements or be captured by the entity's financial reporting information systems; (2) noncompliance may involve acts of concealment such as collusion, management override of controls, or intentional misrepresentation to the auditor; and (3) whether an act constitutes noncompliance is ultimately a matter for a court of law and legal determination.

The more removed an act of noncompliance becomes from events and transactions reflected in the financial statements, the less likely the auditor is to become aware of the noncompliant act. However, if the auditor does detect noncompliance, regardless of its materiality level, other aspects of the audit may be impacted, such as the auditor's consideration of management or employee integrity. AU-C 250 provides the auditor with the guidance to respond to identified or suspected noncompliance with laws or regulations appropriately.

PLANNING AID REMINDER: There are some specific statutory requirements that require the auditor to report on the entity's compliance with certain provisions of laws or regulations as part of the financial statement audit. AU-C 705 addresses the auditor's reporting responsibilities in these circumstances.

Definition

Noncompliance   Acts of intentional or unintentional omission or commission by the entity which are contrary to prevailing laws or regulations. Acts of noncompliance include transactions entered into by the entity, in the name of the entity, or on its behalf by those charged with governance, management, or employees. Noncompliance does not include personal misconduct by those charged with governance, management, or employees of the entity that is unrelated to the entity's business activities.

Requirements

The auditor is presumptively required to perform the following procedures in considering laws and regulations in a financial statement audit:

Consideration of Compliance with Laws and Regulations

1. As part of obtaining an understanding of the entity and its environment, obtain a general understanding of the legal and regulatory framework applicable to the entity and its industry and how the entity is complying with that framework.

2. Obtain sufficient appropriate audit evidence regarding material amounts and disclosures in the financial statements for which the provisions of laws and regulations are generally recognized to have a direct effect on their determination.

3. Perform the following audit procedures that may identify instances of noncompliance with other laws and regulations that may have a material effect on the financial statements:

   a. Inquire of management (and those charged with governance as appropriate) as to whether the entity is in compliance with such laws and regulations

   b. Inspect any correspondence with relevant licensing or regulatory authorities

4. Remain alert during the audit to the possibility that instances of noncompliance or suspected noncompliance may be brought to the auditor's attention through other audit procedures.

5. If noncompliance is not identified or suspected, the auditor is not required to perform additional audit procedures regarding the entity's compliance with laws and regulations.

Audit Procedures When Noncompliance is Identified or Suspected

6. If noncompliance with laws and regulations is identified or suspected, obtain an understanding of the nature and circumstances of occurrence of the act and further information to evaluate the possible effect on the financial statements.

7. If noncompliance is suspected, discuss the matter with management (and those charged with governance as appropriate). Consider the need to obtain legal advice if management or those charged with governance do not provide sufficient information supporting the entity's compliance with laws and regulations and the auditor judges the effect of the suspected noncompliance may be material to the financial statements.

8. If sufficient information about suspected noncompliance cannot be obtained, evaluate the effect of the lack of sufficient appropriate audit evidence on the auditor's opinion.

9. Evaluate the implications of noncompliance on other aspects of the audit, including the auditor's risk assessment and the reliability of written representations, and take appropriate action.

Reporting Identified or Suspected Noncompliance

10. Communicate matters involving identified or suspected noncompliance with laws and regulations that are not clearly inconsequential with those charged with governance unless all of those individuals are involved in the entity's management and already aware of these matters.

11. If the auditor judges identified or suspected noncompliance to be intentional and material, communicate the matter to those charged with governance as soon as practicable.

12. If the auditor suspects management or those charged with governance of being involved in noncompliance, communicate the matter to the entity's next higher existing level of authority. Consider the need to obtain legal advice if no such higher authority exists or the auditor believes the communication may not be acted upon or is unsure of whom to report the matter to.

13. If the auditor concludes that the noncompliance has a material effect on the financial statements that is not adequately reflected in the financial statements, the auditor should express a qualified or adverse opinion on the financial statements.

14. If management or those charged with governance prevent the auditor from obtaining sufficient appropriate audit evidence to evaluate whether potentially material noncompliance has or is likely to have occurred, that is a limitation on the scope of the audit and the auditor should express a qualified opinion or disclaim an opinion on the financial statements.

15. If the auditor is unable to determine whether noncompliance has occurred due to circumstances other than limitations imposed by management or those charged with governance, evaluate the effect on his or her opinion.

16. If noncompliance with laws and regulation is identified or suspected, determine whether the auditor has a responsibility to report this noncompliance to parties outside the entity.

OBSERVATION: The issuance of SAS-122 that icontains the ASB's Clarified SASs included some minor new requirements related to illegal acts. AU-C 250 now specifically requires the auditor to inspect correspondence, if any, with the relevant licensing or regulatory authorities. This procedure was not previously required. Auditing standards have also previously noted that an audit performed in accordance with GAAS provides no assurance that noncompliance with laws and regulations will be detected or that contingent liabilities that may result will be disclosed. However, the Clarified SASs state that because of the inherent limitations in an audit, some material misstatements in the financial statements may not be detected, even though the audit is properly planned and performed with in accordance with GAAS. The concept of "no assurance" is different from the concept described as "inherent limitations of an audit."

Documentation

Document identified or suspected noncompliance with laws and regulations and the results of discussion with management, those charged with governance where applicable, and other parties inside and outside the entity.

Analysis and Application of Procedures

Management Responsibilities

Management, with oversight from those charged with governance, is responsible for ensuring the entity's operations are conducted in accordance with laws and regulations. To prevent and detect noncompliance with laws and regulations, an entity may employ policies and procedures such as monitoring legal requirements; using appropriate internal control systems; and developing, training employees on, and monitoring compliance with a code of conduct. Large entities may support these activities by assigning responsibilities to an audit committee or the internal audit, legal, or compliance function.

PLANNING AID REMINDER: The auditor should request a written representation from the entity stating that no violations or possible violations of laws or regulations have occurred that may require accrual or disclosure in the financial statements. Management should also represent that it has informed the auditor of all possible illegal acts that it is aware of. Written representations provided by management provide audit evidence about management's knowledge of identified or suspected noncompliance with laws and regulations. However, these representations do not provide sufficient appropriate audit evidence on their own and do not affect the nature and extent of other audit evidence the auditor must obtain.

Consideration of Compliance with Laws and Regulations

Obtaining an understanding of the legal and regulatory framework

Procedures the auditor may use to obtain a general understanding of the legal and regulatory framework and the entity's compliance with that framework include the following:

- Using the auditor's existing understanding of the entity's industry, regulatory, and other external factors
- Updating the understanding of laws and regulations that directly determine reported amounts and disclosures in the financial statements
- Inquiring of management as to other laws and regulations that may have a fundamental effect on the entity's operations
- Inquiring of management as to the entity's policies and procedures regarding compliance with laws and regulations and those adopted to identify, evaluate, and account for litigation claims
- Inquiring of management as to the use of management representations and entity-issued directives concerning compliance with laws and regulations
- Considering the auditor's knowledge of the entity's history of noncompliance with laws and regulations

Laws and regulations with direct effects on financial statements

Generally, the auditor takes into consideration laws and regulations that directly apply to the determination of financial statement amounts or disclosures when planning his or her audit procedures. These laws and regulations may include those relating to the form and content of financial statements, industry-specific financial reporting issues, accounting for transactions under government contracts, and the accrual or recognition of expenses for income tax or pension costs. For example, the auditor would likely evaluate compliance with Internal Revenue Code and related regulations when determining whether the provision for income taxes is fairly presented in the financial statements. The auditor's responsibility for detecting illegal acts relating to laws and regulations having a direct and material effect on the financial statements is the same as the responsibility relating to the detection of errors and fraud. The auditor must design the audit to provide reasonable assurance of detecting such acts.

Laws and regulations with indirect effects on financial statements

Most laws and regulations have only an indirect effect on financial statements; that is, when noncompliance related to this type of law or regulation has occurred, the effects are often indirect in that they only require disclosure in the financial statements based on their classification as a contingent liability. Laws and regulations of this type may include those related to securities trading, occupational safety and health, food and drug administration, environmental protection, equal employment, and antitrust violations.

Noncompliant acts of this type are generally related to the operations of the organization rather than to the financial and accounting aspects of the entity and could have a fundamental effect on the entity's operations by causing it to cease operations or creating a going concern. Furthermore, under many circumstances, the auditor lacks sufficient basis for determining whether this type of law or regulation has been violated.

Audit Procedures When Noncompliance is Identified or Suspected

Indicators of Noncompliance

AU-C 250 lists the following as examples of specific information that raises questions about the existence of noncompliance with laws and regulations:

- Unauthorized or improperly recorded transactions
- Investigation by a governmental or regulatory agency, or payment of fines or penalties
- Noncompliance with laws or regulations cited in reports of examinations by regulatory agencies made available to the auditor
- Payments for unspecified services or loans to consultants, affiliates, employees, or government officials or employees
- Sales commissions or agents' fees that appear excessive in relation to those normally paid by the client or to the services actually received
- Unusual payments in cash, purchases of bank cashiers' checks in amounts payable to bearer, or transfers to numbered bank accounts
- Purchases made at prices significantly above or below market price
- Unusual transactions with companies registered in tax havens
- Payments for goods or services made to countries other than those from which the goods or services originated
- Existence of an information system that fails, by design or by accident, to provide an adequate audit trail or sufficient audit evidence
- Unfavorable media comment
- Failure to file tax returns or pay government duties or similar fees common to the entity's industry or the nature of its business

Perform appropriate audit procedures

If it is necessary to obtain a further understanding of the identified or suspected noncompliant act, perform additional procedures such as the following:

- Inspect supporting documentation and compare it with the accounting records
- Confirm information with other parties and intermediaries
- Determine if the transaction has been properly authorized
- Consider whether other, similar transactions have occurred, and attempt to identify them

Further information to consider in evaluating the possible effect of noncompliant acts on the financial statements includes:

- The quantitative and qualitative materiality of the effect of noncompliance on the financial statements

- If the potential financial consequences require accrual or disclosure under the applicable financial reporting framework
- If the potential financial consequences are so serious that the financial statements may not be fairly presented or may be otherwise misleading

When management cannot provide sufficient information to demonstrate that a noncompliant act did not take place, the auditor may consult with the entity's legal counsel or external legal counsel. If it is not appropriate for the auditor to consult with the entity's legal counsel or the auditor is not satisfied with the counsel's opinion, it may be appropriate for the auditor to consult his or her own legal counsel regarding the existence of a noncompliant act, the possible legal consequences including the possibility of fraud, and any further action the auditor should take.

FRAUD POINTER: In November 2004, the AICPA issued a Practice Alert on illegal acts that states that the client is normally expected to perform an investigation if an illegal act might have occurred. (These investigations are typically performed by an outside law firm with the assistance of forensic accountants under the supervision of the audit committee.) The auditor should request that he or she be allowed to attend the presentation of the investigation team's report at the completion of the engagement and discuss the results of the investigation with senior management and the audit committee.

Evaluate the implications of noncompliance

The implications of noncompliant acts on other aspects of the audit are particularly applicable to the evaluation of the reliability of management representations. Such facts as the perpetrators involved, the methods of concealment, and the nature of internal control procedures overridden should be considered in the evaluation. In circumstances where management or those charged with governance do not take remedial actions the auditor considers appropriate, the auditor may question his or her ability to rely on management representations and the potential effects of continuing association with the entity. These circumstances may cause the auditor to seek legal advice in considering withdrawal from the engagement. If withdrawal is prohibited by law or regulation, the auditor may consider alternative actions such as describing the noncompliance in an Other Matter(s) paragraph in the auditor's report.

OBSERVATION: The possible loss arising from the illegal act should be evaluated to determine whether the amount is material. All costs related to the loss, such as penalties and fines, should be considered. The need for accrual and/or disclosure in the financial statements should be evaluated in the context of guidelines codified in ASC 450 (Contingencies). The auditor must consider both quantitative and qualitative factors in evaluating the materiality of the illegal act. Qualitative factors are often more important than the immediate quantitative effect in evaluating the materiality of an illegal act. For example, penalties and fines can sometimes exceed the amount of the illegal act itself.

The illegal act should also be evaluated to determine whether other aspects of the engagement are affected. This is particularly applicable to the evaluation of the reliability of management representations. Such facts as the perpetrators involved, the methods of concealment, and the nature of internal control procedures overridden should be considered in the evaluation.

FRAUD POINTER: The AICPA's Practice Alert on illegal acts states that the auditor is to evaluate management's conclusions after receiving the investigation report. After the auditor considers the results of the special investigation and discusses the investigation report with senior management and the audit committee, he or she must determine (1) whether additional audit procedures need to be performed, (2) the nature of any needed disclosures in the financial statements and notes, (3) whether internal control deficiencies exist and need to be communicated, and (4) whether the audit report needs to be modified. The auditor should also consider whether it is appropriate to withdraw from the engagement.

Reporting Identified or Suspected Noncompliance

The auditor's communication of identified or suspected noncompliance to those charged with governance may include the following:

- Description of the noncompliant act
- Circumstances surrounding the noncompliant act
- Auditor's evaluation of the effects of the noncompliant act on the financial statements

---

FRAUD POINTER: If members of senior management are involved in the illegal act, the auditor should communicate directly with the audit committee (or equivalent individuals). The communication can be written or oral, and in either case it should be adequately documented in the audit files.

The auditor may reach an agreement with those charged with governance in advance regarding the nature of matters to be communicated in order to avoid communicating clearly inconsequential matters.

ENGAGEMENT STRATEGY: If the auditor finds it necessary to issue a qualified or adverse opinion or a disclaimer of opinion on the financial statements and management or those charged with governance refuse to accept this modified opinion, the auditor may withdraw from the engagement and indicate the reasons for withdrawal in writing to those charged with governance.

Notifying parties external to the entity about the occurrence of a noncompliant act is generally not required; however, AU-C 250 notes that under the following circumstances the auditor may be called on to inform another party of a noncompliant act:

- Inquiries received from a successor auditor
- Subpoena issued by a court

- Governmental audit requirements applicable to entities that have received financial aid

---

ENGAGEMENT STRATEGY: Because of the confidential relationship between the entity and the auditor, the auditor may find it advisable to contact legal counsel before noncompliant acts are disclosed to outside parties.

Audits of governmental agencies may have additional reporting requirements relating to compliance with laws, regulations, and provision of contracts or grant agreements and may require communicating instances of noncompliance to appropriate oversight bodies and funding agencies.

SECTION 260

THE AUDITOR'S COMMUNICATION WITH THOSE CHARGED WITH GOVERNANCE

Authoritative Pronouncements

SAS-122—Statements on Auditing Standards: Clarification and Recodification

Overview

Effective governance over the entity's processes, including those related to financial reporting, is a critical element of an entity's internal controls. Persons should be in place who have responsibility for overseeing the strategic direction of the entity and obligations related to the accountability of the entity to its key stakeholders, including oversight of the financial reporting process. Governance structures vary by entity, often depending on the entity's size and organizational structure.

AU-C 260 establishes standards and provides guidance on the auditor's communication with those charged with governance in relation to the audit of financial statements. The intent of AU-C 260 is to provide a framework for an effective two-way communication between the auditor and those charged with governance, and it identifies specific matters to be communicated. Auditors are additionally required to communicate matters that in their judgment are significant and relevant to the responsibilities of those charged with governance for overseeing the financial reporting process. AU-C 260 does not preclude the auditor from communicating other matters in addition to those required.

The principal purposes of the auditor's communications with those charged with governance include the following:

- Communicate clearly the responsibilities of the auditor in relation to the financial statement audit, including an overview of the scope and timing of the audit.
- Obtain information relevant to the audit from those charged with governance.
- Provide those charged with governance with timely information about observations arising from the audit that are relevant to their governance responsibilities in the oversight of the financial reporting processes.
- Promote effective two-way communication between the auditor and those charged with governance.

The intended recipient of the auditor's communication is *those charged with governance*, which may vary across entities. For many, those charged with governance include the board of directors or its audit committee. For others, those charged with governance may reside outside the entity, such as a government agency, or those charged with governance may include those who have management responsibilities. Determination of who those charged with governance are is based on the auditor's judgment.

Definitions

Those charged with governance	The person(s) or organization(s) with responsibility for overseeing the strategic direction of the entity, the obligations related to the accountability of the entity, and the financial reporting process. May include management personnel; for example, executive members or a governance board or an owner-manager.
Management	The person(s) with executive responsibility for the conduct of the entity's operations. May include some or all of those charged with governance.

Requirements

The auditor is required to perform the following procedures related to communications with those charged with governance:

Those Charged with Governance

1. Determine the appropriate people to communicate with in the entity's governance structure.

2. When communicating with a subgroup of those charged with governance, determine if there is an additional need to communicate with the governing body.

3. If matters have been communicated to those involved in managing the entity who also have governance responsibilities, those matters do not need to be communicated again to the same individual in their governance role. This does not preclude the need for all those who would be communicated with in their governance capacity to be adequately informed.

Matters to Be Communicated

4. The auditor's responsibilities in relation to the financial statements should be communicated. This includes the auditor's responsibility for forming and expressing an opinion on whether the financial statements are prepared, in all material respects, in conformity with the applicable financial reporting framework. This also includes communicating that the financial statement audit does not relieve management or those charged with governance of their responsibilities.

5. Communicate an overview of the planned scope and timing of the audit.

6. Communicate any significant findings or issues, including the auditor's views about qualitative aspects of the entity's significant accounting practices, significant difficulties encountered during the audit, and disagreements with management. Also communicate significant findings that in the auditor's judgment are relevant to the responsibilities of those charged with governance for overseeing the financial reporting process.

7. Communicate nontrivial uncorrected misstatements and any effect they may have on the auditor's opinion. Identify any material uncorrected misstatements individually and request they be corrected. Also communicate the effect of any uncorrected misstatements related to prior periods.

8. If there are members of those charged with governance that are not involved in managing the entity, additional information needs to be communicated. These communications should include material, corrected misstatements and significant findings or issues that have been shared with management; the auditor's views on significant matters management discussed with other accountants; and written representations the auditor is requesting.

The Communication Process

9. Communicate the form, timing, and expected general content of communications.

10. Communicate significant findings or issues in writing when, using professional judgment, oral communication is not adequate. This communication does not need to include matters that have been communicated with those charged with governance and satisfactorily resolved.

11. Any written communication related to this standard is a by-product report and should include an indication that its use should be restricted to those charged with governance and, if appropriate, management.

12. Communicate with those charged with governance on a timely basis.

13. Evaluate the adequacy of the two-way communication for the purpose of the audit. If there has been inadequate communication, evaluate any effect on the assessment of risks of material misstatement and ability to obtain sufficient appropriate audit evidence.

Documentation

14. Document any oral communications related to AU-C 260, including when and to whom the communications occurred. Retain a copy of any written communications related to AU-C 260 as part of the audit documentation.

Analysis and Application of Procedures

Those charged with governance

Determine the appropriate recipients of the auditor's communication

The intended recipients of the auditor's communication are those charged with governance, which varies from one entity to another. The auditor's understanding of the entity's governance structure and processes obtained in connection with the requirements in AU-C 315 provides relevant input to his or her determination of the appropriate recipients of his or her communication.

Those charged with governance might include one or more of the following:

- Board of directors or supervisory board
- Subgroup of the board, such as the audit committee
- Partners or proprietors
- Committee of management or trustees
- Owner-manager or sole trustee

AU-C 260 does not establish communication requirements with an entity's management or owners unless they also are charged with a governance role.

In many instances, communication with the audit committee (or another equivalent subgroup of those charged with governance) adequately fulfills the auditor's responsibility to communicate with those charged with governance. Audit committees exist in many entities and are often responsible for oversight of the financial reporting process.

PUBLIC COMPANY IMPLICATION: Both the New York Stock Exchange and the NASDAQ require registrants to have audit committees. The Sarbanes-Oxley Act of 2002 (SOX) specifically mandates that the audit committee of a public company be directly responsible for the appointment, compensation, and oversight of the work of the auditor. In effect, the audit committee, and not the management, of a public company is to be viewed as "the client."

The auditor's determination of whether communication with the audit committee (or equivalent subgroup) fulfills the requirements to communicate with those charged with governance should include consideration of the following:

- The respective responsibilities of the governing body and the subgroup
- The nature of the matter to be communicated
- Relevant legal or regulatory requirements
- The authority of the subgroup to take action in relation to the information communicated
- The ability of the subgroup to provide further information and explanations needed by the auditor
- Whether there are potential conflicts of interest between the subgroup and the other members of the governing body

In making this determination, the auditor should assess how effectively the subgroup communicates relevant information with the governing body. To protect communication channels, the auditor may include an explicit statement in the engagement terms retaining the right to communicate directly with the governing body. For many entities, the auditor will determine that the audit committee constitutes the appropriate communication recipients.

OBSERVATION: In evaluating audit committees or other subgroups of those charged with governance, the auditor should assess whether the audit committee or subgroup exercises good governance principles. Effective audit committee processes include facilitating access between the auditor and the audit committee, including regular meetings with the auditor and the audit committee chair and others on the audit committee, with at least one of those meetings each year occurring without management present.

Matters to Be Communicated

Auditor's responsibilities related to the financial statement audit

The auditor should communicate to those charged with governance the auditor's responsibilities under auditing standards. These communications may include the following responsibilities:

- Performing the audit in accordance with GAAS and designing the audit to obtain reasonable assurance that the financial statements are free from material misstatement

- Considering internal control over financial reporting for purposes of designing audit procedures, but not for purposes of expressing an opinion on the effectiveness of the entity's internal control over financial reporting

- Communicating only those matters related to the financial statement audit that in the auditor's professional judgment are relevant to the financial reporting oversight responsibilities of those charged with governance

- Communicating other matters required by laws or regulations, by agreement with the entity, or by additional engagement requirements

---

ENGAGEMENT STRATEGY: The auditor may communicate these required matters regarding the auditor's GAAS responsibilities through an engagement letter or other form of written agreement, as long as that agreement is provided to those charged with governance.

While the auditor's report affirms the auditor's independence, it may be appropriate to communicate with those charged with governance circumstances or relationships such as financial interests, business or family relationships, or nonaudit services that the auditor considered in concluding that independence was not impaired.

OBSERVATION: It may be particularly appropriate to communicate matters that could bear on independence with those charged with governance in audits of public interest entities. Public interest entities include those subject to Securities and Exchange Commission reporting requirements as well as other entities with audited financial statements directly relied upon by significant numbers of stakeholders or indirectly relied upon through regulatory oversight such that an audit failure involving the entity could cause significant harm to the public.

Overview of the planned scope and timing of the audit

The auditor should communicate with those charged with governance an overview of the planned scope and timing of the audit. Communication of these matters may assist the auditor in better understanding the entity and its environment. These communications also assist those charged with governance in understanding better the consequences of the auditor's work for their oversight activities and help those charged with governance better understand the auditor's consideration of risks and materiality.

The auditor should exercise caution when communicating matters related to the planned scope and timing of the audit. It is important that the auditor's communication of these matters not compromise the effectiveness of the audit. This caution is especially relevant when those charged with governance are involved in managing the entity, such as an owner-manager. The auditor should avoid disclosing information that makes his or her audit procedures predictable.

Typical matters related to the planned scope and timing that the auditor may communicate include the following:

- How the auditor plans to address significant risks of material misstatements
- The auditor's approach to internal control
- The application of materiality in the context of an audit
- The extent to which the auditor will use internal audit, if applicable

Discussions with those charged with governance about the planned scope and timing of the audit may provide the auditor with useful insights about their attitude and actions. For example, the communications may reveal information about the attitudes, awareness, and actions of those charged with governance regarding their responsibilities for the oversight of the financial reporting process, including responsibility for internal control and assessing fraud risk.

Communications may provide the views of those charged with governance regarding issues such as the allocation of responsibilities between management and those charged with governance; the entity's strategies and related risks that could result in material misstatements; matters warranting particular attention during the audit; and significant communications with regulators. Discussions may also cover the actions of those charged with governance in response to previous communications with the auditor and in response to developments in laws, accounting standards, and corporate governance practices.

Significant findings from the audit

A primary component of the required auditor communications is to inform those charged with governance about significant findings from the audit. Communications about significant findings from the audit include matters that directly relate to the financial reporting oversight of those charged with governance. Exhibit AU-C 260-1 summarizes the topics that AU-C 260 states should be communicated with those charged with governance and describes what the nature of those communications may include.

ENGAGEMENT STRATEGY: Audit evidence may include additional information requested from those charged with governance as part of the communication of significant findings. For example, the auditor may want to confirm that he or she has the same understanding of significant issues as those charged with governance.

PLANNING AID REMINDER: If the auditor encounters significant difficulties in the audit, such difficulties may constitute a scope limitation that leads to a modification of his or her opinion.

The Communication Process

Establishing the communication process

Clear communications about the auditor's GAAS responsibilities, the planned audit scope and timing, and the nature of expected communications strengthen the communications between the auditor and those charged with governance. Thus, AU-C 260 requires the auditor to establish a mutual understanding of these matters with those charged with governance.

Clarification of the purpose, form, and process of the required communications with those charged with governance in advance of making the required communications contributes to effective two-way communication. Explicit understanding about the auditor's expectation that the communication is designed to be a two-way communication reinforces to those charged with governance the importance of their providing relevant information to the auditor that might affect the audit of financial statements. AU-C 260 does not preclude the auditor from discussing matters with management or the internal auditor before communicating with those charged with governance when appropriate.

Form of communication

For a matter not required to be communicated in writing, whether to communicate orally or in writing is determined by the auditor's judgment. In making those determinations, the auditor should consider the following matters:

- Significance of the particular matter

- Whether the matter has been satisfactorily resolved

- Whether management previously communicated the matter to those charged with governance

- The size, operating structure, control environment, and legal structure of the entity

- Legal or regulatory requirements to communicate certain audit findings in writing

- Amount of ongoing contact and dialogue the auditor has with those charged with governance and the expectations of those charged with governance

- Whether there have been significant changes in the composition and membership of the governing body

---

ENGAGEMENT STRATEGY: If a matter is discussed with an individual member of those charged with governance, the auditor may summarize the matter in later communications to ensure that all of those charged with governance have full and balanced information.

ENGAGEMENT STRATEGY: Documentation of oral communication may include entity-prepared copies of minutes if they are an appropriate record of the communication.

Timing of communication

The appropriate timing of communications will vary with the circumstances, depending on the significance and nature of the matter and the action expected to be taken by those charged with governance. Matters related to audit planning, such as the overview of the auditor's responsibilities and the planned scope and timing of the audit, are likely to be discussed early in the engagement as part of clarifying the terms of the engagement. Significant findings from the audit may be communicated as they are encountered (for example, significant difficulties) so that they can be overcome in a timely fashion.

Adequacy of communication

The evaluation of the two-way communication between the auditor and those charged with governance can be supported based on observations from audit procedures performed for other purposes. Such observations of those charged with governance may include:

- Appropriateness and timeliness of actions taken in response to matters communicated by the auditor
- Apparent openness in communications with the auditor
- Willingness and capacity to meet with the auditor without management present
- Apparent ability to understand matters raised by the auditor, often exhibited by extent of probing and questioning recommendations
- Difficulty in establishing a mutual understanding of the form, timing, and expected general content of communications
- For those charged with governance also involved in managing the entity, awareness of how matters discussed with the auditor affect their governance and management responsibilities

Inadequate communication may signal an ineffective control environment, which should impact the auditor's assessment of risk of material misstatements, and it may signal an increased risk that the auditor may not have obtained all the audit evidence required to form an opinion on the financial statements. To address concerns about the adequacy of the communications, the auditor may discuss concerns with those charged with governance. If the situation remains unresolved, the auditor may consider modifying the opinion on the financial statements due to a scope limitation, obtaining legal advice, communicating with those outside the entity (e.g. regulators, shareholders, responsible government agencies), or withdrawing from the engagement.

AU-C 260 does not change requirements in other standards to communicate certain matters to those charged with governance. The following communications required by other standards remain in effect:

- Communications with the audit committee or others with equivalent authority and responsibility pertaining to illegal acts that come to the auditor's attention (see AU-C 250)

- Communications to management and the audit committee or others with equivalent authority and responsibility when the auditor becomes aware during the audit that the entity is subject to an audit requirement that may not be encompassed in the terms of the engagement, and that an audit in accordance with generally accepted auditing standards may not satisfy the relevant legal, regulatory, or contractual requirements (see AU-C 935)

- Required direct inquiry of the audit committee (or at least its chair) regarding the audit committee's views about the risk of fraud and whether the audit committee has knowledge of any fraud or suspected fraud affecting the entity (see AU-C 240)

- Communications to those charged with governance about fraud caused by senior management and fraud (whether caused by senior management or others) that causes a material misstatement in the financial statements (see AU-C 240)

- Communications in writing to management and those charged with governance regarding control deficiencies identified during an audit that upon evaluation are considered to be significant deficiencies or material weaknesses (see AU-C 265)

- Consideration of communication of the nature of significant assumptions used in fair value measurements, the degree of subjectivity involved in the development of the assumption, and the relative materiality of the items being measured at fair value to the financial statements as a whole (see AU-C 540)

- Communications with those charged with governance regarding the auditor's responsibility with respect to other information, any procedures performed relating to the other information, and the results (see AU-C 720)

Practitioner's Aids

Exhibit AU-C 260-1 presents examples of significant findings from the audit that generally are communicated by the auditor to those charged with governance.

EXHIBIT AU-C 260-1 TOPIC AND NATURE OF COMMUNICATIONS ABOUT SIGNIFICANT FINDINGS

Topic of Communication	Nature of Communication
Qualitative aspects of entity's significant accounting practices	• Appropriateness and acceptability of accounting policies to the circumstances
	• Initial selection of and changes to accounting policies, including application of new pronouncements

Topic of Communication	*Nature of Communication*
	• Effect of significant accounting policies in controversial or emerging areas
	• Effect of the timing of transactions in relation to the period they are recorded
	• Identification of and process used to make accounting estimates
	• Indicators of possible management bias
	• Risks of material misstatement due to significant accounting estimates
	• Financial statement disclosure of estimation uncertainty
	• Issues involved and judgments made in preparing sensitive financial statement disclosures
	• Overall neutrality, consistency, and clarity of disclosures in financial statements
	• Extent to which financial statements are potentially impacted by significant disclosed uncertainties, unusual transactions, and selective correction of misstatements
	• Factors affecting asset and liability carrying values
Significant difficulties encountered during the audit	• Significant delays in management providing required information
	• Unnecessarily short time frame to complete the audit
	• Extensive unexpected effort required to obtain sufficient, appropriate evidence
	• Restrictions imposed by management on the auditors
	• Unavailability of expected information
	• Management unwilling to provide information about plans to deal with conditions that led the auditor to believe there is substantial doubt about the entity's ability to continue as a going concern
Disagreements with management	• Disagreements with management are required to be communicated (whether or not satisfactorily resolved) about matters that individually or in the aggregate could be significant to the financial statements
	• Significant disagreements with management concerning applicability of accounting principles, scope of the engagement, or wording of the audit report
Uncorrected misstatements	• Information about overall number and monetary effect of individually immaterial uncorrected misstatements
	• Discussion of the implications of failure to correct known and likely misstatements
Corrected misstatements	• Any corrected immaterial misstatements that could indicate a particular bias in financial statement preparation

Topic of Communication	*Nature of Communication*
Significant issues discussed or subject to correspondence with management	• Issues may include business conditions affecting the entity that increase the risk of material misstatement and discussions in connection with the retention of the auditor or discussions about the application of accounting principles and auditing standards
Written representations	• Provision of a copy of management's written representations to those charged with governance

SECTION 265

COMMUNICATING INTERNAL CONTROL RELATED MATTERS IDENTIFIED IN AN AUDIT

Authoritative Pronouncements

SAS-122—Statements on Auditing Standards: Clarification and Recodification

Overview

AU-C 265 provides the auditor with guidance on appropriately communicating internal control deficiencies identified during the audit to those charged with governance and management. The auditor may identify internal control deficiencies while identifying and assessing the risks of material misstatement as well as during other phases of the audit. AU-C 265 specifies which identified deficiencies are required to be communicated to those charged with governance and management. However, the auditor is not precluded from communicating other identified internal control matters that are not required to be communicated.

> **PLANNING AID REMINDER:** AU-C 265 is not applicable if the auditor is engaged to report on the effectiveness of an entity's internal control over financial reporting under AT 501 (*An Examination of an Entity's Internal Control over Financial Reporting That Is Integrated with an Audit of Its Financial Statements*).

> **PUBLIC COMPANY IMPLICATIONS:** Sarbanes-Oxley Act of 2002 (SOX) requires the auditor of an accelerated filer public company to issue a report on the operating effectiveness of its internal control over financial reporting. The audit of internal controls and the audit of the financial statements of a public company are to be integrated. In order to provide reasonable assurance about the operating effectiveness of internal controls, the auditor is to perform tests of controls over financial reporting. Information about significant deficiencies and material weaknesses obtained through work performed as part of the financial statement audit should be considered when reporting on internal controls (and vice versa).

Definitions

Deficiency in internal control	Exists when the design or operation of a control does not allow management or employees, in the normal course of performing their assigned functions, to prevent or detect and correct misstatements on a timely basis.
	A *design* deficiency exists when a control needed to meet the control objective is missing or an existing control is not properly designed such that the control objective would not be met even if the control operated as designed.

	A deficiency in *operation* exists when a properly designed control does not operate as designed or when the person performing the control does not have the necessary authority or competence to effectively perform the control.
Material weakness	A deficiency or combination of deficiencies in internal control such that there is a reasonable possibility that a material misstatement of the entity's financial statements will not be prevented or detected and corrected on a timely basis.
Significant deficiency	A deficiency or combination of deficiencies in internal control that is less severe than a material weakness yet important enough to merit attention by those charged with governance.

Requirements

The auditor is presumptively required to perform the following procedures with respect to the communication of internal control related matters to management and those charged with governance:

1. Determine whether internal control deficiencies have been identified based on the audit work performed.

2. If internal control deficiencies have been identified, determine whether they constitute significant deficiencies or material weaknesses individually or in combination based on audit work performed.

3. If an internal control deficiency or combination of deficiencies is determined to not be a material weakness, consider whether prudent officials using the same facts and circumstances would likely reach the same conclusion.

4. Communicate significant deficiencies and material weaknesses identified during the audit, including those that were remediated during the audit, in writing to those charged with governance on a timely basis.

5. Communicate to management at an appropriate level of responsibility on a timely basis:

   a. In writing, unless doing so is inappropriate, significant deficiencies and material weaknesses communicated or intended to be communicated with those charged with governance

   b. In writing or orally, other internal control deficiencies identified during the audit not otherwise communicated to management that the auditor judges to be sufficiently important to merit management's attention. If these deficiencies are communicated orally, document the communication.

6. Communications to those charged with governance and management should be made no later than 60 days following the report release date.

7. Written communication of significant deficiencies and material weaknesses should include:

   a. The definitions of the terms "material weakness" and, when relevant, "significant deficiency"

    b. A description of the material weaknesses and significant deficiencies and an explanation of their potential effects

    c. Sufficient information for those charged with governance and management to understand the context of the communication, including explanations that (1) the audit's purpose was to express an opinion on the financial statements; (2) the audit included consideration of internal control over financial reporting to design appropriate audit procedures, but not to express an opinion on the effectiveness of internal control; (3) the auditor is not expressing an opinion on internal control effectiveness; and (4) the auditor's consideration of internal control was not designed to identify all deficiencies that might be significant deficiencies or material weaknesses, so unidentified deficiencies, significant deficiencies, or material weaknesses may exist.

    d. A restriction on the use of the communication to those charged with governance, management, others within the organization, and any specified governmental authority to which the auditor is required to report.

8. A written communication issued stating that no material weaknesses were identified during the audit should include the matters described in paragraph 7(a), (c), and (d).

9. A written communication should *not* be issued that states that no significant deficiencies were identified in an audit.

Analysis and Application of Procedures

Identifying deficiencies in internal control and evaluating their severity

The auditor is required to obtain an understanding of internal control relevant to the audit when identifying and assessing the risks of material misstatement. In making those risk assessments and when performing further audit procedures in response to those risks, the auditor may identify deficiencies in internal control. While the purpose of the audit is not to express an opinion on internal controls, the auditor may identify deficiencies that would be appropriate to communicate to those charged with governance. AU-C 265 provides guidance regarding those communications.

The auditor may communicate his or her findings with management when determining whether internal control deficiencies have been identified. It is appropriate to discuss these issues with a level of management familiar with the internal control area in question and with the authority to take remedial actions on any control deficiencies identified. The auditor may obtain other relevant information to consider from these discussions such as:

- Management's understanding of the actual or suspected causes of deficiencies

- Exceptions management may have noted that arose from deficiencies

- Preliminary indications from management of its response to the findings

> **OBSERVATION:** Smaller, less complex entities may have less segregation of duties or more informal controls than larger organizations. However, this may not indicate that control deficiencies exist, because management authority and oversight may act effectively as controls, reducing the need for more detailed control activities.

> **PLANNING AID REMINDER:** An auditor may decide not to test controls and instead perform all substantive audit procedures. AICPA Technical Practice Aid 8200.15 notes that the decision to not test controls does not automatically mean there is a control deficiency that must be evaluated. If the auditor decides not to test a control because it is nonexistent or is not properly designed, then that would represent a control deficiency that needs to be assessed in order to determine whether it is a significant deficiency or material weakness. If the design of the control is appropriate but the auditor decides not to test it for other reasons, then he or she has not identified a control deficiency.

AU-C 265 requires the auditor to determine whether identified control deficiencies, individually or in combination, are significant deficiencies or material weaknesses. The determination of whether a control deficiency constitutes a significant deficiency or material weakness is a matter of professional judgment. When making this determination, the auditor considers the likelihood and magnitude of misstatement.

> **PLANNING AID REMINDER:** The auditor is not obtaining an understanding of internal control for the purpose of expressing an opinion on internal control. Thus, significant deficiencies and material weaknesses may exist even if the auditor has not identified misstatements during the audit.

> **PLANNING AID REMINDER:** Internal control deficiencies might be discovered during various phases of the engagement. Deficiencies can be related to any of the five components of internal control. In addition, deficiencies can arise because of poor design or poor operation of the control. For example, a deficiency could be related to lack of proper segregation of duties and responsibilities (design within internal control) or lack of timely preparation of bank reconciliations (execution within internal control).

Several factors can affect the likelihood that a deficiency might fail to prevent or detect and correct a misstatement. Examples of such factors include the nature of the account or transaction, the susceptibility of assets or liabilities to loss, the subjectivity, complexity, and judgment required to determine the amount involved, the cause and frequency of exceptions due to the control deficiency, the interactions of the control with other controls and other control deficiencies, and the importance of the controls to the financial reporting process.

The magnitude of the misstatement caused by a control deficiency may be affected by size of the financial statement amounts or disclosures impacted by the deficiency and by the volume of activity in an account balance or class of transactions. The magnitude of a potential misstatement is generally limited to overstating an account balance or transaction total by the recorded amount, while understatements could be larger. Some control deficiencies may be individually insignificant; however, when combined with other deficiencies that affect the same account balance or disclosure, the combination of deficiencies can increase the risks of misstatement to the extent that a significant deficiency or material weakness exists.

AU-C 265 identifies specific indicators of material weaknesses in internal control:

- Ineffective oversight of the entity's financial reporting and internal control by those charged with governance

- Restatement of previously issued financial statements to reflect the correction of a misstatement

- Identification by the auditor of a material misstatement in the financial statements not initially identified by the entity's internal control

- Identification of fraud of any magnitude on the part of senior management

Exhibit AU-C 265-1 provides guidance regarding what items may be considered deficiencies in internal control over financial reporting.

Communicating internal control deficiencies

AU-C 265 requires the auditor's communication of significant deficiencies and material weaknesses to be in writing. This communication requirement applies to all significant deficiencies or material weaknesses identified during the current audit in addition to significant deficiencies and material weaknesses communicated in previous audits that have not yet been remediated. If the entity has chosen not to act on a previously identified significant deficiency or material weakness with no rational explanation, that decision could constitute a significant deficiency or material weakness.

The timing of required written communications is best if made by the report release date, although AU-C 265's requirement is that the written communication be made no later than 60 days after the report release date. Some matters may be communicated to management or those charged with governance at an earlier date to allow management the opportunity to remediate the deficiency on a timely basis. The early communication does not have to be in writing; however, the auditor must ultimately communicate all significant deficiencies and material weaknesses in writing.

OBSERVATION: For some significant deficiencies or material weaknesses, management or those charged with governance may make a conscious decision to accept the risk of the deficiency leading to a material misstatement due to the cost or other considerations associated with remediating the deficiency. Despite management's decision, the auditor is still required to communicate all significant deficiencies and material weaknesses.

PUBLIC COMPANY IMPLICATIONS: In the audit of internal control over financial reporting required by SOX for public companies, the presence of one or more material weaknesses prohibits the auditor from concluding that internal control over financial reporting is operating effectively.

The level of detail the auditor communicates regarding identified significant deficiencies and material weaknesses is subject to the auditor's professional judgment. Factors that may impact the level of detail communicated include the nature, size, and complexity of the entity; the nature of the significant deficiencies and material weaknesses identified; the entity's governance composition; and any legal or regulatory requirements about the communication of internal control deficiencies.

In some circumstances, it may not be appropriate for the auditor to communicate significant deficiencies and material weaknesses to management because identified deficiencies may cause the auditor to question management's integrity or competence. In these situations the auditor should, as appropriate, follow the guidance in either AU-C 250 on reporting identified or suspected noncompliance with laws and regulations when those charged with governance are involved in the noncompliance or AU-C 240 on communicating to those charged with governance when fraud or suspected fraud involving management has been identified.

If deficiencies other than significant deficiencies or material weaknesses have been reported to management in a prior period and management has chosen not to remedy the deficiencies, the auditor does not need to communicate the deficiencies again during the current audit. However, if there has been a change in management or new information has arisen affecting the auditor's understanding of the deficiencies, the auditor may find it appropriate to recommunicate these deficiencies. The failure of management to remedy previously communicated internal control deficiencies may constitute a significant deficiency that requires communication with those charged with governance. When reporting on other internal control deficiencies identified in the audit, those charged with governance may wish to be informed of any such deficiencies communicated to management.

OBSERVATION: The appropriate level of management is the one that has responsibility and authority to evaluate the deficiencies in internal control and to take necessary remedial action. For significant deficiencies and material weaknesses, the appropriate level is likely to be the CEO or CFO. Other deficiencies might be appropriately communicated to operational management.

While the auditor should explain the potential effects of the deficiencies in his or her written communication of significant deficiencies and material weaknesses, the effects do not need to be quantified. Other items the auditor may include in the written communication include the following:

- Inherent limitations of internal control, including the potential for management override of controls

- The specific nature and extent of the auditor's consideration of internal control during the audit

- Suggestions for remedial action on identified deficiencies

- Management's actual or proposed responses and a statement about whether the auditor has taken any steps to verify if management's responses have been implemented

Management may prepare a written response to the auditor's communication regarding significant deficiencies and material weaknesses. This response may include information such as a description of corrective actions taken by the entity, the entity's plans to implement new controls, or a statement indicating that management believes the costs of correcting a deficiency outweigh the benefits. If such a response is included in a document containing the auditor's written communication of significant deficiencies and material weaknesses, the auditor may add a paragraph such as the following to his or her written communication disclaiming an opinion on management's response:

> X Corporation's written response to the significant deficiencies [*and material weaknesses*] identified in our audit was not subjected to the auditing procedures applied in the audit of the financial statements and, accordingly, we express no opinion on it.

A written communication stating that no material weaknesses were identified in the audit does not provide any assurance about the effectiveness of an entity's internal control over financial reporting. However, management or those charged with governance may request that this communication be made or it may be required by some governmental entities and the auditor is not precluded from issuing such a communication. The auditor is precluded from issuing a written communication indicating that no significant deficiencies were identified during the audit due to its potential to be misunderstood or misused.

Practitioner's Aids

Exhibit AU-C 265-1 includes examples from AU-C 325 of circumstances that indicate possible control deficiencies, significant deficiencies, or material weaknesses. Exhibit AU-C 325-2 is an example of a written communication encompassing AU-C 325's requirements. Exhibit AU-C 325-3 contains examples of possible material weaknesses for a small business enterprise.

EXHIBIT AU-C 265-1—EXAMPLES OF POSSIBLE DEFICIENCIES

- Deficiencies in internal control design
    - —Inadequate overall internal control design over financial statement preparation
    - —Inadequate design over a significant account or process

—Inadequate documentation of internal control

—Insufficient control consciousness across the organization

—Evidence of ineffective aspects of the control environment

—Evidence of an ineffective entity risk assessment process

—Evidence of an ineffective response to identified significant risks

—Inadequate segregation of duties

—Absent or inadequate controls over safeguarding of assets

—Inadequate design of information technology general and application controls

—Unqualified or inadequately trained employees or management

—Inadequate design of monitoring controls

—Absence of an internal process to report deficiencies in internal control to management on a timely basis

—Absence of a risk assessment process in an entity where one would ordinarily be established

- Failures in the operation of internal control

—Evidence of failure in the operation of an effectively designed control over a significant account or process

—Evidence of failure of the information and communication component of internal control to provide complete and accurate output because of deficiencies in timeliness, completeness, or accuracy

—Evidence of failure of controls designed to safeguard assets from loss, damage, or misappropriation

—Lack of performance of reconciliations of significant accounts

—Presence of undue bias or lack of objectivity by those responsible for accounting decisions

—Misrepresentation by client personnel to the auditor

—Management override of controls

—Failure of an application control caused by a deficiency in the design or operation of an IT general control

—An observed deviation rate exceeding the auditor's expected deviation rate in a test of the operating effectiveness of a control

---

EXHIBIT AU-C 265-2—EXAMPLE OF A WRITTEN COMMUNICATION ABOUT SIGNIFICANT DEFICIENCIES AND MATERIAL WEAKNESSES

To Management and [*identify the body or individuals charged with governance, such as the entity's Board of Directors*] of X Corporation

In planning and performing our audit of the financial statements of X Corporation as of and for the year ended December 31, 20X5, in accordance with auditing standards generally accepted in the United States of America, we considered X Corporation's internal control over financial reporting (internal control) as a basis for designing audit procedures that are appropriate in the circumstances for the purpose of expressing our opinion on the financial statements, but not for the purpose of expressing an opinion on the effectiveness of X Corporation's internal control. Accordingly, we do not express an opinion on the effectiveness of the company's internal control.

Our consideration of internal control was for the limited purpose described in the preceding paragraph and was not designed to identify all deficiencies in internal control that might be [*material weaknesses or significant deficiencies or material weaknesses*] and therefore, [*material weaknesses or significant deficiencies or material weaknesses*] may exist that were not identified. However, as discussed below, we identified certain deficiencies in internal control that we consider to be [*material weaknesses or significant deficiencies or material weaknesses and significant deficiencies*].

A deficiency in internal control exists when the design or operation of a control does not allow management or employees, in the normal course of performing their assigned functions, to prevent, or detect and correct, misstatements on a timely basis. A material weakness is a deficiency, or combination of deficiencies, in internal control, such that there is a reasonable possibility that a material misstatement of the entity's financial statements will not be prevented, or detected and corrected, on a timely basis. [*We consider the following deficiencies in X Corporation's internal control to be material weaknesses:*]

[*Describe the material weaknesses that were identified and explain their potential effects.*]

[*A significant deficiency is a deficiency, or combination of deficiencies, in internal control that is less severe than a material weakness, yet important enough to merit attention by those charged with governance. We consider the following deficiencies in X Corporation's internal control to be significant deficiencies:*]

[*Describe the significant deficiencies that were identified and explain their potential effects.*]

[*If the auditor is communicating significant deficiencies and did not identify any material weaknesses, the auditor may state that none of the identified significant deficiencies are considered to be material weaknesses.*]

This communication is intended solely for the information and use of management, [*identify those charged with governance*], others within the organization, and [*identify any governmental authorities to which the auditor is required to report*] and is not intended to be and should not be used by anyone other than these specified parties.

[*Auditor's Signature*]

[*Date*]

EXHIBIT AU-C 265-3—EXAMPLES OF POSSIBLE MATERIAL WEAKNESSES: SMALL BUSINESS ENTERPRISE

Determining whether a specific condition is a material weakness is based on exercising professional judgment in the context of the existing characteristics of a particular client. The following list includes examples of conditions that the auditor may identify as a material weakness for a small business enterprise. The list is illustrative only and is not intended to be comprehensive. Also, because the assumption is that the client is a small business enterprise, there is an emphasis on cash and related cash transactions, inventory, and property, plant, and equipment.

- *Cash and credit sales*

    —Credit sales are approved by the bookkeeper, who is responsible for the write-off of bad debts.

    —A bookkeeper maintains cash receipts records, opens the mail, and prepares the bank deposit.

    —Cash payments for expenditures using cash receipts for the day.

    —Cash receipts are deposited at the end of the week, net of expenditures paid during the week.

    —Several sales clerks have access to the single cash drawer used during the day to record cash sales.

    —Cash registers used during the day are not read and reconciled after the end of each shift.

    —A bookkeeper is responsible for the purchase of goods and services.

    —There is no formal documentation that shows that goods purchased were received.

    —Documentation to support cash disbursements is maintained on a haphazard basis.

    —The office manager authorizes the payment of invoices, prepares checks, and reconciles the bank statements.

- *Cash and purchases of goods and services*

    —Purchase orders are not used to authorize the acquisition of goods and services.

    —Invoices and other supporting documentation are not marked as "canceled" or "paid."

    —The hiring and firing of employees is not centralized.

    —Paychecks are given to an immediate supervisor for distribution.

    —The number of hours or days worked is not controlled through the use of time clocks or otherwise approved by supervisory personnel.

    —An unusually large amount of petty cash is maintained, and support for expenditures is lacking.

    —Numerous checking accounts are used, and prenumbered checks are not accounted for.

    —Numerous employees are authorized to sign checks.

    —Checks are often written to "cash."

    —Bank reconciliations are seldom prepared.

- *Inventory controls*

    —The periodic inventory count is not under the control of the owner or manager.

    —The inventory is not subject to reasonable limited access (for both employees and customers) based on the characteristics of the business.

—Inventory shipments to customers are not based on appropriate shipping authorization.

—Inventory receipts are not properly counted and inspected.

—The year-end inventory summarization is not analyzed and evaluated by the owner or manager for unusual variations in gross profit percentages, obsolete inventory lines, unreasonable inventory counts, missing items, inappropriate cost data, etc.

- *Property, plant, and equipment*

    —A plant ledger is not maintained.

    —The owner or manager does not periodically verify the existence and condition of property items.

    —The sale of used property items is not approved by the owner or manager.

AU-C 300
Risk Assessment and Response to Assessed Risks

SECTION 300

PLANNING AN AUDIT

Authoritative Pronouncements

SAS-122—Statements on Auditing Standards: Clarification and Recodification

Overview

AU-C 300 recognizes that the successful completion of an audit engagement is a difficult task and, like most difficult tasks, requires proper planning. The auditor's objective is to plan the audit so that it is performed effectively. AU-C 300 primarily considers the auditor's responsibility to plan an audit in the context of a recurring audit. Additional considerations relevant to initial audit engagements are addressed in AU-C 600 (*Special Considerations—Audits of Group Financial Statements (Including the Work of Component Auditors)*).

Adequate planning of an audit benefits the financial statement audit in many ways:

- Helping to identify important areas of the audit and potential problems in a timely manner
- Determining personnel requirements
- Determining how to use a firm's resources in an effective and efficient manner
- Helping in the direction, supervision, and review of the work of engagement team members
- Helping with any necessary coordination of work done by auditors of components and specialists

The nature, timing, and extent of planning depend on (1) the size and complexity of the entity, (2) the auditor's previous experience serving the entity, and (3) changes in circumstances that occur during the audit engagement.

The audit plan must be responsive to the auditor's identification of the risk of material misstatement. Although planning begins before the auditor begins fieldwork, planning is not a discrete process but, rather, is an iterative process that continues until the current audit engagement is completed. As the auditor performs planned audit procedures, he or she considers the need to revise the nature, timing, and extent of audit procedures that were selected during the initial phase of planning the audit.

PUBLIC COMPANY IMPLICATION: In 2010 the PCAOB issued eight auditing standards (AS-8 through AS-5) related to the auditor's assessment of and response to risk. The standards bear many similarities to the eight risk-assessment standards adopted by the Auditing Standards Board in 2006. AS-9 (Audit Planning) and AS-10 (Supervision of the Audit Engagement) are the PCAOB standards that affect audit planning and supervision. AS-9 establishes requirements related to planning the audit, including requirements related to developing an appropriate audit strategy and audit plan. AS-10 describes the auditor's responsibilities for supervising the engagement, and it applies to the engagement partner and other audit team members who assist the partner in supervising others. Although there are a number of differences between the PCAOB's and ASB's risk standards, the risk-assessment concepts contained in the PCAOB standards should be familiar to most auditors. As is currently the case, audit risk is the risk that the auditor will issue an inappropriate opinion on financial statements that are materially misstated. The auditor is to reduce audit risk to a low level through the application of audit procedures. As a result, the amount of audit effort devoted to particular accounts, classes of transactions, and disclosures should vary based on their respective risk.

Requirements

The auditor is presumptively required to perform the following procedures related to planning an audit:

1. The engagement partner and other key engagement team members should be involved in planning the audit. This includes planning and participating in the engagement team member discussion.

2. At the beginning of the current audit engagement, perform the following activities:

   a. Perform procedures regarding continuing the client relationship and the specific audit engagement as required by AU-C 220 (*Quality Control for an Engagement Conducted in Accordance with Generally Accepted Auditing Standards*)

   b. Evaluate compliance with ethical requirements, including independence, as required by AU-C 220

   c. Establish an understanding of the engagement terms as required by AU-C 210 (*Terms of Audit Engagements*)

3. Establish an overall audit strategy setting the scope, timing, and direction of the audit and that guides development of the audit plan. In establishing the audit strategy, the auditor should:

   a. Identify the engagement's characteristics defining its scope

   b. Determine the engagement's reporting objectives in order to plan the audit's timing and the nature of the required communications

   c. Consider significant factors, determined using professional judgment, directing the engagement team's efforts

   d. Consider the results of preliminary engagement activities and whether any knowledge the engagement partner gained on other engagements performed for the entity is relevant

   e. Determine the nature, extent, and timing of resources necessary to perform the engagement

4. Develop an audit plan, including descriptions of:

    a. The nature and extent of planned risk assessment procedures as determined by AU-C 315

    b. The nature, timing, and extent of planned further audit procedures at the relevant assertion level as determined by AU-C 330

    c. Other planned audit procedures that are required for the engagement to comply with GAAS

5. Update and revise the overall audit strategy and plan as necessary during the course of the audit.

6. Plan the nature, timing, and extent of direction and supervision of engagement team members and review of their work.

7. Consider whether specialized skills are needed to perform the audit and, if they are, seek the assistance of an audit staff professional or an outside professional. The auditor should have sufficient knowledge to communicate the objectives of the other professional's work; evaluate whether the specified audit procedures will meet the auditor's objectives; and evaluate the results of the audit procedures applied as they relate to the nature, timing, and extent of further planned audit procedures.

8. Document (1) the overall audit strategy, (2) the audit plan, and (3) any significant changes made during the audit engagement to the overall audit strategy or plan and the reasons for those changes.

9. Perform the following activities prior to starting an initial audit:

    a. Perform procedures regarding the acceptance of the client relationship and specific audit engagement as required by AU-C 220.

    b. Communicate with the predecessor auditor when there is a change of auditors in accordance with AU-C 210.

Analysis and Application of Procedures

Discussion among Key Engagement Team Members

Key engagement team members are required to discuss the risks of material misstatement of the financial statements due to error or fraud. This discussion improves the effectiveness and efficiency of the planning process by drawing on the experience of the engagement partner and other team members and by helping team members understand how the results of audit procedures they perform may affect other aspects of the audit, such as the nature, timing, and extent of further audit procedures.

Preliminary Engagement Activities

The required preliminary engagement activities allow the auditor to assess certain conditions relating to the audit. One important aspect evaluated with these procedures is management integrity. The auditor also needs to ascertain that he or she is independent and that there is no misunderstanding with the client regarding engagement terms before commencing the audit engagement.

    For a continuing engagement, these preliminary procedures often occur shortly after the completion of the previous audit engagement.

PLANNING AID REMINDER: Although the auditor evaluates client continuance, ethical requirements, and independence before commencing the engagement, he or she needs to monitor these aspects throughout the period of the professional engagement.

Develop an Overall Strategy for the Audit Engagement

The specific audit strategy for an engagement is based on the characteristics of the client. Specific factors that the auditor should consider include the following:

- Characteristics of the client's business and the related industry implications (e.g., the financial reporting framework that provide the client's basis of reporting, locations, etc.)
- The nature of reports expected to be rendered, including deadlines and key dates for expected communications and the involvement of other auditors, including internal auditors
- Preliminary judgment of materiality levels, and material locations and account balances (including setting materiality levels for auditors of other locations)
- Conditions where there may be a higher risk of material misstatement
- Whether to test the operating effectiveness of internal control
- Identification of recent events affecting the entity or its industry, including recent financial reporting developments

PLANNING AID REMINDER: The auditor should also consider his or her knowledge gained from performing other engagements for the entity.

In developing an overall audit strategy, the auditor should consider (1) the scope of the audit engagement and (2) the engagement's reporting objectives, timing, and required communications. In determining the scope of the audit engagement, the auditor may consider the following:

- Industry-specific reporting requirements
- Expected audit coverage (e.g., number of client locations where audit procedures are going to be performed)
- Nature of control relationships between a parent and a subsidiary
- Use of other auditors
- The entity's reporting currency
- Any statutory or regulatory audit requirements
- The use of client personnel (e.g., internal audit) in performing the audit engagement
- The client's use of service organizations, and how the auditor will test the design and operating effectiveness of controls at the service organization
- The auditor's planned use of audit evidence obtained in prior periods

- The effect of information technology on audit procedures, including the availability of electronic data and the use of computer-assisted audit techniques
- The availability of client personnel and data
- Engagement budgeting, including allocating sufficient time to audit areas with greater risk
- Audit areas with a higher risk of material misstatement
- The entity's volume of transactions (which may affect whether the auditor decides to test the operating effectiveness of internal control)
- Management's commitment to internal control and the results of previous evaluations of the operating effectiveness of internal control, including management's efforts to remedy significant deficiencies or material weaknesses
- Significant recent developments affecting the entity (e.g., business, industry, legal, regulatory)

In determining the engagement's reporting objectives, timing, and required communications, the auditor may consider

- Due dates of financial reports, including interim reports
- Planned meeting dates with management and those charged with governance
- The expected type and timing of reports to be issued (e.g., audit report, management letter, etc.)
- Periodic updates to management on the progress of the audit throughout the engagement
- The type and timing of reports from other auditors involved in performing the engagement
- The schedule of audit team meetings during the audit and the planned schedule for reviewing audit work
- Whether there are any required communications with third parties

---

PUBLIC COMPANY IMPLICATIONS: SOX and revised SEC rules prohibit the auditor of a public company from performing certain nonaudit services for that company. Many of these services were prohibited under existing SEC rules on independence adopted in November 2000. The new rules clarify many of the existing prohibitions and expand the circumstances in which the services are prohibited. Furthermore, SOX requires that any allowed nonaudit service be preapproved by the audit committee of the public company. There are a number of differences between SEC/PCAOB independence rules and the independence rules that apply to auditors of private (non-SEC registrants) companies.

An outcome of preparing the audit strategy is that it helps the auditor determine the allocation of audit resources; for example:

- The nature of audit staff to assign to specific audit areas (e.g., assign experienced staff to high-risk areas)

- The number of staff to assign to specific audit areas
- The timing of when audit staff are to be assigned
- The supervision, management, and direction of audit staff

ENGAGEMENT STRATEGY: The audit strategy helps in developing the audit plan, but preparing the strategy and developing the plan are not unrelated or sequential processes. The audit strategy and plan are highly interrelated, and changes to one will likely result in changes to the other.

Because the nature, timing, and extent of audit planning depends in part on the size and complexity of the client, the planning for a small entity does not have to be complex or time-consuming. A brief memorandum that outlines issues from the previous audit, updated based on conversations with the owner-manager, can serve as the basis for planning the current audit.

Communications with Management and Those Charged with Governance

The auditor is required to communicate an overview of the audit's planned scope and timing with those charged with governance of the entity. These discussions are intended to facilitate the effective administration of the engagement. Those communication responsibilities are addressed in AU-C 260 (*The Auditor's Communication with Those Charged with Governance*).

ENGAGEMENT STRATEGY: The auditor may discuss aspects of the audit plan with the entity's management; however, the overall audit strategy and plan are the auditor's responsibility. Furthermore, care should be taken in discussions with entity management to maintain the effectiveness of the audit. For example, discussing the details of audit procedures with management could compromise audit effectiveness by making the audit procedures too predictable.

Develop an Audit Plan

The auditor should prepare a detailed audit plan that reflects the overall strategy for performing the audit engagement. The audit plan will include the nature, timing, and extent of further audit procedures to be performed by the engagement team. Planning for these procedures occurs throughout the audit, and may be adjusted as the auditor conducts risk assessment procedures and further audit procedures, such as tests of the operating effectiveness of controls, and substantive procedures.

ENGAGEMENT STRATEGY: The auditor may need to revise the original audit strategy and plan as a result of a change in circumstances or the results of audit procedures that were performed. For example, audit evidence obtained through substantive procedures that contradicts earlier evidence gathered through tests of controls may cause the auditor to revise the assessment of risk and amend the audit strategy and plan.

Planning the nature, timing, and extent of the direction and supervision of engagement team members and the review of their work depends on many factors, such as:

- Entity complexity and size

- Area of the audit

- Assessed risks of material misstatement (i.e., higher assessed risks of material misstatement typically correspond to increased extent and timeliness of supervision and increased review of team member work)

- Competence of team members performing the audit work

In audits carried out by a sole practitioner, there is no direction, supervision, or review of others' work. In these circumstances, the auditor may want to consult with other suitably experienced auditors if complex or unusual issues are involved.

Consider Whether Specialized Skills Are Needed to Perform the Audit Engagement

Specialized skills are often needed in performing an audit (e.g., information technology, valuation, forensic, etc.). The audit engagement team often needs an individual possessing information technology (IT) skills to (1) determine the effect of IT on the audit, (2) understand IT controls, and (3) design and perform tests of IT controls and substantive procedures. An IT professional is more likely to be needed on the engagement if:

- The entity's systems and IT controls are complex

- The entity has made significant changes to existing systems or has implemented new systems

- The entity has significant involvement with electronic commerce

- The entity uses emerging technologies

- Significant audit evidence is available only in electronic form

- Significant data sharing exists among systems

An IT specialist may perform the following audit procedures: (1) analyze how the entity initiates, authorizes, records, processes, and reports transactions; (2) analyze the design of the entity's internal controls; (3) inspect the entity's system documentation; (4) observe the operation of IT controls; and (5) plan and perform tests of IT controls.

Documentation

The auditor's documentation of the overall audit strategy should communicate significant matters to the engagement team and include key decisions made to properly plan the audit, such as the overall scope, timing, and conduct of the audit. This documentation may in the form of a memorandum.

Documentation of the audit plan records the planned nature, timing, and extent of risk assessment procedures and further audit procedures at the relevant assertion level that respond to the assessed risks. For this, the auditor may use standard audit programs or audit completion checklists tailored to the specific audit engagement.

Recording significant changes made to the audit strategy or plan during the audit and the reasons for those changes helps to explain why changes were made, that appropriate responses were taken to changes that occurred, and also describes the final audit strategy and plan adopted.

Considerations Relevant to Initial Audit Engagements

In a first-year audit, the auditor should also consider the following factors in developing the audit strategy and plan:

- The need to make arrangements with the previous auditor to review their documentation; see AU-C 510 (*Opening Balances—Initial Audit Engagements, Including Reaudit Engagements*)

- Any major issues discussed with management before being retained, the need to communicate these issues to those charged with governance, and the effect of these issues on the audit strategy and audit plan

- The need to obtain appropriate audit evidence for account balances as of the beginning of the year

- Other steps required by the firm's system of quality control (e.g., the involvement of a second partner to review the audit plan before work begins)

PLANNING AID REMINDER: The process of planning the audit is typically more extensive in the first year of an engagement than in later years.

AU-C 510 requires the auditor to communicate with the predecessor auditor before accepting an engagement. Inquiry of the predecessor auditor might provide useful information relevant to the successor auditor's decision about whether to accept the engagement.

Practitioner's Aids

Use a planning checklist

The auditor may use an engagement planning checklist to control the planning phase of the audit engagement. Exhibit AU-C 300-1 is an example of such a checklist.

EXHIBIT AU-C 300-1—AUDIT ENGAGEMENT PLANNING CHECKLIST

Use the following checklist as a guide for planning audit procedures in a continuing engagement. The checklist is only a guide, and professional judgment should be exercised to determine how the checklist should be modified by revising the questions listed or adding questions to it where appropriate.

Check the appropriate response. If the question is not relevant to this particular audit engagement, place "N/A" (not applicable) in the space provided for the audit documentation reference. If additional explanation is needed with respect to a question, provide a proper cross-reference to another audit schedule.

Client Name: _____

Date of Financial Statements: _____

	Yes	No	Audit Documentation Reference
1. Is the scope of the audit engagement limited to a single financial statement?	_____	_____	_____
• If yes, have we identified the notes and other disclosures that are appropriate for a single financial statement presentation?	_____	_____	_____
• If yes, are the other financial statements going to be available for our perusal in order to identify events, transactions, and balances that may have implications for the audited financial statements?	_____	_____	_____
2. Are comparative financial statements presented?	_____	_____	_____
• If yes, are we responsible for reporting on the previous year's financial statements?	_____	_____	_____
3. If a predecessor CPA is reporting on the previous year's financial statements, have we:	_____	_____	_____
• Discussed relevant matters with the predecessor CPA before accepting the engagement?	_____	_____	_____
• Considered what matters to discuss with the predecessor CPA?	_____	_____	_____
• Arranged to communicate matters discovered in the current engagement to the predecessor CPA?	_____	_____	_____
• Arranged to provide the predecessor with a preliminary draft of the current and previous year's financial statements and our audit report?	_____	_____	_____

	Yes	No	Audit Documentation Reference
• Considered the format and content of the representation letter to be issued to the predecessor CPA?	_____	_____	_____
4. Have we considered the effect on audit procedures if the client has decided not to present a statement of cash flows?	_____	_____	_____
5. If the client has decided to present supplementary information, which is not part of the basic financial statements, are we engaged to review the supplementary information?	_____	_____	_____
6. If a portion of the financial statements is audited by another CPA, have we determined whether we can serve as the principal CPA?	_____	_____	_____
7. If we can serve as the principal CPA, have we considered whether to refer in our audit report to the work done by the other CPA?	_____	_____	_____
8. Have we identified the bases (operating income, total assets, etc.) and percentages of those amounts that should be used by subordinates to identify material misstatement?	_____	_____	_____
9. In designing the specific inquiries to be made, have we considered:			
• The nature and materiality of items?	_____	_____	_____
• The likelihood of misstatement?	_____	_____	_____
• Knowledge obtained during current and previous engagements?	_____	_____	_____
• The stated qualifications of the entity's accounting personnel?	_____	_____	_____
• The extent to which a particular item is affected by management's judgment?	_____	_____	_____

	Yes	No	Audit Documentation Reference
• The inadequacies in the entity's underlying financial data?	_____	_____	_____
• The potential for related-party transactions	_____	_____	_____
10. Have we acquired an adequate understanding of specialized accounting principles and practices of the client's industry by:			
• Reviewing relevant AICPA Accounting/Audit Guides?	_____	_____	_____
• Reviewing financial statements of other entities in the same industry?	_____	_____	_____
• Consulting with other individuals familiar with accounting practices in the specialized industry?	_____	_____	_____
• Reading periodicals, textbooks, and other publications?	_____	_____	_____
• Performing other procedures? (Describe.)	_____	_____	_____
11. Have we developed an understanding of the client's organization, including:			
• The form of business organization?	_____	_____	_____
• The history of the client?	_____	_____	_____
• The principals involved in the organization by review of the organizational chart or similar analysis?	_____	_____	_____
• Changes in capital structure?	_____	_____	_____
• Other relevant matters? (Describe.)	_____	_____	_____
12. Have we developed an understanding of the client's operating characteristics, including:			
• An understanding of the client's products and services?	_____	_____	_____
• Identification of operating locations?	_____	_____	_____
• An understanding of production methods?	_____	_____	_____

	Yes	No	Audit Documentation Reference
• Degree of reliance on information technology, including the use of outside service centers?	_____	_____	_____
• Other operating characteristics? (Describe.)	_____	_____	_____
13. Have we developed an understanding of the nature of the client's assets, liabilities, revenues, and expenses by:			
• Reviewing the client's chart of accounts?	_____	_____	_____
• Reviewing the previous year's financial statements?	_____	_____	_____
• Considering the relationships between specific accounts and the nature of the client's business?	_____	_____	_____
• Performing other procedures? (Describe.)	_____	_____	_____
14. Have we made inquiries concerning accounting principles, practices, and methods?	_____	_____	_____
15. Have we made inquiries concerning the accounting procedures and processes used by the client, including:			
• Recording transactions?	_____	_____	_____
• Classifying transactions?	_____	_____	_____
• Summarizing transactions?	_____	_____	_____
• Accumulating information for making disclosures in the financial statements?	_____	_____	_____
• Other accounting procedures? (Describe.)	_____	_____	_____
16. Have we obtained an adequate understanding of internal control over financial reporting, including whether to test the operating effectiveness of controls?	_____	_____	_____
17. Have we made inquiries concerning the effect on the financial statements due to actions taken at meetings of:			

	Yes	No	Audit Documentation Reference
• Stockholders?	_____	_____	_____
• The board of directors?	_____	_____	_____
• Other committees? (Describe.)	_____	_____	_____
18. If there were changes in the application of accounting principles:			
• Did the change in accounting principle include the adoption of another acceptable accounting principle?	_____	_____	_____
• Was the change properly justified?	_____	_____	_____
• Were the effects of the change presented in the financial statements, including adequate disclosure, in a manner consistent with GAAP?	_____	_____	_____
• Were there other matters that we took into consideration?	_____	_____	_____
19. Have we made inquiries concerning changes in the client's business activities or industry that may require the adoption of different accounting principles, and have we considered the implication of this change for the financial statements?	_____	_____	_____
20. Have we made inquiries concerning the occurrence of events subsequent to the date of the financial statements that may require:			
• Adjustments to the financial statements?	_____	_____	_____
• Disclosures in the financial statements?	_____	_____	_____
21. Have we considered whether other professional services are needed in order to complete the audit engagement, including:			
• Preparing a working trial balance?	_____	_____	_____

	Yes	No	Audit Documentation Reference
• Preparing adjusting journal entries?	_____	_____	_____
• Consulting matters fundamental to the preparation of acceptable financial statements?	_____	_____	_____
• Preparing tax returns?	_____	_____	_____
• Providing bookkeeping or data-processing services that do not include the generation of financial statements?	_____	_____	_____
• Other services considered necessary before an audit can be performed? (Describe.)	_____	_____	_____
22. Have we performed preliminary analytical procedures as required by AU-C 520?	_____	_____	_____
23. Have we obtained reports from other CPA(s) who reported on the financial statements of components of the client-reporting entity if we have decided to rely on their reports?	_____	_____	_____

Prepared By: _____

Date: _____

SECTION 315

UNDERSTANDING THE ENTITY AND ITS ENVIRONMENT AND ASSESSING THE RISKS OF MATERIAL MISSTATEMENTS

Authoritative Pronouncements

SAS-122—Statements on Auditing Standards: Clarification and Recodification

Overview

The Preface to the Codification of Statements on Auditing Standards notes that the auditor is to obtain a sufficient understanding of the entity and its environment, including its internal control, to identify and assess the risk of material misstatement of the financial statements whether caused by error or fraud. This understanding is also used by the auditor to plan the nature, timing, and extent of further audit procedures (i.e., tests of operating effectiveness of controls and substantive procedures) to respond to the assessed risks of material misstatement.

Definitions

Assertions	Management representations embodied in the financial statements and used by the auditor to consider the different types of potential misstatements that may occur.
Relevant assertion	A financial statement assertion that has a reasonable possibility of containing one or more misstatements that would cause the financial statements to be materially misstated. The determination of relevance is made without regard to the effect of internal controls.
Business risk	A risk resulting from the setting of inappropriate objectives and strategies or from significant conditions, events, circumstances, actions, or inactions that could adversely affect an entity's ability to achieve its objectives and execute its strategies.
Internal control	A process—effected by those charged with governance, management, and other personnel—designed to provide reasonable assurance about the achievement of the entity's objectives with regard to (1) reliability of financial reporting, (2) effectiveness and efficiency of operations, and (3) compliance with applicable laws and regulations. Internal control over safeguarding of assets against unauthorized acquisition, use, or disposition may include controls relating to financial reporting and operations objectives.

Risk assessment procedures	Audit procedures performed to obtain an understanding of the entity and its environment, including the entity's internal control, to identify and assess the risks of material misstatement, whether due to fraud or error, at the financial statement and assertion levels.
Significant risk	An identified and assessed risk of material misstatement that, in the auditor's judgment, requires special audit consideration.

Requirements

The auditor is presumptively required to perform the following procedures in developing an understanding of the entity and its environment and assessing the risks of material misstatements:

Risk Assessment Procedures

1. Perform the following risk assessment procedures to provide a basis for identifying and assessing risks of material misstatements at the financial statement and assertion levels:

    a. Inquiries of management and others within the entity who may have information that could assist in identifying risks of material misstatement

    b. Analytical procedures

    c. Observation and inspection

These procedures alone do not provide sufficient appropriate audit evidence on which to base the audit opinion.

2. Consider whether information obtained from the client acceptance or continuance process is relevant to identifying risks of material misstatement.

3. If the engagement partner has performed other engagements for the entity, that partner should consider any information relevant to identifying risks of material misstatement.

4. If the auditor intends to use information from previous experience with the entity or from procedures performed in previous audits, perform audit procedures to establish the continued relevance of that information to the current audit.

5. During planning, consider the results of the assessed risk of material misstatement due to fraud along with other information gathered in the process of identifying risks of material misstatement.

6. The engagement partner and other key engagement team members should discuss the susceptibility of the entity's financial statements to material misstatement and application of the applicable financial reporting framework to the entity. The engagement partner should determine which matters are communicated to engagement team members who are not involved in the discussion.

Understanding the Entity and Its Environment

7. Obtain an understanding of:

    a. Relevant industry, regulatory, and other external factors, including the applicable financial reporting framework.

    b. The entity's nature, including its operations, ownership and governance structures, types of investments being made and planned, including investments in entities formed to accomplish specific objectives, their structure, and how they are financed.

    c. The entity's selection and application of accounting policies, including the reasons for any changes. Evaluate whether policies are appropriate for its business and consistent with the applicable financial reporting framework and accounting policies used in its industry.

d. The entity's objectives and strategies and related business risks that may result in risks of material misstatement.

e. The measurement and review of the entity's financial performance.

Understanding the Entity's Internal Control

8. Obtain an understanding of internal control relevant to the audit. Whether a control is relevant to the audit is a matter of professional judgment. Most relevant controls are likely relate to financial reporting, but not all controls related to financial reporting will be relevant.

9. Evaluate the design of controls relevant to the audit and determine whether they have been implemented by performing procedures in addition to inquiry of the entity's personnel.

10. Obtain an understanding of the control environment. Evaluate whether (1) management, with the oversight of those charged with governance, has created and maintained a culture of honesty and ethical behavior and (2) strengths in the control environment provide an appropriate foundation for the other internal control components, or if deficiencies in the control environment undermine other components.

11. Obtain an understanding of whether the entity has a process for identifying business risks relevant to financial reporting objectives, estimating their significance, assessing their likelihood of occurrence, and deciding about actions to address those risks.

12. If the entity has established a risk assessment process, obtain an understanding of it and its results. If the auditor identifies risks of material misstatement that management failed to identify, evaluate whether an underlying risk exists that would be expected to be identified by the entity's risk assessment process. If such a risk exists, obtain an understanding of why the process failed to identify it and evaluate whether the process is appropriate to its circumstances or if a significant deficiency or material weakness exists in the process.

13. If the entity has not established a risk assessment process or has an ad-hoc process, discuss with management whether business risks relevant to financial reporting objectives have been identified and how they have been addressed. Evaluate whether the absence of a documented risk assessment process is appropriate in the circumstances or represents a significant deficiency or material weakness in the entity's internal control.

14. Obtain an understanding of the information system, including the related business processes relevant to financial reporting, including the following areas:

a. Classes of transactions in the entity's operations significant to the financial statements.

b. Procedures within manual and IT systems by which those transactions are initiated, authorized, recorded, processed, corrected as necessary, transferred to the general ledger, and reported in the financial statements.

c. Related accounting records, in manual or electronic form, supporting information and specific accounts in the financial statements that are used to initiate, authorize, record, process, correct as necessary, transfer to the general ledger, and report transactions.

d. How the information system captures events and conditions significant to the financial statements other than transactions.

e. The financial reporting process used to prepare the entity's financial statements, including significant accounting estimates and disclosures.

f. Controls surrounding journal entries, including nonstandard journal entries used to record nonrecurring, unusual transactions or adjustments.

15. Obtain an understanding of how the entity communicates financial reporting roles and responsibilities and significant matters relating to financial reporting, including (1) communications between management and those charged with governance and (2) external communications, such as those with regulatory authorities.

16. Obtain an understanding of control activities relevant to the audit. Relevant activities are those the auditor judges necessary to understand in order to assess the risks of material misstatement at the assertion level and design further audit procedures responsive to assessed risks. Obtain an understanding of the entity's process of reconciling detailed records to the general ledger for material account balances and of how the entity has responded to risks arising from IT.

17. Obtain an understanding of the major activities the entity uses to monitor internal control over financial reporting, including those related to control activities relevant to the audit and how the entity initiates corrective actions to its controls.

18. If the entity has an internal audit function, obtain an understanding of the nature of its responsibilities, how it fits in the entity's organizational structure, and the activities it performs or will perform in order to determine the internal audit function's relevance to the audit.

19. Obtain an understanding of the sources of information used in the entity's monitoring activities and the reasons management considers the information to be sufficiently reliable for monitoring.

Identifying and Assessing the Risks of Material Misstatement

20. Identify and assess the risks of material misstatement at (1) the financial statement level and (2) the relevant assertion level related to each material class of transactions, account balance, and disclosure to provide a basis for designing and performing further audit procedures. To do this:

a. Identify risks throughout the process of obtaining an understanding of the entity and its environment, including relevant controls that relate to the risks, and considering the classes of transactions, account balances, and disclosures in the financial statements.

b. Assess identified risks and evaluate whether they relate pervasively to the financial statements as a whole and may affect many assertions.

c. Relate identified risks to what can go wrong at the assertion level, taking into account relevant controls the auditor intends to test.

d. Consider the likelihood of one or more misstatements and whether the potential misstatement is of a magnitude that could result in a material misstatement.

21. Determine whether any risks identified in the risk assessment process are significant risks in the auditor's judgment, excluding the effects of identified

controls related to the risk. Consider the following in determining significant risks:

    a. Whether the risk is a risk of fraud

    b. Whether the risk requires special attention because it is related to significant economic, accounting, or other developments

    c. The complexity of transactions

    d. Whether the risk involves significant transactions with related parties

    e. The degree of subjectivity in the measurement of financial information related to the risk, especially those measurements involving a wide range of measurement uncertainty

    f. Whether the risk involves significant transactions that are outside the entity's normal course of business or are otherwise unusual

22. If it is determined that a significant risk exists, obtain an understanding of the entity's controls, including control activities, relevant to that risk and evaluate whether such controls have been suitably designed and implemented to mitigate such risks.

23. It may not be possible or practicable to obtain sufficient appropriate audit evidence from substantive procedures alone for some risks, such as those relating to the inaccurate or incomplete recording of routine and significant classes of transactions or account balances that often permit highly automated processing with little manual intervention. For such risks, obtain an understanding of the entity's controls over those risks.

24. If new information or audit evidence from performing further audit procedures is obtained that is inconsistent with the audit evidence on which the auditor originally based his or her assessment of risks of material misstatement at the assertion level, revise the assessment and modify the further planned audit procedures accordingly.

Documentation

25. Document:

    a. The required discussion among the engagement team, significant decisions reached, how and when the discussion occurred, and the participating audit team members.

    b. Key elements of the understanding obtained regarding each specified aspect of the entity and its environment and each internal control component, the sources of information from which the understanding was obtained, and the risk assessment procedures performed.

    c. Identified and assessed risks of material misstatement at the financial statement and assertion levels.

    d. Identified significant risks and risks for which substantive procedures alone do not provide sufficient appropriate audit evidence, and related controls about which the auditor has obtained an understanding.

Analysis and Application of Procedures

Risk Assessment Procedures

Although much of the auditor's effort in identifying and assessing risks occurs in planning the audit, the auditor should continue to assess risk throughout the audit and, if necessary, modify his or her overall risk evaluation and the nature, timing, and extent of audit procedures to reflect any modification to his or her initial risk assessments. The extent of the understanding of the entity required is determined by the auditor's professional judgment and should be sufficient to identify and assess the risks of material misstatement, whether due to error or fraud. The auditor's required depth of understanding is less than that of the entity's management.

PLANNING AID REMINDER: In assessing the entity's risks, the auditor should also be mindful of the specific fraud-risk-assessment requirements contained in AU-C 240 (*Consideration of Fraud in a Financial Statement Audit*). For example, AU-C 240 requires the auditor to assess the risk of material misstatement due to fraud and to modify audit procedures in response to this risk. A heightened risk of material misstatement due to fraud might call for an overall response (e.g., more supervision, more experienced staff, greater skepticism); a response tailored to classes of transactions, account balances, or disclosures (e.g., modify the nature, timing, and extent of audit procedures to be performed); or both.

The auditor should (1) perform analytical procedures, (2) make inquiries of management and others within the entity, and (3) observe activities and inspect documents and records in performing risk assessment procedures. Although the auditor should perform all three of these risk assessment procedures, he or she is not required to perform all three of these procedures for every area of risk being assessed.

The auditor may perform other risk assessment procedures in addition to the three types of procedures that are required. For example, the auditor may make inquiries of individuals outside the entity (e.g., the entity's outside counsel, bankers, and valuation experts). The auditor also may examine information developed by outside sources (e.g., analyst reports, reports by credit rating agencies, trade journals, etc.).

ENGAGEMENT STRATEGY: In performing risk assessment procedures the auditor may also gather evidence about the operating effectiveness of controls even though the risk assessment procedures were not specifically designed to accomplish this purpose. Also, due to efficiency concerns, the auditor may choose to perform tests of controls or substantive procedures at the same time that he or she performs risk assessment procedures.

Inquiries of management and others

Auditors direct many of their inquiries to management and to those responsible for the entity's financial reporting process. In addition, an auditor may want to extend his or her inquiries to other parties within the entity. These other parties can often provide a valuable (different) perspective that may be useful in identifying risks of material misstatement. In deciding on other parties to talk with and on what to ask, an auditor should focus on obtaining information that will help him or her identify risks of material misstatement. Other parties that may be uniquely helpful to the auditor, and the types of information they might provide, are as follows:

Internal Party	Type of Risk Information Provided
Those charged with governance	An understanding of the entity's control environment
Internal audit	Results of audits performed during the year, including control deficiencies that were identified and management's responses to these findings
Those involved with initiating, authorizing, processing, or recording complex or unusual transactions	An understanding of the business purpose of the transaction, the accounting policy that was selected, and how it was applied
In-house legal counsel	Pending or threatened litigation, compliance with laws or regulations, any known or suspected fraud, and an understanding of contract terms and provisions with financial reporting implications
Marketing or sales personnel	Changes in marketing strategies, sales trends, or agreements with customers

Analytical procedures

AU-C 520 (*Analytical Procedures*) requires the auditor to perform analytical procedures in planning the audit. These procedures are useful in obtaining an understanding of the entity and its environment and in identifying financial statement risk areas. Analytical procedures may also help the auditor identify unusual transactions and events. In performing analytical procedures, the auditor should develop his or her own independent expectation as to the recorded account balance or ratio. A difference between the auditor's expectation and the entity's recorded account balance (or a ratio computed using recorded account balances) may indicate a higher risk of material misstatement.

FRAUD POINTER: Auditors sometimes perform analytical procedures at a highly aggregated level. For example, an auditor might compare the entity's recorded total revenue amount to his or her expectation of total revenue. Analytical procedures performed at such an aggregated level may not be effective in identifying risks of material misstatement. The auditor should consider performing analytical procedures on a more disaggregated basis (e.g., analyze revenue amounts by quarter or month, by operating unit, by product line, etc.).

Observation and inspection

Auditors typically observe procedures and inspect documents and records in assessing client risks. Examples of these activities include the following:

- Tour some of the entity's locations and plants
- Observe the operations of the entity, including selected control procedures
- Inspect documents, records, and control manuals
- Read reports prepared by management, internal audit, and those charged with governance

Prior-period information

Based on prior experience with the entity, the auditor may have knowledge of the nature of the entity and its environment, its internal control, past misstatements, management's efforts to correct past misstatements, and significant changes the entity has undergone since the prior period. This knowledge is useful in assessing risks in the current year's audit. When performing audit procedures to assess the continued relevance of prior period information, the auditor may make inquiries and perform walk-throughs of relevant systems.

Required discussion among the audit team

The audit team should discuss the risks of material misstatement in the client's financial statements, whether caused by error or fraud. This discussion may occur at the same time as the audit team brainstorming session required by AU-C 240.

PLANNING AID REMINDER: AU-C 240 requires the audit team to brainstorm on where and how an entity's financial statements might be susceptible to material misstatement due to fraud. AU-C 315 extends this requirement—requiring a discussion of where and how the entity's financial statements are susceptible to material misstatement, whether caused by fraud or by error.

All audit members need not take part in the discussion, nor is it necessary for them to be informed of all decisions reached in the discussion. The engagement partner or a delegate may communicate appropriate portions of the discussion to other engagement team members and a communication plan may be useful for this purpose.

ENGAGEMENT STRATEGY: A sole practitioner may be performing the audit. In this case, he or she is responsible for considering the risks of material misstatement in the client's financial statements.

The required audit team discussion provides more experienced engagement team members with an opportunity to share their knowledge, allows an exchange of information among engagement team members, helps team members to identify those aspects of the entity's financial statements that are susceptible to material misstatement that are being assigned to each audit team member, and provides a way for team members to share new information obtained throughout the audit regarding the risk assessment.

Understanding the Entity and Its Environment

PUBLIC COMPANY IMPLICATION: The PCAOB's Staff Audit Practice Alert No. 3 (Audit Considerations in the Current Economic Environment) states that events in the financial markets and the economy may have implications for the valuation, impairment, or recoverability of assets and for the completeness and valuation of liabilities. Staff Audit Practice Alert No. 3 is designed to help auditors identify matters that may affect audit risk and thereby require additional audit effort. Practice Alert 3 provides guidance on (1) overall audit considerations, (2) auditing fair value measurements, (3) auditing accounting estimates, (4) auditing the adequacy of disclosures, (5) the auditor's consideration of an entity's ability to continue as a going concern, and (6) additional audit considerations in other areas. As it relates to overall audit considerations, Practice Alert 3 provides guidance on planning, fraud, internal controls, substantive procedures, and audit committee communications. For example, relating to internal controls, controls over the identification and review of assets for recoverability and impairment and controls over the use of specialists may require additional audit attention. Staff Audit Practice Alert No. 3 emphasizes that Practice Alert No. 2 (Matters Related to Auditing Fair Value Measurements of Financial Instruments and the Use of Specialists) remains applicable in the current environment. The Practice Alert 3 reminds auditors of the sensitivity of various accounting estimates, the approaches that the auditor should consider in auditing estimates, and that the auditor should perform a retrospective review of significant accounting estimates from the prior year. Such a retrospective review may identify deficiencies in the client's estimation process, including possible management bias. With respect to disclosures, the Practice Alert 3 reminds auditors of the client's disclosure obligations related to significant risks and uncertainties. Practice Alert 3 reminds auditors that in a case of the omission of a required disclosure, the auditor should issue a qualified or adverse report. Practice Alert 3 emphasizes the requirements in AU-C 570 (*Going Concern*). In addition to the factors listed in AU-C 570 that relate to management's plans to mitigate the conditions or events that give rise to the going-concern doubt, the auditor may also consider the client's participation in a program of federal assistance. Finally, Practice Alert 3 suggests that audit risk may be elevated in the following areas as a result of the current economic environment: (1) consolidation, (2) contingencies and guarantees, (3) derivatives, especially credit derivatives, (4) debt obligations, (5) deferred tax assets, (6) goodwill, intangibles, and other long-lived assets, (7) inventory, (8) other-than-temporary impairment of investment securities, (9) pension and other postretirement benefits, (10) receivables, (11) restructuring, (12) revenue recognition, and (13) share-based payments.

Industry, regulatory, and other external factors

The auditor should understand the industry and regulatory factors that affect the client. These factors include industry conditions, regulations affecting the client, the legal and political environment, environmental requirements affecting the client, and other factors. Some industries pose unique risks of material misstatements (e.g., financial institutions, high-technology companies), and the auditor should consider whether the engagement is staffed with individuals who possess an appropriate degree of industry expertise. Exhibit AU-C 315-5 provides examples of industry, regulatory, and other external factors.

The regulatory environment in which the entity operates may have an impact on accounting principles and industry-specific factors, laws and regulations, government policies, tax implications, and other regulatory issues that may impact financial reporting and the risk of material misstatement.

Nature of the entity

The auditor should understand the nature of the entity in order to be informed about the classes of transactions, account balances, and disclosures that are likely to appear in the entity's financial statements. For example, an entity with a complex structure (e.g., numerous subsidiaries, a number of which are located in foreign locations) may present issues related to preparing consolidated financial statements, the allocation of goodwill across different operating units, asset impairment testing, and foreign currency translation. Also, understanding the relationships between management, owners, and those charged with governance is useful in identifying related-party transactions. Significant changes the entity has undergone from prior periods may change or increase the risks of material misstatement. Exhibit AU-C 315-6 provides examples of entity-specific factors to consider and their link to relevant standards of financial reporting (GAAP).

OBSERVATION: Entities may be formed by entities to accomplish a specific purpose, such as variable interest entities, and financial reporting frameworks often specify conditions that amount to control or circumstances under which an entity should be considered for consolidation for which a detailed understanding of the agreements involving the entity formed for a specific purpose is involved.

Entity's selection and application of accounting policies

The auditor's understanding of the entity's selection and application of accounting policies may include the following matters:

- Entity's method of accounting for significant and unusual transactions
- Effect of significant accounting policies in areas lacking authoritative guidance or consensus
- Significant changes in the entity's accounting policies and disclosures and the reasons for these changes
- Financial reporting standards, laws, and regulations that are new to the entity and the entity's adoption plans
- Financial reporting competencies of personnel involved in selecting and applying significant new or complex accounting standards

Objectives and strategies of the entity and the resulting business risks

The auditor should obtain an understanding of the entity's objectives and strategies as well as the business risks that result from them. Objectives are management's overall plans for the entity. For governmental entity audits, management objectives may be influenced by legislation, regulation, and public accountability concerns. Strategies are management's detailed approach for accomplishing its objectives. Business risks are those factors that might prevent the entity from achieving its objectives or implementing its strategies, as well as the risk that the entity has designed flawed objectives or strategies. Entity objectives and strategies are dynamic, changing, and evolve over time.

OBSERVATION: The entity's business risks encompass the risk of material misstatement in the financial statements and include risks that may be extend beyond risks related to financial reporting.

The successful identification of client business risks helps the auditor assess the risks of material misstatement in the financial statements; however, the auditor is not expected to identify all business risks. Rather, the auditor focuses on business risks that have financial statement implications. Examples of client strategies and factors affecting the client's business and the related business risks include the following:

Client Strategy or Factor Affecting the Client's Business	Business Risk
Expansion into new markets	The client lacks the expertise and personnel needed to effectively compete in the new markets; failure to accurately forecast demand
Introduction of new products	Lack of customer acceptance; cost overruns in producing the product; lack of historical data on customer returns and warranty claims; increased liability exposure
Issuance of new accounting pronouncements	The client implements the new pronouncement incorrectly or fails to apply it
Changes in industry-specific regulations	Loss of key licenses; increased compliance costs; increased liability exposure
Issuance of new equity or debt securities	Failure to complete the offering in the amount expected; additional restrictions imposed on the entity's operations
Introduction of a new information processing system	Existing systems and processes are not compatible; failure to effectively manage the conversion from the old system to the new system

Financial performance of the entity

The measurement of the entity's financial performance—whether via internal or external measures—creates performance pressure on management. This performance pressure can appropriately cause management to take steps to improve the entity's operating performance but in some instances performance pressure can lead to inappropriate managerial actions that result in material misstatements in the financial statements.

Management may use the following internally generated performance measures in evaluating the entity's financial performance:

- Key performance indicators and operating ratios
- Measures of employee performance
- Actual-to-budget comparisons
- Comparative financial statements
- Department, division, or subsidiary performance reports
- Comparison of the entity's performance with that of competitors

In smaller entities, management inquiry may reveal a lack of processes in place to internally measure and review financial performance, which could indicate an increased risk that misstatements may not be detected and corrected. The auditor's use of performance measures may help him or her identify risks of material misstatement. For example, client growth that significantly outpaces that of the rest of the industry may be a risk factor. Unexplained client growth may be of particular concern when coupled with very aggressive employee compensation plans (a high ratio of variable-based compensation to fixed compensation).

OBSERVATION: Management's measurement, review, and investigation of (unexpected) financial performance are not part of the monitoring element of internal control; rather, such activity is a type of manual detective control activity.

Internal Control Components

The auditor should obtain an understanding of the following five components of internal control:

1. *Control environment* The control environment sets the tone of an organization, which influences the control consciousness of its employees. The control environment is the foundation for all other components of internal control, because it provides discipline and structure.

2. *Risk assessment by the entity* Risk assessment is the process that an entity must conduct in order to identify and assess any relevant risks to its objectives. Once this assessment is performed, management must determine how the risks should be managed.

3. *Information and communication systems* Information and communication systems are used to identify, capture, and exchange the information needed for employees to carry out their responsibilities.

4. *Control activities* Control activities are the policies and procedures that help ensure that management directives are carried out.

5. *Monitoring* Monitoring is a process that an entity uses to assess the quality of its internal control performance over time.

PUBLIC COMPANY IMPLICATION: The Sarbanes-Oxley Act of 2002 (SOX) requires all public companies to issue an "internal control report" that includes the following: (1) a statement that management is responsible for establishing and maintaining adequate internal control over financial reporting and (2) an assessment of the effectiveness of internal control over financial reporting as of the end of the company's fiscal year. Auditors are also required to perform a separate evaluation of the effectiveness of internal control for large, accelerated filers. Related SEC rules require management to explicitly state their responsibility for internal control and to identify material weaknesses in internal control. The framework that management uses as a basis for its evaluation of internal control must be one that has been established by a body or group that followed a due-process procedure that allowed for public comment. Most public companies use COSO's *Internal Control—Integrated Framework*. The concepts in AU-C 315 are based on that framework.

FRAUD POINTER: Gaining an understanding of internal control provides useful information about the presence of one of the three fraud conditions: opportunity.

Nonexistent or deficient internal controls can provide management or employees with opportunities or circumstances that allow them to carry out material misstatements in the financial statements. For this reason, auditors should consider the information they obtain through understanding internal control as they evaluate the presence of other risk factors related to conditions of fraud. The more fraud risk factors the auditor observes, the greater the likelihood of a material misstatement due to the occurrence of fraud.

Control environment

The success or failure of internal control depends on the environment in which the internal control process takes place (i.e., the control environment). The control environment is also referred to as "the tone at the top," and it is the foundation for all the other elements of internal control. AU-C 315 identifies the following as elements that affect an entity's control environment:

- Integrity and ethical values
- Commitment to competence
- Participation of those charged with governance
- Management's philosophy and operating style
- Organizational structure
- Assignment of authority and responsibility
- Human resource policies and practices

Exhibit AU-C 315-1 provides examples of elements of the control environment.

The effectiveness of an entity's controls cannot exceed the integrity and ethical values of those who design, administer, and monitor controls. Given this fact, an entity's control consciousness is heavily influenced by those charged with governance.

FRAUD POINTER: The AICPA's thought paper entitled "Management Override of Internal Controls: The Achilles' Heel of Fraud Prevention" provides guidance to audit committees to help them address the ever-present risk of fraud resulting from management override of internal control. The document notes that the audit committee (or the board where there is no audit committee) plays a vital role in overseeing the actions of management. For many organizations, the audit committee is in the best position to prevent, deter, and detect fraud resulting from management override of controls. The document identifies specific actions an audit committee can take to address the risk of management override of internal controls. Auditors may find the document helpful as they assess the "participation of those charged with governance" element of the control environment.

Risk assessment by the entity

The design of internal control related to financial reporting should include management's identification, analysis, and management of risk factors that may prevent financial statements from being prepared in accordance with GAAP. When designing internal controls, management should consider "external and internal events, and circumstances that may occur and adversely affect an entity's ability to initiate, authorize, record, process, and report financial data consistent with the assertions of management in the financial statements." Risk assessment is an ongoing process, and Exhibit AU-C 315-2 provides examples of factors affecting entity risks.

OBSERVATION: In 2004, the Committee of Sponsoring Organizations of the Treadway Commission (COSO) issued an enterprise risk management framework to assist boards of directors, management, and others within entities to effectively manage risks across the enterprise. The framework builds on the five elements of internal control to create eight elements of effective enterprise risk management. More recently, more organizations have begun to embrace an enterprise risk management process that helps the board and senior management identify, assess, and manage the entity's most significant risk exposures. In 2010, COSO released reports of two surveys of boards of directors and senior executives that COSO commissioned to learn about the current state of enterprise-wide risk oversight in organizations today. Collectively, results from both surveys suggest that while risk oversight is a high priority among boards and senior management, the relative state of maturity of underlying processes to identify, assess, report, and monitor top risks of the organization are relatively immature, especially in light of the increasing complexity of the world today. Practitioners should discuss with boards and senior management the nature of processes an entity's leadership uses to monitor the organizations' most significant risks, including information about the most significant business risk exposures.

PUBLIC COMPANY IMPLICATION: COSO's *Enterprise Risk Management— Integrated Framework* is likely to be particularly useful to auditors of public companies who are assessing an entity's risk assessment process as part of auditing the effectiveness of internal control over financial reporting.

Information and communication systems

The auditor needs to obtain an understanding of the entity's financial reporting system. A financial reporting system generally consists of computer hardware, software, people, automated and manual procedures, and data used by the entity to initiate, authorize, record, process, and report its transactions and events and maintain accountability for assets, liabilities, and equity. The information system may be heavily automated, but it often includes some manual or human-performed processes. Additionally, the information system includes the use of standard and nonstandard journal entries. All these, and other, aspects of the information system should be considered as part of the assessment of risks related to financial reporting.

Exhibit AU-C 315-3 provides a description of information systems' objectives. The quality of information generated by the system affects management's ability to make appropriate decisions and reliably report financial information.

The auditor also needs to understand how the entity communicates to individuals their roles and responsibilities related to the financial reporting process. Communication occurs in written form (e.g., manuals), orally, electronically, and through management actions.

Control activities

Control activities are those policies and procedures that help ensure that management's objectives and strategies are carried out. Within the domain of financial reporting controls, control activities should be designed to address risks of material misstatement to the financial statements. Examples of control activities are authorizations, performance reviews, information processing, physical controls, and segregation of duties. Control activities may be within IT or manual systems. Exhibit AU-C 315-4 provides other examples of control activities germane to internal control over financial reporting. The auditor typically does not obtain an understanding of the control activities related to every relevant assertion or each transaction class, account balance, and disclosure in the financial statements.

ENGAGEMENT STRATEGY: The requirement that the auditor obtain an understanding of all five components of internal control does not suggest that this gathering of information is accomplished as five distinct tasks. The auditor might, for example, develop an understanding of some control activities as part of his or her consideration of the information and communication component of internal control.

Monitoring

Once internal controls are implemented, management must assess the controls (both from a design perspective and an operational perspective) on a timely basis and make modifications when appropriate. Monitoring of controls involves assessing the quality of internal control performance over time, and is accomplished through ongoing activities, separate evaluations, or both.

Ongoing monitoring should be part of the routine activities of effective internal control, and include supervisory and management activities. The entity's internal audit function may be relevant to the audit if its responsibilities and activities are related to the entity's financial reporting, including monitoring of internal controls, and the auditor expects to use some of the internal auditors' work. In these circumstances, the guidance in AU-C 610 applies. In addition, external parties can have an important role in monitoring internal controls. For example, as part of its role, a regulatory agency might evaluate internal control or the client's customers might complain about billing errors or incorrect shipment of materials. All of these factors make up the monitoring component of internal control.

Auditor objectives related to internal control

The auditor's primary objective in understanding internal control is to understand whether and how a control prevents, or detects and corrects, material misstatements in relevant assertions related to classes of transactions, account balances, or disclosures. The primary objective is not necessarily to evaluate each of the five internal control components. Therefore, an auditor may define internal control using different terminology or a different framework as long as the internal control objectives underlying the five internal control components are met.

The auditor should obtain an understanding of internal control over financial reporting sufficient to understand the design of controls and whether the controls have been implemented. The auditor uses this knowledge to (1) identify the types of possible misstatements, (2) identify the factors that affect the risk of material misstatement, and (3) design further audit procedures (tests of the operating effectiveness of controls and substantive procedures).

PLANNING AID REMINDER: AICPA Technical Practice Aid TIS 8200.05 clarifies that the auditor is required to obtain an understanding of internal control in every audit, even if he or she believes that internal control is not effective. This requirement applies even if the auditor intends to design a substantive audit approach and not rely on controls. Additionally, AICPA Technical Practice Aid TIS 8200.11 notes that the auditor cannot skip the evaluation and documentation of controls when he or she believes the controls over financial reporting are nonexistent or ineffective. The auditor is required to obtain a sufficient understanding of internal controls to assess their design and implementation. The purpose of obtaining such an understanding in every audit is to evaluate the design of controls to provide the auditor with information to assess the risk of material misstatements. When the auditor believes, based on his or her understanding of internal controls, that controls do not exist to prevent or detect material misstatements in financial statements, he or she would plan and perform substantive procedures to respond to the assessed risks. The auditor needs to be satisfied that only performing substantive procedures provides sufficient appropriate evidence to support his or her opinion. Additionally, the auditor must evaluate identified control deficiencies to determine whether any are deemed to be significant deficiencies or material weaknesses for communication in writing to management and those charged with governance.

Relevant assertions

The auditor obtains an understanding of the entity and its environment, including internal controls, to assess the risk of material misstatements in the financial statements. Misstatements arise when assertions made by management in the preparation and presentation of financial statements are violated. The assertions are made by management implicitly and explicitly when they prepare and present financial information in accordance with the applicable financial reporting framework. These assertions relate to the recognition, measurement, presentation, and disclosure of the various elements of the financial statements. These assertions encompass the following three categories:

1. Assertions related to classes of transactions

2. Assertions related to account balances at the end-of-period

3. Assertions related to presentation and disclosure

There are five assertions that relate to classes of transactions or events for the period under audit:

1. *Occurrence* The entity has entered into the transactions and events that are recorded.

2. *Completeness* All transactions and events that affected the entity during the period have been recorded.

3. *Accuracy* Transactions and events are recorded at the right amount.

4. *Cutoff* Transactions and events are recorded in the right period.

5. *Classification* Transactions and events are recorded in the right account.

There are four assertions that relate to account balances at the end of the period under audit:

1. *Existence* Assets, liabilities, and owners' interests exist.

2. *Rights and obligations* The entity holds or controls the rights to recorded assets, and recorded liabilities are obligations of the entity.

3. *Completeness* All of the entity's assets, liabilities, and owners' interests have been recorded.

4. *Valuation and allocation* Assets, liabilities, and owners' interests are correctly valued in accordance with GAAP.

There are four assertions that relate to presentation and disclosure:

1. *Occurrence and rights and obligations* Events and transactions that are disclosed have occurred and pertain to the entity.

2. *Completeness* All required disclosures are included in the financial statements.

3. *Classification and understandability* Financial information is appropriately presented and described, and disclosures are understandable.

4. *Accuracy and valuation* Financial and other information is properly disclosed and at appropriate amounts.

OBSERVATION: The auditor may use the list of assertions or develop his or her own list of assertions (as long as the objectives underlying the foregoing assertions are met).

The auditor uses the assertions to form the basis for the assessment of risks of material misstatement and to design and perform further audit procedures. The risk of material misstatement may relate directly to a particular assertion for classes of transactions, account balances, or disclosures or it may pertain to the financial statements taken as a whole. If the risk of material misstatement pertains to the overall financial statements, many assertions will be affected.

Understanding the Entity's Internal Control

The auditor is required to obtain an understanding of internal control in every engagement in order to assess the risks of material misstatement and to have an adequate basis to plan the nature, timing, and extent of audit procedures that are responsive to these risks.

PLANNING AND REMINDER: AU-C 314 requires the auditor to obtain an understanding of internal control. Auditors may perform walk-throughs of transactions to confirm their understanding of internal control relevant to transaction processing. Walk-throughs are considered to be a good practice, and an auditor might (although is not required to) perform a walk-through of significant accounting cycles every year. AICPA Technical Practice Aid TIS 8200.12 notes that a walk-through performed every year might be an effective technique that the auditor performs to update his or her understanding of the control in order to allow him or her to rely on certain audit evidence obtained in prior years that is based on the continued performance of that control in the current fiscal period. In that instance, the walk-through may be an efficient and effective technique to obtain an understanding of the continued relevance of the audit evidence obtained in prior years. Furthermore, when performing a walk-through of controls, the auditor might identify improvements to the controls that the client should consider implementing. A by-product of obtaining an understanding of controls is that suggestions for improvements can be made to the client, which adds value to the audit process.

PUBLIC COMPANY IMPLICATION: SOX requires all public companies to issue an "internal control report" by management. Furthermore, SOX requires that auditors of the larger, accelerated filer public companies issue a separate opinion based on their evaluation of the effectiveness of internal control over financial reporting. Auditors of all entities, including auditors of public companies, must obtain an understanding of internal control over financial reporting. Auditors of accelerated filer public companies must also perform tests of controls in every audit that are sufficient to provide separate assurance about the design and operating effectiveness of internal control over financial reporting.

Limitations and general characteristics of internal control

Internal control is subject to limitations through unintentional means such as faulty decision-making and human error or through intentional means, including collusion to circumvent controls and management override of controls. Because of this, internal control can only provide reasonable assurance, not absolute assurance, that the entity is achieving its financial reporting objectives. In smaller entities, sufficient segregation of duties may not be practicable but this internal control deficiency can be compensated for through more effective oversight than in a larger entity. Finally, a basic concept in the design of internal control is the expectation that controls must be cost-effective. That is, the benefits derived from an internal control procedure should exceed the cost of adopting the procedure. When designing an internal control, an entity cannot measure the cost-benefit relation precisely, but a reasonable analysis combined with appropriate judgment and estimates is useful.

> **FRAUD POINTER:** One of the limitations of internal control is that management is in a unique position to commit fraud because it can override established controls. The risk of management override when the entity is run by an owner-manager depends heavily on the entity's control environment and on the owner-manager's attitude toward internal control. Since the risk of management override of internal control is present in virtually all audits, AU-C 240 mandates that certain audit procedures be performed in every audit to respond to the ever-present risk of management override. Auditors must (1) examine journal entries and other adjustments, (2) review accounting estimates for bias, and (3) evaluate the business reason for significant unusual transactions.

Entities' internal control systems often combine manual and automated elements with characteristics relevant to the auditor's risk assessment and further audit procedures. Manual controls (1) may be independent of IT, (2) may use information generated by the IT system, (3) may be used to monitor IT functioning and automated controls, and (4) may be used to handle exceptions from normal transaction processing. An entity's use of IT may affect internal control components related to financial reporting, operations, or compliance objectives as well as the way in which transactions are initiated, authorized, recorded, processed, and reported. The nature and characteristics of the entity's information system will cause the extent and nature of the risks to internal control to vary among entities.

The use of IT-based controls can benefit internal control because of the following IT system characteristics:

- Predefined business rules and complicated calculations can be consistently applied by IT to a large number of similar transactions
- Information can be processed accurately by IT and be available to internal users in a timely fashion
- A variety of analytical tools can be applied by IT to the processed information
- An entity's IT-based activities and its policies and procedures can be better monitored
- The risk that IT controls can be circumvented can be reduced
- Security controls for applications, databases, and operating systems can be implemented to enhance the effective segregation of duties

On the other hand, the use of IT controls introduces a variety of specific risks related to the internal control environment. Risks that are related to IT-based controls can arise through the following situations:

- A reliance on automated procedures that are incorrectly processing data or that are processing incorrect data
- Changing, destroying, or introducing new data into the system without proper authorization
- IT personnel gaining excess access privileges thereby breaking down segregation of duties

- An unauthorized change of data in a master file
- An unauthorized change to a system or a program
- The failure to make necessary changes to a system or a program
- Inappropriate manual intervention (i.e., override of IT-based processing)
- The potential loss of data

Although IT controls offer many advantages and are increasingly common in today's business environment, manual controls may be more appropriate where judgment and discretion are needed. For example, manual controls are particularly germane in the case of (1) transactions that are large, unusual, or nonrecurring; (2) transactions or events where defining or predicting misstatements is difficult; (3) rapidly changing circumstances where a unique or custom control response may be needed; and (4) monitoring the performance of automated controls. However, manual controls have a number of limitations, and therefore their use may be less suitable for high-volume or recurring transactions. It is easier to bypass, override, or ignore manual controls than IT controls, and manual controls are more prone to error or mistake. The auditor cannot assume that manual controls have been applied on a consistent basis. As a result, the auditor should test a sample of transactions where the manual control is expected to operate to evaluate the operating effectiveness of any manual control that the auditor plans to rely on.

PLANNING AID REMINDER: If the auditor decides to use an outside professional with specialized IT skills to evaluate and test IT systems and controls, the guidance in AU-C 620 (*Using the Work of an Auditor's Specialist*) should be followed.

Controls relevant to the audit

AU-C 315 notes that management develops internal control related to a broad spectrum of objectives ranging from financial reporting matters to the efficient execution of operational activities. However, the auditor's consideration of internal controls in an audit of financial statements is specific. The auditor is concerned with internal control and its components as they relate to the reliability of financial reporting. More specifically, the auditor is concerned with relevant assertions over classes of transactions, account balances, and presentation and disclosure.

The auditor is not required to assess all controls that are designed to reduce the risk of a material misstatement in the financial statements. The determination of which controls to be assessed is a function of the auditor's professional judgment. However, in exercising his or her professional judgment, the auditor should consider the following:

- Materiality of the assertion related to the class of transaction, account balance, or disclosure that the control pertained to
- The entity's size (see Exhibit AU-C 315-7 for examples of the application of internal control concepts to small and midsize entities)

- The nature of the entity's business (e.g., organizational and ownership characteristics) and information systems
- The diversity and complexity of the entity's operations
- Legal and regulatory requirements
- Whether and how a control, alone or in combination with others, prevents or detects and corrects material misstatement

---

PLANNING AID REMINDER: During the planning stage of the audit engagement, the auditor's responsibility to gain an understanding of internal control is limited to understanding the design of the system of controls and determining whether internal controls are in place; it does not include determining whether those controls are operating effectively. (Determining whether controls are operating effectively is part of further audit procedures, which are discussed in AU-C 330.)

The auditor is not primarily concerned with controls related to the efficiency and effectiveness of operations or compliance with laws and regulations; however, these controls may be relevant if they relate to the generation of information or data that the auditor will use in performing other audit procedures. For example, quality control data may be useful for testing the assertion in the financial statements that the allowance for returned goods is properly valued. Likewise, controls related to compliance with laws and regulations are likely to be relevant if noncompliance could have a material and direct effect on financial statement amounts and disclosures (e.g., compliance with income tax laws and regulations).

Determine the extent of internal control understanding needed

The auditor needs to test whether controls have been designed and implemented (i.e., the control exists and is being used). The focus is on determining whether the control is likely to prevent (or detect and correct) material misstatements in the financial statements. A control that is improperly designed may represent a material weakness, and the auditor will have to make this evaluation.

An auditor evaluates the design and implementation of controls by performing a combination of procedures—inquiry, observation, inspection of documents and reports, and tracing transactions through the accounting system. Reliance on inquiry alone is not sufficient. In most cases, obtaining an understanding of the design of a control is not sufficient to conclude that the control is operating effectively. However, if the control is automated, and the entity has strong general computer controls (particularly over computer security and program changes), the auditor's testing of the design and implementation of an automated control may provide evidence of the operating effectiveness of the control.

FRAUD POINTER: AU-C 240 reminds the auditor that as part of gaining an understanding of an entity's internal control, he or she should evaluate whether the internal controls that address identified risks of material misstatement due to fraud have been suitably designed and placed in operation. These controls may be specific controls designed to mitigate specific fraud risks, or they may be broad programs and controls designed to prevent, deter, and detect fraud.

Understanding the internal control component: control environment

The auditor should obtain an understanding of the attitudes, awareness, and actions of management and those charged with governance toward internal control and its importance in the entity. In other words the auditor attempts to assess the entity's "tone at the top"—that is, how important are strong internal controls and reliable financial reporting to those ultimately responsible for the entity's operations and performance? It is this control environment that sets the tone of the organization and provides a foundation for the other internal control components.

PLANNING AID REMINDER: The control environment may be less formal in smaller entities than larger entities. AICPA Technical Practice Aid TIS 8200.08 reminds auditors that auditing standards require the auditor to understand all components of internal control, including the control environment, sufficiently to evaluate the design of the controls and to determine whether they have been placed in operation. Even in smaller entities, auditors may rely on the control environment to determine the nature, timing, and extent of further audit procedures. Thus, auditors are required to understand the control environment even when it is less formal. When auditors rely on aspects of the control environment, they are required to test those controls. Because of the potential impact on audit strategy, auditors are encouraged to evaluate the control environment early in the audit process.

The auditor should evaluate whether control environment elements have been implemented. For example, an entity may claim to have a hotline process, but the auditor should determine whether the hotline has been established, whether employees know about it, and whether it is being used. Also, an entity may state that employees must sign an acknowledgement on a yearly basis that they are in compliance with the entity's code of conduct, but is there any evidence that these employee certifications are taking place and does the entity follow up with employees who fail to provide the certification? The auditor should obtain sufficient, appropriate audit evidence through inquiries, supplemented with observation and inspection, to determine whether control environment elements have been implemented.

Some elements of an entity's control environment have a pervasive effect on assessing the risks of material misstatement, one of which is the role of those charged with governance. The auditor should consider the independence from management of those charged with governance (e.g., the board of directors, audit committee). For example, if management's compensation is highly variable and that variability is tied (directly or indirectly) to reported financial results (e.g., bonuses, stock options, grants, and other awards) there is a tension between management's desire to increase their compensation and the requirement to produce accurate financial statements. Those charged with governance are one of the few checks on management's behavior in this situation; however, the effectiveness of these individuals in acting as a check on management is often dependent on their independence from management.

Other factors that may impact the effectiveness of the control environment include whether those charged with governance understand the entity's business transactions and the extent to which they evaluate whether the financial statements are prepared in accordance with the applicable financial reporting framework. Although nonpublic companies are not required to have financial experts among those charged with governance, the entity's control environment is likely to be stronger if individuals with financial expertise are involved in overseeing the affairs of the entity.

In making an overall evaluation of the control environment component, the auditor should consider the strengths and weaknesses in the various control environment elements. A strong control environment reduces the risk of material misstatement, particularly the risk of material misstatement due to fraud. Because the control environment is the foundation for all the other elements of internal control, this component has a pervasive effect on the risks of material misstatement and therefore the auditor's evaluation of the nature, timing, and extent of further audit procedures. However, the operation of the control environment is not specific enough to provide substantial audit comfort that material misstatements in individual classes of transactions, account balances, or disclosures will be prevented or detected.

Understanding the internal control component: risk assessment by the entity

When the auditor is obtaining an understanding of the entity's risk assessment process, the determination of whether that risk assessment process is appropriate to the entity's circumstances is a matter of judgment.

Understanding the internal control component: information and communication system

Auditors should obtain an understanding of related business processes of the entity to further the understanding of the entity's information system relevant to financial reporting. Related business processes include developing, purchasing, producing, selling, and distributing an entity's products and services, ensuring compliance with laws and regulations, and recording information including financial reporting and accounting information.

ENGAGEMENT STRATEGY: When transaction totals are entered into the general ledger automatically and when financial statements are prepared using IT, there may be little in the way of an audit trail. In these situations, it is important that the auditor be able to rely on the client's IT controls. Also, the auditor may want to consider having a computer audit specialist on the engagement and/or using computer-assisted audit techniques.

FRAUD POINTER: To address the risk of management override of internal controls, AU-C 240 requires the auditor in every audit to examine journal entries and other adjustments for evidence of possible misstatements. The required understanding of both automated and manual procedures related to the process for recording journal entries and adjustments helps the auditor in examining journal entries and other adjustments for evidence of possible misstatements. The auditor's understanding of the entity's financial reporting process can help in identifying the type, number, and monetary value of journal entries and other adjustments that are typically made in preparing the financial statements.

The auditor should understand how the entity communicates financial reporting roles and responsibilities to affected employees and how it communicates matters related to financial reporting to affected parties. Communication often occurs through policy manuals and financial reporting manuals, which the auditor may consider examining. Employees should understand how their roles and responsibilities relate to the work of others, and they should understand the entity's processes for reporting financial reporting exceptions to their supervisors and other levels of management within the entity.

Understanding the internal control component: control activities

In reviewing control activities, the auditor's primary consideration is understanding how a control activity alone or in combination with other control activities either prevents or detects and corrects material misstatements in the financial statements. The focus is on identifying and understanding relevant control activities, which are those related to significant risks and risks for which substantive procedures alone do not provide sufficient appropriate audit evidence as well as those that are relevant in the auditor's judgment, such as those in financial statement areas where a material misstatement is most likely to occur.

To understand how IT affects control activities, the auditor should obtain an understanding of both application controls and general computer controls. Application controls apply to processing transactions by individual applications and help to ensure transactions occurred, are authorized, and are completely and accurately recorded and processed. For example, the review and follow-up of items on a system-generated exception report depends on the accuracy of the underlying system-generated information.

The entity's control activities should be designed to respond to IT-related risks. For example, effective general computer controls reduce the risks associated with relying on application controls. The auditor's focus is on those controls that maintain the integrity and security of system-generated information (i.e., that prevent or detect unauthorized additions, modifications, or deletions to this information).

Understanding the internal control component: monitoring

Management often relies on internally generated information in performing monitoring activities. Management may assume that the information is accurate, but this assumption should not be made unless the controls over the generation of the information are designed and operating effectively or the accuracy of the information has been directly tested. The auditor should understand the information sources used by management in performing monitoring activities, and management's basis for relying on this information.

Identifying and Assessing the Risks of Material Misstatement

Assessment of risks of material misstatement at the financial statement and assertion levels

The auditor uses the assertions described earlier to form the basis for the assessment of risks of material misstatement and to design and perform further audit procedures. The risk of material misstatement may relate directly to a particular assertion for classes of transactions, account balances, or disclosures or it may pertain to the financial statements taken as a whole. If the risk of material misstatement pertains to the overall financial statements, many assertions will be affected. Financial statement risks are often especially relevant to the auditor's assessment of the risks of material misstatement due to fraud. Risks related to the financial statements taken as a whole often may relate to a deficient control environment. Weaknesses in the control environment often have a pervasive effect on the audit and may call for an overall response by the auditor (e.g., assign more experienced personnel to the engagement, devote more partner and manager time to supervising the engagement, increase the overall skepticism that the engagement is performed with).

Risks of material misstatement at the assertion level should also be considered because they help to determine the nature, timing, and extent of further audit procedures necessary in the audit. Management implicitly or explicitly makes assertions about the classes of transaction and events for the period under audit, account balances at the end of the period, and presentation and disclosure. The auditor is then responsible for considering the types of potential misstatements that could occur regarding relevant assertions. Relevant assertions are those that have a reasonable possibility of containing misstatements that would cause the financial statements to be materially misstated.

In gaining an understanding of an entity's internal control, the auditor may develop concerns regarding the integrity of the entity's management or the condition and reliability of an entity's records such that the auditor's opinion may need to be modified or the auditor may need to withdraw from the engagement where doing so is legally allowed.

Auditor's evaluation of controls

In evaluating controls, the auditor primarily focuses on those controls that are likely to prevent or detect and correct material misstatements in relevant assertions. The relevance of an assertion depends on its nature, the volume of transactions or data related to the assertion, and the nature and complexity of the systems the entity uses to process and control information supporting the assertion. In some cases multiple controls must operate effectively to reduce the risk of material misstatement for a particular assertion to an appropriately low level. In other cases a single control activity may be sufficient to achieve a control objective for a relevant assertion. For example, the entity's controls related to completing the count of physical inventory are designed to address the existence and completeness assertions for the inventory account balance.

Some controls are directly related to an assertion, while other controls are indirectly related to an assertion. For example, preventive controls, especially those that are control activities, tend to be directly related to an assertion. Detective controls (e.g., management reviews of business performance) are more likely to be indirectly related to an assertion. In general, more direct controls are more effective in reducing the risk of material misstatement.

OBSERVATION: The auditor may identify deficiencies in internal control as part of the risk assessment process. If these deficiencies rise to the level of significant deficiencies or material weaknesses, they must be communicated in writing to those charged with governance.

Significant risks requiring special audit attention

Significant risks often relate to significant nonroutine transactions and judgmental matters, whereas less complex, routine transactions that are subject to systematic processing are less likely to produce significant risks. Exhibit AU-C 315-8 presents factors that may indicate a heightened risk of material misstatement. Issues requiring the auditor's attention are (2) risks related to nonroutine transactions, (3) risks related to judgmental matters, and (4) management controls over nonroutine transactions and judgmental matters.

Nonroutine transactions are more likely to represent a significant risk when (1) management is involved in specifying the accounting treatment, especially operating management, (2) the transaction involves complex accounting principles or computations, (3) the transaction is with related parties, (4) the transaction is not subject to the entity's normal internal control processes, and (5) there is extensive manual involvement in collecting and processing the data underlying the transaction.

Financial statement amounts and disclosures whose determination involves significant judgment, especially accounting estimates, are more likely to represent a significant risk. In particular, estimates that are dependent on the occurrence or nonoccurrence of future events are more prone to misstatement. In addition, judgments involving revenue recognition for certain types of transactions can be subject to differing interpretations, increasing the likelihood of a misstatement.

Although nonroutine transactions and judgmental matters are less likely to be subject to routine controls, management still needs to develop controls over these issues. The auditor should consider *whether* and *how* management responds to nonroutine transactions and judgmental matters. For example, when assumptions are involved in determining recorded amounts, the assumptions should be reviewed by senior management or experts. In addition, management should have implemented formal processes for developing significant accounting estimates, including review by senior management and, in some instances, those charged with governance.

OBSERVATION: If the entity does not have effective controls over significant risks and the auditor evaluates this deficiency as either a significant deficiency or a material weakness, he or she should communicate this matter to those charged with governance.

Risks for which substantive procedures alone are not sufficient

The auditor may not be able to reduce detection risk to an acceptably low level using only substantive procedures when an entity processes significant classes of business transactions (e.g., revenues, purchases, cash receipts, and cash disbursements) entirely using automated processing. In these instances, audit evidence might exist only in electronic form and the reliability of such electronic evidence depends on the design and operating effectiveness of the controls over the generation of the evidence. There is also a heightened risk that information can be improperly initiated or altered if the initiation, authorization, recording, processing, or reporting of transactions occurs only in electronic form. In these circumstances, the auditor will have to rely on the effectiveness of internal controls, at least to some extent, to reduce detection risk to an appropriately low level.

Assessment of risk throughout the engagement

The auditor assesses the risk of material misstatement in the planning stage of the audit based on his or her understanding of the entity and its environment, including internal control. As the auditor performs further audit procedures, his or her initial assessment may change. For example, the auditor might find that controls that he or she planned to rely on are not operating effectively. The auditor might also find errors in performing substantive tests that are larger and more frequent than he or she expected based on his or her initial risk assessment. In these situations, the auditor should revise his or her risk assessments and modify the nature, timing, and extent of audit procedures as appropriate.

Documentation

The auditor uses his or her professional judgment in determining the nature and extent of documentation. The nature and extent of the auditor's documentation depends on (1) the nature, size, and complexity of the entity and its environment, including its internal control; (2) how much information is available from the entity; (3) the extent of the auditor's procedures; and (4) the auditor's specific audit methodology. Generally, the larger and more complex the entity and the greater the extent of the auditor's procedures, the more extensive the auditor's documentation will be. The extent of documentation sufficient for the auditors to obtain an appropriate understanding of the entity may also be greater if the engagement team is less experienced. Documentation may be carried forward and updated to reflect any changes in a recurring audit.

PLANNING AID REMINDER: Although it is recommended that an entity document its controls so that the auditor can efficiently understand them, assess the risk of material misstatement, and test them for operating effectiveness, controls do not have to be documented by the client for them to be tested. If the entity does not document a control and it is an important control, AU-C 315 requires the auditor to document the control as part of his or her risk assessment procedures to identify and assess the risks of material misstatements.

Practitioner's Aids

The following exhibits may be used as practitioner's aids.

EXHIBIT AU 314-1—EXAMPLES OF ELEMENTS OF THE CONTROL ENVIRONMENT

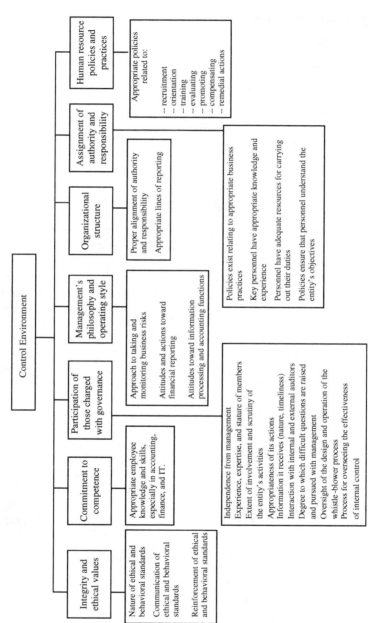

EXHIBIT AU 314-2—EXAMPLES OF FACTORS AFFECTING ENTITY RISKS

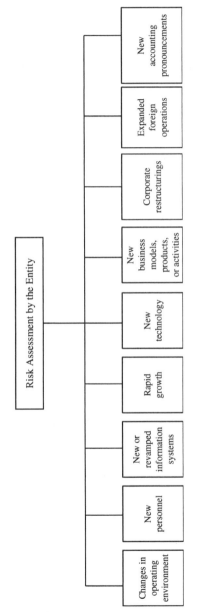

Risk Assessment by the Entity

- Changes in operating environment
- New personnel
- New or revamped information systems
- Rapid growth
- New technology
- New business models, products, or activities
- Corporate restructurings
- Expanded foreign operations
- New accounting pronouncements

EXHIBIT AU 314-3—OBJECTIVES OF INFORMATION SYSTEMS

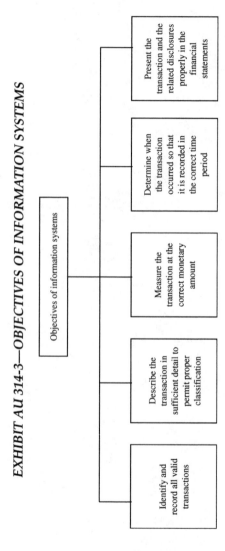

EXHIBIT AU 314-4—EXAMPLES OF CONTROL ACTIVITIES GERMANE TO INTERNAL CONTROL OVER FINANCIAL REPORTING

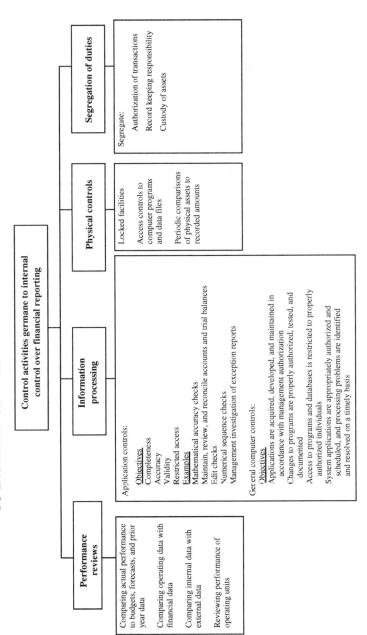

EXHIBIT AU 314-5—EXAMPLES OF INDUSTRY, REGULATORY, AND OTHER EXTERNAL FACTORS

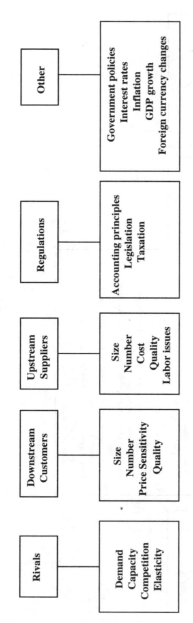

EXHIBIT AU-C 315-6—NATURE OF THE ENTITY AND RELEVANT STANDARDS OF FINANCIAL REPORTING

Nature of the Entity	Examples	Relevant Standards of Financial Reporting[a]
Business operations	Geographic segments	ASC 280
	Joint ventures	ASC 323
	Key customers	ASC 280
	Long-term supply contracts	ASC 440, ASC 470
	Major customers	ASC 280
	Pension, other postretirement benefits, and other postemployment benefits	ASC 715, ASC 712, ASC 958
	Related-party transactions	ASC 850
	Research and development activities	ASC 730, ASC 985
	Sources of revenue	ASC 605
	Stock option plans	ASC 718, ASC 505
	Subsidiaries or divisions	ASC 810, ASC 840
	Warranties	ASC 450
Investments	Acquisitions, mergers, and disposals	ASC 350, ASC 805
	Investments in securities	ASC 320, ASC 323
	Derivatives	ASC 815
	Capital expenditures	ASC 835
Financing	Off-balance-sheet financing	ASC 460
	Leasing	ASC 840
Financial reporting	Revenue recognition	ASC 605
	Fair-value accounting	ASC 820, ASC 825
	Foreign currency transactions and translation	ASC 830

[a] Not a complete list. Readers desiring a more complete list or a detailed discussion of these pronouncements might refer to CCH's *GAAP Guide, Volume I*, by Williams, Carcello, and Neal.

EXHIBIT AU-C 315-7—APPLICATION OF INTERNAL CONTROL CONCEPTS TO SMALL AND MIDSIZED ENTITIES

Internal control is a critical element in helping the client to prepare financial statements that reflect generally accepted accounting principles (GAAP). However, AU-C 315 recognizes that internal control will often be designed and implemented differently for a large company than for a small or even a midsized company. For example, the five components of internal control may not be clearly distinguishable in a smaller entity; rather, the owner-manager in a smaller entity may perform functions that cut across the five components of internal control. Although the internal control objectives underlying the internal control components should be met in every entity regardless of size, how the control objectives are achieved can vary from client to client. For example, the following features of a small or midsized entity's internal control may be as effective as the features adopted by a larger entity:

- *Control environment* Controls related to the control environment might not be as extensively documented in a formal manner but, rather, may be communicated orally and by management example to affected personnel. For example, although a formal code of conduct might not be reduced to written form, the essence of such a code might be part of the culture of the entity. In addition, smaller companies might not have independent or outside members among the group charged with governance of the entity. In fact, in some very small entities, it is often the owner-manager him- or herself who is charged with governance.

- *Risk assessment by entity* Risk assessment related to the preparation of financial statements might be less formal in a small company. However, all entities regardless of size, should have established financial reporting objectives. They may just be implicit rather than explicit in smaller entities. It is often the case that because of their involvement in the day-to-day operations of the entity, key managerial personnel (including owner-managers), are fully aware of the relationship between various operational activities and financial reporting objectives. The auditor should discuss with management how risks are identified and how they are managed.

- *Information and communication systems* Documentation of the information and communication system and related controls might not be as extensive or formal in a small company. The active involvement by a relatively small number of managerial personnel might not require formal accounting manuals or sophisticated accounting records. Also, communication in a smaller entity is often easier to achieve.

- *Control activities* Management involvement might substitute for certain types of control activities in smaller entities (e.g., management may specifically authorize the entity to enter into transactions through its direct involvement). Segregation of duties can often be a challenge in a smaller entity. However, reasonable segregation of duties can often be achieved even in an entity with only a few employees through (1) appropriate assignment of responsibilities to these few individuals, (2) management oversight of incompatible activities, or (3) utilization of embedded controls in packaged software programs.

- *Monitoring* Ongoing monitoring activities in smaller entities are likely to be informal. However, management's day-to-day involvement in operational activities may provide an adequate separate evaluation of the effectiveness of the design and operation of internal control.

The auditor's process of obtaining an understanding of the entity and its environment is also typically different for a small entity than for a midsize or large entity. For example, smaller entities often don't reduce their objectives and strategies to written form. These entities also may not have formal processes for managing business risks. The auditor obtains an understanding of the entity and its environment through discussions with management, and through his or her observation of how the business is run (i.e., what the implicit objectives and strategies are) and risks are managed.

Smaller entities may not have a formal process for measuring and reviewing their financial performance. Management of these entities may nonetheless rely on key indicators that they know from experience are accurate barometers of business performance. The auditor should discuss how management measures and reviews the entity's financial performance and document this discussion in the workpapers.

EXHIBIT AU-C 315-8—FACTORS THAT MIGHT INDICATE A HEIGHTENED RISK OF MATERIAL MISSTATEMENT

Operating Factors

- The entity operates in a region that is economically unstable (e.g., highly inflationary economies, countries with political and economic instability).
- The entity has operations in volatile markets (e.g., derivatives trading).
- The entity is struggling to meet objectives it has set, especially if the entity has publicly committed to meeting the objectives.
- The entity has begun offering new products or services.
- The entity has changed its sales, distribution, and production methods.
- There has been turnover among key personnel, especially among senior executives and individuals with financial reporting oversight responsibilities.
- The entity is subject to complex regulations.
- The entity's industry is subject to rapid changes.

Financing Factors

- The entity's ability to access capital and credit is constrained.
- The entity has completed a large acquisition or divestiture during the period under audit.
- The entity enters into complex alliances, joint venture agreements, special-purpose entities, and other types of off-balance-sheet financing.

Financial Reporting Factors

- There are questions about the ability of the entity to continue as a going concern.
- The entity lacks an adequate number of personnel with accounting and financial reporting skills.
- The entity has implemented a new information system or made significant modification to existing information systems.
- New accounting pronouncements apply to the entity.
- The entity has changed the accounting policies it uses or the methods used to apply an existing accounting policy.
- The entity's financial reports depend on complex measurements and/or highly subjective judgments (e.g., fair-value accounting).
- The entity enters into material related-party transactions.

- There are weaknesses in the entity's internal control over financial reporting.
- The entity has a history of past misstatements and/or significant material audit adjustments.
- Regulators or others are investigating or have alleged financial reporting improprieties.
- The entity faces pending litigation and other types of contingent liabilities.
- The entity has entered into large revenue transactions at the end of the period.
- The entity has entered into nonroutine and nonsystematic transactions that are material.
- The accounting for material transactions depends on management intent.

EXHIBIT AU 314-9—RELATIONSHIP OF ASSESSED RISKS OF MATERIAL MISSTATEMENT AND AUDITOR'S RESPONSES

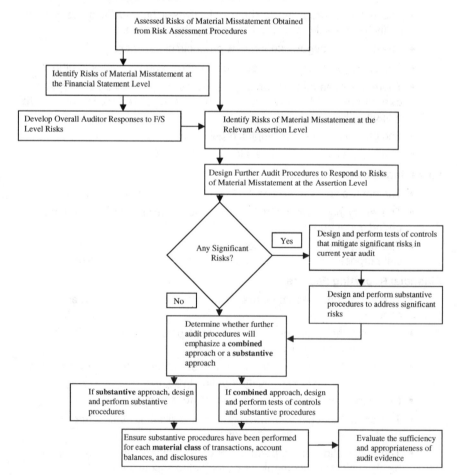

SECTION 320

MATERIALITY IN PLANNING AND PERFORMING AN AUDIT

Authoritative Pronouncements

SAS-122—Statements on Auditing Standards: Clarification and Recodification

Overview

In determining the nature, timing, and extent of audit procedures, the auditor must consider, among other factors, materiality and audit risk. Considering materiality and audit risk helps the auditor in planning and performing the audit. AU-C 450 (*Evaluation of Misstatement Identified during the Audit*) provides the auditor with guidance in evaluating the effect of any identified misstatements on the audit and of any uncorrected misstatements on the financial statements, and in forming the opinion in the auditor's report.

"Materiality" is generally defined by financial reporting frameworks (such as the FASB's Statement of Financial Accounting Concepts No. 2 (CON-2) (Qualitative Characteristics of Accounting Information) as omissions or misstatements of accounting information that, in the light of surrounding circumstances, could reasonably be expected to cause the judgment of a reasonable person relying on the financial statements to be changed or influenced by the omission or misstatement. Judgments about materiality are affected by the circumstances, including the size and nature of the misstatements, as well as by the common needs of the financial statement users.

"Audit risk" is the risk that the auditor may unknowingly fail to appropriately modify his or her opinion on financial statements that are materially misstated and is a function of the risks of material misstatement and detection risk. The concept of audit risk is based on the reality that the audit process can result in only reasonable assurance (not absolute assurance) that the auditor will detect material misstatements in financial statements, whether caused by error or fraud.

OBSERVATION: Materiality in an audit engagement relates to the assertions that are explicitly stated or implied in the financial statements. AU-C 314 outlines three classes of assertions: (1) assertions related to classes of transactions, (2) assertions related to account balances, and (3) assertions related to presentation and disclosure.

An auditor's opinion refers to materiality of the financial statements in the context of the financial statements taken as a whole. AU-C 320 notes that in performing the audit the auditor is concerned with matters that either individually or in the aggregate could be material to the financial statements. The auditor's responsibility is to plan and perform the audit to obtain reasonable assurance that material misstatements, whether caused by error or fraud, are detected. Reasonable assurance is achieved by obtaining sufficient appropriate audit evidence to reduce audit risk to the desired level. Judgments about materiality help the auditor determine the nature and extent of risk assessment procedures, identify and assess the risks of material misstatement, and determine further audit procedures.

ENGAGEMENT STRATEGY: The auditor is concerned with materiality levels during both the planning and evaluation phases of an engagement. Although conceptually it is possible, usually, the assessment of materiality levels will not be the same at the planning stage as at the evaluation stage. Because the auditor will have more complete information to better assess materiality for a particular engagement, the materiality level at the end of the audit can differ from the materiality used in the planning stage. In fact, if the level of materiality is significantly less at the evaluation stage than at the planning stage, the auditor will generally need to reevaluate the sufficiency of the audit procedures he or she has performed. See AU-C 450 for more specific guidance about materiality considerations when evaluating misstatements identified during the audit.

PUBLIC COMPANY IMPLICATION: In 2010 the PCAOB issued eight auditing standards (AS-8 through AS-15) related to the auditor's assessment of and response to risk. The standards bear many similarities to the eight risk-assessment standards adopted by the Auditing Standards Board in 2006. AS-9 (Audit Planning) and AS-10 (Supervision of the Audit Engagement) affect audit planning and supervision. AS-9 establishes requirements related to planning the audit, including requirements related to developing an appropriate audit strategy and audit plan. AS-10 describes the auditor's responsibilities for supervising the engagement, and it applies to the engagement partner and other audit team members who assist the partner in supervising others. Although there are a number of differences between the PCAOB's and ASB's risk standards, the risk-assessment concepts contained in the PCAOB standards should be familiar to most auditors. Audit risk is the risk that the auditor will issue an inappropriate opinion on financial statements that are materially misstated. The auditor is to reduce audit risk to a low level through the application of audit procedures. As a result, the amount of audit effort devoted to particular accounts, classes of transactions, and disclosures should vary based on their respective risk.

Definitions

Performance materiality	Amount(s) set by the auditor at less than materiality to reduce the probability of the aggregate of uncorrected and undetected misstatements exceeding materiality to an appropriately low level. Performance materiality amount(s) can apply to the financial statements as a whole or to particular classes of transactions, account balances, or disclosures. Performance materiality is different from tolerable misstatement.

Requirements

The auditor is presumptively required to perform the following procedures in considering materiality when planning and performing the audit:

1. Determine materiality for the financial statements as a whole when establishing the overall audit strategy. Also determine materiality for particular classes of transactions, account balances, or disclosures for which misstatements in amounts smaller than materiality for the financial statements as a whole could be reasonably expected to be material to financial statement users.

2. Determine performance materiality in order to assess the risks of material misstatement and determine the nature, timing, and extent of further audit procedures.

3. If the auditor becomes aware of information during the audit that would have caused different initial determinations of materiality, revise impacted materiality levels as appropriate.

4. If the auditor concludes a lower materiality level than that initially determined is appropriate for the financial statements as a whole or for particular classes of transactions, account balances, or disclosures, determine if it is necessary to revise performance materiality, and if the nature, timing, and extent of further audit procedures remain appropriate.

5. Documentation should include the following amounts and the factors considered in their determination:

   a. Materiality for the financial statements as a whole

   b. Any applicable materiality levels for particular classes of transactions, account balances, or disclosures

   c. Performance materiality

   d. Any revision of these materiality levels as the audit progressesd.

Analysis and Application of Procedures

Determine materiality during the planning phase of the engagement

The determination of materiality is a matter of professional judgment. Often the auditor applies a percentage to a chosen benchmark as a step in determining materiality for the financial statements as a whole. In identifying an appropriate benchmark, auditors often consider common financial statement elements (e.g., assets, liabilities, pre-tax income, etc.); specific financial statement accounts or elements that will be the focus of financial statement users' attention; the nature of the entity, its industry, and the economic environment; the entity's ownership structure and financing methods; and the relative volatility of the benchmark. Appropriate benchmarks for a profit-oriented entity may be profit before tax, total revenues, or gross profit, while appropriate benchmarks for not-for-profit or governmental entities may be total cost, net cost, or asset value. The percentage to be applied to the chosen benchmark is subject to professional judgment and may vary depending on the benchmark chosen and the type of entity being audited. For example, assume that the auditor has established the following analysis as a preliminary step in establishing materiality levels in an engagement:

Financial Statement Element	Financial Statements Amount (unaudited)	Percentage Misstatement Considered Material	Amount Misstatement Considered Material
Gross profit	$4,000,000	6%	$240,000
Income before taxes from continuing items	3,000,000	7%	210,000
Total assets	4,000,000	10%	400,000
Current assets	3,000,000	8%	240,000

Although the auditor may be concerned with the misstatement of several financial statement elements, generally the smallest materiality level is used in the planning phase of the engagement. This approach is justified because of the interrelationship of the financial statements and the need for audit efficiency. In the current example, the overall materiality level for the financial statements would be $210,000.

ENGAGEMENT STRATEGY: When the auditor uses a single materiality threshold for all of the financial statements, the planned audit risk is lower for those items that have a materiality threshold level higher than the single materiality level selected for planning purposes. In the current example, the planned audit risk is lower for the balance sheet (total assets) because the materiality level is $210,000 rather than $400,000. However, AU-C 320 does allow the auditor to use two different levels of materiality for the income statement and balance sheet as part of the engagement strategy. In this example, the auditor may conclude that misstatements aggregating $210,000 are material to the income statement but that misstatements to the balance sheet would have to aggregate to $400,000, as long as balance sheet misstatements have no impact on the income statement.

Relevant financial data used in calculating the benchmark and materiality level generally include prior-period and period-to-date financial information, current period budgets or forecasts, and changes in the economy or the entity's industry. Determination of materiality levels is also based on the auditor's understanding of user needs and expectations and may be influenced by factors such as financial statement elements with a high degree of estimation uncertainty, or, for audits of governmental entities, by legislative and regulatory requirements. Once the materiality level is established, however, misstatements should be evaluated regardless of any inherent uncertainties. Furthermore, materiality levels relate to the financial reporting period being audited regardless of its length.

The auditor is required to consider whether there are circumstances where misstatements of particular classes of transactions, account balances, or disclosure of lesser amounts than the materiality level determined for the financial statements as a whole might affect economic decisions of users of the financial statements. For example, accounting standards, regulations, or laws may affect user expectations regarding the measurement or disclosure of certain items. Additionally, the industry or environment the entity operates in may place importance on key disclosures. Focus on a particular aspect of an entity's business that is disclosed separately in the financial statements may also affect user expectations. In considering whether establishing materiality levels for transaction classes, account balances, or disclosures is necessary, it may be useful to the auditor to obtain an understanding of the views and expectations of management and those charged with governance.

OBSERVATION: In assessing the significance of a misstatement, the auditor should consider the pervasiveness of the misstatement (such as whether the amounts and presentation of numerous financial statement items are affected), and the effect of the misstatement on the financial statements taken as a whole.

PUBLIC COMPANY IMPLICATION: The SEC Staff has issued guidance about materiality considerations relevant to financial statements for public companies. SEC Staff Accounting Bulletin No. 99 (SAB-99) (Materiality) contains the SEC staff's views that the auditor's exclusive reliance on certain quantitative benchmarks to assess materiality in preparing financial statements and performing audits of those financial statements is inappropriate; misstatements are not immaterial simply because they fall beneath a numerical threshold. SAB-99 emphasizes the importance of evaluating qualitative aspects of materiality and provides guidance to auditors of useful qualitative characteristics to consider. Auditors of public companies should examine SAB-99's guidance.

PLANNING AID REMINDER: There is an inverse relationship between audit risk and materiality, which can be expressed in the following generalizations: (1) the risk that an item could be misstated by an extremely large amount is generally low and (2) the risk that an item could be misstated by an extremely small amount is generally high. Thus, as the planned level of materiality is reduced, the scope of the audit approach must be increased.

Performance materiality considerations

The auditor plans the audit to detect material misstatements, which could arise from an individual misstatement that is material or from the aggregation of individually immaterial misstatements. AU-C 320 requires the auditor to set performance materiality to reduce to an appropriately low level the probability that an aggregate of uncorrected and undetected misstatements exceeds materiality for the financial statements as a whole.

Performance materiality levels are determined using professional judgment. These levels are affected by the auditor's understanding of the entity, which includes information gathered during risk assessment procedures, the nature and extent of misstatements identified in prior audits, and the auditor's expectations regarding misstatements in the current audit. Tolerable misstatement is the application of performance materiality to a particular sampling procedure.

Revision of materiality levels

The auditor should revise materiality levels if it appears that actual financial results will be significantly different from the anticipated results used to initially determine materiality of the financial statements, relevant transactions, account balances, or disclosures. Circumstances that could create a need to revise materiality levels include a change in the entity's circumstances, new information, or a change in the auditor's understanding of the entity and its operations as a result of performing further audit procedures.

PLANNING AID REMINDER: Materiality levels may be determined for planning purposes before financial statements are prepared. In these situations, the auditor may base materiality judgments on annualized interim financial statements or prior-period financial statements, adjusting for any relevant changes in the entity, industry, or economy.

SECTION 330

PERFORMING AUDIT PROCEDURES IN RESPONSE TO ASSESSED RISKS AND EVALUATING THE AUDIT EVIDENCE OBTAINED

Authoritative Pronouncements

SAS-122—Statements on Auditing Standards: Clarification and Recodification

Overview

Auditing standards require the auditor to obtain sufficient appropriate audit evidence by performing audit procedures in response to the risks of material misstatements identified and assessed by the auditor. That audit evidence is obtained to afford a reasonable basis for an opinion regarding the financial statements as a whole. AU-C 330 establishes the standards and procedures to assist the auditor in fulfilling these requirements and provides guidance to assist the auditor with the following:

- Determining the overall response to the risk of material misstatement at the financial statement level.

- Designing and performing further audit procedures in response to risks of material misstatement at the relevant financial statement assertion level.

- Evaluating the sufficiency and appropriateness of audit evidence obtained.

- Satisfying the related documentation requirements.

The auditor's performance of risk assessment procedures should lead to the identification of those account balances, classes of transactions, or disclosures where material misstatements are most likely to occur. The risk assessment procedures should provide the basis for designing and performing further audit procedures. To reduce audit risk to an acceptably low level, the auditor performs further audit procedures, whose nature, timing, and extent are responsive to the assessed risks of material misstatement. AU-C 330 provides guidance to assist auditors in the design and performance of these further audit procedures to address the risks of material misstatement identified. Exhibit AU-C 315-9 provides an overview of the linkage between the assessed level of risk of material misstatements and the auditor's responses to the risks that are identified (described elsewhere in this section).

PUBLIC COMPANY IMPLICATION: In 2010 the PCAOB issued eight auditing standards (AS-8 through AS-15) related to the auditor's assessment of and response to risk. The standards bear many similarities to the eight risk-assessment standards adopted by the Auditing Standards Board in 2006. AS-13 (The Auditor's Responses to the Risks of Material Misstatement) and AS-14 (Evaluating Audit Results) provide guidance to the auditor in performing audit procedures. AS-13 establishes requirements for responding to audit risk, both at the overall level and at the level of significant accounts and disclosures. AS-14 describes the auditor's responsibilities for evaluating audit results. The auditor must evaluate whether he or she has obtained sufficient appropriate audit evidence, and he or she is required to consider (1) uncorrected misstatements and control deficiencies, (2) overall financial statement presentation, including disclosures, and (3) potential management bias in preparing the financial statements. Although there are a number of differences between the PCAOB's and ASB's risk standards, the risk-assessment concepts contained in the PCAOB standards should be familiar to most auditors. As is currently the case, audit risk is the risk that the auditor will issue an inappropriate opinion on financial statements that are materially misstated. The auditor is to reduce audit risk to a low level through the application of audit procedures. As a result, the amount of audit effort devoted to particular accounts, classes of transactions, and disclosures should vary based on their respective risk.

Definitions

Substantive procedure	An audit procedure, including tests of details and substantive analytical procedures, designed to detect material misstatements at the assertion level.
Test of controls	An audit procedure designed to evaluate the operating effectiveness of controls in preventing, or detecting and correcting, material misstatements at the assertion level.

Requirements

The auditor is presumptively required to perform the following procedures regarding audit procedures in response to assessed risks and evaluating the audit evidence obtained:

Overall Responses

1. Design and implement overall responses to address the assessed risks of material misstatement at the financial statement level.

Assertion Level Responses

2. Design and perform further audit procedures with the nature, timing, and extent to respond to the assessed risks of material misstatement at the relevant assertion level.

3. When designing further audit procedures to perform:

   a. Consider the reasons for the assessed risk of material misstatement at the relevant assertion level for each material class of transactions, account balance, and disclosure, including the inherent risk of material misstatement for each item and whether the risk assessment incorporates control risk thereby requiring the auditor to obtain evidence about the operating effectiveness of controls.

   b. Obtain more persuasive audit evidence the higher the assessment of risk.

Tests of Controls

4. Design and perform tests of controls to obtain sufficient appropriate audit evidence about the operating effectiveness of relevant controls at the assertion level when (1) the assessment of risks of material misstatement includes an expectation that controls are operating effectively or (2) substantive procedures cannot provide sufficient appropriate audit evidence alone.

5. Obtain more persuasive audit evidence through the performance of test of controls the greater the reliance on the effectiveness of a control.

6. When designing and performing tests of controls:

　a. Perform inquiry and other procedures to obtain audit evidence about controls' operating effectiveness, including how controls were applied at relevant times during the period under audit, the consistency of application, and by whom or what means they were applied, including whether the person performing the control has the authority and competence necessary to perform the control effectively.

　b. Determine whether the tested controls depend on other indirect controls and, if so, whether it is necessary to obtain audit evidence supporting the indirect controls' operating effectiveness.

7. Test controls for the particular time or throughout the period for which the auditor intends to rely on those controls.

8. When obtaining evidence about the operating effectiveness of controls during an interim period, (a) obtain audit evidence about significant changes to those controls subsequent to the interim period and (b) determine the additional audit evidence to be obtained for the remaining period.

9. Determine if it is appropriate to use audit evidence about the operating effectiveness of controls obtained in previous audits and, if so, the length of time that may elapse before retesting a control, by considering:

　a. The effectiveness of other elements of internal control

　b. Risks arising from the characteristics of the control (e.g., characteristics of manual or automated controls)

　c. The effectiveness of general IT controls

　d. The effectiveness of the control and its application including the nature and extent of deviations previously noted and if there have been personnel changes significantly affecting control application

　e. If the lack of change in a control poses a risk due to changing circumstances

　f. The risks of material misstatement and the extent of reliance on the control

10. If planning to use audit evidence about the operating effectiveness of controls from previous audits, perform audit procedures such as inquiry combined with observation or inspection to establish that information's continuing relevance to the current audit. If changes have occurred affecting the audit evidence's continuing relevance to the current audit, test the controls in the current audit. If such changes have not occurred, test the controls at least once every third audit, rotating testing so some controls are tested during each audit.

11. If planning to rely on controls over a significant risk, test the operating effectiveness of those controls in the current period.

12. When evaluating the operating effectiveness of relevant controls, evaluate whether misstatements detected by substantive procedures indicate the con-

trols are not operating effectively. The absence of detected misstatements does not provide audit evidence that the controls are effective.

13. When deviations from controls the auditor intends to rely on are detected, make specific inquiries to understand the matter and its potential consequences. Determine whether (1) the tests of controls performed provide an appropriate basis for reliance on the controls, (2) additional tests of controls are necessary, or (3) the potential risks of misstatement need to be addressed using substantive procedures.

Substantive Procedures

14. Design and perform substantive procedures for all relevant assertions related to each material class of transactions, account balance, and disclosure regardless of the assessed risks of material misstatement.

15. Consider whether external confirmation procedures should be performed as substantive audit procedures. External confirmations of accounts receivable are often necessary to reduce audit risk to an acceptably low level for the relevant assertion and should be used unless (1) the overall account balance is immaterial, (2) those confirmations would be ineffective, or (3) the assessed level of risk of material misstatement is low and sufficient appropriate audit evidence will be obtained by performing substantive procedures. If the auditor concludes external confirmation procedures for accounts receivable are not necessary, document the basis for that determination.

16. Perform audit procedures related to the financial statement closing process, such as agreeing or reconciling the financial statements with the underlying accounting records and examining material journal entries and other adjustments made during financial statement preparation.

17. If the assessed risk of material misstatement at the relevant assertion level is considered a significant risk, perform substantive procedures specifically responsive to that risk. When the response to a significant risk consists only of substantive procedures, those procedures should include tests of details.

18. When substantive procedures are performed at an interim date, cover the remaining period by performing (1) substantive procedures combined with tests of controls for the intervening period or (2) substantive procedures only if those procedures are sufficient to extend the audit conclusions from the interim date to period end.

19. If unexpected misstatements are detected at an interim date, evaluate whether the related assessment of risks and the planned nature, timing, and extent of substantive procedures covering the remaining period need to be modified.

Selecting Items for Testing

20. Determine a means of selecting items for testing that is effective for the audit procedure when designing tests of controls and tests of details.

Presentation and Disclosure

21. Perform audit procedures to evaluate whether the overall financial statement presentation and related disclosures are in accordance with the applicable financial reporting framework.

Sufficiency and Appropriateness of Audit Evidence

22. Before the audit's conclusion, based on audit procedures performed and audit evidence obtained, evaluate whether the assessments of the risks of material misstatement at the relevant assertion level remain appropriate.

23. Conclude whether sufficient appropriate audit evidence has been obtained. Consider all relevant audit evidence, whether it corroborates or contradicts financial statement assertions.

24. If sufficient appropriate audit evidence about a relevant assertion has not been obtained, attempt to obtain further audit evidence. If unable to obtain such evidence, express a qualified opinion or a disclaimer of opinion.

Documentation

25. Document (a) the overall responses to address the assessed risks of material misstatement at the financial statement level and the nature, timing, and extent of further audit procedures performed; (b) the linkage of those procedures with the assessed risks at the relevant assertion level; and (c) the result of the audit procedures and the conclusions where they are not otherwise clear.

26. If planning to use audit evidence about the operating effectiveness of controls obtained in previous audits, document the conclusions reached about relying on those controls.

27. Documentation should demonstrate that the financial statements agree or reconcile with the underlying accounting records.

Analysis and Application of Procedures

Overall Responses

The auditor's risk assessment procedures may identify risks pervasive to the financial statements. In particular, the auditor's understanding of the control environment obtained as part of the auditor's risk assessment procedures may affect the assessment of the risk of material misstatement at the overall financial statement level. When deficiencies in the control environment exist, the auditor's confidence in internal control and the reliability of evidence generated internally by the client's internal control system may lead the auditor to perform audit procedures closer to period end than at interim and seek more audit evidence from the performance of substantive procedures. Thus, consideration of matters affecting the control environment or other factors that affect the overall risks of material misstatements at the financial statement level has a significant effect on the general approach to the audit.

To respond to assessed risks of material misstatement at the financial statement level, the auditor's response may include the following:

- Emphasizing to the audit engagement team the importance of maintaining professional skepticism in gathering and evaluating audit evidence

- Assigning more experienced staff or those with specialized skills or using specialists

- Providing more supervision

- Incorporating additional elements of unpredictability in the selection of further audit procedures to be performed

- Making general changes to the nature, timing, and extent of audit procedures

Assertion Level Responses

Based on his or her performance of risk assessment procedures, the auditor may identify risks of material misstatements at the relevant assertion level for account balances, classes of transactions, or disclosures. AU-C 330 requires the auditor to design and perform further audit procedures to respond to the assessed risks of material misstatements at the relevant assertion level. This ensures a direct linkage between the risk assessment and the nature, timing, and extent of further audit procedures. Further audit procedures may emphasize the performance of substantive procedures (a substantive approach) or use both tests of controls and substantive procedures (a combined approach).

PLANNING AID REMINDER: Although audit procedures performed in prior audits and example audit procedures in illustrative audit programs may be useful to the auditor, the assessment of the risk of material misstatement in the current period forms the primary basis for designing further audit procedures.

To determine the appropriateness of further audit procedures, the auditor considers several factors:

- The significance of the risk

- The likelihood that a material misstatement will occur

- The characteristics of the class of transactions, account balance, or disclosure involved

- The nature of specific controls used by the entity, in particular, whether they are manual or automated

- Whether the auditor expects to obtain audit evidence from tests of controls (to determine whether the controls are operating effectively to prevent or detect and correct material misstatements)

In some cases, the auditor may respond by only performing substantive procedures and exclude the effect of controls. However, in doing so, he or she must be satisfied that only performing substantive procedures for the relevant assertions is appropriate for effectively reducing detection risk to an acceptable level. Often, however, auditors determine that a combined approach of performing both tests of controls and substantive procedures is most effective.

PLANNING AID REMINDER: Because there are limitations in any system of internal control in preventing or detecting material misstatements, tests of controls do not eliminate the need for the performance of substantive procedures.

Considering the nature of further audit procedures

The nature of the audit procedures is of most importance when designing and performing further audit procedures to respond to risks of material misstatement. The nature of further audit procedures refers to the purpose and type of further audit procedures. The purpose relates to whether the procedures are designed to be tests of controls or to provide substantive evidence about an account balance, class of transaction, or disclosure. The type of further audit procedure relates to whether the procedures involve inspection, observation, inquiry, confirmation, recalculation, reperformance, or analytical procedure.

As the risks of material misstatement for a relevant assertion increase, the auditor may modify the nature of the further audit procedure by changing the purpose from a test of control to a substantive procedure, because evidence from substantive procedures is often more reliable and relevant. The auditor may also modify the type of procedure in order to obtain evidence that is more reliable.

The reasons for the assessment of risk of material misstatement for the relevant assertion should affect the nature of the further audit procedures. Information affecting the auditor's assessment of inherent risk and his or her understanding of internal control will directly affect his or her determination of the appropriate nature of further audit procedures. For example, if the auditor believes internal controls are effectively designed and in operation, he or she may plan to perform tests of controls and modify the nature of substantive procedures accordingly. In other situations when the auditor's assessment of risk of material misstatement is low, the auditor may conclude that the performance of substantive analytical procedures provides sufficient appropriate audit evidence.

Considering the timing of further audit procedures

Timing refers to when the auditor performs further audit procedures or the period or date that the audit evidence applies to. The auditor's decision about the timing of further audit procedures is affected by his or her assessment of the risks of material misstatement at the relevant assertion level. As the risks of material misstatement increase, the auditor may decide to perform substantive procedures closer to the period end, unannounced, or at unpredictable times.

When the auditor performs procedures before period end, he or she should consider the additional evidence that might be necessary for the remaining untested period. In some cases, audit procedures performed at interim periods help the auditor identify important matters at an early stage of the audit. Having determined that further audit tests are to be performed at earlier interim periods, the auditor should consider whether additional testing is required between the interim and period-end time frame.

The timing of the performance of audit procedures may be affected by when the relevant information is available. In some cases, electronic evidence may be overwritten and thus must be examined on a timely basis before that occurs. In other cases, the nature of risks may affect the timing of procedures. For example, if there is a risk of material misstatement related to the cutoff of revenue transactions, the auditor may wait to inspect transactions near period end. Certain audit procedures can only be performed at or after period end, such as reconciling accounting records to the financial statements.

Considering the extent of further audit procedures

The extent of further audit procedures encompasses the sufficiency or quantity of a specific audit procedure to be performed. Several factors affect the auditor's considerations of the extent of further audit procedures:

- Materiality level: Extent increases as materiality decreases.
- The assessed risk of material misstatement: As the risk increases, the extent may need to increase.
- The degree of assurance the auditor plans to obtain from the further audit procedures: The greater the assurance needs, the greater the extent of testing needed.

The increase in the extent of further audit procedures is effective as long as the nature of the test is relevant to the risks identified.

Tests of Controls

Further audit procedures consist of tests of controls and substantive procedures. Tests of controls are only performed on controls that the auditor has determined to be suitably designed to prevent or detect and correct a material misstatement in a relevant assertion. Some controls are directly related to specific assertions, and other controls are related only indirectly to specific assertions. The more direct the relationship between controls and an assertion, the more likely the control can provide a basis for reducing the overall risk of material misstatement. If tests of controls show them to be operating effectively at the relevant assertion level and level of planned reliance, the extent of substantive procedures in the audit may be able to be reduced.

PLANNING AID REMINDER: The auditor performs tests of controls when he or she expects the operating effectiveness of controls to reduce his or her assessment of the risks of material misstatements or when substantive procedures alone will not provide sufficient appropriate evidence. According to AICPA Technical Practice Aid TIS 8200.06, the phrase "expectation of the operating effectiveness of controls" means that the auditor's understanding of all five components of internal control enable him or her to initially assess control risk at less than the maximum. In that case, the auditor's strategy is to perform a combination of tests of controls and substantive procedures. The auditor's initial assessment of control risk is preliminary and subject to satisfactory results from the tests of the operating effectiveness of those controls. An audit is usually more efficient when the auditor can rely to some degree on the client's internal control.

Although the objective of tests of controls differs from the auditor's risk assessment procedures, he or she may determine that testing the operating effectiveness of controls can be efficiently and effectively performed as part of procedures performed to assess their design and implementation. The auditor may also perform dual-purpose tests, performing a test of controls concurrently with a test of details on the same transaction. Dual-purpose tests are designed and evaluated by considering each purpose of the test separately.

Nature and extent of tests of controls

The nature of tests of controls ordinarily includes the following procedures:

- Inquiries of appropriate entity personnel
- Inspection of documents, reports, or electronic files for indication of the performance of the control
- Observation of the application of the control
- Reperformance by the auditor of the application of the control

The nature of the test of controls is affected by the desired assurance to be obtained about the operating effectiveness of the controls. Evidence obtained from inspection or reperformance generally provides more assurance than evidence obtained from inquiry or observation. Furthermore, inquiry alone is not sufficient to obtain evidence about the operating effectiveness of controls. As the desired level of assurance from controls increases, auditors usually change the nature of tests of controls from a combination of inquiry and observation to inspection and reperformance.

The nature of tests of controls is directly affected by the nature of the underlying control. For some controls, operating effectiveness is best evidenced by documentation. In those situations, the auditor's tests of controls most likely involve inspection of documentation. For other controls, such as those related to the control environment, the most reliable and relevant evidence may be obtained through inquiry and observation.

The extent of tests of controls relates to the sufficiency of the tests. Several factors affect the extent of tests of controls:

- The frequency of the performance of the control by the entity during the period
- The length of time during the audit period that the auditor is relying on the control
- The relevance and reliability of the audit evidence to be obtained in supporting that the control prevents or detects and corrects material misstatements at the relevant financial statement level
- The extent to which audit evidence is obtained from tests of other controls related to the relevant assertion
- The extent to which the auditor plans to rely on the operating effectiveness of the control in the assessment of risk
- The expected deviation from the control

Because of the inherent consistency of IT processing, the nature and extent of the auditor's tests of an automated control may be affected by his or her testing of the operating effectiveness of IT general controls, particularly those related to security and program change controls. That is, the automated control might require limited testing because once the control is implemented it functions the same way each time unless the program or underlying data is changed. The auditor may test the automated control once it is implemented and then test the overall effectiveness of general IT controls to ensure that the automated control has not changed since it was implemented and that it continues to function effectively. This evaluation may require the skills of an IT specialist.

Timing of tests of controls

The timing of the auditor's tests of controls depends on the period of time he or she intends to rely on those controls. If the auditor only intends to rely on the performance of controls as of a point in time (for example, relying on controls related to the physical inventory taken as of the balance sheet date), tests of the controls may be conducted as of that particular time. If the auditor intends to rely on the performance of controls throughout the period under audit, the tests of controls should be performed to determine that they operated effectively during that period.

For many controls, the auditor's tests may be performed during an interim period and several factors affect the need for additional evidence about those controls during the remaining untested period:

- The significance of the assessed risks of material misstatements
- The specific controls that were tested during the interim period, the results of those tests, and significant changes to those controls since testing
- The degree to which audit evidence about the operating effectiveness of those controls was obtained
- The length of the remaining period
- The extent to which the auditor intends to reduce further substantive procedures based on the reliance of controls
- The effectiveness of the control environment

Additional evidence may be obtained by extending testing of the operating effectiveness of controls over the remaining period or testing the entity's monitoring of controls.

The auditor may be able to rely on tests of controls performed in prior-year audits. To rely on tests of controls performed in prior audits, the auditor must obtain evidence about whether changes in those specific controls have occurred subsequent to the prior-year audit. If changes have been made since the prior-year testing, the auditor may obtain evidence to determine whether the changes have affected the control's continued effective functioning. The evidence gathered about these changes may support increasing or decreasing the expected audit evidence to be obtained about the operating effectiveness of those controls in the current-year audit.

The auditor uses professional judgment in determining the reliance to be placed on prior-year audit evidence for controls that have not changed since they were last tested and do not mitigate significant risks. More frequent retesting of a control generally occurs when the control environment is weak, there is weak monitoring of controls, there is a significant manual element to the control, personnel changes have occurred that affect the application of the control, there are weak general IT controls, and there are other circumstances that indicate a need for changes in the control. By testing some controls each audit, the auditor obtains information about the continuing effectiveness of the control environment that can affect the decision to rely on evidence obtained in previous audits.

Exhibit AU-C 330-1 provides a summary of decisions auditors make about the timing of the testing of controls for current-year audits.

Operating Effectiveness of Controls

Deviations from controls the auditor intends to rely on may be detected and can be caused by factors such as personnel changes, seasonal fluctuations in transaction volume, and human error. The detected deviation rate may be significant enough to indicate that the control cannot be relied on to reduce risk at the relevant assertion level to the level assessed by the auditor. Furthermore, a material misstatement detected by the auditor's procedures that indicates the misstatement would not have been detected by the entity is an indicator of a material weakness in internal control.

Substantive Procedures

Substantive procedures consist of two types: (1) substantive analytical procedures and (2) tests of details of classes of transactions, account balances, and disclosures.

Generally, the nature, timing, and extent of substantive procedures are affected by the assessed level of risk of material misstatement. However, AU-C 330 notes that the auditor should design and perform substantive procedures for all relevant assertions pertaining to each account balance, disclosure, and material class of transactions. As a result, substantive procedures are required in every audit because (1) the auditor's assessment of risks of material misstatements is judgmental and may not be sufficiently precise to identify all risks of material misstatements and (2) there are inherent limitations in any system of internal control.

Nature and extent of substantive procedures

The nature of substantive procedures is directly affected by whether the procedure is a substantive analytical procedure or a test of details. Substantive analytical procedures are generally more applicable to larger volumes of transactions that tend to be predictable over time, such as income statement accounts. Tests of details are generally more appropriate for obtaining audit evidence about account balances, particularly existence and valuation.

The nature of substantive procedures should be responsive to the level of planned detection risk. In many instances the auditor's planned level of detection risk is affected by his or her tests of controls. Thus, the nature of substantive testing is affected by the audit evidence obtained through tests of controls. For example, substantive analytical procedures may be sufficiently responsive to the planned level of detection risk for some accounts, particularly when the tests of operating effectiveness have reduced the auditor's assessed level of the risk of material misstatements. In other situations, only a test of details or a combination of tests of details and substantive analytical procedures is appropriate to respond to the planned level of detection risk.

The nature of substantive procedures is directly affected by the nature of the relevant assertion. For example, to test the existence assertion, the nature of the auditor's substantive procedures should include the selection of items for testing from those recorded in the accounting records. To test the completeness assertion, the nature of the auditor's substantive procedures should include the selection of items for testing from audit evidence that indicates that an item has occurred and should be recorded in the accounting records. Exhibit AU-C 330-2 provides an example of illustrative substantive procedures linked to the inventory account balance assertions and the inventory presentation and disclosure assertions.

The extent of substantive testing may need to increase to achieve a reduced level of planned detection risk when results from tests of controls are unsatisfactory. The extent of substantive procedures is often addressed through the sample size examined in the substantive procedure. Other matters may also affect the extent of substantive procedures, including whether it is more effective to use other selective means of testing.

In considering whether to perform external confirmation procedures to provide audit evidence, the auditor should consider that confirmations may be relevant when addressing assertions related to many different items, including account balances, agreement terms, contracts, transactions with other parties, and the absence of certain conditions, such as "side agreements." Factors the auditor may consider in determining whether to perform external confirmation procedures include:

- The confirming party's knowledge of the subject matter
- The willingness or ability of the confirming party to respond, which may affect whether the party responds, responds in a casual manner, or attempts to restrict reliance on the response
- The confirming party's objectivity
- The ability of a confirmation performed for one purpose to provide audit evidence about other matters

Confirmation of accounts receivable is a generally accepted auditing procedure, where accounts receivable refers to the entity's claims against customers from the sale of goods or services in the normal course of business and a financial institution's loans. Confirmations can also be effective in auditing many other areas: cash, notes receivable, inventory, consigned merchandise, construction and production contracts, investment securities, market values, accounts payable, notes payable, lines of credit, and actual and contingent liabilities. It is important to recognize that external confirmations provide more relevant audit evidence related to certain assertions such as existence than they do regarding other assertions such as recoverability of accounts receivable. The auditor may determine external confirmations would be ineffective if the auditor has reason to believe response rates would be inadequate or otherwise unreliable.

PLANNING AID REMINDER: The auditor's procedures examining adjustments made during the course of preparing the financial statements refers to journal entries and adjustments prepared by the entity during the process of preparing its financial statements, such as consolidating entries or elimination entries between subsidiaries. It does not refer to journal entries recorded by the entity in the general ledger during the year. However, AU-C 240 reminds auditors that they are required to design audit procedures to test the appropriateness of journal entries recorded by the entity in the general ledger during the year.

FRAUD POINTER: AU-C 240 requires the auditor to respond to the risk of management override of internal controls in every audit by examining journal entries. Thus, the auditor's examination of journal entries and other adjustments as part of his or her substantive procedures should be coordinated with the examination of journal entries required by AU-C 240 to address the ever-present risk of management override of internal control.

In addition to the foregoing required substantive procedures at the financial statement reporting level, AU-C 330 requires the auditor to perform substantive procedures for all significant risks. For example, if the auditor determines that the risk of material misstatement in accounts receivable is high related to the existence assertion, the auditor may not only confirm outstanding account balances of related customer balances but also other details related to transactions affecting customers' account balances.

PLANNING AID REMINDER: In certain instances, the auditor may plan an all-substantive approach even if his or her understanding of internal control causes him or her to believe that controls are designed effectively. After the auditor obtains an understanding of the entity and its environment, including internal controls, and assesses the risk of material misstatement, he or she may consider the cost-benefit to determine the most effective set of further audit procedures. If the auditor believes that the benefit of testing the operating effectiveness of internal controls is less than the costs of testing them, he or she may adopt an audit strategy that consists solely of substantive procedures to respond to the risk of material misstatement.

Timing of substantive procedures

Similar to tests of controls, the auditor may decide to perform substantive procedures at an interim date or at periods close to or as of period end. When substantive procedures are performed at interim dates, there is a risk that material misstatement that exists at the period end will not be detected by the auditor. As the length of the period between interim testing and period end increases, this risk increases. As a result, when the auditor decides to perform substantive tests at an interim date, he or she should perform further substantive procedures, sometimes in combination with tests of controls, to cover the remaining period to provide a basis for extending the audit conclusions from interim substantive procedures to period end. Exhibit AU-C 330-3 provides an illustrative example of how interim substantive procedures can be rolled forward to period end.

Several factors affect the auditor's decision to perform substantive procedures at an interim date:

- The strength of the control environment and other relevant controls

- The availability of information at a later date that is necessary for the auditor's procedures

- The objective of the substantive procedure

- The assessed risk of material misstatement

- The nature of the account balance or class of transactions and relevant assertions

- The ability of the auditor to reduce the risk that misstatements that exist at the period end are not detected by performing appropriate substantive procedures, including those combined with tests of controls.

FRAUD POINTER: When the auditor identifies risks of material misstatements due to fraud, one of his or her responses might include a change in the timing of substantive procedures to perform tests at or closer to the end of the reporting period.

Unlike the auditor's tests of controls, he or she is in most cases unable to rely on substantive procedures performed in prior audits to reduce detection risk in the current audit. Audit evidence obtained from prior audits typically provides little or no evidence to reduce detection risk in the current audit. As a result, substantive procedures should generally be performed during the current audit. However, in some cases the auditor may use audit evidence from a previous audit's substantive procedures if the evidence and subject matter have not fundamentally changed and audit procedures have been performed during the current period to establish its continuing relevance.

Selecting Items for Testing

For a test to be effective, the auditor must obtain audit evidence to the extent that sufficient appropriate audit evidence will be obtained when combined with other audit evidence. Therefore, the items selected to be tested should be relevant, reliable, and sufficient for the auditor to draw valid conclusions, with an acceptable level of risk that the conclusion based on a selected sample may be different from the conclusion reached if the entire population was tested.

There are three methods the auditor can use to select items for testing, and any method may be appropriate given particular circumstances.

1. Select all items in a population: This may occur for tests of details and may be appropriate when the population is a small number of large-value items, there is a significant risk of material misstatement, or a complete examination is cost effective due to its repetitive nature.

2. Select specific items: This method is subject to nonsampling risk and items selected may include high value or key items, all items over a certain amount, or items to obtain information about certain matters. This method does not constitute audit sampling, so the results cannot be projected to the entire population, although they may provide some evidence about the remainder of the population.

3. Audit sampling: This method is designed to enable the auditor to draw conclusions about an entire population based on testing a sample of the population (discussed in AU-C 530).

Sufficiency and Appropriateness of Audit Evidence

Auditing standards require the auditor to obtain sufficient appropriate audit evidence in order to obtain a reasonable basis for his or her opinion about the financial statements. The sufficiency and appropriateness of audit evidence to support the auditor's conclusions made throughout the audit are a matter of professional judgment. Several factors affect the sufficiency and appropriateness of audit evidence:

- Significance of the potential misstatement in the relevant assertion and the likelihood of it having a material effect on the financial statements
- Effectiveness of management's responses and controls to address the risks
- Experience gained during previous audits with respect to similar potential misstatements
- Results of audit procedures performed, including whether such audit procedures identified specific instances of fraud or error
- Source and reliability of audit evidence
- Persuasiveness of audit evidence
- Understanding of the entity and its environment, including its internal control

The auditor's accumulation of audit evidence in an audit is cumulative and iterative. As the auditor performs the audit procedures and obtains related audit evidence, he or she should evaluate whether assessments of the risks of material misstatement at the relevant assertion level remain appropriate.

Evidence obtained from risk assessment procedures or further audit procedures, including tests of controls and substantive procedures, may have an impact on the nature, timing, and extent of audit procedures. For example, information may come to the auditor's attention that differs from the information he or she used to assess the risk of material misstatement or information obtained from tests of controls may identify deviations in those controls. That information may require the auditor to modify the assessed level of risk of material misstatement, in turn requiring changes in the nature, timing, or extent of other planned audit procedures that should be performed.

FRAUD POINTER: A deficiency commonly cited in SEC enforcement actions against auditors is their overreliance on internal controls, particularly their failure to expand testing in light of known control deficiencies. In some cases, auditors actually identified and documented significant control problems in specific areas and then failed to alter the audit testing in response to the heightened risk. In other cases, auditors assumed the presence of a baseline level of internal control despite documenting that the client essentially had no controls in place.

FRAUD POINTER: When the auditor identifies a material misstatement due to fraud, he or she should not assume that the fraud instance is an isolated occurrence. The auditor should consider the implications for the overall financial statement audit and may need to modify his or her overall response to the risk of material misstatements or his or her response at the relevant assertion level.

Documentation

The form and extent of documentation is a matter of professional judgment influenced by the entity's nature, size, complexity, and internal control; availability of information from the entity; and the audit methodology and technology used in the audit.

Practitioner's Aids

The following exhibits may be used as practitioner's aids.

EXHIBIT AU-C 330-1—DECISION TREE FOR DESIGNING AND PERFORMING CURRENT YEAR TESTS OF CONTROLS

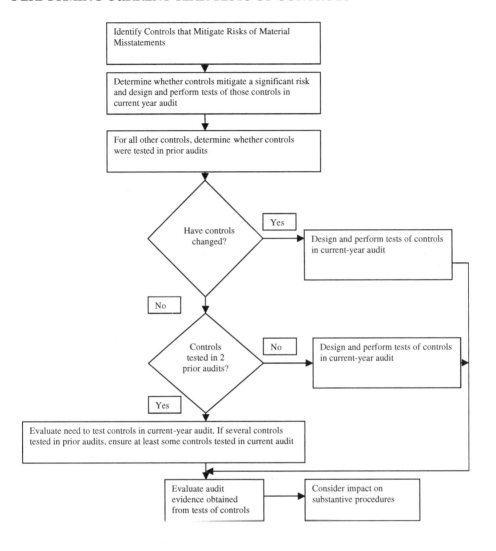

EXHIBIT AU-C 330-2—EXAMPLES OF SUBSTANTIVE PROCEDURES RELEVANT TO INVENTORY ASSERTIONS

Inventory Account Balance Assertions	Examples of Substantive Procedures
Existence Inventories included in the balance sheet physically exist	Conduct a physical examination of inventory items
	Obtain confirmation of inventory items held at outside locations
	Inspect documentation related to the purchase and sale of inventory between the physical inventory date and the balance sheet date
Completeness Inventory items on hand at the balance sheet date are included in the balance sheet.	Conduct a physical examination of inventory items and determine that the items are recorded in the inventory listing
	Inspect shipping and receiving transactions near year-end for recording in the proper period
Valuation Inventories are stated at cost (except when market is lower).	Examine invoices paid to vendors for inventory purchases and compare product unit prices to those appropriate given the underlying selected accounting policy (e.g. LIFO versus FIFO)
	Inspect inventory publications and other market data for current market prices and determine whether unit prices used to value inventory are at lower of cost or market
	Recalculate unit price times quantity for selected items included in the inventory listing
	Watch for evidence of slow-moving items while present for the physical examination of inventory

Inventory Account Balance Assertions	Examples of Substantive Procedures
Rights and obligations The entity has legal title or similar rights of ownership to the inventories.	Obtain confirmation of inventory held at other locations to confirm title of goods held
	Examine vendor invoices for evidence of consignment arrangements
	Examine sales invoices and related shipping documents to ensure inventories exclude items billed to customers or owned by others

Inventory Presentation and Disclosure Assertions	Examples of Substantive Procedures
Rights and obligations Any pledge or assignment of inventories is appropriately disclosed	Obtain confirmation of inventories pledged under loan agreements
Completeness The financial statements include all disclosures related to inventories specified by GAAP	Use a disclosure checklist to determine whether required GAAP disclosures are included in the footnotes

Inventory Account Balance Assertions	Examples of Substantive Procedures
Understandability Inventories are properly classified in the balance sheet as current assets and all related disclosures are understandable	Examine drafts of the financial statements for appropriate balance sheet classification
	Read the inventory footnote disclosures for clarity
Accuracy and valuation The major categories of inventories and their bases of valuation are accurately disclosed in the financial statements.	Examine the drafts of the financial statements for appropriate disclosure

EXHIBIT AU-C 330-3—EXAMPLES OF ROLL FORWARD OF SUBSTANTIVE PROCEDURES FROM INTERIM TO PERIOD END

Professional judgment must be used to determine which balance sheet accounts can be subjected to substantive tests prior to the balance sheet date. To illustrate how this approach may be applied, assume that an auditor has decided to confirm accounts receivable at an interim date. The confirmation procedures normally applied at year-end would be applied to the trial balance of accounts receivable as of the interim date. Returned confirmations would be evaluated, and the auditor would develop various confirmation statistics. For transactions occurring after the interim date, the auditor would rely upon the client's internal control to process data in an acceptable manner. Summary data in the sales journal and cash receipts journal would be reviewed for unusual items. In addition, the client could be requested to prepare an aged trial balance at the end of the year, and the auditor could perform the analysis. During the review, the auditor would look for significant amounts from customers that were not listed on the interim trial balance. Other items that are unusual or that otherwise come to the attention of the auditor could be subject to confirmation as of the year-end date.

The following illustrates an audit schedule format that an auditor could use to document the approach of performing substantive tests on data processed by the client after the interim date:

Averroes Company

Analysis of Accounts Receivable from Interim to Year-End Date 12/31/X6

Accounts Receivable Balance @ 9/30/X6		$450,000
		See audit schedule
		@ AR110
Sales — October[a]	80,000	
November[a]	85,000	
December[a]	82,000	
		247,000
Cash receipts — October[b]	78,000	
November[b]	81,000	
December[b]	79,000	

	238,000
Write-offs — October[c]	450
November[c]	230
December[c]	1,850
	-2,530
Accounts Receivable Balance @ 12/31/X6	$456,470

See audit schedule
@ AR100

---

[a] Traced to Sales Journal—Footed November and December journals
[b] Traced to Cash Receipts Journal—Footed October
[c] Traced to approvals and reviewed with credit manager

Prepared By: JB

Date: 1/29/X7

AR101

SECTION 402

AUDIT CONSIDERATIONS RELATING TO AN ENTITY USING A SERVICE ORGANIZATION

Authoritative Pronouncements

SAS-122—Statements on Auditing Standards: Clarification and Recodification

Overview

The guidance established by AU-C 402 applies to the audit of a client that uses the services of another entity (service organization), whereby those services are considered to be part of the client's information system used to process transactions because they affect one or more of the following:

- Classes of transactions significant to the entity's financial statements

- Procedures used to initiate, record, process, and report transactions in the financial statements

- The client's accounting records, supporting information, and specific accounts in the financial statements

- The procedures, both manual and automated, used to process accounting transactions (from the initiation of a transaction to the impact of the transaction on the financial statements)

- The process used to prepare the client's financial statements (including significant accounting estimates and disclosures)

- Procedures used to capture events and conditions, other than transactions, that are significant to the financial statements

- Controls surrounding journal entries, including nonstandard journal entries used to record nonrecurring, unusual transactions, or adjustments

The activities performed by the service organization may be considered part of the client's internal control and therefore may require that the auditor develop a sufficient understanding of the controls in place at the service organization's facilities. However, it may be costly to have the client's auditor visit the other organization to obtain such an understanding. Also, it could be disruptive to the other organization to have several of its customers' auditors review and test its internal control.

To provide a reasonable solution to this problem, the AICPA issued AU-C 402, which the auditor of a user entity should use in obtaining a sufficient understanding of the services provided by a service organization as well as effects on the user entity's internal control relevant to the audit in order to identify, assess, and respond to the risks of material misstatement. The nature and extent of the user auditor's work regarding the service organization's services depends on the nature and significance of the services to the entity and their relevance to the audit.

OBSERVATION: AU-C 402 provides guidance for the user auditor when a client uses a service organization. Statement on Standards for Attestation Engagements (SSAE) No. 16 (Reporting at a Service Organization) contains the guidance for service auditors.

PLANNING AID REMINDER: The standards established by AU-C 402 are not applicable to the audit of a client's transactions that arise from financial interests in partnerships, corporations, and joint ventures, when the entity's proprietary interest is accounted for and reported. In addition, AU-C 402 would not apply when the service organization executes transactions based on specific authorization granted by the user organization. In that case, the client retains responsibility for authorizing the transactions and maintaining the related accountability. For example, the user auditor would not consider the control procedures of a broker that simply executes security transactions for the user organization.

ROLE OF THE USER AUDITOR

When a user organization employs a service organization, the user organization's ability to institute effective internal controls over the activities performed by the service organization can vary.

In many instances, internal controls of the service organization are an extension of the user organization's accounting system. Generally, transactions authorized by the user organization are transferred to the service organization for additional processing, and internal controls are maintained by both the user and the service organization. In other instances, the service organization may execute transactions and maintain related accountability, and the user organization might not have effective internal controls over such transactions.

Definitions

Complementary user entity controls	Controls the service organization assumes will be implemented by user entities. If these controls are necessary to achieve the control objectives stated in management's description of the service organization's system, they should be identified as such in the description.
Report on management's description of a service organization's system and the suitability of the design of controls (type 1 report)	A report comprising (1) management's description of the service organization's system; (2) a written assertion by the service organization's management about whether in all material respects, based on suitable criteria and as of a specified date, management's description of the service organization's system fairly presents such system's design and implementation, and the controls related to the description's control objectives were suitably designed to achieve those objectives; and (3) a service auditor's report expressing an opinion on these written assertions.
Report on management's description of a service organization's system and the suitability of the design and operating effectiveness of controls (type 2 report)	A report comprising (1) management's description of the service organization's system; (2) a written assertion by the service organization's management about whether in all material respects, based on suitable criteria and throughout the specified period, the description of the service organization's system fairly presents such system's design and implementation, the controls related to the description's control objectives were suitably designed and operated effectively to achieve those objectives; and (3) a service auditor's report expressing an opinion on these written assertions and including a description of the service auditor's tests of controls and their results.
Service auditor	A practitioner who reports on controls at a service organization.
Service organization	An organization or segment of an organization providing services to user entities that are part of those user entities' information and communication systems relevant to financial reporting.
Service organization's system	Policies and procedures designed, implemented, and documented by management of the service organization to provide user entities with the services covered by the service auditor's report. Management's description of the service organization's system identifies the services covered; the period or date to which the description relates; the control objectives specified by management or an outside party, including specification of the outside party; and the related controls.
Subservice organization	A service organization used by another service organization to perform some of the services provided to user entities that are relevant to those user entities' internal control over financial reporting.

| User auditor | An auditor who audits and reports on the financial statements of a user entity. |
| User entity | An entity that uses a service organization and whose financial statements are being audited. |

Requirements

The user auditor is presumptively required to perform the following procedures in the financial statement audit of an entity that uses one or more service organizations:

Obtain an Understanding of the Services Provided by a Service Organization

1. Obtain an understanding of how the user entity uses a service organization in its operations, including the nature and significance of services the service organization provides, including the user entity's internal control; the nature and materiality of transactions processed and accounts or financial reporting processes affected by the service organization; the degree of interaction between the service organization's and user entity's activities; and the nature of the relationship, including the contractual terms, between the organizations.

2. Obtain an understanding of internal control relevant to the audit by evaluating the design and implementation of relevant controls at the user entity, including controls applied to transactions processed by the service organization, relating to services performed by the service organization.

3. Determine whether a sufficient understanding of the user entity's internal control relevant to the audit has been obtained to provide a basis for the identification and assessment of risks of material misstatement. This evidence can be obtained from one or more of the following sources: information about the service organization available at the user entity, a type 1 or type 2 report, specific information obtained by contacting the service organization through the user entity, using another auditor to perform procedures providing the necessary information, or by visiting the service organization and performing these procedures.

Using a Service Auditor's Report

4. The service auditor's professional reputation, competence, and independence from the service organization as well as the adequacy of the standards under which report was issued should be considered in determining the sufficiency and appropriateness of the audit evidence provided by a type 1 or type 2 report.

5. To use a type 1 or type 2 report as audit evidence about the design and implementation of controls at the service organization, evaluate whether the description of the service organization's system is as of or for an appropriate time period; evaluate the sufficiency and appropriateness of the evidence provided for the understanding of internal control relevant to the audit; and determine whether identified complementary user entity controls are relevant, and, if so, obtain an understanding of whether the user entity has designed and implemented such controls.

Responding to the Assessed Risks of Material Misstatement

6. In responding to assessed risks, determine whether sufficient appropriate audit evidence concerning relevant financial statement assertions is available from records held at the user entity and, if not, perform further audit proce-

dures to obtain that evidence or ask the service auditor through the user entity to perform those procedures on the user auditor's behalf.

7. If the risk assessment includes an expectation that controls applied only at the service organization are operating effectively, the user auditor should obtain evidence about this operating effectiveness via one or more of the following procedures: obtaining and reading a type 2 report, performing appropriate tests of controls at the service organization, or using another auditor to perform tests of controls at the service organization on the user auditor's behalf.

8. To use a type 2 report as audit evidence about the operating effectiveness of controls at the service organization, perform the following procedures to determine whether the service auditor's report provides sufficient appropriate audit evidence to support the risk assessment: evaluate whether the report is for an appropriate time period; determine whether identified complementary user entity controls are relevant, and, if so, obtain an understanding of whether the user entity has designed, implemented, and tested the operating effectiveness of such controls; evaluate the adequacy of the period covered by the tests of controls and the time elapsed since the performance of the tests of controls; and evaluate whether the tests of controls and results described in the type 2 report are relevant to assertions in the user entity's financial statements.

9. If the user auditor plans to use a type 1 or type 2 report that excludes the services provided by a subservice organization and those services are relevant to the audit of the user entity's financial statements, apply the requirements of AU-C 402 with respect to the services provided by the subservice organization.

Fraud, Noncompliance, and Uncorrected Misstatements in Relation to Service Organization Activities

10. Inquire of the user entity's management about whether the service organization has reported any fraud, noncompliance with laws and regulations, or uncorrected misstatements. If so, evaluate how such matters affect the nature, timing, and extent of further audit procedures.

Reporting by the User Auditor

11. Modify the user auditor's report opinion in accordance with AU-C 705 (*Modifications to The Opinion in The Independent Auditor's Report*) if unable to obtain sufficient appropriate audit evidence regarding the services provided by the service organization relevant to the audit of the user entity's financial statements.

12. Do not refer to the work of a service auditor in a report containing an unmodified opinion.

13. Reference can be made to the work of a service auditor if the opinion is modified and reference to the work is relevant to an understanding of the modification. This reference should indicate that the user auditor's responsibility for the audit opinion is not diminished.

Analysis and Application of Procedures

Obtain an Understanding of the Services Provided by a Service Organization

Information about relevant controls instituted by a service organization can be identified from a number of sources, including the following:

- User manuals
- System overviews
- Technical manuals
- The contract between the two parties
- Reports by other parties including the service auditor, internal auditors and regulatory authorities

When the activities performed by the service organization are routine and highly standardized, a review of information obtained by the user auditor in previous experience with the service center might be useful in planning the current engagement. Services provided by services organizations that are relevant to the audit include maintaining accounting records, managing assets, and initiating, recording, or processing transactions for user entities.

OBSERVATION: Smaller entities may use external bookkeeping services to process transactions, maintain accounting records, or prepare their financial statements. Use of such a service organization does not relieve management and those charged with governance of their responsibilities for the financial statements.

An understanding of service organization controls that affect a user entity's internal control may be necessary if the nature of the transactions processed is significant, even if the transactions processed and accounts affected do not appear material to the user entity's financial statements. The degree of interaction between the organizations is also important to consider, because the higher the degree of interaction between the organizations, the more likely the user entity will be able to implement effective controls over transactions performed by the service organization. For audits of governmental entities, additional audit procedures may be required such as obtaining and understanding of internal control over compliance, and performing tests of compliance and compliance controls.

Contractual terms or service level agreements between the organizations may provide for matters such as the information to be provided to the user entity, the form of records maintained and access to them, any indemnification to be provided to the user entity in the event of a performance failure, whether a type 1 or type 2 report will be provided, whether the user auditor has rights of access to the user entity's accounting records at the service organization, and whether the agreement allows for direct communication between the user auditor and the service auditor.

PLANNING AID REMINDER: While there are direct relationships between the service organization and user entity and between the service organization and service auditor, there is not a direct relationship between the user auditor and service auditor. Communication between the user auditor and service auditor are typically conducted through the user entity and service organization.

If it is not possible or practicable to obtain sufficient appropriate audit evidence about certain risks from substantive procedures alone, the controls over such risks are relevant to the audit and the user auditor is required to obtain an understanding about those controls. This situation can occur when highly automated processing gives rise to risks of inaccurate or incomplete recording of transactions and balances, a situation often present when a using a service organization.

The procedures the auditor determines are needed to provide a basis for the identification and assessment of the risks of material misstatement related to the user entity's use of the service organization may be influenced by factors such as the size of the organizations, the complexity of transactions and services involved, the service organization's location, whether the procedure will provide the user auditor with sufficient appropriate audit evidence, and the nature of the relationship between the user entity and service organization. In situations where a user entity outsources significant business units or functions and a type 1 or type 2 report is not available, visiting the service organization may be the most effective procedure for the user auditor to gain an understanding of controls at the service organization. In situations where a type 1 or type 2 report has been issued, the user auditor may also choose to use the service auditor to perform procedures to provide the necessary information about relevant controls at the service organization, following the guidance in AU-C 600 about using the work of another auditor.

Using a Service Auditor's Report

The user auditor may make inquiries about the service auditor to the auditor's professional organization and other practitioners and inquire as to whether the service auditor is subject to regulatory oversight. If the service auditor practices in a jurisdiction with different standards, the user auditor may obtain information about those standards from the standard-setting organization in that jurisdiction.

OBSERVATION: A service auditor's report implies that the service auditor is independent of the service organization. However, the service auditor does not need to be independent of user entities.

Type 1 report

A type 1 report can be useful to user auditors, particularly in providing an understanding of:

- Controls at the service organization affecting the user entity's transaction processing

- The flow of transactions through the service organization's system to identify points where material misstatements in the user entity's financial statements could occur

- Service organization control objectives relevant to the user entity's financial statement assertions

- Whether service organization controls are suitably designed and implemented for detecting and correcting processing errors that could result in material misstatements in user entity financial statements

---

PLANNING AID REMINDER: A type 1 report does not provide any evidence of the operating effectiveness of relevant controls.

A type 1 report is "as of" a date, and if that date is outside the user entity's reporting period, the report may still be used to provide the user auditor with a preliminary understanding of service organization controls if it is supplemented by additional current information. Procedures the user auditor may perform to update the information in a type 1 report include discussing changes at the service organization with user entity or service organization personnel or reviewing current documentation and correspondence issued by the service organization.

Type 2 report

The more overlap there is between the period covered by the type 2 report and the user entity's financial statement period, the more evidence a type 2 report typically provides. If there is little overlap between the two periods, additional audit evidence may be provided by an additional type 2 report covering the preceding or subsequent period, by obtaining additional evidence about significant changes in service organization controls outside the period covered by the report, or by performing additional audit procedures. Factors influencing the additional audit evidence obtained for the period not covered by the type 2 report include the following:

- Significance of the assessed risks of material misstatement at the assertion level
- Significant changes to controls since they were tested
- Degree to which audit evidence was obtained about the operating effectiveness of controls
- Length of the remaining period
- Extent to which the user auditor plans to reduce substantive testing based on reliance on controls
- Effectiveness of the user entity's control environment and monitoring controls

If there is no overlap between the period of the type 2 report and the user entity's financial statement period, the user auditor cannot rely on the type 2 report to determine the operating effectiveness of the user entity's controls, because it provides no current period evidence.

If the user auditor believes the type 2 report does not provide sufficient audit evidence, the auditor may contact the service organization through the user entity to discuss the scope and result of the service auditor's work or to request that the service auditor perform additional procedures, or the user auditor may perform additional procedures.

A service auditor's report noting deviations or containing a modified opinion can still be used by the user auditor, and any deviation or modification should be considered in assessing the tests of controls performed by the service auditor.

PUBLIC COMPANY IMPLICATION: The Sarbanes-Oxley Act of 2002 (SOX) requires all public companies to issue an "internal control report" by management. Furthermore, SOX requires the auditor to issue a separate opinion based on his or her evaluation of the effectiveness of internal control over financial reporting. That responsibility includes a requirement for the auditor to arrive at his or her own assessment of the operating effectiveness of the internal controls. When auditing a public company that uses a service organization to process transactions relevant to financial statements, the auditor should consider the guidance contained in AU-C 402. In many cases the auditor is required to obtain a service auditor's report on a description of a service organization's system and the suitability of the design and operating effectiveness of controls.

Communication of significant deficiencies and material weaknesses

If a significant deficiency or material weakness in internal control is identified, the user auditor should communicate these deficiencies in writing on a timely basis to management and those charged with governance, following the guidance in AU-C 265. Control deficiencies that may be identified in an audit of a user entity related to use of a service organization include monitoring controls that are needed but have not been implemented by the user entity, complementary user entity controls identified in a type 1 or type 2 report that have not been implemented by the user entity, and controls needed at the service organization that were not implemented or are not operating effectively. The auditor may also communicate other control-related matters, such as deficiencies that are not significant deficiencies or material weaknesses.

Type 1 and Type 2 Reports that Exclude the Services of a Subservice Organization

If a service organization uses a subservice organization, the service auditor's report may include or exclude the subservice organization's relevant control objectives and controls. These reporting methods are known as the inclusive method and carve-out method, respectively. If the service auditor's report (type 1 or 2) excludes the controls at the subservice organization and the services provided by the subservice organization are relevant to the audit of the entity's financial statement, the user auditor is required to apply the requirements of AU-C 402.

Responding to the Assessed Risks of Material Misstatement

If a service organization maintains material elements of the user entity's accounting records, the user auditor may need direct access to those records to obtain sufficient appropriate audit evidence regarding the operation of controls over those records and to substantiate recorded transactions and balances. The user auditor may perform the following procedures in obtaining audit evidence for financial statement assertions about transactions and balances maintained by the service organization for a user entity:

- Inspect records and documents held by the user entity or service organization

- Obtain confirmations of balances and transactions from the service organization if the user entity maintains independent records

- Perform analytical procedures on records maintained by the user entity or on reports received from the service organization

The user auditor is required to design and perform tests of controls to obtain sufficient appropriate audit evidence concerning the operating effectiveness of relevant controls in a service organization when (1) the user auditor's assessment of risks of material misstatement includes an expectation that the controls at the service organization are operating effectively or (2) substantive procedures alone or in combination with tests of operating effectiveness of controls at the user entity cannot provide sufficient appropriate audit evidence at the assertion level. Risk assessments will be based on combined evidence from the user auditor's procedures and the service auditor's report. Procedures the user auditor may perform to test a user entity's controls over service organization activities include reperformance of items processed by the service organization and tests of the user entity's reconciliation of output reports with source documents.

In some circumstances, the user auditor may require additional information to evaluate how any reported matters affect the nature, timing, and extent of further audit procedures. When this occurs, the user auditor may consider contacting the service organization or service auditor to obtain that information.

Fraud, Noncompliance, and Uncorrected Misstatements in Relation to Service Organization Activities

Some contracts between service organizations and user entities require the service organization to disclose to affected user entities any fraud, noncompliance with laws and regulations, or uncorrected misstatements attributable to the service organization. User auditors are required to make inquiries of the user entity management regarding any such matters that have been disclosed to the user entity by the service organization and the user auditor should evaluate the impact of such disclosures on the nature, timing, and extent of the auditor's further audit procedures.

Reporting by the User Auditor

The user auditor may be unable to obtain sufficient appropriate audit evidence regarding the relevant services provided by the service organization, causing a scope limitation on the audit. The auditor may express a qualified opinion or disclaim an opinion depending on whether he or she considers the potential effects on the financial statements to be material, pervasive, or both. The user auditor may be unable to obtain sufficient appropriate audit evidence when:

- He or she is unable to obtain a sufficient understanding of services provided by the service organization and does not have a basis for identifying and assessing risks of material misstatement
- His or her risk assessment includes an expectation that service organization controls are operating effectively but sufficient appropriate audit evidence to support this cannot be obtained
- Sufficient appropriate audit evidence is only available from service organization records and he or she is unable to obtain direct access to these records

The user auditor's report does not reference the service auditor's report as a basis for the user auditor's opinion on the user entity's financial statements. However, if the user auditor expresses a modified opinion because of a modified opinion in the service auditor's report, he or she is not precluded from referencing the service auditor's report. In these situations, the user auditor may need the consent of the service auditor to make such reference and the service auditor does not need to be referred to by name.

SECTION 450

EVALUATION OF MISSTATEMENTS IDENTIFIED DURING THE AUDIT

Authoritative Pronouncements

SAS-122—Statements on Auditing Standards: Clarification and Recodification

Overview

AU-C 450 guides the auditor in evaluating the effect of any misstatements to the financial statements identified during the audit and the effect of any uncorrected misstatements on the financial statements. AU-C 320 (*Materiality in Planning and Performing an Audit*), addresses the auditor's responsibilities in applying the concept of materiality in planning and performing an audit.

ENGAGEMENT STRATEGY: The auditor is concerned with materiality levels during both the planning phase and the evaluation phase of an engagement. Although conceptually possible, generally, the assessment of materiality levels will not be the same at the planning stage as at the evaluation stage. Because the auditor will have more complete information to better assess materiality for a particular engagement, the materiality level at the end of the audit can differ from the materiality used in the planning stage. In fact, if the level of materiality is significantly less at the evaluation stage than at the planning stage, the auditor will generally need to reevaluate the sufficiency of the audit procedures he or she has performed.

Definitions

Misstatement	Difference between a reported financial statement item's amount, classification, presentation, or disclosure and what is required for it to be in accordance with the applicable financial reporting framework. Misstatements can arise from error or fraud. In the context of the auditor's expressing an opinion on the financial statements, misstatements include adjustments of amounts, classifications, presentations, or disclosures that the auditor judges are necessary for the financial statements to be presented fairly in all material respects.
Uncorrected misstatements	Misstatements the auditor has accumulated during the audit that have not been corrected.

Requirements

The auditor is presumptively required to perform the following procedures in considering materiality when planning and performing the audit:

1. Accumulate misstatements identified during the audit, other than those that are clearly trivial.

2. Determine whether the overall audit strategy and audit plan need to be revised if:

   a. The nature and circumstances of occurrence of identified misstatements indicate that other misstatements may exist that could be material when aggregated with accumulated misstatements, or

   b. The aggregate of accumulated misstatements approaches materiality levels determined for the financial statements as a whole, classes of transactions, account balances, or disclosures

3. Communicate all accumulated misstatements with the appropriate level of management on a timely basis. Request that management correct the misstatements.

4. If management, at the auditor's request, has examined and corrected the detected misstatements, perform the necessary additional audit procedures to determine if any misstatements remain.

5. If management refuses to correct some or all of the misstatements communicated by the auditor, obtain an understanding of management's reasons for not making the corrections and consider those reasons when evaluating whether the financial statements as a whole are free from material misstatement.

6. Prior to evaluating the effect of uncorrected misstatements, reassess the determination of materiality levels for the financial statements as a whole and any classes of transactions, account balances, or disclosures considered to determine whether those levels are still appropriate given the entity's actual financial results

7. Determine whether uncorrected misstatements are material, individually or in the aggregate. Make this determination by considering the size, nature, and circumstances of the misstatements' occurrence and the effect of uncorrected misstatements related to prior periods in relation to the financial statements as a whole, relevant transaction classes, account balances, and disclosures.

8. Documentation should include:

   a. The amount below which misstatements are clearly regarded as trivial

   b. All misstatements accumulated during the audit and whether they have been corrected

   c. The auditor's conclusion about whether uncorrected misstatements are material, individually or in aggregate, and the basis for that conclusion

Analysis and Application of Procedures

Accumulating identified misstatements

Misstatements arise due to error or fraud. They may exist as the result of various means, including inaccurate data gathering or processing, omission of amounts or disclosures, or use or accounting estimates that are clearly incorrect or that the auditor considers unreasonable. There are three types of misstatements the auditor may encounter:

- *Factual misstatements* Misstatements about which there is no doubt

- *Judgmental misstatements* Differences in judgment between management and the auditor concerning appropriate selection and application of accounting estimates and policies

- *Projected misstatements* The auditor's best estimate of misstatements in populations obtained by extrapolating misstatements identified in audit samples to the entire population

When accumulating identified misstatements, the term "clearly trivial" does not have the same meaning as the term "not material." Clearly trivial misstatements will be of a lower order of magnitude than materiality levels and will be of inconsequential amounts whether considered individually or in the aggregate. If there is any uncertainty about the triviality of a misstatement, it is not to be considered clearly trivial.

OBSERVATION: If the auditor has concluded, based on audit procedures employed, that a particular balance likely falls within a range, then the likely misstatement is the difference between the balance recorded in the financial statement and the upper or lower boundary of the range. For example, if the range is likely to be between $200,000 and $300,000 and the recorded balance is $315,000, the misstatement to be aggregated is $15,000 ($315,000-$300,000). However, if the auditor's assessment of the balance is based on a point estimate (say, $290,000) rather than a range, the misstatement to be aggregated is the difference between the point estimate and the financial statement balance [in this case $25,000 ($315,000-$290,000)].

Considering identified misstatements during the audit

The nature and circumstances of occurrence of a misstatement may indicate the misstatement is not the only instance of misstatement. This could be the case if the misstatement occurred due to a breakdown in internal control or from inappropriate assumptions or valuation methods commonly used by the entity.

If the auditor identifies misstatements during the audit that approach materiality levels, the risk that undetected misstatements may exceed materiality levels when combined with identified misstatements may be greater than is acceptable.

OBSERVATION: The current year's financial statements may be affected by misstatements from the prior year's engagement financial statements because such misstatements were not considered material and therefore no adjustment was made in the prior year. If the auditor believes that "there is an unacceptably high risk" that the current year's financial statements are materially misstated when the prior year's misstatements are taken into consideration, the auditor should include the likely misstatement amount due to the prior year's misstatement with the current year's likely misstatement amount to determine whether the current year's financial statements appear to be materially misstated.

Communicating and correcting misstatements

The auditor should communicate all identified misstatements to an appropriate level of management. This communication should be made timely to allow management an opportunity to evaluate whether the items are misstatements and to take any necessary action. The appropriate level of management to receive the communication from the auditor is typically the level of management with the authority to take the appropriate action. In some cases, laws or regulations may prevent the auditor from communicating certain misstatements to management or others within the entity. In these circumstances, the auditor may consider seeking legal advice to understand his or her responsibilities.

Management's correction of all identified misstatements is preferable because it helps to maintain the accuracy of books and records and to prevent the risk of material misstatements in future financial statements due to the accumulation of effects of prior uncorrected misstatements. The auditor should request management to record adjustments needed to correct all factual misstatements, unless they are considered to be trivial, including the effect of prior-period misstatements. For projected material misstatements based on a sample, the auditor should request management to examine the class of transactions, account balance, or disclosure in order to identify and correct misstatements. For judgmental misstatements based on differences in estimates, the auditor should request management to review the assumptions and methods used in developing management's estimate.

If management decides not to correct some or all of the misstatements communicated by the auditor, he or she should consider the qualitative aspects of the entity's accounting practices and indicators of possible bias in management's judgments when determining the implications related to his or her report.

Evaluating the effect of uncorrected misstatements

If the auditor reassesses materiality during the audit and determines lower materiality levels are appropriate, then performance materiality levels as well as the nature, timing, and extent of further audit procedures will need to be reconsidered to ensure that sufficient appropriate audit evidence is obtained for the auditor to formulate an opinion.

There are several factors the auditor should consider in determining whether uncorrected misstatements are material, whether considered individually or in the aggregate. Uncorrected misstatements from different entity locations or found by other auditors performing portions of the audit should be included in evaluating the effects of uncorrected misstatements. Furthermore, the materiality of a misstatement in the audit of a governmental entity may be affected by legislation, regulation, or additional reporting responsibilities. While individual misstatements may be offset by other misstatements, this generally does not offset the misstatements' materiality. However, it may be appropriate to offset misstatements within the same class of transactions or account balance if the auditor determines the risk that further undetected misstatements may exist is acceptable.

The materiality of classification misstatements depends on several qualitative factors, including the effects of the misstatement on debt and contractual covenants, on individual line items or subtotals, and on key ratios. In some circumstances, the auditor may conclude that a classification misstatement is not material even if it exceeds materiality levels. This conclusion may be drawn if, for example, the misclassification amount is small in relation to the size of related balance sheet items and the misstatement does not impact the income statement or key ratios.

The objective of the auditor is to perform the audit to obtain reasonable assurance that misstatements that could be quantitatively material to the financial statements are detected. However, qualitative factors also contribute to the determination of materiality and may cause the auditor to determine a misstatement is material even if the amount of the misstatement is lower than the prescribed materiality levels. Exhibit AU-C 450-1 lists several qualitative factors the auditor may consider in determining a misstatement's materiality. It is important for the auditor to remember that existence of any of these qualitative factors does not necessarily mean a misstatement is material.

FRAUD POINTER: If a misstatement may be the result of fraud, AU-C 240 (*Consideration of Fraud in a Financial Statement Audit*) requires the auditor to consider the implications of the misstatement in relation to other aspects of the audit, even if the misstatement is not material to the financial statements as a whole.

Document audit results relating to misstatements

The auditor's documentation of uncorrected misstatements may consider the following:

- The aggregate effect of misstatements on the financial statements
- Whether any materiality levels for particular classes of transactions, account balances, or disclosures have been exceeded
- The effect of uncorrected misstatements on key ratios or trends and compliance with legal, regulatory, and contractual requirements

Practitioner's Aids

EXHIBIT AU-C 450-1—CHECKLIST OF QUALITATIVE FACTORS IN DETERMINING MATERIALITY

The following qualitative factors may be relevant in determining the materiality of an item:

- Items that have an effect on ratios used to evaluate the entity's financial position, results of operations, or cash flows
- Items that change losses to income or vice versa

- Items that are relevant in determining whether loan covenants and similar items have been violated
- Items that have an effect on materiality thresholds that are established by statute or regulation
- Items that mask a change in earnings or other trends
- Items that increase management's compensation
- Items that are significant given the auditor's understanding of known previous communications to users
- Items involving particular parties (such as related parties)
- Items that affect other information that will be communicated in documents containing the audited financial statements that could be reasonably expected to influence financial statement users
- Items that affect the sensitivity of the financial statements to possible fraud, illegal acts, or other similar situations
- Items that are misclassified (such as misclassification of an item that should be considered operating but is classified as nonoperating)
- The omission of information that is not required by the applicable financial reporting framework but that the auditor judges to be important to the users' understanding of the entity's financial position, financial performance, or cash flows
- The significance of the item in relationship to known user needs
- The character of the misstatement (for example, the degree to which an account balance is based on an estimate)
- The possible motivation of management for the misstatement
- The existence of offsetting effects of individually significant items
- The possibility that an item or incorrect selection or application of an accounting policy that is currently immaterial could have a material impact on subsequent financial statements
- The cost of making a correction
- The risk that other undetected misstatements would affect the auditor's opinion

EXHIBIT AU-C 450-2—SEC STAFF ACCOUNTING BULLETIN (SAB-99): "MATERIALITY"

The Financial Accounting Standards Board (FASB) and the American Institute of Certified Public Accountants (AICPA) have provided little guidance for determining what constitutes a material item in financial statements. The Securities and Exchange Commission (SEC) has addressed this issue in a Staff Accounting Bulletin (SAB) titled "Materiality" (SAB-99). Although the SEC addresses only publicly traded companies, SAB-99, discussed here, provides valuable guidance in the performance of audits in general. This Practitioner's Aid summarizes the guidance in the SAB.

SAB-99 discusses how the auditor of a public company should do the following:

- Assess materiality
- Aggregate and net misstatements
- Consider immaterial misstatements that are intentional

Assessing materiality

FASB Concepts Statement No. 2 (CON-2) (Qualitative Characteristics of Accounting Information) characterizes "materiality" as follows:

> The omission or misstatement of an item in a financial report is material if, in the light of surrounding circumstances, the magnitude of the item is such that it is probable that the judgment of a reasonable person relying upon the report would have been changed or influenced by the inclusion or correction of the item.

While everyone agrees with this description of materiality, applying the concept in practice requires a considerable amount of professional judgment. In many engagements, an auditor establishes a material threshold or a rule of thumb, such as 5% or 10%, and a misstatement(s) that is less than the specific threshold is not considered material. SAB-99 points out that the creation of a specific materiality percentage or dollar value for determining whether a particular item is material "has no basis in the accounting literature or the law."

An auditor deals with two broad types of materiality during an engagement. First, in order to help plan an engagement, the auditor must identify a materiality factor. That is, the auditor must make some determination of what may be material in determining the nature, timing, and extent of audit procedures. Generally, as the materiality threshold falls from, say, 10% to 5%, the extent of audit procedures that are necessary to achieve the auditor's objective is increased. The SEC has no problem with an auditor using preliminary definitions of "materiality" in determining the audit approach in a particular engagement.

The second type of materiality the auditor must address in an engagement involves determining whether specific misstatements are in the aggregate large enough for the auditor to conclude that the financial statements may be materially misstated. The SEC points out that in this phase of the audit engagement, using hard and fast materiality thresholds is not appropriate. That is, concluding whether or not an item is material is not a procedural process (asking whether an item exceeds a specific threshold) but rather an analytical process (asking whether it could affect one's assessment of a particular company). To support the argument that acceptance of the analytical process is the appropriate approach, the SEC refers to the following legal conclusion: "Magnitude by itself, without regard to the nature of the item and the circumstances in which the judgment has to be made, will not generally be a sufficient basis for a materiality judgment." That is, the SEC reminds auditors that both quantitative and qualitative factors must be considered in determining whether an item is material to the financial statements taken as a whole.

SAB-99 points out that the qualitative factors used to evaluate a matter that is below the quantitative threshold should include the following:

- Whether the misstatement arises from an item capable of precise measurement or from an estimate and, if from an estimate, the degree of imprecision inherent in the estimate
- Whether the misstatement masks a change in earnings or other trends
- Whether the misstatement hides a failure to meet analysts' consensus expectations for the enterprise
- Whether the misstatement changes a loss into income or vice versa
- Whether the misstatement concerns a segment or other portion of the registrant's business that has been identified as playing a significant role in the registrant's operations or profitability
- Whether the misstatement affects the registrant's compliance with regulatory requirements
- Whether the misstatement affects the registration's compliance with loan covenants or other contractual requirements
- Whether the misstatement has the effect of increasing management's compensation—for example, by satisfying requirements for the award of bonuses or other forms of incentive compensation
- Whether the misstatement involves concealment of an unlawful transaction

The SEC also notes that an auditor must be particularly careful when audit results suggest that management has intentionally made misstatements in the preparation of its financial statements that appear to have the objective of "managing earnings." In this regard, SAB-99 makes the following observation:

> The staff believes that investors generally would regard as significant a management practice to over- or under-state earnings up to an amount just short of a percentage threshold in order to "manage" earnings. Investors presumably also would regard as significant an accounting practice that, in essence, rendered all earnings figures subject to a management-directed margin of misstatement.

Based on the SEC's reasoning and plain common sense, an auditor should not establish a materiality threshold and then blindly apply it in an engagement. That is not exercising judgment; it is reducing the audit process to a mechanical process that can be more efficiently performed by a computer.

Aggregating and netting misstatements

In determining whether financial statements are materially misstated, the misstatement should be evaluated both individually and in the aggregate. This determination should be made on the basis of both quantitative thresholds and qualitative factors (such as those discussed in the previous section), and the analysis should be directed to "individual line item amounts, subtotals, or totals in the financial statements."

When an individual item by itself is material, it is incorrect to offset its significance with another item that has the opposite impact on the financial statements. For example, if sales are materially overstated and cost of goods sold is materially overstated by more or less the same amount, it would not be proper to suggest that the income statement is not materially misstated because net income is not materially affected by the offsetting misstatements.

SAB-99 warns auditors that they must be careful when aggregating the effects of two or more misstatements that net to a smaller effect on a particular total or subtotal. This is especially true when two misstatements are offset and one is based on an estimate and the other on a precise measurement.

ENGAGEMENT STRATEGY: The auditor must take into consideration in the current engagement misstatements that were made in previous years but were considered immaterial. Those previous years' misstatements could have a material impact on the current year's financial statements, since the quantitative and qualitative factors that are relevant to identifying material items in the current engagement may have changed.

Consider immaterial misstatements that are intentional

SAB-99 raises the question of whether a client can make deliberate adjustments to its financial statements that are inconsistent with generally accepted accounting principles (GAAP) even though the effect is immaterial. The SEC takes the position that such action by a client is inappropriate and may in fact be in violation of securities laws that require that the books and records be accurate in "reasonable detail," a more stringent constraint than the materiality threshold. In determining what is reasonable detail, the auditor should consider the materiality factors (quantitative and qualitative factors discussed earlier) as well as additional factors such as the following:

- *The significance of the misstatement* Though registrants do not need to make finely calibrated determinations of significance with respect to immaterial items, it is "reasonable" to treat misstatements with clearly inconsequential effects differently than more significant ones.

- *How the misstatement arose* It is unlikely that it is ever "reasonable" for registrants to record misstatements or fail to correct known misstatements—even immaterial ones—if these actions are directed by or known to senior management and are for the purposes of "managing" earnings. On the other hand, insignificant misstatements that arise from the operation of systems or recurring processes in the normal course of business generally will not cause a registrant's books to be inaccurate "in reasonable detail."

- *The cost of correcting the misstatement* The books and records provisions of the Exchange Act do not require registrants to make major expenditures to correct small misstatements. However, if there is little cost or delay involved in correcting a misstatement, failing to do so is unlikely to be "reasonable."

- *The clarity of authoritative accounting guidance with respect to the misstatement* If reasonable minds may differ about the appropriate accounting treatment of a financial statement item, a failure to correct it may not cause the registrant's financial statements to be inaccurate "in reasonable detail."

However, if there is little ground for reasonable disagreement, it becomes less reasonable to leave a misstatement uncorrected.

The auditor's response to intentional misstatements

Securities laws and auditing standards (AU-C 240 and AU-C 250 (*Consideration of Laws and Regulations in an Audit of Financial Statements*)) both require that an auditor report fraudulent acts to the appropriate level of management. If the auditor believes that a misstatement is, or may be, the result of fraud, he or she should consider the implications of the misstatement in relation to other aspects of the audit, even if the misstatement is not material to the financial statements.

ENGAGEMENT STRATEGY: In addition to reporting fraudulent acts to the appropriate level of management, the auditor must also consider how the discovery of such facts affects the nature, timing, and extent of audit procedures. In some instances it may be appropriate, after seeking competent legal advice, for the auditor to resign from an engagement.

GAAP precedent over industry practice

When there is a conflict between GAAP and industry accounting practice, clearly GAAP must be observed. Thus, if a client prepares a portion of its financial statements to conform to industry accounting practices that are inconsistent with GAAP, these departures must be evaluated to determine whether the financial statements are materially misstated.

General comments

The SEC recognizes that determining when financial statements are materially misstated can be a complex process. This is especially true when the application of GAAP to a particular transaction or balance is not clear. Under these conditions, a client may account for an item "based on analogies to similar situations or other factors." When these conditions arise, an auditor is encouraged to discuss ambiguous accounting and reporting issues with the SEC staff on a timely basis.

ENGAGEMENT STRATEGY: When the client is not a public company, the auditor should have in place procedures that encourage staff accountants to discuss difficult reporting issues with appropriate personnel within the firm.

AU-C 500
Audit Evidence

SECTION 500

AUDIT EVIDENCE

Authoritative Pronouncements

SAS-122—Statements on Auditing Standards: Clarification and Recodification

Overview

The "Preface to the Codification of Statements on Auditing Standards" notes that to obtain reasonable assurance, the auditor:

> Obtains sufficient appropriate audit evidence about whether material misstatements exist through designing and implementing appropriate responses to assessed risks.

AU-C 500 explains what constitutes audit evidence in a financial statement audit and addresses the auditor's responsibilities to design and perform audit procedures to obtain sufficient appropriate audit evidence to be able to draw reasonable conclusions on which to base the auditor's opinion.

AU-C 500 applies to all audit evidence obtained during the course of the audit. Other AU-C sections supplement this guidance by addressing additional details of audit evidence such as specific aspects of the audit, audit evidence to be obtained in relation to a particular topic, specific procedures to obtain audit evidence, and the evaluation of whether sufficient appropriate audit evidence has been obtained.

Definitions

Accounting records	Records of initial accounting entries and supporting records, including checks, records of electronic fund transfers, invoices, contracts, general and subsidiary ledgers, journal entries, financial statement adjustments not reflected in journal entries, and work sheets and spreadsheets supporting cost allocations, computations, reconciliations, and disclosures.
Appropriateness (of audit evidence)	Measure of the quality of audit evidence and its relevance and reliability in providing support for conclusions on which the auditor's opinion is based.
Audit evidence	Information contained in the accounting records underlying the financial statements and other information used by the auditor in arriving at conclusions on which the auditor's opinion is based.
Management's specialist	A person or organization possessing expertise in a field other than accounting or auditing whose work in that field is used by the entity to assist in preparing the entity's financial statements.
Sufficiency (of audit evidence)	Measure of the quantity of audit evidence. The quantity of audit evidence needed is affected by the auditor's assessment of the risks of material misstatement and by the quality of the audit evidence.

Requirements

The auditor is presumptively required to perform the following procedures in collecting and evaluating audit evidence to support his or her opinion on the client's financial statements:

1. Design and perform audit procedures that are appropriate in the circumstances in order to obtain sufficient appropriate audit evidence.

2. Consider the relevance and reliability of information to be used as audit evidence when designing and performing audit procedures.

3. Evaluate whether information produced by the entity is sufficiently reliable for the purposes of the audit by (1) obtaining audit evidence about the accuracy and completeness of the information and (2) evaluating whether the information is sufficiently precise and detailed.

4. If information to be used as audit evidence has been prepared using the work of a management's specialist, (1) evaluate the specialist's competence, capabilities, and objectivity; (2) obtain an understanding of the specialist's work; and (3) evaluate the appropriateness of the specialist's work as audit evidence for the relevant assertion.

5. If audit evidence obtained from different sources is inconsistent or the auditor has doubts about the reliability of information to be used as audit evidence, the auditor should determine what modifications to audit procedures are necessary to resolve the matter and any effect of the matter on other aspects of the audit.

Analysis and Application of Procedures

Sufficient Appropriate Audit Evidence

Audit evidence is cumulative in nature, and includes evidence from (1) procedures performed during the audit, (2) results from prior-year audits, and (3) the firm's quality control process for client acceptance and continuance. Audit evidence includes both information that supports and information that contradicts management's assertions and in some cases may include the absence of information, such as when management refuses to provide a requested representation. Many types of audit procedures are performed to obtain audit evidence. Inquiry is one of these audit procedures that may provide important audit evidence, but that alone is not sufficient to test the operating effectiveness of controls and generally does not provide sufficient audit evidence of the absence of a material misstatement at the assertion level.

The auditor obtains reasonable assurance regarding his or her audit conclusions when sufficient appropriate audit evidence has been obtained to reduce audit risk to an acceptably low level. The sufficiency and appropriateness of audit evidence are interrelated and, as the relevance and reliability of evidence increases, the quantity of evidence required may decrease. However, increased quantities of audit evidence may not compensate for poor-quality evidence. The reliability of audit evidence depends on its source, its nature, and the circumstances under which it is obtained. Audit judgment is used to determine when the audit evidence obtained is sufficient and appropriate to draw reasonable conclusions on which to base the audit opinion.

PUBLIC COMPANY IMPLICATION: The PCAOB's AS-15 (Audit Evidence) defines what constitutes audit evidence, and it provides guidance to the auditor of a public company in evaluating the sufficiency and appropriateness of audit evidence. Although there are a number of differences between the PCAOB's and ASB's risk standards, the risk-assessment concepts contained in the PCAOB standards should be familiar to most auditors. Audit risk is the risk that the auditor will issue an inappropriate opinion on financial statements that are materially misstated. The auditor is to reduce audit risk to a low level through the application of audit procedures. The guidance in AU-C 500 is largely consistent with AS-15.

FRAUD POINTER: A very common deficiency in enforcement actions against auditors is the auditor's failure to gather adequate audit evidence. In some cases, the SEC has highlighted specific areas where evidence was inadequate, such as auditors' examinations of draft contracts rather than final contracts and auditors' failure to obtain evidence related to all the steps in written audit programs. In these instances, the SEC believed the failure to gather adequate evidence prevented the auditors from detecting material misstatement due to fraud.

Audit evidence is obtained from a variety of sources. Some audit evidence is obtained from audit procedures testing the accounting records to determine that the records are internally consistent and agree to the financial statements. Accounting records alone, however, do not provide sufficient appropriate audit evidence for the auditor's opinion. Additional assurance is typically obtained from consistent or corroborating audit evidence from other sources, such as those independent of the entity. Sources of information independent of the entity that the auditor may use as audit evidence may include third-party confirmations, analysts' reports, and benchmarking data about competitors.

Audit Procedures

The auditor obtains audit evidence by performing three types of procedures: (1) risk assessment procedures, (2) tests of controls, and (3) substantive procedures, which include tests of details and substantive analytical procedures. Tests of controls should be performed when required by auditing standards or when the auditor chooses to perform these tests.

Audit evidence gathering procedures used by the auditor include (1) inspection, (2) observation, (3) external confirmation, (4) recalculation, (5) reperformance, (6) analytical procedures, and (7) inquiry. In some cases, audit evidence gathered in previous years' audits may continue to provide sufficient appropriate audit evidence, but the auditor should perform audit procedures to ascertain the continuing relevance of this evidence from prior years.

PLANNING AID REMINDER: Often the accounting data and corroborating evidence only exist in electronic form, and that evidence may only exist at a certain point in time. As a result, some of that evidence may not be visible in written form and it might not be retrievable after certain points in time. As part of planning the audit, the auditor should identify the time that evidence might exist or is available and consider that timing when planning the audit. In some cases, the auditor might determine that the use of IT specialists is appropriate in performing the audit.

Inspection

Inspection involves examining documents or records or physically examining an asset. The reliability of the audit evidence obtained from inspecting documents or records varies depending on the nature and source of the documents and records, and on the strength of internal control for internally generated documents and records. Inspection of tangible assets can provide useful audit evidence regarding the existence of the asset. It is a less effective procedure for providing evidence related to valuation of an asset and the entity's right to use it. Inspection is sometimes paired with observation as an evidence-gathering technique—for example, auditors often inspect individual assets during a physical inventory observation.

Observation

Observation involves looking at a client-performed process or procedure (e.g., observation of the entity's process for counting inventory, observation of the performance of a control procedure). Observation is limited to providing evidence about the state of a process or procedure at the time its performance is observed. Also, the very act of observing a process or procedure may change its performance—that is, client personnel may perform a process or procedure differently than normal when they know the auditor is watching.

External confirmation

A confirmation is a specific type of inquiry. It involves asking a third party to make a representation through a direct written response to the auditor about certain information or of an existing condition (e.g., confirmation of an accounts receivable balance). Often confirmations are used to provide audit evidence related to account balances, but they can also be used to confirm the existence of any agreements that may affect an account balance (e.g., a side agreement allowing a customer to return goods if the customer is not able to resell them).

Recalculation

Recalculation is a procedure that involves checking the mathematical accuracy of documents or records.

Reperformance

The auditor may reperform a procedure or control that is part of the entity's internal control. For example, an entity may have a control that involves the assistant controller reviewing the account coding for cash disbursements. The auditor could reperform this procedure.

Analytical procedures

Analytical procedures involve analyzing the reasonableness of financial information by comparing it with other financial and nonfinancial data. For example, the auditor might evaluate the reasonableness of the allowance for doubtful accounts by relating the allowance to the ratio of days' sales in receivables. In performing analytical procedures, the auditor should develop his or her own independent expectation of the account balance (or ratio etc.) *before* performing the analytical procedure. The effectiveness of an analytical procedure largely depends on the auditor's subsequent investigation of fluctuations or relationships that are inconsistent with other data or that deviate significantly from the auditor's expectations.

FRAUD POINTER: In some cases the auditor uses the prior year's audited balance as the implicit expectation and then focuses on differences between the recorded amount and the prior year's balance in performing the analytical procedure. In some cases the *lack of a difference* between the recorded amount and the prior year's balance is just as problematic as the existence of a difference.

Scanning is a type of an analytical procedure. Scanning involves reviewing accounting records (e.g., transaction listings, subsidiary ledgers, general ledger control accounts, adjusting entries, suspense accounts, reconciliations) for large or unusual items and then testing them. The effectiveness of scanning depends on the auditor's ability to define unusual items. Scanning is implemented most effectively through the use of electronic auditing procedures.

Inquiry

Inquiry involves asking questions to obtain information from knowledgeable sources. The auditor should consider making inquiries of both financial and nonfinancial personnel and of personnel both inside and external to the entity. Inquiry involves both formal written inquiries and informal oral questions. Inquiry is typically a complementary procedure to another audit evidence-gathering technique, and its effectiveness depends on the auditor's ability to evaluate the responses received.

Responses to inquiries may provide the auditor with new information, corroborative audit evidence, or contradictory audit evidence. The auditor may choose to modify or perform additional audit procedures based on his or her evaluation of these inquiry responses.

Inquiry may be used in assessing management intent where such intent is determinative of the accounting under GAAP (e.g., the classification of securities held as investments). Management may state that it has the positive intent and ability to hold a debt security to maturity, but finding evidence to corroborate this management representation may be difficult. In such cases, management's past history of doing what it says may provide evidence either to support or refute its representations.

FRAUD POINTER: Inquiry of senior management is likely to be particularly ineffective in cases of fraud where top management is involved. Note also that AU-C 240 (*Consideration of Fraud in a Financial Statement Audit*) requires the auditor to make certain inquiries related to the risk of fraud.

ENGAGEMENT STRATEGY: Some responses to inquires are of sufficient importance that the auditor may wish to obtain written representations from management or those charged with governance.

Relevance and Reliability

The relevance and reliability of information impacts the quality of the audit evidence.

Relevance

Relevant audit evidence relates to the specific assertion being tested by the auditor. For example, observation of the client's physical inventory count provides relevant audit evidence related to the existence assertion for the inventory account balance. The direction of testing is a factor that affects the relevance of audit evidence.

The audit procedures used also affect the relevance of audit evidence. Certain audit procedures may provide audit evidence relevant to particular assertions but not others. The auditor should bear in mind that audit evidence provided about one assertion is not a substitute for audit evidence about another assertion. It is also important to remember that audit evidence from different procedures or sources may be relevant to the same assertion.

Reliability

The reliability of audit evidence is determined by referring to its source, its nature, and the circumstances under which it is obtained. Although there are exceptions to these general principles, audit evidence is more reliable when it

- Is obtained from a knowledgeable, independent source external to the entity
- Is produced by a system with effective internal control
- Is obtained directly by the auditor (e.g., observation, reperformance) rather than indirectly (e.g., inquiry)
- Exists in documentary form
- Exists in original form (rather than as a copy, fax, or document that has been transformed into electronic form)

FRAUD POINTER: Although the auditor is expected to evaluate the reliability of audit evidence, he or she is not expected to authenticate the validity of written documents. The auditor is not trained in authenticating documents and auditing standards do not expect auditors to have this expertise. Nonetheless, many frauds are perpetrated through the creation of bogus documentation or the alteration of legitimate documentation. The auditor should be cognizant of this risk, and may want to involve forensic specialists in high risk engagements, particularly where questions about the authenticity of documentation arise.

Entity-Produced Information

The auditor often uses information produced by the entity as the source for other audit procedures. When the auditor uses client-generated information, he or she needs to test whether the information is accurate and complete. The auditor may test the completeness and accuracy of client-generated information at the same time that he or she is performing another audit procedure using that data. Rather than directly testing the accuracy and completeness of client-generated information, the auditor may, alternatively, test the controls over the production and maintenance of the information.

The entity may use a management's specialist to provide expertise in an area other than accounting or auditing that is used to assist in preparing its financial statements. In these situations, the auditor performs audit procedures to evaluate the specialist's work and the nature, timing, and extent of the audit procedures performed may depend on several factors such as:

- The nature and complexity of the matter of the specialist's work
- The risks of material misstatement in the matter
- The availability of alternative sources of audit evidence
- The nature, scope, and objectives of the specialist's work
- Whether the specialist is employed or engaged by the entity
- The extent of management's control or influence over the specialist's work
- Whether the specialist is subject to technical performance standards or other professional or industry requirements
- The nature and extent of entity controls over the specialist's work
- The auditor's knowledge of and experience with the specialist's field of expertise
- The auditor's previous experience with the specialist's work

Information about the competence, capabilities, and objectivity of a management's specialist may come from sources such as personal experience with prior work of the specialist, discussions with the specialist, with an auditor's specialist, or with others familiar with the specialist's work, knowledge of the specialist's qualifications, or works published by the specialist. In evaluating the specialist's competence, capabilities, and objectivity, the auditor may consider:

- If the specialist's work is subject to technical performance standards or other professional or industry requirements
- The relevance of the specialist's competence to the matter for which their work will be used
- The specialist's competence related to relevant accounting requirements

- Whether unexpected events, changes in conditions, or audit evidence obtained from results of audit procedures indicate the auditor's initial evaluation of the specialist's competence, capabilities, and objectivity needs to be reconsidered

If the objectivity of a management's specialist is threatened, safeguards created by external structures or the specialist's work environment may reduce those threats; however, threats to a management's specialist's objectivity cannot be entirely eliminated. To evaluate the specialist's objectivity, the auditor may inquire of the entity and specialist about any interests or relationships between the entity and specialist that may affect objectivity such as financial interests, business and personal relationships, or the provision of other services. The auditor may also discuss any applicable safeguards and professional requirements applying to the specialist to evaluate whether those safeguards are adequate.

The auditor may find the following relevant in obtaining an understanding of the management's specialist's field of expertise:

- Whether the specialist's field has specialized areas that are relevant to the audit

- Whether any professional standards or legal or regulatory requirements apply

- The assumptions, methods, and applicable models used by the specialist and whether they are generally accepted in the specialist's field and appropriate for financial reporting purposes

- The nature of internal and external data or information used by the specialist

If a management's specialist is engaged by the entity, there will likely be a written agreement or engagement letter between the specialist and the entity and evaluation of this agreement may assist the auditor in determining the appropriateness of the nature, scope, and objectives of the specialist's work; the roles and responsibilities of management and the specialist; and the nature, timing, and extent of communication between management and the specialist. If a management's specialist is employed by the entity, it is less likely that there will be such a written agreement and inquiry of management and the specialist may be the best way for the auditor to obtain an understanding of the specialist's work.

When evaluating the appropriateness of a management's specialist's work as audit evidence for the relevant assertion, the auditor may consider:

- The relevance and reasonableness of the specialist's findings or conclusions, their consistency with other audit evidence, and whether they have been appropriately reflected in the financial statements

- The relevance and reasonableness of any significant assumptions and methods used

- The relevance, completeness, and accuracy of any significant source data used

Evidence That Is Inconsistent or of Doubtful Reliability

If the auditor identified information during an audit that is inconsistent with the final conclusion regarding a significant matter, AU-C 230 addresses specific documentation requirements for the auditor.

SECTION 501

AUDIT EVIDENCE—SPECIFIC CONSIDERATIONS FOR SELECTED ITEMS

Authoritative Pronouncements

SAS-122—Statements on Auditing Standards: Clarification and Recodification

Overview

AU-C 501 provides guidance for the auditor in obtaining sufficient appropriate audit evidence in accordance with relevant AU-Cs regarding the:

- Valuation of investments in securities and derivative instruments
- Existence and condition of inventory
- Completeness of litigation, claims, and assessments involving the entity
- Presentation and disclosure of segment information in accordance with the applicable financial reporting framework

Requirements

The auditor is presumptively required to perform the following procedures in obtaining sufficient appropriate audit evidence for the following selected items:

Investments in Securities Valued Based on Investee's Financial Results Excluding Investments Accounted for Using Equity Method of Accounting

1. When investments in securities are valued based on an investee's financial results (excluding investments accounted for using the equity method of accounting), obtain sufficient appropriate audit evidence supporting the investee's financial results by:

   a. Obtaining and reading the available financial statements of the investee and any accompanying audit report and determining if the audit report is satisfactory for this purpose

   b. If the investee's financial statements are not audited or the audit report is not satisfactory, apply (or request the investor arrange with the investee to have another auditor apply) appropriate auditing procedures to the financial statements, considering the materiality of the investment to the investor entity's financial statements

   c. Obtain sufficient appropriate audit evidence if the carrying amount of the investment reflects factors not recognized in the investee's financial statements or fair values of assets that are materially different from the investee's carrying amounts

   d. If there is a time lag between the date of the entity's and the investee's financial statements that could have a material effect on the entity's financial statements, determine if the entity's management has considered the lack of comparability and determine any effect this has on the auditor's report

If sufficient appropriate audit evidence cannot be obtained because the auditor is unable to perform one or more of these procedures, determine the effect on the auditor's opinion in accordance with AU-C 705 (*Modifications to the Opinion in the Independent Auditor's Report*).

2. To address subsequent events and transactions of the investee occurring after the date of the investee's financial statements but before the auditor's report date, obtain and read available interim financial statements of the investee and make appropriate inquiries of the investor's management to identify events and transactions that may be material to the investor's financial statements that need to be recognized or disclosed in the financial statements.

Investments in Derivative Instruments and Securities Measured or Disclosed at Fair Value

3. Determine whether the applicable financial reporting framework specifies the method to be used to determine the fair value of the entity's derivative investments and investments in securities and evaluate whether the determination of fair value is consistent with the specific valuation method.

4. If fair value estimates of derivative instruments or securities are obtained from broker-dealer or other third-party sources based on proprietary valuation models, understand the method used in developing the estimate and consider the applicability of AU-C 500 (*Audit Evidence*).

5. If fair value estimates of derivative instruments or securities are developed by the entity using a valuation model, obtain evidence supporting management's assertions about fair value determined using the model.

Impairment Losses

6. When considering impairment losses, evaluate management's conclusion about the need to recognize an impairment loss for a decline in a security's fair value below its cost or carrying amount and obtain sufficient appropriate audit evidence supporting the amount of any impairment adjustment recorded, including evaluating whether the entity complied with the requirements of the applicable financial reporting framework.

7. Obtain sufficient appropriate audit evidence about the amount of unrealized appreciation or depreciation in the fair value of a derivative that is recognized or disclosed because of the ineffectiveness of a hedge, including evaluating whether the entity complied with the requirements of the applicable financial reporting framework.

FRAUD POINTER: In 2010 the Committee of Sponsoring Organizations of the Treadway Commission (COSO) issued a study entitled "Fraudulent Financial Reporting: 1998-2007, An Analysis of U.S. Public Companies" that found that 51% of the fraudulent financial reporting enforcement actions by the SEC involved asset overstatements. Assets related to fair value measurement and disclosure might involve heightened fraud risk because of the significant opportunities for management to perpetrate fraud related to those accounts. The significant dependence on management assumptions and the related complexities associated with measuring and disclosing fair value instruments can create significant opportunities for management to engage in fraud.

Inventory

8. If inventory is material to the financial statements, obtain sufficient appropriate audit evidence regarding its existence and condition by:

    a. Attending physical inventory counting, unless doing so is impracticable, to evaluate management's instructions and procedures for recording and controlling the results of the entity's physical inventory counting; observe the performance of management's count procedures; inspect the inventory; and perform test counts

    b. Performing audit procedures over the entity's final inventory records to determine whether they accurately reflect actual inventory count results

9. If physical inventory counting is conducted at a date other than the date of the financial statements, also perform audit procedures to obtain audit evidence about whether changes in inventory between the count date and the date of the financial statements are recorded properly.

10. If unable to attend physical inventory counting due to unforeseen circumstances, make or observe some physical counts on an alternative date and perform audit procedures on intervening transactions.

11. If attending physical inventory counting is impracticable, perform alternative audit procedures to obtain sufficient appropriate audit evidence regarding the existence and condition of inventory. If this is not possible, modify the opinion in the auditor's report in accordance with AU-C 705.

12. If there is inventory under custody and control of a third party that is material to the financial statements, obtain sufficient appropriate audit evidence about its existence and condition by requesting confirmation from the third party regarding the quantities and condition of inventory held on the entity's behalf and/or performing inspection or other audit procedures appropriate in the circumstances.

Litigation, Claims, and Assessments

13. Design and perform audit procedures to identify litigation, claims, and assessments involving the entity that may give rise to a risk of material misstatement, including:

    a. Inquiring of management and, where applicable, others within the entity including in-house legal counsel

    b. Obtaining from management a description and evaluation of litigation, claims, and assessments that existed at the date of the financial statements being reported on and during the period between the financial statements' date and the date the information is furnished, including an identification of matters referred to legal counsel

    c. Reviewing minutes of meetings of those charged with governance; documents from management concerning litigation, claims, and assessments; and correspondence between the entity and its external legal counsel

    d. Reviewing legal expense accounts and invoices from external legal counsel

14. For actual or potential litigation, claims, and assessments identified based on the above audit procedures, obtain audit evidence relevant to:

    a. The period in which the underlying cause for legal action occurred

    b. The degree of probability of an unfavorable outcome

    c. The amount or range of potential loss

15. If a risk of material misstatement regarding litigation or claims is identified or audit procedures indicate other material litigation or claims may exist, seek direct communication with the entity's external legal counsel. Communicate through a letter of inquiry, prepared by management and sent by the auditor, requesting the entity's external legal counsel communicate directly with the auditor.

16. In cases when the entity's in-house legal counsel has the responsibility for the entity's litigation, claims, and assessments, the auditor should also seek direct communication with the in-house legal counsel through a letter of inquiry. This communication is not a substitute for seeking direct communication with external legal counsel.

17. Document the basis for any determination not to seek direct communication with the entity's external legal counsel.

18. Request that management authorize the external legal counsel to discuss applicable matters with the auditor.

19. Letters of inquiry should include, but are not limited to, the following matters:

   a. Identification of the entity and its subsidiaries and the date of the audit

   b. A list prepared by management or a request for legal counsel to prepare a list describing and evaluating pending or threatened litigation, claims, and assessments with respect to which the legal counsel has been engaged and has devoted substantive legal consultation or representation on behalf of the entity

   c. A list prepared by management describing and evaluating unasserted claims and assessments management considers to be probable or assertion and that, if asserted, would have at least a reasonable possibility of an unfavorable outcome with respect to which the legal counsel has been engaged and has devoted substantive legal consultation or representation on behalf of the entity

   d. For each pending or threatened litigation, claim, and assessment listed, a request that legal counsel either provide the following information or comment on those matters on which legal counsel's views may differ from management's stated views:

      i. A description of the nature of the matter, the progress of the case to date, and the action the entity intends to take

      ii. An evaluation of the likelihood of an unfavorable outcome and an estimate, if possible, of the amount or range of potential loss

      iii. An identification of the omission of any pending or threatened litigation, claims, and assessments from the list or a statement that the list of such matters is complete

   e. For each unasserted claim and assessment listed, a request that legal counsel comment on those matters on which legal counsel's views may differ from management's stated views

   f. A statement that management understands that legal counsel will advise and consult with the entity concerning disclosure and the requirements of the applicable financial reporting framework if legal counsel forms a professional conclusion that the entity should disclose or consider disclosing an unasserted possible claim or assessment

g. A request that the legal counsel confirm whether the understanding described in item (f) is correct

h. A request that the legal counsel specifically identify the nature of and the reasons for any limitation on the response

i. A request that the legal counsel specify the effective date of the response

20. If the auditor is aware that an entity has changed legal counsel or the entity's legal counsel has resigned, he or she should consider inquiring of management or others about the reasons such legal counsel is no longer associated with the entity.

21. Modify the opinion in the auditor's report in accordance with AU-C 705 if (1) the entity's external legal counsel refuses to respond appropriately to the letter of inquiry and the auditor is unable to obtain sufficient appropriate audit evidence by performing alternative audit procedures or (2) management refuses to give the auditor permission to communicate or meet with the entity's external legal counsel.

Segment Information

22. Obtain sufficient appropriate audit evidence regarding the presentation and disclosure of segment information in accordance with the applicable financial reporting framework by:

a. Obtaining an understanding of management's methods in determining segment information, evaluating whether such methods are likely to result in disclosure in accordance with the applicable financial reporting framework, and testing the methods' application where appropriate

b. Performing analytical procedures or other audit procedures appropriate in the circumstancesb.

Analysis and Application of Procedures

Investments in Securities and Derivative Instruments

Professional judgment may be involved in evaluating audit evidence regarding assertions about investments in securities and derivative instruments, especially valuation. AU-C 540 (*Auditing Accounting Estimates, Including Fair Value Accounting Estimates and Related Disclosures*) addresses the auditor's responsibilities related to accounting estimates, including fair value accounting estimates and related disclosures in a financial statement audit and the AICPA's Audit Guide *Auditing Derivative Instruments, Hedging Activities, and Investments in Securities* provides additional and more detailed guidance related to planning and performing procedures for assertions about derivative instruments, hedging activities, and investments in securities.

To obtain evidence about the cost of securities valued at cost, the auditor may inspect documentation of the purchase price, confirm with the issuer or holder, and test discount or premium amortization using recomputation or analytical procedures.

FRAUD POINTER: The auditor should consider the guidance established in AU-C 240 (*Consideration of Fraud in a Financial Statement Audit*) for the possibility of management override of controls related to fair value information presented in financial statements.

ENGAGEMENT STRATEGY: Although this may be obvious, the Auditing Standards Board recognizes that accounting standards, especially those related to fair value, are becoming sophisticated and that auditors must stay current with financial accounting theory. For example, the valuation and disclosures related to derivatives as codified in ASC 815 (Derivatives and Hedging) and the application of the standards related to goodwill as codified in ASC 350 (Intangibles—Goodwill and Other) can be challenging even to the most seasoned auditor. It is more important than ever that the auditor devote a part of his or her professional life to professional development in order to deliver an audit product that satisfies professional standards. In some instances an effective engagement strategy includes the use of a specialist who is knowledgeable about fair value instruments, measurements, and disclosures.

PLANNING AID REMINDER: Although GAAP requires the investments to be recorded at fair value, a readily determinable fair value may not exist. For example, investments in a hedge fund may be reported at fair value even though fair value is not readily determinable. The hedge fund management might not provide details on how the fair value of its investments is determined, and it might only confirm the aggregate amount of a company's investment in the hedge fund. The receipt by an auditor of a confirmation where investments are confirmed on an aggregate basis is not sufficient. However, the existence assertion is supported if the auditor receives confirmation from the hedge fund as to the individual investments held by the fund. The valuation assertion is not supported even if the fund manager confirms the investments held by the hedge fund on an individual basis. Management, not the hedge fund manager, is responsible for determining the fair values of investments held by the fund. Management needs to develop a process for determining the fair value of investments held in the hedge fund. The auditor needs to (1) understand management's process, (2) evaluate whether the fair value measurements are in conformity with GAAP, and (3) test management's fair value determinations. If the auditor is unable to gather sufficient appropriate audit evidence related to either the existence or valuation assertions, a scope limitation may exist, requiring either a qualified audit opinion or a disclaimer of opinion.

Investments in Securities Valued Based on Investee's Financial Results Excluding Investments Accounted for Using Equity Method of Accounting

To determine whether the auditor's report on an investee's financial statements is satisfactory, the auditor may make inquiries about the professional standing and reputation of the other auditor, visit the other auditor, discuss the audit procedures followed and their results, and review the other auditor's audit plan and documentation.

PLANNING AID REMINDER: If investments are accounted for using the equity method of accounting, the auditor should follow the guidance in AU-C 600 (*Special Considerations—Audits of Group Financial Statements (Including the Work of Component Auditors)*).

The auditor may conclude after reading his or her report on an investee's financial statements that additional audit procedures are necessary to obtain sufficient appropriate audit evidence. Additional evidence could be needed because of significant differences in fiscal year-ends, significant differences in accounting principles, changes in ownership, or the significance of the investment to the investor's financial statements. Procedures the auditor may perform to obtain additional evidence include reviewing the investor's information about the investee such as investee minutes, budgets, and cash flow information, and inquiring of the investor's management about the investee's financial results. The auditor may need to obtain evidence related to transactions between the entity and the investee to evaluate that any unrealized profits and losses on transactions between the entity and investee were properly eliminated and that disclosures about material related-party transactions are adequate.

PLANNING AID REMINDER: The client may have more than one valuation method and identified a range of significantly different estimates of fair value. In that instance, the auditor evaluates how the client has investigated these differences in establishing a particular valuation.

A time lag in reporting between the date of the investor's and investee's financial statements could have a material effect on the investor's financial statements if the time lag is not consistent with the prior period in comparative statements or because a significant transactions occurred during the time lag. If a change in time lag occurs that has a material effect on the investor's financial statements, the auditor may be required to add an emphasis-of-matter paragraph to the auditor's report because the comparability of financial statements between periods has been materially affected by a change in reporting period.

PLANNING AID REMINDER: An entity may hold an interest in a trust that is managed by a third-party trustee. GAAP may require the assets in the trust to be reported at fair value (see ASC 958, Not-for-Profit Entities). The receipt of a confirmation from the trustee, where the investments held are confirmed on an aggregate basis, is not sufficient. However, the existence assertion is supported if the auditor receives confirmation from the trustee as to the individual investments held by the trustee. The valuation assertion is not supported even if the trustee confirms the investments held by the trust on an individual basis. Management, not the third-party trustee, is responsible for determining the fair values of investments held in the trust. Management needs to develop a process for determining the fair value of investments held in a trust. The auditor needs to (1) understand management's process, (2) evaluate whether the fair value measurements are in conformity with GAAP, and (3) test management's fair value determinations. If the auditor is unable to gather sufficient appropriate audit evidence related to either the existence or valuation assertions, a scope limitation may exist, requiring either a qualified audit opinion or a disclaimer of opinion.

Investments in Derivative Instruments and Securities Measured or Disclosed at Fair Value

The fair value of derivative instruments and securities may be available from quoted market prices for instruments and securities listed on national exchanges or over-the-counter markets. Quoted market prices from these sources generally provide sufficient evidence of fair value. Quoted market prices may also come from other sources such as broker-dealers who are market makers in the derivative or security or the National Quotation Bureau; the auditor may need special knowledge to understand the circumstances in which a quote was developed from one of these sources in order to use the quote to test valuation assertions.

PUBLIC COMPANY IMPLICATION: The PCAOB's Staff Audit Practice Alert No. 2 (Matters Related to Auditing Fair Value Measurements of Financial Instruments and the Use of Specialists) is designed to provide guidance related to auditing fair values, particularly in light of the FASB's guidance in ASC 820 (Fair Value Measurements and Disclosures). The auditor needs to understand the company's process for determining fair value measurements and disclosures, including related internal controls. The auditor should also evaluate whether (1) management's assumptions in determining fair value are reasonable and are not inconsistent with market information, (2) management's reliance on historical financial information continues to be justified (e.g., use of historical default rates may not be appropriate when credit markets are deteriorating), and (3) the company's determination of fair value is applied consistently and whether this is appropriate. For example, a company may apply a model consistently in determining fair value, but because of changes in the environment it may be more appropriate for the company to change the relative weights of model inputs. In addition, the auditor should recognize that model inputs based on the company's own data are generally more susceptible to bias and take appropriate audit steps to respond to this increased risk. Finally, GAAP provides many required disclosures relating to fair value measurements. The auditor needs to recognize that material disclosures that depart from GAAP represent a misstatement of the financial statements.

PUBLIC COMPANY IMPLICATION: The PCAOB's Staff Audit Practice Alert No. 4 (Auditor Considerations Regarding Fair Value Measurements, Disclosures, and Other-than-Temporary Impairments) is designed to inform auditors about the potential implications on annual audits and interim reviews of three former FASB Staff Positions (FSPs): (1) FSP FAS 157-4 (Determining Fair Value When the Volume and Level of Activity for the Asset or Liability Have Significantly Decreased and Identifying Transactions That Are Not Orderly), (2) FSP FAS 115-2 and FAS 124-2 (Recognition and Presentation of Other-than-Temporary-Impairment), and (3) FSP FAS 107-1 and APB 28-1 (Interim Disclosures about Fair Value of Financial Instruments). The guidance in these now superseded FSPs is incorporated in ASC 820 (Fair Value Measurements and Disclosures), ASC 320

(Investments—Debt and Equity Securities), and ASC 825 (Financial Instruments), respectively. Staff Audit Practice Alert No. 4 states that the auditor should include inquiries about the application of these FSPs in a review of interim financial information. For audits of financial statements, Practice Alert 4 emphasizes the need for auditors to obtain sufficient appropriate evidence to support accounting estimates, including their measurement and disclosure. For example, in certain cases the guidance in ASC 320 (Investments—Debt and Equity Securities) requires losses from other-than-temporary impairments to be separated between credit losses and other factors. Such a determination involves significant judgment. Practice Alert 4 also reminds auditors of their responsibility to read other information in documents containing interim and annual financial statements. If this other information is inconsistent with the financial statements, either the audit report, the financial statements, or the other information needs to be changed. The application of these FSPs may require communication to the audit committee because their application might involve a change in (1) accounting policy, (2) accounting estimates, (3) the process by which management develops sensitive estimates, and (4) the auditor's judgment about the quality, not just the acceptability, of the client's accounting policies. These required disclosures to the audit committee pertain to both annual audits and interim reviews.

If quoted market values are not available for a derivative instrument or security, fair value estimates may often be obtained from broker-dealers or other third-party sources based on proprietary valuation models or from the entity based on internally or externally developed valuation models. Obtaining an understanding of the valuation method used may include understanding whether a pricing model or cash flow projection was used. The auditor may also find it necessary to obtain estimates from more than one pricing source if, for example, the pricing source has a relationship with the entity that might impair its objectivity or the valuation is based on assumptions that are highly subjective or particularly sensitive to changes in the underlying circumstances.

ENGAGEMENT STRATEGY: Fair value information may be based on sensitive assumptions. That is, a change in an assumption can have a significant impact on the dollar value of fair value information. The auditor may consider encouraging management to use techniques such as sensitivity analysis to help identify particularly sensitive assumptions. If management has not used sensitivity analysis in this manner, the auditor should consider whether to use the approach as part of the engagement strategy to identify such assumptions.

OBSERVATION: When the client uses a valuation model to quantify measurements and disclosures, the auditor neither serves as an appraiser nor substitutes his or her judgment for that of the client. The auditor's role is to review the model and determine whether the client has used reasonable assumptions based on the relevant circumstances.

Impairment Losses

The auditor determines whether an impairment loss has been incurred by making judgments based on knowledge and experience about past and current events and assumptions about future events. These judgments are based on subjective and objective factors, the relevance of which may depend on whether they tend to corroborate or conflict with management's conclusions. Examples of such factors include:

- Fair value is significantly below cost or carrying value and the decline is attributable to adverse conditions specifically related to the security, industry, or geographic area; the decline has existed for an extended period of time; and management has the intent to sell the security or it is more likely than not that it will be required to sell the security before recovery for an equity security or before the security's anticipated recovery of its amortized cost basis for a debt security

- The security has been downgraded by a rating agency

- The financial condition of the issuer has deteriorated

- Dividends have been reduced or eliminated or scheduled interest payments have not been made

- The entity recorded losses from the security subsequent to the end of the reporting period

Obtaining sufficient appropriate audit evidence about the unrealized appreciation or depreciation in the fair value of a derivative that is recognized or disclosed because of the ineffectiveness of a hedge may include understanding the methods used to determine whether the hedge is highly effective and to determine the ineffective portion of the hedge.

Inventory

Attendance at physical inventory counting may serve as a test of control, substantive procedure, or both, depending on the auditor's risk assessment, planned approach, and the specific procedures carried out. The following are examples of relevant matters for the auditor in planning attendance at physical inventory counting or in designing and performing audit procedures related to the existence and condition of inventory:

- The risks of material misstatement and the control risk related to inventory

- Whether adequate procedures are expected to be established and proper instructions issued for physical inventory counting

- The timing of physical inventory counting

- Whether the entity maintains a perpetual inventory system

- To determine at which locations attendance is appropriate, the locations at which inventory is held and the materiality and risks of material misstatement at different locations. AU-C 600 may be relevant if component auditors are involved in attending physical inventory counting at a remote location.

- Whether the assistance of an auditor's specialist is needed

---

FRAUD POINTER: AU-C 240 notes that when the auditor believes there is a risk of material misstatement due to fraud, he or she may consider observing inventory on unexpected dates or at unexpected locations on a surprise basis. For situations in which the risk of material misstatement in inventory due to fraud is perceived to be high, AU-C 240 notes that the auditor's examination of the entity's inventory records might help identify locations or items that require specific attention during or after the physical count. For example, the auditor may decide to count inventory at multiple locations on the same date.

The auditor evaluates management's instructions and procedures for recording and controlling the results of the entity's physical inventory counting by examining whether they address, for example:

- The application of appropriate control activities such as count and recount procedures
- The accurate identification of the stage of completion of work in progress; of slow-moving, obsolete, or damaged items; and of inventory owned by a third party, for example, on consignment
- The procedures used to estimate physical quantities where applicable
- Control over inventory's movement between areas and its shipping and receipt before and after the cutoff date

Observing the performance of management's count procedures assists the auditor in obtaining audit evidence that management's instructions and count procedures are designed and implemented adequately. Inspecting the inventory assists the auditor in verifying the existence of inventory and in identifying obsolete, damaged, or aging inventory. Performing test counts provides the auditor with audit evidence about the completeness and accuracy of management's count records. Exhibit AU-C 501-1 provides an example audit program for an inventory observation.

Entities may use an external firm that specializes in taking physical inventories to perform their inventory count. The auditor may be able to adjust the extent of work on the physical count of inventory because of the work of an outside inventory firm but the use of such a firm does not by itself provide the auditor with sufficient appropriate audit evidence regarding inventory. AU-C 500 requires the auditor to perform certain procedures if information to be used as audit evidence has been prepared using the work of a management's specialist. Procedures the auditor may perform to obtain sufficient appropriate audit evidence regarding inventory in these circumstances include examining the outside firm's program, observing its procedures and controls, evaluating the effectiveness of its procedures, recomputing calculations of the submitted inventory on a test basis, and applying appropriate tests to the intervening transactions. If there is any restriction on the auditor's judgment concerning the extent of the auditor's contact with the inventory, there may be a scope restriction, in which case AU-C 705 requires the auditor to modify the audit opinion due to the scope limitation.

PLANNING AID REMINDER: Some companies are in the business of counting, recording, and pricing inventories. The auditor's responsibility for the count and other tasks performed by an inventory-taking company is similar to the responsibility for tasks normally performed directly by the client. Therefore, the auditor should (1) review the client's inventory-counting program, (2) make or observe a test of physical counts, (3) make appropriate mathematical checks, and (4) test the valuation of the inventory.

If physical inventory counting is performed at a date other than the date of the financial statements, the auditor considers whether this is appropriate by evaluating the effectiveness of the design, implementation, and maintenance of controls over changes in inventory. If the entity has a perpetual inventory system, differences in the perpetual inventory records and actual physical inventory quantities on hand may indicate that the controls over changes in inventory are not operating effectively. Factors to consider when designing audit procedures to obtain audit evidence about whether changes in inventory amounts between the count date and final inventory records are recorded properly include whether the perpetual inventory records are properly adjusted; the reliability of the entity's perpetual inventory system; and the reasons for significant differences between the information obtained during the physical count and the perpetual inventory records.

ENGAGEMENT STRATEGY: If an auditor has not substantiated the existence of inventory based on one of the approaches described above, testing solely the client's inventory records will not be sufficient to satisfy professional standards. Under this circumstance the auditor should observe the client's count or actually make inventory counts of the inventory and test intervening transactions between the count date and the balance sheet date. These procedures should be performed in concert with documentation created and procedures performed by the client.

FRAUD POINTER: AU-C 240 notes that the auditor may request that the client count inventory at year-end or on a date closer to year-end to minimize the risk of inventory balances being manipulated between the count date and the balance sheet date.

Attendance at physical inventory counting may be impracticable due to the nature and location of the inventory. For example, the location may pose a safety threat to the auditor or the auditor may be auditing financial statements covering periods for which he or she has not observed or made some physical counts of prior inventories. However, matters of inconvenience, difficulty, time, or cost are not by themselves valid bases for the auditor to not attend physical inventory counting. If attendance at physical inventory counting is impracticable, the auditor may be able to obtain sufficient appropriate audit evidence about the existence and condition of inventory by performing alternative audit procedures such as inspecting documentation of subsequent sales of specific inventory items owned at the time of the physical inventory count, testing prior transactions, reviewing the records of prior counts, or applying gross profit tests or other analytical procedures. However, if the auditor is unable to obtain sufficient appropriate evidence about the existence of inventory, he or she may need to modify the auditor's report.

When inventory is held by a third party that is material to the financial statements, circumstances such as when there is doubt as to the third party's integrity and objectivity may make it appropriate for the auditor to perform audit procedures in place of or in addition to confirmation with the third party. An example confirmation is shown in Exhibit AU-C 501-2. Other audit procedures may include:

- Attending or arranging for another auditor to attend the third party's physical inventory count

- Obtaining another auditor's report or service auditor's report on the adequacy of the third party's internal control for ensuring that the inventory is properly counted and adequately safeguarded

- Inspecting documentation regarding inventory held by third parties

- Requesting confirmation from other parties when inventory has been pledged as collateral

Litigation, Claims, and Assessments

Litigation, claims, and assessments involving the entity may have a material effect on the financial statements and therefore be required to be disclosed or accounted for in the financial statements. Some legal matters involving the entity may not have a material effect on the financial statements such as matters unrelated to actual or potential litigation, claims, or assessments; matters that management or legal counsel have not devoted substantive attention to; matters for which the entity's insurance exceeds the amount sought from the entity; or matters that are clearly trivial to the financial statements.

Management is responsible for adopting policies and procedures to identify, evaluate, and account for litigation, claims, and assessments in order to prepare the financial statements in conformity with the applicable financial reporting framework. Because management is the primary source of information about events or conditions considered in the financial accounting for and reporting of litigation, claims, and assessments, the auditor's procedures regarding litigation, claims, and assessments may include:

- Discussing with management the policies and procedures adopted for identifying, evaluating, and accounting for litigation, claims, and assessments involving the entity that may give rise to a risk of material misstatement

- Obtaining a written representation from management that they have disclosed and accounted for all known actual or possible litigation and claims whose effects should be considered when preparing the financial statements in accordance with the applicable financial reporting framework

Risk assessment procedures performed while obtaining an understanding of the entity and its environment may assist the auditor in becoming aware of litigation, claims, and assessments involving the entity. Examples of such procedures include reading minutes from meetings of directors and other bodies held during and subsequent to the audit period; reading documents such as contracts, loan agreements, leases, and correspondence from taxing or other governmental agencies; obtaining information concerning guarantees from bank confirmations; and inspecting other documents for possible guarantees by the entity. AU-C 250 details the auditor's responsibilities to obtain an understanding of the entity's legal and regulatory framework applicable to the entity and its industry or sector and how the entity is complying with that framework.

ENGAGEMENT STRATEGY: Audit evidence obtained for the purpose of identifying litigation, claims, and assessments that may give rise to a material misstatement may also provide audit evidence about other relevant considerations, such as valuation or measurement of litigation, claims, or assessments.

The auditor ordinarily lacks the expertise to evaluate litigation, claims, and assessments and therefore must rely a great deal on the client's lawyer regarding these matters. Direct communication with the entity's external legal counsel is the auditor's primary means of obtaining sufficient appropriate audit evidence about whether potentially material litigation, claims, and assessments are known, and management's estimates of the costs and financial implications are reasonable. An entity's inside counsel may provide the auditor with corroborating evidence.

OBSERVATION: The American Bar Association (ABA) has approved *Statement of Policy Regarding Lawyers' Responses to Auditor's Requests for Information* (the ABA Statement), which explains the concerns of the legal counsel and the nature of limitations that an auditor is likely to encounter in connection with seeking direct communication with the entity's legal counsel about litigation, claims, assessments, and unasserted claims. The ABA Statement is provided as an exhibit in AU-C 501.

ENGAGEMENT STRATEGY: Audit inquiry letters should be sent to those lawyers, which may be either inside counsel or outside lawyers, who have the primary responsibility for, and knowledge about, particular litigation, claims and assessments.

PLANNING AID REMINDER: AU-C 501 states that an external legal counsel's response to a letter of inquiry provide the auditor with sufficient appropriate evidence concerning the accounting for and reporting of pending and threatened litigation, claims, and assessments.

FRAUD POINTER: AU-C 240 requires the auditor to consider making inquiries of others separate from management about the risks of fraud. As part of these inquiries, auditors may make inquiries of in-house legal counsel about the risks of fraud.

In some situations, the auditor may find it necessary to meet with the entity's external legal counsel to discuss the likely outcome of litigation or claims or to seek clarification of matters noted by the legal counsel in the response to the auditor. This may occur when the auditor determines a matter is a significant risk, the matter is complex, or a disagreement exists between management and the entity's external legal counsel. These meetings typically require management's permission and are held with a member of management in attendance. Clarifications of matters should be adequately documented in the working papers.

The auditor is responsible for obtaining audit evidence about the status of litigation, claims, and assessments up to the date of the auditor's report. This evidence may be obtained by inquiry of management, including in-house legal counsel, or by obtaining updated information from the entity's external legal counsel.

ENGAGEMENT STRATEGY: The lawyer's response to the auditor's letter of audit inquiry should be addressed to the auditor, should apply to circumstances that existed from the date of the balance sheet through the auditor's report date, and should have an effective date within two or three weeks of the report date. Clearly specifying the earliest acceptable effective date of legal counsel's response to the letter of inquiry to approximate the expected date of the audit report can help alleviate the need to obtain updated information from the entity's legal counsel.

If legal counsel limits the response to the letter of inquiry to matters counsel has given substantive attention to or to matters that are individually or collectively material to the financial statements using materiality limits agreed upon by the entity and auditor, these are not limitations on the scope of the audit. If legal counsel cannot respond about the likelihood of an unfavorable outcome of litigation, claims, and assessments or the amount or range of potential loss because of inherent uncertainties, the auditor may conclude that the financial statements are affected by an uncertainty concerning the outcome of a future event that is not able to be reasonable estimated. In these situations, AU-C 705 addresses any effect of legal counsel's response on the auditor's report.

PLANNING AID REMINDER: If management imposes a scope limitation and the auditor cannot obtain sufficient appropriate audit evidence through alternative audit procedures, AU-C 705 requires the auditor to disclaim an opinion or to withdraw from the audit when practicable.

___

While the auditor would typically consider the inability to review information that could be significant to the audit as a scope limitation, this is not intended to apply to documents subject to the attorney-client privilege. To emphasize this, the letter of inquiry may contain language such as the following:

> We do not intend that either our request to you to provide information to our auditor or your response to our auditor should be construed in any way to constitute a waiver of the attorney-client privilege or the attorney work-product privilege.

This type of language does not constitute a scope limitation of legal counsel's response.

If the auditor believes there may be actual or potential litigation, claims, or assessments and the entity has not engaged legal counsel on these matters, he or she may discuss the possible need to consult legal counsel to assist in determining the appropriate measurement, recognition, or disclosure of related liabilities or loss contingencies in the financial statements. Refusal by management to consult legal counsel in this situation may result in a scope limitation that precludes an unqualified opinion.

___

OBSERVATION: In some situations, legal counsel may be required by relevant ethical requirements to resign if the entity disregards legal counsel's advice concerning financial accounting and reporting for litigation, claims, and assessments.

___

Exhibit AU-C 501-3, which is taken from Appendix A of AU-C 501, illustrates an audit inquiry letter to legal counsel.

Exhibit AU-C 501-4, illustrates an audit inquiry letter whereby management has requested that the lawyer prepare the list of pending or threatened litigation, claims, and assessments.

Segment Information

The auditor is responsible for the presentation and disclosure of segment information as it relates to the financial statements as a whole and so is not required to perform audit procedures necessary to express an opinion on the segment information by itself. When obtaining an understanding of management's methods in determining segment information and evaluating whether those methods are likely to result in disclosure in accordance with the applicable financial reporting framework, the following matters may be relevant:

- Sales, transfers, and charges between segments and elimination of inter-segment amounts
- Comparisons with budgets and other expected results
- The allocation of assets and costs among segments

- Consistency with prior periods and the adequacy of the disclosures with respect to inconsistencies

- Management's process for identifying segments requiring disclosure in accordance with the entity's financial reporting framework

Practitioner's Aids

EXHIBIT AU-C 501-1—AUDIT PROGRAM: INVENTORY OBSERVATION PROCEDURES

Use the following procedures as a guide for the observation of inventories. The audit program is only a guide, and professional judgment should be exercised to determine how the procedures should be modified by revising procedures listed or adding procedures to the audit program.

Initial and date each procedure as it is completed. If the procedure is not relevant to this particular audit engagement, place "N/A" (not applicable) in the space provided for an initial.

Client Name: _____

Date of Financial Statements: _____

Audit Report Date: _____

		Yes	No	*Audit Documentation Reference*
Planning Phase				
1.	Review with appropriate personnel the inventory count procedures to be used by the client.	_____	_____	_____
2.	Attend meetings in which the client instructs personnel concerning the inventory count.	_____	_____	_____
3.	Identify inventory count issues that need special attention (such as the use of a specialist, inventory held by consignees, inventory held for other parties).	_____	_____	_____
4.	Determine the number of staff personnel and level of experience needed to cover the client's inventory count.	_____	_____	_____
Inventory Count Phase				
5.	Meet with client personnel to identify any new issues that need to be addressed before the count begins.	_____	_____	_____

		Yes	No	*Audit Documentation Reference*
6.	Determine whether inventory that should not be counted (such as consigned goods, inventory to be shipped during the day) has been appropriately segregated or otherwise identified.	_____	_____	_____
7.	Obtain inventory control count information (such as range of ticket numbers or count sheet numbers to be used during the count).	_____	_____	_____
8.	Obtain inventory cutoff information from the shipping department (such as bill of lading numbers) and the receiving department (such as receiving report numbers).	_____	_____	_____
9.	Test inventory counts on a sample basis, and determine whether items are being counted and described correctly and identified as obsolete or damaged if appropriate.	_____	_____	_____
10.	Record some test counts that can be used later to test the client's summarization of inventory counts.	_____	_____	_____
11.	Determine whether all inventory items are counted and clearly marked as "counted."	_____	_____	_____
12.	Determine whether inventory that is moved from one location to another is appropriately identified to avoid double counting or omission from the count.	_____	_____	_____
13.	Once the inventory count is completed, obtain inventory control information (such as last ticket or counting sheet number used).	_____	_____	_____

Inventory Count Summary Phase

14.	Trace inventory test counts made during the inventory count to client inventory summarization sheets.	_____	_____	_____

	Yes	No	**Audit Documentation Reference**
15. Determine whether inventory numbers used in the client's summarization sheets are consistent with inventory control information obtained at the conclusion of the physical inventory count.	_____	_____	_____
16. Select inventory amount in the inventory summarization, and trace to either (1) inventory test count information or (2) consistency of ticket control information.	_____	_____	_____
17. Determine whether inventory items identified as damaged or obsolete during the inventory count were appropriately identified in the client's inventory summarization.	_____	_____	_____
18. Determine whether inventory cutoff information obtained during the inventory count is consistent with sales information and purchases information shortly before and after the year-end date.	_____	_____	_____

Reviewed by: _____

Date: _____

EXHIBIT AU-C 501-2—CONFIRMATION REQUEST FOR INVENTORY HELD BY ANOTHER PARTY

[*Client's Letterhead*]

[*Custodian's Name and Address*]

Dear _____:

In accordance with the request of our auditors, please confirm the correctness of the inventory items owned by us but held by your company as of December 31, 20X5. For your convenience we have included with this correspondence a list of these items based on our records.

Also, please answer the following questions:

1. How did you determine the number of inventory items held by you as of December 31, 20X5?

_____

_____

_____

2. Are any of the items held by you for us damaged?

_____

_____

_____

3. Are there any negotiable or nonnegotiable warehouse receipts issued, and if so, to your knowledge have any of the receipts been assigned or pledged?

_____

_____

_____

4. Are there any liens against the inventory?

_____

_____

_____

5. Do we owe you any amount of money as of December 31, 20X5?

_____

_____

_____

If the amounts and descriptions included in the attachment are correct, please sign the space provided and return this letter to our auditor in the enclosed self-addressed envelope.

If the amounts are incorrect or there is other relevant information that you want to communicate to our auditors, sign in the space provided, explain the difference in a separate letter, and return this letter and any other relevant information to our auditor in the enclosed self-addressed envelope.

Thank you for your prompt attention to this matter.

Very truly yours,

_____

[*Client's Signature*]

The above balance at the confirmation date is correct, except as noted on the back of this letter.

_____

[*Custodian's Signature*]

[*Title*]

EXHIBIT AU-C 501-3—ILLUSTRATIVE AUDIT INQUIRY LETTER TO LEGAL COUNSEL

In connection with an audit of our financial statements at [*balance sheet date*] and for the [*period*] then ended, management of the Company has prepared, and furnished to our auditors [*name and address of auditors*], a description and evaluation of certain contingencies, including those set forth below involving matters with respect to which you have been engaged and to which you have devoted substantive attention on behalf of the Company in the form of legal consultation or representation. These contingencies are regarded by management of the Company as material for this purpose [*management may indicate a materiality limit if an understanding has been reached with the auditor*]. Your response should include matters that existed at [*balance sheet date*] and during the period from that date to the date of your response.

[*Alternative wording when management requests the lawyer to prepare the list that describes and evaluates pending or threatened litigation, claims, and assessments is as follows:*

> In connection with an audit of our financial statements as of [*balance sheet date*] and for the [*period*] then ended, please furnish our auditors [*name and address of auditors*], with the information requested below concerning contingencies involving matters with respect to which you have devoted substantive attention on behalf of the Company in the form of legal consultation or representation. [*When a materiality limit has been established based on an understanding between management and the auditor, the following sentence should be added:* This request is limited to contingencies amounting to [*amount*] individually or items involving lesser amounts that exceed [*amount*] in the aggregate.]

Pending or Threatened Litigation [excluding unasserted claims]

[*Ordinarily the information would include the following: (1) the nature of the litigation, (2) the progress of the case to date, (3) how management is responding or intends to respond to the litigation (for example, to contest the case vigorously or to seek an out-of-court settlement), and (4) an evaluation of the likelihood of an unfavorable outcome and an estimate, if one can be made, of the amount or range of potential loss.*] This letter will serve as our consent for you to furnish to our auditor all the information requested herein. Accordingly, please furnish to our auditors such explanation, if any, that you consider necessary to supplement the foregoing information, including an explanation of those matters as to which your views may differ from those stated and an identification of the omission of any pending or threatened litigation, claims, and assessments or a statement that the list of such matters is complete.

[*Alternative wording when management requests the lawyer to prepare the list that describes and evaluates pending or threatened litigation, claims, and assessments is as follows:*

> Regarding pending or threatened litigation, claims, and assessments, please include in your response (1) the nature of the litigation, (2) the progress of the case to date, (3) how the Company is responding or intends to respond (for example, to contest the case vigorously or to seek an out-of-court settlement), and (4) an evalua-

tion of the likelihood of an unfavorable outcome and an estimate, if one can be made, of the amount or range of potential loss.]

Unasserted Claims and Assessments [considered by management to be proba-ble of assertion and that, if asserted, would have at least a reasonable possibility of an unfavorable outcome]

[*Ordinarily, management's information would include the following: (1) the nature of the matter, (2) how management intends to respond if the claim is asserted, and (3) an evaluation of the likelihood of an unfavorable outcome and an estimate, if one can be made, of the amount or range of potential loss.*] Please furnish to our auditors such explanation, if any, that you consider neces-sary to supplement the foregoing information, including an explanation of those matters as to which your views may differ from those stated.

We understand that whenever, in the course of performing legal services for us with respect to a matter recognized to involve an unasserted possible claim or assessment that may call for financial statement disclosure, if you have formed a professional conclusion that we should disclose or consider disclosure concern-ing such possible claim or assessment, as a matter of professional responsibility to us, you will so advise us and will consult with us concerning the question of such disclosure and the applicable requirements of Financial Accounting Stan-dards Board (FASB) *Accounting Standards Codification* (ASC) 450, *Contingen-cies*. Please specifically confirm to our auditors that our understanding is correct.

[*Alternative wording when management requests the lawyer to prepare the list that describes and evaluates pending or threatened litigation, claims, and as-sessments is as follows:*

We have represented to our auditors that there are no unasserted possible claims or assessments that you have advised us are proba-ble of assertion and must be disclosed in accordance with FASB ASC 450. We understand that whenever, in the course of perform-ing legal services for us with respect to a matter recognized to involve an unasserted possible claim or assessment that may call for financial statement disclosure, you have formed a professional con-clusion that we should disclose or consider disclosure concerning such possible claim or assessment, as a matter of professional re-sponsibility to us, you will so advise us and will consult with us concerning the question of such disclosure and the applicable re-quirements of FASB ASC 450. Please specifically confirm to our auditors that our understanding is correct.]

Please specifically identify the nature of and reasons for any limitation on your response.

[*The auditor may request the client to inquire about additional matters—for example, unpaid or unbilled charges—or specified information on certain con-tractually assumed obligations of the company, such as guarantees or indebted-ness of others.*]

[*Alternative wording when management requests the lawyer to prepare the list that describes and evaluates pending or threatened litigation, claims, and assessments is as follows:*

Your response should include matters that existed as of [*balance sheet date*] and during the period from that date to the effective date of your response. Please specifically identify the nature of and reasons for any limitations on your response. Our auditors expect to have the audit complete about [*expected completion date*]. They would appreciate receiving your reply by that date with a specified effective date no earlier than [*ordinarily two weeks before expected completion date*].]

[*Wording that could be used in an audit inquiry letter, instead of the heading and first paragraph, when the client believes that there are no unasserted claims or assessments (to be specified to the lawyer for comment) that are probable of assertion and that, if asserted, would have a reasonable possibility of an unfavorable outcome as specified by FASB ASC 450, is as follows:*

Unasserted claims and assessments—We have represented to our auditors that there are no unasserted possible claims that you have advised us are probable of assertion and must be disclosed, in accordance with FASB ASC 450, *Contingencies*. [*The second paragraph in the section relating to unasserted claims and assessments would not be altered.*]]

EXHIBIT AU-C 501-4—ILLUSTRATIVE AUDIT INQUIRY LETTER TO LEGAL COUNSEL WHEREBY MANAGEMENT HAS REQUESTED THAT THE LAWYER PREPARE THE LIST OF PENDING OR THREATENED LITIGATION, CLAIMS, AND ASSESSMENTS

In connection with an audit of our financial statements as of [*balance sheet date*] and for the [*period*] then ended, please furnish our auditors, [*name and address of auditors*], with the information requested below concerning certain contingencies involving matters with respect to which you have devoted substantive attention on behalf of the Company in the form of legal consultation or representation. [*When a materiality limit has been established based on an understanding between management and the auditor, the following sentence should be added:* This request is limited to contingencies that amount to [*amount*] individually or items involving lesser amounts that exceed [*amount*] in the aggregate.]

Pending or Threatened Litigation, Claims, and Assessments

Regarding pending or threatened litigation, claims, and assessments, please include in your response (1) the nature of each matter; (2) the progress of each matter to date; (3) how the Company is responding or intends to respond (for example, to contest the case vigorously or seek an out-of-court settlement); and (4) an evaluation of the likelihood of an unfavorable outcome and an estimate, if one can be made, of the amount or range or potential loss.

Unasserted Claims and Assessments

We have represented to our auditors that there are no unasserted possible claims or assessments that you have advised us are probable of assertion and must be disclosed in accordance with FASB Statement No. 5 (ASC 450). We understand that whenever, in the course of performing legal services for us with respect to a matter recognized to involve an unasserted possible claim or assessment that may call for financial statement disclosure, you have formed a professional conclusion that we should disclose or consider disclosure concerning such possible claim or assessment, as a matter of professional responsibility to us, you will so advise us and will consult with us concerning the question of such disclosure and the applicable requirements of ASC 450 (Contingencies). Please specifically confirm to our auditors that our understanding is correct.

Other Matters

Your response should include matters that existed as of [*balance-sheet date*] and during the period from that date to the effective date of your response.

Please specifically identify the nature of and reasons for any limitations on your response.

Our auditors expect to have the audit completed about [*expected completion date*]. They would appreciate receiving your reply by that date with a specified effective date no earlier than [*ordinarily two weeks before expected completion date*].

SECTION 505

EXTERNAL CONFIRMATIONS

Authoritative Pronouncements

SAS-122—Statements on Auditing Standards: Clarification and Recodification

Overview

The auditor can obtain audit evidence by confirming with, or acquiring information from, third parties. The confirmation process can be used as part of the audit of a number of account balances, transactions, and other information. For example, accounts receivable and payable may be confirmed with customers and vendors, respectively; a complex transaction may be confirmed with the counterparty; and the relationship between two (related) parties may be explained by the other party. The objective of the auditor in using external confirmation procedures is to design and perform the procedures to obtain relevant and reliable audit evidence.

In general, audit evidence obtained through the external confirmation process is often considered to be appropriate evidence. AU-C 500 reinforces this position, indicating that audit evidence is more reliable when it obtained from sources outside the entity, obtained directly by the auditor, and exists in documentary form, all of which are characteristics of external confirmations.

PLANNING AID REMINDER: AU-C 330 (*Performing Audit Procedures in Response to Assessed Risks and Evaluating the Audit Evidence Obtained*) requires the auditor to use external confirmation procedures for accounts receivable. While confirmation of accounts receivable is a generally accepted auditing procedure, confirmations can be effective in auditing many other areas: cash, notes receivable, inventory, consigned merchandise, construction and production contracts, investment securities, market values, accounts payable, notes payable, lines of credit, and actual and contingent liabilities. Confirmations can also be used to confirm the terms of unusual transactions and transactions with related parties.

Definitions

External confirmation	Audit evidence obtained as a direct written response to the auditor from a third party (the confirming party), in paper form, by electronic or other medium, or through the auditor's direct access to information held by a third party when the auditor is provided the information necessary to access the confirming party's data by the third party. If management provides the information necessary to access the confirming party's data, this does not meet the definition of an external confirmation.
Positive confirmation request	A request that the confirming party respond directly to the auditor providing the requested information or indicating whether the confirming party agrees with the information in the request.
Negative confirmation request	A request that the confirming party respond directly to the auditor only if the confirming party disagrees with the information provided in the request.
Nonresponse	A positive confirmation request the confirming party fails to respond or fully respond to, or a confirmation request returned undelivered.
Exception	A response indicating a difference between the information that is requested to be confirmed or that is contained in the entity's records and information provided by the confirming party.

Requirements

The auditor is presumptively required to perform the following procedures when using external confirmations:

1. Maintain control over confirmation requests by:

   a. Determining the information to be confirmed or requested

   b. Selecting the appropriate confirming party

   c. Designing the confirmation requests and determining that requests are directed to the appropriate confirming party and responses are coming directly to the auditor

   d. Sending the requests including any follow-up requests to the confirming party

2. If management refuses to allow the auditor to send a confirmation request:

   a. Inquire about management's reasons for the refusal and seek audit evidence about the validity and reasonableness of those reasons.

   b. Evaluate the implications of management's refusal on the auditor's assessment of the relevant risks of material misstatement, including the risk of fraud, and on the nature, timing, and extent of other audit procedures.

   c. Perform alternative audit procedures designed to obtain relevant and reliable audit evidence.

3. If the auditor concludes management's refusal to allow the auditor to send a confirmation request is unreasonable or the auditor is unable to obtain reliable audit evidence from alternative audit procedures, communicate with those charged with governance and determine the implications for the audit and the auditor's opinion.

4. If factors are identified causing the auditor to doubt the reliability of a response to a confirmation request, obtain further audit evidences to resolve those doubts.

5. If the auditor determines that a response to a confirmation request is not reliable, evaluate the implications on the assessment of the relevant risks of material misstatement, including the risk of fraud, and on the nature, timing, and extent of other audit procedures.

6. For each nonresponse, perform alternative audit procedures to obtain relevant and reliable audit evidence.

7. If a written response to a positive confirmation request is necessary to obtain sufficient appropriate audit evidence, alternative audit procedures will not provide the required evidence. If confirmation is not obtained, determine the implications for the audit and the auditor's opinion.

8. Investigate exceptions to determine whether they indicate the presence of misstatements.

9. Negative confirmations provide less persuasive audit evidence than positive confirmations and should not be used as the sole substantive audit procedure to address an assessed risk of material misstatement at the assertion level unless the following four factors exist:

   a. The assessed risk of material misstatement is low and sufficient appropriate audit evidence has been obtained regarding the operating effectiveness of controls relevant to the assertion.

   b. The population of items subject to negative confirmation procedures consists of a large number of small, homogeneous account balances, transactions, or conditions.

   c. The expected exception rate is very low.

   d. The auditor is unaware of any circumstances that would cause recipients to disregard the confirmation requests.

10. Evaluate whether the results of the external confirmation procedures provide relevant and reliable audit evidence or if further audit evidence is necessary.

Analysis and Application of Procedures

External Confirmation Procedures

While external confirmation procedures are often used to confirm account balances or disclosures, they may also be used to confirm terms of agreements, contracts, or transactions between parties or to confirm the absence of other conditions, such as "side agreements."

PLANNING AID REMINDER: AU-C 330, (*Performing Audit Procedures in Response to Assessed Risks and Evaluating the Audit Evidence Obtained*) requires the auditor to use external confirmation procedures for accounts receivable. Accounts receivable also encompass notes receivable and other receivables that use descriptive terms, assuming the account balance arose from the sale of goods or services in the normal course of business.

PUBLIC COMPANY IMPLICATION: In 2010 the Public Company Accounting Oversight Board (PCAOB) issued a proposed auditing standard, Confirmation. The proposed standard, if adopted, would supersede the existing guidance in AU-C 330 for audits of public companies. The proposed standard (1) continues to require the use of confirmation procedures for certain specific accounts (e.g., accounts receivable, cash), (2) expands the required use of confirmation procedures, because the PCAOB believes that confirmation procedures provide useful evidence in detecting fraud, (3) requires that confirmation procedures be used in response to significant risks if confirmation procedures are likely to be effective, (4) updates the PCAOB's existing guidance related to confirmations to reflect advances in technology (e.g., electronic confirmations will be acceptable), and (5) enhances requirements when a confirmation response includes disclaimers and other restrictive language. The PCAOB has not reached final conclusion as to the issuance of this as a final standard.

Confirmation requests should be addressed to respondents who, when they respond to the requests, will generate meaningful and appropriate audit evidence. When selecting the appropriate confirming party, the auditor should select a party believed to be knowledgeable about the information to be confirmed.

FRAUD POINTER: The auditor should be aware that under some circumstances the level of professional skepticism should be increased, resulting in a closer scrutiny of the respondent's competence, knowledge, and objectivity. For example, increased skepticism is appropriate when there has been an unusual transaction or a significant balance or transaction. For these as well as other circumstances, the auditor may decide to investigate the characteristics of the respondents more closely or to employ other audit procedures to reduce the risk of material misstatements in the financial statements.

PLANNING AID REMINDER: Auditors must be cautious when confirming the fair value of assets with parties that were originally involved in the acquisition of the assets being investigated. Because the respondent party might not provide objective evidence, the auditor should consider whether it is necessary to communicate with a party that is not involved in the transaction in order to collect appropriate audit evidence concerning the fair value of an asset.

The auditor should determine that external confirmation requests are properly addressed before they are sent out by testing the validity of some or all of the addresses, whether physical or electronic. The nature and extent of the procedures necessary to test addresses' validity depends on the risk associated with the type of confirmation or address.

ENGAGEMENT STRATEGY: Confirmation requests (either positive or negative) may be returned as undeliverable. In this case, it is important for the auditor to corroborate that the intended recipient actually exists. AICPA Practice Alert 03-1 (Audit Confirmations) states that the auditor may want to discuss confirmations returned as undeliverable with a client official not related to the area being audited.

The reliability of the audit evidence obtained and the confirmation response rate may be directly affected by the design of the confirmation request. In designing the confirmation request, factors such as the following should be considered:

- Assertions being addressed
- Identified risks of material misstatements, including fraud risks
- Confirmation request layout and presentation
- Prior auditor experience
- Method of communication
- Management authorization or encouragement to the confirming parties to respond to the auditor; some confirming parties may require management authorization before responding
- The respondent's ability to confirm or provide the requested information

ENGAGEMENT STRATEGY: Although confirming accounts payable is not a generally accepted auditing procedure, accounts payable confirmations can be useful in providing audit evidence related to the existence and completeness assertions. In particular, it may be appropriate to send accounts payable confirmations to major suppliers, including those with small or zero balances. In addition, confirming accounts payable can be useful in detecting round-trip or linked transactions (an entity simultaneously sells to and buys from another party). AICPA Practice Alert 03-1 (Audit Confirmations) states that the following circumstances suggest that confirming accounts payable is appropriate: (1) the client has weak controls over payables and cash disbursements, (2) the client's industry poses a higher risk of unrecorded liabilities or inappropriate accounting, and (3) the complexity of the client's environment increases the risk of unrecorded liabilities. In confirming accounts payable, a blank confirmation request form is generally used. An important aspect of confirming accounts payable is the generation of a reliable and complete vendor list. The auditor should (1) review the accounts payable subsidiary ledger, (2) review invoice files by supplier, (3) review disbursement records by supplier, and (4) ask client personnel for the names of major suppliers. If an accounts payable confirmation is not returned, the auditor should perform alternative procedures, including examining subsequent cash disbursements. Subsequent cash disbursements might indicate amounts that should have been recorded as a liability at the balance sheet date.

One form of confirmation request is the positive external confirmation request and a response to such a request is generally expected to provide reliable evidence. A positive confirmation form may be designed in two ways. The information to be confirmed may be indicated in the confirmation request or the request may be blank, requiring the respondent to fill in the missing information. In either circumstance, audit evidence is dependent on the receipt of responses from the recipients of confirmation requests.

ENGAGEMENT STRATEGY: There is a trade-off between selecting the complete format and selecting the incomplete format as part of the engagement strategy. A risk exists when using the complete format that the confirming party may reply without verifying that the information is correct. When a respondent completes and returns an incomplete form, more appropriate evidence is created than when the respondent is simply asked to sign a complete confirmation form. However, when the incomplete form is used, the response rate will usually be lower and less accurate (sufficiency of evidence matter), and it may be necessary to perform alternative audit procedures to supplement the confirmation process. When a positive confirmation is used and the request is not returned, no evidence is created.

Management Refuses to Allow the Auditor to Send a Confirmation Request

When evaluating the implications of management's refusal to allow the auditor to send a confirmation request, the auditor may find it necessary to revise the assessment of risks of material misstatement at the assertion level and modify planned audit procedures.

FRAUD POINTER: If management's refusal is unreasonable, this may indicate the presence of a fraud risk factor that the auditor should evaluate.

In order to obtain sufficient evidence, the auditor should also perform alternative audit procedures, such as those used by the auditor in the event of nonresponses to confirmation requests.

OBSERVATION: Clients sometimes ask the auditor not to send a confirmation request to a particular party. Often the stated reason is that there is a dispute between the client and the party as to the account balance. Audit Practice Alert 03-1 (Audit Confirmations) states that a dispute is not by itself a sufficient reason not to send a confirmation. Although there may be valid reasons for honoring a management request not to send a confirmation request to a particular party, the auditor should corroborate the reasons management is making this request. Simple reliance on management representations as corroboration is not sufficient. If the auditor concludes that management's request not to send a confirmation is not reasonable, and the restriction significantly limits the audit scope, he or she should normally either disclaim an opinion or withdraw from the engagement.

Reliability of Confirmation Responses

The confirmation process should be executed so that the client does not have an opportunity to intercept requests when they are mailed or when they are returned from respondents. The confirmation process ideally involves the auditor mailing a confirmation request directly to a respondent and receiving the returned confirmation directly from the respondent. However, there is always some risk that confirmation responses may be intercepted, altered, or subject to fraud. Factors that may cause the auditor to doubt the reliability of the confirmation response include the response being received by the auditor indirectly or the response appearing to come from someone other than the intended confirming party. Risks the auditor should consider when determining the reliability of confirmation responses include:

- The information obtained may not be from an authentic source

- A respondent may not be knowledgeable about the information to be confirmed

- The integrity of the information may have been compromised

Electronic responses such as fax or e-mail responses involve reliability risks that can be mitigated by using a secure confirmation environment. Tools such as encryption, electronic digital signatures, and procedures to verify website authenticity may help the auditor to improve the security of the electronic confirmation process. If relying on an electronic confirmation process, the auditor may use an assurance trust services report such as SysTrust to help assess the design and operating effectiveness of the controls related to the process and address reliability risks and concerns.

When the auditor has doubts about the reliability of a confirmation response to be used as audit evidence, he or she may determine additional or modified procedures are needed to resolve those doubts. Under these circumstances, the auditor may employ procedures such as the following:

- Verify the source and content of electronic response through a telephone call to the respondent.

- Request the respondent mail the original confirmation directly to the auditor if the response has been received indirectly.

A response to a confirmation request may contain restrictive language regarding its use. These restrictions may not create doubt about the reliability of the response if the restrictive language does not relate to the assertions being tested by the confirmation or if the restriction appears to be a boilerplate disclaimer of liability. However, if the restrictive language causes the auditor to have doubts about the completeness, accuracy, or reliability of the response, further audit evidence will need to be obtained to resolve those doubts. If the auditor concludes that a response is unreliable, he or she may find it necessary to revise the assessment of risks of material misstatement at the assertion level and modify planned audit procedures.

FRAUD POINTER: If a response is unreliable, this may indicate the presence of a fraud risk factor that the auditor should evaluate.

Oral Responses

An oral response to a confirmation does not meet the definition of a confirmation request, because it is not written. Therefore, if external confirmation is required to provide sufficient appropriate audit evidence and an oral response is all the auditor receives, the auditor has not obtained the evidence needed.

ENGAGEMENT STRATEGY: If an auditor has concluded that a direct written response to a positive confirmation is necessary to obtain sufficient appropriate evidence, the auditor may take the oral response to a confirmation request in consideration when determining the nature, timing, and extent of alternative procedures. An appropriately documented oral response combined with the evidence the original confirmation request was based on may provide sufficient appropriate audit evidence for the auditor in certain circumstances. Appropriate documentation includes details such as the time and date of the conversation, the identity of the person providing the response, and the response provided. The auditor may also wish to perform additional procedures to establish the reliability of the oral confirmation.

Nonresponses

In the case of each nonresponse to a confirmation request, alternative audit procedures must be used. The specific nature of alternative procedures depends on the account balance or transaction and the adequacy of the client's internal control. For example, when a customer will not confirm an account receivable, the existence of the account could be substantiated through the review of a subsequent cash collection(s) or the inspection of documentation for the transaction(s) that created the year-end balance. A nonresponse to a confirmation request may cause the auditor to revise the assessed risk of material misstatement at the assertion level, to modify planned audit procedures, and to evaluate a newly indicated fraud risk factor.

It may be acceptable to omit the use of alternative procedures if both of the following two circumstances exist:

1. Unconfirmed balances do not appear to be unique.
2. Unconfirmed balances are immaterial when projected as 100% misstatements.

Unconfirmed balances do not appear to be unique

The auditor should review those accounts that respondents will not confirm to determine whether they are unusual. Although it is difficult to define "unusual," transactions that are complex and not routine, and balances that do not follow a dollar-value pattern, would increase the level of audit risk and generally preclude the auditor from omitting alternative procedures. For example, most auditors would be skeptical if most of the unconfirmed accounts receivable were from customers who also had other relationships with the client.

Unconfirmed balances are immaterial

The auditor may treat all accounts that respondents do not confirm as misstatements if collectively those misstatements could not have a material effect on the financial statements. In determining the misstatements, the auditor must project the assumed misstatements from the unconfirmed balances to the total population.

PLANNING AID REMINDER: AICPA Practice Alert 03-1 (Audit Confirmations) states that the auditor can increase confirmation response rates by (1) using clear wording, (2) sending the confirmation to a specific person, (3) naming the company being audited, (4) having the client manually sign the confirmation request, (5) providing deadlines for receiving a response, (6) sending second and third requests, and (7) calling the respondent for an oral confirmation and requesting that the written request be subsequently mailed. In addition, accounts receivable confirmation requests may receive greater attention if they are included with the monthly statement sent to the customer.

When a Positive Confirmation Response is Necessary to Obtain Sufficient Appropriate Audit Evidence

Circumstances that could cause a positive confirmation response to be necessary in order to obtain sufficient appropriate audit evidence include:

- Information to corroborate management's assertions is only available outside of the entity
- Specific fraud risk factors prevent the auditor from relying on evidence from the entity. These factors may include the risk of collusion or management override of controls.

Exceptions

Exceptions may be used by the auditor to gauge the quality of confirmation responses from similar parties or accounts or the presence of deficiencies in the entity's internal control over financial reporting. Exceptions in confirmation responses may not indicate misstatements, but may be due to timing, measurement, or clerical errors in the external confirmation process. However, in some instances, exceptions may indicate misstatements or potential misstatements in the financial statements.

FRAUD POINTER: If the auditor identifies a misstatement, he or she is required to evaluate whether that misstatement indicates the presence of fraud.

Negative Confirmations

A negative confirmation form requires the respondent to return the confirmation only if there is disagreement. When negative confirmations are not returned, the evidence generated is different from that generated when positive confirmations are used. That is, the lack of returned negative confirmations provides only implicit evidence that the information is correct.

ENGAGEMENT STRATEGY: Unreturned negative confirmations do not provide explicit evidence that the intended third parties received the confirmation requests and verified that the information contained on them is correct. Auditors should factor this limitation into their engagement strategy.

It is also important for the auditor to consider that confirming parties who disagree with the information on the negative confirmation request may be more likely to respond to the request if the perceived error is not in their favor and less likely to respond if the perceived error is in their favor. For example, negative confirmation requests may be useful in providing evidence about whether balances in account holders' bank deposit accounts are understated, but may be ineffective in providing evidence about whether those accounts are overstated.

Evaluate the Audit Evidence Obtained

FRAUD POINTER: Enforcement actions against auditors often result from deficiencies in the accounts receivable confirmation process. Some cases involved the failure to confirm accounts receivable; other cases involved auditors' failure to control the confirmation process (e.g., allowed the client to handle mailing and receipt of confirmations and the related responses). Finally, a number of auditors were cited for failing to perform alternative procedures when confirmations were not returned or were returned with material exceptions.

Practitioner's Aids

In the confirmation of accounts receivable the auditor may use a positive confirmation or a negative confirmation or a combination of both. An example of a positive confirmation is presented in Exhibit AU-C 505-1. An example of a negative confirmation is presented in Exhibit AU-C 505-2. Positive and negative confirmations may take a variety of forms. For example, the negative confirmation may be a stamp or a sticker placed directly on the monthly statements sent to the client's customers; for a positive confirmation it may be a letter in a format similar to the one used in Exhibit AU-C 505-1.

The standards related to the confirmation process apply to all confirmations, not just those that involve the confirmation of receivables. Exhibits AU-C 505-3 and AU-C 505-4 illustrate other types of confirmations, namely, the confirmation of a lease obligation and a mortgage obligation.

Exhibit AU-C 505-5 illustrates an audit program for the confirmation of accounts receivable.

Exhibit AU-C 505-6 provides an example of an audit schedule that summarizes the results of the accounts receivable confirmation process.

EXHIBIT AU-C 505-1—POSITIVE CONFIRMATION

[*Client's Letterhead*]

[*Customer's Name and Address*]

Dear _____:

In accordance with the request of our auditors, please confirm the correctness of your account as listed below.

Account # _____

Date of Account Balance _____

(Confirmation Date)

Account Balance $ _____

    If the amount is correct, sign in the space provided and return this letter to our auditor in the enclosed self-addressed envelope.

    If the amount is incorrect, sign in the space provided, explain the difference on the back of this letter, and return this letter to our auditor in the enclosed self-addressed envelope.

    This is not a request for payment.

    Thank you for your prompt attention to this matter.

    Very truly yours.

    [*Client's Signature*]

    The above balance at the confirmation date is correct, except as noted on the back of this letter.

    [*Customer's Signature*]

    [*Title*]

EXHIBIT AU-C 505-2—NEGATIVE CONFIRMATION

CONFIRMATION REQUEST

    Please examine this statement carefully. If it is not correct, please notify our auditors of any differences. For your convenience a stamped, self-addressed envelope is enclosed.

    If you do not reply to this request, it will be assumed that the balance is correct.

    This is not a request for payment.

EXHIBIT AU-C 505-3—OBLIGATION UNDER LONG-TERM LEASES

[*Client's Letterhead*]

[*Lessor's Name and Address*]

Dear _____:

In accordance with the request of our auditors, please confirm the correctness of terms of our lease (and related matters) with your company.

Initial date of lease: _____

Monthly payments: $ _____

Number of months covered by the lease: _____

Renewal date (if applicable): _____

Monthly renewal payments $ _____

Period covered by renewal options: From: _____To: _____

Purchase option (if applicable)

Purchase option price: $ _____

Dates covered by purchase option: From: _____To: _____

Date of last lease payment received: _____

Other information:

_____

_____

_____

_____

If the above information is correct, sign in the space provided and return this letter to our auditor in the enclosed self-addressed envelope.

If the above information is incorrect, sign in the space provided, explain the difference on the back of this letter, and return this letter to our auditor in the enclosed self-addressed envelope.

Thank you for your prompt attention to this matter.

Very truly yours,

_____

[*Client's Signature*]

The above information is correct, except as noted on the back of this letter.

_____

[*Lessor's Signature*] [*Title*]

EXHIBIT AU-C 505-4—MORTGAGE OBLIGATION

[*Client's Letterhead*]

[*Mortgagor's Name and Address*]

Dear _____:

In accordance with the request of our auditors, please confirm the correctness of terms of our mortgage (and related matters) with your company.

Initial date of mortgage: _____

Monthly payments: $ _____

Number of months covered by the mortgage: _____

Interest rate: _____%;

Unpaid balance as of (Date): $ _____

Date of last mortgage payment received: _____

Purpose of mortgage:

_____

_____

Description of mortgaged property:

_____

_____

Escrow amount held by you: $ _____

Amount of property taxes paid during (Date): $ _____

Amount of insurance paid during (Date): $ _____

Other information:

_____

_____

If the above information is correct, sign in the space provided and return this letter to our auditor in the enclosed self-addressed envelope.

If the above information is incorrect, sign in the space provided, explain the difference on the back of this letter, and return this letter to our auditor in the enclosed self-addressed envelope.

Thank you for your prompt attention to this matter.

Very truly yours,

_____

[*Client's Signature*]

The above information is correct, except as noted on the back of this letter.

_____

[*Mortgagor's Signature*]   [*Title*]

_____

EXHIBIT AU-C 505-5—AUDIT PROGRAM—CONFIRMATION OF ACCOUNTS RECEIVABLE

Use the following procedures as a guide for confirming accounts receivable. The audit program is only a guide, and professional judgment should be exercised to determine how the procedures should be modified by revising procedures listed or adding procedures to the audit program.

Initial and date each procedure as it is completed. If the procedure is not relevant to this particular audit engagement, place "N/A" (not applicable) in the space provided for an initial.

Client Name: _____

Date of Financial Statements: _____

Audit Report Date: _____

		Yes	No	Audit Documentation Reference
1.	Obtain or prepare an aged trial balance of accounts receivable.	_____	_____	_____
2.	Foot and crossfoot the aged trial balance and trace the total to the general ledger.	_____	_____	_____
3.	Trace a sample of accounts listed on the aged trial balance to the account in the accounts receivable subsidiary ledger.	_____	_____	_____
4.	Trace a sample of accounts in the accounts receivable subsidiary ledger to the aged trial balance.	_____	_____	_____
5.	From the aged trial balance select a sample of account balances for confirmation.	_____	_____	_____
6.	If confirmations are prepared by the client, substantiate the information on the confirmation with information contained in the subsidiary ledger.	_____	_____	_____
7.	Mail confirmations directly with the U.S. Postal Service and include in the mailings a self-addressed return envelope.	_____	_____	_____
8.	Trace returned confirmation to information contained in the list of confirmations mailed.	_____	_____	_____
9.	Investigate exceptions noted in returned confirmation.	_____	_____	_____
10.	Send second requests for confirmations not returned.	_____	_____	_____

	Yes	**No**	**Audit Documentation Reference**
11. Apply alternative procedures (such as review of subsequent cash collection and inspection of documentation that substantiate the original balance) to confirmations not returned.	_____	_____	_____
12. Prepare summary statistics based on confirmations mailed and results of confirmation process.	_____	_____	_____

Reviewed by: _____

Date: _____

EXHIBIT AU-C 505-6—SUMMARY OF ACCOUNTS RECEIVABLE CONFIRMATION STATISTICS

Averroes Company Accounts Receivable Confirmation Statistics 12/31/X5

			Relative to Total Accounts Receivable		Relative to Total Confirmations Sent	
	Dollar Value	**Number of Accounts**	**Dollar Value**	**Number of Accounts**	**Dollar Value**	**Number of Accounts**
Total Accounts Receivable	$351,574.31	426				
Total Confirmations Mailed	223,876.12	235	63.70%	55.20%		
Accounts Confirmed (including exceptions cleared)	184,392.13	177	52.50%	41.60%	82.40%	75.30%
Unconfirmed Accounts Verified through Alternative Procedures	36,726.75	43	10.40%	10.10%	16.40%	18.30%
Exceptions not cleared[a]	2,757.24	15	0.80%	3.50%	1.20%	6.40%
Totals	$223,876.12	235	63.70%	55.20%	100.00%	100.00%

[a] See analysis of exceptions not cleared at AR201.

Prepared By: JB

Date: 2/18/X6   AR200

SECTION 510

OPENING BALANCES—INITIAL AUDIT ENGAGEMENTS, INCLUDING REAUDIT ENGAGEMENTS

Authoritative Pronouncements

SAS-122—Statements on Auditing Standards: Clarification and Recodification

Overview

AU-C 510 addresses the auditor's responsibilities in an initial audit engagement, including a reaudit engagement, with regards to opening balances. In these audit engagements, the auditor's objective is to obtain sufficient appropriate audit evidence about whether:

- Opening balances contain misstatements materially affecting the current period's financial statements

- Appropriate accounting policies reflected in the opening balances are consistently applied in the current period's financial statements and any changes in these policies are properly accounted for, presented, and disclosed in accordance with the applicable financial reporting framework.

PLANNING AID REMINDER: The standards established by AU-C 510 do not apply to an engagement if the most recently audited financial statements are dated more than one year prior to the earliest period being audited.

Requirements to communicate with the predecessor auditor are addressed in AU-C 210 (*Terms of Engagement*).

Definitions

Initial audit engagement	An engagement in which the prior-period financial statements were either (1) not audited or (2) audited by a predecessor auditor.
Opening balances	Account balances existing at the beginning of the period that are based on prior-period closing balances and reflect prior-period events, transactions, and accounting policies. Opening balances include matters requiring disclosure that exist at the beginning of the period such as contingencies and commitments.
Predecessor auditor(s)	The auditor from a different audit firm who reported on the most recent audited financial statements and/or the auditor who was engaged to perform but did not complete an audit of the financial statements.
Reaudit	An initial audit engagement to audit financial statements that have been previously audited by a predecessor auditor.

Requirements

The auditor is presumptively required to perform the following procedures in an initial audit engagement:

Audit Procedures

1. Read the most recent financial statements, if any, and any predecessor auditor's report on those statements for information relevant to opening balances, including disclosures and consistency in the application of accounting policies.

2. If prior-period financial statements were audited by a predecessor auditor, request that the client authorize the predecessor auditor to share his or her audit documentation and to respond fully to inquiries by the current auditor to assist in engagement planning.

3. Obtain sufficient appropriate audit evidence about whether the opening balances contain misstatements materially affecting the current period's financial statements by:

    a. Determining if the prior-period closing balances were correctly brought forward to the current period or restated, if appropriate

    b. Determining whether opening balances reflect application of appropriate accounting policies

    c. Evaluating if audit procedures performed in the current period provide evidence relevant to the opening balances and reviewing the predecessor auditor's documentation when the prior-year financial statements were audited and/or performing specific audit procedures to obtain evidence regarding the opening balances.

4. If the auditor obtains evidence that the opening balances contain misstatements that could materially affect the current-period financial statements, perform appropriate additional audit procedures to determine the effect on the current-period financial statements. If the auditor concludes such misstatements exist in the current-period financial statements, communicate the misstatements to the appropriate level of management and those charged with governance.

5. Obtain sufficient appropriate audit evidence about whether accounting policies reflected in the opening balances are consistently applied in the current period's financial statements and any changes in these policies are properly accounted for, presented, and disclosed in accordance with the applicable financial reporting framework.

6. If prior-period financial statements were audited by a predecessor auditor and the audit opinion was modified by the predecessor auditor, evaluate the effect of the matter causing the modification in assessing the risks of material misstatement in the current-period financial statements.

Possible Misstatements in Financial Statements Reported on by a Predecessor Auditor

7. If the auditor becomes aware of information during the audit leading him or her to believe the financial statements reported on by the predecessor auditor may require revision, request that the client inform the predecessor auditor of the situation and arrange for the three parties to discuss the information and attempt to resolve the matter.

8. Communicate information regarding subsequent discovery of facts that may have affected audited financial statements previously reported on to the predecessor auditor.

9. If the client refuses to inform the predecessor auditor or the auditor is not satisfied with the matter's resolution, evaluate the implications on the current engagement and whether to resign from the engagement or, if law or regulation prevents the auditor from withdrawing, disclaim an opinion on the financial statements.

Audit Conclusions and Reporting

10. Do not make reference in the audit report to the report or work of the predecessor auditor as part of the basis for the opinion.

11. If unable to obtain sufficient appropriate audit evidence regarding opening balances, express a qualified opinion or a disclaimer of opinion as appropriate.

12. If the auditor concludes the opening balances contain a misstatement materially affecting the current-period financial statements and the misstatement's effect is not properly accounted for, presented, or disclosed, express an opinion as appropriate.

13. If the auditor concludes that, in accordance with the applicable financial reporting framework, the current period's accounting policies are not consistently applied in relation to opening balances or a change in accounting policies is not properly accounted for, presented, or disclosed, express a qualified or adverse opinion as appropriate.

14. If the predecessor auditor's opinion regarding the prior-period financial statements was modified and that modification remains relevant and material to the current period financial statements, modify the opinion on the current-period financial statements.

Analysis and Application of Procedures

Audit Procedures

Considerations when there is a predecessor auditor

Communications between the predecessor auditor and the successor auditor may be helpful in planning the audit engagement, but they do not have to be made before the auditor accepts the client. The auditor's communications with the predecessor auditor are guided by relevant ethical and professional requirements.

PLANNING AID REMINDER: When the most recent financial statements have been compiled or reviewed, a predecessor auditor does not exist; however, the current auditor is not prohibited from following the guidance established by AU-C 510.

Before allowing access to audit documentation, the predecessor auditor should reach an understanding with the successor auditor regarding the use of the audit documentation. This understanding may be documented in a letter prepared by the predecessor auditor and acknowledged by the successor. Exhibit AU-C 510-1 is an example of such a letter. In order to further document the process related to the review of the predecessor's audit documentation, the predecessor auditor may request a consent and acknowledgment letter from the client. Exhibit AU-C 510-2 is an example of such a letter.

PLANNING AID REMINDER: If the predecessor auditor denies or limits access to documentation or does not respond fully to inquiries, it may affect the successor auditor's assessment of risk or the nature, timing, and extent of the his or her procedures regarding opening balances.

Although the predecessor auditor must use professional judgment in determining which audit documentation should be made available to the auditor, AU-C 510 points out that generally the predecessor auditor grants access to audit files, such as those documenting (1) the planning of the engagement, (2) risk assessment procedures, (3) further audit procedures, (4) audit results, and (5) matters related to continuing accounting and auditing significance, such as analyses of balances and contingencies. In audits of governmental entities, there may be legal or regulatory restrictions limiting the auditor's access to information from the predecessor auditor. In these situations, audit evidence may need to be obtained through other means, or, if sufficient appropriate audit evidence cannot be obtained, the effect on the auditor's opinion should be considered.

FRAUD POINTER: When assessing the risks of material misstatements due to fraud, the auditor should consider other information obtained in an audit, such as procedures related to the acceptance and continuance of clients. Information obtained from the predecessor auditor about management's integrity, disagreements between management and the predecessor auditor, and the reasons for the change in auditors can provide relevant insights to the successor auditor, particularly when combined with other information gathered by the successor auditor to assess fraud risks.

In addition to review of the predecessor auditor's audit documentation, the auditor may also assess the competence and independence of the predecessor auditor. The nature, timing, and extent of the auditor's audit procedures relating to opening balances and consistency of accounting principles may be affected by review of the predecessor auditor's working papers, but they, as well as the conclusions reached from these procedures, remain the sole responsibility of the current auditor.

OBSERVATION: If the predecessor auditor is owed fees for prior work, he or she does not need to comply with a request until those fees are paid.

Obtain audit evidence to support beginning account balances

The nature and extent of audit procedures the auditor uses to obtain sufficient appropriate audit evidence about opening balances depends on many factors, including:

- The entity's accounting policies

- The nature of the account balances, classes of transactions, and disclosures and the risks of material misstatement in the current-period financial statements

- The significance of the opening balances relative to the current-period financial statements

- Whether the prior-period financial statements were audited and any modification to that audit opinion

Current-period audit procedures may be useful in obtaining evidence about opening balances of some current assets and liabilities; for example, collection or payment during the current period provides some evidence about the opening balances of accounts receivable and accounts payable, respectively. The auditor may also obtain some evidence about the opening balances of noncurrent assets and liabilities through current-period audit procedures; for example, third-party confirmations may provide some evidence about the opening balances of long-term debts and investments. However, for many current and noncurrent asset and liability accounts additional audit procedures may be necessary.

Audit Conclusions and Reporting

When the auditor is unable to obtain sufficient appropriate audit evidence regarding the opening balances, the audit report may need to be modified in one of the following ways as appropriate:

- The auditor may issue a qualified opinion or a disclaimer of opinion

- The auditor may issue an opinion that is qualified or disclaimed regarding the results of operations and cash flows and unmodified regarding financial position.

Practitioner's Aids

Exhibit AU-C 510-1 is an example of a letter of understanding between the predecessor and successor auditors. This letter is reproduced, with minor modifications, from Exhibit C of AU-C 315.

EXHIBIT AU-C 510-1—LETTER OF UNDERSTANDING FROM PREDECESSOR TO SUCCESSOR AUDITOR

We have previously audited, in accordance with auditing standards generally accepted in the United States of America, the December 31, 20X7, financial statements of Averroes Company. We rendered a report on those financial statements and have not performed any audit procedures subsequent to the audit report date. In connection with your audit of Averroes Company's 20X8 financial statements, you have requested access to our audit documentation prepared in connection with that audit. Averroes Company has authorized our firm to allow you to review the audit documentation.

Our audit, and the audit documentation prepared in connection therewith, of Averroes Company's financial statements was not planned or conducted in contemplation of your review. Therefore, items of possible interest to you may not have been specifically addressed. Our use of professional judgment and the assessment of audit risk and materiality for the purpose of our audit mean that matters may have existed that would have been assessed differently by you. We make no representation as to the sufficiency or appropriateness of the information in our audit documentation for your purposes.

We understand that the purpose of your review is to obtain information about Averroes Company and our 20X7 audit results to assist you in planning and performing your 20X8 audit of Averroes Company. For that purpose only, we will provide you access to our audit documentation that relates to that objective.

Upon request, we will provide copies of audit documentation that provides factual information about Averroes Company. You agree to subject any such copies or information otherwise derived from our audit documentation to your normal policy for retention of audit documentation and protection of confidential client information. Furthermore, in the event of a third-party request for access to your audit documentation prepared in connection with your audits of Averroes Company, you agree to obtain our permission before voluntarily allowing any such access to our audit documentation or information otherwise derived from our audit documentation, and to obtain on our behalf any releases that you obtain from such third party. You agree to advise us promptly and provide us with a copy of any subpoena, summons, or other court order for access to your audit documentation that include copies of our audit documentation or information otherwise derived therefrom.

Please confirm your agreement with the foregoing by signing and dating a copy of this letter and returning it to us.

Very truly yours,

[*Predecessor Auditor*]

By:

Accepted:
[*Successor Auditor*]
By:

Date:

An additional paragraph may be added to the letter to provide the predecessor auditor with additional assurance concerning the use of audit documentation in order for the successor auditor to gain broader access to that documentation. An example of such a paragraph is reproduced from AU-C 510:

Because your review of our audit documentation is undertaken solely for the purpose described previously and may not entail a review of all our audit documentation, you agree that (1) the information obtained from the review will not be used by you for any other purpose, (2) you will not comment, orally or in writing, to anyone as a result of that review about whether our audit was performed in accordance with generally accepted auditing standards, (3) you will not provide expert testimony or litigation support services or otherwise accept an engagement to comment on issues relating to the quality of our audit, and (4) you accept sole responsibility for the nature, timing, and extent of audit work performed and the conclusions reached in rendering your opinion on the 20X8 financial statements of Averroes Company.

Exhibit AU-C 510-2 is an example of a consent and acknowledgement letter the predecessor auditor may send to the client (reproduced from AU-C 510).

ENGAGEMENT STRATEGY: Rule 301 of the Code of Professional Conduct prohibits an auditor from disclosing confidential information except when the client agrees to the disclosure. To reconcile the requirements of SAS-84[TP1] with Rule 301, the successor auditor should ask the prospective client to grant permission to discuss the impending engagement with the predecessor auditor. The client should not place any restrictions on the exchange of information between the successor and predecessor auditors. If the successor auditor cannot obtain required information from the predecessor auditor because of client restrictions, the successor auditor should consider the reasons for the restrictions and take the circumstances into consideration when deciding whether to accept the client.

EXHIBIT AU-C 510-2—CLIENT CONSENT AND ACKNOWLEDGMENT LETTER

You have given your consent to allow [*name of successor CPA firm*], as independent auditors for Averroes Company, access to our audit documentation for our audit of the December 31, 20X7, financial statement of Averroes Company. You also have given your consent to us to respond fully to [*name of successor CPA firm*] inquiries. You understand and agree that the review of our audit documentation is undertaken solely for the purpose of obtaining an understanding of Averroes and certain information about our audit to assist [*name of successor CPA firm*] in planning and performing the audit of the December 31, 20X8, financial statement of Averroes Company.

Please confirm your agreement with the foregoing by signing and dating a copy of this letter and returning it to us.

Attached is the form of the letter we will furnish [*name of successor CPA firm*] regarding the use of the audit documentation.

Very truly yours,

[*Predecessor Auditor*]
By:

Accepted:
[*Averroes Company*]
By:

Date:

SECTION 520

ANALYTICAL PROCEDURES

Authoritative Pronouncements

SAS-122—Statements on Auditing Standards: Clarification and Recodification

Overview

Analytical procedures are used to determine whether relationships between information presented in financial statements are consistent with the auditor's expectations. For example, if an auditor is aware that a client has invested heavily in new machinery, depreciation expense would be expected to be significantly greater in the current period than in the prior period. To successfully employ analytical procedures, an auditor must have a thorough knowledge of the client and the industry in which it operates.

AU-C 520 provides guidance to the auditor in using analytical procedures as substantive procedures and in performing analytical procedures near the end of an audit in order to help form an overall conclusion on the financial statements. AU-C 315 addresses the use of analytical procedures as risk assessment procedures and AU-C 330 addresses the nature, timing, and extent of audit procedures, including substantive analytical procedures, in response to assessed risks.

ENGAGEMENT STRATEGY: The auditor must use professional judgment to determine whether analytical procedures should be used as a substantive procedure to collect audit evidence related to account balances or classes of transactions. Although AU-C 520 does not require that analytical procedures be used as part of substantive testing, it does imply that it may be difficult to achieve certain audit objectives efficiently without applying substantive analytical procedures.

Definition

Analytical procedures	Evaluations of financial information through analysis of plausible relationships among both financial and nonfinancial data, including any necessary investigation of identified fluctuations or relationships that are inconsistent with other relevant information or that differ significantly from expected values.

Requirements

The following are presumptively required of the auditor when performing substantive analytical procedures or analytical procedures used near the end of the audit to assist in forming an overall conclusion:

1. When designing and performing substantive analytical procedures, alone or in combination with tests of details:

   a. Determine the suitability of the analytical procedures for the assertions being tested, considering the assessed risks of material misstatement and any tests of details used

   b. Evaluate the reliability of the data the auditor's expectations are developed from, considering factors such as the source, comparability, nature and relevance of available information, and controls over preparation of the data

   c. Develop an expectation of recorded amounts or ratios and evaluate whether the expectation combined with other audit evidence obtained is precise enough to identify a misstatement that, whether alone or with other misstatements, may cause material misstatement of the financial statements

   d. Determine the level of difference of recorded amounts from expected values that is acceptable and does not require any further investigation and compare the recorded amounts or ratios based on recorded amounts with the expectations

2. Design and perform analytical procedures near the end of an audit to assist in drawing reasonable conclusions about whether the financial statements are consistent with the auditor's understanding of the entity.

3. If analytical procedures performed in accordance with AU-C 520 identify fluctuations or relationships that are inconsistent with other relevant information or that differ from expected values by a significant amount, investigate those differences by inquiring of management and obtaining appropriate audit evidence relevant to management's responses and performing any other necessary audit procedures.

4. When using substantive analytical procedures, document:

   a. The expectation of recorded amounts or ratios when the expectation is not otherwise readily determinable from existing documentation

   b. Results of the comparison of the expectation to the recorded amounts or ratios

   c. Any additional auditing procedures performed relating to fluctuations or relationships that are inconsistent with other relevant information or that differ from expected values by a significant amount and the results of such procedures

Analysis and Application of Procedures

Analytical procedures

Analytical procedures operate under the basic premise that plausible relationships among data may be reasonably expected to exist. The reasons for the plausibility of these relationships are important because apparently related data may not be related, which can lead to erroneous conclusions or an unexpected relationship may be able to provide important evidence.

   Analytical procedures include considering comparisons of the entity's financial information with comparable prior-period information, anticipated entity results, and similar industry information. Analytical procedures also involve considering relationships among financial information elements expected to conform to a predictable pattern or between financial and nonfinancial information. Scanning is an analytical procedure used to identify significant or unusual items where the auditor uses professional judgment to review accounting data. Analytical procedures may be performed using many methods, from simple comparisons to complex analyses using statistical techniques, and may be applied at many different levels of aggregation.

PUBLIC COMPANY IMPLICATION: In 2010 the PCAOB issued eight auditing standards (AS-8 through AS-15) related to the auditor's assessment of and response to risk. The standards bear many similarities to the eight risk-assessment standards adopted by the Auditing Standards Board in 2006. The discussion of analytical procedures is integrated across these eight new risk-assessment standards. In particular, analytical procedures are discussed in AS-12, AS-13, AS-14, and AS-15. Although there are a number of differences between the PCAOB's and ASB's risk standards, the risk-assessment concepts contained in the PCAOB standards should be familiar to most auditors. Audit risk is the risk that the auditor will issue an inappropriate opinion on financial statements that are materially misstated. The auditor is to reduce audit risk to a low level through the application of audit procedures. As a result, the amount of audit effort devoted to particular accounts, classes of transactions, and disclosures should vary based on their respective risk.

The AICPA Audit Guide *Analytical Procedures* states that the process of using analytical procedures consists of four phases:

1. Formation of auditor expectations
2. Identification of differences between account balances and auditor expectations
3. Investigation of differences
4. Evaluation of results

Formation of auditor expectations

The auditor incorporates all of his or her experiences, both general and client-specific, to develop expectations of relationships between financial and nonfinancial data. Thus, at this stage the auditor must formulate an expectation about a relationship involving an amount that appears in the client's accounting system. Because of the varying nature of information processed and otherwise developed by a client, the Audit Guide notes that the effectiveness of developing an expectation depends on the following factors:

- Nature of account or assertion
- Reliability and other characteristics of data
- Inherent precision of an analytical procedure

Nature of account or assertion

Auditor expectations must be based on plausible relationships between financial and nonfinancial data. The more predictable a relationship, the more plausible the auditor's expectation. For example, there is a relationship between the amount of interest-bearing debt on the balance sheet (as reported throughout the year) and the interest expense reported on the operating statement. Developing an expected relationship between two amounts such as these is relatively easy to do; however, expectations about other relationships can be more difficult to identify with an acceptable degree of precision. For example, the relationship between accounts receivable and the allowance for uncollectible accounts can be difficult to predict if the client has changed its credit policies or the economics of the client's industry have significantly changed. The Audit Guide lists the following as examples of factors that an auditor may consider in establishing a relationship between accounts (assertions) on the financial statements:

- The degree of subjectivity exercised to develop the account balance (for example, an account may simply be an aggregation of transactions (low degree of subjectivity) or be based on estimates (high degree of subjectivity)
- The product mix
- The client's profile (for example, the manner in which it distributes its products)
- Management's discretion
- Various measurements of the client's environment (for example, changes in economic, technological, or regulatory conditions)
- The type of account (balance sheet or operating account)

Reliability and other characteristics of data

The precision of the auditor's expectation (how close the expectation is to the correct amount, not the reported amount) depends on the quality of the data used to form the expectation. If the reliability of the data is poor, the quality of the audit evidence created by performing an analytical procedure will be poor and perhaps irrelevant. The Audit Guide identifies the following as factors that are useful in determining the usefulness of data used to develop auditor expectations:

- The client's internal control (the stronger the internal control, the more reliable the data)
- The source of data (data based on outside parties are more reliable than internally generated data)
- Audited data (data that have been subjected to audit procedures (generally financial data) are more reliable than data that have not been audited (generally nonfinancial data))
- The degree of aggregation (the more aggregated data, the more difficult it is to develop a precise expectation)

PLANNING AID REMINDER: In addition to financial information, nonfinancial data may be taken into consideration as part of the performance of analytical procedures. For example, quality control reports prepared near year-end may identify production problems, which may suggest that significant amounts of inventory sold during the latter part of the year may be returned or may significantly increase future warranty claims.

Inherent precision of an analytical procedure

The Audit Guide broadly classifies analytical procedures as (1) trend analysis, (2) ratio analysis, (3) reasonableness test, and (4) regression analysis. These broad analytical procedures are not substitutes for one another. The auditor, using professional judgment, selects the appropriate analytical procedure based on the desired level of assurance that the account (assertion) is not materially misstated.

Trend analysis is based on the analysis of changes in a balance over a period of time that can vary from two years (the current year compared with the previous year) to several years. Generally trend analysis is most effective when the client is in a stable environment. For example, the reasonableness of current-year sales may be appropriately tested by comparing that amount to sales in the previous year if there is an absence of increased competition in the area serviced by the client, changing local economic conditions, changing consumer preferences, and an absence of change in a host of other environmental conditions.

The advantage of using trend analysis is its simplicity; however, its effectiveness is limited by the fact that it does not take into consideration changes in the client's environment. In addition, the use of this approach is based on an implicit rather than an explicit expectation. That is, in trend analysis the auditor does not explicitly establish an expected dollar amount but, rather, compares two numbers that because of changed conditions might not be comparable. Trend analysis is also limited to a single predictor and cannot take into consideration operating data or external data.

Ratio analysis can be used to compare the relationship between (1) accounts over time (inventory turnover), (2) an account and nonfinancial information (for example, sales per square foot of space), (3) accounts of the client and data from the client's industry (for example, the percentage of uncollectible accounts), and (4) a combination of the foregoing three items.

Like trend analysis, ratio analysis is most effective when the environmental characteristics of the client are stable; however, the Audit Guide points out that ratio analysis can be more effective than trend analysis "because comparisons between the balance sheet and operating statement can often reveal unusual fluctuations that an analysis of the individual accounts would not." Furthermore using ratio analysis that is based in part on industry data can only be effective if the client's operating and financing activities do not deviate significantly from industry norms.

Reasonableness tests utilize financial and nonfinancial data to determine the acceptability of an account balance or a change in an account balance. For example, the current year's payroll expense expectation may take into consideration last year's account balance and other factors such as the average pay rate change, the timing of pay rate adjustments, and the expansion or contraction of the labor force. The advantage of a reasonableness test over trend analysis and ratio analysis is that in a reasonableness test the auditor takes into consideration a client's changed environment and, using professional judgment, assesses whether the current-year balance appears to be appropriate. In applying a reasonableness test the auditor must be careful to identify all the significant factors that could have an impact on the account balance being investigated.

Regression analysis is the most sophisticated analytical procedure in that it is based on a statistical model to predict the relationship between the account balance and various other factors. Generally the difference between a reasonableness test and regression analysis is that regression analysis produces a quantitative prediction (expressed as a range) of what the current year's balance should be.

The most difficult analytical procedure to employ is regression analysis, but it has all of the advantages of reasonableness tests and, additionally, it provides a measure of statistical precision. That is, the auditor does not attempt to predict a single amount but, rather, estimates a projected amount plus or minus a dollar value.

PLANNING AID REMINDER: The effectiveness of analytical procedures is increased if the data sets are disaggregated. For example, applying a trend analysis approach to divisional information rather than consolidated financial information will generally result in more precise expectations. Be aware that when conducting regression analyses, one needs a sufficient number of data points to obtain a statistically valid result. Usually 18 to 20 data points are sufficient. Quarterly results can be used if the data are accurate. Microsoft Excel and other spreadsheet programs contain easy-to-use statistical analysis programs.

Identification of differences between account balance and auditor expectations

The second phase of the analytical procedure process is the identification of differences, which simply means that the auditor computes the difference between the expectation and the recorded account balance. The computed difference is then compared with the auditor's measure of materiality. When the analytical procedure is part of substantive testing, the auditor will accept the recorded amount balance when the difference is less than the materiality threshold for the account (e.g., the tolerable misstatement). If the difference is greater than the materiality threshold, the difference must be investigated.

Investigation of differences

The Audit Guide points out that differences between the expected amount and the recorded account balance can arise for one or more of the following reasons:

- The recorded account balance is misstated.
- The recorded account balance is affected by inherent factors related to the nature of the account to a degree not anticipated by the auditor.
- The expected amount is affected by the reliability of databases used to establish the expected amount to a degree not anticipated by the auditor.

Initially the auditor should evaluate the expectation results by determining whether there is an apparent problem with the precision of the estimate (the second and third items listed above). If it is concluded that the analytical procedure created a too imprecise expectation, then the auditor must decide whether the cost related to employing a more precise analytical procedure can be justified. For example, the auditor might have used trend analysis to develop an implicit expectation about a client's current sales figure, but if the difference between the expected amount and the recorded sales amount is too great, it may be concluded that regression analysis should be used to test the acceptability of the sales figure.

If the auditor concludes that the level of precision does not appear to be the reason for the unacceptable difference between the expected amount and the recorded amount, the investigation should consider whether there is a plausible explanation for the difference. Generally a plausible explanation is related to unexpected events, changes in the business environment, or accounting changes. The Audit Guide states that a plausible explanation should be evaluated in the context of such factors as the following:

- The development of audit evidence in other parts of the engagement, especially evidence obtained that relates to the database used to formulate the original expectation.
- Reports by management or the board of directors that identify and explain significant variances between budgeted and actual results.
- Relevant information identified in the minutes of the board of directors.
- Information about unusual events that occurred in previous years that may have reoccurred in the current period.

When an analytical procedure is performed as part of substantive testing, reasons that support a plausible explanation must be investigated and corroborated. The specific form of corroboration will depend on the nature of the account and the plausible explanation, but the Audit Guide notes that one or more of the following procedures may be useful to an auditor:

- Confirm related factors with outside parties.
- Make inquiries of internal personnel who did not provide the plausible explanation to the auditor.
- Perform other auditing procedures (perhaps on the data that were used to establish the expectation).
- Inspect documents that support the plausible explanation.

  If the auditor cannot corroborate the plausible explanation, the difference must be evaluated as unexplained.

Evaluation of results

The final step in the analytical procedures process is the evaluation of results arising from the application of the procedure. Professional judgment must be exercised to determine how the results of applying an analytical procedure affect the audit engagement. The Audit Guide points out that "the auditor should attempt to quantify that portion of the difference for which plausible explanations can be obtained and, where appropriate, corroborate and determine that the amount that cannot be explained is sufficiently small to enable him or her to conclude on the absence of material misstatement." More specifically when a plausible explanation cannot be supported, the auditor should aggregate misstatements that the entity has not corrected in a way that enables him or her to consider whether, in relation to individual amounts, subtotals, or totals in the financial statements, they materially misstate the financial statements taken as a whole. Qualitative considerations also influence the auditor in reaching a conclusion as to whether misstatements are material.

Substantive analytical procedures

In determining whether and to what extent analytical procedures should be used, an auditor should consider the relative effectiveness and efficiency of analytical procedures as compared to tests of details in reducing the risk of material misstatement and identifying potential misstatements. The effectiveness and efficiency of substantive analytical procedures depend on the following factors:

- Nature of the assertion being tested
- Plausibility and predictability of the relationship
- Reliability and availability of the data used to develop the expectation
- Precision of the expectation

ENGAGEMENT STRATEGY: Analytical data prepared by management may be effective if the auditor is satisfied that the data are properly prepared.

The applicability of analytical procedures for given assertions depends on the nature of the assertion and the risk of material misstatement. Because the auditor desires more persuasive audit evidence, a more predictable relationship is generally required. The following generalizations may be useful in identifying predictable relationships:

- Relationships in a relatively stable environment tend to be more predictable than those in an unstable environment. (For example, bad debts expense and credit sales tend to be closely related to a stable economic environment.)
- Relationships among data on the income statement tend to be more predictable than relationships among data on the balance sheet. (For example, sales and sales commission expense tend to be more closely related than trade accounts payable and inventories.)
- Relationships that are subject to management discretion are more difficult to evaluate. (For example, loss contingency accruals associated with the number of pending lawsuits tend not to be predictable.)

Substantive analytical procedures may be used in conjunction with tests of details to provide sufficient audit evidence on a particular assertion. In these circumstances, less persuasive analytical procedures may still be useful in providing corroborating evidence. Widely recognized trade ratios can also often be used effectively in substantive analytical procedures to support the reasonableness of recorded amounts.

PLANNING AID REMINDER: Many relationships between financial statement items that may be used in the audit of business entities may not be relevant for audits of governmental entities. For example, governmental entities may have little direct relationship between revenue and expenditure.

For the auditor to be able to draw an inference about an account balance or a class of transactions based on applying analytical procedures, the data from which the inference is made must be reliable and available. In evaluating the reliability of data, the following generalizations are useful:

- Audited data (current or prior years) are more reliable than unaudited data.

- Internal data tend to be more reliable when developed under an effective system of internal control.

- Data from an external source tend to be more reliable than data from an internal source.

- Data tend to be more reliable when they are comparable to other available information.

- Data tend to be more reliable when the auditor is satisfied as to their nature and relevance.

The auditor may consider testing the operating effectiveness of controls over the entity's preparation of information used in substantive analytical procedures. When these controls are effective, the auditor may have greater confidence in the reliability of the data and, therefore, in the results of the analytical procedures.

Because analytical procedures generally lead to fairly broad conclusions about assertions in the financial statements, an auditor should consider the precision of the established expectation. In some instances, an auditor may be satisfied with a fairly imprecise expectation. For example, expectations concerning the relationship between warranty expense and sales subject to warranty may be imprecise (say, from 1% to 8% of sales) if significant changes in warranty expenses are unlikely to have a material effect on the financial statements. On the other hand, a more precise expectation may be demanded for sales returns when the client is in an industry that experiences significant returns and a change of a percentage point or two could have a material effect on the financial statements.

A less precise expectation may be appropriate when the evidence from the substantive analytical procedure will be combined with audit evidence from tests of details. However, a more precise expectation is needed if the substantive analytical procedure is the only procedure planned to address a risk of misstatement for a relevant assertion.

The precision of an expectation is also affected by the level of aggregation of the information. Expectations developed at a disaggregated level increase the auditor's change of detecting material misstatements by decreasing the risk that offsetting factors may obscure material misstatements. The appropriate level of aggregation to use for analytical procedures is influenced by the entity's nature, size, and complexity.

When planning analytical procedures, the auditor should set the materiality thresholds for acceptable deviations from expected amounts. The amount of an acceptable deviation from the expected amount should be less than what is considered material when those deviations are combined with other errors in other account balances and classes of transactions. As the auditor's assessment of the risk of material misstatement increases, the persuasiveness of the audit evidence obtained should also increase. Therefore, as the assessed risk increases, the auditor's level of acceptable deviation from the expected amount will decrease.

Analytical procedures performed to assist in forming an overall conclusion

Analytical procedures performed near the end of the audit to assist the auditor in forming an overall conclusion may be similar to those used as risk assessment procedures. These procedures may include reading the financial statements, considering the adequacy of evidence obtained related to unusual or unexpected balances identified during the audit, and considering unusual or unexpected balances or relationships that were not previously identified. If the results of these analytical procedures reveal a previously unidentified risk of material misstatement, the auditor is required to revise his or her assessment of the risks of material misstatement and modify further planned audit procedures as appropriate.

Investigating results of analytical procedures

When the auditor is investigating differences between identified relationships and their expected values, he or she may obtain audit evidence relevant to management's responses by evaluating those responses in the context of the understanding of the entity and its environment and other audit evidence obtained during the course of the audit. Circumstances in which the auditor may find it necessary to perform other audit procedures may occur when management is unable to provide an explanation or when management's explanation combined with the evidence obtained relevant to management's response is not sufficient.

Practitioner's Aids

Exhibit AU-C 520-1 and Exhibit AU-C 520-2 are examples of audit documentation that could be used to document the performance and results of analytical procedures. Exhibit AU-C 520-3 illustrates an approach to the performance of final analytical review.

EXHIBIT AU-C 520-1—DOCUMENTATION OF THE EFFECT OF ANALYTICAL PROCEDURES ON THE PLANNING OF SUBSTANTIVE AUDIT PROCEDURES

Use this audit schedule to document the effect of analytical procedures on planned substantive audit procedures. The evaluation of the preliminary condition's effect on planned substantive audit procedures is preliminary, and the nature, extent, and timing of audit procedures may be revised based on additional information obtained during the engagement.

Client   Name:

_____

Date of Financial Statements: _____

Preliminary Condition	*Implication of Preliminary Condition on Planning Substantive Audit Procedures*	*Substantive Audit Documentation Reference*
• **Account Balance/Transaction:**	Nature of Procedure:	
Description of preliminary condition:		
	Timing of Procedure:	
	Extent of Procedure:	
• **Account Balance/Transaction:**	Nature of Procedure:	
Description of preliminary condition:		
	Timing of Procedure:	
	Extent of Procedure:	
• **Account Balance/Transaction:**	Nature of Procedure:	
Description of preliminary condition:		
	Timing of Procedure:	
	Extent of Procedure:	
• **Account Balance/Transaction:**	Nature of Procedure:	
Description of preliminary condition:		
	Timing of Procedure:	
	Extent of Procedure:	
• **Account Balance/Transaction:**	Nature of Procedure:	
Description of preliminary condition:		
	Timing of Procedure:	
	Extent of Procedure:	

Analysis Performed by: _____

Date: _____

Reviewed by: _____

Date: _____

EXHIBIT AU-C 520-2—PERFORMANCE OF ANALYTICAL PROCEDURES

Use this form to document the performance of analytical procedures. The form is only a guide, and professional judgment should be exercised to determine how the form should be modified by omitting or adding analytical procedures.

Client Name: _____

Date of Financial Statements: _____

COMPARISON OF CURRENT FINANCIAL STATEMENTS WITH COMPARABLE PRIOR-PERIOD FINANCIAL STATEMENTS

The following ratios were computed:

_____ Using financial data that reflect adjustments proposed to date.

_____ Using financial data that do not reflect adjustments.

	Formula
LIQUIDITY RATIOS	
1. Current ratio	Current Assets
	Current Liabilities
2. Acid-test ratio	Quick Assets
	Current Liabilities
3. Days' sales in accounts receivable	Average Accounts Receivable × 365 Days
	Net Credit Sales
4. Current liabilities to total assets	Current Liabilities
	Total Assets
ACTIVITY RATIOS	
1. Inventory turnover	Cost of Goods Sold
	Average Inventory
2. Receivable turnover	Net Credit Sales
	Average Accounts Receivable
OTHER RATIOS	
1. Asset turnover	Net Sales
	Average Total Assets
2. Gross profit percentage	Gross Profit
	Net Sales
PROFITABILITY RATIOS	
1. Bad debt to sales	Bad Debt Expense
	Net Sales
2. Return on assets	Net Income
	Average Total Assets
3. Return on equity	Net Income
	Average Total Equity
4. Net margin	Net Income
	Net Sales
COVERAGE RATIOS	
1. Debt to total assets	Total Debt
	Total Assets
2. Interest expense to sales	Interest Expense
	Net Sales
3. Number of times interest earned	Income before Interest and Taxes

Formula

OTHER RATIOS

	Ratio	Formula
1.	Effective tax rate	$\dfrac{\text{Income Taxes}}{\text{Income Before Taxes}}$
2.	Bad debt rate	$\dfrac{\text{Allowance for Bad Debts}}{\text{Accounts Receivable}}$
3.	Depreciation rate	$\dfrac{\text{Depreciation Expense}}{\text{Average Depreciable Property}}$
4.	Accounts payable to purchases	$\dfrac{\text{Accounts Payable}}{\text{Purchases}}$
5.	Dividend rate	$\dfrac{\text{Dividends}}{\text{Common Stock (Par)}}$
6.	Interest rate	$\dfrac{\text{Interest Expense}}{\text{Average Interest - Bearing Debt}}$
7.	Payroll rate	$\dfrac{\text{Payroll Expense}}{\text{Net Sales}}$
8.	Dividend return	$\dfrac{\text{Dividend Income}}{\text{Average Equity Investments}}$
9.	Interest income return	$\dfrac{\text{Interest Income}}{\text{Average Debt Investments}}$

OTHER

COMPARISON OF CURRENT FINANCIAL STATEMENTS WITH ANTICIPATED RESULTS

			20XX	
Acct #	Account Name	Actual	Budgeted	Difference
	Cash in bank—name			
	Petty cash			
	Cash in bank—payroll			
	Investment—marketable equity securities (current)			
	Allowance for decline in market value—marketable equity securities (current)			
	Accounts receivable			
	Allowance for doubtful accounts			
	Other receivables (current)			
	Accrued interest receivable			
	Notes receivable (current)			
	Discount on notes receivable			
	Dividends receivable			
	Inventory (year-end balance)			
	Prepaid insurance			
	Prepaid rent			
	Prepaid advertising			
	Land			
	Buildings			
	Accumulated depreciation—buildings			

Acct #	Account Name	Actual	20XX Budgeted	Difference
	Delivery equipment			
	Accumulated depreciation—delivery equipment			
	Fixtures			
	Accumulated depreciation—fixtures			
	Office equipment			
	Accumulated depreciation—Office equipment			
	Property—capital leases			
	Investment—marketable equity securities (noncurrent)			
	Allowance for decline in market value—marketable equity securities (noncurrent)			
	Deferred bond issuance costs			
	Other receivables (noncurrent)			
	Investment—convertible bonds			
	Land held for investment			
	Accounts payable			
	Accrued liabilities			
	Payroll taxes and other withholdings			
	Interest payable			
	Notes payable			
	Discounts/premiums—notes payable			
	Obligations—capital leases (current)			
	Dividends payable			
	Income taxes payable			
	Notes payable (noncurrent)			
	Bonds payable			
	Discounts/premiums—bonds payable			
	Obligations—capital leases (noncurrent)			
	Common stock			
	Paid-in capital in excess of par			
	Unappropriated retained earnings			
	Appropriated retained earnings			
	Unrealized loss—marketable equity securities (noncurrent)			
	Sales			
	Sales returns and allowances			
	Sales discounts			
	Cost of goods sold			
	Purchases			
	Freight-in			
	Bad debt expense			
	Utilities expense			
	Travel expense			
	Advertising expense			
	Delivery expense			
	Miscellaneous expense			
	Insurance expense			
	Rent expense			
	Professional fees expense			
	Salaries and wages expense			
	Payroll taxes expense			
	Depreciation expense—buildings			
	Depreciation expense—delivery equipment			
	Depreciation expense—fixtures			
	Depreciation expense—office equipment			
	Depreciation expense—capital leases			
	Repairs and maintenance expense			
	Miscellaneous income			
	Extraordinary items			
	Dividend income			

Acct #	Account Name	Actual	20XX Budgeted	Difference
	Interest income			
	Interest expense			
	Loss/gain on sale of assets			
	Unrealized loss—marketable equity securities			
	Recovery of market reduction of marketable equity securities (current) recorded in prior years			
	Loss on exchange of assets			
	Loss due to permanent decline in value of security investments			
	Loss/gain on sale of investments			
	Income tax expense			
	Totals			

Prepared   By:

_____

Reviewed   By:

_____

STUDY OF FINANCIAL STATEMENT ELEMENTS AND UNEXPECTED RELATIONSHIPS

Unexpected Relationships   Summary of Analysis

     _____   _____

     _____   _____

     _____   _____

     _____   _____

     _____   _____

     _____   _____

OTHER ANALYTICAL PROCEDURES

Summary of findings: _____

_____

_____

_____

_____

Prepared By: _____

Date: _____

Reviewed By: _____

Date: _____

EXHIBIT AU-C 520-3—EXAMPLE OF FINAL ANALYTICAL REVIEW

Client: _____

Name: _____

At this stage of the engagement it is important to consider the financial statements as a whole in light of the audit evidence that has been accumulated and in light of known and likely user expectations. The objective of this phase of the audit is to answer one very important question about the statement as they are presented:

Do these financial statement make sense?   Yes _____   No _____

Consider the following broad significant financial statement categories (please check):

Cash	_____
Accounts receivable	_____
Inventory	_____
Fixed assets	_____
Investments	_____
Accounts payable & accrued expenses	_____
Notes payable	_____
Equity	_____
Revenues	_____
Cost of goods sold	_____
Payroll	_____
Other expenses	_____

		Yes	No	N/A
1.	Do they appear reasonable compared to			
	a. Prior years?	_____	_____	_____
	b. Industry norms?	_____	_____	_____
	c. Current budget?	_____	_____	_____
2.	Do related data within the statement appear to be congruent? For example	_____	_____	_____
	a. Cost of sales compared to sales?	_____	_____	_____
	b. Cost of sales compared to inventory?	_____	_____	_____
	c. Payroll taxes, benefits, workers' compensation, compared to payroll?	_____	_____	_____
	d. Current assets compared to current liabilities?	_____	_____	_____
	e. Percent relations of income statement amounts to gross income?	_____	_____	_____
	f. Percent relations of significant expenses to total expenses?	_____	_____	_____
	g. Percent relation of significant assets/liabilities to total assets?	_____	_____	_____

	Yes	No	N/A
3. Is there known nonfinancial information that corroborates financial data in the statements?	_____	_____	_____

Explain:

_____

_____

_____

4. Attach a draft copy of statements to this workpaper and make notations on them as appropriate.

SECTION 530

AUDIT SAMPLING

Authoritative Pronouncements

SAS-122—Statements on Auditing Standards: Clarification and Recodification

Overview

Auditors obtain appropriate audit evidence by performing audit procedures sufficient to afford a reasonable basis for an opinion on the financial statements. "Audit evidence" represents all the information used by an auditor in arriving at the conclusions that support his or her audit opinion.

Examining the documentation for every transaction of a business is costly and time-consuming. Because most audit objectives do not require that amount of evidence, auditors frequently use sampling techniques and procedures. AU-C 530 provides guidance regarding the auditor's use of statistical and non-statistical sampling when designing and selecting the audit sample, performing test of controls and tests of details, and evaluating sample results. The auditor's objective in using audit sampling is to provide a reasonable basis for drawing conclusions about the population from which the sample is selected.

PLANNING AID REMINDER: AU-C 530 notes that there may be reasons other than performing sampling why an auditor would examine fewer than all of the items in a given population and that under these circumstances, the guidelines established in AU-C 530 are not applicable. One example is the auditor's performance of risk-assessment procedures to obtain an understanding of the entity and its environment, including its internal controls. Another example is an auditor deciding to confirm all receivables that have a balance of $1,000 or more. Previous AICPA Audit Risk Alerts point out that in this case the results of the confirmed items cannot be projected to the total balance of accounts receivable, because the auditor has not drawn a sample from all of the receivables. Sampling results cannot be projected to the population as a whole unless all of the items in the total population have had some chance for selection.

AU-C 530 endorses both a non-statistical approach and a statistical approach to sampling by concluding that either approach can provide sufficient audit evidence, as required by the third standard of fieldwork. Both non-statistical and statistical sampling are based on judgment, and the same factors are used in both approaches in order to determine the appropriate sample size and to evaluate the sample results.

PLANNING AID REMINDER: For additional guidance, auditors may wish to reference the AICPA Audit Guide *Audit Sampling*, which provides practical guidance for auditors on the use of non-statistical and statistical sampling in auditing.

Definitions

Audit sampling (sampling)	Selection and evaluation of a sample of items from a population of relevance to the audit (i.e., less than 100 percent of the population) such that the auditor expects the sample to be representative of the population and likely to provide a reasonable basis for conclusions about the population. A representative sample will result in conclusions that, subject to sampling risk limitations, are similar to those that would be drawn if the same procedures were applied to the population.
Population	The entire set of data from which a sample is selected and about which the auditor wishes to draw conclusions.
Sampling risk	The risk that the auditor's conclusion based on a sample may be different from the conclusion if the entire population was subjected to the same audit procedure. Sampling risk can lead to two types of erroneous conclusions:

1. The conclusion that controls are more effective than they actually are in a test of controls or that a material misstatement does not exist when it actually does in a test of details. This is the type of erroneous conclusion of primary concern to the auditor because it affects audit effectiveness and is more likely to lead to an inappropriate audit opinion.

2. The conclusion that controls are less effective than they actually are in a test of controls or that a material misstatement exists when it actually does not in a test of details. This type of erroneous conclusion affects audit efficiency as it usually leads to additional work to establish that initial audit conclusions were incorrect, but audit effectiveness is not impacted.

Nonsampling risk	The risk that the auditor reaches an erroneous conclusion for any reason not related to sampling risk.
Sampling unit	Individual items constituting a population (may be physical items or monetary units).
Statistical sampling	An approach to sampling characterized by random selection of the sample items and the use of an appropriate statistical technique to evaluate sample results, including measurement of sampling risk. A sampling approach without these characteristics is considered non-statistical sampling.
Stratification	The process of dividing a population into subpopulations, each of which is a group of sampling units intended to have similar characteristics (often monetary value).
Tolerable misstatement	A monetary amount set by the auditor for which the auditor seeks to obtain an appropriate level of assurance that the set amount is not exceeded by the population's actual misstatement.
Tolerable rate of deviation	A rate of deviation set by the auditor for which the auditor seeks to obtain an appropriate level of assurance that the set deviation rate is not exceeded by the population's actual deviation rate.

Requirements

The auditor is presumptively required to use the following procedures when using audit sampling:

1. Consider the purpose of the audit procedure and the characteristics of the population from which the sample will be drawn when designing an audit sample.

2. Determine a sample size that will reduce sampling risk to an acceptably low level.

3. Select items for the sample such that there is a reasonable expectation that the sample is representative of the relevant population and likely to provide a reasonable basis for conclusions about the population.

4. Perform appropriate audit procedures on each item selected.

5. If an audit procedure is not applicable to a selected item, perform the procedure on a replacement item.

6. If unable to apply designed or suitable alternative audit procedures to a selected item, treat that item as a deviation from the prescribed control in a test of controls or a misstatement in a test of details.

7. Investigate the nature and cause of any identified deviations or misstatements and evaluate their possible effect on the purpose of the audit procedure and on other areas of the audit.

8. Project audit sampling results to the population.

9. Evaluate sample results, sampling risk, and whether the use of audit sampling provided a reasonable basis for conclusions about the population tested.

Analysis and Application of Procedures

Sample Design

The auditor considers the purpose to be achieved and the combination of audit procedures likely to achieve that purpose when designing an audit sample. Considering this information helps the auditor to determine what population to sample and what conditions constitute a deviation or misstatement. The auditor is required to perform audit procedures to obtain evidence that the population from which the sample is drawn is complete. By considering the conditions constituting a deviation or misstatement, the auditor helps ensure that his or her evaluation of deviations or projection of misstatements contains all the deviations and misstatements and only conditions representing deviations or misstatements.

ENGAGEMENT STRATEGY: Even if the auditor finds a condition during an audit procedure that does not constitute a deviation or misstatement, that condition may have an important effect on other areas of the audit.

When considering the characteristics of the population from which the sample will be drawn, the auditor may determine that the expected rate of deviation for a test of controls or the expected misstatement in a test of details is high. If the expected rate of deviation is unacceptably high, the auditor normally chooses not to perform the test of controls. If the expected misstatement is high, the auditor may use a larger sample size or examine the entire population in a test of details.

Nonsampling risk is a factor to be considered in the audit that cannot be measured, but it can be reduced to an acceptable level if an effective quality control system is implemented and the audit is adequately planned and supervised. Examples of nonsampling risk are (1) the selection of inappropriate auditing procedures and (2) the failure to identify an error on a document that the auditor is examining.

Sample Size

The auditor is responsible for obtaining sufficient appropriate audit evidence to reduce audit risk to an acceptably low level, allowing the auditor to draw reasonable conclusions on which to base the audit opinion. Sampling risk occurs because fewer than 100% of the sample units in a population are reviewed. For this reason, the auditor can reduce sampling risk by increasing the size of the sample. As detection risk for a specific audit objective decreases, the auditor's allowable risk of incorrect acceptance for the test of details decreases and the required sample size for the test increases.

FRAUD POINTER: AU-C 240 notes that one of the auditor's overall responses to the risk of material misstatement due to fraud is to change the extent of audit procedures applied. When the risk of material misstatement due to fraud is considered high, auditors may decide to increase sample sizes or test the entire population instead of using a sample.

Sample size determination is influenced by many factors, such as the following.

For test of controls:

- Tolerable rate of deviation
- Expected rate of deviation for the population to be tested
- The desired level of assurance that the population's actual deviation rate does not exceed the tolerable deviation rate, which may be determined based on the extent to which the auditor's risk assessment takes relevant controls into account
- The number of sampling units in a very small population (for example, fewer than 500 sampling units)

For substantive tests of details:

- The desired level of assurance that the actual population misstatement does not exceed the tolerable misstatement, which may be determined based on the auditor's assessment of the risk of material misstatement and assurance obtained from other substantive procedures relating to the same assertion

- To determine the desired level of assurance, the auditor would consider:

  - Tolerable misstatement

  - Expected misstatement for the population

  - Stratification of the population when performed

  The number of sampling units in each stratum (for some sampling methods)

The auditor should not decide between using statistical or non-statistical sampling approaches based on sample size. Both approaches generally result in a similar sample size and the auditor using a non-statistical approach need not compute the corresponding sample size using statistical techniques. If the auditor uses a statistical approach, sample size will be determined from formulas or tables based on the factors described above. If a non-statistical approach is used, the auditor uses professional judgment to apply the above factors in determining sample size.

Selecting Items for Testing

When selecting items for testing, the auditor may first examine items that have a higher risk of material misstatement and then use sampling to estimate some characteristic for the rest of the population. Statistical sampling selects items using random selection methods, including simple random, systematic random, monetary unit, and probability weighted selection. Non-statistical sampling uses haphazard or random-based selection to select sample items. The methods of selecting samples most frequently used are random, systematic, and haphazard selection.

Performing Audit Procedures

When the auditor is unable to perform an audit procedure on a selected item, a replacement item may be used if the inability to perform the procedure does not represent a deviation from appropriate procedures by the entity. However, if the auditor's inability to perform an audit procedure on a selected item occurs because of a lack of evidence the entity should have, the auditor will need to evaluate the effect on the audit. The auditor should consider the items unable to be examined as deviations or misstatements and evaluate the effect on the sample results. If sample results do not change, examination of the items may not be necessary; if sample results do change such that the auditor would conclude there is a material misstatement or rate of deviation, the auditor is required to perform alternative audit procedures that would provide sufficient appropriate audit evidence to form a conclusion.

FRAUD POINTER: In these circumstances, the auditor should also consider whether the reasons for his or her inability to examine the selected items have implications on the assessment of risks of material misstatement due to fraud, the assessed level of control risk the auditor expects to be supported, or the degree of reliance on management representations.

Nature and Cause of Deviations and Misstatements

In examining the nature and causes of identified deviations and misstatements, the auditor should consider the qualitative aspects of the misstatements, including whether they were caused by fraud or error. Deviations and misstatements caused by fraud require a broader consideration of potential implications than those caused by error. The auditor may also notice a common feature in identified deviations or misstatements that may cause the auditor to extend his or her audit procedures to all the items in the population with that common feature.

ENGAGEMENT STRATEGY: The auditor may also request that management examine a class of transactions, account balance, or disclosure to understand the cause of an identified misstatement, determine the actual misstatement amount, and adjust the financial statements appropriately.

Projecting Misstatements

The auditor projects misstatements found in the sample in a test of details to the population, which provides an impression of the scale of the misstatement but may not be sufficient to determine an amount to be recorded. For tests of controls, the sample deviation rate represents the projected deviation rate for the population so no projection is necessary.

Evaluating Audit Sample Results

If, in a test of controls, there is an unexpectedly high sample deviation rate, the assessed risks of material misstatement may be increased unless additional audit evidence is obtained supporting the initial assessment. If, in a test of details, there is an unexpectedly high misstatement amount in the sample, the auditor may conclude that a class of transactions or account balance is materially misstated unless further audit evidence is obtained that no material misstatement exists.

The tolerable misstatement amount set by the auditor is related to performance materiality. Performance materiality levels are determined to address the risk that when immaterial misstatements are aggregated, they may cause a material misstatement of the financial misstatements if a margin for potential undetected misstatements is not provided. Tolerable misstatement is the auditor's application of performance materiality to a particular sampling procedure and it may be the same or lower than the performance materiality level.

The projected misstatement is the auditor's best estimate of misstatement in a population in a test of details. As the projected misstatement amount approaches or exceeds the tolerable misstatement, the likelihood that the population's actual misstatement exceeds the tolerable misstatement increases. Also, if the projected misstatement is higher than the auditor's expectations, this could mean there is an unacceptable sampling risk that the actual population misstatement exceeds the tolerable misstatement. Under these circumstances, the auditor may consider the results of other audit procedures to assess the risks that the actual population misstatement exceeds the tolerable misstatement, and additional audit evidence may be obtained to reduce that risk.

If the auditor concludes that audit sampling has not provided a reasonable basis for conclusions about the tested population, the auditor may:

- Request management investigate identified misstatements and the potential for further misstatements and make any necessary adjustments; or

- Tailor the nature, timing, and extent of further audit procedures to best achieve the required assurance.

Sampling Tests of Controls (Non-Statistical and Statistical Sampling Approaches)

As stated earlier, attribute sampling measures the frequency of a specific occurrence in a particular population. This sampling technique is used to discover how often exceptions occur in the population under examination. Thus, attribute sampling is concerned with the qualitative characteristics of a sample—with tests of controls, which the auditor must perform in order to assess control risk at less than the maximum level.

Promulgated Procedures Checklist

1. Determine the objectives of the test.
2. Define the deviation conditions.
3. Define the population:
   a. Define the period covered by the test.
   b. Define the sampling unit.
   c. Consider the completeness of the population.
4. Determine the method of selecting the sample:
   a. Random-number sampling
   b. Systematic sampling
   c. Other sampling
5. Determine the sample size:
   a. Consider the allowable risk of assessing control risk too low.
   b. Consider the maximum rate of deviations from prescribed internal controls that would support the auditor's planned assessed level of control risk (tolerable rate).
   c. Consider the expected population deviation rate.
   d. Consider the effect of the population size.
   e. Consider statistical or non-statistical sampling methods.
6. Perform the sampling plan.
7. Evaluate the sample results:

    a. Calculate the deviation rate.

    b. Consider the sampling risk.

    c. Consider the qualitative aspects of the deviations.

    d. Reach an overall conclusion.

  8. Document the sampling procedures.

Analysis and Application of Procedures

Step 1—Determine the objectives of the test

Generally, the use of sampling techniques in tests of controls applies only to those internal controls that generate documentary evidence. Thus, sampling techniques generally cannot be used in tests of controls for segregation of duties or the competency of personnel.

Tests of controls are concerned with determining whether a client's internal control operates in accordance with prescribed policies. Each internal control procedure has an objective and prescribed rules to obtain that objective. For example, in the credit department of a business, a control might state that orders must be appropriately approved for acceptance of credit risk before being processed. The objective of this control is to ensure that credit is approved before an order is accepted. This control must also include the prescribed rules for attaining the objective. One of the rules for attaining this particular objective for the credit department might be that no additional credit may be extended to any customer who has an outstanding balance more than sixty days old. The head of the credit department is responsible for ensuring that this control and its pre-scribed rules are consistently followed.

Every control objective must have one or more stated control techniques, which are designed to achieve the control objective.

Controls may be classified as preventive or detective. Preventive controls are established to prevent errors from occurring. Detective controls are established to detect errors that have occurred.

When performing tests of controls, the auditor must determine whether a specific internal control operates as designed and whether the control objective is being achieved. In this respect the auditor might be concerned with (1) who performed the control, (2) where the control was performed, and (3) whether the control was performed in accordance with prescribed policy.

The audit objective must be defined in terms of specific compliance charac-teristics that can be tested.

FRAUD POINTER: To address the ever-present risk of management override of internal control, AU-C 240 requires the auditor to examine journal entries and other adjustments for evidence of possible material misstatement due to fraud. One objective of the auditor's examination of journal entries is to determine the effectiveness of internal controls over journal entries and other adjustments. In light of the volume of journal entries to be examined as part of testing controls related to the journal entry process, auditors are likely to base their testing on samples of journal entries. Thus, the auditor's objective in this sample application is to obtain evidence that the internal controls over the journal entry process operate effectively.

PUBLIC COMPANY IMPLICATIONS: Sarbanes-Oxley Act of 2002 (SOX) requires all accelerated filer public companies to issue a report by the auditor on the effectiveness of the entity's internal control over financial reporting. To provide the basis for the auditor's report on internal control, he or she performs tests of controls over financial reporting. In many circumstances, the auditor performs tests of controls of samples selected from the population of transactions subject to the internal controls being examined. Thus, the guidance in this section is especially relevant to public company auditors.

Step 2—Define the deviation conditions

A *deviation* is a departure from the prescribed internal control. The auditor must identify any significant deviation conditions that exist in a control. A significant deviation condition exists when a necessary step to achieve a particular internal control objective is not performed as prescribed. The auditor might consider that some internal controls, such as multiple approvals, are unimportant and need not be tested.

Step 3—Define the population

The population selected for examination must be complete and must provide the auditor with the opportunity to satisfy the established audit objective. A sample should be selected in a manner that is representative of the population from which it is selected. If the population is not complete in all respects, the selected sample will not be representative of the complete population. For example, the audit objective may be to determine whether all goods that are shipped are properly billed. For this audit objective, the auditor should define the population as bills of lading or other shipping records prepared during the audit period—rather than sales invoices, which may or may not represent goods that have been shipped.

Step 3a—Define the period covered by the test

A conclusion can be drawn about a population only if all items in the population have a chance of being selected for examination. The population from which the sample is selected should include all transactions for the accounting period under examination. However, professional standards recognize that it may be appropriate to perform tests of controls at interim dates and review subsequent transactions when the auditor performs year-end audit procedures.

Step 3b—Define the sampling unit

A population consists of a number of sampling units, such as canceled checks or sales invoices. For example, if the audit objective is to determine whether vouchers have been properly approved, the sampling items may be the line items in the voucher register rather than the checks used to pay the vouchers. Once the auditor adequately defines the population, the sample unit should not be difficult to define.

Step 3c—Consider the completeness of the population

The physical representation of the population must be consistent with the definition of the population. For example, the auditor might be concerned with all cash disbursements made during the period and define the population as all canceled checks during the period. The auditor must determine that the defined population is complete; otherwise, a representative sample cannot be drawn from the population.

Step 4—Determine the method of selecting the sample

Sampling units must be selected from the defined population so that each sampling unit has a chance of being selected. AU-C 530 requires that a representative sample be selected for both non-statistical sampling and statistical sampling. When statistical sampling is used, the sample must be selected on an unbiased basis (usually a random selection).

ENGAGEMENT STRATEGY: AU-C 530 notes that auditors should select sample items so that the sample is representative of the population. A representative sample is one in which all items in a population have an equal opportunity of being included in the sample. A randomly selected sample meets that definition, and random selection is often the technique used to select samples for statistical sampling applications. However, auditors also often use random selection techniques for non-statistical sampling plans to increase the likelihood that those samples are representative of the population. The use of a representative sample reduces sampling risk.

Step 4a—Random-number sampling

A sample may be selected from the population on a random basis using random numbers generated by a computer or numbers chosen from a random-number table.

Step 4b—Systematic sampling

The auditor may select a random sample using the systematic-selection method, whereby every n th item is selected. Systematic selection is also referred to as sequential sampling. The following steps should be followed when systematic selection is used:

1. Determine the population (N).
2. Determine the sample size (n).
3. Compute the interval size by dividing N by n.
4. Select a random start (a random-number table can be used to determine the starting point).

5. Determine the sample items selected by successively adding the interval to the random starting point.

To illustrate the systematic-selection method, assume that the auditor has defined the population as 3,000 sales invoices listed in the sales journal (*N*) and would like to select 100 sales invoices for testing (*n*). Thus, the interval is every thirtieth sales invoice (3,000/100). If it is assumed that the auditor selects the number 12 as a random starting point, the first sales invoice selected would be the twelfth invoice, the second would be the forty-second invoice (12 + 30), and so on, until the sample of 100 items is selected.

A client might summarize or group a population in a specific order, and thus such a population would not be random. A sample selected from a non-random population using the systematic-selection method might not be appropriate for drawing statistical conclusions about a population, unless the auditor takes steps to solve the randomness problem. The auditor should examine the population to determine whether it has been grouped or summarized in a particular order. Inquiries of client personnel may also be made to ascertain how individual transactions are accumulated or individual balances listed. If the population is in a specific order, it should be stratified and proportional samples should be drawn from each stratum. In this event, the auditor might want to test one or more of the strata more extensively.

Even if the population is not in a specific order, it usually is advisable for the auditor to have two or more random starts.

Step 4c—Other sampling

Block sampling refers to selecting contiguous sampling units, such as all checks numbered from 420 to 440. Block sampling cannot be used when the auditor uses a statistical sampling approach. When the auditor uses only a few blocks to select the sample, block sampling also would be inappropriate for a non-statistical sampling approach.

Haphazard sampling consists of selecting sampling units without any conscious bias. For example, the selection would be biased if the auditor had a tendency to select vendor folders that had the most vendor invoices in them. If properly applied, haphazard sampling can be used for non-statistical sampling but not for a statistical sampling approach.

Step 5—Determine the sample size

A considerable amount of professional judgment is necessary to determine the proper sample size. The method for reaching a decision for determining the sample size is the same for non-statistical sampling as it is for statistical sampling. In statistical sampling, the auditor will quantify the factors that are used to determine the sample size; in non-statistical sampling, the factors will be described in subjective terms. For example, in statistical sampling, the auditor may conclude that a 10% factor should be assigned to the risk of assessing control risk too low. In non-statistical sampling, the auditor may conclude that the client's internal controls appear to be well-designed. Both conclusions are highly subjective and are based on the same fundamental analysis, although the conclusion associated with statistical sampling is more precise.

EXHIBIT AU-C 530-1—AUDIT JUDGMENT FACTORS USED IN NON-STATISTICAL AND STATISTICAL SAMPLING TO DETERMINE SAMPLE SIZE FOR TESTS OF CONTROLS

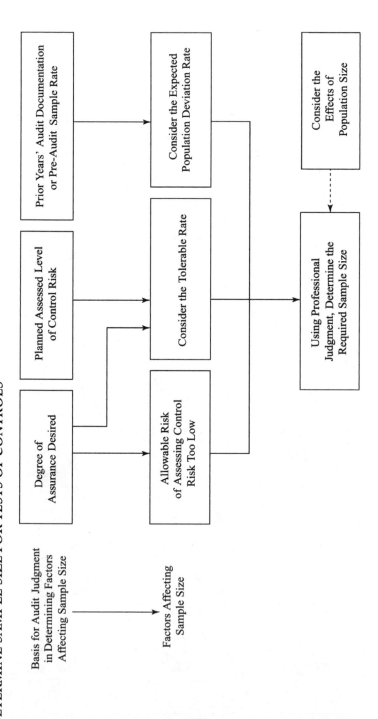

The audit decision process as described in SAS-39 is summarized in Exhibit AU 350-1.

Step 5a—Consider the allowable risk of assessing control risk too low

The level of sampling risk is influenced by the size of the sample. There is always a risk that the auditor will not draw a representative sample. The larger the sample, the more audit hours it takes to test the sample. Achieving an acceptable level of sampling risk is the result of a trade-off between trying to avoid overauditing on the one hand and underauditing on the other.

Establishing an allowable risk of assessing control risk too low is a function of the degree of assurance indicated by the audit evidence selected as part of the sample process. If the auditor desires a high degree of assurance, it is necessary to establish a relatively small risk of assessing control risk too low. Establishing a small risk of assessing control risk too low will require that (assuming all other factors remain constant) the auditor increase the size of the sample. The larger the sample size, the higher the degree of assurance the auditor can offer about the effectiveness of internal control. For example, if using a non-statistical sample, the auditor must select a larger sample in order to establish a low risk of underestimating control risk rather than establishing a moderate risk of assessing control risk too low. When using statistical sampling, the auditor must select a larger sample size in order to make a statement about the maximum error rate at a 99% confidence level (or a 1% allowable risk of assessing control risk too low) rather than at a 90% confidence level.

Step 5b—Consider the tolerable rate

The "tolerable rate" is the maximum percentage of deviations (errors) in a population that an auditor will tolerate without changing the planned assessed level of control risk. The establishment of a tolerable rate in an engagement is based on (1) the planned assessed level of control risk and (2) the degree of assurance indicated by the audit evidence in the sample.

The planned assessed level of control risk results from obtaining an understanding of the client's internal control. Having gained an understanding of the client's internal control, the auditor then establishes the planned level of control risk, which in turn is a factor in determining the sample size for tests of control. For example, if an internal control is considered highly relevant to a critical financial statement assertion, the auditor would initially plan to rely relatively heavily on the control procedure and there would be a tendency to establish a small tolerable rate.

Step 5c—Consider the expected population deviation rate

The purpose of attribute sampling for non-statistical as well as statistical sampling is to provide some insight into the deviation rate of a particular characteristic in a population. For example, the auditor may be interested in the rate of pricing errors the client made in preparing customer invoices. However, before sampling can begin, the auditor must make a preliminary estimate of the deviation rate. The expected population deviation rate is the anticipated deviation rate in the entire population. Ideally, the estimate should be based on the results of audits of prior years, taking into consideration any subsequent modifications of the client's internal control. The auditor may review audit documentation for the last few years to obtain an idea of the expected population deviation rate. In a new engagement, the auditor can estimate the expected population deviation rate by selecting and auditing a preliminary sample of about 25 items. The results of the test should be properly documented, because the preliminary sample becomes part of the final sample.

As the expected population deviation rate approaches the tolerable rate that the auditor established, the required sample size increases because the auditor must make an allowance for sampling risk. That is, if the auditor establishes a tolerable rate of 5% but the preliminary estimate of the deviation rate is 4%, in most situations the risk is too great that the actual deviation rate is more than 5%. In non-statistical and statistical sampling it is misleading to think of estimating a single error rate. It is more useful to think of estimating an error range. In the current example, if the auditor is using non-statistical sampling, it is better to think of the preliminary estimate of the deviation rate of being somewhere around 4%. If statistical sampling is used, the auditor may state that the estimated deviation rate is 4% plus or minus 2% (a range between 2% and 6%). Clearly, when the expected population deviation rate for a particular internal control is equal to or greater than the tolerable rate, the auditor should establish the control risk at its maximum level and generally not complete the test of controls, at least for the particular control(s) under investigation.

Step 5d—Consider the effect of the population size

In most circumstances, the size of the population has little and sometimes no effect on the determination of the required sample size in attribute sampling.

Step 5e—Consider a statistical or non-statistical sampling method

The auditor may use either a non-statistical sampling method or a statistical sampling method.

Sample size and non-statistical sampling When using non-statistical sampling, the auditor takes into consideration the risk of assessing control risk too low, the tolerable rate, and the expected population deviation rate, and determines the sample size by professional judgment. The auditor should observe the following generalizations in determining the sample size when non-statistical sampling is employed:

- As the risk of assessing control risk too low increases, the required sample size decreases.
- As the risk of assessing control risk too low decreases, the required sample size increases.
- As the tolerable rate increases, the required sample size decreases.
- As the tolerable rate decreases, the required sample size increases.
- As the expected population deviation rate increases, the required sample size increases.

- As the expected population deviation rate decreases, the required sample size decreases.

Sample size and statistical sampling For statistical sampling, the auditor can use tables or computer applications to determine the appropriate sample size. To use either tables or computer applications, the following must be established by the auditor:

- The risk of assessing control risk too low
- The tolerable error rate
- The expected population deviation rate

For example, if an auditor established (1) the risk of assessing control risk too low at 5%, (2) a tolerable error rate of 9%, and (3) an expected population deviation rate of 4%, the required sample size would be about 100.

Step 6—Perform the sampling plan

After the sample has been selected, the auditor should apply audit procedures to each sampling unit to determine whether there has been a deviation from the established internal control procedure. Usually, a deviation occurs if the auditor is unable to perform an audit procedure or apply alternative audit procedures to a sampling unit. As a general rule, sampling units that are selected but not examined, such as voided transactions or unused documents, should be replaced with new sampling units. Voided transactions or unused documents are not considered deviations if the established procedure of accounting for these items has been properly followed.

Step 7—Evaluate the sample results

After the audit procedures have been applied to each sampling unit, and the deviations, if any, from the prescribed internal controls have been summarized, the auditor must evaluate the results of the sampling.

Step 7a—Calculate the deviation rate

The deviation rate is computed by dividing the number of deviations by the number of units in the sample. The sample deviation rate is the auditor's best estimate of the population deviation rate.

Step 7b—Consider the sampling risk

The auditor must consider the degree of sampling risk involved in the sample results. Sampling risk arises because the auditor does not examine all of the sampling units in a population. An auditor can reach an entirely different conclusion on the basis of sample results than if the entire population is examined. When the auditor's estimate of the population deviation is less than the tolerable rate for the population, there is still a possibility that the true deviation rate in the population (maximum population deviation) is greater than the tolerable rate. The auditor can determine the degree of sampling risk in the sample results by computing the maximum population deviation rate.

Sampling risk and non-statistical sampling When the auditor employs non-statistical sampling, the sampling risk cannot be quantified; the auditor should nonetheless take that risk into consideration in determining whether the potential error rate in the population is unacceptable. The auditor should observe the following generalizations when evaluating the results of non-statistical sampling:

- The auditor may rely on the planned assessed level of control risk when the auditor's best estimate of the population deviation rate (based on the sample results) is equal to or less than the expected population deviation rate.

- The auditor cannot rely on the planned assessed level of control risk when the auditor's best estimate of the population deviation rate is greater than the expected population deviation rate.

When the deviation rate is greater than the tolerable rate, the planned assessed level of control risk is not justified. Thus, the auditor may, for example, decide not to rely on the client's internal control (assess control risk at the maximum) in the performance of substantive procedures.

Sampling risk and statistical sampling When using statistical sampling, the auditor can use tables or computer applications to measure the allowance for sampling risk. To use either tables or computer applications, the following must be established by the auditor:

- The risk of assessing control risk too low
- The number of actual deviations found in the sample
- The sample size
- The expected deviation rate

To illustrate the above procedures, assume that the risk the auditor has established for assessing control risk too low is 5%, the sample size established by the auditor is 100, the tolerable rate established by the auditor is 9%, and the expected population deviation rate established by the auditor is 4%. If the auditor examines the 100 sample units and discovers two errors, the maximum population deviation rate (obtained from tables in Appendix A of the AICPA's *Audit Sampling* Guide) is 6.2%. The maximum population deviation rate is also referred to as the upper limits or the upper precision limits.

In the above illustration, the auditor can be 95% certain that the maximum population deviation rate is 6.2%. The 95% certainty percentage is the complement of the 5% risk factor (100% minus 5%). Since the maximum deviation rate of 6.2% is less than the tolerable rate of 9% established by the auditor, the planned assessed level of control risk is not changed. However, when the maximum population deviation rate is greater than the tolerable rate established by the auditor, the planned assessed level of control risk is not justified.

Step 7c—Consider the qualitative aspects of the deviations

The auditor should consider the qualitative aspects of each deviation. The nature and cause of each deviation should be analyzed and deviations should be classified into unintentional deviations (errors) or intentional deviations (acts of fraud). The auditor should make a determination about whether the deviation resulted from a misunderstanding of instructions or from carelessness. The discovery of an act of fraud would require more attention from the auditor than the discovery of an error.

Step 7d—Reach an overall conclusion

The auditor must determine whether the overall audit approach supports the planned assessed level of control risk. To make this overall evaluation, the auditor should consider the following factors:

- Sample results of tests of controls
- Results of inquiries about controls that do not leave an audit trail
- Results of observations concerning control procedures that are based on the segregation of responsibilities

Professional judgment is required in reaching a conclusion on how the results of the tests of controls will affect the nature, timing, and extent of the subsequent substantive procedures.

Step 8—Document the sampling procedures

The auditor should consider the following matters for documentation in the audit files:

- Description of internal controls tested
- Objective of the tests of controls
- Definition of population and sampling unit
- Definition of deviation conditions
- Method of determining sample size
- Method of sample selection
- Description of audit procedures employed and list of deviations discovered by the auditor [deviations should be classified as unintentional and (suspected) intentional acts]
- Evaluation of sample results and overall conclusions

Sampling in Tests of Details (Non-Statistical and Statistical Sampling Approaches)

Variable sampling (which is used in the performance of substantive tests of transactions and balances) is used to estimate the dollar value of a population and determine the reasonableness of financial statement balances. The purpose of substantive procedures is to obtain evidence of the validity and propriety of accounting balances and classes of transactions.

Promulgated Procedures Checklist

The auditor may use the following steps to apply variable sampling to substantive procedures:

1. Determine the audit objective of the test.
2. Define the population:

    a. Define the sampling unit.

    b. Consider the completeness of the population.

    c. Identify individually significant items.

3. Choose an audit sampling technique.

4. Determine the sample size:

    a. Consider variations within the population.

    b. Consider the acceptable level of risk.

    c. Consider the tolerable misstatement.

    d. Consider the expected amount of error.

    e. Consider the population size.

5. Determine the method of selecting the sample.

6. Perform the sampling plan.

7. Evaluate the sample results:

    a. Project the misstatement to the population and consider sampling risk.

    b. Consider the qualitative aspects of misstatements and reach an overall conclusion.

8. Document the sampling procedures.

Analysis and Application of Procedures

Step 1—Determine the audit objective of the test

The audit objective of performing substantive procedures is to determine whether the dollar value assigned by management to an account balance or group of transactions is reasonable.

Step 2—Define the population

The population the auditor defines must include all items that are related to the audit objective of the procedures. If items relevant to the audit objective are omitted from the population, the audit objective of the procedure will not be achieved. For example, the audit objective may be to determine whether the repairs and maintenance expense account is reasonably stated. The definition of the population could be all line items that make up the detail of the account, but such a definition would probably be deficient because other accounts—especially property, plant, and equipment—could contain expenditures that were capitalized when they should have been expensed. A better definition of the population would be all repairs and maintenance work orders authorized during the period.

Step 2a—Define the sampling unit

The population is made up of individual sampling units that may be individual transactions, documents, customer or vendor balances, or an individual entry. The auditor must consider the efficiency of the audit when selecting the sampling unit. For example, it may be more efficient to define the sampling unit as the individual sales invoice—rather than as the individual accounts receivable, which may be made up of several invoices.

Step 2b—Consider the completeness of the population

The physical representation of the population must be consistent with the definition of the population. For example, the auditor may be concerned with all cash disbursements made during the period and define the population as all canceled checks during the period. The auditor must determine that the defined population is complete; otherwise, a representative sample cannot be drawn from the population.

Step 2c—Identify individually significant items

The population should be reviewed for items that should be individually examined because of the audit exposure related to these items. Items that should be examined individually include large-dollar items, related-party transactions, and accounts with a history of errors. When items are examined individually, they are not part of the sampling results; however, these items must be considered in determining the possible misstatement in the population. There is, therefore, no sampling risk associated with these items.

Step 3—Choose an audit sampling technique

Initially, the auditor must determine whether a non-statistical or a statistical sampling approach should be employed. As stated earlier, AU-C 530 indicates no preference of one over the other. Whether a non-statistical or a statistical sampling approach is used, many different types of sampling techniques are used in practice. Irrespective of the sampling approach or specific sampling technique the auditor uses, he or she must observe the following steps in the performance of substantive procedures based on sampling.

Step 4—Determine the sample size

The auditor must use professional judgment to determine the sample size. The decision process for determining the sample size is the same for non-statistical sampling as it is for statistical sampling. In statistical sampling the auditor will quantify the relevant factors, whereas in non-statistical sampling the factors will be described in a less structured manner.

The audit decision process for determining the sample size as described in AU-C 530 is summarized in Exhibit AU-C 530-2.

Step 4a—Consider variations within the population

A basic concept in sampling is the need to obtain a representative sample from the population. If the population is composed of various items, the auditor must examine a sufficiently large sample to be reasonably assured that a representative sample has been selected.

For accounting populations, the variation within a population may be expressed in dollar amounts. It is not unusual for an accounting population to be composed of a few large balances, several medium balances, and numerous smaller balances. The required sample size increases as the variability in the population increases.

EXHIBIT AU-C 530-2—AUDIT JUDGMENT FACTORS USED TO DETERMINE SAMPLE SIZE FOR SUBSTANTIVE PROCEDURES

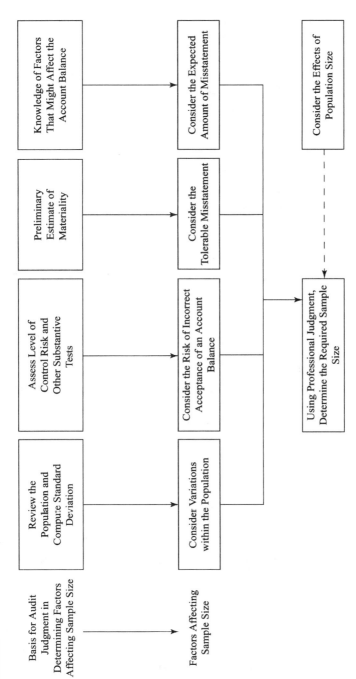

When nonstatistical sampling is employed, the auditor may review the population or the prior years' audit documentation to acquire an understanding of the variation within the population. When a classical variable statistical sampling technique is employed, the auditor measures the variation in the population by computing the estimate of the standard deviation of the sample mean.

It may be efficient to stratify a population with a high degree of variation. "Stratification" simply means that the population is divided into groups (strata) of sampling units that have the same or approximately the same dollar values, and samples are selected from each group. Stratification is necessary to reduce the effect of the variation in the population on the size of the sample. (In both nonstatistical sampling and statistical sampling, as the variation increases, the auditor needs to select a larger sample size.)

ENGAGEMENT STRATEGY: When probability proportional to size (PPS) sampling is used, there is no need to consider the variation within the population, because this technique automatically considers that factor since it is a combination of both attribute sampling and variable estimation.

Step 4b—Consider the acceptable level of risk

When considering whether to accept or reject the results of a sample, the auditor is faced with the risks of (1) incorrect rejection of a balance and (2) incorrect acceptance of a balance. The risk of incorrect rejection of a balance is the risk that the results of a sample will lead the auditor to conclude that the recorded account balance is materially misstated when, in fact, the recorded account balance is not materially misstated. The risk of incorrect acceptance of a balance is the risk that the results of a sample will lead the auditor to conclude that the recorded account balance is not materially misstated when, in fact, the recorded account balance is materially misstated.

In determining an acceptable level of risk of incorrect acceptance for tests of details, the auditor should consider (1) the assessed risk of material misstatement (inherent risk and control risk) and (2) the risk that other relevant substantive procedures (including substantive analytical procedures) would not detect a material misstatement. These risk factors and interrelationships must be considered in non-statistical sampling plans as well as in statistical sampling plans. These relationships are in the following manner:

$$TD = AR/(IR \times CR \times AP)$$

where:

- AR = the allowable audit risk that monetary misstatements equal to tolerable misstatement might remain undetected for the account balance or class of transactions and related assertions after the auditor has completed all audit procedures deemed necessary.

- IR = the susceptibility of an assertion to a material misstatement assuming there are no related internal controls.

- CR = the risk that a material misstatement that could occur in an assertion will not be prevented or detected on a timely basis by the entity's internal controls. (The auditor assesses control risk on the basis of the sufficiency of audit evidence obtained to support the effectiveness of internal controls.)

- AP = the risk that analytical procedures and other relevant substantive procedures would fail to detect misstatements that could occur in an assertion equal to tolerable misstatement, given that such misstatements occur and are not detected by the internal control.

- TD = the allowable risk of incorrect acceptance for the test of details, given that misstatements equal to tolerable misstatement occur in an assertion and are not detected by internal control or analytical procedures and other relevant substantive procedures.

The above equation emphasizes relationships among the various factors that the auditor must consider when determining the allowable risk of incorrect acceptance. For example, as control risk rises, the allowable risk of incorrect acceptance must decrease to achieve a stated level of audit risk. That relationship is based on the simple logic that as the perceived effectiveness of internal control decreases, the auditor is less willing to establish a high allowable risk of incorrect acceptance of an account balance. Stated in terms of its effect on sample size, it is necessary to increase the size of the sample as control risk increases to reduce the level of risk of incorrect acceptance. Thus, from the perspective of sample size and all other factors remaining constant, there is an inverse relationship between control risk and the allowable risk of incorrect acceptance.

Although the relationships established in the above equation are intuitive, it is unlikely that an auditor would assign an absolute value to audit risk; rather he or she would evaluate the risk in an abstract manner. Even when statistical sampling is employed, most auditors would use the relationships established by the equation as a guide, avoiding a strict and comprehensive quantitative approach arrived at by simply plugging in risk factors. Even if an auditor insists on a strictly quantitative approach, that does not imply that judgment has been removed from the process. In a strictly quantitative approach, the process may appear to be unbiased but, as discussed in this section, the risk factors are based on a number of decisions that depend heavily on professional judgments. Those judgments are the same for non-statistical sampling and statistical sampling.

Step 4c—Consider the tolerable misstatement

The tolerable misstatement is an estimate of the maximum monetary misstatement that may exist in an account balance or group of transactions when combined with misstatement in other accounts, without causing the financial statements to be materially misstated. The tolerable misstatement is based on the auditor's definition of "materiality," or the maximum amount by which the financial statements could be misstated and still be in accordance with generally accepted accounting principles. There is an inverse relationship between the tolerable misstatement and the required sample size. Thus, the sample size must be increased when the tolerable misstatement is decreased.

Tolerable misstatement is related to the auditor's planned level of materiality for the financial statements as a whole such that tolerable misstatement when combined for all planned audit procedures does not exceed materiality for the financial statements. Thus, auditors should set tolerable misstatement for a specific audit procedure at an amount less than the financial statements so that when the results are aggregated, the required level of overall assurance is obtained.

Step 4d—Consider the expected amount of misstatement

An estimate of the expected amount of misstatement in a particular account balance or group of transactions is based on the following factors:

- Understanding of the entity's business
- Prior years' tests of the population
- Results of a pre-audit sample
- Results of tests of controls

The required sample size increases as the auditor's estimate of the expected amount of misstatement in the population increases.

PLANNING AID REMINDER: In practice it is often difficult to determine the expected amount of misstatement, but this can be overcome by combining the effects of the tolerable misstatement and the expected amount of misstatement. This can be accomplished by establishing a materiality threshold and then dividing that amount by "about 2" in order to establish the tolerable misstatement. For example, if materiality is established at $100,000, then the tolerable misstatement would be about $50,000 ($100,000/2). Then only the (adjusted) tolerable misstatement would be used to determine the required sample size.

Step 4e—Consider the population size

The population size generally has an effect on the sample size, depending on which sampling technique the auditor employs.

Step 5—Determine the method of selecting the sample

The auditor must select sampling units from the defined population in such a way that each sampling unit has a chance of being selected. The auditor's objective is to select a representative sample of all items from the population. If statistical sampling is used, the sample selection must be random.

Step 6—Perform the sampling plan

Once the sample has been selected, the auditor should apply appropriate audit procedures. If the auditor is unable to perform an audit procedure on a sampling unit selected for examination, alternative audit procedures should be considered. If the sampling unit does not have an effect on the conclusion the auditor reaches concerning the acceptability of the population, alternative audit procedures do not have to be applied, and the sampling unit may be treated as a misstatement for evaluation purposes. In addition, the auditor should determine whether the inability to apply an audit procedure has an effect on the assessed level of control risk or the assessment of risk on representations made by the client.

Step 7—Evaluate the sample results

After testing the sample units, the auditor should evaluate the sample results to determine whether the account balance or group of transactions is correct and in accordance with generally accepted accounting principles.

Step 7a—Project the misstatement to the population and consider sampling risk

The misstatements discovered in the sampling units should be projected to the total population. In its simplest form, a $2,000 misstatement in a sample that represents 20% of the population would be projected as a total misstatement of $10,000 ($2,000/20%). The method of projecting the misstatement to the total population will depend on the type of sampling technique the auditor uses.

If the projected misstatement is greater than the tolerable misstatement, the account balance cannot be accepted as correct. If the projected misstatement is significantly less than the tolerable misstatement, the auditor may conclude that the account balance is not materially misstated. For example, if the projected misstatement is $10,000 and the tolerable misstatement is $50,000, in most instances the risk of accepting an incorrect balance would be acceptable. As the projected misstatement approaches the tolerable misstatement, the risk of accepting an incorrect balance increases, and the auditor must use professional judgment in deciding whether to accept a balance as correct. For example, if the projected misstatement is $40,000 and the tolerable misstatement is $50,000, in most instances the risk of accepting an incorrect balance would not be acceptable.

Step 7b—Consider the qualitative aspects of misstatements and reach an overall conclusion

Each misstatement the auditor discovers by testing the sample should be evaluated to determine why the misstatement was made and whether the misstatement has an effect on other phases of the engagement. For example, the discovery of a fraudulent act would have broader implication to the auditor than the discovery of a routine error.

The results of the substantive procedures may suggest that the assessed level of control risk was too low. Such a condition would require the auditor to consider whether substantive procedures should be expanded.

Step 8—Document the sampling procedures

The auditor should consider the following matters for documentation in the audit files:

- Description of audit procedures and objectives tested
- Definition of population and sampling unit
- Definition of a misstatement
- Basis for establishment of risk of incorrect acceptance, incorrect rejection, tolerable misstatement, and expected misstatement

- Audit sampling technique used
- Method of sampling selection
- Description of sampling procedures performed and list of misstatements discovered [deviations should be classified as unintentional and (suspected) intentional acts]
- Evaluation of sample and summary of overall conclusions

NON-STATISTICAL SAMPLING FOR TESTS OF DETAIL

This section is based on the discussion in the previous section, but it focuses exclusively on non-statistical sampling for tests of detail. The guidance provided here is based on material in Chapter 5 of the AICPA's Audit Guide *Audit Sampling* (a new edition of this Guide was released by the AICPA on May 1, 2008).

Promulgated Procedures Checklist

The auditor may use the following steps to apply non-statistical sampling concepts to tests of details:

- Identify individually significant items
- Determine the sample size
- Select the sample
- Evaluate the sample results

Analysis and Application of Procedures

Identify individually significant items

Initially the auditor should review the items that make up the population to determine whether certain items should be tested 100% rather than sampled. The items selected for 100% testing might be based on the dollar value of the item or unusual characteristics of the item. For example, an auditor may review the trial balance of accounts receivable and decide that all receivables that exceed $1,000 should be selected for confirmation. Generally larger-dollar amounts within a population are selected for 100% testing based on the auditor's judgment.

Determine the sample size

The size of the sample in non-statistical sampling is based on professional judgment. The auditor cannot simply decide to use a rule of thumb in all engagements and expect to satisfy professional standards or to perform an effective engagement. For example, if the auditor has a rule of thumb that he or she always confirms 10% of the dollar value of accounts receivable, that approach is a violation of generally accepted auditing standards.

The Audit Guide *Audit Sampling* points out that when an auditor uses non-statistical sampling to perform test of details, the following four factors (discussed in the previous section) must be taken into consideration:

1. Population variation

2. Risk of incorrect acceptance

3. Tolerable misstatement and expected misstatement

4. Population size

Although these factors sound like concepts that are found in a statistics course, they are actually based on common sense.

PLANNING AID REMINDER: Although the auditor must take the four factors listed above into consideration in determining the size of the sample, he or she does not have to quantify these factors. Also, some auditors believe that there is some simple solution to determining sample size that does not have to take into consideration the four factors listed above. There is no simple rule-of-thumb solution. An auditor must take these factors into consideration and use professional judgment to determine the size of a sample, even when non-statistical sampling is used.

Population variation

In general, the more homogenous the population, the smaller the sample size can be. That is, for example, if the trial balance of accounts receivable is made up of balances that range from $150 to $220, there is little variation in the population. For this reason, an auditor can test relatively few items in order to get a representative sample of the accounts receivable. On the other hand, if the range of balances in accounts receivable is from $5 to $25,000, this population exhibits more variability and it would be necessary to test a larger number of accounts receivable.

ENGAGEMENT STRATEGY: In practice it is unlikely that an accounting population will have as small degree of variation as suggested in the above paragraph; however, it is possible to divide the population into groupings (population stratification) and thus significantly reduce the degree of variation in each grouping. Also, it should be remembered that a group of the population may be tested 100% and evaluated separately. Stratification and testing some of the items 100% will almost always reduce the overall size of the sample.

The auditor can get a feel for the variation within a population by reviewing the items that make up the population. For example, a simple review of the trial balance of accounts receivable should give the auditor a reasonable impression of the variability of the population. A more precise measurement of variability can be determined quickly if the trial balance is digitized and can be subjected to analysis by various file analyzers. For example, if the trial balance of accounts receivable is maintained in a spreadsheet file, such as an Excel spreadsheet, it might be possible to create statistics such as the variance or standard deviation of the population.

Risk of incorrect acceptance

As discussed earlier in this section, an interplay exists among audit risk, inherent risk, and control risk. These relationships can be summarized as follows:

- When the combined inherent and control risks are assessed at a lower level, a greater risk of incorrect acceptance for planned substantive procedures can be established. Under this circumstance, the required sample size is decreased.

- When the combined inherent and control risks are assessed at a higher level, a lower risk of incorrect acceptance for planned substantive procedures can be established. Under this circumstance, the required sample size is increased.

- When the auditor relies more heavily on other substantive procedures (including analytical procedures) to achieve the same audit objective, a greater risk of incorrect acceptance for planned substantive procedures can be established. Under this circumstance, the required sample size is decreased.

- When the auditor relies less heavily on other substantive procedures (including analytical procedures) to achieve the same audit objective, a lesser risk of incorrect acceptance for planned substantive procedures can be established. Under this circumstance, the required sample size is increased.

Tolerable misstatement and expected misstatement

The establishment of a sample size in non-statistical sampling must take into consideration the tolerable misstatement (the size of the error that the auditor considers to be tolerable) and the expected misstatement. In general, as the size of the tolerable misstatement increases, the required sample size decreases. For example, if the auditor believes that a tolerable misstatement in the accounts receivable balance is $30,000 rather than $10,000, the number of items that must be in the sample is decreased.

In determining the size of a sample, the auditor should also take into consideration the expected misstatement in the population. As the expected misstatement in the population increases, the required sample size must be increased. That is, if an auditor does not have much faith in the balances under investigation, common sense would require an auditor to test more items from the population.

Population size

The size of the population has little effect on the size of the sample. Thus, if one trial balance of accounts receivable has 2,000 line items and another trial balance has 4,000 line items, assuming all other factors are equal, both populations would require essentially the same sample size.

ENGAGEMENT STRATEGY: It is easy for auditors to overemphasize the size of the population in determining the required sample size for a particular balance. For example, if the auditor has a rule of thumb that he or she samples 10% of the items of the population, the result is a misapplication of auditing standards. In the previous example, the auditor would select 200 items from the first population and 400 items from the second, but that doubling of the sample size in the second population is not supported by sampling concepts. It is far more important for the auditor to thoughtfully look at the other three factors discussed above, rather than population size, in determining the required sample size for a population.

Consider the interplay of the four factors The auditor uses professional judgment to evaluate the four factors described above and, based on this evaluation, determines the required sample size. There is no single approach that an auditor should use to make this determination; however, for illustrative purpose the AICPA *Audit Sampling* Guide describes the following as an approach that an auditor may consider:

- Consider the level of inherent risk
- Consider the effectiveness of controls related to the financial statement assertions
- Establish the risk of incorrect acceptance
- Establish a tolerable misstatement level
- Evaluate the effect of other related tests of details
- Determine the population reported amount
- Compute the preliminary sample size
- Adjust the preliminary sample size

ENGAGEMENT STRATEGY: The AICPA Audit Guide *Audit Sampling* is careful not to endorse any particular method for determining sample size but describes the usefulness of the approach described above as follows: The model is provided only to illustrate the relative effect of different planning considerations on sample size; it is not intended as a substitute for professional judgment. The auditor can find this approach useful to get a feel for how various assessments of the four factors described earlier can have on the required sample size.

Consider the level of inherent risk Initially the auditor assesses the level of inherent risk related to the particular assertions in the financial statements that will be tested once the sample is selected. Inherent risk is the susceptibility of an assertion to a material misstatement, assuming that there are no related controls. AU-C 500 (*Audit Evidence*) attempts to provide the logical framework for the audit process by identifying the following broad assertions that must be tested:

- Assertions for classes of transactions
- Assertions for account balances
- Assertions for presentation and disclosure

Consider the effectiveness of controls related to the financial statement assertions Once the specific financial statement assertions are identified, the auditor should consider the effectiveness of the controls related to the prevention and detection of material misstatements related to the assertions. Control risk is the risk that a material misstatement that could occur in an assertion will not be prevented or detected on a timely basis by the entity's internal control.

Establish the risk of incorrect acceptance The judgments made in the first two steps should be combined and the auditor should determine the risk of incorrect acceptance (which was described earlier in this section). That is, inherent risk and control risk related to specific assertions included in the financial statements provide insight into how much risk the auditor is willing to accept for those particular assertions. Although there are innumerable levels that could be identified in practice, some auditors think about the risk of incorrect acceptance using quantitative measures such as 5%, 10%, 15%, and so forth, whereas other auditors qualitatively express the risk of incorrect acceptance using the following categories:

- Maximum
- Slightly below maximum
- Moderate
- Low

If the auditor believes that particular assertions have a high inherent risk and that the controls related to the assertions are weak, the maximum level of incorrect acceptance should be established. On the other hand, if there is relatively low inherent risk related to assertions and the related controls are effective, a low level of incorrect acceptance should be established.

Establish a tolerable misstatement level The tolerable misstatement is an estimate of the maximum monetary misstatement that may exist in an account balance or group of transactions when combined with misstatement in other accounts, without causing the financial statements to be materially misstated.

Evaluate the effect of other related tests of details When a single audit procedure is performed, the results of that procedure often test the validity of more than one assertion that appears in the financial statements. For this reason, the auditor should assess the risk that other audit procedures may have an impact on the assertions that are the focus of the current sample determination using the following framework:

- *Maximum risk* No other substantive procedures are performed to test the same assertions
- *Moderate risk* Other substantive procedures that are performed to test the same assertions are expected to be moderately effective in detecting material misstatements in those assertions
- *Low risk* Other substantive procedures that are performed to test the same assertions are expected to be highly effective in detecting material misstatements in those assertions

Determine the population reported amount The dollar value of the population is simply the amount reported in the financial statements less items that make up this value that are to be tested 100%.

Compute the preliminary sample size The preliminary sample size is a function of the auditor's determination of the risk of incorrect acceptance, expected rate of misstatement in the population, tolerable misstatement, and the reported population amount. Tolerable misstatement, the reported population amount, and the risk of incorrect acceptance were discussed earlier. The expected rate of misstatement is the expected monetary misstatement that may exist in an account balance or group of transactions. The illustrative sample sizes in Exhibit AU-C 530-3 are based on Table 4.5 from the Audit Guide.

EXHIBIT AU-C 530-3—ILLUSTRATIVE SAMPLE SIZES

Risk of Incorrect Acceptance	Ratio of Expected Misstatement to Tolerable Misstatement	Tolerable Misstatement as % of Population	Sample Size
5%	0	5%	60
5%	.20	5%	93
5%	.20	2%	232
10%	0	5%	47
10%	.20	5%	69
10%	.20	3%	114
15%	0	5%	38
15%	.20	5%	55
15%	0	2%	95

As Exhibit AU-C 530-3 illustrates, holding other factors constant, the sample size increases given (1) a lower risk of incorrect acceptance, (2) a larger ratio of expected misstatement to tolerable misstatement, and (3) a smaller ratio of tolerable misstatement as a percentage of the reported population amount.

Adjust the preliminary sample size The preliminary sample size must be adjusted upward because non-statistical rather than statistical sampling is used. The AICPA Audit Guide *Audit Sampling* notes that "auditors typically adjust the sample size from 10% to 50% if the sample is not selected in a statically efficient manner." For example, if a population that has a great deal of variation has not been stratified, the auditor should increase the preliminary sample size.

To illustrate this approach, assume an auditor is trying to decide the sample size for the confirmation of accounts receivable under the following conditions:

- *Consider the level of inherent risk* This particular audit procedure is concerned with the existence of accounts receivable, and the level of inherent risk is considered to be moderate based on the nature of accounts receivable and other factors related to the client.

- *Consider the effectiveness of controls related to the financial statement assertions* Based on the evaluation of the client's internal control related to the processing of accounts receivable and cash receipts, the auditor has concluded that internal controls are weak and control risk is assessed at the maximum level.

- *Evaluate the effect of other related tests of details* The auditor has identified another audit procedure that will help to determine the existence of accounts receivable (for example, the review of subsequent cash receipts) and has assessed the risk that other substantive procedures will fail to detect a material misstatement as *moderate.*

- *Establish the risk of incorrect acceptance* The auditor considers the assessed level of inherent risk (moderate), control risk (maximum), and the effect of other related tests of details (moderate) in determining the risk of incorrect acceptance. The auditor decides to assess the risk of incorrect acceptance at 10% (or, qualitatively, at a level *slightly below maximum*).

- *Establish a tolerable misstatement level* Based on the assessment of materiality, the auditor decides to establish a tolerable misstatement level of $11,500.

- *Estimate the expected misstatement level* Based on the auditor's previous experience auditing accounts receivable for this client, expected misstatement is $2,000.

- *Determine the population reported amount* The general ledger balance of accounts receivable is reported at $250,000 but accounts receivable that exceed $4,000 will be tested 100%. The accounts that will be tested 100% are reported at $20,000. Thus, the population subject to sampling has a reported amount of $230,000.

- *Compute the preliminary sample size* The auditor has established the risk of incorrect acceptance at 10%. Expected misstatement, $2,000, is approximately 20% of tolerable misstatement, $11,500. And tolerable misstatement is 5% of the population balance subject to sampling ($11,500 / $230,000). Using the table in Exhibit AU-C 530-3, the preliminary sample size is 69 sample items (i.e., customer accounts receivable balances to be confirmed).

- *Adjust the preliminary sample size* The auditor, based on the review of the trial balance of accounts receivable, decided not to stratify the sample (except for the items that are tested 100%), even though there was a moderate amount of variation in the account balances. For this reason, the auditor decided to increase the size of the sample by 30%. Thus, the required sample size is 90 (69 × 1.3).

Select the sample

Once the sample size has been determined, the sample itself should be selected so that each item in the population has a chance of selection (representative sample). One way to select the sample is to divide the population into categories based on dollar values, selecting more items from the category with the greatest dollar value. The allocation in Exhibit AU-C 530-4 illustrates this approach based on the example presented earlier in this section.

EXHIBIT AU-C 530-4—SELECTING THE SAMPLE

Category	Reported Amount	Allocation Fraction	Total Required Sample Size	Sample Size for Category
$1 to $500	100,000	100/230	90	39
$501 to $2,000	80,000	80/230	90	31
$2,001 to $4,000	50,000	50/230	90	20
Totals	$230,000			90

Thus, 39 receivables will be selected from those receivables that have a balance of $500 or less, and so on. Within each category, the specific items selected for confirmation could be selected on a random basis or an interval basis.

OBSERVATION: In this example, the population has been stratified for sample selection purposes but not for sample evaluation purposes.

Evaluate the sample results

In order to evaluate the sample results when a non-statistical sampling approach is used, the auditor must do the following:

- Project the misstatement in the population
- Consider the sampling risk
- Consider qualitative characteristics

Project the misstatement in the population

Once the specific items are selected for testing, the appropriate audit procedures are performed. Based on the performance of the audit procedures, the auditor would determine the amount of the misstatements found in the sample items. This misstatement must then be projected to the total population. To continue with the current illustration, assume the 90 accounts selected for confirmation have a total account balance of $23,000 and assume that the auditor discovered misstatements equal to $600. The projected total misstatement for the sampled population would be $6,000 ($600 / [$23,000 / $230,000]).

When the auditor has tested a segment of the population 100%, the misstatement found for these items must be added to the projected total misstatement for the sampled item in order to determine the projected total misstatement for the total population. For example, in the current illustration all receivables with a balance greater than $4,000 were tested. If the misstatement discovered in this group of receivables was $1,000, the projected total misstatement for the population would be $7,000 ($6,000 + $1,000).

Consider sampling risk

Once the auditor has determined the projected total misstatement for the population, he or she must be careful not to draw a conclusion about the population based on this single estimate. That is, the auditor cannot say that the best estimate of the misstatement is a specific amount ($7,000 in the current example), but rather he or she must recognize that sampling risk must be considered. Sampling risk arises because not all the items in the population were tested; therefore, the best estimate of the misstatement is not a single amount but a range around that single amount.

Determining, based on the sampling results, whether a population's dollar value is probably not misstated involves a considerable amount of professional judgment. The focus of the judgment is the relationship between the tolerable misstatement and the projected misstatement. The broad generalizations in Exhibit AU-C 530-5 are helpful in making that judgment.

EXHIBIT AU-C 530-5—MISSTATEMENTS AND PROFESSIONAL JUDGMENT

Relationship of Projected Misstatement and Tolerable Misstatement for the Sample	Examples	Analysis and Judgment
The projected misstatement is significantly less than the tolerable misstatement.	Assume the projected misstatement is $1,000 and the tolerable misstatement is $9,000.	The projected misstatement is so much less than the tolerable misstatement, it is probably unlikely that the actual misstatement (if the entire population were sampled) would be greater than the tolerable misstatement. *Conclusion:* The auditor is reasonably assured that the population balance is not misstated.
The projected misstatement is equal to or greater than the tolerable misstatement.	Assume the projected misstatement is $10,000 and the tolerable misstatement is $9,000.	The projected misstatement implies that the balance is materially misstated. *Conclusion:* The auditor may request that the client review the population for possible adjustment. Once adjustments are made, the auditor should reevaluate the balance to determine whether it is acceptable.
The projected misstatement is neither close to nor far from the tolerable misstatement.	Assume the projected misstatement is $7,500 and the tolerable misstatement is $9,000.	When the projected misstatement is neither close to nor far from the tolerable misstatement, the decision process becomes more difficult because the conclusion that can be drawn is not as obvious as it is in the two situations described above.
		Conclusion: Under this circumstance, the auditor might want to (1) increase the sample size (concluding that the original sample might not have been representative) or (2) perform alternative audit procedures in order to obtain additional evidence concerning the possible misstatement of the population.

Consider qualitative characteristics

When a misstatement is discovered, an auditor should not mechanically respond to the misstatement as simply part of the projection of the total misstated amount in the population. Each misstatement should be analyzed to determine whether it arose from an error (an unintentional action) or from possible fraud (an intentional action). If fraud is suspected, the auditor should follow the guidance established in AU-C 240 (*Consideration of Fraud in a Financial Statement Audit*).

Practitioner's Aids

EXHIBIT AU-C 530-6—REQUIRED SAMPLE SIZE FOR NON-STATISTICAL TESTS OF DETAILS

Use the following procedures as a guide for determining the required sample size for the performance of tests of details based on a non-statistical sampling approach. The checklist is only a guide, and professional judgment should be exercised to determine how it should be modified by revising or adding procedures. Initial and date each procedure as it is completed. Each procedure should be cross-referenced to an audit schedule that is the basis for the judgment or factor that is used to determine the required sample size.

Client Name: _____

Account Balance or Transactions Tested: _____

Date of Financial Statements: _____

		Initials	*Date*	*Audit Documentation Reference*
1.	Establish the level of inherent risk.	_____	_____	_____
	——Maximum			
	——Slightly below maximum			
	——Moderate			
	——Low			
2.	Consider the effectiveness of controls related to the financial statement assertions (control risk).	_____	___ ___	_____
	——Maximum			
	——Slightly below maximum			
	——Moderate			
	——Low			
3.	Establish the risk of incorrect acceptance.	_____	_____	_____
	——Maximum			
	——Slightly below maximum			
	——Moderate			
	——Low			

	Initials	Date	Audit Documentation Reference
4. Establish a tolerable misstatement level, both as a dollar amount and as a percentage of the population amount subject to sampling procedures.	_____	_____	_____
5. Estimate the expected misstatement amount, both as a dollar amount and as a percentage of tolerable misstatement.			
6. Evaluate the effect of other related tests of details.	_____	_____	_____

——Maximum

——Slightly below maximum

——Moderate

——Low

	Initials	Date	Audit Documentation Reference
7. Determine the population reported amount subject to sampling procedures.	_____	_____	_____

$ _____

	Initials	Date	Audit Documentation Reference
8. Compute the preliminary sample size using the table in Exhibit AU-C 530-3 or using Table 4.5 in the AICPA's *Audit Sampling* Guide.			

Preliminary sample size:

_____

	Initials	Date	Audit Documentation Reference
9. Adjust the preliminary sample size.	_____	_____	_____

Required sample size:

_____

Reviewed by: _____

Date: _____

SECTION 540

AUDITING ACCOUNTING ESTIMATES, INCLUDING FAIR VALUE ACCOUNTING ESTIMATES AND RELATED DISCLOSURES

Authoritative Pronouncements

SAS-122—Statements on Auditing Standards: Clarification and Recodification

Overview

AU-C 540 describes the auditor's responsibilities related to accounting estimates, including fair value accounting estimates and related disclosures. During the audit, the auditor's objective is to obtain sufficient appropriate audit evidence about whether accounting estimates, including fair value accounting estimates and related disclosures, in the financial statements are adequate and reasonable. Accounting estimates are approximations of financial statement elements, items, or accounts that are made to measure past transactions or events (loss contingency arising from pending lawsuits) or to measure assets (net realizable value of accounts receivable) or liabilities (accrual related to warranty contracts). Many factors, such as the availability of reliable data, the required complexity of the evaluation process, and the extent to which assumptions must be made by management, can increase the likelihood of accounting estimates leading to material misstatement in the financial statements and affect their susceptibility to management bias.

FRAUD POINTER: As described in AU-C 240 (*Consideration of Fraud in a Financial Statement Audit*), one of the three conditions of fraud is the presence of "opportunities," or circumstances that allow fraud to be perpetrated. The presence of accounting estimates in financial statements can create significant opportunities for management to materially misstate financial statements due to the complexity involved in the estimation process and the need for assumptions to be made by management when developing an estimate. As auditors identify and evaluate factors related to fraud risks, they should consider the extent to which estimates are required in client financial statements and identify whether indicators of potential unintentional or intentional management bias exist.

Accounting estimates involve the use of judgment based on information available when the financial statements are prepared and may involve assumptions regarding matters that are uncertain at the time the estimate is made. While uncertainty about matters may exist, the auditor is not responsible for predicting future events that could have impacted the estimates made had they been known at the time of the audit.

OBSERVATION: A difference between an accounting estimate and the amount originally recognized or disclosed in the financial statements does not necessarily indicate a misstatement of the financial statements; the difference could be due to estimation uncertainty.

Auditing estimates that are part of financial statements can often prove to be a significant engagement challenge because they often require a considerable amount of professional judgment. The AICPA has published the Audit Practice Guide *Auditing Estimates and Other Soft Accounting Information,* which is summarized in a Practitioner's Aid at the end of this section.

- The fair value of an asset or liability might have to be estimated depending on the information available regarding that value. Determining the fair value of an asset that is held or a liability that exists is relatively easy if there is an established public market. For example, the fair value of an investment in the equity securities of a public company is generally readily determinable based on prices reflected in public markets. However, the more an item is unique and less like a commodity, the less likely it is that there is an established market with a large number of buyers and sellers to provide reliable information about the item's fair value at a particular point in time.

PLANNING AND REMINDER: AU-C 540 does not identify audit procedures for specific types of assets and liabilities that must be measured or disclosed at their estimated fair values. The auditor must be aware of other standards (for example, AU-C 501, *Audit Evidence—Specific Considerations for Selected Items*) that provide guidance that is more specific.

PUBLIC COMPANY IMPLICATION: The PCAOB's Staff Audit Practice Alert No. 2 (Matters Related to Auditing Fair Value Measurements of Financial Instruments and the Use of Specialists) is designed to provide guidance related to auditing fair values, particularly in light of the FASB's ASC 820 (Fair Value Measurements). The auditor needs to understand the company's process for determining fair value measurements and disclosures, including related internal controls. The auditor should also evaluate whether (1) management's assumptions in determining fair value are reasonable and not inconsistent with market information, (2) management reliance on historical financial information continues to be justified (e.g., use of historical default rates may not be appropriate when credit markets are deteriorating), and (3) the company's determination of fair value is applied consistently and whether this is appropriate. For example, a company may apply a model consistently in determining fair value but because of changes in the environment it may be more appropriate for the company to change the relative weights of model inputs. In addition, the auditor should recognize that model inputs based on the company's own data are generally more susceptible to bias and take appropriate audit steps to respond to this increased risk. Finally, GAAP provides for many required disclosures relating to fair value measurements. The auditor needs to recognize that material disclosures that depart from GAAP represent a misstatement of the financial statements.

PUBLIC COMPANY IMPLICATION: The PCAOB's Staff Audit Practice Alert No. 4 (Auditor Considerations Regarding Fair Value Measurements, Disclosures, and Other-than-Temporary Impairments) is designed to inform auditors about the potential implications on annual audits and interim reviews of three former FASB Staff Positions (FSPs): (1) FSP FAS 157-4 (Determining Fair Value When the Volume and Level of Activity for the Asset or Liability Have Significantly Decreased and Identifying Transactions That Are Not Orderly), (2) FSP FAS 115-2 and FAS 124-2 (Recognition and Presentation of Other-than-Temporary-Impairments), and (3) FSP FAS 107-1 and APB 28-1 (Interim Disclosures about Fair Value of Financial Instruments). The guidance in these now superseded FSPs is incorporated in ASC 820 (Fair Value Measurements and Disclosures), ASC 320 (Investments—Debt and Equity Securities), and ASC 825 (Financial Instruments), respectively. PCAOB Staff Audit Practice Alert No. 4 states that the auditor should include inquiries about the application of these FSPs in a review of interim financial information. For audits of financial statements, Practice Alert 4 emphasizes the need for auditors to obtain sufficient appropriate evidence to support accounting estimates, including their measurement and disclosure. For example, in certain cases the guidance in ASC 320 (Investments—Debt and Equity Securities) requires losses from other-than-temporary impairments to be separated between credit losses and other factors. Such a determination involves significant judgment. Practice Alert 4 also reminds auditors of their responsibility to read other information in documents containing interim and annual financial statements. If this other information is inconsistent with the financial statements, either the audit report, financial statements, or the other information needs to be changed. The application of these FSPs may require communication to the audit committee because their application might involve a change in (1) accounting policy, (2) accounting estimates, (3) the process by which management develops sensitive estimates, and (4) the auditor's judgment about the quality, not just the acceptability, of the client's accounting policies. These required disclosures to the audit committee pertain to both annual audits and interim reviews.

Definitions

Accounting estimate	An approximation of a monetary amount, including an amount measured at fair value, in the absence of a precise means of measurement.
Auditor's point estimate or auditor's range	The amount (point estimate) or range of amounts (auditor's range) derived from audit evidence for use in evaluating management's point estimate.
Estimation uncertainty	The susceptibility of an accounting estimate and related disclosures to an inherent lack of precision in its measurement.
Management bias	A lack of neutrality by management in the preparation and presentation of information.

Management's point estimate	The amount selected by management for recognition or disclosure in the financial statements as an accounting estimate.
Outcome of an accounting estimate	The actual monetary amount resulting from the resolution of the underlying transactions, events, or conditions addressed by the accounting estimate.

Requirements

The auditor is presumptively required to perform the following procedures with respect to accounting estimates in an audit of a client's financial statements:

Risk Assessment and Related Procedures

1. Obtain an understanding of the following to provide a basis for identifying and assessing risks of material misstatement for accounting estimates:

The applicable financial reporting framework's requirements relevant to accounting estimates and related disclosures.

  a. How management identifies transactions, events, or conditions requiring recognition or disclosure of accounting estimates. To do this, inquire of management about changes in circumstances that may create the need for new or revised accounting estimates.

  b. How management makes accounting estimates and the data estimates are based on, including the method used for estimation, relevant controls, use of a specialist, assumptions underlying the estimates, if a change in the estimation method is needed and why, and any assessment by management of the effect of estimation uncertainty.

This understanding should be obtained when performing risk assessment and related procedures to obtain an understanding of the entity and its environment.

2. Review the outcome of accounting estimates from prior-period financial statements or re-estimates made by management during the current period to identify any relevant information for identifying and assessing risks of material misstatement for accounting estimates made in the current period financial statements. This review is not intended to question the auditor's prior judgments made based on the information available at that time.

Identifying, Assessing, and Responding to the Risks of Material Misstatement

3. Evaluate the degree of estimation uncertainty associated with an accounting estimate when identifying and assessing the risks of material misstatement.

4. Using judgment, determine whether any accounting estimates with a high level of estimation uncertainty give rise to significant risks.

5. Determine, based on the assessed risks of material misstatement, whether (1) management has appropriately applied the applicable financial reporting framework's requirements relevant to the accounting estimate and (2) the estimation methods used are appropriate and consistently applied, and whether any changes in estimates or estimation methods are appropriate.

6. To respond to the assessed risks of material misstatement, perform one or more of the following procedures depending on the nature of the accounting estimate:

  a. Determine if events occurring up to the date of the auditor's report provide audit evidence regarding the accounting estimate.

b. Test how management made the estimate and the data on which the estimate is based by evaluating if the measurement method used is appropriate, management's assumptions are reasonable given the measurement objectives of the applicable financial reporting framework, and the data on which the estimate is based are sufficiently reliable for the auditor's purposes.

c. Test the operating effectiveness of controls over how management made the estimate and use appropriate substantive procedures.

d. Develop a point estimate or range to evaluate management's point estimate. If using different assumptions or methods from management, obtain a sufficient understanding of management's assumptions and methods to establish that the auditor's point estimate or range accounts for relevant variables and to evaluate any significant differences from management's point estimate. If using a range, narrow the range based on available audit evidence until all outcomes in the range are considered reasonable.

7. When responding to assessed risks of material misstatement for accounting estimates, consider whether specialized skills or knowledge are needed to obtain sufficient appropriate audit evidence.

Responding to Significant Risks

8. Evaluate the following matters for accounting estimates that create significant risks:

a. a. How management considered and rejected alternative assumptions or outcomes or otherwise addressed estimation uncertainty in making the estimate

b. If significant assumptions used by management are reasonable; a significant assumption is one for which a reasonable variation in the assumption would materially affect the measurement of the accounting estimate

c. Management's intent and ability to carry out specific courses of action as relevant to the reasonableness of significant assumptions or the appropriate application of the applicable financial reporting framework

9. If, in the auditor's judgment, management has not adequately addressed the effects of estimation uncertainty for estimates creating significant risks, develop a range to use to evaluate the estimates' reasonableness if necessary.

10. Obtain sufficient appropriate audit evidence for accounting estimates that create significant risks about whether management's decision regarding recognition of the estimates in the financial statements and the measurement basis selected for the estimates are in accordance with the requirements of the applicable financial reporting framework.

Evaluating Reasonableness of Accounting Estimates

11. Evaluate whether the audit evidence demonstrates that accounting estimates in the financial statements are reasonable or misstated given the applicable financial reporting framework.

Disclosures

12. Obtain sufficient appropriate audit evidence about whether disclosures related to accounting estimates in the financial statements are in accordance with the requirements of the applicable financial reporting framework.

13. For accounting estimates that create significant risks, evaluate the adequacy of disclosure in the financial statements of their estimation uncertainty given the applicable financial reporting framework.

Management Bias

14. Review management judgments and decisions in making accounting estimates to identify any indicators of management bias. Indicators of management bias do not in themselves constitute misstatements for purposes of concluding as to the reasonableness of individual accounting estimates.

Documentation

15. Document:

   a. The basis for conclusions about the reasonableness of accounting estimates that create significant risks and their disclosure

   b. Any indicators of possible management bias

Analysis and Application of Procedures

Risk Assessment and Related Procedures

The auditor is required to perform certain procedures to provide a basis for identifying and assessing the risks of material misstatement for accounting estimates. However, these procedures may not need to be performed if events occurring after management's estimate was made, such as settlement of litigation, sale of an impaired asset, or collection of receivables, have significantly reduced the risk of material misstatement related to the accounting estimate.

Obtain an understanding of the applicable financial reporting framework requirements

Obtaining an understanding of the applicable financial reporting framework assists the auditor in understanding how the entity develops its accounting estimates. The framework's requirements may detail certain conditions for recognizing accounting estimates, methods for measuring accounting estimates, and conditions requiring or allowing measurement at fair value or disclosure. The framework may also guide management's determination of point estimates when alternatives exist; for example, a framework may require management to select a point estimate that is the most likely outcome or to use a discounted probability-weighted expected value. Some frameworks may not allow entities to recognize accounting estimates in the financial statements if a high degree of estimation uncertainty exists.

Obtain an understanding of how management identifies the need for accounting estimates

To obtain an understanding of how management identifies transactions, events, and conditions that require recognition or disclosure of accounting estimates, the auditor may predominantly use management inquiry if management identifies these events using their knowledge and experience. If management has a more structured process for identifying these events, the auditor may perform risk assessment procedures directed at that process. If the auditor identifies a need for an accounting estimate during the audit that management failed to identify, he or she should determine if this constitutes a significant deficiency or material weakness in internal control of the entity's risk assessment process. Exhibit AU-C 540-2 lists common financial statement estimates that require evaluation by an auditor.

The auditor also inquires of management about changes in circumstances that may create the need for new or revised accounting estimates. These inquiries may include questions about whether:

- The entity has engaged in new types of transactions that could require accounting estimates

- Terms of transactions or accounting policies relating to accounting estimates have changed

- Regulatory changes or new events or conditions have occurred that may create the need for new or revised accounting estimates

Obtain an understanding of how management makes accounting estimates

The auditor is required to obtain an understanding of how management makes accounting estimates and the data on which the estimates are based. In addition to the required considerations, the auditor may also consider the types of accounts or transactions the estimates relate to, management's use of recognized measurement techniques in making estimates, and how management has taken into account the effect of any changes in circumstances occurring between the date of the estimate and the period end.

The method of measurement management uses to form accounting estimates is often not prescribed by the applicable financial reporting framework. In these situations, the auditor may evaluate management's consideration of the nature of the item being estimated in selecting an estimation method and whether the entity's industry has commonly used estimation methods. If management has internally developed a method of making an accounting estimate or departs from a commonly used industry method, there may be a greater risk of material misstatement.

In obtaining an understanding of relevant controls, the auditor may consider:

- The competence and experience of those making the accounting estimates

- How the completeness, relevance, and accuracy of data used to develop estimates is determined and how accounting estimates are reviewed and approved, including the assumptions and inputs

- The segregation of duties between those making the accounting estimates and those committing the entity to the underlying transactions

- The extent to which the entity uses a service organization to provide accounting estimates or the data supporting those estimates

- The design and development, or selection, of a particular model for making a particular estimate

- The use, maintenance, periodic validation of integrity, and security controls over unauthorized changes of a model used to make accounting estimates

When obtaining an understanding about the assumptions underlying the accounting estimates, the auditor may consider:

- The nature and significance of the assumptions

- How management assesses if assumptions are relevant, complete, and internally consistent

- Whether assumptions relate to matters within, or outside of, management's control

- The nature and extent of documentation supporting the assumptions

Because management supports assumptions with information from different sources of varying relevance and reliability, the reliability of assumptions will also vary depending on the degree of subjectivity involved. When considering fair value accounting estimates, assumptions rely on what knowledgeable and willing arm's-length parties would use to determine fair value. These assumptions may be based on observable inputs, such as independent market data, or unobservable inputs, such as the entity's own judgments. The auditor's assessment of the risks of material misstatement for an accounting estimate increases as the estimation uncertainty increases, and estimation uncertainty increases as subjectivity related to the estimate increases.

In obtaining an understanding of any changes in management's methods for making accounting estimates, the auditor should evaluate whether these changes are reasonable. When considering management's assessment of the effect of estimation uncertainty, the auditor may examine whether management has considered alternative assumptions or outcomes, how management determines an estimate when there are several outcome scenarios, and whether management monitors and responds to the outcome of prior-period accounting estimates.

Reviewing prior-period accounting estimates

The nature and extent of the auditor's review of prior-period accounting estimates is a matter of professional judgment and the outcome of every prior-period accounting estimate is not required to be reviewed. The extent of review may increase for estimates with high estimation uncertainty or those that changed significantly since the prior period audit. This review can provide the auditor with:

- Information about the effectiveness of management's prior-period estimation process, which can help the auditor judge the likely effectiveness of the current process

- Audit evidence pertinent to the current period re-estimation of prior-period accounting estimates

- Audit evidence of matters that may require disclosure in the financial statements

- Information identifying circumstances that increase the susceptibility of accounting estimates to possible management bias

A difference between the outcome of an accounting estimate and the amount recognized in prior-period financial statements does not necessarily represent a misstatement. However, it may represent a misstatement if the difference exists due to information that was available to management or that could be reasonably expected to have been obtained and taken into account when the prior period financial statements were finalized.

FRAUD POINTER: To address the ever-present risk of management override of internal control, AU-C 240 requires the auditor in every audit to review accounting estimates for biases that could result in material misstatements due to fraud. As part of that review, AU-C 240 requires the auditor to perform a retrospective review of significant accounting estimates reflected in the financial statements of the prior year. The purpose of this retrospective review is to determine whether management judgments and assumptions related to the estimates indicate possible management bias. The management judgments and assumptions examined by the auditor should include those estimates that are based on highly sensitive assumptions or are otherwise significantly impacted by management's judgment. In performing this retrospective review, the auditor is able to take advantage of the benefit of hindsight to determine the extent of bias on the part of management in developing the prior-year estimate. When bias is detected, the auditor should evaluate whether it indicates a risk of material misstatement due to fraud.

Identifying, Assessing, and Responding to the Risks of Material Misstatement

In assessing the risks of material misstatement, the auditor may consider:

- The actual or expected magnitude of an accounting estimate
- The difference between management's recorded accounting estimate and that expected by the auditor
- If management used a specialist in making the accounting estimate
- The outcome of the review of prior-period accounting estimates

Estimation uncertainty

The auditor is also required to evaluate the degree of estimation uncertainty associated with an accounting estimate. The degree of estimation uncertainty may influence the estimate's susceptibility to bias. Estimation uncertainty may be influenced by several factors:

- The extent to which the estimate depends on judgment
- The sensitivity of the estimate to changes in assumptions
- The existence of recognized measurement techniques that may mitigate the estimation uncertainty
- The forecast period's length and the relevance of data from past events in forecasting future events
- The availability of reliable data from external sources
- The extent to which the estimate is based on observable or unobservable inputs

An accounting estimate may be material to the financial statements even if the estimate is for a seemingly small amount if there is a high degree of estimation uncertainty associated with the estimate. Under some circumstances, the estimation uncertainty may be so high that it gives rise to significant risks. When a significant risk related to an accounting estimate is identified, the auditor should obtain an understanding of the entity's controls, including control activities.

In some cases the estimation uncertainty is so high that a reasonable accounting estimate cannot be made, thereby precluding recognition of the item in the financial statements or the measurement of its fair value. In these situations, the auditor may question whether the applicable financial reporting framework permits recognition of the item in the financial statements.

Management's adherence to applicable financial reporting framework and basis for changes

The auditor's consideration of management's application of the requirements of the applicable financial reporting framework as it relates to accounting estimates is focused on those aspects that may result in misapplication or differing interpretations. The auditor may use his or her understanding of the entity and its environment, perform additional audit procedures, or obtain additional evidence in determining whether the framework's requirements were applied appropriately.

The auditor also considers management's reasons for making any changes in accounting estimates or in methods for making accounting estimates to ensure that changes are not arbitrary and are based on a change in circumstances or new information. This is because an arbitrary change can result in inconsistent financial statements, give rise to a financial statement misstatement, or be an indicator of possible management bias. The auditor uses professional judgment to determine whether management's reasons for any changes are sound and adequate.

Procedures responding to assessed risks of material misstatement

The auditor may decide which procedures to perform to respond to the assessed risks of material misstatement related to an accounting estimate depending on the nature of the accounting estimate, if the procedure is expected to provide the auditor with sufficient appropriate audit evidence, the assessed risk of material misstatement, and whether the assessed risk is a significant risk. Some accounting estimates may only require the auditor to perform one procedure, while others may necessitate a combination of procedures to obtain sufficient appropriate audit evidence.

Considering events occurring up to the date of the auditor's report

The auditor may consider events occurring up to the date of the auditor's report to respond to the assessed risks of material misstatement for an accounting estimate if those events are expected to occur and to provide audit evidence confirming or contradicting the accounting estimate. If events contradict the accounting estimate, this may be an indication that management has ineffective processes for making estimates or that management bias exists in making accounting estimates. For fair value accounting estimates, this procedure may not be an appropriate response, because events occurring after the date of the estimate may not be relevant to the measurement of fair value at the balance sheet date.

PLANNING AID REMINDER: The auditor is required under AU-C 560 to perform audit procedures to obtain sufficient appropriate audit evidence that any events occurring between the financial statement date and auditor's report date that require financial statement identification or disclosure have been identified and are appropriately reflected in the financial statements. Therefore, even if the auditor does not use this procedure to consider specific accounting estimates, he or she may still consider many accounting estimates when following AU-C 560 procedures because their measurement depends on events occurring during this time.

Testing how management made the accounting estimate

It may be appropriate for the auditor to test how management made an accounting estimate and the data on which the estimate is based if the accounting estimate is (1) a fair value estimate based on observable and unobservable inputs, (2) derived from routine data processing of the entity's accounting system, (3) based on a large population of similar items that are not significant individually, (4) or if the auditor's review of similar prior-period accounting estimates suggests that management's current-period process is likely to be effective. The auditor is required to evaluate whether the data on which the estimate is based are sufficiently reliable by obtaining evidence about the accuracy and completeness of the data and evaluating whether the data are sufficiently precise and detailed.

Testing of how management made the accounting estimate may involve:

- Testing whether the data on which the estimate is based is accurate, complete, and relevant, and whether the estimate has been properly determined using such data and management assumptions

- Determining how management accounted for the effect of any events occurring between the date of the estimate and the reporting date

- Recalculating the accounting estimate and reviewing information about the estimate for internal consistency

- Considering management's review and approval process

In testing how management made an accounting estimate, the auditor evaluates whether the method used to make the estimate was appropriate in the circumstances. Absent any requirements by the applicable financial reporting framework, a method or model's appropriateness depends on the auditor's professional judgment. Factors the auditor may consider in determining the appropriateness of management's methods or models include whether management has a reasonable rationale for selecting the method; management sufficiently evaluated and appropriately applied any criteria provided to support the selected method; the method is appropriate and the data are sufficient given the nature of the estimate and the requirements of the applicable financial reporting framework; and the method is appropriate in relation to the entity's business, industry, and operating environment.

If the entity uses a model to make accounting estimates (which may be particularly likely for fair value accounting estimates), the auditor may consider some of the following factors such as whether:

- The model is commercially available or proprietary.

- The model is validated prior to usage and periodically reviewed, ensuring continued validity for its intended use. Validation may involve evaluating the model's theoretical soundness, the completeness and consistency of its inputs with market practices, and its output compared to actual transactions.

- Appropriate change control policies and procedures exist.

- The model is periodically tested for validity.

- Adjustments are made to the model's output.

- The model is adequately documented.

The auditor does not offer an opinion on the assumptions, valuation models, or the underlying data themselves. Rather, the auditor's tests are performed in the context of auditing the client's financial statements. If the auditor identifies significant assumptions used by management to make accounting estimates, these may indicate a high degree of estimation uncertainty related to the estimate, which may give rise to a significant risk. The auditor may consider many factors in evaluating the reasonableness of management's assumptions, such as if the assumptions:

- Appear reasonable, both individually and in conjunction with other assumptions

- Are interdependent and internally consistent

- Appropriately reflect observable market assumptions for fair value estimates

- Are reasonable in light of other assumptions

- Are consistent with the entity's plans and the economic environment

- Are consistent with the entity's prior experience as it may relate to future events, any relevant assumptions made in prior periods, and any other assumptions relating to the financial statements

The auditor should pay attention to the consistency of management's assumptions and valuation approaches and to any changes in these approaches or assumptions to ensure that changes in circumstances are reflected in the appropriate changes in management approaches and assumptions.

Management's intent and ability to carry out particular courses of action may affect the auditor's judgment of the reasonableness of the assumptions used. However, this information may not be permitted to be taken into account when using certain financial reporting frameworks or for fair value accounting estimates. When the auditor is obtaining audit evidence about management's intents and abilities, his or her procedures may include:

- Review of management's history of carrying out its stated intentions

- Review of written plans and other documentation

- Inquiry of management about its reasons for a particular course of action
- Review of events occurring between the date of the financial statements and the auditor's report date
- Evaluation of the entity's ability to carry out a particular course of action given its economic circumstances

The auditor may consider additional factors when evaluating the reasonableness of management's assumptions related to fair value accounting estimates, including how management incorporated market-specific inputs into developing its assumptions; if assumptions are consistent with observable market conditions and the characteristics of the item being measured; the relevance and reliability of the sources of market-participant assumptions and how management selected the assumptions to use when several assumptions exist; and how management considered assumptions used for comparable transactions, assets, or liabilities.

If the auditor is evaluating the reasonableness of assumptions related to fair value accounting estimates based on unobservable inputs, he or she may consider how management identified characteristics of market participants relevant to the accounting estimate, modified assumptions to reflect its view of assumptions market participants would use, whether the best information available in the circumstances was incorporated, and how the assumptions used account for comparable transactions, assets, or liabilities. If there are unobservable inputs, the auditor will likely need to combine evaluation of management's assumptions with other response procedures to assessed risks in order to obtain sufficient appropriate audit evidence.

Testing the operating effectiveness of controls

The auditor may test the operating effectiveness of controls over how management made the accounting estimate when management uses a well-designed, implemented, and maintained process for making estimates. Examples of this include when controls exist for management or those charged with governance to review and approve accounting estimates or when the accounting estimate is derived from routing data processing by the entity's accounting system.

PLANNING AID REMINDER: AU-C 330 requires the auditor to test the operating effectiveness of controls when the auditor's assessment of risks of material misstatement at the relevant assertion level include an expectation that controls over the process are operating effectively or when substantive procedures alone do not provide sufficient appropriate audit evidence at the relevant assertion level.

Developing a point estimate or range

Developing a point estimate or range to evaluate management's point estimate may be useful to the auditor when:

- An estimate is not derived from routine data processing by the accounting system

- The auditor's review of similar prior-period accounting estimates suggests management's current-period process is unlikely to be effective

- The entity lacks well-designed or properly implemented controls over management's process for making accounting estimates

- Management's point estimate is contradicted by events occurring between the financial statement date and the auditor's report date

- Alternative sources of data are available to the auditor to make a point estimate or range

The auditor's decision as to whether to develop a point estimate or a range may depend on what is most effective in the circumstances, what is prescribed by the applicable financial reporting framework, the availability of data, the estimation uncertainty involved with the accounting estimate, and the model used. Actual development by the auditor of a point estimate or range may occur by using a commercially available or proprietary model; further developing management's consideration of alternative assumptions or outcomes; engaging a specialist; or making reference to other comparable conditions, transactions, events, or markets for comparable assets or liabilities.

When using a range to evaluate the reasonableness of management's point estimate, the auditor should ensure the range is sufficiently narrow to enable a conclusion about whether the accounting estimate is misstated. To ensure that all range outcomes are considered reasonable, the auditor may narrow the range based on available audit evidence until all outcomes in the range are considered reasonable and may eliminate range outliers that are judged by the auditor to be unlikely to occur. For the auditor's range to be adequate for this evaluation, the range generally has to be narrowed to be less than or equal to performance materiality. However, this is not possible in some circumstances, and in those cases, the accounting estimate may still be able to be recognized but the estimation uncertainty associated with the estimate may be so high that is gives rise to a significant risk.

Considering the need for specialized skills or knowledge

For the majority of accounting estimates, it is unlikely that specialized skills or knowledge will be needed; however, the auditor may decide there is a need for those specialized skills or knowledge in some circumstances. Matters that may affect the auditor's decision include:

- The nature of the underlying asset, liability, or equity component in a particular business or industry

- The degree of estimation uncertainty

- The involvement of complex calculations or specialized models

- The complexity of the requirements of the applicable financial reporting framework relevant to accounting estimates, including whether there are areas subject to differing interpretations or inconsistent or developing practices

- The procedures the auditor intends to undertake to respond to assessed risks

Responding to Significant Risks

The auditor's substantive procedures in auditing accounting estimates that give rise to significant risks are focused on how management assessed the effect of estimation uncertainty on the estimate, the effect that uncertainty may have on the appropriateness of the estimate's recognition in the financial statements, and the adequacy of related disclosures. Management's method for dealing with alternative outcomes or assumptions of accounting estimates is not as important as whether management has assessed how estimation uncertainty may affect the estimates. If management has not considered alternative outcomes or assumptions, the auditor may need to discuss how the effects of estimation uncertainty on the accounting estimate have been addressed with management.

PLANNING AID REMINDER: An assumption may be considered to be significant if a reasonable variation in the assumption would materially affect the measurement of the accounting estimate. The auditor may be able to evaluate the assumptions through inquiries of, and discussions with, management, along with the other audit procedures to obtain sufficient appropriate evidence. Information derived from management's strategic analysis and risk management may provide additional input for the auditor.

Circumstances in which the auditor may determine management's consideration of the effects of estimation uncertainty on the accounting estimates giving rise to significant risks is inadequate include:

- Sufficient appropriate audit evidence could not be obtained through the auditor's evaluation of how management addressed the effects of estimation uncertainty and it is unlikely that other audit evidence can be obtained.

- Further exploration of the degree of estimation uncertainty related to an accounting estimate is needed, such as when the auditor is aware of a wide variation of outcomes for similar estimates.

- Indicators of management bias in making accounting estimates may exist.

OBSERVATION: When evaluating the appropriateness of recognizing or not recognizing specific accounting estimates in the financial statements, the auditor may determine in the case of an estimate not requiring financial statement recognition that there is a need to draw the reader's attention to a significant uncertainty by adding an emphasis-of-matter paragraph to the auditor's report.

Evaluating Reasonableness of Accounting Estimates

If the auditor has developed a point estimate, the difference between the auditor's point estimate and management's point estimate is a misstatement. If the auditor has developed a range, the difference between management's point estimate and the nearest point of the auditor's range is a misstatement. A misstatement may also occur if the auditor concludes that management made an arbitrary change in an estimate or the method of making the estimate. Furthermore, evaluation of the reasonableness of accounting estimates and related disclosures included in the notes to the financial statements, whether required by the applicable financial reporting framework or disclosed voluntarily, involves the same considerations as when auditing an accounting estimate recognized in the financial statements.

OBSERVATION: The purpose of the audit of accounting estimates is to determine whether estimates are reasonable. Thus, an auditor might conclude that an estimate is reasonable even though it is not the best estimate. The difference between the reasonable estimate and the best estimate should not necessarily be treated as a misstatement; however, if most estimates appear to reflect a particular bias, such as the tendency to understate expenses, the auditor should consider whether all misstatements combined could result in a material misstatement.

PLANNING AID REMINDER: The auditor is required under AU-C 260 (*The Auditor's Communication with Those Charged with Governance*) to communicate with those charged with governance about the qualitative aspects of the entity's significant accounting practices, including accounting estimates and to inform those charged with governance about management's process for forming sensitive accounting estimates and the basis for the auditor's conclusions regarding the reasonableness of those estimates.

Disclosures

Disclosures related to accounting estimates in the financial statements may be required by the applicable financial reporting framework or disclosed voluntarily. Disclosures may include information about the assumptions and estimation method used, the basis for selecting the estimation method, the effect of any changes to the estimation method from the prior period, and the sources and implications of estimation uncertainty.

For accounting estimates giving rise to significant risks, additional disclosure about their estimation uncertainty may be required the greater the range is of possible outcomes of the accounting estimate in relation to materiality. In some cases, the auditor may ask management to describe the circumstances related to estimation uncertainty in the notes to the financial statements. If the auditor believes management's disclosure of estimation uncertainty in the financial statements is inadequate or misleading, modifications to his or her opinion may be appropriate.

Management Bias

If the auditor becomes aware of indicators of management bias, the conclusion about the appropriateness of the auditor's risk assessment and related responses may be affected and the auditor may need to consider the implications for the rest of the audit. These indicators may also affect the auditor's evaluation of whether the financial statements as a whole are free from material misstatement.

Indicators of possible management bias with respect to accounting estimates include:

- Changes in an accounting estimate or method for making the estimate based on management's subjective assessment that there has been a change in circumstances

- Use of an entity's own assumptions for fair value accounting estimates when those assumptions are inconsistent with observable market assumptions

- Selection or construction of significant assumptions that yield a point estimate favorable for management objectives

- Selection of a point estimate that may indicate a pattern of optimism or pessimism

---

FRAUD POINTER: In 2010 the Committee of Sponsoring Organizations of the Treadway Commission (COSO) issued a study entitled "Fraudulent Financial Reporting: 1998-2007, An Analysis of U.S. Public Companies" that found that 51% of the fraudulent financial reporting enforcement actions by the SEC involved asset overstatements. Assets related to fair value measurement and disclosure might involve heightened fraud risk because of the significant opportunities for management to perpetrate fraud related to those accounts. The significant dependence on management assumptions and the related complexities associated with measuring and disclosing fair value instruments can create significant opportunities for management to engage in fraud.

Practitioner's Aids

Exhibit AU-C 540-1 discusses nonauthoritative guidance that is helpful in the audit of so-called soft accounting information (estimates). This exhibit summarizes an approach explained in the AICPA's Audit Practice Guide *Auditing Estimates and Other Soft Accounting Information*. The Audit Practice Guide is available for purchase from the AICPA.

EXHIBIT AU-C 540-1—NONAUTHORITATIVE GUIDANCE FOR AUDITING SOFT ACCOUNTING INFORMATION

The AICPA's Audit Practice Guide *Auditing Estimates and Other Soft Accounting Information* provides the following broad guidelines for the audit of accounting estimates:

- Auditing soft accounting information and engagement planning

- Evaluating the persuasiveness of audit evidence related to soft accounting information

- Communicating the nature of soft accounting information

Auditing soft accounting information and engagement planning

Financial statements are based on a variety of accounting estimates ranging from the percentage of accounts receivable expected to be uncollectible to actuarial assumptions required by ASC 715 (Compensation—Retirement Benefits) in order to recognize pension expense. The client needs to understand and appreciate the role of estimates in the financial reporting process and that the determination of those estimates is the responsibility of the client, not the auditor.

For the planning phase of the engagement the Audit Practice Guide addresses the following issues:

- Identify estimates with high risk.
- Determine the client's involvement in accounting estimates.
- Advise and support the client in making accounting estimates.

Identify estimates with high risk

Financial statements incorporate a variety of estimates. During the planning stage of an engagement the auditor should identify areas where there is a high degree of risk for specific estimates. One factor that can help mitigate the risk related to a particular estimate is the client's established procedures. For example, internal reports that are timely reviewed and are the basis of managerial action can help ensure that an estimate is well understood and to some degree controlled. On the other hand, poorly designed procedures increase the likelihood that an estimate that has not received an appropriate amount of attention harbors a relatively high degree of risk. The Audit Practice Guide identifies the following as conditions that can increase the audit risk related to estimates:

- The client might be new and its previous years' financial statements might have been compiled or audited and the client might not have given adequate attention to the role of estimates in financial reporting.
- The client might have switched from another comprehensive basis of accounting to GAAP-based reporting. For example, many estimates are based on the accrual accounting concept and if a cash or modified accrual basis has been used by the client, procedures related to the development of estimates might be nonexistent.
- There has been an issuance of new accounting standards that contain accounting and reporting requirements that rely on client estimates. For example, ASC 360 (Property, Plant, and Equipment) requires under certain conditions the estimate of future net cash flows to determine whether a long-lived asset has a cost-recoverability problem.
- The operations of the client have changed in a manner whereby previous years' experience with estimating account balances is no longer relevant or is less relevant to current estimates. For example, the client has added a line of electronic components that is characterized by rapid technological change compared to previously manufactured components. Previously employed procedures for identifying inventory that needs to be written down might not be appropriate for the new components.

- The customer base of the client has been modified. For example, the client might have decided to sell its products in foreign markets and has limited experience with collection issues related to accounts receivable.

Determine the client's involvement in accounting estimates

The Audit Practice Guide notes that once the estimates that have a higher degree of audit risk are identified, the next step is to determine the extent to which the client has developed an information base to address the estimation issue. This approach should include asking the following questions:

- What are the specific procedures used by the client to develop the data?

- Are the data collected by the client relevant to the account estimate and sufficient to make a reliable estimate?

- What are the procedures (model) used by the client to convert the data into the account estimate?

- Are the procedures used logical and does the process represent a reasonable approximation of the existing conditions?

In the audit of some clients, especially small or newly organized companies, it is possible that the client's procedures do not address many, if any, accounting estimates. This could be especially true of companies dominated by a manager-owner. The Audit Practice Guide points out that under this condition the auditor must determine whether the lack of procedures requires the auditor to withdraw from the engagement or remain in the engagement and help the client develop reasonable estimates for the preparation of the financial statements.

The Audit Practice Guide states that "when the estimates or soft accounting information are vital to the management of the business and are pervasive throughout the financial statements, the client's lack of a process for making these estimates should lead you to consider whether the entity is even auditable." For example, assume that a client manufactures a component for a large computer manufacturer and the controls in the supply chain are so deficient that the client often has fairly large quantities of inventory that become obsolete and of nominal value. If the client has maintained no records from previous years' inventory obsolescence experience, it is possible that the engagement is not auditable if current levels of inventory are material.

OBSERVATION: If the client has essentially no procedures related to the development of an estimate fundamental to the financial statements but still believes that the financial statements are auditable, the auditor should consider whether the condition gives rise to a significant deficiency or material weakness in internal control.

Advise and support the client in making accounting estimates

On the other hand, the client's lack of procedures related to estimating account balances does not always imply that a prudent auditor should withdraw from an engagement. In many small engagements the client lacks the in-house expertise to fully understand the role of estimations in financial reporting or develop appropriate data to make those estimations. Obviously the auditor cannot simply walk away from these engagements (assuming they are auditable) but, rather, must develop a commonsense approach to the situation. The Audit Practice Guide describes the following as an approach that could be useful under this circumstance:

- Explain the role of estimates to the client.
- Assist the client in developing an estimation model.
- Assist the client in developing relevant key assumptions.
- Assist the client in obtaining relevant information about key assumptions.
- Let the client make the final assumptions.
- Assist the client in making the final estimate.

Explain the role of estimates to the client

Many individuals with a limited financial background (including businesspeople) see accounting as black and white with no room for estimates; it can be a challenge to explain to such individuals the accrual basis of accounting. The way an auditor conveys the explanation is personal and dependent upon his or her imagination. It is often best to leave out all of the jargon and technical references and find an everyday, close-to-home context to explain the need for estimates. In the final analysis an auditor must take time to educate the client and make sure they are committed to "getting the numbers right."

Assist the client in developing an estimation model

All estimates are based on a model (mathematical equation), some of which are simple and some of which are elaborate. For example, the aging of accounts receivable in order to estimate the amount of uncollectible accounts is based on a model with two or more variables (the bad-account percentage increases with the age of the account).

The key to developing a successful model (one that represents more or less the real world) is inquisitiveness in the context of the client's operations. The client brings to this project a thorough understanding of its operations and should be able to rely on in-house expertise to be reasonably certain that all of the relevant factors are considered. An auditor brings to this project a more limited knowledge of the client but a great deal of experience with various other clients and industries. Furthermore, the auditor brings a degree of rigor that might not always be the domain of the client. For example, the auditor can analyze factors raised by the client and determine which are relevant, how they interrelate with one another, and the possible financial outcome of their interplay.

Finally an auditor should be careful not to restrict the scope of the information that may be gathered to deal with the estimation issue. The Audit Practice Guide notes that "many practitioners make the mistake of building a model based only on the information they know exists." With the explosion of information and data-retrieval tools, the client and auditor need to be willing to spend an adequate amount of time considering relevant data sources.

Assist the client in developing relevant key assumptions

The auditor should discuss with the client the key assumptions that are likely to be the basis for developing an acceptable account estimate. The assumptions may include a variety of factors such as management's desire to maintain strong customer relations (the liberal application of a warranty clause), reliable costs estimates (for pending lawsuits), and business strategies that relate to future cash flow assumptions (in applying the cost recoverability test to various assets).

Assist the client in obtaining relevant information about key assumptions

Often a client needs help in the collection of information that relates to the key assumptions identified by the client. This is a research task that can include searching databases and other sources of information maintained by industry trade associations, business libraries, and reference sources maintained by the client. As sources of information are identified the auditor must determine whether the information is relevant to the estimate that needs to be made by the client. Like all accounting information, the information must be relevant to the estimation that needs to be made, reliable, and sufficient to support the assertions that will be made in the financial statements.

Let the client make the final assumptions

Even though the auditor is involved in developing the procedures used to make an account estimate, professional standards require that the client, not the auditor, make the assumptions related to the estimation. This is often a very difficult phase of the process. Up to this point the auditor has worked with the client to develop the approach and suddenly the auditor must tell the client that the client has the responsibility for developing an estimate that is included in the financial statements. The client knows that the estimates he or she develops must be acceptable to the auditor and often asks "What is the correct number?" The auditor should point out that it is not so much the specific number that an auditor is concerned with but, rather, the client's approach in developing the number. After all, the estimate is just that, an estimate. The Audit Practice Guide notes that it may be helpful to explain to the client the thought process that the auditor goes through in determining whether the process and assumptions used by the client are acceptable. For example, the auditor would raise the following questions as part of the audit process:

- Are the assumptions internally consistent with one another and consistent with other information developed?

- Do the assumptions reflect current changes and trends that are likely to have an effect on the eventual payments or write-downs related to the estimate?

- Are the assumptions consistent with the client's future plans?

Assist the client in making the final estimate

The final estimate made by the client must satisfy the client as well as the auditor and is fundamentally a trade-off between the cost of developing a highly precise estimate and the materiality of the estimate to the financial statements. If the estimate is clearly not material to the financial statements, a minimum amount of time should be devoted to the process. As the materiality of the estimate increases the auditor must be prepared to expend more audit effort in order to reduce the audit risk to an acceptable level.

Only a seasoned auditor who is familiar with the client and the client's industry should make the decision on how important an estimate is and how much audit time should be allocated to the process. The Audit Practice Guide points out that the auditor should also realize that becoming familiar with a particular estimation process should not be limited to the context of the client. For example, building expertise in a particular area can (1) benefit other audit engagements who have a similar issue or (2) build "valuable skills that later clients will pay for."

PLANNING AID REMINDER: The auditor might not have the expertise to develop an estimation process or evaluate the process used by the client, in which case the guidance established by AU-C 620 (*Using the Work of a Specialist*) should be observed.

Evaluating the persuasiveness of audit evidence related to soft accounting information

Audit evidence related to estimates is different from that which supports historical cost transactions reflected in the financial statements. Past transactions can be corroborated by inspecting documentation, confirming specifics related to the transactions, or performing other, similar audit procedures that generally created high-quality audit evidence. Estimates are future related because they are based on subsequent decisions, events, or transactions and the quality of audit evidence to corroborate estimates will be somewhat limited. The Audit Practice Guide states that in order to be comfortable with an estimate the following two factors are important to the audit process:

1. The reliability of the estimation process
2. The quality of the assumptions used in the estimation process

The reliability of the estimation process

There is an inverse relationship between the time and effort expended by management to develop an estimate and the audit risk related to the estimate. That is, if management has little interest in a particular estimate, the level of audit risk is greater than when management's approach to the estimate is both thoughtful and rigorous. The Audit Practice Guide points out that the following are factors of a reliable estimation process:

- Management's good faith effort
- The appropriateness of the estimation model

    The quality of information used to make the estimate

Management's good faith effort

In determining whether the estimation process is reliable, management's attitude toward the process should be considered. The Audit Practice Guide notes that good faith effort includes (1) being diligent in developing appropriate assumptions, (2) being cautious so as not to include misleading information in the financial statements, and (3) incorporating information that is consistent with management's plans and strategies.

The appropriateness of the estimation model

An appropriate balance can only be created when the model used is a reasonable representation of the real-world conditions that affect the estimate. Key elements of the model should be investigated to determine whether they are consistent with the existing conditions. For example, if a warranty liability is being estimated and one of the key elements of the estimation model is that only parts and not repair service are covered by the warranty, the auditor should determine whether in practice service costs are also covered depending on the nature of the relationship between the client and its customers.

The quality of information used to make the estimate

Obviously the auditor must be reasonable in determining the quality of information that is acceptable in developing an estimate. Professional judgment must be exercised based on the costs to the client and the benefits of producing financial statements that are not materially misstated.

The quality of the assumptions used in the estimation process

The Audit Practice Guide identifies the following as techniques that can be used to evaluate the appropriateness of estimates made by the client:

- Use of hindsight
- Identify ranges of estimates
- Use alternative approaches

Use of hindsight In limited situations an auditor may be able to review transactions and events that occur during the stub period (after the date of the financial statements but before the financial statements are released). For example, if a client made an estimate for returned goods that were shipped before the end of the year, a review of returned goods during the stub period might provide important insight into whether the estimate was reasonable.

Identify ranges of estimates One thing that is almost always certain about a point estimate is that it will be wrong. In most situations the auditor develops an acceptable range for the estimate, and if the client's estimate falls within that range, the auditor might be satisfied with the account balance.

OBSERVATION: The Audit Practice Guide warns that "the process used to develop a range should be as rigorous" as the process used to develop a point estimate.

Use alternative approaches Often the auditor can use alternative ways to determine whether an estimation process used by the client is acceptable. For example, an estimate for warranty costs for a new product could have been made by the client using assessments made by its engineering staff. As an alternative approach, the auditor could select a previously introduced product and review the warranty cost pattern for that product to see if it is reasonably consistent with the one developed by the client. The Audit Practice Guide notes that "wide differences in the results obtained from two or more valid models should be a red flag that causes you to investigate further."

OBSERVATION: The Audit Practice Guide points out that there are three types of estimates that are required by financial accounting standards, namely (1) management's ability and intent, (2) estimates of future cash flows, and (3) fair value estimates. For example, (1) ASC 320 (Investments—Debt and Equity Securities) requires that management classify investments into three possible portfolios that are accounted for in three different ways, (2) ASC 360 (Property, Plant, and Equipment) requires a client to estimate future cash flows for certain long-lived assets, and (3) ASC 718 (Compensation—Stock Compensation) requires that the fair value of compensatory stock option plans be determined. All of these estimation approaches present challenges for the auditor in determining whether the soft accounting information is not misleading as reported in the financial statements.

Communicating the nature of soft accounting information

The inherent nature of estimates constrains the precision and effectiveness of financial reporting. No matter how sophisticated the client's procedure for constructing estimates or how rigorous the auditor's evaluation of those estimates, the information in the current financial statements that is based on estimates is tentative to some degree. The uncertainty related to estimates needs to be communicated to users in a way that allows them to build that uncertainty into their decision making process. The Audit Practice Guide lists the following two broad techniques that can help users better understand this uncertainty:

1. Required disclosures
2. Optional disclosures

Required disclosures

Financial reporting mandates a variety of required disclosures that specifically focus on uncertainties related to financial reporting. ASC 275 (SOP 94-6, Disclosure of Certain Significant Risks and Uncertainties) provides the "primary guidance on disclosures related to estimates and soft accounting information." ASC 275 requires certain disclosures when the following conditions are present:

- It is at least reasonably possible that the estimate of the effect on the financial statements of a condition, situation, or set of circumstances that existed at the date of the financial statements will change in the near term due to one or more future confirming events.
- The effect of the change would have a material effect on the financial statements.

If the above conditions are present, the following disclosures should be made:

- If an estimate requires disclosure under ASC 450 (Contingencies) or another pronouncement, an indication also shall be made that it is at least reasonably possible that a change in the estimate will occur in the near term.

- An estimate that does not require disclosure under ASC 450 (Contingencies) (such as estimates associated with long-term operating assets and amounts reported under profitable long-term contracts) may meet the standards described above and, if so, require the following: (1) disclosure of its nature and (2) an indication that it is reasonably possible that a change in the estimate will occur in the near term.

The scope of ASC 275 (Risks and Uncertainties) is general and can apply to a variety of financial reporting issues as indicated by the following examples that are included in the pronouncement:

- Inventory subject to rapid technological obsolescence
- Specialized equipment subject to technological obsolescence
- Valuation allowances for deferred tax assets based on future taxable income
- Capitalized motion picture film product costs
- Capitalized computer software costs
- Deferred policy acquisition costs of insurance enterprises
- Valuation allowances for commercial and real estate loans
- Environmental remediation-related obligations
- Litigation-related obligations
- Contingent liabilities for obligations of other entities
- Amounts reported for long-term obligations (e.g., pensions and other postretirement benefits)
- Estimated net proceeds recoverable, the provisions for expected loss to be incurred, etc., on disposition of a business or assets
- Amounts reported for long-term contracts

Optional disclosures

Disclosures are not limited to those required by specific accounting pronouncements. The general disclosure principle requires that financial statements include information that could reasonably make a difference in assessments made by financial statement users. This general disclosure principle provides both management and the auditor with an opportunity to step back from the promulgated standards and ask whether the financial statements convey a reasonable description of the financial position and results of operations of the client. The Audit Practice Guide points out that the following optional disclosures may be helpful in portraying the risks and uncertainties related to soft accounting information:

- Disclose significant estimates.
- Describe limitations of estimates.
- Describe models used to make estimates.
- Describe the basis used to make assumptions.
- Describe recognition criteria.

- Explain why an estimate cannot be made.
- Disclose the time period related to future cash flow estimates.

Disclose significant estimates

The listing of estimates used by a client in the preparing of financial statements has become boilerplate and for that reason not very informative. As a supplement, the auditor may encourage the client to disclose and explain significant estimates that are fundamental to presentation of the financial statements.

Describe limitations of estimates

One of the misconceptions of financial reporting is the implication that a number presented is correct with no room for imprecision. This impression can be remedied to some extent by the client's describing the uncertainty related to specific significant estimates used to prepare the financial statements. Management should supplement boilerplate language with a succinct description of the risks that management is aware of and planned strategies to address these issues.

Describe models used to make estimates

The Audit Practice Guide points out that in some instances, such as one-time events, it is helpful to describe in a note to the financial statements "significant features of the process, the key assumptions made, and the rationale for such assumptions." These disclosures could remind the readers of the financial statements of the uncertainty associated with a particular account balance and the practical difficulties with making a reasonable estimate based on existing conditions.

Describe the basis used to make assumptions

Along with describing the elements related to the model used to make an estimate it may be equally insightful to the financial statement reader to be informed of "the rationale, the sources of information, and the thought process" used to construct assumptions that were fundamental to making the estimate.

Describe recognition criteria

In some instances it is not apparent or obvious to a financial statement user the criteria that were used to make an estimate. For example, ASC 450 (Contingencies) uses terms such as "probable," "reasonably possible," and "remote" in determining whether a loss contingency is to be recorded, disclosed in a note, or omitted from the financial statements. Descriptions of these terms in the context of the specific estimates may assist the user in understanding the degree of uncertainty related to certain account balances.

Explain why an estimate cannot be made

In some instances management is unable to make a reasonable estimate because of the lack of relevant information even after an appropriate estimation process has been constructed and executed. Rather than simply state in a note to the financial statements that an estimate cannot be made, the disclosure may "explain why a particular estimate cannot be made and give some indication of when an estimate will be possible."

Disclose the time period related to future cash flow estimates

Accounting estimates may be in part based on estimates of future cash flows. Disclosing the period of time used for the estimate and why a particular length of time was used can better convey to the financial statement user the degree of uncertainty surrounding an estimate.

EXHIBIT AU-C 540-2—COMMON FINANCIAL STATEMENT ESTIMATES REQUIRING AUDITOR EVALUATION

Assets

- Allowance for doubtful accounts
- Allowance for sales returns and allowances
- Evaluation of when a software vendor has established technological feasibility for the purpose of capitalizing computer software development costs
- Estimates of fair-market value of available-for-sale and trading securities (not traded in an active market)
- Impairment of long-lived assets and intangible assets
- Inventory obsolescence reserve
- Recoverability of deferred tax assets (more likely than not)
- Useful lives and salvage values of fixed assets
- Useful lives of intangible assets (those without an indefinite useful life)

Liabilities

- Discount rate, assumed return on plan assets, among other assumptions, for defined benefit pension plans
- Discount rate, health-care-cost trend rate, among other estimates, for retiree health-care-benefit plans
- Salvage value for leased assets, implicit rate of return in a lease contract, among other estimates, for lease contracts
- Warranty obligations

Revenues

- Percentage-of-completion for long-term construction contracts
- Sales discounts
- Sales returns

Expenses

- Amortization expense
- Bad debts expense
- Cost of goods sold
- Depreciation expense
- Income tax expense
- Pension expense (income)
- Postretirement benefit expense other than pension
- Warranty expense

Gains and Losses

- Loss on asset impairment
- Unrealized gains and losses on nonpublic or thinly traded securities

SECTION 550

RELATED PARTIES

Authoritative Pronouncements

SAS-122—Statements on Auditing Standards: Clarification and Recodification

Overview

An audit of financial statements cannot be expected to provide assurance that all related-party transactions were identified. However, an auditor must be alert for the possible occurrence of related party transactions and should evaluate them with a higher degree of skepticism than transactions that are executed by parties that are not related. AU-C 550 establishes guidelines for evaluating related-party relationships and transactions that are discovered during an audit engagement.

While related-party transactions may occur in the normal course of business and carry no higher a risk of material misstatement than an arm's length transaction, in some circumstances, related-party transactions may give rise to higher risks of material misstatement of the financial statements. This increased risk of material misstatement associated with related-party transactions may be due to increased complexity, ineffective transaction identification or tracking, transaction terms or conditions different from the market, or management motivations to engage in or conceal fraud.

The auditor is responsible for identifying, assessing, and responding to risks of material misstatement that arise from the entity's failure to account for or disclose related-party relationships or transactions according to the applicable financial reporting framework. These procedures are important because the auditor should be able to conclude, based on the audit evidence obtained, whether related-party relationships and transactions prevent the financial statements from being fairly presented. Professional guidelines for related-party transactions are contained in AU-C 550 and ASC 850 (Related Party Disclosures).

Definitions

Arm's length transaction	A transaction conducted on such terms and conditions between a willing buyer and seller who are unrelated, acting independently of each other, and pursuing their own best interests.
Related party	This term is defined by GAAP as an entity affiliate; an entity for which the investing entity should account for its investments using the equity method; beneficial employee trusts that are managed by entity management; principal owners and management of the entity and their immediate families; any party that may, or does, deal with the entity and has ownership, control, or significant influence over the management or operating policies of another party to the extent that an arm's-length transaction might not be achieved..

Requirements

The auditor is required to perform the following procedures with respect to related-party relationships and transactions:

Risk Assessment and Related Procedures

1. Obtain information relevant to identifying the risks of material misstatements associated with related-party relationships and transactions.

2. As part of the required engagement team discussion, consider the susceptibility of the financial statements to material misstatement due to fraud or error that could result from the entity's related-party relationships and transactions.

3. Inquire of management about:

   a. The identity of the entity's related parties, including any changes from the prior period

   b. The nature of the relationships between the entity and related parties

   c. If any transactions occurred between the entity and related parties during the period and, if so, the type and purpose of the transactions

4. Inquire of management and others within the entity and perform other appropriate risk assessment procedures to obtain an understanding of any controls management has established to:

   a. Identify, account for, and disclose related-party relationships and transactions

   b. Authorize and approve significant transactions and arrangements outside the normal course of business or with related parties

5. Remain alert during the audit for information indicating the existence of related-party relationships or transactions not previously identified or disclosed to the auditor when inspecting records or documents, in particular, the following: bank and legal confirmations, minutes of meetings of shareholders and those charged with governance, and other records or documents the auditor considers necessary in the entity's circumstances.

6. If significant transactions outside the entity's normal course of business are identified when performing audit procedures, inquire of management about the nature of the transactions and whether related parties could be involved.

7. Share relevant information about the entity's related parties with engagement team members.

Identification and Assessment of the Risks of Material Misstatement

8. Identify and assess the risks of material misstatement associated with related-party relationships and transactions and determine whether any of those risks are significant risks. Identified significant related-party transactions outside the entity's normal course of business should be considered as giving rise to significant risks.

9. When identifying and assessing risks of material misstatement due to fraud, incorporate consideration of related parties as part of the auditor's consideration of fraud risk factors when performing risk assessment and related procedures.

Responses to the Risks of Material Misstatement

10. Design and perform further audit procedures to obtain sufficient appropriate audit evidence about the assessed risks of material misstatement associated with related-party transactions.

11. If arrangements or information are identified suggesting the existence of related-party relationships or transactions that management has not previously identified or disclosed to the auditor, determine whether the underlying circumstances confirm their existence.

12. If previously unidentified or undisclosed related parties or significant related-party transactions are identified:

   a. Promptly communicate the relevant information to other engagement team members.

   b. Request that management identify all transactions with those related parties for the auditor's further evaluation.

   c. Inquire why the entity's controls over related-party relationships and transactions failed to enable their identification or disclosure.

   d. Perform appropriate substantive audit procedures relating to the newly identified related parties or significant related-party transactions.

   e. Reconsider the risk that other related parties or significant related-party transactions may exist that management has not identified or disclosed to the auditor and perform any necessary additional audit procedures.

   f. Evaluate the implications for the audit if management's nondisclosure appears intentional.

13. For identified significant related-party transactions outside the entity's normal course of business:

   a. Inspect any underlying contracts or agreements and evaluate whether the business rationale or lack thereof suggests the transactions may have been entered into to engage in or conceal fraud; the transactions' terms are consistent with management's explanations; and the transactions have been appropriately accounted for and disclosed.

   b. Obtain audit evidence that the transactions have been appropriately authorized and approved.

14. If management asserts in the financial statements that a related-party transaction was conducted on terms equivalent to an arm's length transaction, obtain sufficient appropriate audit evidence about the assertion.

Evaluation of Identified Related-Party Relationships and Transactions

15. In forming an opinion on the financial statements, evaluate whether identified related-party relationships and transactions are appropriately accounted for and disclosed and whether the effects of related-party relationships and transactions prevent fair presentation of the financial statements.

Communication with Those Charged with Governance

16. Unless all of those charged with governance are involved in managing the entity, communicate significant matters arising during the audit in connection with the entity's related parties.

Documentation

17. Include the names of identified related parties and the nature of related-party relationships in the audit documentation.

Analysis and Application of Procedures

Nature of Related-Party Relationships and Transactions

While requirements for the accounting treatment and disclosure of related-party relationships and transactions are prescribed by financial reporting frameworks and accounting pronouncements, related-party transactions are typically not required to be accounted for differently than transactions with unrelated parties. It is important, however, to ensure that the substance rather than the form of related-party transactions is recognized in the financial statements.

In addition to relationships that may lead to the auditor's identification of a related-party transaction, certain transactions suggest that the parties may be related. AU-C 550 lists the following as examples:

- Contracts that carry no interest rate or that carry an unrealistic interest rate
- Real estate transactions that are made at a price significantly different from appraised values
- Nonmonetary transactions that involve the exchange of similar assets
- Loan agreements that contain no repayment schedule

PUBLIC COMPANY IMPLICATIONS: Because related-party transactions are not conducted at arm's length, there is often a lack of independence and objectivity between management and the related party. In light of this, SOX prohibits related-party transactions that involve personal loans to executives of public companies. It is now illegal for any public company to extend or maintain credit, to arrange for the extension of credit, or to renew the extension of credit in the form of a personal loan to any director or executive officer of the company. These restrictions do not apply to any loan, such as a home loan or credit card agreement, made by a bank or other insured financial institution under normal banking operations using market terms. Auditors of public companies should be alert for prohibited loans to executives and deal with them as illegal acts.

Finally, certain conditions may increase the possibility that a related-party transaction may occur. These conditions include the following:

- Inadequate working capital or lines of credit
- Earnings forecast that was too optimistic
- Too great a dependence on one or a few products or customers
- A declining industry
- Excess capacity
- Significant legal problems
- Exposure to technological changes

OBSERVATION: Although these conditions do not usually result in related-party transactions, they indicate that the auditor must be more alert to the increased possibility.

FRAUD POINTER: AU-C 240 notes that the presence of significant related-party transactions not in the ordinary course of business or with related parties who are not audited or who are audited by another firm can create opportunities for management or others to engage in fraudulent financial reporting. When evaluating business transactions involving previously unidentified related parties, auditors should exercise appropriate professional skepticism.

Risk Assessment and Related Procedures

Understanding related-party relationships and transactions

As part of the engagement team discussion considering the financial statements' susceptibility to misstatements that could result from the entity's related-party relationships or transactions, matters such as the following may be addressed:

- The nature and extent of the entity's related-party relationships and transactions
- The importance of maintaining professional skepticism regarding those risks of material misstatement
- Records, documents, or circumstances that could indicate the existence of unidentified or undisclosed related-party relationships or transactions
- The importance management and those charged with governance place on proper accounting for and disclosure of such relationships and transactions
- Circumstances or conditions that may give rise to related parties that might not be identified by management or disclosed to the auditor
- Specific considerations of how related parties may be involved in fraud

PLANNING AID REMINDER: The principal auditor and other auditors of related entities should exchange information on the names of known related parties in the early stages of their examinations.

Information regarding the identity of the entity's related parties may be readily available to the auditor if the entity has an information system that tracks this information to enable the entity to meet disclosure requirements; however, this is not always the case. The auditor's inquiries regarding the identity of related parties may occur as part of the engagement acceptance or continuance process or as part of the risk assessment procedures and related activities performed to obtain information about the entity and its environment. Information about the identity of related parties is also obtained through management's written representations disclosing the identity of related parties that management is aware of and asserting that such related-party relationships and transactions have been appropriately accounted for and disclosed.

ENGAGEMENT STRATEGY: Management is more likely to be aware of relationships of economic significance to the entity so inquiries may be more effective if the auditor focuses on significant transactions the entity engages in and asks if those parties are related parties.

Management is responsible for designing, implementing, and monitoring controls over related-party relationships and transactions so that they are appropriately accounted for and disclosed and those charged with governance are responsible for overseeing management's performance of this responsibility. To obtain an understanding of controls over related-party relationships and transactions, the auditor makes inquiries of management and others within the entity such as those charged with governance, internal auditors, legal counsel, the chief ethics officer, the chief compliance officer, and personnel who initiate, authorize, process, or record significant transactions outside the entity's normal course of business or those who supervise or monitor such personnel.

FRAUD POINTER: Management override of controls is often involved in fraudulent financial reporting when controls appear to be operating effectively. The risk of management override is increased with related parties because management may be presented with greater incentives and opportunities to perpetrate fraud.

AU-C 550 lists factors the auditor may consider in obtaining his or her understanding of internal control over related-party relationships and transactions:

- Communication and enforcement of internal ethics codes
- Policies and procedures for the disclosure of management's and those charged with governance's interests in related-party transactions
- Assignment of responsibilities for initiating, recording, summarizing, and disclosing related-party transactions
- Disclosure and discussion between management and those charged with governance of significant related-party transactions outside the entity's normal course of business, including whether those charged with governance questioned the business rationale for such transactions
- Guidelines approval of for related-party transaction when actual or perceived conflicts of interest exist
- Periodic reviews by internal auditors
- Proactive action taken by management to resolve related-party disclosure issues
- The existence of whistle-blowing policies and procedures

ENGAGEMENT STRATEGY: If controls over related-party transactions and relationships are deficient or nonexistent, sufficient appropriate audit evidence may not be able to be obtained. In these circumstances, the auditor should consider the implications for the audit and the opinion in the auditor's report.

Reviewing documents or records for related-party information and arrangements

Entity documents and records that may provide information about related-party relationships and transactions not previously identified or disclosed to the auditor include: income tax returns; information supplied to regulatory authorities; shareholder registers identifying principal shareholders; statements of conflicts of interest from or contracts and agreements with management and those charged with governance; records of investments and benefit plans; significant contracts and agreements not in the ordinary course of business; invoices and correspondence from professional advisors; life insurance policies acquired; significant contracts renegotiated during the period; capital financing arrangements with entities other than financial institutions; economic development arrangements for capital additions; and prior year audit documentation.

Third party confirmations and prior years' audit documentation are additional documentation that may provide the auditor with relevant information. The auditor may also obtain relevant information by inquiring of a predecessor auditor regarding that auditor's knowledge of existing relationships and the extent of management involvement in material transactions.

An arrangement is a formal or informal agreement between an entity and one or more other parties for reasons such as establishing a business relationship, conducting certain types of transactions, or providing designated services or financial support. Arrangements may indicate the presence of related-party relationships or transactions in certain circumstances, including participation in unincorporated partnerships with other parties, agreements for provision of services to certain parties under terms and conditions outside the entity's normal course of business, or guarantees and guarantor relationships.

When the auditor is identifying significant transactions outside the entity's normal course of business, such transactions may include the following as listed in AU-C 550:

- Complex equity transactions such as corporate restructurings or acquisitions

- Transactions with offshore entities in jurisdictions with less rigorous corporate laws or regulations

- Leases or provision of services to another party with no consideration exchanged

- Sales transactions with unusually large discounts or returns

- Transactions with circular arrangements such as a commitment to repurchase

- Transactions under contracts when terms are changed before expiration

Sharing information with the engagement team

When sharing relevant information obtained about the entity's related parties with other members of the engagement team, the auditor may share information about the nature of related-party relationships and transactions and about significant or complex related-party relationships or transactions that may require special audit consideration, especially if management or those charged with governance are financially involved. This sharing of information is most useful in the beginning stages of an audit.

Identification and Assessment of the Risks of Material Misstatement

If a related party exerts dominant influence over an entity or its management, that is a fraud risk factor which, when combined with other fraud risk factors, may indicate significant risks of material misstatement due to fraud. Factors indicating a related party may be exerting dominant influence include the following:

- The related party has vetoed business decisions of management or those charged with governance.
- Significant transactions are referred to the related party for final approval.
- Business proposals by the related party receive little debate.
- Transactions involving the related party are rarely independently reviewed and approved.
- The related party helped found the entity and still participates in managing the entity.

Responses to the Risks of Material Misstatement

The nature, timing, and extent of the auditor's further audit procedures to respond to the risks of material misstatement associated with related-party relationships and transactions will depend on the nature of those risks and the entity's circumstances.

If there is a significant risk that certain related-party transactions have not been properly accounted for or disclosed, the auditor may perform substantive audit procedures such as:

- Confirming transaction details with the related parties
- Inspecting evidence held by other parties to the transaction
- Confirming or discussing significant transaction information with intermediaries
- Referring to public information sources when there is reason to believe that significant transactions with unfamiliar parties may lack substance
- Obtaining information about the financial capability of other parties to the transaction

---

ENGAGEMENT STRATEGY: Since the audit risk associated with management's assertions concerning related-party transactions is generally higher than the audit risk associated with other transactions, the audit procedures that are applied to related-party transactions should be more extensive or effective. For example, to obtain additional evidence or a better understanding of a related-party transaction, the auditor may apply selected audit procedures to, or may actually audit, the financial statements of the related party as part of the engagement strategy.

PLANNING AID REMINDER: In some circumstances, substantive audit procedures will not provide the auditor with sufficient appropriate audit evidence and testing the entity's controls over related-party relationships and transactions will be required.

If there is a significant risk of material misstatement due to fraud because of a related party with dominant influence, the auditor may perform the following procedures to identify any need for further substantive audit procedures: inquire of management, those charged with governance, and the related party; inspect significant contracts with the related party; perform appropriate background research; and review any employee whistle-blowing reports.

Newly identified related-party relationships or transactions

Substantive audit procedures that may be appropriate for the auditor to perform related to newly identified related-party relationships and transactions include the following:

- Inquiring about the nature of the entity's relationships with the newly identified related parties and other external parties presumed to have significant knowledge of the entity and its business

- Analyzing accounting records for transactions with the newly identified related parties

- Verifying terms and conditions of transactions with newly identified related parties and evaluating whether those transactions have been appropriately accounted for and disclosed

---

FRAUD POINTER: If management appears to have intentionally failed to disclose related-party relationships or transactions, the auditor should consider whether to reevaluate the reliability of management's representations and responses to the auditor's inquiries.

Significant related-party transactions outside the entity's normal course of business

The auditor considers the business rationale of significant related-party transactions outside the entity's normal course of business to evaluate whether these transactions indicate the presence of any fraud risk factors. In evaluating the business rationale of these transactions, the auditor may consider whether: the transaction is overly complex, has unusual terms, lacks an apparent logical business reason for its occurrence, involves previously unidentified related parties, or is processed in an unusual manner. The auditor may also consider whether management has discussed the transaction's nature and accounting with those charged with governance and whether management is emphasizing a particular accounting treatment instead of following the underlying economics of the transaction.

PLANNING AID REMINDER: The auditor is required to understand the business rationale for significant related-party transactions. AICPA Practice Alert 03-1 (Audit Confirmations) states that confirmation of the terms of related-party transactions can help auditors obtain this understanding. Specifically, the auditor might confirm the transaction amount and terms, including any guarantees, with the other party to the transaction. Because client management may be on both sides of a related-party transaction, the auditor should consider confirming the terms of the transaction with intermediaries (e.g., agents, attorneys, banks, guarantors).

A transaction that appears inconsistent with the nature of the related party's business or that is materially inconsistent with management's explanations may represent a fraud risk. Furthermore, if management's explanations are inconsistent with the transaction, the auditor is required to consider the reliability of management's explanations and representations on other significant matters.

Proper authorization and approval of such significant related-party transactions by management, those charged with governance, or shareholders may provide audit evidence that these transactions have been appropriately considered and reflected in the financial statements. However, authorization and approval may not be sufficient to conclude whether risks of material misstatement due to fraud are absent because they may be ineffective in circumstances when there is collusion between related parties or the entity is subject to the dominant influence of a related party.

Assertions regarding the terms of related-party transactions

It is typically difficult for the auditor to substantiate an assertion by management that the terms of a transaction were equivalent to those prevailing in an arm's length transaction. Even if audit evidence is available supporting the price of a transaction, other terms and conditions of the transaction may be impracticable to confirm. Therefore, there may be a risk that management's assertion regarding such a transaction is materially misstated.

Management may support an assertion that the terms of a related-party transaction are equivalent to those of an arm's length transaction by having an external specialist determine and confirm a market value, terms, and conditions for the transaction or by comparing the transaction's terms to those of an identical or similar transaction with an unrelated party or to known market terms from broadly similar transactions on an open market. The auditor may evaluate management's support for such an assertion by considering the appropriateness of management's process for supporting the assertion or by verifying the source of and testing the data supporting the assertion for accuracy, completeness, and relevance.

ENGAGEMENT STRATEGY: If the auditor believes management's assertion that the terms of a related-party transaction are equivalent to an arm's length transaction is unsubstantiated or sufficient appropriate audit evidence to support the assertion cannot be obtained, he or she should consider the implications for the audit and the audit opinion in accordance with AU-C 705.

ENGAGEMENT STRATEGY: If management does not adequately substantiate its representation with respect to the related-party transaction, the auditor should express a qualified or adverse opinion on the financial statements if the matter is considered material.

Evaluation of Identified Related-Party Relationships and Transactions

Appropriate disclosure of related-party transactions may not be achieved if the disclosures are not understandable, which could occur if the business rationale and effects of the transaction on the financial statements are unclear or misstated or key terms, conditions, or other elements of the transactions necessary to understand them are not appropriately disclosed.

Communication with Those Charged with Governance

Significant related-party matters the auditor may communicate with those charged with governance include the following listed in AU-C 550:

- Nondisclosure by management of related-party relationships or transactions
- Significant related-party transactions identified that have not been appropriately authorized and approved
- Disagreement with management regarding the accounting for and disclosure of significant related-party transactions
- Noncompliance with applicable laws or regulations prohibiting or restricting specific types of related-party transactions
- Difficulties in identifying the entity that ultimately controls the entity

PLANNING AID REMINDER: The auditor should consider obtaining written representations from senior management of an entity and its board of directors regarding whether they or other related parties were involved in transactions with the entity.

Determine whether the client has made appropriate disclosures for related-party transactions that have been identified

The Financial Accounting Standards Board (FASB) requires disclosure of related-party transactions that (1) are not eliminated in consolidated or combined financial statements and (2) are necessary to understand the entity's financial statements.

If separate financial statements of an entity that has been consolidated are presented in a financial report that includes the consolidated financial statements, duplicate disclosure of the related-party transactions is not necessary. Thus, disclosure of the related-party transactions in the consolidated statements is all that is required. However, disclosure of related-party transactions is required in separate financial statements of (1) a parent company, (2) a subsidiary, (3) a corporate joint venture, or (4) an investee that is less than 50% owned. The minimum financial statement disclosures required by ASC 850 (Related Parties) for related-party transactions that (1) are not eliminated in consolidation or combination and (2) are necessary to the understanding of the financial statements are as follows:

1. The nature of the related-party relationship. The name of the related party should also be disclosed if it is essential to the understanding of the relationship.

2. A description of the related-party transactions, including amounts and other pertinent information for each period in which an income statement is presented.

3. Related-party transactions of no amount, or of nominal amounts, must also be disclosed. In other words, all information that is necessary for an understanding of the effects of the related-party transactions on the financial statements must be disclosed, assuming this information is material.

4. The effects of any change in terms between the related parties from terms used in prior periods. In addition, the dollar amount of transactions for each period in which an income statement is presented must be disclosed.

5. If not apparent in the financial statements, (1) the terms of related-party transactions, (2) the manner of settlement to related-party transactions, and (3) the amount due to, or due from, related parties must all be disclosed.

6. The nature of any control relationship, even if there were no transactions between the related parties, must be disclosed in all circumstances.

The amount of information disclosed for related-party transactions must be sufficient for the user of the financial statements to be able to understand the related-party transaction. Thus, the disclosure of the total amount of a specific type of related-party transaction, or the effects of the relationship between the related parties, may be all that is necessary. The auditor must determine whether the related-party transaction affects the financial statements to such a degree that they are materially misstated and must modify the report accordingly.

OBSERVATION: One cannot assume that a related-party transaction is consummated in the same manner as an arm's-length transaction. Disclosures or other representations of related-party transactions in financial statements should not, under any circumstances, indicate that the transaction was made on the same basis as an arm's-length transaction.

SECTION 560

SUBSEQUENT EVENTS AND SUBSEQUENTLY DISCOVERED FACTS

Authoritative Pronouncements

SAS-122—Statements on Auditing Standards: Clarification and Recodification

Overview

AU-C 560 addresses the auditor's responsibilities relating to subsequent events and subsequently discovered facts in a financial statement audit. The responsibilities of a predecessor auditor for subsequent events and subsequently discovered facts when reissuing an auditor's report on prior period financial statements are also addressed.

There are two types of subsequent events generally identified by financial reporting frameworks:

1. Those providing evidence of conditions that existed at the date of the financial statements

2. Those providing evidence of conditions that arose after the date of the financial statements but before the date of the auditor's report.

The auditor seeks to obtain sufficient appropriate audit evidence about whether subsequent events are appropriately reflected in the financial statements in accordance with the applicable financial reporting framework. Another objective of the auditor is to respond appropriately to subsequently discovered facts. For predecessor auditors, the objective is to determine if reissuing a previously issued auditor's report on prior period financial statements to be presented with audited financial statements of a subsequent period on a comparative basis is still appropriate.

The auditor's report should be dated no earlier than the date on which the auditor has gathered sufficient audit evidence to support the opinion. The auditor has not obtained sufficient audit evidence to support the opinion until (1) the audit documentation has been reviewed, (2) the financial statements, including required disclosures have been prepared, and (3) management and those charged with governance (as appropriate) have accepted responsibility for the financial statements. Accordingly, the date of the auditor's report on amended financial statements cannot be earlier than the date of approval of the amended financial statements.

The term "audited financial statements" refers to the financial statements together with the auditor's report on the financial statements. While AU-C 560 describes the auditor's responsibilities for subsequent events and subsequently discovered facts in a financial statement audit, the auditor may have additional responsibilities related to subsequent events when audited financial statements are included in other documents subsequent to their issuance. These responsibilities are not addressed in AU-C 560, but may relate to legal or regulatory requirements involving private placement offerings, exempt public offerings, or other public offerings in jurisdictions outside the United States.

Definitions

Date of the auditor's report	The date that the auditor dates the report on the financial statements.
Date of the financial statements	The date of the end of the latest period covered by the financial statements.
Subsequent events	Events occurring between the date of the financial statements and the date of the auditor's report.
Subsequently discovered facts	Facts that become known to the auditor after the date of the auditor's report that, had they been known to the auditor at that date, may have caused the auditor to amend the auditor's report.

Requirements

The auditor is presumptively required to perform the following procedures related to subsequent events and subsequently discovered facts:

Subsequent Events

1. Perform audit procedures designed to obtain sufficient appropriate audit evidence that all subsequent events have been identified. If previously performed audit procedures provide satisfactory conclusions about a matter, additional audit procedures do not need to be performed.

2. Audit procedures should cover the period from the date of the financial statements to the date of the auditor's report as much as is practicable. The nature and extent of audit procedures should take the auditor's risk assessment into account and include the following:

   a. Obtain an understanding of procedures management established to identify subsequent events

   b. Inquire of management and those charged with governance (as appropriate) about whether any events occurred after the date of the financial statements that might affect the statements

   c. Read any minutes of meetings of the entity's owners, management, and those charged with governance held after the date of the financial statements and inquire about matters discussed at any such meeting if minutes are not yet available

   d. Read the latest of any subsequent interim financial statements of the entity

3. Determine if each subsequent event that is identified and requires adjustment of, or disclosure in, the financial statements is appropriately reflected in the financial statements in accordance with the applicable financial reporting framework.

Subsequently Discovered Facts

4. After the date of the auditor's report, the auditor is not obligated to perform any audit procedures regarding the financial statements. If the auditor becomes aware of a subsequently discovered fact before or after the report

release date, (1) discuss the matter with management and those charged with governance (as appropriate) and (2) determine if the financial statements need amendment and, if so, inquire how management intends to address the matter in the financial statements.

5. If management amends the financial statements, perform the necessary audit procedures on the revision and either:5.

    a. Date the auditor's report as of a later date; extend the audit procedures performed for subsequent events to the date of the new auditor's report; and request written representations from management as of the new date of the auditor's report; or

    b. Include an additional date in the auditor's report on the amended financial statements limited to that amendment, indicating the audit procedures on subsequently discovered facts are limited to that amendment, and request written representations from management as of the additional date about whether any information has come to management's attention that would cause management to believe any previous representations should be modified, or any other events have occurred subsequent to the financial statements date that would require adjustment to, or disclosure in, the financial statements.

    c. If a subsequently discovered fact became known to the auditor after the report release date and the audited financial statements had already been made available to third parties, the auditor should assess whether steps taken by management are timely and appropriate to ensure that anyone receiving those financial statements is informed of the situation, including that the audited financial statements are not to be relied on.

    d. If a subsequently discovered fact became known to the auditor after the report release date and the opinion on the amended financial statements is different from the opinion previously expressed, an emphasis-of-matter or other-matter paragraph should be included disclosing (1) the date of the auditor's previous report, (2) the type of opinion previously expressed, (3) the substantive reasons for the different opinion, and (4) that the auditor's opinion on the amended financial statements is different from the auditor's previous opinion.

6. If management does not amend the financial statements and the auditor believes the statements need to be amended:

    a. If a subsequently discovered fact becomes known to the auditor before the report release date, express a modified (qualified or adverse) opinion as required and release the auditor's report.

    b. If a subsequently discovered fact becomes known to the auditor after the report release date and the audited financial statements have not been made available to third parties, notify management and those charged with governance not to make the audited financial statements available until amendments have been made and a new auditor's report has been provided. If the audited financial statements are made available to third parties without the necessary amendments, take appropriate action to seek to prevent reliance on the auditor's report.

    c. If a subsequently discovered fact becomes known to the auditor after the report release date and the audited financial statements have been made available to third parties, assess whether steps taken by management are timely and appropriate to ensure that anyone receiving those financial statements is informed of the situation, including that the audited financial statements are not to be relied on. If the necessary steps are not taken by management, inform management and those charged with governance that the auditor will seek to prevent future reliance on the auditor's report. If the necessary steps are still not taken despite such notification, take appropriate action to seek to prevent reliance on the auditor's report.

Predecessor Auditor's Reissuance of the Auditor's Report in Comparative Financial Statements

7. A predecessor auditor may be requested to reissue a previously issued auditor's report on prior period financial statements when those financial statements are to be presented on a comparative basis with audited financial statements of a subsequent period. In this situation, the predecessor auditor should perform the following procedures to determine if the previously issued auditor's report is still appropriate before reissuing the report:

a. Read the subsequent period financial statements being presented on a comparative basis.

b. Compare the prior period financial statements reported on with the subsequent period financial statements to be presented on a comparative basis.

c. Inquire of and obtain a representation letter from management of the former client at or near the date of reissuance stating (1) whether any information has come to management's attention that would cause them to believe any previous representations should be modified and (2) whether any events have occurred after the date of the most recent prior period financial statements reported on by the predecessor auditor that would require adjustment to or disclosure in the financial statements.

d. Obtain a representation letter from the successor auditor stating whether the successor auditor's audit revealed any matters that in his or her opinion might have a material effect on or require disclosure in the financial statements reported on by the predecessor auditor.

8. If, in performing the above procedures, a subsequently discovered fact becomes known to the predecessor auditor, follow the guidance for auditors becoming aware of subsequently discovered facts after the report release date. However, in circumstances where management amends the financial statements and the predecessor auditor does not plan to issue a new auditor's report or if management does not revise the financial statements when the predecessor auditor believes they need to be revised, the only step the auditor must take is to assess whether the steps taken by management are timely and appropriate to ensure that anyone receiving those financial statements is informed of the situation, including that the audited financial statements are not to be relied on.

Analysis and Application of Procedures

Subsequent Events

The specified audit procedures that the auditor is required to perform relating to subsequent events are not necessarily the only procedures the auditor will perform to obtain sufficient appropriate audit evidence. The auditor may perform audit procedures for other purposes in the audit that also provide evidence about subsequent events. The auditor's risk assessment may be such that he or she includes procedures such as review or testing of accounting records or transactions occurring between the date of the financial statements and the auditor's report date in order to obtain sufficient appropriate audit evidence.

Furthermore, the audit procedures performed to obtain evidence about subsequent events may depend on the availability of information, the manner in which the entity's accounting records have been maintained, and the extent to which information has been prepared since the date of the financial statements. For example, the entity may not have prepared interim financial statements or minutes of meetings of management or those charged with governance. In this instance, the auditor may inspect the entity's books and records. In addition to the required audit procedures, the auditor may consider it necessary to apply additional audit procedures, such as reading the most recent available budgets, cash flow forecasts, and other related management reports for periods after the date of the financial statements.

PLANNING AID REMINDER: The auditor should request written representation from management and those charged with governance (as appropriate) as of the date of the auditor's report that all subsequent events have been adjusted or disclosed in the financial statements.

When inquiring of management or those charged with governance about whether any subsequent events have occurred, the auditor may make specific inquiries on particular matters:

- The current status of items accounted for on the basis of preliminary or inconclusive data

- Any new commitments, borrowings, or guarantees entered into

- Any planned or executed sales or acquisitions of assets

- Any increases in capital, issuance of debt instruments, or plans for or existence of a merger or liquidation agreement

- Any assets that have been appropriated by the government or destroyed

- Any developments regarding contingencies

- Any unusual accounting adjustments that are planned or performed

- Any events likely to occur or that have occurred bringing the appropriateness of accounting policies used in the financial statements into question

- Any events that occurred relevant to the measurement of estimates or provisions made in the financial statements

- Any events that occurred relevant to the recoverability of assets

ENGAGEMENT STRATEGY: When agreeing to the terms of the audit engagement, the auditor may include that management will inform the auditor of subsequent events and subsequently discovered facts.

Subsequently Discovered Facts that Become Known to the Auditor before the Report Release Date

When an amendment to the financial statements is made and the auditor limits the audit procedures performed to that amendment, the auditor's report will be dual-dated. Under this approach, the report is dated based on the original audit report date and an additional date is noted in the report:

March 3, 20X5, except as to Note X, which is as of March 15, 20X5.

If the auditor dual-dates the report, that informs users of the financial statements that the procedures he or she performed after the original date of the auditor's report are limited to the amendment of the financial statements. The auditor is allowed to dual-date the report in certain circumstances, but is never required to dual-date the report and may always extend audit procedures on subsequent events to the date of the auditor's report on the amended financial statements if desired. If the financial statements are revised, management's written representations are required as of the later auditor's report date. In these situations, the auditor may request management provide a new representation letter or may agree to accept a written representation that addresses whether there are any changes to the previously provided written representations and what those changes are.

OBSERVATION: If the financial statements are revised by disclosing an event that arose after the original audit report date in a separate financial statement note labeled as unaudited, the auditor is not required to perform any procedures on the revision and the auditor's report date stays the same.

Subsequently Discovered Facts that Become Known to the Auditor after the Report Release Date

The auditor's responsibility to investigate whether subsequently discovered information existed at the date of the auditor's report does not change even when he or she has resigned or been discharged from the engagement. However, the specific procedures the auditor performs may vary depending on factors such as the time elapsed since the report release date and any legal implications such as those regarding confidentiality.

If management amends the financial statements to reflect a subsequently discovered fact, the steps taken to ensure that anyone in receipt of the financial statements is informed of this amendment may depend on the circumstances:

- Issue amended financial statements with appropriate disclosure of the matter as soon as practicable.

- If the issuance of amended financial statements and a new auditor's report is not imminent, notify anyone known or likely to be relying on the financial statements and auditor's report that they are not to be relied upon and that amended financial statements and a new auditor's report will be issued.

- If issuance of the subsequent period's financial statements is imminent, include appropriate disclosure of the matter in those financial statements.

PLANNING AID REMINDER: Additional requirements exist for audits performed under *Government Auditing Standards* in circumstances where management amends the financial statements to reflect a subsequently discovered fact. These requirements include procedures such as reporting directly to appropriate officials when management does not take the necessary steps.

If the auditor notifies management not to make the financial statements available to third parties and management does so or the auditor notifies management or those charged with governance to take necessary steps to prevent reliance by third parties on the auditor's report on the financial statements and these steps are not taken, the auditor's course of action depends on his or her legal rights and obligations. The auditor may consider it appropriate to seek legal advice under these circumstances.

The auditor may take the following steps, depending on the circumstances, to prevent reliance on the auditor's report to the extent applicable:

- Notify management and those charged with governance that the auditor's report is not to be associated with the financial statements or to be relied upon.

- Notify any applicable regulatory agencies that the auditor's report should no longer be relied on and request that the agency take the appropriate steps to accomplish the necessary disclosure.

- Notify persons known or likely to be relying on the financial statements that the auditor's report should no longer be relied on to the extent practicable.

The notifications by the auditor to third parties may contain different information depending on the circumstances. If the auditor is able to determine that the financial statements need amendment, notification may include: (1) a description of the nature of the matter and its effects on the financial statements and (2) a description of the effect on the auditor's report if the matter had been known to the auditor at the date of the report and not reflected in the financial statements. The notification should avoid comments concerning the conduct or motives of any person. If the auditor is unable to determine if the financial statements need amendment, a notification may indicate that information became known to the auditor that, if true, causes the auditor to believe that the auditor's report should not be relied on. The notification does not need to describe the specific matter.

Predecessor Auditor's Reissuance of the Auditor's Report in Comparative Financial Statements

A request by an entity's management or those charged with governance that the predecessor auditor provide additional copies of the auditor's report after the report release date does not constitute a reissuance of the report. Therefore, the auditor is not responsible for performing any procedures regarding events that may have occurred between the date of the auditor's report and the date of the release of additional copies.

While a predecessor auditor may agree to reissue an audit report on prior period financial statements to be presented in comparative financial statements with audited financial statements of a subsequent period, the auditor is not required to reissue the auditor's report. The predecessor auditor may decline reissuing the report if circumstances such as the current form or manner of presentation of the prior period financial statements make the predecessor's previous audit report inappropriate.

Practitioner's Aids

Exhibit AU-C 560-1 illustrates an audit program for subsequent events.

EXHIBIT AU-C 560-1—SUBSEQUENT EVENTS AUDIT PROGRAM

Use the following procedures as a guide to identify subsequent events that occur after the date of the financial statements but before the date of our audit report. This audit program is only a guide, and professional judgment should be exercised to determine how it should be modified by revising or adding procedures.

Initial and date each procedure as it is completed. If the procedure is not relevant to this particular engagement, place "N/A" (not applicable) in the space provided for an initial.

Client Name: _____

Date of Financial Statements: _____

Audit Report Date: _____

		Initials	Date	Audit Documentation Reference
1.	Inquire of and discuss with appropriate management personnel whether any material contingent liabilities or commitments existed at the date of the balance sheet or shortly thereafter.	_____	_____	_____
2.	Inquire of and discuss with appropriate management personnel whether any significant change in owners' equity, long-term debt, or working capital has occurred since the date of the balance sheet.	_____	_____	_____
3.	Inquire of and discuss with appropriate management personnel whether any material adjustments have been made during the subsequent period.	_____	_____	_____

	Initials	Date	Audit Documentation Reference
4. Inquire of and discuss with appropriate management personnel the status of items that were accounted for in the financial statements on the basis of tentative or preliminary data.	_____	_____	_____
5. Read the latest minutes of stockholders', directors', and other committee meetings that occurred during the subsequent period.	_____	_____	_____
6. Obtain from the client's legal counsel a description and evaluation of any impending litigation, claims, and contingent liabilities.	_____	_____	_____
7. Obtain a letter of representation from management regarding any events occurring during the subsequent period that require adjustment or disclosure.	_____	_____	_____
8. Read the latest interim financial statements and compare them to (a) the year-end financial statements and (b) the interim financial information for the previous year.	_____	_____	_____
9. Review journal entries made after the end of the year for unusual amounts, unusual activity, or other unusual characteristics.	_____	_____	_____
10. Determine whether the client is considering changing any of its accounting policies or procedures.	_____	_____	_____
11. Perform any other procedures deemed appropriate depending on the results of the procedures described above.	_____	_____	_____

Reviewed by: _____

Date: _____

_____

Practitioner's Aids

EXHIBIT AU-C 560-2—DISCOVERY OF FACTS AFTER THE DATE OF THE REPORT

Use the following procedures, which are adapted from guidance found in AU-C 560, as a guide for evaluating the discovery of facts after the date of the report. The program is only a guide, and professional judgment should be exercised to determine how the guidance established in the auditing standard should be adapted to a particular engagement.

Initial and date each procedure as it is completed. If the procedure is not relevant to this engagement, place "N/A" (not applicable) in the space provided for an initial.

Client Name: _____

Date of Financial Statements: _____

	Initials	Date	Audit Documentation Reference
1. Determine whether the discovered facts are relevant to the financial statements by considering the following factors:			
• The report would have been affected if the CPA had known the information at the date of the audit report,	_____	_____	_____
• The matter would have been reflected in the financial statements, and	_____	_____	_____
• The CPA believes that there are third-party users relying on or likely to rely on the financial statements who would attach importance to the subsequently discovered information.	_____	_____	_____
2. If the conditions described in 1 above exist, advise the client to inform third-party users currently relying or likely to rely on the financial statements, following the general guidance:			
• When the effects of the subsequently discovered information can be determined quickly, and the issuance of more current financial statements is not imminent, revised financial statements and a revised report should be issued. (Both the financial statements and the report should describe the reason for the revision.)	_____	_____	_____
• When the issuance of more recent financial statements is imminent, the disclosure of the revision can be made in the more recent financial statements; the earlier financial statements need not be reissued.	_____	_____	_____
• When the effects of the subsequently discovered information cannot be determined without a prolonged investigation, third-party users who are currently relying or likely to rely on the financial statements and the associated report should be notified not to rely on them and should be informed that revised financial statements and a revised audit report will be issued when an investigation is completed.	_____	_____	_____
3. If the client refuses to make appropriate disclosures to third-party users, inform each member of the board of directors of the refusal.	_____	_____	_____
4. If the board of directors is notified but appropriate disclosures to third-party users still are not made, discuss the matter with legal counsel.	_____	_____	_____

	Initials	Date	Audit Documentation Reference

5. If it appears there are or will be third-party users who will rely on the financial statements, consider the following:

  - Notify the client that the CPA's report should no longer be associated with the client's financial statements. _____ _____ _____

  - Notify regulatory agencies having jurisdiction over the client that the CPA's report should no longer be associated with the client's financial statements. _____ _____ _____

  - To the extent practical, the CPA should notify each third-party user known to be relying on the financial statements that the auditor's report should no longer be relied upon. _____ _____ _____

6. If the matters have been satisfactorily investigated and the subsequent information considered reliable, disclosures to regulatory authorities and third-party users should include the following:

  - The nature of the subsequently acquired information and the effects on the financial statements. _____ _____ _____

  - The effects of the subsequently acquired information on the CPA's report, if the information had been known to him or her at the date of the report and it had not been reflected in the financial statements. _____ _____ _____

7. If a satisfactory investigation is not conducted, make the following disclosure to regulatory authorities and third-party users:

  - Describe the general nature of the problem (specific details are not required). _____ _____ _____

  - State that the effects of the problem cannot be substantiated because the client did not cooperate in the investigation of the matter. _____ _____ _____

  - State that if the information is correct, the CPA believes that his or her report should no longer be associated with the client's financial statements. No disclosure should be made unless the CPA believes that the financial statements are likely to be misleading and that his or her audit report should no longer be relied upon. _____ _____ _____

8. Other engagement procedures: _____
    _____

Reviewed by: _____

Date: _____

_____

SECTION 570

THE AUDITOR'S CONSIDERATION OF AN ENTITY'S ABILITY TO CONTINUE AS A GOING CONCERN

Authoritative Pronouncements

IMPORTANT NOTICE FOR 2012: At the time the 2013 *GAAS Guide* went to press, the Auditing Standards Board had not issued a redrafted SAS to supersede SAS-59, *The Auditor's Consideration of an Entity's Ability to Continue as a Going Concern*. The guidance in SAS-59, as amended, was contained in the earlier editions of the *Codification of Statements on Auditing Standards* as AU 341. SAS-122 designates Section 570 for the codification of a subsequent clarified SAS that will be issued to supersede SAS-59 when it is redrafted for clarity and convergence with ISA 570, *Going Concern*, as part of the Clarification and Convergence project of the ASB. For purposes of the 2013 *GAAS Guide*, the guidance in SAS-59, as amended (old section AU 341) is provided in this section.

SAS-59—The Auditor's Consideration of an Entity's Ability to Continue as a Going Concern

SAS-64—Omnibus Statement on Auditing Standards—1990

SAS-77—Amendments to Statements on Auditing Standards No. 22, "Planning and Supervision," No. 59 "The Auditor's Consideration of an Entity's Ability to Continue as a Going Concern," and SAS-62, "Special Reports"

SAS-103—Audit Documentation

SAS-113—Omnibus Statement on Auditing Standards—2006

SAS-114—The Auditor's Communication with Those Charged with Governance

Auditing Interpretation No. 1 of AU 341 (August 1995)—Eliminating a Going Concern Explanatory Paragraph from a Reissued Report

Overview

Financial statements are usually prepared on the assumption that the entity will continue as a going concern. When a company decides or is forced to liquidate, the going-concern concept is not appropriate, and assets should be presented at their estimated net realizable values and legally enforceable liabilities should be classified according to priorities established by law.

SAS-59 (The Auditor's Consideration of an Entity's Ability to Continue as a Going Concern) states that as part of an audit, the auditor should evaluate conditions or events discovered during the engagement that raise questions about the appropriateness of the going-concern assumption. The auditor may identify such conditions or events at various points during the engagement, including during the performance of analytical procedures, when reading of responses received from the entity's legal counsel, and when evaluating the entity's compliance with restrictions imposed by loan agreements.

PLANNING AID REMINDER: Information that raises questions about going concern generally relates to the entity's ability to meet its maturing obligations without selling operating assets, restructuring debt, or revising operations based on outside pressures or similar strategies. SAS-59 states that the projection of the going-concern concept is limited to a "reasonable period of time," which is defined by SAS-59 as not exceeding one year beyond the date of the financial statements being audited.

Promulgated Procedures Checklist

The auditor should perform the following procedures when considering an entity's ability to continue as a going concern:

- Evaluate relevant information obtained during the course of the engagement.
- Identify and evaluate management's plans related to going concern.
- Consider the effect of the evidence on disclosures and the audit report.
- Document audit results.

Analysis and Application of Procedures

Evaluate relevant information obtained during the course of the engagement

Although the auditor is not specifically required to employ procedures to identify conditions or events that might raise substantial doubt, he or she should be sensitive to implications pertaining to going concern in the audit evidence collected during the audit.

SAS-59 provides the examples in Exhibit AU-C 570-1 as conditions and events that may raise substantial doubt about an entity's ability to continue as a going concern.

EXHIBIT AU-C 570-1—CONDITIONS AND EVENTS THAT MAY RAISE A SUBSTANTIAL-DOUBT QUESTION

Condition or Event	Specific Example
Negative trends	• Recurring operating losses
	• Working capital deficiencies
	• Negative cash flows from operations
	• Adverse key financial ratios
Other indications of possible agreements	• Default on loan or similar financial difficulties
	• Arrearages in dividends
Other indications of possible financial difficulties	• Denial of usual trade credit from vendors

Condition or Event	Specific Example
	• Restructuring of debt
	• Noncompliance with statutory capital requirements
	• Need to seek new sources of financing
	• Need to sell substantial assets
Internal matters	• Labor difficulties, such as work stoppages
	• Substantial dependence on the success of a particular project
	• Uneconomic long-term commitments
	• Need to significantly revise operations
External matters or similar matters that might affect the entity's ability to continue operations	• Legal proceedings, legislation
	• Loss of key franchise, license, or patent
	• Loss of principal customer or vendor
	• Occurrence of uninsured catastrophe

When the audit evidence raises substantial doubt, the auditor might consider obtaining additional evidence that could remove the auditor's substantial doubt.

FRAUD POINTER: The Committee of Sponsoring Organizations of the Tread-way Commission (COSO) issued a study in 2010 entitled "Fraudulent Financial Reporting: 1998 – 2007, An Analysis of U.S. Public Companies" that analyzed SEC enforcement actions alleging violations of the antifraud provisions of the securities acts. The study found that many of the companies involved in fraud were financially distressed in periods preceding the fraud. Over a quarter of the companies faced net losses, and several experienced downward trends in net income preceding the first year of the fraud. As auditors observe conditions affecting an entity's ability to continue as a going concern, they should consider whether those conditions create significant incentives or pressures that might lead management to perpetrate fraudulent financial reporting.

Identify and evaluate management's plans related to going concern

If the auditor concludes that there is substantial doubt about the continued existence of the entity as a going concern for a reasonable period of time, he or she should identify and evaluate management's plans to mitigate the effects of the adverse conditions or events. SAS-59 identifies the examples in Exhibit AU-C 570-2 as plans and factors that are relevant to the evaluation of those plans.

EXHIBIT AU-C 570-2—PLANS AND FACTORS RELEVANT TO THE EVALUATION OF MANAGEMENT'S PLANS

Planned Action	Factors Relevant to Evaluation of Planned Action
Sale of assets	• Restrictions on the sale of assets • Likely marketability of assets • Effects from sale of assets
Borrow or restructure debt	• Likelihood of raising funds based on existing or committed debt arrangements • Existing or committed arrangements for restructuring debt or obtaining guarantees for loans • Restrictions on ability to borrow or use assets as collateral
Reduce or delay expenditures	• Feasibility of reducing or postponing expenditures • Effects of reducing or postponing expenditures
Increase ownership equity	• Feasibility of increasing equity based on existing or committed arrangements • Flexibility of dividend policy • Ability to raise funds from affiliates or other investors

The auditor should consider obtaining audit evidence to support planned actions that are significant to the substantial-doubt question.

Some management strategies may in part be evaluated through the auditor's investigation of management's prospective financial statements. Specific audit procedures that the auditor may employ include the following:

- Read the prospective financial statements.

- Identify fundamental assumptions used to prepare the prospective financial statements.

- Evaluate the prospective financial statements on the basis of the auditor's familiarity with the client's operations.

- Compare the prospective financial statements for prior periods with actual results.

- Compare the prospective financial statements for the current period with actual results to date.

During the evaluation of fundamental assumptions used to prepare the prospective financial statements, the auditor should direct special emphasis to the following assumptions:

- Assumptions that have a material effect on the prospective financial statements

- Assumptions that have a high degree of uncertainty

- Assumptions that are inconsistent with past patterns

OBSERVATION: If the auditor discovers material factors that are not reflected in the preparation of the prospective financial statements, such discoveries should be discussed with management with the understanding that the statements may have to be revised.

Consider the effect of the evidence on disclosures and the audit report

Once the auditor has evaluated management's strategies designed to mitigate the adverse effects of conditions or events that raise substantial doubt about continued existence, the auditor must determine whether substantial doubt exists about the going-concern concept.

When events or conditions exist that, when considered in the aggregate, indicate there could be substantial doubt about the entity's ability to continue as a going concern for a reasonable period of time, the auditor is required to communicate certain matters to those charged with governance. These required communications include the nature of the events or conditions identified, the possible effect on the financial statements and the adequacy of related disclosures in the financial statements, and the effects on the auditor's report.

If substantial doubt does not exist, there is no need to modify the auditor's report. However, the auditor should consider whether the conditions or events that originally created the question about going concern should be disclosed in the financial statements. The disclosure might include the possible effect of the conditions or events and mitigating factors (including management's plans).

If the auditor concludes that substantial doubt exists, the effects of conditions or events should be considered as they relate to (1) adequate disclosures in the financial statements and (2) modification to the auditor's report.

Adequate disclosures

If the auditor concludes that substantial doubt exists about the client's ability to continue in existence, care must be taken to ensure that presentations and related disclosures in the financial statements properly reflect the (1) recoverability and classification of assets and (2) amount and classification of liabilities. In addition, the auditor should consider whether disclosures related to the possible discontinuation of operations are adequate in the financial statements. SAS-59 notes that the disclosure might include the following:

- Conditions or events that gave rise to the substantial doubt concerning continued existence
- Possible effects of the conditions or events
- Management's assessments concerning the significance of the conditions or events
- Other factors that may aggravate or mitigate the conditions or events
- Management's strategies that will attempt to deal with the adverse conditions or events

- Possible discontinuance of operations

Report modifications

If an auditor concludes that substantial doubt exists about the continued existence of the client, the audit report should be modified by adding an explanatory paragraph. When the auditor believes that the financial statements can still be relied on, the report modification is limited to a reference to the going-concern matter in the report, but the opinion expressed is unqualified.

The substantial-doubt question is discussed in an explanatory paragraph following the opinion paragraph. SAS-64 (AU 341, AU 508, AU 543) (Omnibus Statement on Auditing Standards—1990) requires that the explanatory paragraph include the phrase "substantial doubt about its [the entity's] ability to continue as a going concern," or similar wording. If similar wording is used, the terms "substantial doubt" and "going concern" must be used in the phrase.

When an auditor concludes that there is substantial doubt about an entity's ability to continue as a going concern, the audit report should not use language that suggests that the conclusion is conditional on future events. Specifically, SAS-77 (AU 311, AU 341, AU 623) notes that the use of conditional terminology—such as "if the company is unable to obtain re-financing, there may be substantial doubt about the company's ability to continue as a going concern"—is precluded.

The introductory, scope, and opinion paragraphs make no reference to the explanatory paragraph. An example of an explanatory paragraph based on a substantial-doubt question is presented below:

> The accompanying financial statements have been prepared assuming that the Company will continue as a going concern. As discussed in Note X to the financial statements, the Company is involved in litigation concerning alleged patent infringement. Because operations of the Company could be substantially impeded if the charges are upheld, the pending litigation raises substantial doubt about its ability to continue as a going concern. Management's plans in regard to the litigation are also described in Note X. The financial statements do not include any adjustments that might result from the outcome of this uncertainty.

When the auditor concludes that the uncertainty related to the substantial-doubt question is so significant that an opinion cannot be expressed on the financial statements, a disclaimer of opinion may be expressed.

The modification of the auditor's report because of a substantial-doubt question in the current year does not imply that the auditor's report on a prior year's financial statements (presented on a comparative basis) should also be modified.

During the current year, a question of substantial doubt contained in an auditor's report on a prior year's financial statements may no longer be applicable. Under this circumstance, the explanatory paragraph should not be repeated in the auditor's report on the comparative financial statements.

ENGAGEMENT STRATEGY: To not include the explanatory paragraph is not a change in the opinion expressed by the auditor; therefore, not including the paragraph does not require that the auditor observe the report guidelines concerning changes of opinions.

Although the auditor is responsible for including an explanatory paragraph in the auditor's report when a substantial-doubt question arises, the auditor is not responsible for predicting the outcome of future events. Thus, the liquidation of an entity (even within one year of the date of the financial statements) does not imply that the audit was substandard when an explanatory paragraph has not been included in the auditor's report. Similarly, the lack of including an explanatory paragraph in the auditor's report should not be taken as an assurance that the entity will continue as a going concern within a reasonable period of time. The auditor's evaluation is based on his or her knowledge of relevant conditions and events that exist at or have occurred prior to the date of the auditor's report.

SAS-77 (AU 311, AU 341, AU 623) prohibits the use of conditional language when a substantial-doubt explanatory paragraph is presented. Two examples of unacceptable language that are provided by SAS-77 (AU 311, AU 341, AU 623) are as follows:

If the company continues to suffer recurring losses from operations and continues to have a net capital deficiency, there may be substantial doubt about its ability to continue as a going concern.

The company has been unable to renegotiate its expiring credit agreements. Unless the company is able to obtain financial support, there is substantial doubt about its ability to continue as a going concern.

The going-concern paragraph should be included in subsequent auditor's reports as long as substantial doubt about the entity's existence continues. If the substantial-doubt condition ceases in a future period, there is no need to include the substantial-doubt explanatory paragraph for reports that cover previous periods in which the substantial-doubt condition was originally applicable.

After the auditor has issued a report that refers to a going-concern issue, the client may request the auditor to reissue the report and remove the going-concern reference because the client believes the circumstances that led to the uncertainty have been changed. Because the request by the client constitutes a new engagement, the auditor is not obligated to accept it. If the auditor accepts the engagement, the circumstances related to the going-concern issue should be examined to determine whether it is appropriate to revise the report.

Auditing Interpretation No. 1 of AU 341 (August 1995) titled "Eliminating a Going-Concern Explanatory Paragraph from a Reissued Report" notes that the auditor is not obligated to reissue a report; however, if the auditor decides to do so, he or she should perform the following procedures:

- Audit the event or transaction that prompted the request to delete the going-concern paragraph.

- Perform procedures related to subsequent events as described in AU 560.11–AU 560.12.

- Consider the factors related to the going-concern concept as described in AU 341.06–AU341.11.

ENGAGEMENT STRATEGY: In addition to the listed procedures, the auditor should conduct other procedures he or she deems appropriate. Based on the results of applying those procedures, the auditor should reassess the going-concern status of the client.

Document audit results

The auditor should document the following in the audit files when a going-concern issue has been raised and investigated based on the standards discussed in AU 341:

- Conditions or events that are the basis for the going-concern substantial doubt

- Elements of management's plans that have a significant effect on overcoming the adverse effects of the conditions or events identified above

- Audit procedures performed and evidence gathered related to the significant elements of management's plans

- The auditor's conclusion about the ability of the client to continue as a going concern for a reasonable period of time

- If the auditor concludes that there is substantial doubt about the client continuing as a going concern, document the possible effects on the financial statements (including disclosures)

- If the auditor concludes that the substantial doubt issue has been alleviated, document the conclusion regarding the need for disclosure of the conditions or events

- The conclusion regarding whether an explanatory paragraph should be included in the audit report

- If disclosures in the financial statements concerning the going-concern issue are inadequate, document the conclusion regarding whether the audit report should be qualified or an adverse opinion should be expressed

---

FRAUD POINTER: The Committee of Sponsoring Organizations of the Treadway Commission (COSO) issued a study in 2010 entitled "Fraudulent Financial Reporting: 1998-2007, An Analysis of U.S. Public Companies" that analyzed SEC enforcement actions alleging fraud. The study found that a large portion of the companies engaging in fraud filed for Chapter 11 bankruptcy, were defunct, taken over by a regulator, delisted from a stock exchange, or sold within two years of the SEC investigation. Auditors of companies where fraud has allegedly occurred should be sensitive to conditions affecting going concern in periods after the alleged fraud has been revealed.

Practitioner's Aids

EXHIBIT AU-C 570-3—EVALUATING AN ENTITY'S ABILITY TO CONTINUE AS A GOING CONCERN

Use the following procedures, which are adapted from guidance found in SAS-59 (The Auditor's Consideration of an Entity's Ability to Continue as a Going Concern), as a guide for evaluating an entity's ability to continue as a going concern. The program is only a guide, and professional judgment should be exercised to determine how the guidance established should be adapted to a particular engagement.

Initial and date each procedure as it is completed. If the procedure is not relevant to this engagement, place "N/A" (not applicable) in the space provided for an initial.

Client Name: _____

Date of Financial Statements: _____

		Initials	*Date*	*Audit Documentation Reference*
1.	Evaluate relevant information obtained during the course of the engagement.	_____	_____	_____
2.	Identify and evaluate management's plans related to going concern.	_____	_____	_____
3.	Consider the effect of the evidence on disclosures and the engagement report.	_____	_____	_____
4.	Consider whether the following disclosures in the financial statements are appropriate:	_____	_____	_____
	• Factors that are the basis for raising the question of going concern	_____	_____	_____
	• Possible effects on the financial statements of the factors that raised the question of going concern	_____	_____	_____
	• Management's assessment of the significance of the factors and any mitigating circumstances	_____	_____	_____
	• Possible discontinuance of operations	_____	_____	_____

	Initials	Date	Audit Documentation Reference

- Management's plans to deal with the current circumstances (including relevant prospective information) _____ _____ _____
- Information related to asset recoverability and classification and the amount and classification of liabilities _____ _____ _____

Other   engagement   procedures:

_____

_____

_____

_____

_____

Reviewed by: _____

Date: _____

OBSERVATION: If through performing other audit procedures the auditor identifies conditions and events that may raise questions about the entity's ability to continue as a going concern and management has not developed plans to address the issue, he or she would ordinarily conclude that doubts about the going-concern issue are valid and would consider modifying his or her report in a manner required by SAS-59.

SECTION 580

WRITTEN REPRESENTATIONS

Authoritative Pronouncements

SAS-122—Statements on Auditing Standards: Clarification and Recodification

Overview

During the course of an engagement, the client's personnel make a variety of representations in response to questions raised by the auditor. Generally accepted auditing standards require that in order to reduce the likelihood of misunderstandings between the client and the auditor, written representations be obtained from the client to confirm explicit and implicit representations made by management during the engagement. Providing written rather than oral representations may prompt more rigorous consideration of matters by management and improve the quality of the representation.

Written representations received from management are audit evidence, and they often support other audit evidence the auditor obtains. For example, the auditor may inspect client documentation to determine whether there are liens against certain capital assets; however, the auditor should obtain a written representation from management stating that no liens exist. In other instances, written representations by management may be a source of audit evidence to support an assertion stated or implied in the financial statements. For example, certain current liabilities may be classified as noncurrent based on the guidance established by ASC 470 (*Debt*). Part of that guidance requires that management must intend to refinance the obligation on a long-term basis. Under this circumstance, the auditor's support for management's intent may be management's written representation in addition to other sources of audit evidence. In general, written representations are not a substitute for other auditing procedures necessary to form the basis for the auditor's opinion and do not provide sufficient appropriate audit evidence about matters on their own.

PLANNING AID REMINDER: Because of the importance of written representations as a source of audit evidence, if management modifies or does not provide a requested written representation it may alert the auditor to the existence of a significant issue.

FRAUD POINTER: In enforcement actions against auditors, an overreliance on inquiry as a form of evidence often has/been mentioned. Auditors have/often cited for a failure to corroborate management's explanations with other evidence. Instead, auditors relied on only management's representations or failed to challenge inconsistent explanations or explanations that were refuted by other evidence.

AU-C 580 details the auditor's responsibilities to obtain written representations from management and those charged with governance, as appropriate, in a financial statement audit. Other AU-Cs, listed in Exhibit AU-C 580-2 contain subject matter-specific requirements for written representations. The requirements of these other AU-Cs do not limit AU-C 580's application. The auditor's objectives in applying AU-C 580 are to obtain written representations from management and those charged with governance indicating they believe they have fulfilled their responsibility for the preparation and fair presentation of financial statements and for the completeness of information provided to the auditor; to support other audit evidence relevant to the financial statements or financial statement assertions with written representations if required by the auditor or other AU-C sections; and to respond appropriately to written representations that are provided or are not provided as requested.

Definitions

Written representation	A written statement by management provided to the auditor to confirm certain matters or to support other audit evidence; this does not include financial statements, the assertions therein, or supporting books and records.
Management	In AU-C 580, the term "management" should be read as "management and, when appropriate, those charged with governance."

Requirements

The auditor is presumptively required to adhere to the following guidance in obtaining written representations from management in an audit of the financial statements:

Management from Whom Written Representations are Requested

1. Request written representations from management with appropriate responsibilities for the financial statements and knowledge of the matters concerned.

Written Representations Requested about Management's Responsibilities

2. Management should represent in writing that it has fulfilled its responsibility for preparing and fairly presenting the financial statements in accordance with the applicable financial reporting framework and for the design, implementation, and fair presentation of financial statements that are free from material misstatement, whether due to fraud or error.

3. Management should represent in writing that it has provided the auditor with all relevant information and access as agreed upon in the audit engagement terms and all transactions have been recorded and are reflected in the financial statements.

Other Written Representations Requested

Written representations should address the following:

4. Management acknowledges its responsibility for the design, implementation, and maintenance of internal control to prevent and detect fraud and has disclosed to the auditor (1) the results of its assessment of the risk that the financial statements may be materially misstated due to fraud; (2) its knowledge of fraud or suspected fraud involving management, employees with significant internal control roles, and others where fraud could have a material effect on the financial statements, and (3) its knowledge of any communicated allegations of fraud or suspected fraud.

5. Management has disclosed to the auditor all known or suspected instances of noncompliance with laws and regulations that have effects that should be considered when preparing the financial statements.

6. Representation about management's belief of whether the effects of uncorrected misstatements are immaterial individually or in the aggregate to the financial statements as a whole, including a summary of those items.

7. Management has disclosed to the auditor and accounted for and disclosed all actual or possible litigation and claims of which it has knowledge that have effects that should be considered when preparing the financial statements in accordance with the applicable financial reporting framework.

8. Representation about management's belief regarding whether significant assumptions it used in making accounting estimates are reasonable.

9. Management has disclosed to the auditor the identity of the entity's related parties and all the related party transactions and relationships it is aware of and has appropriately accounted for and disclosed such relationships and transactions.

10. Management has made the adjustments or disclosures required by the applicable financial reporting framework regarding events occurring subsequent to the date of the financial statements.

11. The auditor should request other written representations determined to be necessary to support other audit evidence relevant to the financial statements or specific financial statement assertions.

Date and Form of Written Representations

12. The date of written representations should be as of the date of the auditor's report on the financial statements and cover all financial statements and periods referred to in the auditor's report.

13. Written representations should be in the form of a representation letter addressed to the auditor.

Written Representations with Doubtful Reliability or Not Provided

14. Determine the effect any concerns about management's competence, integrity, ethical values, diligence, or its commitment to and enforcement of these qualities may have on the reliability of representations and audit evidence in general.

15. If written representations are inconsistent with other audit evidence, perform audit procedures to attempt to resolve the matter. If the matter remains unresolved, reconsider the assessment of management's competence, integrity, ethical values, diligence, and its commitment to and enforcement of these qualities and the effect this may have on the reliability of representations and audit evidence in general.

16. If the auditor concludes the written representations are not reliable, appropriate action should be taken, including determining the possible effect

on the opinion in the auditor's report in accordance with AU-C 705 (*Modifications to the Opinion in the Independent Auditor's Report*).

17. Disclaim an opinion on the financial statements in accordance with AU-C 705 (*Modifications to the Opinion in the Independent Auditor's Report*) or withdraw from the engagement if management does not provide the required written representations about its responsibilities or there is sufficient doubt about management's integrity to make the auditor conclude that those representations provided are unreliable.

18. If one or more requested written representations are not provided by management, (1) discuss the matter with management, (2) reevaluate management's integrity and the effect this may have on the reliability of representations and audit evidence in general, and (3) take appropriate action, including determining the possible effect on the opinion in the auditor's report in accordance with AU-C 705.

Analysis and Application of Procedures

Management from Whom Written Representations are Requested

The auditor requests representations from those within the entity who have sufficient knowledge of and responsibility for the matters covered in the representations. Individuals with this knowledge are typically the management of an entity, but may also include those charged with governance or other individuals within the entity with specialized knowledge regarding representation matters such as actuaries, staff engineers, or internal counsel. The auditor may request that management confirm in its representations that it has inquired of others as appropriate to gain sufficient knowledge about the matters represented.

Management may include qualifying language in its representations indicating that representations are made to the base of its knowledge of belief. This type of qualification is reasonable for the auditor to accept if he or she believes the representations are being made by those with sufficient knowledge of and responsibilities for the matters included.

Written Representations Requested about Management's Responsibilities

Written representations about management's responsibilities are important to the audit because the auditor is not able to obtain sufficient appropriate audit evidence about management's fulfillment of its responsibilities without obtaining confirmation from management. These written representations act to confirm that management has fulfilled the responsibilities it agreed to and acknowledged in the terms of the audit engagement. In the case of audits of governmental entities with broader mandates than other entities, management may be responsible for additional written representations confirming that transactions and events have been carried out in accordance with law, regulation, or other authority.

When management represents that it has provided the auditor with all relevant information, this includes matters such as:

- The completeness and availability of all minutes of meetings of stockholders, directors, and committees of directors

- The completeness of communications from regulatory agencies concerning noncompliance with or deficiencies in financial reporting practices

The auditor may also request that management reconfirm its acknowledgement and understanding of its responsibilities in its written representations, especially when certain conditions exist: those signing the audit engagement terms no longer have the relevant responsibilities, the audit engagement terms were prepared in a previous year, there is an indication that management misunderstands its responsibilities, or changes in circumstances make reconfirmation appropriate. Any reconfirmation should be unconditional.

Other Written Representations Requested

When management makes representations about uncorrected misstatements, they may not believe some of those items are misstatements and may add wording to this effect along with their reasons for this belief in the representations.

PLANNING AID REMINDER: Even though the auditor obtains written representations from management about uncorrected misstatements, he or she still needs to form a conclusion on the effect of uncorrected misstatements in accordance with AU-C 450 (*Evaluation of Misstatements Identified during an Audit*).

Management's representations about whether its assumptions used in making accounting estimates are reasonable may include the following matters for accounting estimates recognized or disclosed in the financial statements:

- The appropriateness of the measurement processes used in determining accounting estimates in the context of the applicable financial reporting framework and the consistency in the processes' application

- That assumptions appropriately reflect management's intent and ability to carry out specific courses of action on the entity's behalf

- That accounting estimate disclosures are complete and appropriate under the applicable financial reporting framework

- That no subsequent event requires adjustment to the accounting estimates and disclosures included in the financial statements

For accounting estimates not recognized or disclosed in the financial statements, representations may include the following regarding the appropriateness of the basis used by management:

- Determination that the recognition of disclosure criteria of the applicable financial reporting framework have not been met

- Overcoming a presumption regarding the use of fair value set forth under the entity's applicable financial reporting framework for those accounting estimates not measured or disclosed at fair value

When evaluating management's judgments and intentions, the auditor may consider factors such as the entity's history in carrying out its stated intentions, its reasons for choosing and ability to pursue a particular course of action, and whether other information obtained during the course of the audit exists that may be inconsistent with management's judgment and intent.

The auditor may request written representations from those charged with governance regarding related parties in certain circumstances: when they have approved related party transactions that materially affect the financial statements or involve management; when they have represented details of certain related party transactions orally to the auditor; or when they have financial or other interests in the related parties or related party transaction. The auditor is also required to communicate the written representations requested from management with those charged with governance.

The auditor may request additional written representations from management beyond those required about matters such as:

- Whether the selection and application of accounting policies are appropriate
- Whether certain matters have been recognized, measured, presented, or disclosed in accordance with the applicable financial reporting framework when they are relevant
  - The existence of plans or intentions that may affect the carrying value or classification of assets or liabilities
  - Actual and contingent liabilities
  - The existence of satisfactory title to assets, liens, or encumbrances on assets, and assets pledged as collateral
- Compliance with aspects of contractual agreements that may affect the financial statements
- Whether management has communicated all internal control deficiencies it is aware of
- Specific assertions in the financial statements to provide support about management's judgment or intent regarding those assertions

---

FRAUD POINTER: AU-C 240 requires the auditor to make specific inquiries of management related to the risk of material misstatements due to fraud and written representations related to these inquiries are important to obtain regardless of the entity's size because of the nature of fraud and the difficulty for the auditor in detecting material misstatements due to fraud.

Representations made by management may be limited to items that are material to the client's financial statements, if "management and the auditor have reached an understanding on materiality for this purpose." That understanding, expressed either in quantitative or qualitative terms, may be part of the management representation letter. However, some items that are the basis for management representations do not relate to dollar values and therefore are not affected by materiality considerations. For example, the management representation that all financial records and related data have been made available to the auditor is not subject to a materiality threshold.

FRAUD POINTER: AU-C 580 specifically notes that materiality does not apply to representations related to management's acknowledgement regarding its responsibility for the design, implementation, and maintenance of internal control to prevent and detect fraud.

Date and Form of Written Representations

Written representations are required audit evidence so the auditor's report date cannot be dated before the date of the written representations. If the auditor has obtained a written representation about a specific assertion during the course of the audit, he or she may need to request an updated written representation as of the date of the auditor's report. Although management needs to make written representations about all periods referred to in the auditor's report, the auditor and management may agree to a form of written representation that addresses whether there are any changes to written representations about prior periods and what those changes are. In some situations, management will not have been present during all the periods referred to in the auditor's report; however this does not diminish their responsibilities for making written representations covering the entire relevant period.

PUBLIC COMPANY IMPLICATIONS: SOX requires the auditor of a public company to issue an audit report on the financial statements and a report on the effectiveness of internal control over financial reporting. The audit of financial statements and the audit of internal controls are to be integrated and the report dates should be the same. As a result, auditors may consider combining representations from management related to the audit of financial statements with representations made by management about internal control matters. Management representations required by AS-5 should be included in the combined representation letter.

In some circumstances, management does not provide a signed representation letter to the auditor by the date of the auditor's report. In these situations, the auditor may accept management's oral confirmation that they have reviewed and will sign the representation letter without exception as of the date of the auditor's report as sufficient evidence to date the report. However, the report may not be released before the signed representation letter is obtained.

PLANNING AID REMINDER: AU-C 560 provides guidance for situations in which the auditor's report should be "dual-dated." AU-C 580 points out that the auditor should consider whether it is appropriate to obtain updated written representations when a subsequent event creating a dual-dating situation occurs.

Written Representations with Doubtful Reliability or Not Provided

When a management representation contradicts evidence the auditor has obtained, the auditor may consider whether the risk assessment remains appropriate or needs revision and the nature, timing, and extent of further audit procedures to respond to the revised risks.

FRAUD POINTER: AU-C 200 provides practical insight into the auditor's reliance on statements made by management. It states, "The auditor neither assumes that management is dishonest nor assumes unquestioned honesty . . . a belief that management and those charged with governance are honest and have integrity does not relieve the auditor of the need to maintain professional skepticism or allow the auditor to be satisfied with less than persuasive audit evidence when obtaining reasonable assurance."

The auditor may be sufficiently concerned about the competence, integrity, ethical values, or diligence of management or about its commitment to or enforcement of these qualities that the risk of management misrepresentation is such that an audit cannot be conducted. In these situations, the auditor may consider withdrawing from the engagement where permitted by law or regulation unless those charged with governance put appropriate corrective measures in place. Even if such measures are put in place, they may not be sufficient for the auditor to issue an unmodified audit opinion.

If the auditor concludes that written representations made by management regarding fulfillment of its responsibilities are not reliable due to doubts about management integrity or if management does not provide those representations, he or she should disclaim an opinion on the financial statements because the possible effects on the financial statements are pervasive. Modification of the written representation that was requested does not necessarily mean that the representation was not provided and the reasons for the modification may affect the opinion in the auditor's report. Furthermore, based on the nature of the representations not obtained or the circumstances of management's refusal to provide written representations, the auditor, rather than disclaiming an opinion or withdrawing from the engagement, may conclude that a qualified opinion is appropriate.

Practitioner's Aids

EXHIBIT AU-C 580-1—MANAGEMENT REPRESENTATION LETTER

Exhibit AU-C 580-1 illustrates a management representation letter similar to the one included in Exhibit 1 of AU-C 580, in which there are no exceptions to the written representations requested.

(Entity letterhead)

(To Auditor) (Date)

This representation letter is provided in connection with your audit of the financial statements of XYZ Company, which comprise the balance sheet as of December 31, 20X5, and the related statements of income, changes in stockholders' equity and cash flows for the year then ended, and the related notes to the financial statements, for the purpose of expressing an opinion as to whether the financial statements are presented fairly, in all material respects, in accordance with the accounting principles generally accepted in the United States (U.S. GAAP).

Certain representations in this letter are described as being limited to matters that are material. Items are considered material, regardless of size, if they involve an omission or misstatement of accounting information that, in the light of surrounding circumstances, makes it probable that the judgment of a reasonable person relying on the information would be changed or influenced by the omission or misstatement.

Except where otherwise stated below, immaterial matters less tha $[*amount*] collectively are not considered to be exceptions that require disclosure for the purpose of the following representations. This amount is not necessarily indicative of amounts that would require adjustment to or disclosure in the financial statements.

We confirm, [*to the best of our knowledge and belief, having made such inquiries as we considered necessary for the purpose of appropriately informing ourselves*] [as of (date of auditor's report)]:

Financial Statements

- We have fulfilled our responsibilities, as set out in the terms of the audit engagement dated [*date*] for the preparation of the financial statements in accordance with U.S. GAAP.

- We acknowledge our responsibility for the design, implementation, and maintenance of internal control relevant to the preparation and fair presentation of financial statements that are free from material misstatement, whether due to fraud or error

- We acknowledge our responsibility for the design, implementation, and maintenance of internal control to prevent and detect fraud

- Significant assumptions used by us in making accounting estimates, including those measured at fair value, are reasonable.

- Related party relationships and transactions have been appropriately accounted for and disclosed in accordance with the requirements of U.S. GAAP.

- All events subsequent to the date of the financial statements and for which U.S. GAAP requires adjustment or disclosure have been adjusted or disclosed.

- The effects of uncorrected misstatements are immaterial, both individually and in the aggregate, to the financial statements as a whole. A list of the uncorrected misstatements is attached to the representation letter.

- [Any other matters the auditor may consider appropriate.]

Information Provided

- We have provided you with:

- Access to all information, of which we are aware that is relevant to the preparation and fair presentation of the financial statements such as records, documentation and other matters;

- Additional information that you have requested from us for the purpose of the audit; and

- Unrestricted access to persons within the entity from whom you determined it necessary to obtain audit evidence.

• All transactions have been recorded in the accounting records and are reflected in the financial statements.

• We have disclosed to you the results of our assessment of the risk that the financial statements may be materially misstated as a result of fraud.

• We have [no knowledge of any][disclosed to you all information that we are aware in relation to] fraud or suspected fraud that affects the entity and involves (a) management, (b) employees who have significant roles in internal control, or (c) others where the fraud could have a material effect on the financial statements.

• We have [no knowledge of any][disclosed to you all information in relation to] allegations of fraud or suspected fraud affecting the entity's financial statements communicated by employees, former employees, analysts, regulators, or others.

• We have disclosed to you all known instances of non-compliance or suspected non-compliance with laws and regulations whose effects should be considered when preparing financial statements.

• We [have disclosed to you all known actual or possible][are not aware of any pending or threatened] litigation and claims whose effects should be considered when preparing the financial statements [and we have not consulted legal counsel concerning litigation or claims].

• We have disclosed to you the identity of the entity's related parties and all the related party relationships and transactions of which we are aware.

[Any other matters that the auditor may consider necessary.]

[Name of Chief Executive Officer and Title]

[Name of Chief Financial Officer and Title]

EXHIBIT AU-C 580-2—ADDITIONAL REQUIREMENTS FOR WRITTEN REPRESENTATIONS

Exhibit AU-C 580-2 identifies other AU-C sections that have requirements for specific written representations if relevant to the audit as well as written representations recommended by AICPA Audit Guides for use in certain situations if the auditor decides that a written representation to provide corroborative audit evidence is necessary.

AU-C Sections with Written Representation Requirements

• AU-C 560, *Subsequent Events and Subsequently Discovered Facts* (paragraph 19)

• AU-C 570, *Going Concern*

- AU-C 700, *Forming an Opinion and Reporting on Financial Statements* (paragraph 52)
- AU-C 935, *Compliance Audits* (paragraph 23)

Conditions AICPA Audit Guides Recommend May Require Written Representations

General

- Unaudited interim financial information accompanies the financial statements
- The effect of a new accounting principle is unknown
- Financial circumstances are strained and management discloses its intentions and the entity's ability to continue as a going concern
- The value of specific significant long lived assets or identifiable intangibles may be impaired
- The entity has a variable interest in another entity
- A specialist's work has been used by the entity

Assets

- Disclosure of compensating balances or other arrangements involving restrictions on cash balances, lines of credit, or similar arrangements is required
- Management intends to and has the ability to hold to maturity debt securities classified as held-to-maturity
- Management considers the decline in value of debt or equity securities to be temporary
- Management has determined the fair value of significant financial instruments that do not have readily determinable market values
- There are financial instruments with off-balance-sheet risk and concentrations of credit risk
- There are unusual circumstances in determining the application of equity accounting
- There are loans to executive officers, nonaccrued loans, or zero interest rate loans

Liabilities

- Short term debt can be refinanced on a long term basis and management intends to do so
- Tax-exempt bonds have been issued
- Management intends to reinvest undistributed earnings of a foreign subsidiary
- An actuary has been used to measure pension liabilities and cost
- There is involvement with a multiemployer plan
- Postretirement benefits have been eliminated
- Employee layoffs that would otherwise lead to curtailment of a benefit plan are intended to be temporary
- Management intends to continue to make or not make frequent amendments to its pension or other postretirement benefit plans, which may

affect the amortization period of prior service cost, or has expressed a substantive commitment to increase benefit obligations

Equity

- Capital stock repurchase options or agreements or capital stock reserved for options, warrants, conversions, or other requirements exist

SECTION 585

CONSIDERATION OF OMITTED PROCEDURES AFTER THE REPORT RELEASE DATE

Authoritative Pronouncements

SAS-122—Statements on Auditing Standards: Clarification and Recodification

Overview

AU-C 585 provides guidance when the auditor concludes, subsequent to the report release date, that one or more procedures necessary given the circumstances existing at the time of the audit were omitted from an engagement. AU-C 585 does not apply when an auditor's work is at issue in a threatened or pending legal proceeding or regulatory investigation. When the auditor becomes aware of a fact after the report release date that may have caused the auditor to amend his or her report had it been known at that date, the guidance in AU-C 560 (*Subsequent Events and Subsequently Discovered Facts*) is applicable.

> **OBSERVATION:** Disclosure that procedures were omitted often comes as a result of a quality review or peer review of the auditor's engagement.

Definition

Omitted procedure	An auditing procedure considered necessary to be performed in the circumstances existing at the time of the financial statement audit, which was not performed

Requirements

The auditor is presumptively required to perform the following procedures when considering the omission of audit procedures after the report release date:

1. When the auditor concludes subsequent to the report release date there is an omitted procedure, he or she should assess any effect of the omitted procedure on the auditor's current ability to support the previously expressed audit opinion.

2. If the auditor concludes an omitted procedure impairs his or her current ability to support the previously expressed audit opinion and the auditor believes there are users relying or likely to rely on the previously released report, the omitted procedure or alternative procedures should be performed to determine whether there is a satisfactory basis for the auditor's previously expressed opinion. The procedures performed should be documented in accordance with AU-C 230 (*Audit Documentation*), including the circumstances encountered; new or additional procedures performed, audit evidence obtained, conclusions reached, and

their effect on the auditor's report; and when and by whom the changes to audit documentation were made and reviewed.

3. When subsequent performance of an omitted procedure or alternative procedure causes the auditor to becomes aware of facts about the financial statements that existed at the report date that would have affected the auditor's opinion had he or she been aware of them, the auditor should follow the requirements in AU-C 560 regarding subsequently discovered facts that become known to the auditor after the report release date.

Analysis and Application of Procedures

Initially, the auditor should assess the importance of the omitted audit procedure within the context of the engagement to determine any effect is has on his or her current ability to support the previously expressed audit opinion. This assessment may include a review of the audit documentation, discussions with other personnel within the firm, and reevaluation of the audit's overall scope. An omitted procedure may be compensated for by other audit procedures applied or a subsequent audit may provide evidence supporting a previously expressed opinion.

OBSERVATION: After the report release date, even though the auditor has no responsibility to perform a retrospective review of audit work performed, there may be circumstances in which the auditor becomes aware of an omitted procedure.

If the auditor is unable to apply an omitted or alternative audit procedure, he or she may consult an attorney and discuss the appropriateness of the following actions:

- Notification of regulatory authorities (SEC etc.)
- Notification of persons relying, or likely to rely, on the financial statements

Practitioner's Aids

EXHIBIT AU-C 585-1—OMISSION OF ENGAGEMENT PROCEDURES DISCOVERED AFTER THE REPORT RELEASE DATE

Use the following procedures, as a guide for evaluating the omission of engagement procedures discovered after the report release date. The program is only a guide, and professional judgment should be exercised to determine how the guidance established in the auditing standards should be adapted to a particular engagement.

Initial and date each procedure as it is completed. If the procedure is not relevant to this engagement, place "N/A" (not applicable) in the space provided for an initial.

Client Name: _____

Date of Financial Statements: _____

		Initials	*Date*	*Audit Documentation Reference*
1.	Establish the level of inherent risk.	_____	_____	_____
2.	Assess the significance of omitted procedures and consider whether to apply audit procedures.	_____	_____	_____
3.	If doing so is appropriate, apply the omitted procedures and consider the effect that the evidence gathered has on the auditor's conclusions.	_____	_____	_____
4.	Determine the proper course of action if significant procedures or alternative procedures cannot be performed.	_____	_____	_____

Other engagement procedures: _____

Reviewed by: _____

Date: _____

AU-C 600
Using the Work of Others

SECTION 600

SPECIAL CONSIDERATIONS—AUDITS OF GROUP FINANCIAL STATEMENTS (INCLUDING THE WORK OF COMPONENT AUDITORS)

Authoritative Pronouncements

SAS-122—Statements on Auditing Standards: Clarification and Recodification

Overview

As part of an audit of group financial statements, the group engagement partner must abide by the requirements in AU-C 220, *Quality Control for an Engagement Conducted in Accordance with Generally Accepted Auditing Standards*. The guidance in AU-C 600 helps the group engagement partner to meet these requirements when component auditors are involved in the audit. This guidance can also be useful to the auditor when adapted to situations other than group audits where other auditors are involved in an audit (e.g., observing an inventory count at a remote location).

AU-C600 helps the auditor decide whether to act as the auditor of the group financial statements. It also provides guidance to the auditor in communicating with component auditors. The auditor is to obtain sufficient appropriate audit evidence regarding the components' financial information and the consolidation process to express a group audit opinion. The evidence needed is affected by audit risk, which in a group audit includes the risk that the component auditor and group engagement team may not detect a misstatement in the component information that could cause a material misstatement of the group financial statements.

AU-C 600 also assists the auditor is determining whether reference should be made to the audit of a component auditor in the auditor's report on the group financial statements. If the group engagement partner assumes responsibility for the work of component auditors, the group auditors should be involved in the work of the component auditors as it relates to expressing a group audit opinion; if the group engagement partner does not assume responsibility for the component auditors' work, reference should be made to the audit of a component auditor in the group auditor's report.

OBSERVATION: AU-C 600 replaces what was previously AU 543, *Part of an Audit Performed by Other Independent Auditors.* The scope of AU-C 600 is broader than the scope of AU 543. In addition, the term "principal auditor" from AU 543 has been replaced by the terms "group engagement partner," "group engagement team," or "auditor of the group financial statements," depending on the context.

Definitions

Component	An entity or business activity for which group or component management prepares financial information that is required by the applicable financial reporting framework to be included in the group financial statements.
Component auditor	An auditor who performs work on the financial information of a component that will be used as evidence for the group audit. A component auditor can be part of the same firm as the group engagement partner; it can be a firm that belongs to the same network as the group engagement partner's firm; or it can be another firm.
Component management	Management responsible for preparing the financial information of a component.
Component materiality	The materiality for a component determined by the group engagement team for the purposes of a group audit.
Consolidation process	Includes the recognition, measurement, presentation, and disclosure of components' financial information in the group financial statements through inclusion, consolidation, proportionate consolidation, the equity or cost methods of accounting, or aggregation in combined financial statements of the financial information of components that have no parent but are under common control.
Group	All the components (always more than one) whose financial information is included in the group financial statements.
Group audit	The audit of group financial statements.
Group audit opinion	The audit opinion of the group financial statements.
Group engagement partner	The partner or other person in the firm responsible for the group audit engagement, its performance, and the group audit opinion issued on behalf of the firm; this may include joint engagement partners when joint auditors conduct a group audit.
Group engagement team	The group engagement partner, partners, and staff who establish the overall group audit strategy, communicate with component auditors, perform work on the consolidation process, and evaluate the conclusions drawn from the audit evidence in order to form an opinion on the group financial statements.
Group financial statements	Financial statements that include the financial information of more than one component, or combined financial statements aggregating the financial information prepared by components that have no parent but are under common control.
Group management	Management responsible for preparing and presenting group financial statements.
Group-wide controls	Controls over financial reporting designed, implemented, and maintained by group management.
Significant component	A component identified by the group engagement team that is of individual financial significance to the group or, due to its nature or circumstances, is likely to include significant risks of material misstatement of the group financial statements.

Requirements

The group engagement team is presumptively required to perform the following procedures in audits of group financial statements:

Responsibility

1. The group engagement partner is responsible for the direction, supervision, and performance of the group audit engagement in compliance with professional standards, legal and regulatory requirements, and the firm's policies and procedures and for determining if the issued audit report is appropriate in the circumstances.

Acceptance and Continuance

2. The group engagement partner should determine whether sufficient appropriate audit evidence will be able to be obtained about the consolidation process and the financial information of components for the group engagement team to serve as the auditor of the group financial statements and formulate a group audit opinion. For this determination, the group engagement team should obtain a sufficient understanding of the group, its components, and their environments to identify components that are likely to be significant.

3. The group engagement partner should determine whether the work of the group engagement team and the work of component auditors will be sufficient for the group engagement team to serve as the group auditor.

4. If the group engagement partner concludes that sufficient appropriate audit evidence will not be able to be obtained through the group engagement team's work or involvement in the work of component auditors due to restrictions imposed by group management or other reasons, and this may result in a disclaimer of a group audit opinion, the partner should:

    a. Not accept the engagement if it is a new engagement

    b. Withdraw from the engagement if it is a continuing engagement

    c. Disclaim an opinion on the group financial statements if prohibited from declining or withdrawing from the engagement due to law or regulation

5. The group financial statements auditor is required to agree upon the terms of the group audit engagement. This is a mandatory requirement (rather than a presumptively mandatory requirement).

Overall Audit Strategy and Audit Plan

6. The group engagement team should establish and the group engagement partner should review and approve an overall group audit strategy and audit plan. In developing the group audit plan, the group engagement partner should assess the extent to which the work of component auditors will be used and whether the group audit report will reference the audit of a component auditor.

Obtaining an Understanding

7. Identify and assess the risks of material misstatement by obtaining an understanding of the entity and its environment through (1) enhancing the understanding of the group, its components, their environments, and group-wide controls obtained during acceptance and continuance; and (2) an understanding of the consolidation process, including the instructions issued by group management to components. This understanding should be sufficient to confirm or revise the initial identification of components likely to be significant and to assess the risks of material misstatement of the group financial statements whether due to fraud or error.

8. Obtain an understanding of:

a. A component auditor's independence, professional competence, and understanding and willingness to comply with the ethical requirements relevant to the group audit

b. The extent the group engagement team will be able to be involved in the work of the component auditor

c. Whether the group engagement team will be able to obtain information affecting the consolidation process from a component auditor

d. If a component auditor operates in a regulatory environment that actively oversees auditors

9. If a component auditor is not independent, or the auditor is seriously concerned that the component auditor does not understand or will not comply with ethical requirements or lacks professional competence, obtain sufficient appropriate audit evidence relating to the financial information of the component without using the work of or making reference to the audit of the component auditor in the group auditor's report.

Whether to Make Reference to a Component Auditor in the Group Audit Report

10. The group engagement partner should decide whether to make reference to a component auditor in the group audit report.

11. Reference should not be made to the audit of a component auditor unless: (1) the component and group financial statements are prepared using the same financial reporting framework, and (2) the component auditor has performed a financial statement audit of the component in accordance with GAAS, or Public Company Accounting Oversight Board (PCAOB) auditing standards when required, and issued an unrestricted auditor's report.

OBVERSATION: If the component auditor performed the audit using auditing standards other than GAAS or, where applicable, PCAOB standards, the engagement partner may evaluate whether these standards meet the requirements of GAAS. In general, International Auditing Standards (IASs), promulgated by the International Auditing and Assurance Standards Board, are more likely to meet the requirements of GAAS than are other auditing frameworks.

---

12. If reference will be made to the audit of a component auditor in the group audit report, obtain sufficient appropriate audit evidence about those components by:

a. Performing all of the required procedures except those applicable when assuming responsibility for the work of a component auditor

b. Identifying significant findings and issues by reading the components' financial information and any component auditor's report and, if necessary, communicating with the component auditor

13. If reference is made to the audit of a component auditor in the group audit opinion, the group audit report should clearly indicate the division of responsibility between the component auditor and group engagement team. Disclose in the report the magnitude of the portion of the financial statements audited by the component auditor.

14. If the component auditor is named in the group audit report, the express permission of the component auditor should be obtained and the component auditor's report should be presented with the group auditor's report.

15. If the component auditor's opinion is modified or includes an emphasis-of-matter or other-matter paragraph, the group engagement partner should

determine the effect this may have on the group auditor's report, and, where appropriate, should modify the opinion or include an emphasis of matter or other matter paragraph in the group auditor's report.

16. If assuming responsibility for the work of a component auditor, do not make reference to the component auditor in the group auditor's report.

Materiality

17. Determine:

    a. Materiality, including performance materiality, for the group financial statements as a whole when establishing the overall group audit strategy.

    b. Materiality to be applied to any particular classes of transactions, account balances, or disclosures in the group financial statements for which misstatements less than materiality for the statements as a whole could be reasonably expected to influence the economic decisions of users taken on the basis of the group financial statements.

    c. Component materiality for components on which an audit or review will be performed, which should be lower than materiality for the group financial statements as a whole to reduce the risk that aggregate detected and undetected misstatements exceed materiality.

    d. The threshold above which misstatements cannot be regarded as clearly trivial to the group financial statements.

Response to Assessed Risks

18. Design and implement appropriate responses to address the assessed risks of material misstatement of the financial statements. The group or component auditor should test the operating effectiveness of controls if the procedures to be performed on the consolidation process or the components' financial information is based on an expectation that group-wide controls are operating effectively or substantive procedures alone cannot provide sufficient appropriate audit evidence at the assertion level.

Consolidation Process

19. Design and perform further audit procedures on the consolidation process to respond to the assessed risks of material misstatement of the group financial statements arising from the consolidation process, including evaluating whether all components have been included in the group financial statements.

20. Evaluate the appropriateness, completeness, and accuracy of consolidation adjustments and reclassifications and the existence of any fraud risk factors or indicators of possible management bias.

21. If a component's financial information has not been prepared in accordance with the same accounting policies as the group financial statements, evaluate whether that financial information has been appropriately adjusted for purposes of preparing and presenting group financial statements.

22. Determine whether the financial information the component auditor identifies as reporting on is the information that is incorporated in the group financial statements.

23. If the group financial statements contain the financial statements of a component with a different financial reporting period-end, evaluate whether appropriate adjustments have been made to those financial statements in accordance with the applicable financial reporting framework.

Subsequent Events

24. When audits are performed on the financial information of components, procedures should be performed that are designed to identify events at those components that occur between the date of the financial information of the components and the group auditor's report date that may require adjustment or disclosure in the group financial statements.

Communication with the Component Auditor

25. Communicate requirements to the component auditor on a timely basis and include:

   a. A request that the component auditor confirm their cooperation with the group engagement team knowing the context in which the component auditor's work will be used

   b. Relevant ethical and independence requirements

   c. A list of related parties prepared by group management and any other related parties the group engagement team is aware of. Request the component auditor communicate on a timely basis any related parties not previously identified. The group engagement team should identify such additional related parties to other component auditors.

   d. Identified significant risks of material misstatement of the group financial misstatements due to fraud or error that are relevant to the component auditor.

26. Request that component auditors communicate matters relevant to the conclusion for the group audit, including:

   a. Whether the component auditor complied with relevant ethical requirements, including independence and professional competence

   b. Identification of the financial information of the component the component auditor is reporting on

   c. The component auditor's overall findings, conclusions, or opinion

Evaluating Audit Evidence

27. Evaluate a component auditor's communication, discuss significant findings and issues arising from that evaluation with the component auditor, component management, or group management as appropriate.

28. Evaluate whether sufficient appropriate audit evidence to base the group audit opinion on has been obtained from the audit procedures performed on the consolidation process and the work performed by the group and component auditors on the financial information of the components.

29. The group engagement partner should evaluate the effect on the group audit opinion of any uncorrected misstatements and any instances in which sufficient appropriate audit evidence has been unable to be obtained.

Communication with Management and Those Charged with Governance of the Group

30. Communicate material weaknesses and significant deficiencies in internal control identified by the group auditor or component auditors to group management and those charged with governance of the group.

31. Communicate identified fraud or information indicating a fraud may exist on a timely basis to the appropriate level of group management.

32. When a component auditor is engaged to audit a component's financial statements and the group engagement team becomes aware of a matter that may be significant to the component's financial statements but that component management may not be aware of (such as potential litigation, plans for abandonment of material operating assets, subsequent events, or significant legal agreements), request that group management inform component management of the matter. If group management refuses to communicate this information, discuss the matter with those charged with governance of the group. If the matter remains unresolved, consider whether, given legal and professional responsibility considerations, to advise the component auditor not to issue the auditor's report on the component's financial statements until the matter is resolved and whether to withdraw from the engagement.

33. Communicate the following matters with those charged with governance of the group:

    a. An overview of the type of work to be performed on the financial information of the components, including the basis for a decision to make reference to the audit of a component auditor in the group auditor's report

    b. An overview of the nature of the planned involvement by the group auditor in the work to be performed by component auditors on the financial information of significant components

    c. Instances in which evaluation of the work of a component auditor gives rise to a concern about the quality of that auditor's work

    d. Any limitations on the group audit (e.g., restrictions on access to information)

    e. Fraud or suspected fraud involving group or component management, employees with significant roles in group-wide controls, or others in which a material misstatement of the group financial statements has or may have resulted from fraud

Documentation

34. Document:

    a. An analysis of components indicating significant components and the type of work performed on the components' financial information

    b. Components for which the auditor's report on the group financial statements refers to the reports of component auditors

    c. Written communications between the group engagement team and the component auditors about the group engagement team's requirements

    d. For components for which the auditor is making reference to the audit of a component auditor, the financial statements of the component and the auditor's report on the component

Additional Requirements Applicable When Assuming Responsibility for the Work of a Component Auditor

35. Evaluate the appropriateness of performance materiality at the component level.

36. Determine the type of work to be performed by the group or component auditors on the financial information of components and the nature, timing, and extent of involvement in the work of component auditors.

37. If a component is significant due to its individual financial significance to the group, the group or component auditor should perform an audit of the financial information of the component to meet the needs of the group engagement team, using component materiality.

38. If a component is significant because it is likely to include significant risks of material misstatement of the group financial statements due to qualitative factors, the group or component auditor should use component materiality and perform one or more of the following:

    a. An audit of the component's financial information to meet group engagement team needs

    b. An audit of one or more account balances, classes of transactions, or disclosures, or specified audit procedures relating to the likely significant risks of material misstatement

39. If a component is not a significant component, perform analytical procedures at the group level.

40. If sufficient appropriate audit evidence cannot be obtained from work performed on the financial information of significant components, group-wide controls and the consolidation process, and from analytical procedures performed at the group level, select additional non-significant components and the group or component auditor should perform one or more of the following on the selected components:

    a. A review or audit of the component's financial information to meet the group engagement team's needs, using component materiality

    b. An audit of one or more account balances, classes of transactions, or disclosure

    c. Specified audit procedures

Vary the selection of individual components over a period of time.

41. If a component auditor audits or performs audit procedures on the financial information of a significant component, the group auditor should be involved in the component auditor's assessment of significant risks of material misstatement to the group financial statements, although the nature, timing, and extent of involvement will vary based on the understanding of the component auditor. Involvement should, at a minimum, include:

    a. Discussing the component's business activities of significance to the group with the component auditor or component management

    b. Discussing the susceptibility of the component to material misstatement of the financial information through fraud or error with the component auditor

    c. Reviewing the component auditor's documentation of identified significant risks of material misstatement of the group financial statements

42. If significant risks of material misstatement to the group financial statements have been identified in a component, evaluate the appropriateness of further audit procedures to be performed to respond to those identified significant risks and determine if it is necessary to be involved in the further audit procedures depending on the group auditor's understanding of the component auditor.

43. If component auditors perform work other than audits of components' financial information at the request of the group engagement team, request that the component auditors notify the group engagement team if they become aware of subsequent events that may require adjustment or disclosure in the group financial statements.

44. Communication between the group auditor and the component auditor should include:

a. The nature of the work to be performed by the component auditor, and the nature and content of the component auditor's communication with the group auditor at the conclusion of this work

b. When the component auditor performs an audit or review: (1) component materiality (2) any amounts lower than component materiality for particular account balances, transaction classes, and disclosures; and (3) the threshold above which misstatements cannot be viewed as clearly trivial

c. Whether the component auditor has complied with the group engagement team's requirements

d. Information on instances of noncompliance with laws or regulations at the component or group level that could lead to a material misstatement of the group financial statements

e. Significant risks of material misstatement of the group financial statements due to fraud or error in the component and the component auditor's responses to those risks

f. A list of corrected and uncorrected misstatements (does not need to include clearly trivial misstatements) of the financial information of the component

g. Indicators of possible management bias regarding accounting estimates and the application of accounting principles

h. Description of any identified material weaknesses and significant deficiencies in internal control at the component level

i. Other significant findings and issues the component auditor communicated or expects to communicate to those charged with governance of the component, including fraud or suspected fraud involving component management, employees with significant roles in internal control at the component level, or others in which a material misstatement of the financial information of the component has resulted from fraud

j. Any other matters that may be relevant to the group audit or that the component auditor wishes to draw to the attention of the group engagement team, including exceptions noted in the written representations the component auditor requested from component management

45. If the component auditor's work is concluded to be insufficient, determine additional procedures to be performed and whether they will be performed by the component or group auditor.

46. The group auditor should evaluate material weaknesses and significant deficiencies in internal control identified by a component auditor, and determine which of these items to communicate to group management and those charged with governance of the group.

47. Document the nature, timing, and extent of the involvement in the work performed by the component auditors on significant components including any review of relevant parts of the component auditors' audit documentation and conclusions of that review.

Analysis and Application of Procedures

Components and Component Auditors

Components are entities or business activities for which management prepares financial information. This is often based on organizational structure, and components may be subsidiaries of a parent, joint ventures, or investees accounted for by the cost or equity method of accounting; however, components may be also identified based on function, process, product or service, or geographical location. Furthermore, there may be different levels of components within a group financial reporting system such that components may be identified at aggregated levels rather than individually. These aggregated components may constitute a component for the purposes of a group audit and may constitute a group for preparation of group financial statements incorporating all of the encompassed individual components. Therefore, there may be multiple group audits that occur within one group financial reporting system.

When identifying significant components, the auditor considers quantitative and qualitative factors. The auditor may, using professional judgment, apply a percentage to a chosen benchmark to identify components of individual financial significance.

Component auditors may include auditors working for a network firm, auditors working in a different office of the group engagement partner's firm, or even group engagement team members working on a component's financial information at the request of the group engagement team. However, an auditor performing work on a component that will not be used to provide evidence for the group audit is not a component auditor.

Responsibility

Group engagement partners are responsible for the group audit opinion; however, component auditors remain responsible for their overall findings, conclusions, and opinions on the components' financial information.

Acceptance and Continuance

The group engagement team obtains an understanding of the group, its component, and their environments as part of the decision to accept or continue the engagement. This understanding may be obtained from information provided by or communication with group management or from communication with component management, component auditors, or the previous group engagement team when applicable. The auditor's understanding may incorporate matters such as:

- Group structure
- Component business activities that are significant to the group
- Use of service organizations
- A description of group-wide control
- Complexity of the consolidation process
- If there will be any component auditors outside of the group engagement partner's firm or network and group management's rationale for that decision
- If the group engagement team will have unrestricted access to the necessary people and information and will be able to perform necessary work on the components' financial information.

If the engagement is a continuing engagement, the ability to obtain sufficient appropriate audit evidence may be affected by significant changes, such as changes in group structure, components' business activities significant to the group, the composition of management or those charged with governance of the group or of significant components, group-wide controls, the applicable financial reporting framework, or concerns of the group engagement team regarding the integrity and competence of group or component management.

Determination of whether to act as the group financial statement auditor may include factors such as the group engagement team's involvement in significant components, and the extent of the group engagement team's knowledge of the overall financial statements. If a group does not contain any significant components, the auditor should be able to act as the group financial statement auditor if the group engagement team will be able to perform the work on the financial information of some of the components and be involved in the work of component auditors on the financial information of other components to the extent necessary to obtain sufficient appropriate audit evidence.

PLANNING AID REMINDER: In determining whether to act as the auditor for governmental group financial statement audits, the auditor also considers his or her engagement by the primary government as the auditor of the financial reporting entity and his or her responsibility for auditing the primary government's general or other primary operating fund.

The group engagement team may have restricted access to information due to group management or other circumstances. If information access is restricted because of circumstances, sufficient appropriate audit evidence may still be able to be obtained if the component is not significant. However, if the component is significant and reference will not be made to the component auditor in the group auditor's report, sufficient appropriate audit evidence about that component will not be able to be obtained. If information is restricted because of group management and the component is significant, the group engagement team will not be able to obtain sufficient appropriate audit evidence. Sufficient appropriate audit evidence may be able to be obtained about a component that is not significant even if information is restricted by group management, but the reason for the restriction may affect the group audit opinion because it may affect the reliability of group management responses and representations.

OBSERVATION: The group engagement team uses professional judgment to determine the materiality and pervasiveness of an inability to obtain sufficient appropriate audit evidence about a significant component. If the effect of this inability is material but not pervasive, a qualified opinion should be expressed. However, if the effect of this inability is material and pervasive, a disclaimer of opinion should be expressed.

The terms of engagement agreed upon by the group engagement partner identify the applicable financial reporting framework and may include matters such as whether reference to the component auditor's audit will be made in the auditor's report on the group financial statements; the group engagement team's need for unrestricted communication between the group engagement team and component auditors; having any important communications between component auditors, management, and those charged with governance, or between regulatory authorities and components related to financial reporting matters communicated; necessary access to components' management, those charged with governance, auditors, and information; and permission to perform work or request a component auditor perform work on components' financial information as necessary.

Obtaining an Understanding

Understanding the entities and their environments

When obtaining an understanding of the entity and its environment to identify and assess the risks of material misstatement, specific matters to consider that may be relevant to a group audit engagement include group-wide controls and matters relating to the applicable financial reporting framework, the consolidation process, consolidation adjustments, and the instruction issued by group management to components.

The instructions from group management to components often cover the accounting policies to be applied, a reporting timetable, and statutory and disclosure requirements applicable to the group financial statements such as segment identification and reporting, related party relationships and transactions, and intragroup account balances, transactions, and unrealized profits. The auditor's understanding of these instructions may include:

- The clarity and practicality of the instructions for completing the reporting package, which consists of a standard format for providing financial information for incorporation into the group financial statements

- Whether the instructions adequately describe the characteristics of the applicable financial reporting framework

- Whether the instructions provide for disclosure sufficient to comply with applicable financial reporting framework requirements, identification of consolidation adjustments, and the approval of the financial information by component management

The auditor should obtain an understanding sufficient to identify and assess the risks of material misstatement of the group financial statements, whether due to error or fraud. Information used to identify the risks of material misstatement due to fraud may include:

- Group management's assessment of the risks of the group financial statements being materially misstated due to fraud

- Group management's process for identifying and responding to identified or likely fraud risks, how those charged with governance of the group monitor that process, and controls that group management has established to mitigate those risks

- Whether particular components are likely to have a fraud risk

- Responses of group or component management, those charged with governance of the group, internal audit, or component auditors to inquiries of the group engagement team regarding knowledge of any actual, suspected, or alleged fraud affecting a component or group

There are many conditions and events that may indicate risks of material misstatement of the group financial statements. Examples of these conditions that are specific to a group audit engagement include: a complex group structure, nonexistent or ineffective group-wide controls, uncertainties regarding which components' financial information to consolidate in the group financial statements, prior occurrences of intragroup account balances not balancing or reconciling on consolidation, complex transactions accounted for in multiple components, use of different accounting policies in component and group financial statements, components with different financial year-ends, and prior occurrences of incomplete consolidation adjustments.

The required discussion among key members of the engagement team about the susceptibility of an entity to material misstatement of the financial statements, emphasizing the risks due to fraud, may include component auditors based on the group engagement partner's determination. This discussion provides auditors with the opportunity to share information and ideas about the group and its components and business risks, the potential for management bias or override and the existence of fraud risk factors, and identified or indicated instances of fraud or noncompliance with laws or regulations.

Understanding the component auditor

The group engagement partner's decision about whether to use the component auditor's work to provide audit evidence for the group audit and whether to make reference to the component auditor's audit in the auditor's report on the group financial statements may be influenced by factors such as differences in the financial reporting framework or auditing or other standards applied in preparing the component and group financial statements, whether the component's financial statement audit will be completed in time to meet the group reporting timetable, and whether the group engagement team is able to be involved in the work of the component auditor.

PLANNING AID REMINDER: It is not necessary to obtain an understanding of auditors of components for which the group engagement team only plans to perform analytical procedures at a group level.

The nature, timing, and extent of the group engagement team's procedures to obtain an understanding of a component auditor depend on previous knowledge of or experience with the component auditor and the degree to which the group engagement team and component auditor are subject to the same policies and procedures, laws and regulations, education and training, professional oversight and standards, and language and culture.

In the first year working with a component auditor, this understanding may be obtained by:

- Determining that the component auditor is aware that : the component's financial statements will be included in the group financial statements; the component auditor's report will be relied upon; the group financial statement auditor will make reference to the component auditor's report in the opinion on the group financial statements or the group engagement team will be involved in the work of the component auditor; and matters affecting the elimination of intercompany transactions and accounts and the uniformity of accounting practices among the components in the group financial statements will be reviewed

- Evaluating results of the quality control monitoring system if the group engagement team and component auditor are under common monitoring policies and procedures at a firm or network

- Visiting a component auditor or requesting a component auditor to confirm or complete questionnaires about matters that the group engagement team is required to obtain an understanding of

- Discussing a component auditor with colleagues in the group engagement partner's firm or with a reputable third party with knowledge of the component auditor

In later years, the group engagement team's previous experience may provide sufficient understanding of the component auditor. Then, the group engagement team may just request that the component auditor confirm any changes in matters they are required to obtain an understanding.of

The understanding of a component auditor's professional competence may include whether the component auditor possesses: a sufficient understanding of the standards applicable to the group audit, the special skills necessary to perform the work on a particular component's financial information, and a sufficient understanding of the applicable financial reporting framework. Inquiries about the professional competence of a component auditor may be made of the AICPA, the component auditor's state board of accountancy or state or local CPA society, or the corresponding foreign professional organization.

If the group engagement team has less than serious concerns about a component auditor's professional competence or the component auditor is operating in an environment that does not actively oversee auditors, by being involved in the work of the component auditor or performing additional risk assessment or further audit procedures on the component's financial information, that auditor's work may still be able to be used. However, greater involvement by the group auditor cannot remedy a lack of independence on the part of a component auditor. If the component auditor is not subject to the AICPA Code of Professional Conduct, compliance with the International Federation of Accountants *Code of Ethics for Professional Accountants* will suffice.

OBSERVATION: In some foreign jurisdictions, the group auditor may be precluded from accessing the workpapers of a component auditor. This problem can be addressed by having the component auditor prepare a memorandum discussing the matters documented in the aforementioned workpapers.

Whether to Make Reference to a Component Auditor in the Group Audit Report

The decision about whether to refer to the audit of a component auditor in the group audit report is made separately for each component auditor such that none, some, or all of the component auditors may be referred to in the group audit report. If the group engagement partner assumes responsibility for the work of a component auditor, no reference to the component auditor should be made in the group audit report because it could cause a reader to misinterpret the degree of responsibility the group auditor is assuming.

OBSERVATION: While the group audit report typically may not refer to the audit of a component auditor if the component's financial statements were prepared using a different financial reporting framework than the group financial statements, this restriction does not apply to group financial statements prepared in accordance with a reporting framework that provides for the inclusion of component financial statements prepared in accordance with a different financial reporting framework. Both the Governmental Accounting Standards Board and Federal Accounting Standards Advisory Board reporting frameworks have such provisions.

PUBLIC COMPANY IMPLICATION: PCAOB Auditing Standard No. 3 (AS-3) (Audit Documentation and Amendment to Interim Auditing Standards) provides documentation guidelines involving the use of principal and other auditors for public companies. AS-3 specifies appropriate audit documentation when the principal auditor does not refer to the work of the other auditors. The principal auditor must obtain and review the following prior to issuing his or her audit report: (1) an engagement completion document; (2) a list of significant fraud risk factors, the other auditor's response, and the results from these procedures; (3) information on any matters that are inconsistent with or contradict the auditor's final conclusions; (4) any findings that affect the consolidating or combining of accounts in the consolidated financial statements; (5) the information necessary for the principal auditor to reconcile the amounts audited by the other auditor to the consolidated financial statements; (6) a schedule of audit adjustments, including the nature and cause of each adjustment; (7) a listing of all significant deficiencies and material weaknesses in internal control, with each group listed separately; (8) management representation letters; (9) any matters to be communicated to the audit committee. In addition to these documentation requirements, the principal auditor should consider discussing the other auditors' audit procedures and related results, and consider reviewing the audit programs used by other auditors.

When reference is made to the audit of a component auditor in the group audit report, the magnitude of the portion of the financial statements audited by the component auditor may be disclosed by stating the dollar amounts or percentages of total assets, total revenues, and other criteria as appropriate. If multiple component auditors participated, the portion of the financial statements covered by their work may be stated as an aggregate amount. Exhibit AU-C

600-1 displays an example of a group audit report that makes reference to a component auditor.

OBSERVATION: Reference to a component auditor in the group audit report reflects that the group financial statement auditor is not assuming responsibility for the component auditor's work and the source of the audit evidence referenced for such components; it does not indicate a qualified opinion.

Materiality

The component materiality levels determined by the group engagement team to assist in establishing the overall audit strategy for a component may be different for different components and, when added together, component materiality levels may exceed group materiality.

For components that require work performed at the component level in order to obtain sufficient appropriate audit evidence for the group audit opinion, component materiality levels should be communicated to and used by the component auditor if the work of the component auditor will not be referred to in the group audit report. Any misstatements identified in components' financial information that exceed the threshold above which they cannot be regarded as clearly trivial should be communicated to the group engagement team.

Consolidation Process

When evaluating the appropriateness, completeness, and accuracy of consolidation adjustments and reclassifications, the group engagement team may:

- Evaluate if significant adjustments appropriately reflect their underlying events and transactions
- Determine whether significant adjustments are properly supported, sufficiently documented, and correctly calculated, processed, and authorized by group and component management as appropriate
- Check the reconciliation and elimination of intragroup account balances, transactions, and unrealized profits
- Communicating with the component auditor, regardless of whether the group financial statement audit report references the audit of the component auditor

Subsequent Events

When the group audit report on the financial statements references the audit of a component auditor, procedures to identify subsequent events between the date of the component auditor's report and the group auditor's report may include:

- Obtaining an understanding of procedures group management has established to identify such subsequent events
- Requesting that the component auditor update subsequent event procedures to the date of the group financial statements auditor's report

- Obtaining written representations from component management regarding subsequent events

- Reading the component's interim financial information and inquiring of group management

- Reading board meeting minutes for meeting held since the financial statement date

- Reading the subsequent year's capital and operating budgets

- Inquiring of group management about currently known facts, decisions, or conditions expected to have a significant effect on financial position or results of operations for subsequent event items

- Considering the implications for the group financial statements auditor's report if the group engagement team is unable to obtain sufficient appropriate audit evidence regarding subsequent events

Additional Requirements Applicable When Assuming Responsibility for the Work of a Component Auditor

Performance materiality levels are determined to reduce the risk that the aggregated detected and undetected misstatements in a component's financial information exceed component materiality. The group engagement team may set component materiality at the level of performance materiality for the component. The component auditor uses component materiality to evaluate the individual or aggregate materiality of uncorrected detected misstatements.

An audit of a component's financial information adapted to meet group engagement team needs may refer to an audit performed in accordance with GAAS with the exception of performing audit procedures on tax and other accounts for which procedures will be performed at a group financial statement level. Another adaptation may be that the results of the component audit will be communicated in a form to meet the group engagement team's needs.

The group engagement team's determination of the type of work to be performed on a component's financial information and the nature, timing, and extent of involvement in the work of a component auditor will depend on many factors, such as:

- The component's significance

- Identified significant risks of material misstatement of the group financial statements

- Evaluation of design and implementation of group-wide controls

    Understanding of the component auditor

The group engagement team's involvement in the work of a component auditor may include the following procedures:

- Obtaining an understanding of the component and its environment by meeting with component management or auditors

- Reviewing the overall audit strategy and plan of the component auditors

- Performing risk assessment procedures to identify and assess the risks of material misstatement at the component level alone or with the component auditors

- Designing and performing further audit procedures alone or with the component auditors

- Participating in key meetings between component auditors and component management

- Reviewing relevant parts of component auditors' audit documentation

For a component identified as significant because it is likely to include significant risks of material misstatement due to qualitative factors, the group engagement team may be able to identify and perform or request that a component auditor perform an audit solely of account balances, classes of transactions, or disclosures affected by those risks.

In some circumstances, work is required to be performed on components that are not significant in order to obtain sufficient appropriate audit evidence to base the group audit opinion on. In some group audits, there may be no significant components and it is likely that in these circumstances additional work will be required to be performed at the component level to obtain sufficient appropriate audit evidence. The group engagement team's decision regarding which and how many components to select and what work to perform on these components may be affected by factors such as:

- The extent of audit evidence expected from significant components' financial information

- If the component is newly formed or acquired

- If significant changes have occurred in the component

- If any work has been performed at the component by internal audit and its effect on the group audit

- If components apply common systems and processes

- The operating effectiveness of group-wide controls

- Abnormal fluctuations identified by analytical procedures performed at the group level

- The individual financial significance of, or risk posed by, the component compared to other non-significant components

- Whether the component is otherwise already subject to an audit

An audit of a non-significant component may have already been performed for component management, in which case the group engagement partner may decide to use that work to provide audit evidence. If this occurs, the decision about whether to make reference to the work of the component auditor in the group audit report must be made.

Communication with the Component Auditor

Communication of the group engagement team's requirements to the component auditor is often accomplished using a letter of instruction. A letter of instruction may contain guidance on required communications as well as additional matters that may be relevant to the planning or conduct of the work of the component auditor. The component auditor often communicates with the group engagement team using a memorandum or report of work performed. However, required communication between the group engagement team and component auditor may not need to be written; for example, communication may be accomplished through visits to the component auditor or review of the component auditor's audit documentation. Required communication is also often accomplished through means other than writing when a member of the group engagement team is also a component auditor.

Practitioner's Aid

Exhibit AU-C 600-1 illustrates an auditor's report in which reference is made to the work of a component auditor.

EXHIBIT AU-C 600-1—REFERENCE TO THE WORK OF ANOTHER AUDITOR IN THE AUDIT REPORT

We have audited the accompanying consolidated financial statements of X Company and its subsidiaries, which comprise the consolidated balance sheets as of December 31, 20X5 and 20X4, and the related consolidated statements of income, changes in stockholders' equity, and cash flows for the years then ended, and the related notes to the financial statements.

Management's Responsibility for the Financial Statements

Management is responsible for the preparation and fair presentation of these consolidated financial statements in accordance with accounting principles generally accepted in the United States of America; this includes the design, implementation, and maintenance of internal control relevant to the preparation and fair presentation of consolidated financial statements that are free from material misstatement, whether due to fraud or error.

Auditor's Responsibility

Our responsibility is to express an opinion on these consolidated financial statements based on our audits. We did not audit the financial statements of Z Company, a wholly owned subsidiary, whose statements reflect total assets constituting 15% and 12%, respectively, of consolidated assets at December 31, 20X5 and 20X4, and total revenues constituting 18% and 14%, respectively, of consolidated revenues for the years then ended. Those statements were audited by other auditors whose report has been furnished to us, and our opinion, insofar as it relates to the amounts included for Z Company, is based solely on the report of the other auditors. We conducted our audits in accordance with auditing standards generally accepted in the United States of America. Those standards require that we plan and perform the audit to obtain reasonable assurance about whether the consolidated financial statements are free of material misstatement.

An audit involves performing procedures to obtain audit evidence about the amounts and disclosures in the consolidated financial statements. The procedures selected depend on the auditor's judgment, including the assessment of the risks of material misstatement of the consolidated financial statements, whether due to fraud or error. In making those risk assessments, the auditor considers internal control relevant to the entity's preparation and fair presentation of the consolidated financial statements in order to design audit procedures that are appropriate in the circumstances, but not for the purpose of expressing an opinion on the effectiveness of the entity's internal control. Accordingly, we express no such opinion. An audit also involves evaluating the appropriateness of accounting policies used and the reasonableness of significant estimates made by management, as well as evaluating the overall presentation of the consolidated financial statements.

We believe that the audit evidence we have obtained is sufficient and appropriate to provide a basis for our audit opinion.

Opinion

In our opinion, based on our audit and the report of other auditors, the consolidated financial statements referred to above present fairly, in all material respects, the financial position of X Company and its subsidiaries as of December 31, 20X5 and 20X4, and the results of their operations and their cash flows for the year then ended in accordance with accounting principles generally accepted in the United States of America.

[Auditor's signature]

[Auditor's city and state]

[Date of the auditor's report]

SECTION 610

THE AUDITOR'S CONSIDERATION OF THE INTERNAL AUDIT FUNCTION IN AN AUDIT OF FINANCIAL STATEMENTS

Authoritative Pronouncements

IMPORTANT NOTICE FOR 2013: At the time the 2013 *GAAS Guide* went to press, the Auditing Standards Board had not issued a redrafted SAS to supersede SAS 65, *The Auditor's Consideration of the Internal Audit Function in an Audit of Financial Statements.* The guidance in SAS-65 was contained in the earlier editions of the *Codification of Statements on Auditing Standards* as AU 322. SAS-122 designates AU-C 610 for the codification of a subsequent clarified SAS that will be issued to supersede SAS-65 when it is redrafted for clarity and convergence with ISA 610, *Using the Work of Internal Auditors,* as part of the Clarification and Convergence project of the ASB. For purposes of the 2013 *GAAS Guide*, the guidance in SAS-65 (old section AU 322) is provided in this section.

SAS-65—The Auditor's Consideration of the Internal Audit Function in an Audit of Financial Statements

Overview

An internal audit function, if it exists, is part of the client's internal control. SAS-65 describes how the auditor should evaluate the internal audit function in order to plan the audit engagement (designing the nature, timing, and extent of subsequent audit procedures).

An internal audit function may consist of a variety of activities, some or all of which might not be related to the recording, processing, and reporting of financial information. The auditor should obtain an understanding of the internal audit function as part of obtaining an understanding of the entity and its environment, including its internal controls. Although the special circumstances of each engagement will dictate the specific audit approach, the auditor should make inquiries to gain an understanding of the following issues:

- Internal audit's status within the organizational hierarchy of the entity
- Internal audit's application of professional standards, such as professional internal auditing standards
- Internal audit's audit plan, including the nature, timing, and extent of its work
- Internal audit's ability to assess records and any restrictions on the scope of their activities

Certain internal audit activities might not be relevant to the audit of financial statements, such as operational audits performed by internal audit. If after gaining an understanding of the internal audit function the auditor determines that internal audit's activities are not relevant to the audit of financial statements, he or she does not have to further consider the internal audit function.

PUBLIC COMPANY IMPLICATION: In 2003, the New York Stock Exchange (NYSE) changed its listing requirements to mandate that all NYSE registrants have an internal audit function.

Promulgated Procedures Checklist

If the auditor concludes that relevant activities are being performed by internal auditors, and it appears that it would be efficient to rely on those activities in lowering the assessment of control risk, the auditor should perform the following:

- Assess the objectivity and competence of the internal audit function
- Determine the effect of the internal audit function on understanding the internal control
- Determine the effect of the internal audit function on the assessment of the risk of material misstatement
- Determine the degree of reliance on the internal audit function
- Evaluate internal audit's work

PLANNING AID REMINDER: SAS-65 requires that in all engagements the auditor develop some understanding of the internal audit function and determine whether that function is relevant to the assessment of control risk. Thus, if there is an internal audit function, it must be evaluated. The evaluation is not optional.

Analysis and Application of Procedures

Assess the objectivity and competence of the internal audit function

The auditor should evaluate the objectivity of internal auditors by determining the organizational status of the internal audit function and by examining the policies that may enhance the likelihood that the internal auditors are objective.

OBSERVATION: The standard of objectivity is different from the standard of independence. Although it could be argued that it is simply a matter of semantics, the differentiation is based on the reasonable assumption that an internal auditor cannot achieve independence, because he or she is an employee of the client.

SAS-65 states that factors relevant to determining organizational status of the internal audit function include the following:

- Direct reporting to an officer, which implies broad audit coverage and adequate consideration of audit findings

- Direct access and reporting to the board of directors, the audit committee, or the owner/manager
- For internal audit employment decisions, oversight responsibility that rests with the board of directors, the audit committee, or the owner/manager

In addition, policies that minimize the placement of internal auditors in situations where they have an existing relationship (for example, auditing a department where a spouse works) or may have a future relationship (possible assignment to a department once the internal audit stint is completed) can contribute to the objectivity of the internal audit function and should be considered by the auditor.

In assessing the competence of the internal auditors, the auditor should review background information on the internal auditors, such as their educational achievements (degrees, certifications, continuing education) and professional experience. In addition, the auditor should consider operational practices such as the assignment of internal auditors, supervision and review of personnel within the department, quality of audit documentation, and specific performance evaluations. Audit policies, programs, and procedures are also relevant, when evaluating the internal audit functions.

SAS-65 states that in some instances it is necessary to test the effectiveness of the client's controls on objectivity and competency. For example, rather than simply accepting an assertion that the audit committee is involved in the hiring of internal auditors, the auditor may decide to interview members of the committee and ask them specifically about their roles in hiring and overseeing internal audit staff.

ENGAGEMENT STRATEGY: The degree to which the effectiveness of controls will be tested should be based on the anticipated degree to which the internal audit function will be a factor in the planning of subsequent audit procedures: The greater the reliance on the internal audit function, the greater the degree to which the controls should be tested.

If the auditor concludes that the internal audit function possesses an acceptable level of objectivity and competence, the auditor should determine the effect of the function on (1) the understanding of the internal control, (2) the assessment of risk, and (3) the design of substantive procedures.

Determine the effect of the internal audit function on understanding the internal control

The auditor's responsibility with regard to the client's internal control generally consists of obtaining an understanding of the design and determining whether controls have been placed in operation. Work performed by internal auditors may affect one or both of these phases of the engagement. For example, internal auditors may have documented the cash disbursements system by preparing a flowchart and supportive narrative descriptions. In addition, the internal auditors may have inspected canceled voucher packages to determine whether certain specific control procedures depicted on the flowchart were followed. The auditor could rely on this documentation to gain an initial understanding of the cash disbursement system (understanding design phase) and could review the number and types of control deviations discovered by the internal auditors (placed in operation phase).

Determine the effect of the internal audit function on the assessment of risk of material misstatement

The auditor assesses risk at the financial statement level and at the account balance or class-of-transaction level. Risk at the financial statement level is broad in nature in that it applies to assessing the risk of material misstatement in many financial statement assertions. Generally, factors related to the control environment have a broad effect on numerous accounts. Thus, an evaluation of the internal audit function as an element of the client's internal control can have an effect on the auditor's assessment of risk at the financial statement level because internal audit can affect many account assertions.

Risk at the account balance or class-of-transaction level is directed to specific control activities and the related assertions that appear in the financial statements. Having internal auditors perform tests of controls may influence the level of risk assessed at the account balance level or class-of-transaction level. For example, if internal auditors have tested specific assertions in the cash disbursement system, the auditor reviewing internal audit's tests may decide that control risk as it relates to assertions concerning certain operating expenses (such as advertising expense and utilities expense) can be assessed at a level less than maximum.

FRAUD POINTER: AU-C 240 requires auditors to inquire of internal audit personnel, if there is an internal audit function, about internal audit's views related to the risks of fraud. Auditors must also inquire about whether internal audit has performed any procedures to identify or detect fraud during the year and whether management has responded satisfactorily to internal audit's findings regarding fraud risks. Auditors must also ask internal audit whether they have knowledge of any fraud or suspected fraud.

Determine the degree of reliance on the internal audit function

Although the role of the internal audit function should be considered as part of understanding internal control, assessing risk, and designing substantive procedures, the independent auditor is solely responsible for the opinion expressed on the financial statements. For this reason, the auditor should carefully consider the extent to which the internal audit function should influence the audit approach. The fundamental guidance for determining the role the internal audit function should play in the audit is simple: Audit evidence obtained indirectly from an internal auditor is less reliable than the same audit evidence developed directly by the independent auditor.

OBSERVATION: SAS-65 states that the auditor should consider three factors: (1) the materiality of balances or classes of transactions, (2) the degree of inherent risk and control risk that affects assertions, and (3) the degree of subjectivity needed to evaluate evidence to support assertions in the financial statements—in determining the degree of reliance on the internal audit function. As each one of these factors increases, the degree of reliance on work performed by internal auditors should decrease (and vice versa).

SAS-65 reiterates that when assertions related to material amounts are characterized by a high risk of material misstatement or a high degree of subjectivity (or both), the auditor must be in a position to accept sole responsibility for satisfying the standards of fieldwork with respect to these assertions and the related internal control. Furthermore, the work of the internal auditors cannot solely be used as a basis for eliminating the auditor's performance of substantive procedures on those assertions. SAS-65 suggests that the following assertions have either a high degree of risk or a high degree of subjectivity in the evaluation of audit evidence:

- Significant accounting estimates that are the basis for valuing assets or liabilities
- Existence and disclosure of related-party transactions
- Existence and disclosure of contingencies and other uncertainties
- Existence and disclosure of subsequent events

Although the work of internal auditors may be used in a variety of circumstances, SAS-65 states that the following judgments should be made by the auditor and not by internal auditors:

- Assessments of inherent risk and control risk
- Sufficiency of audit tests performed
- Evaluation of significant accounting estimates

Other similar judgments also should be made exclusively by the auditor. SAS-65 states that if the internal auditors are requested to directly assist in the audit, the auditor should follow the guidelines listed below:

- Assess the competence and objectivity of the internal auditors
- Supervise, review, evaluate, and test the work performed by the internal auditors
- Describe to the internal auditors their responsibilities
- Describe the objective of the work that is being performed by internal audit
- Describe circumstances that could affect the nature, timing, and extent of audit procedures
- Direct internal auditors to inform the auditor of all significant accounting and auditing issues that arise during the performance of their work

Evaluate internal audit's work

When the auditor concludes that the work of internal auditors may be used to determine an understanding of internal control, to assess risk, or as substantive procedures, the auditor should evaluate the quality of that work. Factors that might be considered in assessing the work of internal auditors are the following:

- Whether the scope of the work is consistent with audit objectives
- Adequacy of internal audit programs
- Adequacy of audit documentation, including evidence of supervision and review
- Appropriateness of conclusions drawn
- Whether the internal audit reports are consistent with the nature of the work performed

The auditor's evaluation of the effectiveness of the procedures conducted by internal auditors should include the testing of the internal auditors' work related to significant financial statement assertions. The auditor can satisfy the need for such evaluation either by (1) examining controls, transactions, or balances examined by the internal auditors or by (2) examining similar controls, transactions, or balances not actually examined by the internal auditors. The auditor should then compare his or her own results to those of the internal auditors. The degree to which the auditor performs such tests is a matter of professional judgment.

SECTION 620

USING THE WORK OF AN AUDITOR'S SPECIALIST

Authoritative Pronouncements

SAS-122—Statements on Auditing Standards: Clarification and Recodification'

Overview

In some instances the dollar amounts reflected in the financial statements are based on audit evidence that an auditor is not capable of evaluating. For example, pension costs depend on an actuarial analysis that is usually beyond the expertise of an auditor. AU-C 620 provides guidance in engagements that require the services of an auditor's specialist. An auditor's specialist is a person or firm that possesses specialized knowledge or skill in a nonaccounting or nonauditing field, whose work is used by the auditor to assist in obtaining sufficient appropriate audit evidence.

The guidance in AU-C 620 does not apply when the auditor consults someone with expertise in a specialized area of accounting or auditing, as these circumstances are addressed in AU-C 220, *Quality Control for an Engagement Conducted in Accordance with Generally Accepted Auditing Standards,* and AU-C 300, *Planning an Audit.* AU-C 620 also does not apply when the auditor uses the work of someone with expertise other than accounting or auditing when that specialist's work is used by the entity to assist in preparing its financial statements, a situation covered by the guidance in AU-C 500, *Audit Evidence.*

PLANNING AND REMINDER: AU-C 336 did not change the requirement established by SOP 92-4 (Auditing Insurance Entities' Loss Reserves) that a "loss reserve specialist," not an employee or officer of the client, must be used to audit the loss reserve for property and liability insurance companies.

ENGAGEMENT STRATEGY: An entity's use of information technology is likely to have a significant impact on internal control. AU-C 315 notes that the auditor should consider whether specialized IT skills are needed for the auditor to understand the effect of IT on the audit. In some instances, an outside IT specialist is needed to inquire of client IT personnel about IT-based transaction processing and related automated controls, including examination of system documentation and planning and performance of tests of IT controls. An auditor who engages an IT specialist should have sufficient IT-related knowledge to communicate the audit objectives to the specialist, to evaluate whether the specialist's procedures satisfy audit objectives, and to evaluate the results of the specialist's work.

FRAUD POINTER: As part of the auditor's mandated responses to address the risk of management override of internal controls, AU-C 240, *Consideration of Fraud in a Financial Statement Audit,* requires the auditor to examine journal entries and other adjustments for evidence of possible material misstatements due to fraud. AU-C 240 notes that journal entries and other adjustments might only exist in electronic form for entities that use IT in the financial reporting process. In some circumstances, an IT specialist might be needed to extract electronic evidence needed by the auditor to test journal entries and other adjustments.

While the auditor may use the work of an auditor's specialist as appropriate audit evidence, the audit opinion expressed is the sole responsibility of the auditor. Therefore, the auditor must decide whether to use the work of an auditor's specialist and if that work is adequate for the auditor's purposes.

Definitions

Auditor's specialist	An individual or organization possessing expertise in a field other than accounting or auditing, whose work in that field is used by the auditor to assist in obtaining sufficient appropriate audit evidence. The specialist may be an internal specialist who is a partner, staff, or temporary staff member of the auditor's firm or a network firm or an external specialist.
Expertise	Skills, knowledge, and experience in a particular field.
Management's specialist	An individual or organization possessing expertise in a field other than accounting or auditing, whose work in that field is used by the entity to assist in preparing its financial statements.

Requirements

The auditor is presumptively required to perform the following procedures when using the work of an auditor's specialist in an audit engagement:

1. Determine whether to use the work of an auditor's specialist if expertise in an area other than accounting or auditing is needed to obtain sufficient appropriate audit evidence.

2. Determine the nature, timing, and extent of audit procedures related to the auditor's specialist and his or her work, considering matters such as:

   a. The nature of and risks of material misstatement in the matter of the specialist's work

   b. The significance of the specialist's work in the context of the audit

   c. The auditor's knowledge of and experience with prior work of the specialist

   d. Whether the specialist is subject to the auditor's firm's quality control policies and procedures

3. Evaluate whether the auditor's specialist's competence, capability, and objectivity are adequate for the auditor's purposes. If the specialist is

external, inquire about interests and relationships that could threaten the specialist's objectivity.

4. Obtain a sufficient understanding of the specialist's field of expertise to determine the nature, scope, and objectives of the specialist's work and to evaluate the adequacy of that work for the auditor's purposes.

5. When appropriate, agree in writing with the auditor's specialist regarding:

    a. The nature, scope, and objectives of the specialist's work

    b. The respective roles and responsibilities of the auditor and the specialist

    c. The nature, timing, and extent of communication between the auditor and specialist, including the form of any report to be provided by the specialist

    d. The need for the auditor's specialist to observe confidentiality requirements

6. Evaluate the adequacy of the auditor's specialist's work for the auditor's purposes, including:

    a. The relevance and reasonableness of the specialist's findings or conclusions and their consistency with other audit evidence

    b. Obtaining an understanding and evaluating the relevance and reasonableness of any significant assumptions and methods used considering the specialist's rationale and support as well as the auditor's other findings and conclusions

    c. The relevance, completeness, and accuracy of any significant source data used

7. If the auditor determines the work of the auditor's specialist is not adequate for the auditor's purposes, he or she should agree with the specialist on the nature and extent of further work to be performed by the specialist or perform additional audit procedures appropriate to the circumstances.

8. An auditor's specialist's work should not be referred to in an auditor's report with an unmodified opinion.

9. The auditor should not refer to the work of the auditor's specialist in a report containing an unmodified opinion. But, if an auditor's external specialist's work is referred to in an auditor's report to help understand a modification to the audit opinion, the auditor's report should indicate that such reference does not reduce the auditor's responsibility for the audit opinion.

Analysis and Application of Procedures

Auditor's Specialist

An auditor's specialist has expertise in fields other than accounting or auditing, such as:

- The valuation of complex financial instruments, land and buildings, plants and machinery, jewelry, works of art, antiques, intangible assets, assets and liabilities assumed in business combinations, and assets that may have been impaired
- The actuarial calculation of liabilities associated with insurance contracts or employee benefit plans
- The estimation of oil or gas reserves
- The valuation of environmental liabilities and site cleanup costs
- The interpretation of contracts, laws, and regulations
- The analysis of complex or unusual tax compliance issues
- The determination of physical characteristics relating to quantity on hand or condition

While it is often clear whether a specialist has expertise in accounting or auditing or in another field, in some cases making this distinction will require the use of professional judgment. In these situations, the auditor may use applicable professional rules and standards regarding education and competency requirements for accountants and auditors to help make these decisions. Sometimes a specialist may possess expertise in accounting or auditing as well as in another field. In these circumstances, the decision about whether that individual is an auditor's specialist depends on the nature of the work performed by the individual that the auditor is using for the audit.

OBSERVATION: An auditor's specialist may be an individual or an organization, so the auditor may consider the personal attributes of the individual and the managerial attributes of the organization, such as its system of quality control, in evaluating the competence, capabilities, and objectivity of the specialist.

Need for an Auditor's Specialist

The auditor may determine an auditor's specialist is needed to assist in one or more phases of the audit. The decision to use the work of an auditor's specialist may help the auditor fulfill requirements under AU-C 220 that the engagement team and any external auditor's specialists have the appropriate competence and capabilities to perform the audit and under AU-C 300 to determine the nature, timing, and extent of resources necessary to perform the engagement.

Even if an auditor is not a specialist in a relevant field other than accounting or auditing, he or she may be able to obtain a sufficient understanding of the field to perform the audit without an auditor's specialist. Experience auditing entities requiring this type of expertise or education or professional development in the relevant field may contribute to this understanding.

When deciding whether to use an auditor's specialist, the auditor may consider the following: if management used a specialist to prepare the financial statements; the nature, significance, complexity, and risks of material misstatement of the matter; and the expected nature of the procedures to respond to identified risks, including the auditor's knowledge of and experience with specialists' work in such matters and the availability of alternative sources of evidence.

PUBLIC COMPANY IMPLICATION: The PCAOB has issued Staff Audit Practice Alert No. 2 (Matters Related to Auditing Fair Value Measurements of Financial Instruments and the Use of Specialists), which includes a discussion of the auditor's use of a specialist in auditing fair values. The auditor should consider using a specialist when he or she lacks the necessary skill and knowledge to plan and perform audit procedures relating to fair value measurements in the financial statements. The auditor should be more likely to use a specialist given a greater client use of unobservable inputs, greater complexity in valuation techniques, and fair value amounts that are large. If the auditor chooses to rely on the work of a specialist, he or she must obtain an understanding of the specialist's methods and evaluate whether they will result in a measurement that is in accordance with GAAP. In addition, the auditor needs to evaluate the specialist's assumptions. Finally, the auditor should evaluate the specialist's qualifications, including his or her experience in performing the type of work that the auditor is considering relying upon.

Management's specialists may be used to address the increased risks of material misstatement that can occur when expertise other than accounting is needed for management to prepare the financial statements. If a management's specialist has been used, the auditor's decision about whether to use an auditor's specialist may also include the nature, scope, and objectives of the management's specialist's work; if the specialist is employed by the entity; the extent to which entity management can influence or control their work; the specialist's competence and capabilities; whether the specialist is subject to technical performance standards or other professional or industry requirement; any entity controls over their work; and the auditor's ability to evaluate the work of management's specialists without the use of an auditor's specialist.

Auditor's Firm's Quality Control Policies and Procedures

In accordance with SQCS-8, *A Firm's System of Quality Control*, if an auditor's specialist is part of the auditor's firm or part of a network firm, he or she is subject to the quality control policies and procedures of the firm. However, if the auditor's specialist is external to the auditor's firm, he or she is not a member of the engagement team and is not subject to the firm's quality control policies and procedures.

AU-C 220 guidance allows engagement teams to rely on the firm's system of quality control unless the engagement partner determines it is inappropriate to do so. The extent of the auditor's reliance depends on the nature, timing, and extent of the audit procedures with respect to matters such as: competence and capabilities, objectivity, the auditor's evaluation of the adequacy of the auditor's specialist's work, adherence to regulatory and legal requirements through monitoring processes, and agreement with the auditor's specialist.

PLANNING AID REMINDER: Reliance on the firm's system of quality control does not reduce the auditor's responsibility to meet AU-C 620's requirements.

Competence, Capabilities, and Objectivity of the Auditor's Specialist

Information about the competence, capabilities, and objectivity of an auditor's specialist may come from sources such as: personal experience with prior work of the specialist, discussions with the specialist or with others familiar with the specialist's work, knowledge of the specialist's qualifications and works published by the specialist, or the auditor's firm's quality control policies and procedures. In evaluating the specialist's competence, capabilities, and objectivity, the auditor may consider:

- If the specialist's work is subject to technical performance standards or other professional or industry requirements
- The relevance of the specialist's competence to the matter his or her work will be used for
- The specialist's competence related to relevant accounting and auditing requirements
- Whether unexpected events, changes in conditions, or audit evidence obtained from results of audit procedures indicate the auditor's initial evaluation of the specialist's competence, capabilities, and objectivity needs to be reconsidered

If the objectivity of an auditor's specialist is threatened, safeguards created by external structures, the specialist's work environment, or the audit engagement may eliminate or reduce those threats. The role of the auditor's specialist and the significance of his or her work to the audit impact the evaluation of the significance of threats to their objectivity. In some situations, such as when the auditor's specialist is also a management's specialist, safeguards may not be sufficient to reduce these threats to an acceptable level.

To evaluate the specialist's objectivity, the auditor may inquire of the entity and specialist about any interests or relationships between the entity and specialist that may affect objectivity such as financial interests, business and personal relationships, the provision of other services, as well as any applicable safeguards that could reduce objectivity threats to an acceptable level. If the auditor believes the relationship between the entity and the specialist may impair the specialist's objectivity, additional procedures may be performed to determine if the specialist's findings are reasonable.

Obtaining an Understanding of the Auditor's Specialist's Field of Expertise

The auditor may find the following relevant in obtaining an understanding of the auditor's specialist's field of expertise:

- Whether the specialist's field has specialized areas relevant to the audit
- Whether any professional standards or legal or regulatory requirements apply

- The assumptions, methods, and applicable models used by the auditor's specialist and whether they are generally accepted in the specialist's field and appropriate for financial reporting purposes

- The nature of internal and external data or information used by the specialist

Agreement with the Auditor's Specialist

Regardless of whether the auditor's specialist is internal or external, the nature, scope and objectives of the specialist's work, the respective roles and responsibilities of the auditor and specialist, and the nature, timing, and extent of communication between the auditor and specialist should be agreed upon.

Agreement on the nature, scope, and objectives of the specialist's work may include discussion of relevant technical performance standards or other professional or industry requirements the specialist will adhere to. Agreement on the roles and responsibilities of the auditor and specialist may include who will perform detailed testing of the source data, consent for the auditor to discuss the specialist's findings or conclusions with the entity and others and to include details of these finding or conclusions in the basis for a modified opinion in the auditor's report if needed.

ENGAGEMENT STRATEGY: The auditor may need to inform the specialist that his or her work will be used to substantiate certain assertions in the financial statements. It generally would be necessary to ensure that the specialist understands the need to provide a "usable link" between the specialist's work and the assertions to be substantiated. Essentially, the prudent auditor must make sure that the technical nature of the specialist's work makes sense in the context of the audit engagement. This should be determined early in the strategy planning for the engagement.

This agreement may also determine access to and retention of each party's working papers, as the working papers of a specialist who is part of the engagement team are part of the audit documentation but the working papers of an external auditor's specialist are not part of the audit documentation absent an agreement otherwise. Agreement on the nature, timing, and extent of communication between the auditor and specialist is also important and, in situations when the specialist's work relates to the auditor's conclusions regarding a significant risk, both a formal written report at the conclusion of the specialist's work and oral reports as the work progresses may be appropriate.

The auditor's specialist should abide by the same confidentiality provisions of relevant ethical requirements as the auditor. Law or regulation may impose additional requirements. Additionally, the entity may request that auditor's external specialists agree to specific confidentiality provisions.

The agreement between the auditor and auditor's specialist may or may not be written. If there is no written agreement, evidence of the agreement may be included in the auditor's planning documentation or the policies and procedures of the auditor's firm. No documentation may be required if, for example, the auditor's firm has protocols detailing the circumstances in which the work of a specialist is used. In establishing an agreement with the auditor's specialist, it is important to consider the implications of any reservation, limitation, or restriction on the specialist's work. A more detailed or written agreement may be preferred if some of the following factors exist:

- The specialist will have access to sensitive or confidential entity information
- The auditor and specialist have different roles and responsibilities than would normally be expected
- Multijurisdictional legal or regulatory requirements apply
- The matter the specialist's work relates to is highly complex
- The auditor has not previously used work performed by the specialist
- The specialist's work is extensive and significant in the context of the audit

A written agreement between the auditor and auditor's external specialist is often in the form of an engagement letter. Exhibit AU-C 620-1 provides a listing of matters the auditor may consider including in an engagement letter or other agreement with an auditor's external specialist.

Evaluating the Adequacy of an Auditor's Specialist's Work

The nature, timing, and extent of the auditor's procedures to evaluate the adequacy of the auditor's specialist's work are affected by the auditor's: evaluation of the specialist's competence, capabilities, and objectivity; familiarity with the specialist's field of expertise; and the nature of work performed by the specialist. To evaluate the adequacy of the specialist's work, the auditor may:

- Make inquiries of the specialist
- Review the specialist's working papers and reports
- Perform corroborative procedures such as observing the specialist's work, examining published data, confirming relevant matters with third parties, performing detailed analytical procedures, and reperforming calculations
- Discuss with another specialist with relevant expertise when the auditor's specialist's findings or conclusions are not consistent with audit evidence
- Discuss the specialist's report with management

When the auditor considers the relevance and reasonableness of the specialist's findings or conclusions, he or she may include whether the findings and conclusions are: presented in a manner consistent with the specialist's profession or industry; clearly expressed, referring to the agreed objectives, scope of work performed, and standards applied; based on an appropriate period taking into account subsequent events as appropriate; and based on appropriate consideration of any errors or deviations encountered.

If the auditor's specialist is evaluating management's underlying assumptions and methods, the auditor primarily performs procedures to evaluate whether the specialist has adequately reviewed those methods. If the specialist is developing an estimate or range for the auditor to compare with management's estimate, the auditor primarily performs procedures to evaluate the assumptions and methods used by the specialist.

OBSERVATION: The guidance in AU-C 540, *Auditing Accounting Estimates, Including Fair Value Accounting Estimates and Related Disclosures*, about the auditor obtaining sufficient appropriate audit evidence regarding management's assumptions and methods may also assist the auditor in evaluating a specialist's assumptions and methods.

If a specialist's work uses significant assumptions and methods, the auditor's evaluation of those assumptions and methods may include whether they are:

- Generally accepted in the specialist's field
- Consistent with the requirements of the applicable financial reporting framework
- Dependent on the use of specialized models
- Consistent with management's assumptions and methods, and the reason for and effect of any inconsistencies

When the auditor considers the relevance, completeness, and accuracy of source data significant to the specialist's work, he or she may test the data by verifying the origin of the data, obtaining an understanding of and possibly testing the internal controls over the data and its transmission to the specialist, and reviewing the data for completeness and internal consistency. In some situations, such as when the data is highly technical in relation to the specialist's field, the specialist may test the source data. When this occurs, the auditor may inquire of the specialist or supervise or review the specialist's test to evaluate the data's relevance, completeness, and accuracy.

If the auditor's specialist's work is not adequate for the auditor's purposes and additional work performed by the auditor or specialist cannot resolve the matter, a modified opinion may need to be expressed in the auditor's report because the auditor has not obtained sufficient appropriate audit evidence.

If Applicable, Consider Using A Specialist's Work to Determine Whether There Has Been a Transfer of Financial Assets as Defined by ASC-860

ASC 860 (Accounting for Transfers of Financial Assets) provides the following guidance for determining when the transfer of financial assets may be treated as a sale:

> The transferred financial assets have been isolated from the transferor—put presumptively beyond the reach of the transferor and its creditors, even in bankruptcy or other receivership.

Determining whether the above condition (the isolation criterion) has been satisfied is "largely a matter of law." The need for the work of a specialist (lawyer) generally depends on the complexity of the transfer. When the transfer is routine and there is no continuing involvement in the assets by the transferor, the use of a lawyer may not be necessary. On the other hand, if the transfer involves complex legal structures, the opinion of a legal specialist may be required.

When it is concluded that the opinion of a legal specialist is needed, the following factors should be considered in assessing the adequacy of the legal opinion:

- The legal experience of the specialist in the area (including exposure to the U.S. Bankruptcy Code and other relevant statutes)
- An understanding by the auditor of the assumptions that are used by the legal specialist
- The performance by the auditor of appropriate tests on relevant information that has been provided to the specialist by management

---

OBSERVATION: The specialist's work is usually expressed "in the form of a reasoned legal opinion that is restricted to particular facts and circumstances relevant to the specific transaction." If the auditor concludes that the legal opinion provided by the specialist is inadequate or inappropriate, the auditor must determine how the audit report should be modified.

Practitioner's Aids

EXHIBIT AU-C 620-1—CONSIDERATIONS FOR INCLUSION IN AN AGREEMENT BETWEEN THE AUDITOR AND AN AUDITOR'S EXTERNAL SPECIALIST

Nature, Scope, and Objectives of the Specialist's Work

- Nature and scope of procedures the specialist will perform
- Specialist's objectives in the context of materiality and risk considerations concerning the matter of the specialist's work and the applicable financial reporting framework when relevant
- Relevant technical performance standards or professional or industry requirements the specialist will follow
- The assumptions, methods, and models the specialist will use and their authority
- The effective date or testing period for the matter of the specialist's work and requirements regarding subsequent events

Roles and Responsibilities of the Auditor and the Auditor's External Specialist

- Relevant auditing and accounting standards and regulatory or legal requirements
- The specialist's consent to the auditor's intended use of the specialist's report including any reference to or disclosure of it to others
- The nature and extent of the auditor's review of the specialist's work
- Whether the auditor or specialist will test source data

- The specialist's access to the entity's records, files, personnel, and specialists engaged by the entity

- Procedures for communication between the specialist and the entity

- Access of the auditor and the specialists to each other's working papers

- Ownership and control of working papers during and after the engagement

- The specialist's responsibility to perform work with due skill and care

- The specialist's competence and capability to perform the work

- The expectation that the specialist will use all his or her knowledge that is relevant to the audit

- Any restriction on the specialist's association with the auditor's report

- Any agreements to inform the specialist of the auditor's conclusions regarding the specialist's work

Communications and Reporting

- Methods and frequency of communication including how the specialist's findings or conclusions will be reported and identification of engagement team members who will communicate with the specialist

- When the specialist will complete the work and report findings or conclusions to the auditor

- The specialist's responsibility to communicate promptly any potential delay in completing the work, any potential reservation or limitation on his or her findings or conclusions, and any instances of the entity restricting the specialist's access to records, files, personnel, or specialists engaged by the entity

- The specialist's responsibility to communicate to the auditor all information the specialist believes may be relevant to the audit

- The specialist's responsibility to communicate circumstances that may threaten his or her objectivity and any relevant safeguards that may eliminate or reduce such threats to an acceptable level

Confidentiality

- The need for the specialist to observe confidentiality requirements, including the confidentiality provisions of relevant ethical requirements that apply to the auditor and any additional requirements that may be imposed by law or regulation

AU-C 700
Audit Conclusions and Reporting

SECTION 700

FORMING AN OPINION AND REPORTING ON FINANCIAL STATEMENTS

Authoritative Pronouncements

SAS-122—Statements on Auditing Standards: Clarification and Recodification

Overview

AU-C 508 provides the auditor with guidance regarding forming an opinion on financial statements in addition to the form and content of the auditor's report on the financial statement audit. AU-C 508 guidance covers audits of complete sets of financial statements prepared in accordance with a fair presentation framework.

The auditor's objectives in adhering to AU-C 508 are to form an opinion on the financial statements based on an evaluation of the audit evidence obtained and to express that opinion clearly through a written report that includes a description of the opinion's basis. An additional aim of this standard is to promote consistency in the auditor's report, which increases the credibility of audit reporting and promotes the user's understanding and identification of any unusual circumstances that have occurred.

PUBLIC COMPANY IMPLICATION: In 2008, the Advisory Committee on the Auditing Profession, a committee established to advise the Treasury Department, issued its final report. The Advisory Committee made one recommendation that will affect the auditor's report if adopted; namely, it recommends that the SEC and PCAOB clarify in the auditor's report the auditor's responsibility for detecting fraud. Partially as a response to the Advisory Committee's work, the PCAOB has a standard-setting item on its agenda related to the form and content of the standard audit report. It is likely that any revised reporting standard adopted by the PCAOB will clarify in the auditor's report the auditor's responsibility for detecting fraud.

Definitions

Comparative financial statements	A complete set of financial statements for one or more prior periods that is included for comparison with the current period financial statements.
Comparative information	Prior period information presented for purposes of comparison with current period amounts or disclosures that is not in the form of a complete set of financial statements (e.g., condensed financial statements or summarized financial information).
General purpose financial statements	Financial statements prepared in accordance with a general purpose framework.

General purpose framework	A financial reporting framework designed to meet the common financial information needs of a wide range of users.
Unmodified opinion	The opinion expressed by the auditor when the auditor concludes that the financial statements are presented fairly, in all material respects, in accordance with the applicable financial reporting framework.

Requirements

The auditor is presumptively required to perform the following procedures when forming an opinion and reporting on financial statements:

Forming an Opinion

1. Form an opinion on whether the financial statements are presented fairly, in all material respects, in accordance with the applicable financial reporting framework.

2. Reach a conclusion as to whether reasonable assurance has been obtained that the financial statements as a whole are free from material misstatement, whether due to fraud or error. The conclusion should take into account the auditor's conclusions about whether sufficient appropriate audit evidence has been obtained and whether uncorrected misstatements are material either individually or in the aggregate, as well as the evaluations detailed in requirements 3 through 6 that the auditor makes in forming an opinion on the financial statements.

3. Evaluate whether the financial statements are prepared, in all material respects, in accordance with the applicable financial reporting framework. Consider the qualitative aspects of the entity's accounting practices, including indicators of possible bias in management's judgments.

4. Evaluate whether, given the requirements of the applicable financial reporting framework:

    a. Financial statements adequately disclose the significant accounting policies selected and applied

    b. Accounting policies selected and applied are appropriate and consistent with the applicable financial reporting framework

    c. Accounting estimates are reasonable

    d. Financial statement information presented is relevant, reliable, comparable, and understandable

    e. Financial statements provide adequate disclosures to enable the intended users to understand the effect of material transactions and events on the information conveyed in the statements

    f. Appropriate titles and terminology are used in the financial statements

5. Evaluate whether the financial statements achieve fair presentation by considering the overall presentation, structure, and content of the statements and whether the financial statements and related notes represent the underlying transactions and events in a manner that achieves fair presentation.

6. Evaluate whether the financial statements adequately refer to or describe the applicable financial reporting framework.

Form of Opinion

7. Express an unmodified opinion when the auditor concludes that the financial statements are presented fairly, in all material respects, in accordance with the applicable financial reporting framework.

8. Modify the opinion in the auditor's report if the auditor (1) concludes that the financial statements as a whole are materially misstated based on the audit evidence obtained or (2) is unable to obtain sufficient appropriate audit evidence to conclude that the financial statements as a whole are free from material misstatement.

9. If the auditor concludes that the financial statements do not achieve fair presentation, discuss the matter with management and, depending on how the matter is resolved, determine whether a modification of the auditor's opinion is necessary.

Auditor's Report

10. The report should be in writing.

11. The report should have a title that includes the word independent.

12. The report should be addressed as required by the engagement circumstances.

13. There should be an introductory paragraph identifying the entity whose financial statements have been audited, stating that the financial statements have been audited, identifying the title of each statement comprising the financial statements, and specifying the date or period covered by each financial statement.

14. A section with the heading, "Management's Responsibility for the Financial Statements" should be included. This section should describe management's responsibility for the preparation and fair presentation of the financial statements in accordance with the applicable financial reporting framework, including its responsibility for the design, implementation, and maintenance of internal control relevant to the preparation and fair presentation of financial statements that are free from material misstatement, whether due to fraud or error. The auditor's report should not refer to any separate management statement about management's responsibilities if a description of management's responsibilities is included in a document containing the auditor's report.

OBSERVATION: Unlike AU 508 (the predecessor standard to AU-C 700), AU-C 700 recommends that the audit report contain section headings to clearly define each section of the report.

---

15. A section with the heading "Auditor's Responsibility" should be included. This section should include the following statements:

a. The auditor's responsibility is to express an opinion on the financial statements based on the audit.

b. The audit was conducted in accordance with GAAS and the U.S. is the country of origin of those standards, which require that the auditor plan and perform the audit to obtain reasonable assurance about whether the financial statements are free from material misstatement.

c. An audit involves performing procedures to obtain audit evidence about the amounts and disclosures in the financial statements and the procedures selected depend on the auditor's judgment, including the assessment of the risks of material misstatement of the financial statements, whether due to fraud or error. Risk assessments involve consideration of internal control relevant to the entity's preparation and fair presentation of the financial statements in order to design audit procedures that are appropriate in the circumstances, but not for the purpose of expressing an opinion on the effectiveness of the entity's internal control, and accordingly, no such opinion is expressed. If the auditor is responsible for expressing an opinion on the effectiveness of internal control in conjunction with the financial statement audit, omit the phrase in the audit report that the auditor's consideration of internal control is not for the purpose of expressing an opinion on the effectiveness of the entity's internal control, and accordingly, no such opinion is expressed.

d. An audit includes evaluating the appropriateness of the accounting policies used and the reasonableness of significant accounting estimates made by management, as well as the overall presentation of the financial statements.

e. A statement about whether the auditor believes that the audit evidence obtained is sufficient and appropriate to provide a basis for the auditor's opinion.

16. A section with the heading "Opinion" should be included. If an unmodified opinion is expressed, the opinion should state that the financial statements present fairly, in all material respects, the financial position of the entity as of the balance sheet date and results of its operations and its cash flows for the period then ended in accordance with the applicable financial reporting framework, which should be identified along with its origin.

17. If reporting responsibilities in addition to those under GAAS to report on the financial statements are addressed in the auditor's report on the financial statements, address those responsibilities in a separate section in the auditor's report subtitled, "Report on Other Legal and Regulatory Requirements," or another title as appropriate for the section's content.

18. If the audit report includes a separate section on other reporting responsibilities, the report should contain a subtitle, "Report on the Financial Statements," encompassing the main section of the audit report, which should precede the section on other reporting responsibilities.

19. The manual or printed signature of the auditor's firm should be included.

20. The city and state where the auditor practices should be included.

21. The report should be dated no earlier than the date on which the auditor has obtained sufficient appropriate audit evidence on which to base the opinion on the financial statements, including evidence that the audit documentation has been reviewed, all the statements and related notes comprising the financial statements have been prepared, and management has asserted that they have taken responsibility for the financial statements.

22. If an audit is conducted in accordance with GAAS and another set of auditing standards, the auditor may indicate that the audit was also conducted in accordance with that other set of auditing standards in the report. This reference should not be made unless the audit was conducted in accordance with both sets of standards in their entirety. If the report refers to another set of auditing standards, identify the set of auditing standards and their country of origin.

Comparative Financial Statements

23. If comparative financial statements are presented, whether due to requirements of the applicable financial reporting framework or because management elected to provide the information, the auditor's report should refer to each period for which financial statements are presented and on which an audit opinion is expressed.

24. If expressing an opinion on all periods presented, a continuing auditor should update the report on the financial statements of the prior comparative periods with those of the current period. The auditor's report on comparative financial statements should not be dated earlier than the date on which the auditor has obtained sufficient appropriate audit evidence on which to support the opinion for the most recent audit.

25. If comparative information is presented but not covered by the auditor's opinion, the auditor should clearly indicate in the auditor's report the nature of any work performed by the auditor and the degree of responsibility the auditor is taking.

OBSERVATION: Comparative information, rather than comparative financial statements, typically denotes condensed financial statements or summarized financial information.

---

26. If comparative information for prior periods is presented and the auditor is requested to express an opinion on all periods presented, he or she should consider whether the information included for prior periods is sufficiently detailed to constitute a fair presentation in accordance with the applicable financial reporting framework.

27. Determine whether the comparative financial statements or comparative information has been prepared in accordance with the relevant requirements of the applicable financial reporting framework.

28. Evaluate whether (1) the comparative financial statements or comparative information agrees with the amounts and disclosures presented in the prior period or has been restated for the correction of a material misstatement or adjusted for the retrospective application of an accounting principle when applicable and (2) the accounting policies reflected in the comparative financial statements or comparative information are consistent with those applied in the current period or, if there have been changes in accounting policies, if those changes have been properly accounted for and adequately presented and disclosed.

29. If the auditor becomes aware of a possible material misstatement in the comparative financial statements or comparative information while performing the current period audit, perform any additional audit procedures necessary in the circumstances to obtain sufficient appropriate audit evidence to determine whether a material misstatement exists. If the auditor audited the prior period's financial statements and becomes aware of a material misstatement in those financial statements, also follow the relevant requirements in AU-C 560. If the prior period financial statements are restated, determine that the comparative financial statements or comparative information agrees with the restated financial statements.

30. Request written representations for all periods referred to in the auditor's opinion. Obtain a specific written representation regarding any restatement made to correct a material misstatement in a prior period that affects the comparative financial statements.

31. If reporting on prior period financial statements in connection with the current period audit and the auditor's opinion on the prior period statements differs from the opinion the auditor previously expressed, disclose the following matters in an emphasis-of-matter or other-matter paragraph:

   a. The date of the auditor's previous report

   b. The type of opinion previously expressed

   c. The substantive reasons for the different opinion

   d. That the auditor's opinion on the amended financial statements is different from the auditor's previous opinion

32. If prior period financial statements were audited by a predecessor auditor and the predecessor auditor's report on those statements is not reissued, state in an other-matter paragraph that the prior period financial statements were audited by a predecessor auditor, the type of opinion that was expressed and the reasons for any modification of the opinion, the nature of any emphasis-of- matter or other-matter paragraph included in the predecessor's report, and the date of that report.

33. If prior period financial statements were reported on by a predecessor auditor without modification and the auditor concludes that a material misstatement exists that affects the prior period statements, follow the communication requirements in AU-C 315, *Opening Balances—Initial Audit Engagements, Including Reaudit Engagements.* If the prior period financial statements are amended and the predecessor auditor agrees to issue a new auditor's report on the amended statements, express an opinion only on the current period.

34. If prior period financial statements were compiled or reviewed and are presented comparatively with current period financial statements without the report on the prior period being reissued, an other-matter paragraph should be included in the current period auditor's report with:

   a. The service performed in the prior period

   b. The date of the report on that service

   c. A description of any material modification noted in that report

   d. A statement that the service was less in scope than an audit and does not provide the basis for the expression of an opinion on the financial statements

35. If prior period financial statements were not audited, reviewed, or compiled, state in an other-matter paragraph that the auditor has not audited, reviewed, or compiled the prior period financial statements and assumes no responsibility for them.

Other Information Presented in the Financial Statements

36. Information that is presented as part of the basic financial statements even though it is not required by the applicable financial reporting framework should be covered by the auditor's opinion if it cannot be clearly differentiated.

Analysis and Application of Procedures

Forming an Opinion

The auditor considers qualitative aspects of accounting practices in evaluating whether the financial statements are prepared in all material respects in accordance with the requirements of the applicable financial reporting framework.

The auditor may identify indicators of a lack of neutrality that cause the financial statements as a whole to be materially misstated. Possible indicators include the selective correction of misstatements brought to management's attention during the audit and possible management bias in making accounting estimates.

The auditor also evaluates whether the financial statements achieve fair presentation. In making this evaluation, the auditor applies his or her judgment about the fairness of presentation in the context of the applicable financial reporting framework.

The financial statements should adequately refer to or describe the applicable financial reporting framework. It is only appropriate to state that the financial statements are prepared in accordance with an applicable financial reporting framework if the statements comply with all framework requirements that are effective during the period covered by the statements. Describing the applicable financial reporting framework with imprecise qualifying or limiting language, such as "in substantial compliance with," is not adequate because it may mislead financial statement users.

The financial statements may be prepared in accordance with one financial reporting framework and contain sufficient description in the notes to the financial statements to also comply with another framework. In this situation, the information is considered an integral part of the financial statements if it cannot be clearly differentiated and is therefore covered by the auditor's opinion.

Form of Opinion

If the financial statements do not achieve fair presentation even though they were prepared in accordance with the requirements of a fair presentation framework, fair presentation may be able to be achieved by providing additional disclosures in the financial statements beyond those specifically required or, in rare circumstances, departing from a framework requirement.

Rule 203 of the AICPA Code of Professional Conduct describes the requirements for the auditor in situations where a departure from a framework requirement has a material effect on the financial statements as a whole, but the financial statements would have been misleading without the departure. Under these circumstances, the auditor may still issue an unqualified opinion but should describe the departure, its approximate effects if practicable, and the reasons why compliance with the principle would result in a misleading statement in an emphasis of matter paragraph in the auditor's report. The other paragraphs in the audit report are not modified, and no reference is made to the emphasis of matter paragraph in the opinion paragraph.

OBSERVATION: Although Rule 203 may be needed to provide flexibility in the application of accounting principles, the rule must be used with a great deal of caution. When the rule is used, the auditor is, in effect, promulgating an accounting rule for a specific client, which is a heavy responsibility to undertake. Not surprisingly, there are very few examples where Rule 203 has been employed concerning the adaptation of different accounting methods.

Auditor's Report

Including the word "independent" in the title of the auditor's report indicates that the auditor has met all of the relevant ethical requirements regarding independence.

The auditor's report may be addressed to the client, its board of directors, or its stockholders. For an unincorporated client, the report may be addressed to the partners or the sole proprietor. When an audit is performed at the request of a party other than the management or owners of the audited entity, the report may be addressed to the party that requested the audit.

PUBLIC COMPANY IMPLICATION: Under SOX, the audit committee of the client's board of directors is directly responsible for the appointment, compensation, and oversight of the auditor. As such, the client in a public company audit is now the audit committee. Therefore, public company audit reports should no longer be addressed to the company or to the company's management.

Because the introductory paragraph should identify each statement comprising the financial statements, if a statement of changes in stockholders' equity accounts or statement of comprehensive income is included, those statements should be identified in the introductory paragraph. However, these statements do not need to be reported on separately in the opinion paragraph because changes in stockholders' equity accounts and comprehensive income are part of the presentation of financial position, results of operations, and cash flows.

The auditor may include the page numbers containing the financial statements in the audit report to help users identify the statements to which the audit report relates if the statements will be included in a document containing other information.

The auditor should not make additional references beyond those required to be made in the management responsibility section of the audit report because such references may lead users to erroneously believe that the auditor is providing assurances regarding management representations about their responsibilities contained in the management report.

In the auditor's responsibility section of the audit report, the auditor should only state that the audit was conducted in accordance with GAAS if the auditor has complied with the requirements of all AU-C sections relevant to the audit.

PUBLIC COMPANY IMPLICATION: For public companies, PCAOB Auditing Standard No. 1, *References in Auditors' Reports to the Standards of the Public Company Accounting Oversight Board*, requires that the scope paragraph of the audit report state that the audit was conducted "in accordance with the standards of the Public Company Accounting Oversight Board (United States)."

PUBLIC COMPANY IMPLICATION: The auditor's opinion relates to whether the financial statements are fairly presented. Auditors have historically assumed that if the financial statements are in accordance with GAAP, then the financial statements are fairly stated. This assumption might no longer be valid for public company audits. For example, Section 302 of SOX requires management to certify whether the financial statements fairly present in all material respects the financial condition and results of operations of the entity. There is no reference to compliance with GAAP in evaluating whether the financial statements are fairly stated. All auditors, but particularly public company auditors, should only issue an unqualified report if the client's financial statements accurately represent the economics of the client's financial position and results of operations, regardless of compliance with GAAP.

Financial statements are fairly presented in accordance with GAAP if the statements are in accordance with either U.S. GAAP or International Financial Reporting Standards (IFRS) as issued by the International Accounting Standards Board (IASB). This reflects the fact that AICPA Council has designated the IASB as the body to promulgate international financial reporting standards under Rules 202 and 203 of the AICPA's Code of Professional Conduct. The auditor would state in the management responsibility and opinion paragraphs of the audit report that the financial statements were prepared in accordance with IFRS as issued by the IASB rather than in accordance with U.S. GAAP.

The auditor may have the responsibility to report on matters in addition to his or her responsibility under GAAS to report on the financial statements. Other reporting responsibilities are addressed in a separate section of the auditor's report in order to provide clear differentiation. Relevant laws and regulations will dictate whether the auditor is required or permitted to report on these other responsibilities within the auditor's report on the financial statements or in a separate report. Additional reporting responsibilities may include requirements under *Government Auditing Standards* to report on internal control over financial reporting and on compliance with laws, regulations, and provisions of contracts or grant agreements.

The auditor's signature in some circumstances may be required by law or regulation to include the personal name and signature of the auditor in addition to the auditor's firm. Also, in some situations, the auditor may be required to declare his or her professional accountancy designation or the auditor or firm's recognition by the appropriate licensing agency in the audit report.

In audits involving an engagement quality control review, the audit report may not be released before the review is completed. Some audits require final approval of the financial statements by governmental legislative bodies before the statements are issued; this approval is not necessary for the auditor to reach the conclusion that sufficient appropriate audit evidence has been obtained. The date of financial statement approval for the purposes of GAAS in these situations is the earlier of the date that those with the recognized authority determine that all financial statements and related notes have been prepared and the date that those with recognized authority assert that they have taken responsibility for the statements.

An audit may be performed in accordance with GAAS and another set of auditing standards such as International Standards on Auditing (ISAs), PCAOB auditing standards, or *Government Auditing Standards*. If an audit is conducted in accordance with another set of auditing standards in addition to U.S. GAAS, then the auditor's responsibility paragraph of the standard audit report is modified to read as follows (for illustrative purposes it is assumed that the other set of auditing standards satisfied were those established by the International Auditing and Assurance Standards Board):

> We conducted our audit in accordance with auditing standards generally accepted in the United States of America and in accordance with International Standards on Auditing.

PLANNING AID REMINDER: If an audit is performed in accordance with GAAS and ISAs, the auditor may reference Appendix B of AU-C 700, "Analysis of International Standards of Auditing" of the AICPA's *Codification of Statements on Auditing Standards*. This appendix identifies ISA sections that may require documentation and procedures in addition to GAAS to help the auditor plan and perform the audit in accordance with the ISAs.

Comparative Financial Statements

In an audit report on comparative financial statements, the auditor may express differing opinions on the financial statements of different periods. The auditor may issue an updated report on prior period financial statements in conjunction with the auditor's report on the current period financial statements. An updated report is different from a reissued report in that it considers information the auditor has become aware of during the current period financial statement audit.

OBSERVATION: If comparative information is presented that is not in the form of a complete set of financial statements, it is not considered comparative financial statements and the auditor does not need to issue an opinion on the information.

If only summarized comparative financial information for prior periods is presented, the auditor is not required to report on that summarized information. If the client requests the auditor to express an opinion on summarized comparative financial information for prior periods, additional detail may need to be added to that information or the opinion in the audit report may need to be modified.

The auditor may express a different opinion on the prior period financial statements than the opinion previously expressed due to circumstances or events the auditor becomes aware of during the current period audit that materially affect the prior period financial statements. In these situations, the auditor may have additional reporting responsibilities detailed in AU-C 560 that are designed to prevent future reliance on the auditor's previously issued report on the prior period financial statements.

If the prior year's financial statements have been restated and the predecessor auditor previously reporting on those statements is unable or unwilling to reissue the audit report on those statements, an other-matter paragraph of the successor auditor's report may state that the predecessor auditor reported on the prior year's financial statements before they were restated. When the successor auditor has been engaged to audit the restatement adjustments, and has applied sufficient procedures to determine that the adjustments are appropriate, the following paragraph may be added to the successor auditor's report in the other-matter paragraph section:

> As part of our audit of the 20X5 financial statements, we also audited the adjustments described in Note X that were applied to restate the 20X4 financial statements. In our opinion, such adjustments are appropriate and have been properly applied. We were not engaged to audit, review, or apply any procedures to the 20X4 financial statements of the Company other than with respect to such adjustments and, accordingly, we do not express an opinion or any other form of assurance on the 20X4 financial statements taken as a whole.

PLANNING AID REMINDER: In determining the nature, timing, and extent of audit procedures related to the restatement or amendment adjustments, the successor auditor should consider the guidance established by AU-C 560.

PUBLIC COMPANY IMPLICATION: The PCAOB staff has issued a series of questions and answers surrounding auditor reporting responsibilities when prior-period financial statements are adjusted. Adjustments to prior-period financial statements can relate to reporting a discontinued operation, restatements to correct errors, and retrospective applications of changes in accounting principles. Either the predecessor or successor auditor may audit the adjustments to the prior-period financial statements, as long as the auditor is independent and registered with the PCAOB. If the predecessor auditor audits the adjustments, the predecessor auditor should dual date his or her report and the successor auditor should obtain an understanding of the adjustments and their effects on the current-period financial statements. In deciding whether the successor auditor can audit the adjustments or has to re-audit the prior-period financial statements, the successor auditor should consider (1) the extent of the adjustments, (2) the reason for the adjustments, and (3) the cooperation of the predecessor auditor. In addition, the successor auditor must have completed the audit of the current-period financial statements to audit adjustments to prior-period financial statements.

If the prior period financial statements were not audited, but were reviewed, the other-matter paragraph may read as follows:

> The 20X4 financial statements were reviewed by us (other accountants) and our (their) report thereon, dated March 1, 20X5, stated we (they) were not aware of any material modifications that should be made to those statements for them to be in conformity with accounting principles generally accepted in the United States of America. However, a review is substantially less in scope than an audit and does not provide a basis for the expression of an opinion on the financial statements as a whole.

If the prior period financial statements were compiled, the other matter paragraph may read as follows:

> The 20X4 financial statements were compiled by us (other accountants) and our (their) report thereon, dated March 1, 20X5, stated we (they) did not audit or review those financial statements and, accordingly, express no opinion or other form of assurance on them.

If the prior period financial statements were not audited, reviewed, or compiled, the other matter paragraph may read as follows:

> The accompanying balance sheet of X Company as of December 31, 20X4, and the related statements of income and cash flows for the year then ended were not audited, reviewed, or compiled by us and, accordingly, we do not express an opinion or any other form of assurance on them.

PLANNING AID REMINDER: A successor auditor can report on restated financial statements previously audited by a predecessor auditor in the manner described above only when reporting on comparative financial statements. Thus, a successor auditor cannot report only on the restatement adjustments.

Other Information Presented in the Financial Statements

Additional information may be presented in the financial statements that is not required by the applicable financial reporting framework, but that is not able to be clearly differentiated from the financial statements because of its nature and manner of presentation. This information should typically be covered by the auditor's opinion; however, if the information is clearly differentiated and is not necessary to fairly present the financial position, operating results, or cash flows on which the auditor is reporting, it may be identified as *unaudited* or *not covered by the auditor's report.*

Practitioner's Aids

EXHIBIT AU-C 700-1—STANDARD UNMODIFIED AUDITOR'S REPORT

INDEPENDENT AUDITOR'S REPORT

[Appropriate Addressee]

Report on the Financial Statements

We have audited the accompanying consolidated financial statements of X Company and its subsidiaries, which comprise the consolidated balance sheets as of December 31, 20X5 and 20X4, and the related consolidated statements of income, changes in stockholders' equity, and cash flows for the years then ended, and the related notes to the financial statements.

Management's Responsibility for the Financial Statements

Management is responsible for the preparation and fair presentation of these consolidated financial statements in accordance with accounting principles generally accepted in the United States of America; this includes the design, implementation, and maintenance of internal control relevant to the preparation and fair presentation of consolidated financial statements that are free from material misstatement, whether due to fraud or error.

Auditor's Responsibility

Our responsibility is to express an opinion on these consolidated financial statements based on our audits. We conducted our audits in accordance with auditing standards generally accepted in the United States of America. Those standards require that we plan and perform the audit to obtain reasonable assurance about whether the financial statements are free of material misstatement.

An audit involves performing procedures to obtain audit evidence about the amounts and disclosures in the financial statements. The procedures selected depend on the auditor's judgment, including the assessment of the risks of material misstatement of the consolidated financial statements, whether due to fraud or error. In making those risk assessments, the auditor considers internal control relevant to the entity's preparation and fair presentation of the financial statements in order to design audit procedures that are appropriate in the circumstances, but not for the purpose of expressing an opinion on the effectiveness of the entity's internal control. Accordingly, we express no such opinion. An audit also includes evaluating the appropriateness of accounting policies used and the reasonableness of significant accounting estimates made by management, as well as evaluating the overall presentation of the financial statements.

We believe that the audit evidence we have obtained is sufficient and appropriate to provide a basis for our audit opinion.

Opinion

In our opinion, the consolidated financial statements referred to above present fairly, in all material respects, the financial position of X Company and its subsidiaries as of December 31, 20X5 and 20X4, and the results of their operations and cash flows for the years then ended in accordance with accounting principles generally accepted in the United States of America.

Report on Other Legal and Regulatory Requirements

[*Form and content of this section of the auditor's report will vary depending on the nature of the auditor's other reporting responsibilities.*]

[Auditor's signature]

[Auditor's city and state]

[Date of the auditor's report]

SECTION 705

MODIFICATIONS TO THE OPINION IN THE INDEPENDENT AUDITOR'S REPORT

Authoritative Pronouncements

SAS-122—Statements on Auditing Standards: Clarification and Recodification

SAS-123—Omnibus Statement on Auditing Standards—2011

Overview

AU-C 705 addresses the auditor's responsibilities to issue an appropriate report and clearly express an appropriately modified opinion when he or she concludes that a modification to the auditor's opinion on the financial statements is necessary. A modified opinion is necessary if the auditor concludes that the financial statements as a whole are materially misstated, or if the auditor is unable to obtain sufficient appropriate evidence to form an opinion on the financial statements. The three types of modified opinions that may be issued are a qualified opinion, adverse opinion, and disclaimer of opinion. The type of modification issued depends on the nature of the matter causing the modification and the auditor's judgment about the pervasiveness of the effects or possible effects of the matter on the financial statements.

OBSERVATION: The guidance in AU-C 706 should be followed if the auditor considers it necessary or is required to include additional communications in the auditor's report that are not audit opinion modifications.

Definitions

Modified opinion	A qualified opinion, adverse opinion, or disclaimer of opinion
Pervasive	Effects or possible effects on the financial statements of misstatements that, in the auditor's judgment are not confined to specific financial statement elements, accounts, or items, if so confined, represent or could represent a substantial proportion of the financial statements, or are fundamental disclosures to users' understanding of the financial statements

Requirements

The auditor is presumptively required to perform the following procedures when deciding whether to issue a modified opinion and, if a modified opinion is to be issued, in issuing the modified opinion in the independent auditor's report:

Audit Opinion Modifications

1. Modify the audit report opinion when:

    a. The auditor concludes that, based on the audit evidence obtained, the financial statements as a whole are materially misstated; or

    b. The auditor is unable to obtain sufficient appropriate audit evidence to conclude that the financial statements as a whole are free from material misstatement.

2. Express a qualified opinion when (1) sufficient appropriate audit evidence has been obtained to conclude that misstatements, individually or in the aggregate, are material but not pervasive to the financial statements, or (2) sufficient appropriate audit evidence is unable to be obtained on which to base the opinion, but the auditor concludes that the possible effects of undetected misstatements could be material but not pervasive to the financial statements.

3. Express an adverse opinion when sufficient appropriate audit evidence has been obtained to conclude that misstatements, individually or in the aggregate, are material and pervasive to the financial statements.

4. Disclaim an opinion when sufficient appropriate audit evidence is unable to be obtained on which to base the opinion, but the auditor concludes that the possible effects of undetected misstatements could be material and pervasive to the financial statements.

5. If, after accepting an engagement, management limits the scope of the audit such that the auditor considers the need to express a qualified opinion or to disclaim an opinion likely, request that management remove the limitation. If management refuses to remove the limitation, communicate the matter to those charged with governance (unless all of those charged with governance are part of management) and determine if it is possible to obtain sufficient appropriate audit evidence by performing alternative procedures.

6. If a management imposed limitation causes an inability to obtain sufficient appropriate audit evidence and the possible effects of undetected misstatements could be material and pervasive to the financial statements, disclaim an opinion or withdraw from the audit when practicable. Before withdrawal from the audit, communicate to those charged with governance any matters regarding misstatements identified during the audit that would have caused a modification of the opinion.

7. If expressing an adverse opinion or disclaiming an opinion on the financial statements as a whole, the audit report should not include an unmodified opinion with respect to the same financial reporting framework on a single financial statement or specific financial statement element, account, or item because to do so would be contradictory.

8. If the auditor expects to modify the opinion in the auditor's report, communicate with those charged with governance the circumstances leading to the expected modification and the proposed wording of the modification.

9. If the auditor is not independent but is required by law or regulation to report on the financial statements, the auditor should disclaim an opinion and indicate that he or she is not independent. The auditor has the option as to whether or not to disclose the reason(s) for his or her lack of independence, but if the auditor discloses the reasons for a lack of independence all of the relevant reasons should be disclosed.

Reporting on Audit Opinion Modifications

10. Directly before the opinion paragraph, include a basis for modification paragraph in the audit report describing the matter giving rise to the modification appropriately entitled "Basis for Qualified Opinion," "Basis for Adverse Opinion," or "Basis for Disclaimer of Opinion."

11. The basis for modification paragraph should include a description and quantification of the financial effects of material misstatements relating to specific financial statement amounts or quantitative disclosures if practicable; or, if not practicable, that should be stated in the paragraph.

12. The basis for modification paragraph should include an explanation of how material misstatements of financial statements related to narrative disclosures are misstated.

13. If a material financial statement misstatement relates to the omission of information required to be presented or disclosed: discuss the omission with those charged with governance; describe the nature of the omitted information in the basis for modification paragraph; and include the omitted information if sufficient appropriate audit evidence about the information has been obtained and it is practicable to do so.

14. If the modification is due to an inability to obtain sufficient appropriate audit evidence, the basis for modification paragraph should include the reasons for that inability.

15. If an adverse opinion is expressed or an opinion is disclaimed, the auditor should:

   a. Describe in the basis for modification paragraph any other matters the auditor is aware of that would have required a modification of opinion and their effects

   b. Consider the need to describe in an emphasis-of-matter or other-matter paragraph any other matters that would have resulted in additional communications but not opinion modifications in the audit report.

16. The opinion paragraph should be titled "Qualified Opinion," "Adverse Opinion," or "Disclaimer of Opinion" when the opinion is modified.

17. If the opinion is qualified due to a material misstatement in the financial statements or an inability to obtain sufficient appropriate audit evidence, the opinion paragraph should state that, in the auditor's opinion, except for the effects (possible effects if the qualification is due to lack of sufficient evidence) of the matter(s) described in the basis for qualified opinion paragraph, the financial statements are presented fairly, in all material respects, in accordance with the applicable financial reporting framework.

18. If an adverse opinion is expressed, the opinion paragraph should state that, in the auditor's opinion, because of the significance of the matter(s) described in the basis for adverse opinion paragraph, the financial statements are not presented fairly in accordance with the applicable reporting framework.

19. If an opinion is disclaimed, the opinion paragraph should state that, because of the significance of the matter(s) described in the basis for disclaimer of opinion paragraph, the auditor has not been able to obtain sufficient appropriate audit evidence to provide a basis for an audit opinion, and, accordingly, an opinion is not expressed on the financial statements.

20. If a qualified or adverse opinion is expressed, the description of the auditor's responsibility in the audit report should be amended to state that the auditor believes that the audit evidence obtained is sufficient and appropriate to provide a basis for the auditor's modified opinion.

21. If there is a disclaimer of opinion, the introductory paragraph of the audit report should be amended to state that the auditor was engaged to audit the financial statements. The description of the auditor's responsibility and the scope of the audit should be amended to state only that "Our responsibility is

to express an opinion on the financial statements based on conducting the audit in accordance with auditing standards generally accepted in the United States of America. Because of the matter(s) described in the basis for disclaimer of opinion paragraph, however, we were not able to obtain sufficient appropriate audit evidence to provide a basis for an audit opinion."

Analysis and Application of Procedures

Audit Opinion Modifications

One reason for an audit opinion modification is that the auditor concludes, based on the audit evidence obtained, that the financial statements as a whole are materially misstated. This conclusion takes into account the auditor's evaluation of any uncorrected misstatements in the financial statements that were identified when following the guidance in AU-C 450. Material misstatements may be related to the appropriateness or application of the selected accounting policies or the appropriateness of the adequacy of disclosures in the financial statements or the presentation of the financial statements.

The appropriateness of the selected accounting policies is evaluated based on whether the selected policies are in accordance with the applicable financial reporting framework or the financial statements and related notes represent the underlying transactions and events in a manner achieving fair presentation. Material misstatements related to the appropriateness of accounting policies may also occur when the entity has changed accounting policies and not complied with the requirements of the applicable financial reporting framework in accounting for and disclosing this change.

Material misstatements related to the application of the selected accounting policies may occur due to the method of application (e.g., due to an unintentional error in applying the policy), or when management has not applied the selected policies in accordance with the applicable financial reporting framework, or has not applied policies consistently between periods or to similar transactions or events.

Material misstatements related to the appropriateness of financial statement presentation or adequacy of disclosures in the financial statements may occur due to several factors: the financial statements may not provide all the disclosures required by the applicable financial reporting framework or all those necessary to achieve fair presentation; the disclosures may not be presented in accordance with the applicable financial reporting framework; or information required to be presented by the applicable financial reporting framework may be omitted due to lack of a required statement or other lack of disclosure in the financial statements.

Another reason the auditor may modify the audit opinion is due to a scope limitation, or an inability to obtain sufficient appropriate audit evidence to conclude that the financial statements as a whole are free from material misstatement. A scope limitation does not arise from an inability to perform a specific procedure if the auditor is able to obtain sufficient appropriate audit evidence by performing alternative procedures. Scope limitations may arise from the following three sources:

1. *Circumstances beyond the entity's control* The entity's accounting records have been destroyed or seized indefinitely by governmental authorities

2. *Circumstances relating to the nature or timing of the auditor's work* The timing of the auditor's appointment prevents the observation of the physical inventory count and the auditor is unable to perform other appropriate procedures, substantive procedures alone are determined to be insufficient but the entity's controls are not effective, or the auditor is unable to obtain an investee's audited financial statements when accounting for long-term investments, or the auditor is not able to obtain sufficient appropriate audit evidence for an investee accounted for by the investor (client) using the equity method of accounting

3. *Limitations imposed by management* Management prevents the auditor from observing the physical inventory count or from requesting external confirmation of specific account balances

---

PLANNING AID REMINDER: Management limitations may have additional audit implications related to the auditor's assessment of fraud risks and consideration of engagement continuance.

When the auditor is unable to obtain sufficient appropriate audit evidence due to a management-imposed limitation and is considering either disclaiming an opinion or withdrawing from the engagement, his or her ability to withdraw may depend on several factors. It may not be practical to withdraw from the audit if the auditor has already substantially completed the audit and the auditor may instead decide to disclaim an opinion. In some circumstances, law or regulation or an audit appointment prohibiting withdrawal before audit completion or the end of a certain period may prevent withdrawal.

OBSERVATION: There are circumstances in which an auditor may disclaim an opinion or express an adverse opinion on certain portions of the audit and still express an unmodified opinion on other portions of the audit. The auditor may express an unmodified opinion on the financial position and disclaim an opinion on the results of operations and cash flows of an entity because this does not constitute disclaiming an opinion on the financial statements as a whole. In audits of governmental entities, the auditor expresses or disclaims an opinion for each opinion unit, so the audit report may include an unmodified opinion about one or more opinion units and a modified opinion about one or more other opinion units.

By communicating with those charged with governance about the circumstances leading to an expected audit opinion modification and the proposed wording of the modification: the auditor gives notice to those charged with governance of any intended modifications and the reasons for those modifications; the auditor seeks agreement of those charged with governance about the facts of the matter causing the expected modification or confirms matters of disagreement with management as such; and, those charged with governance have an opportunity to provide the auditor with further information and explanations about the matter causing the expected modification.

Reporting on Audit Opinion Modifications

Including a basis for modification paragraph before the opinion paragraph when the opinion is modified helps to promote consistency in the form and content of the audit report, which increases users' understanding and helps identify unusual circumstances when they occur. When describing the quantification of the financial effects of the material misstatement causing a modified opinion in the basis for modification paragraph, the auditor may reference the notes to the financial statements if they include such a disclosure. As one example, if inventory is overstated, the financial effects of the material misstatements that the auditor describes in the basis for modification paragraph may include the effects on income before taxes, income taxes, net income, and equity.

PLANNING AID REMINDER: Rule 301, *Confidential Client Information*, of the AICPA Code of Professional Conduct states that the auditor should not disclose any confidential client information without the client's specific consent. The auditor uses confidential client information in the audit, but may not disclose that information unless it is required to be disclosed or presented in order for the financial statements to comply with the applicable financial reporting framework.

If an opinion is being modified because of omitted information, the auditor should include that omitted information in the report as long as it is practicable to do so. Practicable means that the information has been prepared by management or is otherwise readily available to the auditor or, that in the auditor's judgment, the information is not too long in relation to the auditor's report. However, the auditor should not assume the role of a preparer of financial information — for example, the auditor should not prepare a basic financial statement that is otherwise missing.

OBSERVATION: When the audit opinion is modified due to an inability to obtain sufficient appropriate audit evidence, it is not appropriate for the scope of the audit to be explained in a note to the financial statements because the description of audit scope is the auditor's responsibility, not management's.

When an audit opinion is qualified, phrases such as "with the foregoing explanation" or "subject to" are not appropriate for the opinion paragraph because they are not sufficiently clear or forceful. Wording such as "fairly presented, in all material respects, when read in conjunction with Note X" is also not appropriate because it is likely to be misunderstood. If an audit opinion is qualified due to a scope limitation, wording such as "In our opinion, except for the above-mentioned limitation on the scope of our audit" is unacceptable because it bases the qualification on the restriction rather than the possible effects on the financial statements.

Practitioner's Aids

The following exhibits related to modified auditor's reports are presented in this section:

- Exhibit AU-C 705-1 —Qualified Auditor's Report Due to Material Misstatement
- Exhibit AU-C 705-2—Qualified Auditor's Report Due to Inadequate Disclosure
- Exhibit AU-C 705-3—Adverse Auditor's Report
- Exhibit AU-C 705-4—Qualified Auditor's Report Because of a Scope Limitation
- Exhibit AU-C 705-5—Disclaimer Report
- Exhibit AU-C 705-6—Auditor's Report on Comparative Financial Statements with Unmodified Prior-Year Opinion and Modified Current-Year Opinion

Exhibits AU-C 705-1 and AU-C 705-5 provide examples of complete auditor's reports with modified opinions. Exhibits AU-C 705-2, AU-C 705-3, AU-C 705-4, and AU-C 705-6 provide examples of changes to the auditor's responsibility paragraph, the basis for modification and opinion paragraphs of auditor's reports with modified opinions.

EXHIBIT AU-C 705-1—QUALIFIED AUDITOR'S REPORT DUE TO MATERIAL MISSTATEMENT

INDEPENDENT AUDITOR'S REPORT

[Appropriate Addressee]

Report on the Financial Statements

We have audited the accompanying financial statements of X Company, which comprise the balance sheets as of December 31, 20X5 and 20X4, and the related statements of income, changes in stockholders' equity, and cash flows for the years then ended, and the related notes to the financial statements.

Management's Responsibility for the Financial Statements

Management is responsible for the preparation and fair presentation of these financial statements in accordance with accounting principles generally accepted in the United States of America; this includes the design, implementation, and maintenance of internal control relevant to the preparation and fair presentation of financial statements that are free from material misstatement, whether due to fraud or error.

Auditor's Responsibility

Our responsibility is to express an opinion on these financial statements based on our audit. We conducted our audits in accordance with auditing standards generally accepted in the United States of America. Those standards require that we plan and perform the audit to obtain reasonable assurance about whether the financial statements are free of material misstatement.

An audit involves performing procedures to obtain audit evidence about the amounts and disclosures in the financial statements. The procedures selected depend on the auditor's judgment, including the assessment of the risks of material misstatement of the financial statements, whether due to fraud or error. In making those risk assessments, the auditor considers internal control relevant to the entity's preparation and fair presentation of the financial statements in order to design audit procedures that are appropriate in the circumstances, but not for the purpose of expressing an opinion on the effectiveness of the entity's internal control. Accordingly, we express no such opinion. An audit also includes evaluating the appropriateness of accounting policies used and the reasonableness of significant accounting estimates made by management, as well as evaluating the overall presentation of the financial statements.

We believe that the audit evidence we have obtained is sufficient and appropriate to provide a basis for our qualified audit opinion.

Basis for Qualified Opinion

The company has stated inventories at cost in the accompanying balance sheets. Accounting principles generally accepted in the United States of America require inventories to be stated at the lower of cost or market. If the company stated inventories at the lower of cost or market, a write down of $xxx and $xxx would have been required as of December 31, 20X5 and 20X4, respectively. Accordingly, cost of sales would have been increased by $xxx and $xxx, and net income, income taxes, and stockholders' equity would have been reduced by $xxx, $xxx, $xxx, and $xxx, $xxx, $xxx, as of and for the years ended December 31, 20X5 and 20X4, respectively.

Qualified Opinion

In our opinion, except for the effects of the matter described in the Basis for Qualified Opinion paragraph, the financial statements referred to above present fairly, in all material respects, the financial position of X Company as of December 31, 20X5 and 20X4, and the results of its operations and cash flows for the years then ended in accordance with accounting principles generally accepted in the United States of America.

Report on Other Legal and Regulatory Requirements

[*Form and content of this section of the auditor's report will vary depending on the nature of the auditor's other reporting responsibilities.*]

[Auditor's signature]

[Auditor's city and state]

[Date of the auditor's report]

EXHIBIT AU-C 705-2—QUALIFIED AUDITOR'S REPORT DUE TO INADEQUATE DISCLOSURE

We believe that the audit evidence we have obtained is sufficient and appropriate to provide a basis for our qualified audit opinion.

Basis for Qualified Opinion

The Company's financial statements do not disclose [*describe the nature of the omitted information that it is not practicable to present in the auditor's report*]. In our opinion, disclosure of this information is required by accounting principles generally accepted in the United States of America.

Qualified Opinion

In our opinion, except for the omission of the information described in the Basis for Qualified Opinion paragraph, the financial statements referred to above present fairly, in all material respects, the financial position of X Company as of December 31, 20X5 and 20X4, and the results of its operations and cash flows for the years then ended in accordance with accounting principles generally accepted in the United States of America.

EXHIBIT AU-C 705-3—ADVERSE AUDITOR'S REPORT

We believe that the audit evidence we have obtained is sufficient and appropriate to provide a basis for our adverse audit opinion.

Basis for Adverse Opinion

As described in Note X, the Company has not consolidated the financial statements of subsidiary ABC Company it acquired during 20X5 because it has not yet been able to ascertain the fair values of certain of the subsidiary's material assets and liabilities at the acquisition date. This investment is, therefore, accounted for on a cost basis by the Company. Under accounting principles generally accepted in the United States of America, the subsidiary should have been consolidated because it is controlled by the Company. Had ABC been consolidated, many elements in the accompanying consolidated financial statements would have been materially affected. The effects on the consolidated financial statements of the failure to consolidate have not been determined.

Adverse Opinion

In our opinion, because of the significance of the matter discussed in the Basis for Adverse Opinion paragraph, the consolidated financial statements referred to above do not present fairly the financial position of X Company and its subsidiaries as of December 31, 20X5, or the result of its operations or its cash flows for the year then ended.

EXHIBIT AU-C 705-4—QUALIFIED AUDITOR'S REPORT BECAUSE OF A SCOPE LIMITATION

We believe that the audit evidence we have obtained is sufficient and appropriate to provide a basis for our qualified audit opinion.

Basis for Qualified Opinion

X Company's investment in ABC Company, a foreign affiliate acquired during the year and accounted for under the equity method, is carried at $xxx on the balance sheet at December 31, 20X5, and X's share of ABC's net income of $xxx is included in X's net income for the year then ended. We were unable to obtain sufficient appropriate audit evidence about the carrying amount of X's investment in ABC as of December 31, 20X5 and X's share of ABC's net income for the year then ended because we were denied access to the financial information, management, and the auditors of ABC Company. Consequently, we were unable to determine whether any adjustments to these amounts were necessary.

Qualified Opinion

In our opinion, except for the possible effects of the matter described in the Basis for Qualified Opinion paragraph, the financial statements referred to above present fairly, in all material respects, the financial position of X Company as of December 31, 20X5, and the results of its operations and cash flows for the year then ended in accordance with accounting principles generally accepted in the United States of America.

EXHIBIT AU-C 705-5—DISCLAIMER REPORT

INDEPENDENT AUDITOR'S REPORT

[Appropriate Addressee]

Report on the Financial Statements

We were engaged to audit the accompanying financial statements of X Company, which comprise the balance sheet as of December 31, 20X5, and the related statements of income, changes in stockholders' equity, and cash flows for the year then ended, and the related notes to the financial statements.

Management's Responsibility for the Financial Statements

Management is responsible for the preparation and fair presentation of these financial statements in accordance with accounting principles generally accepted in the United States of America; this includes the design, implementation, and maintenance of internal control relevant to the preparation and fair presentation of financial statements that are free from material misstatement, whether due to fraud or error.

Auditor's Responsibility

Our responsibility is to express an opinion on these financial statements based on conducting the audit in accordance with auditing standards generally accepted in the United States of America. Because of the matter described in the Basis for Disclaimer of Opinion paragraph, however, we were not able to obtain sufficient appropriate audit evidence to provide a basis for an audit opinion.

Basis for Disclaimer of Opinion

The company's investment in ABC Company, a joint venture, is carried at $xxx on the company's balance sheet, which represents over 90 percent of the company's net assets as of December 31, 20X5. We were not allowed access to the management and the auditors of ABC Company. As a result, we were unable to determine whether any adjustments were necessary relating to the company's proportional share of ABC's assets that it controls jointly, its proportional share of ABC's liabilities for which it is jointly responsible, its proportional share of ABC's income and expenses for the year, and the elements making up the statements of changes in stockholders' equity and cash flows.

Disclaimer of Opinion

Because of the significance of the matter described in the Basis for Disclaimer of Opinion paragraph, we have not been able to obtain sufficient appropriate audit evidence to provide a basis for an audit opinion. Accordingly, we do not express an opinion on these financial statements.

Report on Other Legal and Regulatory Requirements

[*Form and content of this section of the auditor's report will vary depending on the nature of the auditor's other reporting responsibilities.*]

[Auditor's signature]

[Auditor's city and state]

[Date of the auditor's report]

EXHIBIT AU-C 705-6—AUDITOR'S REPORT ON COMPARATIVE FINANCIAL STATEMENTS WITH UNMODIFIED PRIOR-YEAR OPINION AND MODIFIED CURRENT-YEAR OPINION

We believe that the audit evidence we have obtained is sufficient and appropriate to provide a basis for our audit opinion.

Basis for Qualified Opinion

The Company has excluded, from property and debt in the accompanying 20X5 balance sheet, certain lease obligations that were entered into in 20X5 which, in our opinion, should be capitalized in accordance with accounting principles generally accepted in the United States of America. If these lease obligations were capitalized, property would be increased by $XXX, long-term debt by $XXX, and retained earnings by $XXX as of December 31, 20X5, and net income and earnings per share would be increased (decreased) by $XXX and $XXX, respectively, for the year then ended.

Qualified Opinion

In our opinion, except for the effects on the 20X5 financial statements of not capitalizing certain lease obligations as described in the Basis for Qualified Opinion paragraph, the financial statements referred to above present fairly, in all material respects, the financial position of X Company as of December 31, 20X5 and 20X4, and the results of its operations and cash flows for the years then ended in accordance with accounting principles generally accepted in the United States of America.

SECTION 706

EMPHASIS-OF-MATTER PARAGRAPHS AND OTHER-MATTER PARAGRAPHS IN THE INDEPENDENT AUDITOR'S REPORT

Authoritative Pronouncements

SAS-122—Statements on Auditing Standards: Clarification and Recodification

Overview

AU-C 706 provides the auditor with guidance on the use of emphasis-of-matter paragraphs and other-matter paragraphs in the auditor's report. These paragraphs are additional communications included when the auditor judges it is necessary to, in an emphasis-of-matter paragraph, draw users' attention to a matter that is appropriately presented or disclosed in the financial statements but is of such importance that it is fundamental to users' understanding of the financial statements or, in an other-matter paragraph, to draw users' attention to any other-matter relevant to users' understanding of the audit, the auditor's responsibilities, or the auditor's report as appropriate.

Some AU-Cs contain specific requirements for the auditor to include an emphasis-of-matter paragraph or other-matter paragraph in the auditor's report. See Exhibit AU-C 706-1 for a listing of these AU-Cs. The guidance in AU-C 706 applies regarding the form and placement of these required paragraphs.

OBSERVATION: AU-C 706 addresses emphasis-of-matter paragraphs and other-matter paragraphs included due to the auditor's judgment; however, the other AU-Cs listed in Exhibit AU-C 706-1 require the use of emphasis-of-matter and other-matter paragraphs and do not leave their inclusion up to the auditor's discretion.

Definitions

Emphasis-of-matter paragraph	A paragraph included in the auditor's report at the auditor's discretion or as required by GAAS that refers to a matter appropriately presented or disclosed in the financial statements that, in the auditor's judgment, is of such importance that it is fundamental to users' understanding of the financial statements
Other-matter paragraph	A paragraph included in the auditor's report at the auditor's discretion or as required by GAAS that refers to a matter other than those presented or disclosed in the financial statements that, in the auditor's judgment, is relevant to users' understanding of the audit, the auditor's responsibilities, or the auditor's report

Requirements

The auditor is presumptively required to perform the following procedures when including an emphasis-of-matter paragraph or other-matter paragraph in the auditor's report:

1. An emphasis-of-matter paragraph should be included only if sufficient appropriate audit evidence has been obtained that the matter is not materially misstated in the financial statements and should refer only to information presented or disclosed in the financial statements.

2. An emphasis-of-matter paragraph should: (1) be included immediately after the opinion paragraph in the auditor's report, (2) have an appropriate heading such as "Emphasis of Matter," (3) clearly reference the matter being emphasized and where relevant disclosures fully describing the matter can be found in the financial statements, and (4) state that the auditor's opinion is not modified regarding the emphasized matter.

3. An other-matter paragraph should be have an appropriate heading such as "Other Matter" and should be included immediately after the opinion paragraph and any emphasis-of-matter paragraph or elsewhere if the paragraph's content is relevant to the "Other Reporting Responsibilities" section.

4. If the auditor expects to include an emphasis-of-matter or other-matter paragraph in the report, communicate this expectation and the paragraph's proposed wording with those charged with governance.

Analysis and Application of Procedures

Emphasis-of-matter Paragraph

The following are matters that the auditor may want to emphasize (in addition to those matters in Exhibit AU-C 706-1 that are required to be emphasized):

- There is uncertainty as to the future outcome of exceptional litigation or regulatory action.

- A major catastrophe has had or continues to have a significant effect on the entity's financial position.

- There have been significant transactions with a related party.

- A significant subsequent event has taken place.

PLANNING AID REMINDER: An emphasis-of-matter paragraph should not contain more information than the related financial statement presentation or disclosure because this may imply that the matter was not appropriately presented or disclosed.

Including an emphasis-of-matter paragraph does not affect the auditor's opinion and does not act as a substitute for either (1) the auditor expressing a qualified or adverse opinion or disclaiming an opinion when required or (2) financial statement disclosures that the applicable financial reporting framework requires management to make.

Other-Matter Paragraph

There are several circumstances in which inclusion of an other-matter paragraph may be necessary or desired. When the auditor is unable to withdraw from an engagement even though the possible effect of a management-imposed scope limitation is pervasive, an other-matter paragraph may be needed to explain why withdrawal is not permitted. If the auditor reports on two sets of financial statements prepared by the same entity in accordance with different financial reporting frameworks, an other-matter paragraph may be included referring to the entity's preparation of another set of financial statements in accordance with another general purpose framework and the auditor's issuance of a report on those financial statements. Further explanation of the auditor's responsibilities or of the auditor's report may be included in an other-matter paragraph where required or permitted by law, regulation, or generally accepted practice.

PLANNING AID REMINDER: An other-matter paragraph is not used to address an auditor's additional reporting responsibilities in addition to the responsibilities under GAAS to report on the financial statements, an auditor's performance of and reporting on additional specified procedures, or the expression of an opinion on specific matters.

An other-matter paragraph clearly indicates that the matter discussed is not required to be presented and disclosed in the financial statements. Information that should not be included in an other-matter paragraph includes information the auditor is prohibited by law, regulation, or other professional standards from including or information that is required to be provided by management.

The placement of an other-matter paragraph in the auditor's report depends on the nature of the information being communicated. If the other-matter paragraph relates to the audit of the financial statements, it should be included immediately after the opinion paragraph and any emphasis-of-matter paragraph. If the other-matter paragraph relates to other reporting responsibilities addressed in the auditor's report, it may be included in the section subtitled "Report on Other Legal and Regulatory Requirements." If the other-matter paragraph relates to all the auditor's responsibilities or the users' understanding of the auditor's report, it may be included in a separate section following the main content of the auditor's report.

PLANNING AID REMINDER: If an other-matter paragraph on a particular matter continues to recur on successive engagements, the auditor may determine it is unnecessary to repeat the required communications with those charged with governance on each engagement.

Practitioner's Aids

EXHIBIT AU-C 706-1—AUDITING STANDARDS REQUIRING EMPHASIS-OF-MATTER PARAGRAPHS AND OTHER-MATTER PARAGRAPHS

AU-Cs with Requirements for Emphasis-of-matter Paragraphs

- AU-C 560, *Subsequent Events and Subsequently Discovered Facts* (paragraph 16c)
- AU-C 570, *The Auditor's Consideration of an Entity's Ability to Continue as a Going Concern* (paragraphs 12 and 16)
- AU-C 708, *Consistency of Financial Statements* (paragraphs 8–9 and 11–13)
- AU-C 800, *Special Considerations—Audits of Financial Statements Prepared in Accordance with Special Purpose Frameworks* (paragraph 19 and 21)

AU-Cs with Requirements for Other-matter Paragraphs

- AU-C 560, *Subsequent Events and Subsequently Discovered Facts* (paragraph 16c)
- AU-C 700, *Forming an Opinion and Reporting on Financial Statements* (paragraphs 53–54 and 56–57)
- AU-C 720, *Other Information in Documents Containing Audited Financial Statements* (paragraph 11)
- AU-C 725, *Supplementary Information in Relation to the Financial Statements as a Whole* (paragraph 9)
- AU-C 730, *Required Supplementary Information* (paragraph 7)
- AU-C 800, *Special Considerations—Audits of Financial Statements Prepared in Accordance with Special Purpose Frameworks* (paragraph 20)
- AU-C 806, *Reporting on Compliance with Aspects of Contractual Agreements or Regulatory Requirements in Connection with Audited Financial Statements* (paragraph 13)
- AU-C 905, *Alert that Restricts the Use of the Auditor's Written Communication* (paragraph 1)

EXHIBIT AU-C 706-2—AUDITOR'S REPORT WITH EMPHASIS-OF-MATTER PARGRAPH

INDEPENDENT AUDITOR'S REPORT

[Appropriate Addressee]

Report on the Financial Statements

We have audited the accompanying financial statements of X Company, which comprise the balance sheet as of December 31, 20X5, and the related statements of income, changes in stockholders' equity, and cash flows for the year then ended, and the related notes to the financial statements.

Management's Responsibility for the Financial Statements

Management is responsible for the preparation and fair presentation of these financial statements in accordance with accounting principles generally accepted in the United States of America; this includes the design, implementation, and maintenance of internal control relevant to the preparation and fair presentation of financial statements that are free from material misstatement, whether due to fraud or error.

Auditor's Responsibility

Our responsibility is to express an opinion on these financial statements based on our audit. We conducted our audit in accordance with auditing standards generally accepted in the United States of America. Those standards require that we plan and perform the audit to obtain reasonable assurance about whether the financial statements are free of material misstatement.

An audit involves performing procedures to obtain audit evidence about the amounts and disclosures in the financial statements. The procedures selected depend on the auditor's judgment, including the assessment of the risks of material misstatement of the financial statements, whether due to fraud or error. In making those risk assessments, the auditor considers internal control relevant to the entity's preparation and fair presentation of the financial statements in order to design audit procedures that are appropriate in the circumstances, but not for the purpose of expressing an opinion on the effectiveness of the entity's internal control. Accordingly, we express no such opinion. An audit also includes evaluating the appropriateness of accounting policies used and the reasonableness of significant accounting estimates made by management, as well as evaluating the overall presentation of the financial statements.

We believe that the audit evidence we have obtained is sufficient and appropriate to provide a basis for our audit opinion.

Opinion

In our opinion, the financial statements referred to above present fairly, in all material respects, the financial position of X Company as of December 31, 20X5, and the results of its operations and cash flows for the year then ended in accordance with accounting principles generally accepted in the United States of America.

Emphasis of Matter

We draw attention to Note X to the financial statements, the Company is a defendant in a lawsuit [*briefly describe the nature of the litigation consistent with the Company's description in the note to the financial statements*]. Our opinion is not modified with respect to this matter.

Report on Other Legal and Regulatory Requirements

[*Form and content of this section of the auditor's report will vary depending on the nature of the auditor's other reporting responsibilities.*]

[Auditor's signature]

[Auditor's city and state]

[Date of the auditor's report]

EXHIBIT AU-C 706-3—AUDITOR'S REPORT WITH OTHER-MATTER PARAGRAPH

INDEPENDENT AUDITOR'S REPORT

[Appropriate Addressee]

Report on the Financial Statements

We have audited the accompanying financial statements of X Company, which comprise the balance sheets as of December 31, 20X5 and 20X4, and the related statements of income, changes in stockholders' equity, and cash flows for the years then ended, and the related notes to the financial statements.

Management's Responsibility for the Financial Statements

Management is responsible for the preparation and fair presentation of these financial statements in accordance with accounting principles generally accepted in the United States of America; this includes the design, implementation, and maintenance of internal control relevant to the preparation and fair presentation of financial statements that are free from material misstatement, whether due to fraud or error.

Auditor's Responsibility

Our responsibility is to express an opinion on these financial statements based on our audits. We conducted our audits in accordance with auditing standards generally accepted in the United States of America. Those standards require that we plan and perform the audit to obtain reasonable assurance about whether the financial statements are free of material misstatement.

An audit involves performing procedures to obtain audit evidence about the amounts and disclosures in the financial statements. The procedures selected depend on the auditor's judgment, including the assessment of the risks of material misstatement of the financial statements, whether due to fraud or error. In making those risk assessments, the auditor considers internal control relevant to the entity's preparation and fair presentation of the financial statements in order to design audit procedures that are appropriate in the circumstances, but not for the purpose of expressing an opinion on the effectiveness of the entity's internal control. Accordingly, we express no such opinion. An audit also includes evaluating the appropriateness of accounting policies used and the reasonableness of significant accounting estimates made by management, as well as evaluating the overall presentation of the financial statements.

We believe that the audit evidence we have obtained is sufficient and appropriate to provide a basis for our audit opinion.

Opinion

In our opinion, the financial statements referred to above present fairly, in all material respects, the financial position of X Company as of December 31, 20X5 and 20X4, and the results of its operations and cash flows for the years then ended in accordance with accounting principles generally accepted in the United States of America.

Other Matter

In our report dated March 1, 20X5, we expressed an opinion that the 20X4 financial statements did not fairly present financial position, results of operations, and cash flows of X Company in accordance with accounting principles generally accepted in the United States of America because of two departures from such principles: (1) X Company carried its property, plant, and equipment at appraisal values, and provided for depreciation on the basis of such values and (2) X Company did not provide for deferred income taxes with respect to differences between income for financial reporting purposes and taxable income. As described in Note X, the Company has changed its method of accounting for these items and restated its 20X4 financial statements to conform with accounting principles generally accepted in the United States of America. Accordingly, our present opinion on the restated 20X4 financial statements, as presented herein, is different from that expressed in our previous report.

Report on Other Legal and Regulatory Requirements

[*Form and content of this section of the auditor's report will vary depending on the nature of the auditor's other reporting responsibilities.*]

[Auditor's signature]

[Auditor's city and state]

[Date of the auditor's report]

SECTION 708

CONSISTENCY OF FINANCIAL STATEMENTS

Authoritative Pronouncements

SAS-122—Statements on Auditing Standards: Clarification and Recodification

Overview

AU-C 708 provides guidance to the auditor in evaluating the consistency of financial statements and applying the effect of that evaluation on the auditor's report. The auditor should communicate in the report when the comparability of financial statements is materially affected by a change in accounting principle or by adjustments to correct a material misstatement in previously issued financial statements.

PUBLIC COMPANY IMPLICATION: The PCAOB's AS-6 (Evaluating Consistency of Financial Statements and Conforming Amendments) requires the auditor to evaluate whether financial statements between periods are comparable. Financial statements might not be comparable because of a change in accounting principle or an adjustment to correct a misstatement in previously issued financial statements. If there is a change in accounting principle, the auditor should evaluate whether (1) the new accounting principle is generally accepted, (2) the accounting for the change in accounting principle is in accordance with GAAP, (3) the disclosures surrounding the change are adequate, and (4) the change in accounting principle is preferable. Assuming these four criteria are met, the auditor should add an explanatory paragraph to the audit report describing the lack of consistency in the financial statements. If the four criteria are not met, the financial statements are not in accordance with GAAP and the auditor should issue either an adverse opinion or a qualified opinion.

If the financial statements are not comparable because of a change in accounting principle due to the adoption of a new FASB standard, the explanatory paragraph should state that the company has changed its method of accounting due to the adoption of the specific FASB standard and refer the reader to the particular note describing the change. If the financial statements are not comparable because of a voluntary change in accounting principle, the explanatory paragraph should refer to the elective nature of the change and refer the reader to the particular note describing the change.

In addition, if the financial statements are adjusted to correct a material misstatement in previously issued financial statements, the auditor's report should include an explanatory paragraph describing the lack of consistency due to the correction of the previously issued financial statements (i.e., the financial statements for earlier years included for comparative purposes in the current year's filing will differ from previously filed statements). Finally, a change in how items are classified in the financial statements does not need to be recognized in the auditor's report unless it represents a change in accounting principle or the correction of a material misstatement.

Definition

Current period   The most recent year upon which the auditor is reporting.

Requirements

The auditor is presumptively required to perform the following procedures when considering the consistency of financial statements:

Evaluating Consistency

1. Evaluate whether financial statement comparability between periods has been materially affected by a change in accounting principle or adjustments to correct a material misstatement in previously issued financial statements.

    a. If the auditor's opinion is only on the current period's financial statements, the auditor's evaluation should address the consistency between the current period and the preceding period (regardless of whether the financial statements for the preceding period are included).

    b. If the auditor's opinion covers two or more periods, the auditor's evaluation should address the consistency between the periods presented and covered by the auditor's report, as well as the consistency between the earliest period reported on and the prior period if financial statements for the prior period are included with the financial statements that the auditor is reporting on.

2. Evaluate whether the financial statements for the periods reported on are consistent with previously issued financial statements for the respective periods. This evaluation is particularly important when a change in accounting principle is retrospectively applied to earlier periods presented for comparative purposes.

Change in Accounting Principle

3. Evaluate a change in accounting principle to determine whether:

    a. The newly adopted accounting principle and the method of accounting for the effect of the change are in accordance with the applicable financial reporting framework

    b. Disclosures related to the change are appropriate and adequate

    c. The entity has justified that the alternative accounting principle is preferable

4. If the criteria in the preceding paragraph are met and the effect of the change on the financial statements is material, include an emphasis-of-matter paragraph in the auditor's report describing the change in accounting principle and referring to the entity's disclosure. If the criteria in the preceding paragraph are not met, evaluate whether the accounting change results in a material misstatement and if there is a need for the auditor's opinion to be modified.

5. Include an emphasis-of-matter paragraph relating to a change in accounting principle in the auditor's report in the period of change and all subsequent periods until the new accounting principle is applied in all periods presented. An emphasis-of-matter paragraph is only needed in the period of change if

the change is accounted for by retrospective application to the financial statements of all prior periods presented.

6. Evaluate and report on a change in accounting estimate inseparable from the effect of a related change in accounting principle in the same manner as a change in accounting principle.

7. If a change in reporting entity results in financial statements that are, in effect, those of a different reporting entity, include an emphasis-of-matter paragraph in the auditor's report describing the change in reporting entity and referring to the entity's disclosure, unless the change in reporting entity is due to a transaction or event. The requirements in paragraph 5 also apply to a change in the reporting entity.

8. If an entity's financial statements contain an investment accounted for by the equity method, evaluate the consistency of the investee's financial statements. If the investee has made a change in accounting principle that is material to the investing entity's financial statements, an emphasis-of-matter paragraph should be included in the auditor's report describing that change. The requirements in paragraph 5 apply in this case as well.

Correction of a Material Misstatement in Previously Issued Financial Statements

9. Include an emphasis-of-matter paragraph in the auditor's report when financial statements are restated to reflect adjustments to correct a material misstatement in previously issued financial statements. This paragraph does not need to be repeated in subsequent periods.

10. The emphasis-of-matter paragraph should (*a*) state that the previously issued financial statements have been restated for the correction of a material misstatement in the respective period and (*b*) refer to the entity's disclosure of the correction of the material misstatement.

11. If the financial statement disclosures relating to the restatement correcting a material misstatement in previously issued financial statements are not adequate, address this inadequacy as described in AU-C 705 (*Modifications to the Opinion in the Independent Auditor's Report*).

Change in Classification

12. Evaluate a material change in financial statement classification and the related disclosure to determine whether that change is also a change in accounting principle or an adjustment to correct a material misstatement in previously issued financial statements, in which case the applicable requirements described above should be followed.

OBSERVATION: Under current GAAS, changes and material reclassifications in previously issued financial statements to improve comparability with the current year's financial statements do not have to be referred to in the auditor's report. Under AU-C 708, the auditor needs to evaluate whether a material change in financial statement classification is a change in accounting principle or a correction of a material misstatement.

Analysis and Application of Procedures

Evaluating Consistency

The auditor's report implies that the auditor is satisfied as to the comparability of the financial statements presented unless the report explicitly states otherwise. Therefore, if no change in accounting principle has occurred or a change in accounting principle or its method of application has occurred but the effect is immaterial, consistency does not need to be referred to in the auditor's report.

Change in Accounting Principle

A change in accounting principle is a change in accounting principle or a change in the method of applying an accounting principle, in accordance with the applicable financial reporting framework, when (*a*) two or more accounting principles apply or (*b*) the accounting principle formerly used is no longer in accordance with the applicable financial reporting framework. The applicable financial reporting framework generally provides the method of accounting for the change in accounting principle and the related disclosures.

An entity's justification for a change in accounting principle is generally adequate if an accounting pronouncement is issued that requires the use of a new principle, interprets an existing principle, expresses a preference for an accounting principle, or rejects a specific principle, so long as the change is made in accordance with the applicable financial reporting framework.

An example of an emphasis-of-matter paragraph for a change in accounting principle due to the adoption of a new accounting pronouncement follows:

> As discussed in Note X to the financial statements, in [*insert year(s) of financial statements that reflect the accounting method change*], the entity adopted new accounting guidance [*description of new accounting guidance*]. Our opinion is not qualified with respect to this matter.

An example of an emphasis-of-matter paragraph for a voluntary change in accounting principle not due to the adoption of a new accounting pronouncement follows:

> As discussed in Note X to the financial statements, the entity has elected to change its method of accounting for [*describe accounting method change*] in [*insert year(s) of financial statements that reflect the accounting method change*]. Our opinion is not qualified with respect to this matter.

ENGAGEMENT STRATEGY: If a change in accounting principle does not have a material effect on the financial statements in the current year but is expected to have a material effect in later years, the auditor is not required to recognize this change in his or her report. However, the applicable financial reporting framework may include a requirement to disclose this situation in the notes to the financial statements.

A change in reporting entity that would not require recognition in the auditor's report is one resulting from a "transaction or event, such as the creation, cessation, or complete or partial purchase or disposition of a subsidiary or other business unit." The auditor should include an emphasis-of-matter paragraph for changes in the reporting entity that are not the result of a transaction or event, including:

- Consolidated or combined financial statements are presented in the current year, but individual financial statements were presented in the previous year.

- Consolidated financial statements for the current year do not include the same subsidiaries that were used to prepare the previous year's consolidated financial statements.

- Combined financial statements for the current year do not include the same companies that were used to prepare the previous year's combined financial statements.

Correction of a Material Misstatement in Previously Issued Financial Statements

The correction of a material misstatement includes a change in accounting principle from one that is not in accordance with the applicable financial reporting framework to one that is in accordance with that framework. If adjustments have been made to correct a material misstatement in previously issued financial statements, AU-C 560 (*Subsequent Events and Subsequently Discovered Facts*) provides guidance as to the auditor's responsibilities.

An example of an emphasis-of-matter paragraph when there has been a correction of a material misstatement in previously issued financial statements follows:

> As discussed in Note X to the financial statements, the 20X5 financial statements have been restated to correct a misstatement. Our opinion is not modified with respect to this matter.

Change in Classification

Changes in classification that would require recognition in the auditor's report include reclassifications in previously issued financial statements occurring because the items were classified incorrectly in the previously issued statements. In situations where reclassifications in previously issued financial statements are due to changes in the entity's business or operating structure, the auditor may need to obtain further understanding of the underlying business rationale for these changes to determine whether the changes require recognition in the auditor's report.

SECTION 720

OTHER INFORMATION IN DOCUMENTS CONTAINING AUDITED FINANCIAL STATEMENTS

Authoritative Pronouncements

SAS-118—Other Information in Documents Containing Audited Financial Statements

Overview

The auditor's report may be included in a document that contains other information. For example, a company's annual report may include a message from the chief executive officer and descriptions of operations and future plans, as well as a variety of charts and graphs accompanied by explanations.

AU-C 550 establishes the responsibilities of the independent auditor with respect to other information in (*a*) annual reports sent to holders of securities, (*b*) annual reports of government and charitable or philanthropic organizations available to the public, and (*c*) other documents reviewed by the auditor at the client's request.

PLANNING AID REMINDER: A designated accounting standard setter such as the Financial Accounting Standards Board (FASB) may have issued guidance or standards regarding the form and content of other information. AU-C 720 addresses this other information when it is voluntarily presented in a document containing the audited financial statements and auditor's report, but if the other information is required to be included by a designated accounting standard setter, the auditor should follow the guidance in AU-C 730.

Although not required to audit the other information, the auditor must read it to determine whether—compared with the information presented in the financial statements—there is (*a*) a material inconsistency or (*b*) a material misstatement of fact. By reading the other information, the auditor can respond appropriately if other information is presented that could undermine the credibility of the audited financial statements and the auditor's report.

Definitions

Other information	Financial and nonfinancial information (other than the financial statements, auditor's report, and required supplementary information) that is included in a document containing audited financial statements and the auditor's report.
Inconsistency	Other information that conflicts with information in the audited financial statements. A material inconsistency may raise doubt about the audit conclusions drawn and the basis for the auditor's opinion on the financial statements.
Misstatement of fact	Other information unrelated to matters appearing in the audited financial statements that is incorrectly stated or presented. A material misstatement of fact may undermine the credibility of the document containing audited financial statements.

Requirements

The auditor is presumptively required to perform the following procedures on other information in documents containing audited financial statements:

Reading Other Information

1. Read other information in documents containing audited financial statements and the auditor's report to identify any material inconsistencies with the audited financial statements.

2. Arrange with management or those charged with governance to obtain other information prior to the report release date, or, if that is not possible, read other information as soon as practicable.

3. Communicate with those charged with governance regarding the auditor's responsibility for other information as well as any procedures performed related to other information and their results.

Material Inconsistencies

4. If a material inconsistency is identified when reading the other information, determine whether revision of the audited financial statements or other information is needed.

5. If the auditor discovers information prior to the report release date requiring revision of the audited financial statements and management refuses to make the revision, modify the auditor's report in accordance with AU-C 705.

6. If revision of the other information is necessary and management refuses to make the revision, communicate the matter to those charged with governance and: include an explanatory paragraph in the auditor's report describing the material inconsistency in accordance with AU-C 700; withhold the auditor's report; or withdraw from the engagement where withdrawal is legally permitted.

7. If the auditor becomes aware of other information subsequent to the report release date, and there is a material inconsistency between this other information and the audited financial statements necessitating a revision of the audited financial statements, refer to the guidance in AU-C 560 (*Subsequent Events and Subsequently Discovered Facts*).

8. If revision of the other information obtained subsequent to the report release date is necessary and management agrees to make the revision, carry out the necessary procedures under the circumstances. If management refuses

to make the revision, the auditor should notify those charged with governance of his or her concerns and take further appropriate action.

Material Misstatements of Fact

9. If the auditor becomes aware of an apparent material misstatement of fact when reading the other information, discuss the matter with management.

10. If the auditor still considers there to be an apparent material misstatement of fact after such discussions, request management consult with a qualified third party such as legal counsel and the auditor should consider the advice the entity receives.

11. If the auditor concludes there is a material misstatement of fact in the other information that management refuses to correct, the auditor should notify those charged with governance of his or her concerns and take appropriate further action.

Analysis and Application of Procedures

Other Information

Items that may comprise other information include the following:

- A report on operations by management or those charged with governance
- Financial summaries or highlights
- Employment data
- Planned capital expenditures
- Financial ratios
- Names of officers and directors
- Selected quarterly data

"Other information" does not include information on a company's website, information contained in analyst briefings, or a press release or cover letter accompanying the document containing audited financial statements and the auditor's report.

Reading Other Information

The other information is not required to be referenced in the auditor's report on the financial statements. However, an explanatory paragraph disclaiming an opinion on the other information may be included to prevent users from inferring an unintended level of assurance on the other information. An example of such an explanatory paragraph follows:

> Our audit was conducted for the purpose of forming an opinion on the basic financial statements as a whole. The [identify the other information] is presented for purposes of additional analysis and is not a required part of the basic financial statements. Such information has not been subjected to the auditing procedures applied in the audit of the financial statements, and, accordingly, we do not express an opinion or provide any assurance on it.

The auditor may find an agreement with management helpful in obtaining the other information on a timely basis. The auditor may also consider delaying release of his or her report until the client provides the auditor with the other information.

Material Inconsistencies

When material inconsistencies are identified in other information obtained prior to the report release date and management refuses to make revisions, the auditor may use legal counsel's advice to decide on further appropriate action. In instances where withdrawal from the engagement is not legally permitted, the auditor may issue a report to those charged with governance and the appropriate statutory body detailing the identified inconsistency.

When material inconsistencies are identified in other information obtained subsequent to the report release date and management agrees to make revisions, the auditor's procedures may include reviewing steps taken by management to inform recipients of the issued financial statements, auditor's report, and other information of the revision. If management refuses to make revisions the auditor deems necessary, the auditor may take further action including obtaining advice from legal counsel.

Material Misstatements of Fact

It is more difficult to identify a material misstatement of fact in an annual report, because the nature of much of the other information will be nonaccounting and beyond the expertise of the auditor. The auditor may conclude valid differences of judgment or opinion exist if he or she is unable to evaluate the validity of some disclosures in the other information or of management's responses to inquiries.

FRAUD POINTER: AU-C 720 is vague in this area of material misstatement, because it relies on the auditor's limited expertise in relation to the other information. In other words, the auditor must proceed with caution. However, if the auditor discovers a material misstatement of fact and the client refuses to change the other information but the auditor still issues a report, it might be wise for the auditor to follow the reporting format prescribed when a material misstatement is encountered in the financial statements or accompanying notes.

If the auditor concludes there is a material misstatement of fact that management refuses to correct, the auditor may take further actions including obtaining advice from legal counsel, withholding his or her report if not already issued, or withdrawing from the engagement.

SECTION 725

SUPPLEMENTARY INFORMATION IN RELATION TO THE FINANCIAL STATEMENTS AS A WHOLE

Authoritative Pronouncements

SAS-118—Other Information in Documents Containing Audited Financial Statements

SAS-119—Supplementary Information in Relation to the Financial Statements as a Whole

Overview

AU-C 725 applies to engagements where the auditor expresses an opinion on whether supplementary information is fairly stated, in all material respects, in relation to the financial statements as a whole. The supplementary information that this AU-C 725 applies to is not required in order for the financial statements to be fairly presented in accordance with the applicable financial reporting framework.

This guidance may also be applied if the auditor is engaged to express an opinion on whether required supplementary information is fairly stated in all material respects in relation to the financial statements as a whole. However, AU-C 720 addresses the auditor's responsibilities for information other than the financial statements, auditor's report and required supplementary information, and AU-C 730 addresses the auditor's responsibilities for information required by a designated accounting standard setter to accompany an entity's basic financial statements. Furthermore, if the auditor is engaged to express an opinion on specified elements, accounts, or items of financial statements for the purpose of a separate presentation, the guidance in AU-C 805 applies. An engagement to examine supplementary information or an assertion related to the supplementary information may also be performed in accordance with AT 101.

Definitions

Supplementary information	Information other than the financial statements, auditor's report, and required supplementary information that is not considered necessary for the financial statements to be fairly presented in accordance with the applicable financial reporting framework. This information includes details, explanations, or historical summaries of financial statement items, consolidating information, statistical data, and other information which may come from sources outside the accounting system or the entity. This information may be presented with or separate from the audited financial statements. Supplementary information may be prepared in accordance with an applicable financial reporting framework, management's criteria, or by regulatory, contractual, or other requirements.

Requirements

The auditor is presumptively required to apply the following procedures for reporting on supplementary information in relation to the financial statements as a whole:

Procedures

1. Determine the following in order to express an opinion on whether supplementary information is fairly stated in all material respects in relation to the financial statements as a whole:

    a. Supplementary information relates to the same period as the financial statements and was derived from and directly relates to the underlying accounting and other records used to prepare those statements

    b. The financial statements were audited, an adverse opinion or disclaimer or opinion was not issued, and the auditor served as the principal auditor in the engagement

    c. The supplementary information will accompany the audited financial statements or the entity will make those statements readily available

2. Obtain management's agreement that it acknowledges and understands its responsibility:

    a. To prepare the supplementary information in accordance with the applicable criteria

    b. To provide the auditor with the written representations described in requirement 3f

    c. To include the auditor's report on the supplementary information in any document containing the supplementary information and indicate the auditor has reported on that information

    d. To present the supplementary information with the audited financial statements or make the audited financial statements readily available to the supplementary information's intended users no later than the date the supplementary information and auditor's report on that information are issued

3. Perform the following procedures in addition to procedures performed during the financial statement audit, using the same materiality level used in the financial statement audit, in order to express an opinion on whether supplementary information is fairly stated in all material respects in relation to the financial statements as a whole:

    a. Inquire of management about the purpose of supplementary information and the criteria used to prepare that information

    b. Obtain an understanding about the methods of preparing the information including whether those methods have changed from prior periods and the reasons why as well as whether the form and content of the information complies with established criteria

    c. Compare and reconcile the information to the financial statements or to the underlying accounting and other records used in preparing the financial statements

    d. Inquire of management about any significant assumptions or interpretations underlying the information's measurement or presentation

    e. Evaluate the appropriateness and completeness of the information, considering procedures performed and other knowledge obtained during the financial statement audit

f. Obtain written representations from management: acknowledging responsibility for the supplementary information; stating that the information's form and content is in accordance with prescribed guidelines; stating that measurement and presentation methods have not changed from the prior period or the reasons for any such changes; about any significant assumptions or interpretations underlying information measurement or presentation; and that when supplementary information is not presented with the audited financial statements those statements will be made readily available to the supplementary information's intended users no later than the date the supplementary information and auditor's report are issued.

4. The auditor has no responsibility for considering subsequent events with respect to the supplementary information. However, if information comes to the auditor's attention before or after the auditor's report on the financial statements is released regarding events that affect the financial statements, he or she should follow the guidance in AU-C 560.

Reporting

5. If the auditor expresses an opinion on the supplementary information in relation to the financial statements as a whole that is presented with the financial statements, include an other-matter paragraph in the auditor's report on the financial statements with the following statements:

a. The audit was conducted for the purpose of forming an opinion on the financial statements as a whole

b. Supplementary information is presented for additional analysis purposes and is not a required part of the financial statements

c. Supplementary information is management's responsibility and was derived from and directly relates to the underlying accounting and other records used to prepare the financial statements

d. Supplementary information has been subjected to the auditing procedures applied in the financial statement audit and certain additional procedures, including comparing and reconciling such information directly to the underlying accounting and other records used to prepare the financial statements and other additional procedures as prescribed by auditing standards generally accepted in the United States of America

e. If the financial statement opinion is unqualified and the supplementary information is fairly stated, include a statement that, in the auditor's opinion, the other supplementary information is fairly stated in all material respects, in relation to the financial statements as a whole.

f. If the financial statement opinion is qualified and the qualification has an effect on the supplementary information, include a statement that, in the auditor's opinion, except for the effects on the supplementary information of (refer to the paragraph in the auditor's report explaining the qualification), such information is fairly stated in all material respects in relation to the financial statements as whole.

6. If the auditor expresses an opinion on supplementary information and the audited financial statements are not presented with the supplementary information, the report on the supplementary information should include all of the above elements and: a reference to the financial statement report, the date of that report, the opinion expressed on the financial statements, and any report modifications.

7. If an adverse opinion or disclaimer of opinion is issued on the financial statements, the auditor may not express an opinion on the supplementary information and may withdraw from the engagement to report on such information where permitted by law or regulation. If the auditor does not withdraw from the engagement, the report on the supplementary information should state that because of the significance of the matter disclosed in the auditor's report, it is inappropriate to and the auditor does not express an opinion on the supplementary information.

8. The date of the auditor's opinion on the supplementary information should not be earlier that the date on which the auditor completed the required procedures.

9. If the auditor concludes the supplementary information is materially misstated in relation to the financial statements as a whole, he or she should discuss the matter with management and propose appropriate revision of such information. If management does not revise the supplementary information, the auditor should modify the auditor's opinion on such information and describe the misstatement in the auditor's report, or, if a separate report is being issued on the supplementary information, withhold the auditor's report on the supplementary information.

Analysis and Application of Procedures

Reporting on Supplementary Information

While the auditor is not obligated to report on supplementary information presented outside the basic financial statements, he or she may choose to apply auditing procedures to such information in order to express an opinion on that information. Management information not directly related to the basic financial statements is not ordinarily subjected to auditing procedures. However, when that information has been obtained or derived from accounting records the auditor has tested, the auditor may be in a position to express an opinion on such information in relation to the financial statements as a whole.

Procedures

To express an opinion on other supplementary information in relation to the financial statements as a whole, the auditor is not required to obtain a separate understanding of internal control or assess fraud risk. The auditor may consider testing accounting or other records through observation or examination of source documents or other procedures ordinarily performed in a financial statement audit to evaluate the appropriateness and completeness of the supplementary information.

PLANNING AID REMINDER: The materiality level used for the supplementary information is the overall audit materiality used in the financial statement audit, or, for the entire governmental entity in a government audit. Therefore, the procedures required to express an opinion on the supplementary information in relation to the financial statements as a whole do not need to be as extensive as if the auditor was expressing an opinion on the supplementary information by itself.

Other guidance the auditor may follow in determining whether supplementary information is fairly stated in relation to the financial statements as a whole includes:

- Obtaining an updating representation letter in accordance with AU-C 580
- Performing subsequent events procedures in accordance with AU-C 560
- Sending the client's lawyer a letter of inquiry regarding supplementary information in accordance with AU-C 501

Audited financial statements are considered readily available if a third party user can obtain the statements without any further action by the entity. For example, financial statements available on an entity's website are readily available, but if the statements are only available upon request they are not readily available.

ENGAGEMENT STRATEGY: The auditor may consider restricting the use of a separate report on supplementary information to avoid potential misinterpretation or misunderstanding of supplementary information that is not presented with the financial statements (see AU-C 905 for further guidance).

Practitioner's Aids

Exhibit AU-C 725-1 provides an example of an explanatory paragraph that may be used in the auditor's report on the financial statements when the auditor is engaged to report on supplementary information in relation to the financial statements as a whole, an unqualified opinion is being issued on the financial statements, and the auditor has concluded that the supplementary information is fairly stated, in all material respects, in relation to the financial statements as a whole.

EXHIBIT AU-C 725-1—EXPLANATORY PARAGRAPH USED WHEN REPORTING ON SUPPLEMENTARY INFORMATION

Our audit was conducted for the purpose of forming an opinion on the financial statements as a whole. The [*identify accompanying supplementary information*] is presented for purposes of additional analysis and is not a required part of the financial statements. Such information is the responsibility of management and was derived from and relates directly to the underlying accounting and other records used to prepare the financial statements. The information has been subjected to the auditing procedures applied in the audit of the financial statements and certain additional procedures, including comparing and reconciling such information directly to the underlying accounting and other records used to prepare the financial statements or to the financial statements themselves, and other additional procedures in accordance with auditing standards generally accepted in the United States of America. In our opinion, the information is fairly stated in all material respects in relation to the financial statements as a whole.

Exhibit AU-C 725-2 provides a reporting example the auditor may use when reporting separately on supplementary information in relation to the financial statements as a whole, an unqualified opinion has been issued on the financial statements, and an unqualified opinion is being issued on the supplementary information.

EXHIBIT AU-C 725-2—REPORTING ON SUPPLEMENTARY INFORMATION SEPARATELY FROM THE FINANCIAL STATEMENTS AS A WHOLE

We have audited the financial statements of ABC Entity as of and for the year ended December 31, 20X5, and have issued our report thereon dated [*date of the auditor's report on the financial statements*] which contained an unqualified opinion on those financial statements. Our audit was performed for the purpose of forming an opinion on the financial statements as a whole. The [*identify accompanying supplementary information*] is presented for purposes of additional analysis and is not a required part of the financial statements. Such information is the responsibility of management and was derived from and relates directly to the underlying accounting and other records used to prepare the financial statements. The information has been subjected to the auditing procedures applied in the audit of the financial statements and certain additional procedures, including comparing and reconciling such information directly to the underlying accounting and other records used to prepare the financial statements or to the financial statements themselves, and other additional procedures in accordance with auditing standards generally accepted in the United States of America. In our opinion, the information is fairly stated in all material respects in relation to the financial statements as a whole.

SECTION 730

REQUIRED SUPPLEMENTARY INFORMATION

Authoritative Pronouncements

SAS-120—Required Supplementary Information

Overview

Although required supplementary information is not part of the basic financial statements, certain designated entities must disclose such information. The required supplementary information is considered to be an essential part of the financial report for these designated entities. Although this information does not have to be audited, certain prescribed procedures established by AU-C 730 must be applied. The auditor's objective in performing these procedures is to communicate through his or her report whether any of the required supplementary information has not been presented and whether any material modifications have been identified that should be made to the required supplementary information for it to conform with guidelines established by a designated accounting standard setter. AU-C 720 specifies the auditor's responsibilities for other information that is not required supplementary information.

Definitions

Required supplementary information	Information a designated accounting standard setter required to accompany an entity's basic financial statements. This differs from other types of information outside the basic financial statements because a designated accounting standards setter considers the information an essential part of the financial reporting of certain entities and because authoritative guidelines for the measurement and presentation of the information have been established.
Designated accounting standard setter	A body designated by the AICPA council to establish GAAP pursuant to Rule 202 (*Compliance with Standards*) and Rule 203 (*Accounting Principles*). Designated bodies are the Federal Accounting Standards Advisory Board (FASAB), Financial Accounting Standards Board (FASB), Governmental Accounting Standards Board (GASB), and the International Accounting Standards Board (IASB).
Basic financial statements	Financial statements presented in accordance with an applicable financial reporting framework as established by a designated accounting standard setter, excluding required supplementary information.

Applicable financial reporting framework	The financial reporting framework used by management and those charged with governance in preparing the financial statements that is acceptable given the nature of the entity and the objective of the financial statements, or that is required by law or regulation.
Prescribed guidelines	The authoritative guidelines established by the designated accounting standard setter for the methods of measurement and presentation of the required supplementary information.

Requirements

The auditor is presumptively required to perform the following procedures in fulfilling responsibilities related to required supplementary information:

Procedures

1. Apply the following procedures to required supplementary information:

    a. Inquire of management about methods of preparing the information, including whether it has been prepared according to prescribed guidelines, whether any significant assumptions or interpretations underlie its measurement or presentation, and whether measurement or presentation methods have changed since the prior period and reasons for the changes.

    b. Compare the information for consistency with management's responses to the foregoing inquiries, the audited financial statements, and other knowledge obtained during the financial statement audit.

    c. Obtain written representations from management regarding the topics of management inquiry in item 1a and acknowledging responsibility for the required supplementary information.

2. If unable to complete these procedures, consider whether management contributed to the inability to complete the procedures, and, if so, inform those charged with governance.

Reporting

3. Include an other-matter paragraph after the opinion paragraph in the auditor's report referring to the required supplementary information. If some or all of the required supplementary information is presented, the explanatory paragraph should include the following elements:

    a. A statement that [identify the applicable financial reporting framework] require that the [identify the required supplementary information] be presented to supplement the basic financial statements.

    b. A statement that such information, although not a part of the basic financial statements, is required by [identify designated accounting standard setter], who considers it to be an essential part of financial reporting for placing the basic financial statements in an appropriate operational, economic, or historical context.

    c. If the auditor is able to complete the prescribed procedures related to the required supplementary information: (1) a statement that the auditor has applied limited procedures, which consisted of inquiries of management and other limited procedures, as prescribed by auditing standards generally accepted in the United States of America regarding the methods of measurement and presentation of the required supplementary information; and (2) a statement that the limited procedures do not provide the auditor with evidence sufficient to

express an opinion or any other form of assurance on the
information.

d. If the auditor is unable to complete the prescribed procedures related
to the required supplementary information: (1) a statement that the
auditor was unable to apply to the information certain limited procedures prescribed by auditing standards generally accepted in the
United States of America because [state the reasons]; and (2) a
statement that the auditor does not express an opinion or any other
form of assurance on the information.

e. If some of the required supplementary information is omitted: (1) a
statement that management has omitted [description of the missing
required supplementary information] that [identify the applicable
financial reporting framework] require to be presented to supplement
the basic financial statements; (2) a statement that such missing
information, although not a part of the basic financial statements, is
required by [identify designated accounting standard setter] who
considers it to be an essential part of financial reporting for placing
the basic financial statements in an appropriate operational, economic, or historical context; and (3) a statement that the auditor's
opinion on the basic financial statements is not affected by the
missing information.

f. If the measurement or presentation of the required supplementary
information departs materially from prescribed guidelines, a statement that the auditor's opinion on the basic financial statements is
not affected but that material departures from prescribed guidelines
exist [describe the material departures from the applicable financial
reporting framework].

g. If the auditor has unresolved doubts about whether the required
supplementary information conforms to prescribed guidelines, a
statement that although the auditor's opinion on the basic financial
statements is not affected, the results of the limited procedures have
raised doubts regarding whether material modifications should be
made to the information for it to conform with guidelines established
by [identify designated accounting standard setter].

4. If all of the required supplementary information is omitted, the explanatory
paragraph should just include the statements described in requirement 3e.

Analysis and Application of Procedures

Reporting

Required supplementary information is not part of the basic financial statements,
so the auditor's opinion on the financial statements is not affected by the entity's
presentation or lack of presentation of the required supplementary information.
If the entity omits presentation of required supplementary information, the
auditor does not have a responsibility to present that information.

Practitioner's Aid

Exhibit AU-C 730-1 provides an example of an explanatory paragraph that can be
used in the auditor's report when the required supplementary information is
included, the auditor has applied the specified procedures, and no material
departures from the prescribed guidelines have been identified.

EXHIBIT AU-C 730-1—EXPLANATORY PARAGRAPH WHEN REPORTING ON SUPPLEMENTARY INFORMATION

[*Identify the applicable financial reporting framework (for example,* accounting principles generally accepted in the United States of America)] require that the [*identify the required supplementary information*] on page XX be presented to supplement the basic financial statements. Such information, although not a part of the basic financial statements, is required by [*identify designated accounting standard setter*], who considers it to be an essential part of financial reporting for placing the basic financial statements in an appropriate operational, economic, or historical context. We have applied certain limited procedures to the required supplementary information in accordance with auditing standards generally accepted in the United States of America, which consisted of inquiries of management about the methods of preparing the information and comparing the information for consistency with management's responses to our inquiries, the basic financial statements, and other knowledge we obtained during our audit of the basic financial statements. We do not express an opinion or provide any assurance on the information, because the limited procedures do not provide us with sufficient evidence to express an opinion or provide any assurance.

AU-C 800
Special Considerations

SECTION 800

SPECIAL CONSIDERATIONS—AUDITS OF FINANCIAL STATEMENTS PREPARED IN ACCORDANCE WITH SPECIAL PURPOSE FRAMEWORKS

Authoritative Pronouncements

SAS-122—Statements on Auditing Standards: Clarification and Recodification

Overview

An auditor may be engaged to audit financial statements that are not prepared in accordance with GAAP, but rather are prepared in accordance with a special purpose framework. Special purpose frameworks as contemplated by AU-C 800 are those involving a cash, tax, regulatory, or contractual basis of accounting. The auditor's objectives in these situations are to appropriately address the special considerations relevant to engagement acceptance, engagement planning and performance, and forming an opinion and reporting on the financial statements.

OBSERVATION: The cash, tax, and regulatory bases of accounting are often referred to as an other comprehensive basis of accounting (OCBOA). The term "OCBOA" has been replaced by the term "special purpose framework" as part of the clarification and recodification project.

Definitions

Special purpose financial statements	Financial statements prepared in accordance with a special purpose framework.
Special purpose framework	A financial reporting framework other than GAAP, which is one of the following bases of accounting:
• Cash basis	The cash receipts and disbursements basis of accounting, and modifications of the cash basis having substantial support, such as recording depreciation on fixed assets.
• Tax basis	The basis of accounting the entity uses to file its income tax return for the period covered by the financial statements.
• Regulatory basis	A basis of accounting the entity uses to comply with the requirements or financial reporting provisions of a regulatory agency with jurisdiction over the entity.
• Contractual basis	A basis of accounting the entity uses to comply with an agreement between the entity and one or more third parties other than the auditor.

Requirements

The auditor is presumptively required to perform the following procedures when performing an audit of financial statements prepared in accordance with a special purpose framework:

Engagement Acceptance

1. Determine the acceptability of the financial reporting framework applied in preparing the financial statements. Obtain an understanding of the purpose for which the financial statements are prepared, the intended users, and the steps management has taken to determine that the applicable financial reporting framework is acceptable in the circumstances.

2. Establish whether the preconditions for an audit are present. Obtain management's agreement that it acknowledges and understands its responsibility to include all informative disclosures that are appropriate for the special purpose framework used to prepare the entity's financial statements including:

   a. A description of the special purpose framework, a summary of significant accounting policies, and how the framework differs from GAAP (the effects of differences do not need to be quantified)

   b. Informative disclosures similar to those required by GAAP if the financial statements contain items similar or the same as those in financial statements prepared in accordance with GAAP

   c. If prepared in accordance with a contractual basis of accounting, a description of any significant interpretations of the contract on which the financial statements are based

   d. Additional disclosures beyond those specifically required by the framework that may be necessary for the financial statements to achieve fair presentation

Engagement Planning and Performance

3. Comply with all AU-C sections relevant to the audit, adapting all relevant AU-C sections as necessary in the engagement circumstances.

4. Obtain an understanding of the entity's selection and application of accounting policies. If the financial statements are prepared in accordance with a contractual basis of accounting, understand any significant interpretations of the contract management made in preparing the special purpose financial statements. Interpretations are significant if adoption of another reasonable interpretation would have produced a material difference in the information presented in the financial statements.

Audit Opinion and Reporting

5. Apply the requirements in AU-C 700 (*Forming an Opinion and Reporting on Financial Statements*) when forming an opinion and reporting on special purpose financial statements. If the auditor concludes a modification to the opinion is necessary, apply the requirements in AU-C 705 (*Modifications to the Opinion in the Independent Auditor's Report*).

6. Evaluate whether the financial statements adequately refer to or describe the applicable financial reporting framework. This involves an evaluation of whether the financial statements (1) are suitably titled, (2) include a summary of significant accounting policies, (3) adequately describe how the special purpose framework differs from GAAP although quantification of effects of

the differences is not required, and (4) if the financial statements have been prepared in accordance with a contractual basis of accounting, whether any significant interpretations of the contract on which the financial statements are based are adequately described.

7. Evaluate whether the financial statements achieve fair presentation. In audits of special purpose financial statements containing the same or similar items to those in financial statements prepared in accordance with GAAP, evaluate whether the financial statements include informative disclosures similar to those required by GAAP. Evaluate whether additional disclosures beyond those specifically required by the framework, related to matters not specifically identified in the financial statements, are necessary to fairly present the financial statements.

8. The auditor's report on special purpose financial statements should follow the guidance in AU-C 700, but also should include:

    a. If management has a choice of financial reporting frameworks in preparing the financial statements, the explanation of management's responsibility for the financial statements should also reference its responsibility for determining that the applicable financial reporting framework is acceptable in the circumstances.

    b. If the financial statements are prepared in accordance with a regulatory or contractual basis of accounting, the report should describe the purpose for which the financial statements are prepared or refer to a note in the financial statements containing that information.

9. Unless the auditor is reporting on financial statements prepared in accordance with a regulatory basis that are intended for general use, the auditor's report should contain an emphasis-of-matter paragraph under an appropriate heading that (1) alerts users of the auditor's report that the financial statements are prepared in accordance with the [special purpose framework], (2) refers to the note to the financial statements that describes that framework, and (3) states that the special purpose framework is a basis of accounting other than GAAP.

10. Unless the auditor is reporting on financial statements prepared in accordance with a regulatory basis that are intended for general use, if the financial statements are prepared in accordance with a contractual or regulatory basis of accounting, the auditor's report should include an other-matter paragraph under an appropriate heading restricting use of the report to those within the entity, parties to the contract or agreements, or regulatory agencies with jurisdiction over the entity.

11. If the special purpose financial statements are prepared in accordance with a regulatory basis of accounting and those statements and the auditor's report are intended for general use, express an opinion on whether the financial statements are prepared in accordance with GAAP. In a separate paragraph, express an opinion on whether the financial statements are prepared in accordance with the special purpose framework.

12. If required by law or regulation to use a specific layout, form, or wording of the auditor's report, the report should refer to GAAS only if it includes, at a minimum, each of the following elements:

    a. A title

    b. An addressee

    c. An introductory paragraph identifying the financial statements audited

    d. A description of management's responsibility for preparing the financial statements

e. When management has a choice of financial reporting frameworks, a reference to management's responsibility for determining that the applicable financial reporting framework is acceptable

f. When the financial statements are prepared in accordance with a regulatory or contractual basis of accounting, a description of the purpose for which the financial statements are prepared

g. A description of the auditor's responsibility to express an opinion on the special purpose financial statements and the scope of the audit including a reference to GAAS and the law or regulation and a description of the audit in accordance with those standards

h. An opinion paragraph containing an expression of opinion on the special purpose financial statements and a reference to the special purpose financial statements used to prepare the financial statements including identifying the origin of the framework and, when the financial statements are prepared in accordance with a regulatory basis of accounting intended for general use, an opinion on whether the special purpose financial statements are prepared in accordance with GAAP

i. Except when the financial statements are prepared in accordance with a regulatory basis of accounting intended for general use, an emphasis-of-matter paragraph indicating the financial statements are prepared in accordance with a special purpose framework

j. Except when the financial statements are prepared in accordance with a regulatory basis of accounting intended for general use, an other-matter paragraph restricting the use of the auditor's report

k. The auditor's signature

l. The auditor's city and state

m. The date of the auditor's report

13. If the specific layout, form, or wording of the auditor's report is not acceptable or would cause an auditor to make a statement that the auditor has no basis to make, reword the prescribed form of the report or attach an appropriately worded separate report.

OBSERVATION: A contractual or regulatory basis of accounting that is based on U.S. GAAP, but that does not require compliance with all of GAAP, cannot be described as conforming to GAAP but rather must be described as a contractual or regulatory basis of accounting.

Analysis and Application of Procedures

Engagement Acceptance

Financial reporting frameworks applied in preparing the financial statements are presumed to be acceptable if the framework is prescribed by law or regulation or it encompasses standards established by an organization authorized to promulgate standards for special purpose financial statements. In other situations, the auditor will need to use professional judgment to evaluate the acceptability of the financial reporting framework.

In evaluating whether the financial statements achieve fair presentation according to the applicable financial reporting framework, consider the overall presentation, structure, and content of the financial statements and whether the financial statements and related notes represent the underlying transactions and events in a manner that achieves fair presentation.

OBSERVATION: The auditor may want to discuss with management and with those charged with governance how an audit of special purpose financial statements differs from an audit of general purpose financial statements.

Engagement Planning and Performance

An AU-C section is relevant to the audit and to be complied with when the AU-C section is in effect and the circumstances addressed by the AU-C exist. However, requirements of various AU-C sections may need to be adapted to suit the circumstances of a particular engagement. For example, judgments about materiality are generally considered based on the common financial information needs of users as a group, while for special purpose financial statements considering the financial information needs of the intended users may be sufficient.

OBSERVATION: The requirements of AU-C 260, *The Auditor's Communication with Those Charged with Governance*, apply when those charged with governance are responsible for overseeing the preparation of the financial statements. However, in the case of special purpose financial statements, those charged with governance may not have this responsibility so the requirements of AU-C 260 may not be relevant to the audit unless the auditor is also auditing the general purpose financial statements or has otherwise agreed to such communications.

Audit Opinion and Reporting

When financial statements based on a special purpose framework are prepared, the auditor should determine whether the financial statements are properly labeled. Care must be taken in titling financial statements so that a reader of the statements will not infer that the financial statements are prepared in accordance with GAAP. When GAAP-based financial statements are presented, the financial statements are referred to as balance sheet (or statement of financial position), statement of income (or statement of operations), and statement of cash flows. When special purpose financial statements are presented, it would be inappropriate to refer to a financial statement as a balance sheet or a statement of financial position. Instead, for example, if the financial statements are prepared on a modified cash basis, the title might be "Statement of Assets and Liabilities— Modified Cash Basis." If the financial statements are prepared on a regulatory accounting basis an appropriate name would be "Balance Sheet—Regulatory Accounting Basis."

PLANNING AID REMINDER: In describing how the special purpose framework differs from GAAP, only material differences are ordinarily addressed.

PUBLIC COMPANY IMPLICATION: For public companies, an audit report on special purpose financial statements must state that the audit was conducted in accordance with standards of the Public Company Accounting Oversight Board.

In order for special purpose financial statements to achieve fair presentation, all informative disclosures that are appropriate for the applicable financial reporting framework should be included. Disclosures in special purpose financial statements may differ from GAAP disclosures by providing information that communicates the substance of the requirements or by substituting qualitative information for some of the quantitative information required by GAAP. For example, disclosing repayment terms of significant long-term borrowings without providing the summary of principal reduction during each of the next five years may be sufficient to communicate information about future principal reduction.

PLANNING AID REMINDER: There is no comprehensive list of minimum disclosures for special purpose financial statements. Professional judgment must be used to determine whether the basic concept of adequate disclosure has been achieved in the special purpose financial statements.

Special purpose financial statements prepared in accordance with a regulatory framework are intended for general use when the financial statements and auditor's report are intended to be used by parties other than those within the entity and regulatory agencies with jurisdiction over the entity or when the financial statements and auditor's report are distributed by the entity to parties other than the regulatory agencies with jurisdiction over the entity. In this instance, an emphasis-of-matter paragraph indicating that the financial statements are prepared in accordance with a special purpose framework and an other-matter paragraph restricting the use of the auditor's report are not required. However, the auditor is required to opine on whether the special purpose financial statements are prepared in accordance with GAAP as well as in accordance with the special purpose framework.

If the auditor wishes to preclude general use of the report, he or she may, in agreeing with the terms of the engagement, reach an understanding with and obtain agreement from management that the use of the auditor's report will be restricted to those identified in the report. When issuing a restricted use report, if the auditor decides after the audit report has been released to add parties other than the parties originally specified in the report, the auditor should follow the guidance in AU-C 905.

PLANNING AID REMINDER: In some circumstances, the auditor may consider it appropriate to restrict the use of the auditor's report for a report on financial statements prepared in accordance with a cash or tax basis of accounting.

Practitioner's Aids

Examples of reporting on special purpose frameworks are included to illustrate of the requirements of AU-C 800.

Exhibit AU-C 800-1 includes the various special purpose frameworks and reporting requirements that apply to each.

EXHIBIT AU-C 800-1—SPECIAL PURPOSE FRAMEWORKS AND REPORTING REQUIREMENTS

	Cash Basis	Tax Basis	Regulatory Basis (Restricted Use)	Regulatory Basis (General Use)	Contractual Basis
Opinion(s)	Single opinion on special purpose framework	Single opinion on special purpose framework	Single opinion on special purpose framework	Dual opinion on special purpose framework and GAAP	Single opinion on special purpose framework
Description of purpose for which special purpose financial statements are prepared	No	No	Yes	Yes	Yes
Emphasis-of-matter paragraph required (emphasizing use of the special purpose framework)	Yes	Yes	Yes	No	Yes
Other-matter paragraph required (restricting the use of the report)	No	No	Yes	No	Yes

Exhibit AU-C 800-2 contains an example of an independent auditor's report on cash-based financial statements.

EXHIBIT AU-C 800-2—INDEPENDENT AUDITOR'S REPORT ON CASH-BASED FINANCIAL STATEMENTS

INDEPENDENT AUDITOR'S REPORT

[Appropriate Addressee]

Report on the Financial Statements

We have audited the accompanying financial statements of XYZ Partnership, which comprise the statement of assets and liabilities arising from cash transactions as of December 31, 20X5 and the related statement of revenues collected and expenses paid for the year then ended, and the related notes to the financial statements.

Management's Responsibility for the Financial Statements

Management is responsible for the preparation and fair presentation of these financial statements in accordance with the cash basis of accounting described in Note X; this includes determining that the cash basis of accounting is an acceptable basis for the preparation of the financial statements in the circumstances. Management is also responsible for the design, implementation, and maintenance of internal control relevant to the preparation and fair presentation of financial statements that are free from material misstatement, whether due to fraud or error.

Auditor's Responsibility

Our responsibility is to express an opinion on these financial statements based on our audit. We conducted our audit in accordance with auditing standards generally accepted in the United States of America. Those standards require that we plan and perform the audit to obtain reasonable assurance about whether the financial statements are free of material misstatement.

An audit includes involves performing procedures to obtain audit evidence about the amounts and disclosures in the financial statements. The procedures selected depend on the auditor's judgment, including the assessment of the risks of material misstatement of the financial statements, whether due to fraud or error. In making those risks assessments, the auditor considers internal control relevant to the partnership's preparation and fair presentation of the financial statements in order to design audit procedures that are appropriate in the circumstances, but not for the purpose of expressing an opinion on the effectiveness of the partnership's internal control. Accordingly, we express no such opinion. An audit also includes evaluating the appropriateness of accounting principles used and the reasonableness of significant accounting estimates made by management, as well as evaluating the overall presentation of the financial statements.

We believe that the audit evidence we have obtained is sufficient and appropriate to provide a reasonable basis for our audit opinion.

Opinion

In our opinion, the financial statements referred to above present fairly, in all material respects, the assets and liabilities arising from cash transactions of XYZ Partnership as of December 31, 20X5, and its revenue collected and expenses paid during the year then ended in accordance with the cash basis of accounting described in Note X.

Basis of Accounting

We draw attention to Note X of the financial statements, which describes the basis of accounting. The financial statements are prepared on the cash basis of accounting, which is a basis of accounting other than accounting principles generally accepted in the United States of America. Our opinion is not modified with respect to this matter.

Report on Other Legal and Regulatory Requirements

[*Form and content of this section of the auditor's report will vary depending on the nature of the auditor's other reporting responsibilities.*]

[Auditor's signature]

[Auditor's city and state]

[Date of the auditor's report]

Exhibit AU-C 800-3 provides an example of an independent auditor's report on financial statements prepared in accordance with a regulatory basis of accounting and intended for general use.

EXHIBIT AU-C 800-3—INDEPENDENT AUDITOR'S REPORT ON FINANCIAL STATEMENTS PREPARED IN ACCORDANCE WITH A REGULATORY BASIS OF ACCOUNTING AND INTENDED FOR GENERAL USE

INDEPENDENT AUDITOR'S REPORT

[Appropriate Addressee]

Report on the Financial Statements

We have audited the accompanying financial statements of XYZ City, Any State, which comprise cash and unencumbered cash for each fund as of June 30, 20X8 and the related statements of cash receipts and cash disbursements and disbursements-budget and actual for the year then ended, and the related notes to the financial statements.

Management's Responsibility for the Financial Statements

Management is responsible for the preparation and fair presentation of these financial statements in accordance with the financial reporting provisions of Section Y of Regulation Z of Any State. Management is also responsible for the design, implementation, and maintenance of internal control relevant to the preparation and fair presentation of financial statements that are free from material misstatement, whether due to fraud or error.

Auditor's Responsibility

Our responsibility is to express an opinion on these financial statements based on our audit. We conducted our audit in accordance with auditing standards generally accepted in the United States of America. Those standards require that we plan and perform the audit to obtain reasonable assurance about whether the financial statements are free of material misstatement.

An audit involves performing procedures to obtain audit evidence about the amounts and disclosures in the financial statements. The procedures selected depend on the auditor's judgment, including the assessment of the risks of material misstatement of the financial statements, whether due to fraud or error. In making those risk assessments, the auditor considers internal control relevant to the entity's preparation and fair presentation of the financial statements in order to design audit procedures that are appropriate in the circumstances, but not for the purpose of expressing an opinion on the effectiveness of the company's internal control. Accordingly, we express no such opinion. An audit also includes evaluating the appropriateness of accounting principles used and the reasonableness of significant accounting estimates made by management, as well as evaluating the overall presentation of the financial statements.

We believe that the audit evidence we have obtained is sufficient and appropriate to provide a reasonable basis for our audit opinions.

Basis for Adverse Opinion on U.S. Generally Accepted Accounting Principles

As described in Note X of the financial statements, the financial statements are prepared by XYZ City on the basis of the financial reporting provisions of Section Y of Regulation Z of Any State, which is a basis of accounting other than accounting principles generally accepted in the United States of America, to meet the requirements of Any State.

The effects on the financial statements of the variances between the regulatory basis of accounting described in Note X and accounting principles generally accepted in the United States of America, although not reasonably determinable, are presumed to be material.

Adverse Opinion on U.S. Generally Accepted Accounting Principles

In our opinion, because of the significance of the matter discussed in the "Basis for Adverse Opinion on U.S. Generally Accepted Accounting Principles" paragraph, the financial statements referred to above do not present fairly, in accordance with accounting principles generally accepted in the United States of America, the financial position of each fund of XYZ City as of June 30, 20X8, or changes in financial position or cash flows thereof for the year then ended.

Opinion on Regulatory Basis of Accounting

In our opinion, the financial statements referred to above present fairly, in all material respects, the cash and unencumbered cash of each fund of XYZ City as of June 30, 20X8, and their respective cash receipts and disbursements, and budgetary results for the year then ended in accordance with the financial reporting provisions of Section Y of Regulation Z of Any State described in Note X.

Report on Other Legal and Regulatory Requirements

[*Form and content of this section of the auditor's report will vary depending on the nature of the auditor's other reporting responsibilities.*]

[Auditor's signature]

[Auditor's city and state]

[Date of the auditor's report]

SECTION 805

SPECIAL CONSIDERATIONS—AUDITS OF SINGLE FINANCIAL STATEMENTS AND SPECIFIC ELEMENTS, ACCOUNTS OR ITEMS OF A FINANCIAL STATEMENT

Authoritative Pronouncements

SAS-122—Statements on Auditing Standards: Clarification and Recodification

Overview

An auditor may be engaged to audit a single financial statement or a specific element, account, or item of a financial statement. The financial statement or financial statement element audited may be prepared in accordance with either a general or special purpose framework. The auditor's objective in performing this type of audit is to appropriately address the special considerations relevant to engagement acceptance, engagement planning and performance, and forming an opinion and reporting on the financial statement or financial statement element audited.

OBSERVATION: AU-C 805 does not apply to a component auditor's report that is issued based on work performed on a component's financial information at a group engagement team's request for the purposes of an audit of group financial statements.

Definitions

Element of a financial statement	Element, account, or item of a financial statement, including its related notes. Examples include: accounts receivable, allowance for doubtful accounts receivable, inventory, the liability for accrued benefits of a private pension plan, the recorded value of identified intangible assets, the liability for "incurred but not reported" claims in an insurance portfolio, schedules of externally managed assets and income of a private pension plan, schedules of disbursements in relation to a lease property, and schedules of profit participation or employee bonuses.
Single financial statement	Single financial statements include the related notes. Examples include statements of income, operations, retained earnings, cash flows, assets and liabilities, changes in owner's equity, revenue and expenses, operations by product lines, and balance sheet.

Requirements

The auditor is presumptively required to perform the following procedures when auditing a single financial statement or a specific element of a financial statement:

Engagement Acceptance

1. Comply with all AU-C sections relevant to the audit.

2. If not also engaged to audit the entity's complete set of financial statements, determine whether the audit of a single financial statement or a specific financial statement element in accordance with GAAS is practicable. Also determine whether procedures on interrelated items will be able to be performed as necessary to meet the audit objective.

3. Obtain an understanding of the purpose for which the single financial statement or specific element of a financial statement is prepared, the intended users, and the steps management has taken to determine that the application of the financial reporting framework is acceptable.

4. Determine the acceptability of the financial reporting framework applied in preparing the single financial statement or element, including whether (1) the framework's application will result in a presentation with adequate disclosures to enable intended users to understand the information conveyed in the financial statement or financial statement element and (2) the effect of material transactions and events on the information conveyed in the financial statement or element.

Engagement Planning and Performance

5. Adapt all AU-C sections relevant to the audit as necessary in the engagement circumstances.

6. Perform procedures on interrelated items as necessary to meet the objective of the audit. Many financial statement items are interrelated — for example, sales and receivables, inventory and payables, fixed assets and depreciation. If auditing a specific financial statement element and the element is, or is based upon, the entity's stockholders' equity or net income or the equivalent, perform procedures necessary to obtain sufficient appropriate audit evidence to enable expressing an opinion about financial position (and results of operations in the case of net income), excluding classification or disclosure matters that are not relevant to the audit of that element.

7. If auditing a single financial statement, determine materiality for the single financial statement as a whole. If auditing one or more specific elements of a financial statement, determine materiality for *each* individual element reported on rather than the aggregate of the elements or the complete financial statements as a whole.

Audit Opinion and Reporting

8. Apply the requirements in AU-C 700 (*Forming an Opinion and Reporting on Financial Statements*) when forming an opinion and reporting on a single financial statement or a specific financial statement element.

9. If auditing a single financial statement or a specific financial statement element in conjunction with an audit of the entity's complete set of financial statements, issue a separate auditor's report and express a separate opinion for each engagement. The auditor also should indicate the date of the audi-

tor's report on the complete set of financial statements and the nature of opinion expressed on those statements under an appropriate heading.

10. Unless the auditor issues an adverse opinion or disclaims an opinion on the complete set of financial statements, an audited single financial statement or specific financial statement element may be published together with the entity's audited complete set of financial statements if its presentation is sufficiently differentiated from the complete set of financial statements. If the auditor concludes these presentations are not sufficiently differentiated, he or she should ask management to remedy the situation and not release the auditor's report on the single financial statement or specific financial statement element until the auditor is satisfied with the differentiation. The auditor's report on the single financial statement or specific financial statement element should also be differentiated from the report on the complete set of financial statements.

11. If the opinion in the auditor's report on the complete set of financial statements is modified, determine the effect this may have on the opinion on a single financial statement or specific financial statement element.

12. In the audit of a specific financial statement element, if the modified opinion on the complete set of financial statements is relevant to the audit of the specific element or an interrelated item of the specific element:

    a. Express an adverse opinion on the specific element when the modification on the complete set of financial statements is due to a material misstatement.

    b. Disclaim an opinion on the specific element when the modification on the complete set of financial statements is due to an inability to obtain sufficient appropriate audit evidence.

13. If the auditor expresses an adverse opinion or disclaims an opinion on the complete set of financial statements, an unmodified opinion on an audit of a specific element included in those financial statements should only be expressed if (1) that opinion is expressed in an auditor's report that is not published together with and does not otherwise accompany the auditor's report containing the adverse opinion or disclaimer of opinion and (2) the specific element does not constitute a major portion of the entity's complete set of financial statements and is not, or is not based upon, the entity's stockholders' equity or net income or the equivalent.

14. If the auditor expresses an adverse opinion or disclaims an opinion on the complete set of financial statements, an unmodified opinion should not be expressed on a single financial statement that is part of that complete set of financial statements because a single financial statement is deemed to constitute a major portion of a complete set of financial statements.

15. If the auditor's report on a complete set of financial statements includes an emphasis-of- matter or other-matter paragraph that is relevant to the audit of the single financial statement or specific element, include an emphasis-of-matter or other-matter paragraph in the auditor's report in accordance with AU-C 706 (*Emphasis-of-Matter Paragraphs and Other-Matter Paragraphs in the Independent Auditor's Report*).

16. When reporting on an incomplete presentation that is otherwise in accordance with generally accepted accounting principles, include an emphasis-of-matter paragraph in the auditor's report that (1) states the purpose for which the presentation is prepared and refers to a financial statement note describing the basis for the presentation and (2) indicates that the presentation is not intended to be a complete presentation of the entity's assets, liabilities, revenues, or expenses.

> **OBSERVATION:** A practitioner could be engaged to review or to perform agreed-upon procedures to a single financial statement or specific element. In these cases, the guidance in AT 101 and AT 201, respectively, would apply.

Analysis and Application of Procedures

Engagement Acceptance

The auditor is required to comply with all relevant ethical requirements as well as all AU-C sections relevant to the audit. Each requirement in a relevant AU-C section should be complied with unless the requirement is conditional and the condition does not exist. In rare circumstances, the auditor may judge it necessary to depart from a presumptively mandatory requirement in a relevant AU-C section by performing alternative audit procedures to achieve the intent of that requirement.

In determining whether an audit of a single financial statement or a specific financial statement element in accordance with GAAS is practicable, the auditor may find that the relevant AU-C sections require an amount of audit effort disproportionate to the element being audited. For example, considering the going concern status of the entity may be relevant even when retained to audit a specific element. In these circumstances, the auditor may discuss with management whether another type of engagement, such as an agreed-upon procedures or review engagement may be more practicable.

A single financial statement or specific financial statement element may be prepared using a financial reporting framework established by an authorized or recognized standards setting organization for the preparation of a complete set of financial statements. In these circumstances, the auditor needs to determine if that framework is acceptable for presenting the single financial statement or financial statement element with adequate disclosures. In making this determination, the auditor may consider:

- Whether the framework is explicitly or implicitly restricted to preparing complete sets of financial statements
- Whether the single financial statement or financial statement element will fully comply with each framework requirement relevant to that statement or element and whether the presentation will include the related notes
- Whether the single financial statement or financial statement element, if necessary to achieve fair presentation, will need disclosures beyond those specifically required by the framework (or, in rare cases, will need to depart from a requirement of the framework)

The auditor may be requested to audit an incomplete presentation that is otherwise in accordance with GAAP. This incomplete presentation may be requested by an entity or required by a regulatory agency, contract, or agreement and is generally regarded as a single financial statement. If the incomplete presentation is required by a regulatory agency, contract, or agreement, the auditor may determine it is more appropriate for the description of the applicable financial reporting framework to refer to the regulatory or contractual basis of accounting rather than to refer to GAAP. If the auditor makes this determination, AU-C 800 would also be relevant.

Engagement Planning and Performance

AU-C sections relevant to the audit include AU-C sections that are in effect that address circumstances existing in the audit. AU-C sections such as AU-C 240, AU-C 550, and AU-C 570 are relevant even in audits of financial statement elements because the element could, in principle, be misstated or impacted due to fraud, related party transactions, or the incorrect application of the going concern assumption.

ENGAGEMENT STRATEGY: In audits of single financial statements or financial statement elements when the auditor is also engaged to audit the entity's complete set of financial statements, audit evidence obtained as part of the audit of the entity's complete set of financial statements may be able to be used in the single financial statement or financial statement element audit.

Because the auditor determines materiality for the audit of a single financial statement or financial statement element separately from materiality for the complete set of financial statements, the nature, timing, and extent of audit procedures will typically be more extensive for the element audited than if that element was being considered in an audit of the complete financial statements as a whole.

Audit Opinion and Reporting

If the opinion in an auditor's report on an entity's complete set of financial statements is modified and that modification is relevant to the audit of a single financial statement or financial statement element, the modification is considered material and pervasive with respect to that financial statement or element. Modifications the auditor may consider not relevant to the audit of a single financial statement or financial statement element include those solely related to classification or disclosure.

OBSERVATION: If the auditor is retained to audit accounts receivable and if the auditor's report on the financial statements as a whole is modified related to revenues, this modification would be relevant to the audit of the specific element, accounts receivable, because of the interrelated nature of revenues and accounts receivable.

The auditor may decide it is appropriate to include an other-matter paragraph in the audit report on a financial statement or financial statement element describing the modification to the opinion on the entity's complete set of financial statements even when that modified opinion, emphasis-of-matter paragraph, or other-matter paragraph does not relate to the audited financial statement or financial statement element. This may be done if the auditor judges it to be relevant to the users' understanding of the audited financial statement, financial statement element, or the related auditor's report.

OBSERVATION: In the auditor's report on a complete set of financial statements, the auditor is permitted to express a disclaimer of opinion on the results of operations and cash flows and an unmodified opinion on the financial position since the disclaimer is not being issued on the financial statements as a whole.

If an auditor reports on an incomplete presentation that is otherwise in accordance with GAAP and is prepared in accordance with a regulatory or contractual basis of accounting, the requirement to include an emphasis of matter paragraph in the auditor's report does not apply and the auditor should follow the guidance in AU-C 800.

Practitioner's Aids

Examples of auditor's reports on a single financial statement and on a specific financial statement element are illustrated in the following exhibits.

Exhibit AU-C 805-1 contains an auditor's report on a single financial statement.

EXHIBIT AU-C 805-1 — AUDITOR'S REPORT ON A SINGLE FINANCIAL STATEMENT

INDEPENDENT AUDITOR'S REPORT

[Appropriate Addressee]

Report on the Financial Statements

We have audited the accompanying balance sheet of X Company as of December 31, 20X5, and the related notes (the financial statement).

Management's Responsibility for the Financial Statement

Management is responsible for the preparation and fair presentation of this financial statement in accordance with accounting principles generally accepted in the United States of America; this includes the design, implementation, and maintenance of internal control relevant to the preparation and fair presentation of the financial statement that is free from material misstatement, whether due to fraud or error.

Auditor's Responsibility

Our responsibility is to express an opinion on the financial statement based on our audit. We conducted our audit in accordance with auditing standards generally accepted in the United States of America. Those standards require that we plan and perform the audit to obtain reasonable assurance about whether the financial statement is free of material misstatement.

An audit involves performing procedures to obtain audit evidence about the amounts and disclosures in the financial statement. The procedures selected depend on the auditor's judgment, including the assessment of the risks of material misstatement of the financial statement, whether due to fraud or error. In making those risk assessments, the auditor considers internal control relevant to the entity's preparation and fair presentation of the financial statement in order to design audit procedures that are appropriate in the circumstances, but not for the purpose of expressing an opinion on the effectiveness of the entity's internal control. Accordingly, we express no such opinion. An audit also includes evaluating the appropriateness of accounting policies used and the reasonableness of significant accounting estimates made by management, as well as evaluating the overall presentation of the financial statement.

We believe that the audit evidence we have obtained is sufficient and appropriate to provide a basis for our audit opinion.

Opinion

In our opinion, the financial statement referred to above presents fairly, in all material respects, the financial position of X Company as of December 31, 20X5, in accordance with accounting principles generally accepted in the United States of America.

Report on Other Legal and Regulatory Requirements

[*Form and content of this section of the auditor's report will vary depending on the nature of the auditor's other reporting responsibilities.*]

[Auditor's signature]

[Auditor's city and state]

[Date of the auditor's report]

Exhibit AU-C 805-2 contains an auditor's report on a specific element, account, or item of a financial statement when the audit was performed in conjunction with an audit on the entity's complete set of financial statements.

EXHIBIT AU-C 805-2 — AUDITOR'S REPORT ON A SPECIFIC ELEMENT, ACCOUNT, OR ITEM OF A FINANCIAL STATEMENT

INDEPENDENT AUDITOR'S REPORT

[Appropriate Addressee]

Report on the Schedule

We have audited the accompanying schedule of accounts receivable of X Company as of December 31, 20X5, and the related notes (the schedule).

Management's Responsibility for the Schedule

Management is responsible for the preparation and fair presentation of this schedule in accordance with accounting principles generally accepted in the United States of America; this includes the design, implementation, and maintenance of internal control relevant to the preparation and fair presentation of the schedule that is free from material misstatement, whether due to fraud or error.

Auditor's Responsibility

Our responsibility is to express an opinion on the schedule based on our audit. We conducted our audit in accordance with auditing standards generally accepted in the United States of America. Those standards require that we plan and perform the audit to obtain reasonable assurance about whether the schedule of accounts receivable is free of material misstatement.

An audit involves performing procedures to obtain audit evidence about the amounts and disclosures in the schedule. The procedures selected depend on the auditor's judgment, including the assessment of the risks of material misstatement of the schedule, whether due to fraud or error. In making those risk assessments, the auditor considers internal control relevant to the entity's preparation and fair presentation of the schedule in order to design audit procedures that are appropriate in the circumstances, but not for the purpose of expressing an opinion on the effectiveness of the entity's internal control. Accordingly, we express no such opinion. An audit also includes evaluating the appropriateness of accounting policies used and the reasonableness of significant accounting estimates made by management, as well as evaluating the overall presentation of the schedule.

We believe that the audit evidence we have obtained is sufficient and appropriate to provide a basis for our audit opinion.

Opinion

In our opinion, the schedule referred to above presents fairly, in all material respects, the accounts receivable of X Company as of December 31, 20X5, in accordance with accounting principles generally accepted in the United States of America.

Other Matter

We have audited, in accordance with auditing standards generally accepted in the United States of America, the financial statements of X Company for the year ended December 31, 20X5, and our report thereon dated March 15, 20X6 expressed an unmodified opinion on those financial statements.

Report on Other Legal and Regulatory Requirements

[*Form and content of this section of the auditor's report will vary depending on the nature of the auditor's other reporting responsibilities.*]

[Auditor's signature]

[Auditor's city and state]

[Date of the auditor's report]

SECTION 806

REPORTING ON COMPLIANCE WITH ASPECTS OF CONTRACTUAL AGREEMENTS OR REGULATORY REQUIREMENTS IN CONNECTION WITH AUDITED FINANCIAL STATEMENTS

Authoritative Pronouncements

SAS-122—Statements on Auditing Standards: Clarification and Recodification

Overview

An auditor may be asked to provide assurance on an entity's compliance with aspects of contractual agreements or regulatory requirements in connection with a financial statement audit (often referred to as a by-product report). The relevant financial statement audit may be of either general purpose or special purpose financial statements. Financial statement users, such as banks and regulatory agencies, may request that an entity's auditor specifically state whether the entity has observed a particular contract clause, covenant requirement, or administrative regulation. For example, a loan agreement may require that the entity's working capital not be less than a certain dollar amount.

In these situations, the auditor may provide negative assurance about the entity's compliance based on the financial statement audit. Negative assurance consists of a statement that nothing came to the auditor's attention as a result of performing procedures for the financial statement audit that caused the auditor to believe the entity did not comply with specified aspects of contractual agreements or regulatory requirements.

PLANNING AID REMINDER: If engaged to perform a compliance audit, the auditor should follow the guidance in AU-C 935 (*Compliance Audits*). If engaged to provide assurance on compliance with specific laws, regulations, rules, contracts, or grants that are not related to the financial statements, or to report on the effectiveness of internal control with respect to compliance, the auditor should follow the guidance in AT 601.

Requirements

The auditor is presumptively required to perform the following procedures when reporting on compliance with aspects of contractual agreements or regulatory requirements in connection with audited financial statements:

1. Only include a statement in the auditor's report on compliance that nothing came to the auditor's attention causing the auditor to believe that the entity failed to comply with specified aspects of the contractual

agreements or regulatory requirements as they relate to accounting matters when:

  a. The auditor has not identified any instances of noncompliance

  b. The applicable covenants or regulatory matters relate to matters that have been subjected to audit procedures in the financial statement audit

  c. The auditor expressed an unmodified or qualified opinion on the financial statements related to the applicable covenants or regulatory requirements

2. If instances of noncompliance are identified, describe those instances in the report on compliance.

3. If the auditor expressed an adverse opinion or disclaimed an opinion on the financial statements, a report on compliance should only be issued when instances of noncompliance are identified and the wording of the report should be appropriately modified.

4. Notwithstanding the requirements in the foregoing items 1 through 3, the auditor is not precluded from issuing a report on compliance if such a report is required by another set of auditing standards and the auditor has been engaged to audit the financial statements in accordance with GAAS and the other set of auditing standards.

5. Provide the report on compliance in writing as either (1) a separate report or (2) one or more paragraphs included in the auditor's report accompanying the financial statements.

6. If reporting on compliance with aspects of contractual agreements or regulatory requirements in a separate report, include:

  a. A title with the word "independent," indicating the report is from an independent auditor

  b. An appropriate addressee

  c. A paragraph stating that the financial statements were audited in accordance with GAAS, that the United States is the country of origin of those standards, and the date of the auditor's report on those financial statements

  d. If the auditor's report on the financial statements is modified, a statement describing the nature of the modification

  e. A reference to the specific covenants or paragraphs of the contractual agreement or regulatory requirement and (1) if no instances of non-compliance are identified, a statement that nothing came to the auditor's attention causing him or her to believe that the entity failed to comply with specified aspects of the contractual agreements or regulatory requirements related to accounting matters, or, (2) if instances of noncompliance are identified, a description of the con-tractual agreements or regulatory requirements and the identified areas of noncompliance

f. A statement that the report is being provided in connection with the financial statement audit

g. A statement that the audit's primary focus was not obtaining knowledge about compliance and had the auditor performed additional procedures, other matters regarding noncompliance with the specific covenants or paragraphs of the contractual agreement or regulatory requirement may have come to the auditor's attention

h. A paragraph including a description and the source of any significant interpretations made by the entity's management relating to the provisions of a relevant agreement

i. A paragraph restricting the report's use to management, those charged with governance, others within the organization, the regulatory agency responsible for the provisions, or other parties to the contract or agreement

j. The manual or printed signature of the auditor's firm, and the city and state where the auditor practices

k. The date of the report, which should be the same date as the auditor's report on the financial statements

7. If reporting on compliance with aspects of contractual agreements or regulatory requirements within the auditor's report on the financial statements, include:

a. An other-matter paragraph referencing the specific covenants or paragraphs of the contractual agreement or regulatory requirement and (1) if no instances of noncompliance are identified, a statement that nothing came to the auditor's attention causing him or her to believe that the entity failed to comply with specified aspects of the contractual agreements or regulatory requirements related to accounting matters, or, (2) if instances of noncompliance are identified, a description of those identified instances

b. A statement that the communication is being provided in connection with the financial statement audit

c. A statement that the audit was not primarily directed toward obtaining knowledge about compliance and, had the auditor performed additional procedures, other matters regarding noncompliance with the specific covenants or paragraphs of the contractual agreement or regulatory requirement may have come to the auditor's attention

d. A paragraph with a description and source of any significant interpretations of contractual provisions or regulatory requirements made by the entity's management

e. A paragraph restricting the report's use to management, those charged with governance, others within the organization, the regulatory agency responsible for the provisions, or other parties to the contract or agreement

Analysis and Application of Procedures

A restriction on the use of the report is necessary because the aspects of the contractual agreements or regulatory requirements being reported on are developed for and directed to only those parties to the agreement or contract or the regulatory agency responsible for the requirements.

OBSERVATION: If the auditor's report on compliance with aspects of contractual agreements or regulatory requirements is included in his or her report on the financial statements, the restriction on the report's use to specified parties applies to the entire auditor's report. However, if a separate report on compliance with aspects of contractual agreements or regulatory requirements is issued, then only that report will be restricted as to use by the specified parties.

When there are identified instances of noncompliance and the entity has obtained a waiver for the noncompliance, the auditor may include a statement that a waiver has been obtained in the report on compliance. Regardless of whether a waiver has been obtained, all instances of noncompliance are required to be described in the report on compliance.

If the auditor has included an emphasis-of-matter paragraph in the report on the financial statements as a whole (e.g., a going-concern paragraph), the auditor may include that same paragraph in the report on compliance.

Exhibit AU-C 806-1 is an example of a separate auditor's report on compliance when there are no identified instances of noncompliance.

Practitioner's Aids

EXHIBIT AU-C 806-1—SEPARATE AUDITOR'S REPORT ON COMPLIANCE WITH ASPECTS OF CONTRACTUAL AGREEMENTS

INDEPENDENT AUDITOR'S REPORT

We have audited, in accordance with auditing standards generally accepted in the United States of America, the financial statements of X Company, which comprise the balance sheet as of December 31, 20X5, and the related statements of income, changes in stockholders' equity, and cash flows for the year then ended, and the related notes to the financial statements, and have issued our report thereon dated February 20, 20X6.

In connection with our audit, nothing came to our attention that caused us to believe that X Company failed to comply with the terms, covenants, provisions, or conditions of the restrictive terms of the loan agreement dated March 4, 20X0, as explained in Section A of the agreement with First State Bank insofar as they relate to accounting matters. However, our audit was not directed primarily toward obtaining knowledge of such noncompliance. Accordingly, had we performed additional procedures, other matters may have come to our attention regarding the Company's noncompliance with the above-referenced terms, covenants, provisions, or conditions of the loan agreement, insofar as they relate to accounting matters.

This report is intended solely for the information and use of the board of directors and management of X Company and First State Bank and is not intended to be and should not be used by anyone other than these specified parties.

[Auditor's signature]

[Auditor's city and state]

[Date of the auditor's report]

SECTION 810

ENGAGEMENTS TO REPORT ON SUMMARY FINANCIAL STATEMENTS

Authoritative Pronouncements

SAS-122—Statements on Auditing Standards: Clarification and Recodification

Overview

AU-C 810 is applicable to engagements to report separately on summary financial statements that are derived from financial statements audited in accordance with GAAS by the same auditor. The auditor issues an opinion as to whether the summary financial statements are materially consistent with the audited financial statements from which they are drawn. In these situations, the auditor's objectives are: to determine if it is appropriate to accept such an engagement; if the engagement is accepted, to form an opinion on the summary financial statements based on an evaluation of the conclusions drawn from the audit evidence obtained; and to clearly express that opinion through a written report with a description of the basis for that opinion.

In some instances, summary financial statements are required to accompany the basic financial statements by the standard setter responsible for the financial reporting framework being used. In this instance, the requirements of AU-C 730 (*Required Supplementary Information*) are applicable.

OBSERVATION: When an auditor reports on financial statements that present comparative information with summarized prior period financial information, the applicable reporting guidance is described in AU-C 700 (*Forming an Opinion and Reporting on Financial Statements*).

Definitions

Applied criteria	Criteria applied by management in preparation of the summary financial statements.
Summary financial statements	Historical financial information derived from, but containing less detail than, the financial statements that provides a structured representation consistent with that provided by the financial statements of the entity's economic resources or obligations at a point in time or the changes therein for a period of time. These statements are separately presented, and are not shown as comparative information.

Requirements

The auditor is presumptively required to observe the following guidelines in an engagement to report on summary financial statements:

Engagement Acceptance

1. An auditor should only accept an engagement to report on summary financial statements in accordance with AU-C 810 if that auditor has been engaged to conduct an audit in accordance with GAAS of the financial statements from which the summary financial statements are derived.

2. Before accepting an engagement to report on summary financial statements:

   a. Determine whether the applied criteria are acceptable, including whether the criteria (1) are unbiased so summary financial statements are not misleading; (2) permit reasonably consistent qualitative or quantitative measurements so information in the summary financial statements agrees with or can be recalculated from the related information in the audited financial statements; (3) are sufficiently complete so the summary financial statements contain the necessary information and are at an appropriate level of aggregation to not be misleading; and (4) are relevant to the summary financial statements in view of their purpose.

   b. Obtain management's agreement that it acknowledges and understands its responsibility (1) for preparing the summary financial statements in accordance with the applied criteria; (2) to provide the auditor with written representations; (3) to make the audited financial statements readily available to the intended users of the summary financial statements; and (4) to include the auditor's report on the summary financial statements in any document containing the summary financial statements and indicates the auditor has reported on them.

   c. Obtain management's written agreement about the expected form and content of the report on summary financial statements, including that circumstances may cause the report to differ from this expectation.

3. Do not accept the engagement to report on the summary financial statements if the applied criteria are not acceptable or management's agreement is unable to be obtained.

Engagement Procedures

4. Perform the following procedures, and any other procedures considered necessary, on the summary financial statements to provide the basis for the auditor's opinion on those statements:

   a. Evaluate whether the statements' summarized nature is adequately disclosed and the audited financial statements are identified.

   b. If not accompanied by the audited financial statements, evaluate whether the summary financial statements clearly describe where the audited financial statements are available and whether the audited financial statements are readily available to the intended users of the summary financial statements.

   c. Evaluate whether the applied criteria are adequately disclosed.

   d. Compare the summary statements with the audited statements to determine if the summary financial statements agree with or can be recalculated from the related information in the audited financial statements.

e. Evaluate whether the summary statements are prepared in accordance with the applied criteria.

f. Evaluate whether the necessary information in included at the appropriate level of aggregation to not be misleading in view of the purpose of the summary financial statements.

Written Representations

5. Request management provide written representations in the form of a representation letter addressed to the auditor for all summary financial statements and periods referred to in the auditor's report on the summary financial statements for the following matters:

a. Management has prepared the summary financial statements in accordance with the applied criteria and believes the applied criteria to be acceptable.

b. Management will make the audited financial statements readily available to the intended users of the summary financial statements upon issuance of the summary financial statements, if the summary financial statements will not be accompanied by the audited financial statements.

c. If the date of the auditor's report on the summary financial statements is later than the date of the auditor's report on the audited financial statements: (1) whether any information has come to management's attention causing it to believe any previous representations on the audited financial statements need to be modified and (2) whether any events have occurred subsequent to the date of the audited financial statements that may require adjustment of, or disclosure in, the audited financial statements.

6. The date of the written representations should be as of the date of the auditor's report on the summary financial statements.

Audit Opinion and Reporting

7. If the auditor concludes an unmodified opinion on the summary financial statements is appropriate, the auditor's opinion should state that the summary financial statements are consistent, in all material respects, with the audited financial statements from which they have been derived, in accordance with the applied criteria.

8. If the summary financial statements are not consistent, in all material respects, with the audited financial statements, in accordance with the applied criteria, and management does not agree to make the necessary changes, express an adverse opinion on the summary financial statements.

9. If the auditor's opinion on the audited financial statements contains an adverse opinion or a disclaimer of opinion, the auditor should withdraw from the engagement where permissible under applicable law or regulation. If the auditor is not able to withdraw and issues an auditor's report on the summary financial statements, the auditor's report should:

a. State that the auditor's report on the audited financial statements contains an adverse opinion or disclaimer of opinion

b. Describe the basis for that adverse opinion or disclaimer of opinion

c. State that because of that adverse opinion or disclaimer of opinion it is inappropriate to express, and the auditor does not express, an opinion on the summary financial statements. In this case, the report is not required to include the reporting elements described in paragraph 10c (4–5), 10e, and 10f.

10. The auditor's report on the summary financial statements should include the following elements:

a. Title clearly indicating it as the report of an independent auditor

b. Addressee

c. Introductory paragraph: (1) identifying the summary financial statements on which the auditor is reporting, including the title of each statement included; (2) identifying the audited financial statements; (3) referring to the auditor's report on the audited financial statements, the date of that report, and, if it is the case, the fact that an unmodified opinion is expressed on the audited financial statements; (4) stating that, if the date of the auditor's report on the summary financial statements is later than the date of the auditor's report on the audited financial statements, the summary and audited financial statements do not reflect the effect of any events occurring subsequent to the date of the auditor's report on the audited financial statements; and (5) indicating that the summary financial statements do not contain all the disclosures required by the financial reporting framework applied in preparing the audited financial statements, and that reading the summary financial statements is not a substitute for reading the audited financial statements

d. Description of management's responsibility for the summary financial statements including its responsibility for preparing the summary financial statements in accordance with the applied criteria

e. Statement that the auditor is responsible for expressing an opinion on the summary financial statements based on procedures required by GAAS and that the United States is the country of origin of those standards, including that: (1) procedures consist principally of comparing the summary financial statements with the related information in the audited financial statements from which the summary statements have been derived and evaluating whether the summary financial statements are prepared in accordance with the applied criteria and (2) if the date of the auditor's report on the summary financial statements is later than the date of the auditor's report on the audited financial statements, the auditor did not perform any audit procedures regarding the audited financial statements after the date of the report on the audited statements

f. A paragraph clearly expressing an opinion

g. Auditor's signature

h. Auditor's city and state

i. Date of the auditor's report

11. Date the auditor's report on the summary financial statements no earlier than:

a. The date on which sufficient appropriate audit evidence has been obtained on which to base an opinion, including evidence that management and those charged with governance as appropriate have prepared and taken responsibility for the summary financial statements.

b. The date of the auditor's report on the audited financial statements.

12. If the auditor's report on the summary financial statements is dated later than the date of the auditor's report on the audited financial statements and the auditor becomes aware of subsequently discovered facts, do not release the auditor's report on the summary financial statements until consideration of those facts in relation to the audited financial statements has been completed in accordance with AU-C 560.

13. If the auditor's report on the audited financial statements contains a qualified opinion, an emphasis of matter paragraph, or an other matter paragraph, the auditor's report on the summary financial statements should (1) state that the auditor's report on the audited financial statements contains such an opinion or paragraph, (2) describe the basis for that opinion or paragraph, and (3) describe any effect that has on the summary financial statements.

Other Matters

14. If the auditor's report on the audited financial statements is for restricted use or alerts readers that the audited financial statements are prepared in accordance with a special purpose framework, a similar restriction or alert should be included in the auditor's report on the summary financial statements.

15. If the audited financial statements contain comparative financial statements but the summary financial statements do not, determine if this omission is reasonable in the circumstances of the engagement. Determine the effect of an unreasonable omission on the auditor's report on the summary financial statements.

16. If the summary financial statements contain comparative financial statements, and if the prior year summary statements were reported on by another auditor and the predecessor auditor's report on the prior period's summary financial statements is not reissued the auditor's report on the summary financial statements should state:

   a. Summary financial statements of the prior period were audited by a predecessor auditor

   b. The type of opinion expressed by the predecessor auditor and the reasons for any modified opinion

   c. The date of that report

17. If the summary financial statements contain comparative summary financial statements that were not reported on by any auditor, the auditor's report on the summary financial statements should state that the comparative summary financial statements were not reported on by the auditor and therefore the auditor does not express an opinion on the comparative summary financial statements.

18. Evaluate whether any unaudited information presented with the summary financial statements is clearly differentiated from the summary financial statements. If the auditor concludes unaudited information is not clearly differentiated, he or she should ask management to change the presentation of the unaudited information. If management refuses to do so, the auditor should explain in the auditor's report on the summary financial statements that such information is not covered by the report and accordingly, the auditor does not express an opinion on the information.

19. Read other information included in a document containing the summary financial statements and related auditor's report to identify any material inconsistencies with the summary financial statements or the audited financial statements. If a material inconsistency or material misstatement of fact is

identified, he or she should discuss the matter with management and consider appropriate further action in the circumstances. And, in the case of a material inconsistency, the auditor should determine if the summary financial statements or the other information needs to be revised.

20. If an entity intends to state that the auditor has reported on summary financial statements in a document containing the statements but not the auditor's report, the auditor should request management include the auditor's report in the document. If management refuses, the auditor should take appropriate action to prevent being inappropriately associated with the summary financial statements in that document.

21. If the auditor reports on an entity's financial statements but not its summary financial statements and the entity plans to refer to the auditor and the fact that summary financial statements are derived from the audited financial statements, the auditor should be satisfied that the reference to the auditor applies to the auditor's report on the audited financial statements, and the statement does not give the impression that the auditor has reported on the summary financial statements. If the auditor is not satisfied that this is the case, he or she should request management to:

a. Change the statement to satisfy these criteria,

b. Not refer to the auditor in the document, or

c. Engage the auditor to report on the summary financial statements and include the related auditor's report in the document.

If management refuses, the auditor should advise the entity that he or she disagrees with the reference to the auditor and carry out appropriate actions to prevent from being inappropriately associated with the summary financial statements in that document.

Analysis and Application of Procedures

Engagement Acceptance

If the auditor has not also audited the financial statements from which the summary financial statements are derived, application of the guidance in AU-C 810 will not provide sufficient appropriate evidence on which to base an opinion on the summary financial statements and the auditor should not accept the engagement.

In many cases, the criteria for preparing summary financial statements may be established by an authorized or recognized standards setting organization or by law or regulation, in which case the auditor may presume the criteria used are acceptable. In circumstances when the auditor must determine whether the applied criteria are acceptable, however, he or she may consider the nature of the entity, the purpose of the summary financial statements, the information needs of the intended users of the summary financial statements, and whether the applied criteria will result in summary financial statements that are not misleading in the circumstances. In the absence of established criteria for summary financial statements, management will have to develop the criteria. Reference to industry practice may be appropriate in this instance.

Summary financial statements are aggregated versions of the audited financial statements with limited disclosures so they contain an increased risk that information necessary for the statements to not be misleading is not there, especially when there are no existing criteria established for the preparation of summary financial statements.

Because of these limitations, reading summary financial statements is not a substitute for reading the audited financial statements. Therefore, the auditor must obtain management's agreement acknowledging its responsibility for making the audited financial statements readily available to the intended users of the summary financial statements. Audited financial statements are considered readily available if a third party user can obtain the statements without any further action by the entity. For example, indicating that the audited financial statements are available upon request is not consistent with these statements being readily available.

Engagement Procedures

Adequate disclosure of the summarized nature of summary financial statements and the identity of the audited financial statements may be provided by a title such as "Summary Financial Statements Prepared from the Audited Financial Statements as of and for the Year Ended December 21, 20X5."

Audit Opinion and Reporting

The very nature of summary financial statements is that they are presented in less detail than audited financial statements. For this reason, they do not fairly present the financial position or results of operation of an entity. When an auditor is engaged to report on summary financial statements derived from audited financial statements, the auditor should report in a different manner than when he or she reports on the complete financial statements to prevent users from assuming all the disclosures necessary for complete financial statements are included. In some cases, if the auditor expresses a qualified opinion on financial statements, he or she may decide it is inappropriate to express an opinion on the summary financial statements. If so, the auditor should follow the reporting guidance from paragraph 9.

Summary financial statements, due to their summarized nature, are either consistent or not consistent in all material respects with the audited financial statements in accordance with the applied criteria. If the summary financial statements are consistent with the audited financial statements, an unmodified opinion is appropriate; if the statements are not consistent and management refuses to make the necessary changes then an adverse opinion is appropriate.

OBSERVATION: Because of the summarized nature of summary financial statements, a qualified opinion on the summary statements is not appropriate.

Other Matters

When comparative financial statements are included in the audited financial statements, it is presumed that the summary financial statements will also contain comparatives. However, if the summary financial statements do not contain comparatives, the auditor should determine whether that omission is reasonable. This decision may be affected by the nature and objective of the summary financial statements, the applied criteria, or the information needs of the intended users of the summary financial statements.

Auditor Association

Management may indicate in a document including summary financial statements that the auditor has reported on these summary statements but not include the auditor's report, or management may refer to the auditor in a document containing the summary financial statements even though the auditor was not engaged to audit the summary statements. The auditor should request management to remedy either of these situations (see paragraphs 20 and 21 for additional details). In situations where management does not take the action the auditor requests, the auditor may inform the intended users and other known third-party users of inappropriate reference to the auditor including that the auditor did not report and does not express an opinion on the summary financial statements. The auditor may also consider it appropriate to seek legal advice.

Practitioner's Aid

Exhibit AU-C 810-1 is an example of a report on summary financial statements containing an unmodified opinion that is dated after the date of the auditor's report on the audited financial statements.

EXHIBIT AU-C 810-1—REPORT ON SUMMARY FINANCIAL STATEMENTS WITH AN UNMODIFIED OPINION DATED AFTER THE DATE OF THE AUDITOR'S REPORT ON THE AUDITED FINANCIAL STATEMENTS

INDEPENDENT AUDITOR'S ON SUMMARY FINANCIAL STATEMENTS

[Appropriate Addressee]

The accompanying summary financial statements, which comprise the summary balance sheet as of December 31, 20X5, the summary income statement, summary statement of changes in stockholders' equity and summary cash flow statement for the year then ended, and related notes, are derived from the audited financial statements of X Company as of and for the year ended 20X5. We expressed an unmodified audit opinion on those audited financial statements in our report dated February 15, 20X5. The audited financial statements, and the summary financial statements derived therefrom, do not reflect the effects of events, if any, that occurred subsequent to the date of our report on the audited financial statements.

The summary financial statements do not contain all the disclosures required by [*describe financial reporting framework applied in the preparation of the audited financial statements of X Company*]. Reading the summary financial statements, therefore, is not a substitute for reading the audited financial statements of X Company.

Management's Responsibility for the Summary Financial Statements

Management is responsible for the preparation of the summary financial statements on the basis described in Note X.

Auditor's Responsibility

Our responsibility is to express an opinion about whether the summary financial statements are consistent, in all material respects, with the audited financial statements based on our procedures, which were conducted in accordance with auditing standards generally accepted in the United States of America. The procedures consist principally of comparing the summary financial statements with the related information in the audited financial statements from which the summary financial statements have been derived, and evaluating whether the summary financial statements are prepared in accordance with the basis described in Note X. We did not perform any audit procedures regarding the audited financial statements after the date of our report on those financial statements.

Opinion

In our opinion, the summary financial statements of X Company as of and for the year ended December 31, 20X5 referred to above are consistent, in all material respects, with the audited financial statements from which they have been derived, on the basis described in Note X.

[Auditor's signature]

[Auditor's city and state]

[Date of the auditor's report]

AU-C 900
Special Considerations in the United States

SECTION 905

ALERT THAT RESTRICTS THE USE OF THE AUDITOR'S WRITTEN COMMUNICATION

Authoritative Pronouncements

SAS-125—Alert That Restricts the Use of the Auditor's Written Communication

Overview

AU-C 905 provides the auditor with guidance on when to include an alert as to the intended use of the auditor's report or other written communication, such as letters communicating internal control related matters or presentations addressing communications with those charged with governance, issued in connection with an engagement conducted in accordance with GAAS. While several AU-Cs contain requirements for the auditor to include such an alert, nothing precludes the auditor from including such an alert in other circumstances as he or she considers it necessary. Such an alert restricts the use of the auditor's written communication, and is included in an other-matter paragraph.

The auditor's written communication is to be restricted when the risk exists that the written communication will be misunderstood when taken out of the context in which the communication was intended to be used.

Definition

Specified parties   The intended users of the auditor's written communication

Requirements

The auditor is presumptively required to perform the following procedures related to an alert as to the intended use of the auditor's written communication:

1. Include an alert as to the intended use of a written communication when that communication's subject matter is based on:
   a. Measurement or disclosure criteria the auditor determines are suitable only for a limited number of users presumed to have an adequate understanding of the criteria,
   b. Measurement or disclosure criteria available only to the specified parties, or
   c. Matters identified by the auditor during the course of the engagement that are not the primary objective of the engagement, known as a by-product report.
2. The alert should, unless otherwise specified by other relevant AU-Cs:
   a. State that the written communication is intended for the information and use of the specified parties only

   b. Identify the specified parties, which, in the case of a by-product report, should include only management, those charged with governance, others within the entity, parties to the contract or agreement, or the regulatory agencies with jurisdiction over the entity as appropriate

   c. State that the written communication is not intended to be and should not be used by anyone other than the specified parties

3. If the auditor is requested to add other specified parties to an alert, he or she should determine whether to add these parties. In the case of a by-product report, the auditor should not agree to add any specified parties not described in requirement 2b, above.

4. If the auditor agrees to add other parties as specified parties (i.e., permitting these parties to rely on the auditor's written communication), obtain affirmative written acknowledgement from the other parties of their understanding of the nature of the engagement and the measurement or disclosure criteria in the written communication and of the related auditor's written communication.

5. If other parties are added after the release of the auditor's written communication, in addition to the requirements in item 4, above, take one of the following actions:

   a. Amend the written communication to add the other parties but do not change the date of the written communication.

   b. Provide a written acknowledgement to management and the other parties that such parties have been added as specified parties, stating that no procedures were performed after the date of the written communication or the date the engagement was completed as appropriate

6. When an engagement is also performed in accordance with *Government Auditing Standards* and the auditor's written communication is issued under requirements in AU-C 265 (*Communicating Internal Control Related Matters Identified in an Audit*), AU-C 806 (*Reporting on Compliance with Aspects of Contractual Agreements or Regulatory Requirements in Connection with Audited Financial Statements*), or AU-C 935 (*Compliance Audits*), the alert language should not be that stated in requirement 2, above, but should instead describe the purpose of the written communication and state that the written communication is not suitable for any other purpose.

OBSERVATION: AU-C 905 defines certain audit reports as "intended use" reports. The previous language in GAAS referred to "restricted use" reports; the term restricted use reports no longer appears in AU-C 905.

Analysis and Application of Procedures

An alert as to the intended use of the auditor's written communication may be used due to the purpose of the written communication, the nature of procedures applied or the basis of assumptions used in its preparation, the extent to which the procedures performed are generally known or understood, and the potential for the written communication to be misunderstood when taken out of its intended context.

OBSERVATION: The auditor is not precluded from including an alert as to the intended use of his or her written communication in situations where such an alert is not required. For example, the auditor may want to indicate that an audit report related to general purpose financial statements for use in an acquisition is intended only for the use of specified parties.

The auditor is required to issue an alert as to the intended use of a by-product report because the report may be based on matters that were not his or her primary objective during the engagement, so only limited procedures may have been conducted related to the subject of the by-product report and its intended purpose may be misinterpreted or misunderstood.

The alert as to the intended use of the auditor's written communication may list the specified parties or refer to a listing of the specified parties elsewhere in the written communication. An example of an alert is as follows:

> This [*report, letter, presentation, or communication*] is intended solely for the information and use of [*list or refer to the specified parties*] and is not intended to be and should not be used by anyone other than these specified parties.

Other AU-Cs with requirements for the auditor to include an alert as to intended use in the auditor's written communication, listed in Exhibit AU-C 905-1, may include specific requirements relating to the matters to be included in the alert, including identifying the specified parties (for example, see AU-C 920, *Letters for Underwriters and Certain Other Requesting Parties*).

The intended use of a general-use communication is not affected if:

- A written communication that includes an alert as to its intended use is included in a document that also contains a written communication for general use, or

- The auditor issues a single combined written communication covering communications that include an alert as to intended-use and general-use communications.

OBSERVATION: The auditor is not responsible for controlling distribution of the written communication, but he or she may consider informing the entity that the written communication is not intended for distribution to other than the specified parties. The auditor may want to, as part of establishing the engagement terms, obtain an agreement that the entity and specified parties will not distribute the auditor's report to any other parties.

> **OBSERVATION:** The combining of written communications intended for general use with communications intended for specified parties does not, as discussed above, restrict the use of the general purpose report. This guidance in AU-C 905 differs from the guidance in the former AU 532, which required the combined report to be restricted to specified parties.

When following *Government Auditing Standards*, the engagement's written communication is generally required by law or regulation to be publicly available. An example of the type of alert to use in these situations follows:

> The purpose of this [*report, letter, presentation, or communication*] is to [*describe the purpose of the written communication*]. This [*report, letter, presentation, or communication*] is an integral part of an audit conducted in accordance with Government Auditing Standards in considering [*describe what is being assessed—e.g., internal control over financial reporting*]. Accordingly, this [*report, letter, presentation, or communication*] is not intended to be and should not be used for any other purpose.

Practitioner's Aid

EXHIBIT AU-C 905-1—LIST OF STATEMENTS ON AUDITING STANDARDS CONTAINING REQUIREMENTS FOR AN ALERT AS TO THE INTENDED USE OF AN AUDITOR'S WRITTEN COMMUNICATION

- AU-C 260, *The Auditor's Communication with Those Charge with Governance* (paragraph 17)
- AU-C 265, *Communicating Internal Control Related Matters Identified in an Audit* (paragraphS 14(d), A32, and A38–A39)
- AU-C 725, *Supplementary Information in Relation to the Financial Statements as a Whole* (paragraph A16)
- AU-C 800, *Special Considerations—Audits of Financial Statements Prepared in Accordance with Special Purpose Frameworks* (paragraphs 20, A26–A27, and A33)
- AU-C 806, *Reporting on Compliance with Aspects of Contractual Agreements or Regulatory Requirements in Connection with Audited Financial Statements* (paragraphs 12, 13, and A6–A8)
- AU-C 915, *Reports on Application of Requirements of an Applicable Financial Reporting Framework* (paragraphs 14(f) and A6)
- AU-C 920, *Letters for Underwriters and Certain Other Requesting Parties* (paragraphs 33 and A34)
- AU-C 935, *Compliance Audits* (paragraphs 30, 31(i), and A33)

SECTION 910

FINANCIAL STATEMENTS PREPARED IN ACCORDANCE WITH A FINANCIAL REPORTING FRAMEWORK GENERALLY ACCEPTED IN ANOTHER COUNTRY

Authoritative Pronouncements

SAS-124—Financial Statements Prepared in Accordance with a Financial Reporting Framework Generally Accepted in Another Country

Overview

AU-C 910 provides guidance to auditors practicing in the United States who are engaged to report on financial statements prepared in accordance with a financial reporting framework that is generally accepted in another country but is not adopted by a body designated by the Council of the AICPA to establish generally accepted accounting principles (GAAP) when those audited financial statements are intended for use outside the United States, although this does not preclude the use of these financial statements in the United States. AU-C 910 does not apply to financial statements prepared in accordance with financial reporting frameworks established by any of the bodies designated by the Council of the AICPA to establish U.S. GAAP.

OBSERVATION: AU-C 910 states that the guidance in AU-C 700 (*Forming an Opinion and Reporting on Financial Statements*), rather than in AU-C 910, applies when the auditor is engaged to opine on financial statements prepared in accordance with International Financial Reporting Standards (IFRS) as issued by the IASB. If, however, the financial statements use IFRS as modified by a foreign country (i.e., they deviate from IFRS as originally issued by the IASB), then AU-C 910 applies.

OBSERVATION: AU-C 910 does not apply to engagements to report on financial statements of a U.S. subsidiary of a foreign registrant parent company that are presented in that parent company's filing with the U.S. Securities and Exchange Commission when the subsidiary's financial statements have been prepared in accordance with a financial reporting framework used by the parent company and audited in accordance with GAAS.

The auditor's objective in an engagement to report on financial statements prepared in accordance with a financial reporting framework generally accepted in another country when the audited financial statements are intended for use outside the United States is to appropriately address the special considerations relevant to engagement acceptance, engagement planning and performance, and forming an opinion and reporting on the financial statements.

Requirements

The auditor is presumptively required to perform the following procedures when reporting on financial statements prepared in accordance with a financial reporting framework generally accepted in another country:

1. In considering acceptance of an audit engagement, determine the acceptability of the financial reporting framework applied in the preparation of the financial statements. Obtain an understanding of:

   a. The purpose for which the financial statements are prepared and whether the financial reporting framework applied is a fair presentation framework

   b. The intended users of the financial statements

   c. The steps management has taken to determine the financial reporting framework is acceptable in the circumstances

2. If planning to issue a standard report of another country, obtain an understanding of the legal responsibilities in the other country.

3. Comply with U.S. GAAS if financial statements are prepared for use only outside the United States, except for requirements related to report form and content. Determine whether U.S. GAAS application requires special consideration in the circumstances of the engagement.

4. Obtain an understanding of the financial reporting framework applied as part of obtaining an understanding of the entity's selection and application of accounting policies.

5. If the agreed-upon terms of an audit engagement require the auditor to apply another country's auditing standards or the International Standards on Auditing (ISAs), obtain an understanding of and apply the relevant auditing standards as well as U.S. GAAS (except for requirements related to report form and content if the financial statements are prepared for use only outside the United States).

6. If financial statements are intended for use only outside the United States, report using either:

   a. A U.S. form of report reflecting that the financial statements being reported on have been prepared in accordance with a financial reporting framework generally accepted in another country including the elements required by AU-C 700 (*Forming an Opinion and Reporting on Financial Statements*) and a statement referring to the note to the financial statements describing the basis of presentation of the financial statements on which the auditor is reporting, including identification of the nationality of the accounting principles

   b. The standard report form and content of the other country, or that set forth in the ISAs if applicable, provided that such a report would be issued by auditors in the other country in similar circumstances, the auditor understands and has obtained sufficient appropriate audit evidence to support the statements contained in such a report, and he or she has complied with the reporting standards of that country and identifies that country in the report.

7. If financial statements prepared in accordance with a financial reporting framework generally accepted in another country are also intended for use in the United States, report using the U.S. form of the report and include an emphasis-of-matter paragraph in the report (1) identifying the accounting framework used in preparing the financial statements, (2) referring to the note that describes the framework, and (3) indicating that the framework differs from U.S. GAAP.

Analysis and Application of Procedures

Audit Planning and Performance

In auditing financial statements prepared in accordance with a financial reporting framework generally accepted in another country that are prepared for use only outside the United States, GAAS should be complied with excepting requirements related to form and content. However, the procedures applied to perform a GAAS audit may need to be modified to reflect differences in the accounting principles used to prepare the financial statements. For example, some financial reporting frameworks used in foreign countries require, or permit, the revaluation of assets. Auditing such revaluations would differ from an audit of U.S. GAAP-based financial statements.

PLANNING AID REMINDER: If the financial statements prepared in accordance with a framework generally accepted in another country are likely to be used in the United States, the auditor may consider whether U.S. users are likely to understand the differences between the foreign accounting framework and U.S. GAAP. For example, it may not be appropriate to report on financial statements prepared in accordance with a foreign framework if these statements are going to be included in a private placement memorandum that will be used extensively in the United States.

When the auditor is required to comply with auditing standards of another country, both those standards and GAAS must be observed during the engagement. Thus, some audit procedures will be employed to comply with GAAS, whereas other potentially additional audit procedures will be performed to satisfy auditing standards of the foreign country.

PLANNING AID REMINDER: An understanding of a financial reporting framework generally accepted in another country or the auditing standards of another country or the ISAs may be obtained by reading the statutes or professional literature establishing or describing the framework or standards or by consulting with others with appropriate expertise and experience in applying such framework or standards.

Preparing an Appropriate Audit Report

The reporting standards that must be observed in the preparation of the auditor's report on financial statements prepared in accordance with accounting principles of another country are dependent on the purpose of the financial statements. These purposes may be classified as (1) foreign GAAP/foreign use and (2) dual statements (foreign GAAP/U.S. GAAP).

Foreign GAAP/Foreign Use

When financial statements of a U.S. entity that are prepared in accordance with accounting principles of another country are to be used exclusively outside the United States, the auditor may use either (1) the U.S.-style auditor's report with a statement referencing the note to the financial statements describing the basis of presentation of the financial statements and identifying the nationality of the accounting principles or (2) the standard auditor's report of the foreign country. An example of a U.S.-style auditor's report on financial statements intended for use only outside the United States is presented in Exhibit AU-C 910-2.

The assertions in the standard auditor's report of another country may be different from those in the U.S.-style standard auditor's report. The fundamental assertion in the U.S.-style standard auditor's report is that the financial statements are prepared in accordance with generally accepted accounting principles. On the other hand, a foreign country's standard auditor's report may imply or state that the financial statements are prepared in compliance with existing statutory regulations. Thus, before issuing a foreign country's standard auditor's report, the U.S. auditor must fully understand the auditing standards, accounting principles, and laws that are applicable in the foreign country. To gain the appropriate understanding, the U.S. auditor might need to consult with persons who are familiar with the auditing standards, accounting principles, and laws of the particular foreign country.

Dual Statements (Foreign GAAP/U.S. GAAP)

One set of financial statements may be prepared in accordance with GAAP and a second set in accordance with accounting principles acceptable in a foreign country, to provide relevant information to users in both countries. For the financial statements presented in accordance with GAAP, the auditor should observe GAAS in preparing the auditor's report. For the financial statements prepared in accordance with accounting principles acceptable in a foreign country and to be used outside of the United States, the auditor may prepare either type of report that is permitted for statements using foreign GAAP for use outside the United States.

Some confusion may arise when the same financial statements of a U.S. entity are prepared on two different accounting bases. AU-C 910 suggests that to reduce the possibility of a misunderstanding, one or both of the audit reports may contain a statement advising the reader of the other audit report, which has been issued on the same financial statements but is based on the accepted accounting principles of another country. The auditor's report also may refer to the note to the financial statements, if presented, that describes the significant differences between the two bases of accounting. An example of the auditor's reference to such a note is as follows:

> We also have reported separately on the financial statements of Company X for the same period presented in accordance with [*specify the financial reporting framework generally accepted*] in [*name of country*]. (The significant differences between the [*specify the financial reporting framework*] and accounting principles generally accepted in the United States of America are summarized in Note 1.)

Practitioner's Aids

Exhibit AU-C 910-1 is an example of a U.S. form of auditor's report on financial statements prepared in accordance with a financial reporting framework generally accepted in another country that are also intended for use in the U.S.

EXHIBIT AU-C 910-1—U.S. FORM OF AUDITOR'S REPORT ON FINANCIAL STATEMENTS THAT ARE ALSO INTENDED FOR USE IN THE U.S.

INDEPENDENT AUDITOR'S REPORT

[Appropriate Addressee]

Report on the Financial Statements

We have audited the accompanying financial statements of X Company, which comprise the balance sheet as of December 31, 20X5, and the related statements of income, changes in stockholders' equity, and cash flows for the year then ended, and the related notes to the financial statements, which, as describe in note X to the financial statements, have been prepared on the basis of [*specify the financial reporting framework generally accepted*] in [*name of country*].

Management's Responsibility for the Financial Statements

Management is responsible for the preparation and fair presentation of these financial statements in accordance with [*specify the financial reporting framework generally accepted*] in [*name of country*]; this includes the design, implementation, and maintenance of internal control relevant to the preparation and fair presentation of financial statements that are free from material misstatement, whether due to fraud or error.

Auditor's Responsibility

Our responsibility is to express an opinion on these financial statements based on our audit. We conducted our audit in accordance with auditing standards generally accepted in the United States of America (and in [*name of country*]). Those standards require that we plan and perform the audit to obtain reasonable assurance about whether the financial statements are free of material misstatement.

An audit involves performing procedures to obtain audit evidence about the amounts and disclosures in the financial statements. The procedures selected depend on the auditor's judgment, including the assessment of the risks of material misstatement of the financial statements, whether due to fraud or error. In making those risk assessments, the auditor considers internal control relevant to the entity's preparation and fair presentation of the financial statement in order to design audit procedures that are appropriate in the circumstances, but not for the purpose of expressing an opinion on the effectiveness of the entity's internal control. Accordingly, we express no such opinion. An audit also includes evaluating the appropriateness of accounting policies used and the reasonableness of significant accounting estimates made by management, as well as evaluating the overall presentation of the financial statements.

We believe that the audit evidence we have obtained is sufficient and appropriate to provide a basis for our audit opinion.

Opinion

In our opinion, the financial statements referred to above present fairly, in all material respects, the financial position of X Company as of December 31, 20X5, and the results of its operations or its cash flows for the year then ended in accordance with [*specify the financial reporting framework generally accepted*] in [*name of country*].

Emphasis of Matter

As discussed in note X to the financial statements, the Company prepares its financial statements in accordance with [*specify the financial reporting framework generally accepted*] in [*name of country*], which differ(s) from accounting principles generally accepted in the United States of America. Our opinion is not modified with respect to this matter.

[*Auditor's signature*]

[*Auditor's city and state*]

[*Date of the auditor's report*]

Exhibit AU-C 910-2 is an example of a U.S. form of auditor's report on financial statements prepared in accordance with a financial reporting framework generally accepted in another country that is intended for use only outside the United States.

EXHIBIT AU-C 910-2—U.S. FORM OF AUDITOR'S REPORT ON FINANCIAL STATEMENTS INTENDED FOR USE ONLY OUTSIDE THE U.S.

INDEPENDENT AUDITOR'S REPORT

[Appropriate Addressee]

Report on the Financial Statements

We have audited the accompanying financial statements of X Company, which comprise the balance sheet as of December 31, 20X5, and the related statements of income, changes in stockholders' equity, and cash flows for the year then ended, and the related notes to the financial statements, which, as described in Note X to the financial statements, have been prepared on the basis of [*specify the financial reporting framework generally accepted*] in [*name of country*].

Management's Responsibility for the Financial Statements

Management is responsible for the preparation and fair presentation of these financial statements in accordance with [*specify the financial reporting framework generally accepted*] in [*name of country*]; this includes the design, implementation, and maintenance of internal control relevant to the preparation and fair presentation of financial statements that are free from material misstatement, whether due to fraud or error.

Auditor's Responsibility

Our responsibility is to express an opinion on these financial statements based on our audit. We conducted our audit in accordance with auditing standards generally accepted in the United States of America (and in [*name of country*]). Those standards require that we plan and perform the audit to obtain reasonable assurance about whether the financial statements are free of material misstatement.

An audit involves performing procedures to obtain audit evidence about the amounts and disclosures in the financial statements. The procedures selected depend on the auditor's judgment, including the assessment of the risks of material misstatement of the financial statements, whether due to fraud or error. In making those risk assessments, the auditor considers internal control relevant to the entity's preparation and fair presentation of the financial statements in order to design audit procedures that are appropriate in the circumstances, but not for the purpose of expressing an opinion on the effectiveness of the entity's internal control. Accordingly, we express no such opinion. An audit also includes evaluating the appropriateness of accounting policies used and the reasonableness of significant accounting estimates made by management, as well as evaluating the overall presentation of the financial statements.

We believe that the audit evidence we have obtained is sufficient and appropriate to provide a basis for our audit opinion.

Opinion

In our opinion, the financial statements referred to above present fairly, in all material respects, the financial position of X Company as of December 31, 20X5, and the results of its operations and its cash flows for the year then ended in accordance with [*specify the financial reporting framework generally accepted*] in [*name of country*].

[*Auditor's signature*]

[*Auditor's city and state*]

[*Date of the auditor's report*]

SECTION 915

REPORTS ON APPLICATION OF REQUIREMENTS OF AN APPLICABLE FINANCIAL REPORTING FRAMEWORK

Authoritative Pronouncements

SAS-122 — Statements on Auditing Standards: Clarification and Recodification

SAS-123 — Omnibus Statement on Auditing Standards — 2011

Overview

Accountants are often requested to give an informal opinion on how a transaction should or could be accounted for or what type of opinion would be appropriate for a particular set of financial statements. Requests of this nature are frequently associated with prospective clients who are "shopping for an opinion." Unfortunately, such requests have resulted in a significant amount of adverse publicity for the accounting profession. AU-C 915 provides guidance in this sensitive area. AU-C 915 points out that an accountant may be asked by management or other interested parties (1) to explain how an applicable financial reporting framework applies to specific transactions or (2) to increase their knowledge of specific financial reporting issues.

The standards established by AU-C 915 apply to the reporting accountant and help him or her to appropriately address engagement acceptance, planning, performance, and reporting under the following circumstances:

- A written report is prepared on the application of the requirements of an applicable financial reporting framework to specific transactions

- A written report is prepared on the type of opinion that may be expressed on a specific entity's financial statements

- Oral advice is offered that the accountant believes is intended to be used by a principal to the transaction as an important factor to be considered in reaching a decision on the application of the requirements of an applicable financial reporting framework to a specific transaction

- Oral advice is offered by the reporting accountant on the type of opinion that may be expressed on a specific entity's financial statements

---

OBSERVATION: The scope of AU-C 915 includes oral advice so that the reporting accountant cannot circumvent professional standards simply by not preparing a written report.

OBSERVATION: With the increased visibility of accountants in the press and the related close scrutiny of the profession as well as the possibility of litigation, accountants should be particularly careful in accepting engagements covered by AU-C 915.

The standards established by AU-C 915 do not apply to the following circumstances:

- A continuing accountant with respect to the specific entity whose financial statements are being reported upon by the continuing accountant

- An accountant assisting in litigation or providing expert testimony involving accounting matters

- An accountant providing professional advice to another accountant in public practice

- An accountant preparing other communications such as position papers (newsletters, articles, texts, lectures, etc.) on the application of the requirements of an applicable financial reporting framework to an issue unless the guidance is rendered on a specific transaction

---

OBSERVATION: The standards established by AU-C 915 do not provide guidance for a continuing accountant (except as discussed later with respect to the communication between the reporting accountant and the continuing accountant), because the continuing accountant discusses the application of accounting principles to various transactions and the effect of the accounting for such transactions on the auditor's report as part of the normal audit process.

Definitions

Continuing accountant	An accountant who has been engaged to report on the financial statements of a specific entity.
Hypothetical transaction	A transaction or financial reporting issue that does not involve facts or circumstances of a specific entity.
Reporting accountant	An accountant, other than a continuing accountant, in the practice of public accounting who prepares a written report or provides oral advice on the application of the requirements of an applicable financial reporting framework to a specific transaction, or on the type of report that may be issued on a specific entity's financial statements.
Specific transaction	A completed or proposed transaction or financial reporting issue involving facts and circumstances of a specific entity.
Written report	Any written communication expressing a conclusion on the appropriate application of the requirements of an applicable financial reporting framework to a specific transaction, or on the type of report that may be issued on a specific entity's financial statements.

Requirements

The reporting accountant is presumptively required to observe the following performance standards when reporting on the application of requirements of an applicable financial reporting framework:

1. Consider (1) the circumstances under which the written report or oral advice is requested, (2) the purpose of the request, and (3) the intended use of the written report or oral advice in determining whether to accept the engagement. The reporting accountant is not required to be independent.

2. Only accept engagements to issue written reports or provide oral advice on the application of requirements of an applicable financial reporting framework to a specific transaction when the transaction involves facts and circumstances of a specific entity. Engagements to report on hypothetical transactions should not be accepted.

3. Establish an understanding with the entity that management:

   a. Is responsible for the proper accounting treatment and is expected to consult with its continuing accountant

   b. Acknowledges that the reporting accountant may need to consult with the continuing accountant and that management will authorize the continuing accountant to respond fully to the reporting accountant's inquiries upon request

   c. Will notify those charged with governance and the continuing accountant regarding the nature of the engagement

   If management refuses to authorize the continuing accountant to respond fully to the reporting accountant's inquiries, inquire about the reasons and consider the implications in determining whether to accept the engagement.

4. In planning and performing an engagement:

   a. Obtain an understanding of the form and substance of the specific transactions or the conditions relevant to the type of report that may be issued on a specific entity's financial statements

   b. Review the relevant requirements of the applicable financial reporting framework as necessary

   c. Consult with other professionals, specialists, or regulators as necessary

   d. Perform research or other procedures as appropriate to identify and consider existing creditable precedents or analogies

   e. Except as noted in item 5, request permission from the entity's management to consult with the continuing accountant and request the entity's management to authorize the continuing accountant to respond fully to the reporting accountant's inquiries

   f. Except as noted in item 5, consult with the continuing accountant to determine the available facts relevant to forming a conclusion

5. Consultation with the continuing accountant as described above is not required when the reporting accountant is engaged to issue a written report or provide oral advice on the application of the requirements of an applicable financial reporting framework to a specific transaction and

is engaged to provide accounting and reporting advice to the entity on a recurring basis and:

a. Does not believe a second opinion is being requested

b. Has full access to management, and

c. Believes that the relevant information has been obtained in order to provide advice regarding the application of the requirements of an applicable financial reporting framework to that entity's specific transaction.

PLANNING AID REMINDER: The reporting accountant should document its reasons for not consulting with the continuing accountant.

---

6. The written report should be addressed to the requesting entity such as management or those charged with governance and should include:

a. A brief description of the nature of the engagement and a statement that the engagement was performed in accordance with AU-C 915

b. Identification of the specific entity, a description of the specific transaction, and a statement of the relevant facts, circumstances, and assumptions and the source of such information

c. A statement describing the appropriate application of the requirements of an applicable financial reporting framework (including the country of origin) to the specific transaction or type of report that may be issued on the entity's financial statements and a description of the reasons for the accountant's conclusion if appropriate

d. A statement that the preparers of the financial statements are responsible for the proper accounting treatment and should consult with their continuing accountant

e. A statement that differences in the facts, circumstances, or assumptions presented may change the report

f. A separate paragraph at the end of the report including a statement indicating that the report is intended solely for the information and use of the specified parties, identification of the specified parties to whom use is restricted, and a statement that the report is not intended to be and should not be used by anyone other than the specified parties.

g. If applicable, an indication that the reporting accountant is not independent. The reporting accountant has the discretion as to whether or not to disclose the reasons for his or her lack of independence. However, if any reason for a lack of independence is disclosed, all such reasons must be disclosed.

Analysis and Application of Procedures

Engagement Planning and Performance

A continuing accountant's responsibilities to respond to the inquiries of a reporting accountant are the same as a predecessor auditor's responsibilities to respond to inquiries of a successor auditor as addressed in AU-C 210, *Terms of Engagement*. The continuing accountant may be able to provide the reporting accountant with information related to the form and substance of the specific transaction that is otherwise unavailable to the reporting accountant such as the following:

- How management has applied the requirements of an applicable financial reporting framework to similar transactions

- Whether management disputes the method of accounting recommended by the continuing accountant

- The continuing accountant's conclusion on the application of the requirements of an applicable financial reporting framework to the specific transaction or the type of opinion that may be rendered on the entity's financial statements.

Engagement of the reporting accountant on a recurring basis may involve financial reporting advisory services or the effective outsourcing of controllership or other financial reporting functions that may allow the accountant to have complete access to management. When the reporting accountant is determining whether consultation with the continuing accountant is necessary, he or she may consider:

- The nature of the engagement

- Whether full knowledge of the form and substance of the transaction has been obtained

- How management has applied the requirements of the applicable financial reporting framework to similar transactions in the past

- Whether this method of accounting has been discussed with the continuing accountant.

Reporting

An example from AU-C 915 of an accountant's report on the application of the requirements of accounting principles to a specific transaction is presented in Exhibit AU-C 915-1. The restriction of use on the written report is not intended to preclude distribution of the report to the continuing accountant.

ENGAGEMENT STRATEGY: AU-C 915 notes that the reporting standards apply only to written reports but that accountants may find this guidance useful in providing oral advice.

Practitioner's Aids

Exhibit AU-C 915-1 is an example based on the reporting standards established by AU-C 915 of an accountant's report on the application of accounting principles to a specific transaction.

EXHIBIT AU-C 915-1—ACCOUNTANT'S REPORT ON THE APPLICATION OF ACCOUNTING PRINCIPLES

[*Introduction*]

We have been engaged to report on the appropriate application of accounting principles generally accepted in the United States of America to the specific transaction described below. This report is being issued to ABC Company for assistance in evaluating accounting principles for the described specific transaction. Our engagement has been conducted in accordance with Statement on Auditing Standards No. 122, section 915 *Reports on Application of Requirements of an Applicable Financial Reporting Framework.*

[*Description of Transaction*]

The facts, circumstances, and assumptions relevant to the specific transaction as provided to us by the management of ABC Company are as follows: [*describe the transaction*]

[*Appropriate Accounting Principles*]

[*Discuss accounting principles generally accepted in the United States of America and how they apply to the described transaction*]

[*Concluding Comments*]

The ultimate responsibility for the decision on the appropriate application of accounting principles generally accepted in the United States of America for an actual transaction rests with the preparers of financial statements, who should consult with their continuing accountants. Our conclusion on the appropriate application of the requirements of accounting principles generally accepted in the United States of America for the described specific transaction is based solely on the facts provided to us as described above; should these facts and circumstances differ, our conclusion may change.

[*Restricted Use*]

This report is intended solely for the information and use of those charged with governance and management of ABC Company and is not intended to be and should not be used by anyone other than these specified parties.

SECTION 920

LETTERS FOR UNDERWRITERS AND CERTAIN OTHER REQUESTING PARTIES

Authoritative Pronouncements

SAS-122 — Statements on Auditing Standards: Clarification and Recodification

Overview

AU-C 920 provides guidance to auditors in performing engagements to provide (1) letters to requesting parties in conjunction with a nonissuer entity's financial statements included in registration statements filed with the Securities and Exchange Commission (SEC) under the Securities Act of 1933 (the 1933 Act) and (2) letters to a requesting party in conjunction with other securities offerings. AU-C 920 assists the auditor in ensuring a letter with the appropriate form and content is issued to the requesting parties.

PLANNING AID REMINDER: While auditors are often requested to issue comfort letters to requesting parties, generally accepted auditing standards do not require the auditor to accept these engagements.

As part of the registration of securities under the 1933 Act, underwriters of the securities often ask an accountant to provide them with a comfort letter. The comfort letter is not a requirement of the 1933 Act and is not included in the registration statement. However, underwriters request it to assist them in discharging their duty of reasonable investigation and to help establish their affirmative defense under Section 11 of the 1933 Act (often referred to as "Section 11 investigation" or "due diligence"). Therefore, obtaining the accountant's comfort letter is one of many activities that underwriters undertake to respond to the liability imposed on them under Section 11 of the 1933 Act.

A comfort letter may cover subjects such as:

- The auditor's independence
- Whether the form of the audited financial statements included in the securities offering complies in all material respects with the applicable accounting requirements of the 1933 Act and the related rules and regulations adopted by the SEC
- Unaudited financial statements, condensed interim financial information, capsule financial information, pro forma financial information, financial forecasts, management's discussion and analysis, and changes in selected financial statement items during a period subsequent to the date and period of the latest financial statements included in the securities offering

- Tables, statistics, and other financial information included in the securities offering

- Negative assurance about whether the form of certain nonfinancial statement information included in the securities offering complies in all material respects with Regulation S-K.

AU-C 920 states that, in addition to underwriters, the auditor may also provide comfort letters to other requesting parties listed below that are conducting a review process substantially consistent with the due diligence process performed if the securities offering were being registered pursuant to the 1933 Act:

- To a selling shareholder, sales agent, or other party with a statutory due diligence defense under Section 11 of the 1933 Act

- To a broker-dealer or other financial intermediary in connection with the following types of securities offerings:

  — For foreign offerings (e.g., Regulation S, Eurodollar, and other offshore offerings)

  — For transactions that are exempt from the registration requirements of Section 5 of the 1933 Act, including those pursuant to Regulation A, Regulation D, and Rule 144A

  — For offerings of securities issued or backed by governmental, municipal, banking, tax-exempt, or other entities that are exempt from registration under the 1933 Act

- To a buyer or a seller, or both, in connection with acquisition transactions involving an exchange of stock (e.g., Form S-4 or merger proxy situation)

OBSERVATION: AU-C 920 does not cover an auditor's report on a preliminary investigation in connection with a proposed transaction such as a merger or acquisition. The guidance in AT 201 may apply to such engagements.

Definitions

Capsule financial information	Unaudited summarized interim information for periods subsequent to the periods covered by the audited financial statements or unaudited condensed interim financial information included in the securities offering. This information is presented in narrative or tabular form and is often provided for the most recent interim period and for the corresponding period of the prior year.
Change period	The period for which the auditor gives negative assurance ordinarily beginning immediately after the date and period of the latest financial statements included in the securities offering and ending on the cutoff date.
Closing date	The date on which the issuer or selling security holder delivers the securities to the underwriter in exchange for the proceeds of the offering.

Comfort letter	A letter issued by an auditor to requesting parties in connection with an entity's financial statements included in securities offerings.
Comparison date and comparison period	The dates and periods for which data at the cutoff date and data for the change period are to be compared.
Cutoff date	The date through which certain procedures described in the comfort letter are to relate.
Effective date	The date on which the securities offering becomes effective.
Entity	The party whose financial statements are the subject of the engagement.
Negative assurance	A statement that, based on the procedures performed, nothing has come to the auditor's attention causing the auditor to believe that specified matters do not meet specified criteria. For example, there is nothing causing the auditor to believe that material modifications should be made to the unaudited financial statements for them to be in accordance with generally accepted accounting principles.
Requesting party	One of the following specified parties requesting a comfort letter, who has negotiated an agreement with the entity: (1) an underwriter or (2) other parties conducting a review process that is or will be substantially consistent with the due diligence process performed when the securities offering is, or if the securities offering were, being registered pursuant to the 1933 Act.
Securities offerings	One of the following types of securities offerings: (1) registration of securities with the SEC under the 1933 Act; (2) foreign offerings, including Regulation S, Eurodollar, and other offshore offerings; (3) transactions that are exempt from the registration requirements of section 5 of the 1933 Act, including those pursuant to Regulation A, Regulation D, and Rule 144A; (4) offerings of securities issued or backed by governmental, municipal, banking, tax-exempt, or other entities that are exempt from registration under the 1933 Act; or (5) acquisition transactions in which there is an exchange of stock.
Underwriter	A person who has purchased from or offers or sells for an issuer or a person directly or indirectly controlling, in common control with, or controlled by the issuer in connection with the distribution of any security, or who directly or indirectly participates in any such undertaking or the underwriting of any such undertaking. This does not include a person whose interest is limited to a commission from an underwriter or dealer not in excess of the usual and customary distributors' or sellers' commission. For the purposes of AU-C 920, underwriter describes the lead underwriter who negotiates the underwriting or purchase agreement for a group of underwriters whose composition is not determined until shortly before a securities offering becomes effective.

Requirements

The auditor is presumptively required to perform the following procedures with respect to letters for underwriters and certain other requesting parties:

Engagement Acceptance

1. Determine whether to accept the engagement. The auditor is not required to accept an engagement to issue a comfort letter.

2. Only provide a comfort letter in connection with financial statements included in securities offerings to the following requesting parties: (1) underwriters or (2) other parties meeting the definition of a requesting party.

3. Request that the requesting party provide either:

   a. A written opinion from external legal counsel that the requesting party has a statutory due diligence defense under Section 11 of the 1933 Act, or

   b. A representation letter addressed to the auditor and signed by the requesting party that contains the statement "The review process applied to the information relating to the issuer, is, or will be, substantially consistent with the due diligence process that we would perform if this securities offering were being registered pursuant to the Securities Act of 1933. We are knowledgeable with respect to the due diligence process."

4. If a requesting party other than an underwriter requests a comfort letter but does not provide a legal opinion or representation letter, the auditor should not provide negative assurance on the financial statements as a whole, or on any specified elements, accounts, or items of the financial statements and should include the following statements in the comfort letter:

   a. It should be understood that we have no responsibility for establishing and did not establish the scope and nature of the procedures enumerated in the preceding paragraphs; rather, the procedures enumerated therein are those that the requesting party asked us to perform. Accordingly, we make no representations regarding questions of legal interpretation or regarding the sufficiency for your purposes of the procedures enumerated in the preceding paragraphs; also, such procedures would not necessarily reveal any material misstatement of the amounts or percentages previously listed as set forth in the offering circular. Further, we have addressed ourselves solely to the foregoing data and make no representations regarding the adequacy of disclosures or whether any material facts have been omitted. This letter relates only to the financial statement items previously specified and does not extend to any financial statement of the company taken as a whole.

   b. The foregoing procedures do not constitute an audit conducted in accordance with generally accepted auditing standards. Had we performed additional procedures or had we conducted an audit or a review of the company's [*give dates of any interim financial statements*] consolidated financial statements in accordance with auditing standards generally accepted in the United States of America, other matters might have come to our attention that would have been reported to you.

   c. These procedures should not be taken to supplant any additional inquiries or procedures that you would undertake in your consideration of the proposed offering.

    d. This letter is solely for your information and to assist you in your inquiries in connection with the offering of the securities covered by the offering circular. It is not to be used, circulated, quoted, or otherwise referred to for any other purpose, including but not limited to the registration, purchase, or sale of securities, nor is it to be filed with or referred to in whole or in part in the offering document or any other document, except that reference may be made to it in any list of closing documents pertaining to the offering of the securities covered by the offering document.

    e. We have no responsibility to update this letter for events and circumstances occurring after [*cutoff date*].

5. A comfort letter should not be provided to any party other than a requesting party as defined in AU-C 920.

6. When issuing a letter in accordance with AU-C 920, the auditor should not issue any additional letters or reports to a requesting party in connection with the securities offering he or she is commenting on if commenting on those items is otherwise precluded by AU-C 920.

Agreeing Upon the Scope of Services

7. Obtain an understanding of the specific matters to be addressed in the comfort letter.

8. Ask to meet with the requesting party and the entity to discuss the procedures to be followed in connection with a comfort letter and clearly state that any assurance regarding the sufficiency of procedures for the requesting party's purposes cannot be provided.

9. The auditor should provide a draft of the form of the letter he or she expects to furnish that covers all matters and uses exactly the same terms that will be used in the final letter, with the understanding that the comments in the final letter cannot be determined until the procedures underlying it have been performed. Identify the draft letter as a draft to avoid giving the impression that the described procedures have already been performed.

10. In the draft and final comfort letter, clearly describe the procedures the auditor followed. Do not state or imply that the procedures being carried out are those that the auditor considers necessary in order to avoid misunderstandings about the responsibility for the sufficiency of the procedures for the requesting party's purposes.

11. If the auditor is unable to discuss his or her planned procedures with the underwriter, describe in the draft letter those procedures specified in the draft underwriting agreement that the auditor is willing to perform.

12. When the comfort letter relates to group financial statements, the auditor of the group financial statements should read the comfort letters of the component auditors reporting on significant components. State in the comfort letter that (a) reading the component auditors' letters was one of the procedures followed and (b) the other procedures performed by the auditor of the group financial statements relate solely to entities he or she audited and to the group financial statements.

13. AU-C 920 requirements apply to each auditor from whom a comfort letter is requested.

14. In competitive bidding situations where the requesting party's legal counsel acts as the requesting party's representative prior to opening and acceptance of the bid, carry out the discussions and other communications required by AU-C 920 with the legal counsel until the requesting party is selected. In

these situations, do not agree to provide a comfort letter addressed to the client, legal counsel, or a nonspecific addressee such as "any or all underwriters to be selected." If the auditor agrees to provide a draft comfort letter, it should include a legend describing the letter's purpose and limitations.

Comfort Letter Format and Contents

Date

15. The letter should state that the inquiries and other procedures described in the letter did not cover the period from the cut-off date to the date of the letter.

16. If an additional letter, dated at or shortly before the closing date, is requested, carry out the specified procedures and inquiries as of the cut-off date for each letter. The subsequent letter should only relate to information in the most recently amended securities offering.

Addressee

17. Address the letter to the requesting party, or the requesting party and the entity, and do not provide the letter to any other parties.

Introductory paragraph

18. Include an introductory paragraph in the letter identifying the financial statements and the securities offering.

Auditor's reports

19. The comfort letter should not repeat the report on the audited financial statements included in the securities offering but it should reference this report.

20. If the auditor's report on the audited financial statements included in the securities offering contains an emphasis-of-matter or other-matter paragraph, refer to that fact and discuss the subject matter of that paragraph in the comfort letter. In situations where the SEC accepts a modified opinion on historical financial statements, refer to the modification and discuss its subject matter in the comfort letter's opening paragraph.

21. Do not provide negative assurance about the auditor's report or audited financial statements reported on in the securities offering by other auditors.

22. If the comfort letter's introductory paragraph refers to reports the auditor previously issued other than the report on the audited financial statements included in the securities offering, do not repeat the reports in the comfort letter or otherwise imply that the auditor is reporting as of the date of the comfort letter or assuming responsibility for the sufficiency of the procedures for the underwriter's purposes.

23. Do not mention in a comfort letter reports issued in accordance with AU-C 265 or any restricted use reports issued to a client in connection with procedures performed on the client's internal control over financial reporting in accordance with AT 501.

24. Do not refer to or attach to the comfort letter any restricted use report. An example of a restricted use report is a report on agreed upon procedures.

Representations

25. Refer to the requesting party's representations in the comfort letter when the representation letter has been provided.

Independence

26. State in the comfort letter that the auditor is independent with respect to the entity or state the date through which the auditor was independent and identify the applicable independence rules.

Compliance with SEC requirements

27. If the auditor is requested to express an opinion on whether the form of the financial statements covered by the auditor's report comply in all material respects with the pertinent accounting requirements adopted by the SEC, state that such compliance is with the applicable accounting requirements of the 1933 Act and the related rules and regulations adopted by the SEC.

28. If financial statements are incorporated in a 1933 Act registration statement by referring to filings under the Securities Exchange Act of 1934 (the 1934 Act), the auditor may refer to whether the form of the audited financial statements included in the registration statement comply in all material respects with the applicable accounting requirements of the 1934 Act and the related rules and regulations adopted by the SEC. However, the auditor should not refer to compliance with the 1934 Act provisions regarding internal control over financial reporting.

29. If the auditor has been asked to include an opinion in the comfort letter on whether the financial statements covered by the auditor's report comply as to form with the pertinent accounting requirements of the SEC, disclose any existing material departures in the comfort letter.

30. The auditor should only express an opinion about the compliance as to form with requirements under the SEC's adopted rules and regulations for financial statements he or she has audited. If financial statements or financial statement schedules have not been audited, the auditor is limited to providing negative assurance regarding compliance as to form.

31. Do not comment in a comfort letter on compliance as to form of MD&A with the SEC's adopted rules and regulations.

Comments on information other than audited financial statements

32. When commenting on information other than audited financial statements in a comfort letter, describe the procedures performed by the auditor, describe the criteria specified by the requesting party, and state that procedures performed with respect to interim periods may not disclose matters of significance regarding matters about which negative assurance is requested.

33. In the comfort letter, do not:

    a. State or imply that the auditor determined that the applied procedures are necessary or sufficient for the requesting party's purposes

    b. Use terms with uncertain meanings such as general review, limited review, reconcile, check, or test in describing the work unless the procedures encompassed by these terms are described in the comfort letter

    c. Make a statement that nothing else has come to the auditor's attention that would be of interest to the requesting party as a result of carrying out the specified procedures.

34. If the report on the audited financial statements in the securities offering is a modified report, consider the effect on providing negative assurance in the comfort letter regarding subsequent interim financial information included in the securities offering or regarding an absence of specified subsequent changes and follow the procedures describe in requirement 20 (above).

35. Obtain an understanding of a client's internal control over financial reporting for both annual and interim periods when commenting in a comfort

letter on (a) unaudited interim or condensed interim financial information; (b) capsule financial information; (c) a financial forecast when historical financial statements provide a basis for one or more significant assumptions for the forecast; or (d) changes in selected financial statements items (e.g., capital stock, long-term debt).

36. Provide negative assurance on unaudited interim financial information included in the securities offering only if the auditor has reviewed the interim financial information in accordance with AU-C 930. If the auditor has not conducted a review in accordance with AU-C 930, he or she is limited to reporting procedures performed and findings obtained. Negative assurance provided should be about whether:

    a. Any material modifications should be made to the unaudited interim financial information for it to be in accordance with the applicable financial reporting framework, and

    b. The form of the unaudited interim financial information complies in all material respects with the applicable accounting requirements of the 1933 Act and the related rules and regulations adopted by the SEC, if applicable.

37. If the comfort letter states that the auditor has issued a review report, attach the review report to the letter unless the review report is already included in the securities offering.

38. The letter should specifically identify any unaudited interim financial information and should state that the auditor has not audited the interim financial information in accordance with generally accepted auditing standards and does not express an opinion concerning such information.

39. When the requesting party requests that the auditor provide negative assurance on the unaudited interim financial information or information extracted therefrom, for a monthly period ending after the latest financial statements included in the securities offering, requirements 36–38 (above) apply and a copy of the unaudited interim financial information should be attached to the comfort letter.

40. Only provide negative assurance about whether selected capsule financial information is in accordance with the applicable financial reporting framework if (a) the auditor has reviewed the financial statements underlying the capsule financial information in accordance with AU-C 930, and (b) the selected capsule financial information is in accordance with minimal disclosure requirements of the applicable financial reporting framework. If these conditions are not met, the auditor is limited to reporting procedures performed and findings obtained.

41. Only provide negative assurance on selected capsule financial information regarding whether the dollar amounts were determined on a basis substantially consistent with that of the corresponding amounts in the audited financial statements if the auditor has reviewed the financial statements underlying the capsule financial information in accordance with AU 930. Otherwise, the auditor is limited to reporting procedures performed and findings obtained.

42. The auditor should not comment in a comfort letter on pro forma financial information unless he or she has an appropriate level of knowledge of the entity's accounting and financial reporting practices.

43. Only provide negative assurance in a comfort letter on pro forma financial information, including negative assurance on the application of pro forma adjustments to historical amounts, the compilation of pro forma financial information, or whether the form of the pro forma financial information

complies in all material respects with the applicable accounting requirements of Rule 11-02 of Regulation S-X, if the auditor has obtained the required knowledge of the entity's accounting and financial reporting practices and has performed:

a. An audit of the annual financial statements, or

b. A review in accordance with AU-C 930 of the interim financial statements of the entity to which the pro forma adjustments were applied.

If these conditions are not met, the auditor is limited to reporting procedures performed and findings obtained.

44. When performing procedures agreed to with the requesting party on a financial forecast and commenting on them in a comfort letter:

a. Obtain an understanding of the entity's internal control over financial reporting for both annual and interim periods

b. Perform procedures required by AT 301, paragraph 69, for reporting on compilation of a forecast

c. Issue a report on the compilation of prospective financial information in accordance with AT 301 paragraphs 18–19 and attach that report to the comfort letter, and

d. Perform additional procedures as requested by the underwriter (or other requesting party) and report on the findings in the comfort letter.

45. Do not provide negative assurance on the results of procedures performed on a financial forecast.

46. The auditor should not provide negative assurance regarding compliance of the forecast with Rule 11-03 of Regulation S-X unless he or she has performed an examination of the forecast in accordance with AT 301.

47. A comfort letter should not be issued if the forecast is included in the securities offering unless the forecast is accompanied by an indication that the auditor has not examined the forecast and, therefore, does not express an opinion on it.

48. Base comments regarding subsequent changes in specified financial statement items only on the limited procedures performed with respect to the change period as determined by the requesting party.

49. Provide negative assurance in the comfort letter regarding subsequent changes in specified financial statement items only as of a date less than 135 days from the end of the most recent period for which the auditor has performed an audit or review.

50. If the requesting party requests negative assurance regarding subsequent changes in specified financial statement items as of a later date, then the auditor is limited to reporting procedures performed and findings obtained.

51. Subsequent changes should not be characterized using ambiguous terms (e.g., "adverse"). The auditor should note in the comfort letter if there has been a change in the application of the requirements of the applicable financial reporting framework.

52. The auditor should only comment on the occurrence of changes in specified financial statement items that are not included in the securities offering. If the auditor is aware of a change, increase, or decrease that has occurred during the change period and the amount of the change, increase, or decrease is included in the securities offering, he or she should include the phrase "except for changes, increases, or decreases that the securities offering discloses have occurred or may occur" in the comfort letter. This phrase is not needed when no changes, increases, or decreases in the specified financial statement items are disclosed in the securities offering.

53. Identify in the draft and final form of the comfort letter the dates and periods for which data at the cut-off date and for the change period are to be compared, regardless of specification in the underwriting agreement.

54. If the requesting party requests the use of change periods other than beginning immediately after the date of the latest balance sheet and the latest period presented in the securities offering and ending on the cutoff date, explain the implications of using an earlier date to the requesting party. If the requesting party still desires the use of such change periods, the auditor is permitted to use the periods requested.

Comments on tables, statistics, and other financial information

55. Do not comment in a comfort letter on tables, statistics, and other financial information, unless that information is expressed in dollars or percentages and is derived from amounts that have been obtained from accounting records subject to internal control over financial reporting, or information that has been derived directly from such accounting records by analysis or computation.

56. Do not comment in a comfort letter on quantitative information that has been obtained from an accounting record unless the information is subject to the same controls over financial reporting as the dollar amounts.

57. The auditor should not comment on tables, statistics, and other financial information relating to an unaudited period unless he or she has performed an audit of the client's financial statements for a period including or immediately prior to the unaudited period or completed an audit for a later period, or otherwise obtained knowledge of the client's internal control over financial reporting.

58. The auditor should not use the term *presents fairly* in comments concerning tables, statistics, and other financial information and should not comment on information subject to legal interpretation, nonfinancial data presented in MD&A unless the auditor has examined or reviewed the MD&A in accordance with AT 701, or on other matters solely because he or she is capable of reading, counting, measuring, or performing other applicable functions.

59. Comments in the comfort letter about tables, statistics, and other financial information included in the securities offering should clearly identify the specific information commented on, include a description of the procedures performed and the findings, expressed in terms of agreement between items compared.

60. The auditor should only comment on the acceptability of allocation methods used in deriving the figures commented on to the extent to which the allocation is made in or can be directly derived by analysis or computation from the client's accounting records. Such comments should clarify that such allocations are arbitrary to a substantial extent, the allocation method used is not the only acceptable one, and other acceptable allocation methods might produce significantly different results.

61. The letter should state that the auditor makes no representations regarding any matter of legal interpretation, the completeness or adequacy of disclosure, and the adequacy of the procedures followed, and that such procedures would not necessarily disclose material misstatements or omissions in the information to which the comments relate.

Compliance as to form with Regulation S-K

62. Do not provide negative assurance about whether certain financial information in registration statements that is included because of specific requirements of regulation S-K is in conformity with the Regulation's disclosure requirements unless the information is derived directly or by analysis or

computation from the accounting records subject to internal control over financial reporting and this information is capable of evaluation against reasonable criteria that have been established by the SEC.

63. Do not express an opinion on conformity with Regulation S-K's disclosure requirements.

Concluding paragraph

64. The comfort letter should include a concluding paragraph restricting the use of the comfort letter for the information of the addressees and to assist the requesting parties in connection with the securities offering.

Disclosure of subsequently discovered matters

65. Inform the entity when matters are discovered that require mention in the final comfort letter that were not mentioned in the draft letter provided to the requesting party. If the entity decides that disclosure will not be made in the securities offering, inform the entity that the matters will be mentioned in the comfort letter and recommend that the requesting party be informed promptly.

Analysis and Application of Procedures

Engagement Acceptance

Exhibit AU-C 920-1 illustrates a representation letter from requesting parties. A letter from an attorney indicating that a party "may" be deemed to be an underwriter or has liability substantially equivalent to that of an underwriter under the securities laws would not meet the AU-C 920 requirement to be considered a "requesting party."

PLANNING AID REMINDER: Although the auditor is not permitted to provide a comfort letter to any party other than a requesting party, he or she may follow the guidance in AT 201 to provide a report on agreed-upon procedures to such parties.

Agreeing Upon the Scope of Services

While comfort letters are not required under the 1933 Act, receipt of a comfort letter from the auditor is a common condition of the underwriting agreement. In requiring comfort letters from auditors, underwriters are seeking assistance in performing a reasonable investigation of data (unaudited financial information and other data) on the authority of an expert. Unfortunately, what constitutes a reasonable investigation of unaudited data sufficient to satisfy an underwriter's purpose has never been authoritatively established. Therefore, it is only the underwriter who can determine the amount of work sufficient to satisfy his or her due diligence requirement. Accordingly, the auditor carries out procedures that are within his or her professional expertise that will aid underwriters in discharging their responsibility for exercising due diligence, but cannot furnish any assurance on whether those procedures are sufficient for the underwriter's purpose, which paragraph 4 of the sample comfort letter in Exhibit AU-C 920-2 illustrates.

PLANNING AID REMINDER: If the requesting party refuses to meet together with the entity, the auditor may consider the implications in determining whether to accept the engagement.

Acceptance of the draft comfort letter by the requesting party indicates to the auditor that the requesting party considers the procedures described in the letter to be sufficient for its purposes. However, the auditor may wish to further emphasize the point that the requesting party and not the auditor is responsible for the sufficiency of the comfort procedures by including a legend or a concluding paragraph on the draft letter to the underwriter to address its functions and limitations. AU-C 920 contains the following example of such a paragraph:

> This draft is furnished solely for the purpose of indicating the form of letter that we would expect to be able to furnish [*name of requesting party*] in response to their request, the matters expected to be covered in the letter, and the nature of the procedures that we would expect to carry out with respect to such matters. Based on our discussions with [*name of requesting party*], it is our understanding that the procedures outlined in this draft letter are those they wish us to follow. Unless [*name of requesting party*] informs us otherwise, we shall assume that there are no additional procedures they wish us to follow. The text of the letter itself will depend, of course, on the results of the procedures, which we would not expect to complete until shortly before the letter is given and in no event before the cutoff date indicated therein.

In the absence of any discussions with the requesting party, the second sentence of the above paragraph should be revised as follows:

> In the absence of any discussions with [*name of requesting party*], we have set out in this draft letter those procedures referred to in the draft underwriting agreement (of which we have been furnished a copy) that we are willing to follow.

A shelf registration statement enables an entity to register securities under the 1933 Act and then issue these securities over a period of time. At the effective date of the registration statement, an underwriter or lead underwriter may not have been named, although the auditor may have been asked to issue a comfort letter. In these situations, the auditor may issue a draft comfort letter to the entity or the legal counsel representing the underwriter group based on the actual procedures the auditor has performed and include a legend in the draft comfort letter addressing the letter's functions and limitations. The following is an example of such a paragraph as illustrated in AU-C 920:

> This draft describes the procedures that we have performed and represents a letter we would be prepared to sign if the managing underwriter had been chosen and requested such a letter. The text of the final letter will depend, of course, on whether the managing underwriter who is selected requests that these and other procedures be performed to meet his or her needs and whether the managing underwriter requests that any of the procedures be updated to the date of issuance of the signed letter.

A signed comfort letter may be issued to the underwriter selected for the portion of the issue then being offered when the underwriting agreement for an offering is signed and on each closing date.

Comfort Letter Format and Contents

AU-C 920 provides a variety of sample comfort letters, one of which represents a typical comfort letter and is presented in Exhibit AU-C 920-2.

Date

Ordinarily, the comfort letter is dated on or shortly after the underwriting agreement is signed. Usually the underwriting agreement specifies the date to which the procedures described in the letter are to relate. This date, commonly referred to as the cutoff date, is customarily within five business days before the effective date of the registration statement.

PLANNING AID REMINDER: The auditor should consider whether the period between the cut-off date and the date of the letter provides the auditor with sufficient time to perform the procedures and prepare the letter when deciding whether to accept the engagement.

Auditor's reports

The requesting party may request that the auditor put the report on the audited financial statements included in the registration statement in the comfort letter, but the auditor is not permitted to do this because of the significance of the date of the auditor's report. The comfort letter's opening paragraph may refer to matters addressed in emphasis-of-matter or other-matter paragraphs in the auditor's report that do not affect the opinion on the basic financial statements, such as interim financial information accompanying or included in the notes to the audited financial statements or required supplementary information described in AU-C 730.

A requesting party may request that the auditor comment in the comfort letter on unaudited interim financial information required by item 302(a) of Regulation S-K or required supplementary information. AU-C 930 and AU-C 730 provide guidance for these respective items regarding when the auditor is required to modify the auditor's report on the audited financial statements to refer to such information. If the auditor's report in the registration statement is modified, it is generally referred to in the comfort letter's opening paragraph. If the requesting party requests that the auditor perform procedures with regard to such information in addition to those performed for the review or audit as per AU-C 930 and AU-C 730, the auditor may do so and report the findings.

The auditor may have previously reported on any of the following:

- Summarized financial statements derived from audited financial statements, in accordance with AU-C 810 (*Engagements to Report on Summary Financial Statements*)

- Interim financial information, in accordance with AU-C 930 (*Interim Financial Information*)

- Pro forma financial information, in accordance with AT 401 (*Reporting on Pro Forma Financial Information*)

- A financial forecast, in accordance with AT 301 (*Financial Forecasts and Projections*)

- Management's discussion and analysis (MD&A), in accordance with AT 701 (*Management's Discussion and Analysis*)

In these situations, in the introductory paragraph of the comfort letter the accountant may refer to the previously issued reports and, if the reports are not included in the securities offering, they may be attached to the comfort letter.

Independence

In conjunction with SEC filings, the underwriting agreement customarily requests that the auditor represent in the comfort letter that he or she is independent. A simple statement, such as the following, suffices:

> We are independent certified public accountants with respect to [*name of client*], within the meaning of the 1933 Act and the applicable rules and regulations thereunder adopted by the SEC.

In a non-SEC filing, a statement such as the following suffices:

> We are independent certified public accountants with respect to [*name of client*], under Rule 101 of the AICPA's Code of Professional Conduct and its interpretations and rulings.

Auditors for previously nonaffiliated companies recently acquired by the registrant are not required to have been independent with respect to the company whose shares are being registered. In this situation, the statement regarding independence should be modified, as follows:

> As of [*date of the auditor's most recent report on the financial statements of the client*] and during the period covered by the financial statements on which we reported, we were independent certified public accountants with respect to [*name of client*] under Rule 101 of the AICPA's Code of Professional Conduct and its interpretations and rulings.

Compliance with SEC requirements

Usually, the underwriting agreement requests that the auditor comment on whether the financial statements comply with SEC requirements. The auditor may do so in the comfort letter by adding a paragraph like the following:

> In our opinion [*include phrase* "except as disclosed in the registration statement," *if applicable*], the [*identify the financial statements and financial statement schedules*] audited by us and included in the registration statement comply as to form in all material respects with the applicable accounting requirements of the 1933 Act and the related rules and regulations adopted by the SEC.

If there is a material departure from the pertinent published SEC requirements, the auditor should disclose such departure in the comfort letter. Normally, representatives of the SEC will have agreed to such a departure. The following is an example of wording to be used in the comfort letter when the SEC has agreed to a departure from its published accounting requirements:

> In our opinion [*include phrase* "except as disclosed in the registration statement," *if applicable*], the consolidated financial statements and financial statement schedules audited by us and included [incorporated by reference] in the registration statement comply as to form in all material respects with the applicable accounting requirements of the Act and the related rules and

regulations adopted by the SEC; however, as agreed to by representatives of the SEC, separate financial statements and financial statement schedules of ABC Company (an equity investee) as required by rule 3-09 of Regulation S-X have been omitted.

ENGAGEMENT STRATEGY: While the auditor should not use the comfort letter to comment on compliance of MD&A's form with rules and regulations adopted by the SEC, he or she may accept an engagement to examine or review MD&A in accordance with AT 701.

Comments on information other than audited financial statements

The auditor's comfort letter often refers to information other than audited financial statements such as

- Unaudited interim financial information
- Capsule financial information
- Pro forma financial information
- Financial forecasts
- Subsequent changes in specified financial statement items.

The comfort letter should refer to the agreed-upon procedures when commenting on such information with the following exception: when the auditor has been asked to provide negative assurance on interim or capsule financial information, he or she does not need to specify the procedures involved in an AU-C 930 review.

While the auditor is responsible for obtaining a sufficient understanding of internal control over financial reporting for annual and interim periods when commenting in a comfort letter on information described in requirement 35 (above), he or she may have already obtained this understanding through the audit of the entity's financial statements.

The requirements in AU-C 920 related to unaudited condensed interim financial information also apply to complete financial statements and the interim statements may be for a 12-month period ending on a date other than the entity's normal year-end. Exhibit AU-C 920-2 illustrates how the auditor may appropriately comment on unaudited condensed interim financial information when he or she has conducted a review of the information in accordance with AU-C 930. If a review of interim financial information was conducted in accordance with AU-C 930, the auditor may state in the comfort letter that he or she:

1. Performed the procedures identified in AU-C 930 or
2. Issued a report on the review of the interim financial information.

PLANNING AID REMINDER: The auditor may have sufficient knowledge of the entity's accounting and financial reporting practices to comment on pro forma financial information from his or her audit or review of the entity's historical financial statements for the most recent annual or interim period for which the pro forma financial information is presented.

When the auditor performs a compilation on a financial forecast for an entity whose securities are subject to SEC regulation, the SEC's views regarding independence are relevant and independence may be considered impaired when services include preparation or assembly of financial forecasts.

The underwriter often asks the auditor to comment in the comfort letter on subsequent changes in certain financial statement items during the change period. These comments usually relate to (1) changes in capital stock, (2) increases in long-term debt, (3) decreases in net current assets, (4) decreases in stockholders' equity, (5) decreases in net sales, and (6) decreases in total and per-share amounts of income before continuing operations and of net income.

PLANNING AID REMINDER: The auditor should base his or her comments on subsequent changes solely on the limited procedures performed, which may include inquiries of company officials and the reading of minutes. (Paragraph 6 of the sample comfort letter in Exhibit AU-C 920-2 illustrates this requirement.)

When the auditor is providing negative assurance regarding the absence of subsequent changes, he or she may express this negative assurance as illustrated in paragraphs 5b and 6 of the sample comfort letter provided in Exhibit AU-C 920-2.

PLANNING AID REMINDER: In the comfort letter the accountant should use the terms "change," "increase," and "decrease" rather than "adverse change." The term "adverse change" implies that the accountant is making a judgment about the change, which might be misinterpreted by the underwriter.

When the auditor is commenting on subsequent changes, he or she is commenting on the change period as a whole; therefore, changes within the change period that offset each other would not be reported. When more than one auditor is involved in the audit of the financial statements of the entity, the auditor of the group financial statements may comment that there were not changes in consolidated financial statement items even if changes were reported by component auditors. In these situations, the auditor of the group financial statements should make appropriate modifications to the comfort letter commenting on subsequent changes. The modifications consist of an addition to paragraph 4, a substitute for the applicable part of paragraph 5, and an addition to the last sentence of paragraph 6 of the sample comfort letter at the end of this section.

4c. We have read the letter dated [*date*] of [*the other auditors*] with regard to [*the related company*].

5. Nothing came to our attention as a result of the foregoing procedures (which, so far as [*the related company*] is concerned, consisted solely of reading the letter referred to in 4c), however, that caused us to believe that . . .

6. On the basis of these inquiries and our reading of the minutes and the letter dated [*date*] of [*the other auditors*] with regard to [*the related company*], as described in 4, nothing came to our attention that caused us to believe that there was any such change, increase, or decrease, except in all instances for changes, increases, or decreases that the registration statement discloses have occurred or may occur.

Comments on tables, statistics, and other financial information

The auditor's comments in the comfort letter regarding the procedures performed and findings obtained concerning tables, statistics, and other financial information may be presented by:

- Individually describing each item of specific information commented on

- Grouping or summarizing descriptions as long as the procedures and findings are adequately described, the applicability of the descriptions to items in the securities offering is clear, and the descriptions do not imply that the auditor assumes responsibility for the adequacy of the procedures

- Presenting a matrix that lists the financial information and common procedures used and indicates the procedures applied to the specific items

- Identifying procedures performed with specified symbols and identifying items to which those procedures have been applied directly on a copy of the prospectus, which is attached to the comfort letter.

Compliance as to form with Regulation S-K

Items that generally meet the requirements for auditors to be able to provide negative assurance about whether that information is in conformity with the disclosure requirements of Regulation S-K include:

- Item 301, "Selected Financial Data"

- Item 302, "Supplementary Financial Information"

- Item 402, "Executive Compensation"

- Item 503(d), "Ratio of Earnings to Fixed Charges"

Item 305, "Quantitative and Qualitative Disclosure about Market Risk," does not meet the criteria for the auditor to provide either negative assurance on its conformity with Regulation S-K's disclosure requirements or comments on its qualitative disclosures in the comfort letter because the disclosures are not derived from accounting records subject to internal control over financial reporting. The quantitative disclosures required by Item 305 may be presented in the form of a tabular presentation, sensitivity analysis, or value-at-risk disclosures and the auditor may perform limited procedures related to tabular presentation to the extent that such information is derived from the accounting records subject to internal control over financial reporting.

PLANNING AID REMINDER: Even though the auditor cannot express an opinion on conformity with the disclosure requirements of Regulation S-K, he or she is permitted to perform procedures and report findings with respect to this information.

Concluding paragraph

Paragraph 7 of the sample comfort letter in Exhibit AU-C 920-2 illustrates appropriate wording for a concluding paragraph.

Practitioner's Aids

Exhibit AU-C 920-1 is an example of a representation letter as illustrated in AU-C 920. Exhibit AU-C 920-2 is an example of a sample comfort letter for a 1933 Act offering as illustrated in AU-C 920.

EXHIBIT AU-C 920-1—REPRESENTATION LETTER FROM REQUESTING PARTIES

[*Date*]

Dear ABC Accountants:

[*Name of requesting party*], as principal or agent, in the placement of [*identify securities*] to be issued by [*name of issuer*], will be reviewing certain information relating to [*issuer*] that will be included [*incorporated by reference*] in the document [*if appropriate, the document should be identified*], which may be delivered to investors and utilized by them as a basis for their investment decision. This review process, applied to the information relating to the issuer, is [will be] substantially consistent with the due diligence review process that an underwriter would perform if this placement of securities [*or issuance of securities in an acquisition transaction*] were being registered pursuant to the Securities Act of 1933 (the Act). We are knowledgeable with respect to the due diligence review process that would be performed if this placement of securities were being registered pursuant to the Act. We hereby request that you deliver to us a "comfort" letter concerning the financial statements of the issuer and certain statistical and other data included in the offering document. We will contact you to identify the procedures we wish you to follow and the form we wish the comfort letter to take.

Very truly yours,

[*Name of requesting party*]

EXHIBIT AU-C 920-2—SAMPLE COMFORT LETTER FOR A 1933 ACT OFFERING

June 28, 20X6

[*Addressee*]

Dear Ladies and Gentlemen:

We have audited the consolidated balance sheets of The Blank Company, Inc. (the company) and subsidiaries, which comprise the consolidated balance sheets as of December 31, 20X5 and 20X4, and the related consolidated statements of income, changes in stockholders' equity, and cash flows for each of the three years in the three-year period ended December 31, 20X5, and the related notes to the consolidated financial statements, all included in the registration statement (no. 33-00000) on Form S-1 filed by the registrant under the Securities Act of 1933 (the Act); our report with respect thereto is also included in that registration statement.[1] The registration statement, as amended on June 28, 20X6, is herein referred to as the registration statement.[2]

In connection with the registration statement:

1. We are independent certified public accountants with respect to the company within the meaning of the 1933 Act and the applicable rules and regulations thereunder adopted by the SEC.

2. In our opinion [*included the phrase* "except as disclosed in the registration statement," *if applicable*], the consolidated financial statements audited by us and included in the registration statement comply as to form in all material respects with the applicable accounting requirements of the Act and the related rules and regulations adopted by the SEC.

3. We have not audited any financial statements of the company as of any date or for any period subsequent to December 31, 20X5; although we have conducted an audit for the year ended December 31, 20X5, the purpose (and therefore the scope) of the audit was to enable us to express our opinion on the consolidated financial statements as of December 31, 20X5, and for the year then ended, but not on the financial statements for any interim period within that year. Therefore, we are unable to and do not express any opinion on the unaudited condensed consolidated balance sheet as of March 31, 20X6, and the unaudited condensed consolidated statements of income, stockholders' equity, and cash flows for the three-month periods ended March 31, 20X6 and 20X5, included in the registration statement, or on the financial position, results of operations, or cash flows as of any date or for any period subsequent to December 31, 20X5.

4. For purposes of this letter we have read the 20X6 minutes of meetings of the stockholders, the board of directors, and [include other appropriate committees, if any] of the company and its subsidiaries as set forth in the minute books at June 23, 20X6, officials of the company having advised us that the minutes of all such meetings through that date were set forth therein and having discussed with us the unapproved minutes of meetings held on [*dates*], we have carried out other procedures to

---

[1] The example includes financial statements required by SEC regulations to be included in the filing. If additional financial information is covered by the comfort letter, appropriate modifications should be made.

[2] The example assumes that the auditors have not previously reported on the interim financial information. If the accountants have previously reported on the interim financial information, they may refer to that fact in the introductory paragraph of the comfort letter as follows:

Also, we have reviewed the unaudited condensed consolidated financial statements as of March 31, 20X6 and 20X5, and for the three-month periods then ended, as indicated in our report dated May 15, 20X6, which is included (incorporated by reference) in the registration statement. The report may be attached to the comfort letter although restricted use reports should not be attached. The auditors may agree to comment in the comfort letter on whether the interim financial information complies as to form in all material respects with the applicable accounting requirements of the published rules and regulations of the SEC.

June 23, 20X6, as follows (our work did not extend to the period from June 24, 20X6, to June 28, 20X6, inclusive):

a. With respect to the three-month periods ended March 31, 20X6 and 20X5, we have:

    (i) Performed the procedures specified for a review in accordance with auditing standards generally accepted in the United States of America applicable to reviews of interim financial information, on the unaudited condensed consolidated balance sheet as of March 31, 20X6, and unaudited condensed consolidated statements of income, stockholders' equity, and cash flows for the three-month periods ended March 31, 20X6 and 20X5, included in the registration statement.

    (ii) Inquired of certain officials of the company who have responsibility for financial and accounting matters whether the unaudited condensed consolidated financial statements referred to in a(i) comply as to form in all material respects with the applicable accounting requirements of the Act and the related rules and regulations adopted by the SEC.

b. With respect to the period from April 1, 20X6, to May 31, 20X6, we have:

    (i) Read the unaudited consolidated financial statements of the company and subsidiaries for April and May of both 20X5 and 20X6 furnished us by the company, officials of the company having advised that no such financial statements as of any date or for any period subsequent to May 31, 20X6, were available. [*If applicable:* The financial information for April and May is incomplete in that it omits the statements of cash flows and other disclosures.]

    (ii) Inquired of certain officials of the company who have responsibility for financial and accounting matters whether the unaudited consolidated financial statements referred to in b(i) are stated on a basis substantially consistent with that of the audited consolidated financial statements included in the registration statement.

    The foregoing procedures do not constitute an audit conducted in accordance with generally accepted auditing standards. Also, they would not necessarily reveal matters of significance with respect to the comments in the following paragraph. Accordingly, we make no representations regarding the sufficiency of the foregoing procedures for your purposes.

5. Nothing came to our attention as a result of the foregoing procedures, however, that caused us to believe that:[3]

    a.

        (i) Any material modifications should be made to the unaudited condensed consolidated financial statements described in 4a(i), included in the registration statement, for them to be in conformity with generally accepted accounting principles.[4]

        (ii) The unaudited condensed consolidated financial statements described in 4a(i) do not comply as to form in all material respects with the applicable accounting requirements of the Act and the related rules and regulations adopted by the SEC.

    b.

        (i) At May 31, 20X6, there was any change in the capital stock, increase in long-term debt, or decrease in consolidated net current assets or stockholders' equity of the consolidated companies as compared with amounts shown in the March 31, 20X6, unaudited condensed consolidated balance sheet included in the registration statement, or

        (ii) for the period from April 1, 20X6, to May 31, 20X6, there were any decreases, as compared to the corresponding period in the preceding year, in consolidated net sales or in the total or per-share amounts of income before extraordinary items or of net income, except in all instances for changes, increases, or decreases that the registration statement discloses have occurred or may occur.

6. As mentioned in 4b, company officials have advised us that no consolidated financial statements as of any date or for any period subsequent to May 31, 20X6, are available; accordingly, the procedures carried out by us with respect to changes in financial statement items after May 31, 20X6, have, of necessity, been even more limited than those with respect to the periods referred to in 4. We have inquired of certain officials of the company who have responsibility for financial and accounting matters whether (*a*) at June 23, 20X6, there was any change in the capital stock, increase in long-term debt or any decreases in consolidated net current assets or stockholders' equity of the consolidated companies as compared with amounts shown on the March 31, 20X6, unaudited condensed consolidated balance sheet included in the registration statement or (*b*) for the period from April 1, 20X6, to June 23, 20X6, there were any decreases, as compared with the corresponding period in the preceding year, in consolidated net sales or in

---

[3] If there has been a change in accounting principle during the interim period, a reference to that change should be included therein.

[4] AU-C 930 does not require the accountants to modify the report on a review of interim financial information for a lack of consistency in the application of accounting principles provided that the interim financial information appropriately discloses such matters.

the total or per-share amounts of income before extraordinary items or of net income. On the basis of these inquiries and our reading of the minutes as described in 4, nothing came to our attention that caused us to believe that there was any such change, increase, or decrease, except in all instances for changes, increases, or decreases that the registration statement discloses have occurred or may occur.

7. This letter is solely for the information of the addressees and to assist the underwriters in conducting and documenting their investigation of the affairs of the company in connection with the offering of the securities covered by the registration statement, and it is not to be used, circulated, quoted, or otherwise referred to within or without the underwriting group for any purpose, including but not limited to the registration, purchase, or sale of securities, nor is it to be filed with or referred to in whole or in part in the registration statement or any other document, except that reference may be made to it in the underwriting agreement or in any list of closing documents pertaining to the offering of the securities covered by the registration statement.

Note to Exhibit AU-C 920-2: This letter assumes the following circumstances: The prospectus includes audited consolidated balance sheets as of December 31, 20X5 and 20X4, and audited consolidated statements of income, stockholders' equity, and cash flows for each of the three years in the period ended December 31, 20X5. The prospectus also includes an unaudited condensed consolidated balance sheet as of March 31, 20X6, and unaudited condensed consolidated statements of income, stockholders' equity, and cash flows for the three-month periods ended March 31, 20X6 and 20X5, reviewed in accordance with AU-C 930 but not previously reported on by the auditor. The cutoff date is June 23, 20X6, and the letter is dated June 28, 20X6. The effective date is June 28, 20X6. Each of the comments in the letter is in response to a requirement of the underwriting agreement. For purposes of this example, the income statement items of the current interim period are to be compared with those of the corresponding period of the preceding year.

> **PUBLIC COMPANY IMPLICATION:** Because comfort letters are associated with filings under the federal securities laws, references in Exhibit AU-C 920-2 to "independent certified public accountants" are to be changed to "independent registered public accounting firm" ; references to "generally accepted auditing standards" are to be changed to "standards of the Public Company Accounting Oversight Board (United States)"; and references to "procedures of the American Institute of Certified Public Accountants" are to be changed to "standards of the Public Company Accounting Oversight Board."

SECTION 925

FILINGS WITH THE U.S. SECURITIES AND EXCHANGE COMMISSION UNDER THE SECURITIES ACT OF 1933

Authoritative Pronouncements

SAS-122 — Statements on Auditing Standards: Clarification and Recodification

Overview

AU-C 925 provides the auditor with guidance regarding his or her responsibilities in connection with financial statements of a nonissuer included or incorporated by reference in a registration statement filed with the U.S. Securities and Exchange Commission (SEC) under the Securities Act of 1933, as amended. The auditor's objective is to perform procedures to indicate that the auditor has performed a reasonable investigation as referred to in Section 11(b)(3)(B) of the Securities Act of 1933. These procedures are performed at, or shortly before, the effective date of the registration statement.

Definitions

Auditor's consent	A statement signed by the auditor indicating that the auditor consents to the inclusion of the audit report and other references to the auditor in a registration statement filed under the Securities Act of 1933
Awareness letter	A letter signed and dated by the auditor acknowledging the auditor's awareness that the auditor's review report on unaudited interim financial information is included in a registration statement filed under the Securities Act of 1933. This letter is not part of the registration statements and is often called an acknowledgement letter.
Effective date of the registration statement	The date on which the registration statement becomes effective for purposes of evaluating the auditor's liability under Section 11 of the Securities Act of 1933

Requirements

The auditor is presumptively required to perform the following procedures related to filings with the SEC under the Securities Act of 1933.

Effective Date of the Registration Statement

1. The effective date of a registration statement is not necessarily the same as the filing date. Therefore, the auditor should request that management advise the auditor of the registration proceedings' progress through the registration statement's effective date.

Audited Financial Statements

2. If the auditor's report on audited financial statements is included in a registration statement filed with the SEC under the Securities Act of 1933,

perform the procedures described in AU-C 720 (*Other Information in Documents Containing Audited Financial Statements*) on the prospectus and pertinent portions of the registration statement, including material that is included by reference. Determine that the auditor's name is not being used in a way that indicates a greater responsibility than he or she intends.

3. If the auditor has audited the most recent period for which separate audited financial statements of the entity are included in the registration statement, then he or she should perform the following procedures at or shortly before the registration statement's effective date (these procedures are derived from AU-C 560, (*Subsequent Events and Subsequently Discovered Facts*):

    a. Perform audit procedures to identify subsequent events through a date at or near the effective date of the registration statement that require adjustment or disclosure in the financial statements. The nature and extent of audit procedures should take the auditor's risk assessment into account and should include (1) obtaining an understanding of procedures management established to identify subsequent events, (2) inquiring of management and those charged with governance (as appropriate) about whether any events occurred after the date of the financial statements that might affect the statements, (3) reading any minutes of meetings of the entity's owners, management, and those charged with governance held after the date of the financial statements and inquiring about matters discussed at any such meeting if minutes are not yet available, and (4) reading the latest of any subsequent interim financial statements of the entity.

    b. Obtain an updated written representation letter from management responsible for financial and accounting matters as of a date at or near the effective date of the registration statement and determine that the updated letter addresses whether any information has come to management's attention that would cause them to believe any previous representations should be modified or any events have occurred after the date of the most recent financial statements that would require adjustment to or disclosure in the financial statements.

4. If the auditor has audited the most recent period for which separate audited financial statements of the entity are included in the registration statement and (1) the entity has been acquired by another entity, (2) the acquirer's audited financial statements included in the registration statement reflect a period that includes the date of acquisition, and (3) the auditor is a predecessor auditor because the auditor is not the continuing auditor of the entity, then the auditor may not be able to perform the procedures in requirement 3 (above). Alternatively, the auditor should obtain, through a date at or near the registration statement's effective date:

    a. A representation letter from management of the former client stating whether any information has come to management's attention that would cause them to believe any previous representations should be modified or any events have occurred after the date of the most recent prior period financial statements reported on by the predecessor auditor that would require adjustment to or disclosure in the financial statements, and

    b. A letter from the successor auditor stating whether his or her audit revealed any matters that might, in the successor auditor's opinion, have a material effect on or require disclosure in the financial statements reported on by the predecessor auditor.

5. If a predecessor auditor audited the entity's separate financial statements for a prior period included in the registration statement but not for the most

recent period for which the entity's audited financial statements are included in the registration statement, he or she should read the financial statements of the subsequent period to be presented on a comparative basis, compare the prior period financial statements the predecessor auditor reported on with the subsequent period's financial statements to be presented on a comparative basis, and perform the procedures listed in requirement 4a and 4b (above) through a date at or near the registration statement's effective date.

6. If the auditor becomes aware of subsequently discovered facts, the auditor should not consent to the inclusion of his or her report in the registration statement until all of the procedures specified by AU-C 560, *Subsequent Events and Subsequently Discovered Facts*, have been performed. If the auditor believes the audited financial statements need to be revised and management does not revise the statements, he or she should determine whether to withhold the auditor's consent.

Unaudited Financial Statements or Unaudited Interim Financial Information

7. If the auditor concludes that unaudited interim financial information or unaudited annual financial statements included in a registration statement filed under the Securities Act of 1933 are not in conformity with the requirements of the applicable financial reporting framework, he or she should request that management revise the information or statements appropriately.

8. If management does not revise the unaudited annual financial statements or unaudited interim financial information appropriately and (1) the auditor has reported on a review of the unaudited annual financial statements or unaudited interim financial information, (2) the auditor's review report is included in the registration statement, and (3) the subsequently discovered facts would have affected the report had they been known to the auditor at the date of the report, then the auditor should follow the guidance in AU-C 560, *Subsequent Events and Subsequently Discovered Facts*.

9. If management does not revise the unaudited annual financial statements or unaudited interim financial information appropriately and (1) the auditor has not reported on a review of the unaudited annual financial statements or unaudited interim financial information or (2) the auditor's review report is not included in the registration statement, then the auditor should follow the guidance in AU-C 930 to modify the report on the audited financial statements to describe the departure from the requirements of the applicable financial reporting framework contained in the unaudited annual financial statements or unaudited interim financial information.

10. Determine whether to withhold the auditor's consent and, if applicable, the awareness letter.

Analysis and Application of Procedures

Audited Financial Statements

The auditor is responsible for performing a reasonable investigation as described in Section 11(c) of the Securities Act of 1933, and reading the entire prospectus including any documents such as Forms 10-K, 10-Q, and 8-K that are incorporated by reference in the document helps to fulfill this responsibility.

PLANNING AID REMINDER: The auditor may not need to perform the procedures described in AU-C 925 if the filing of a prospectus supplement does not create a new effective date for the auditor even if the filing creates a new effective date for other parties (e.g., the issuing entity).

If the auditor has audited the most recent period for which separate audited financial statements of the entity are included in the registration statement, then in addition to the procedures required, the auditor may consider whether it is appropriate or necessary to inquire of the entity's legal counsel concerning litigation, claims, and assessments.

OBSERVATION: When making the determination as to whether to withhold the auditor's consent, the auditor may consider the need to obtain legal advice.

An entity is only required by the SEC to include an auditor's review report on unaudited interim financial information in the registration statement if the statement states that the unaudited interim financial information has been reviewed by an independent auditor. If an auditor's review report on unaudited interim financial information is included in the registration statement, the auditor should determine that the issuer discloses the fact that an interim review report is not a report on or a part of a registration statement prepared or certified by the auditor within the meaning of Sections 7 and 11 of the Securities Act of 1933 and that the auditor's liability under Section 11 does not extend to the auditor's review report.

Securities Act of 1933

AU-C 925 states that generally an accountant's responsibility for filings under federal securities statutes is no different from the accountant's responsibility in any other reporting engagement. However, Section 11(a) of the Securities Act of 1933 imposes civil liability on an auditor who has consented to the use of the auditor's report on audited financial statements as part of a registration statement filed under the Securities Act of 1933. Management's disclosure stating that audited financial statements are included in the registration statement in reliance on the auditor's report on the audited financial statements is typically included in the "Experts" section of the registration statement. This disclosure cannot imply that the auditor prepared the financial statements or that the financial statements are not the direct representations of management. An example of this disclosure is provided in Exhibit AU-C 925-1. Section 7 of the Securities Act of 1933 requires an issuer to provide the consent of the auditor whose report on audited financial statements is included in a Securities Act of 1933 registration statement.

An accountant's report on a review of interim financial information is not a report under Section 11. Therefore the auditor does not have the same statutory responsibility for such a report as of the effective date of the registration statement. Management's disclosure that the registration statement includes the auditor's review report on unaudited interim financial information is not included in the "Experts" section of the registration statement. The disclosure may be included in the same section as disclosures on the auditor's report on the audited financial statements under a section titled "Independent Auditors" or something similar or may be included in a separate section. An example of this disclosure is provided in Exhibit AU-C 925-2. The issuer is required to file an awareness letter from an auditor if the auditor's review report on interim financial statements is included in a Securities Act of 1933 registration statement.

Shelf registration occurs when issuers register securities under the Securities Act of 1933 to be offered and sold on a delayed or continuous basis. A base prospectus is included in a shelf registration statement at the time it becomes effective, which generally relies entirely on documents incorporated by reference to make issuer-related disclosures. The base prospectus generally omits information relating to the specific amount of each security to be offered and pricing information, providing that information in a prospectus supplement filed at the time the securities are sold. Information that the issuer does not include in the base prospectus and information provided at a later date may be conveyed to investors by a posteffective amendment to the registration statement, by a prospectus supplement filed pursuant to the Securities Act of 1933 Rule 424(b), or through the incorporation by reference of the information from a report filed under the Securities Exchange Act of 1934 such as Forms 10-K or 8-K.

The effective date for the auditor in connection with a Securities Act of 1933 registration statement is the latest of the below dates:

- The date the original registration statement becomes effective

- The effective date of any posteffective amendment

- The filing date of a prospectus supplement if the supplement's filing creates a new effective date for the auditor because it has information the auditor is an expert about requiring a new auditor's consent

- The filing date of any report that includes or amends audited financial statements and is incorporated by reference into the already effective registration statement

The term "expert" is specifically defined in the Securities Act of 1933, so when an issuer refers to the auditor's role in an offering document in connection with a securities offering that is not registered under the Securities Act of 1933, the disclosure is generally in a section labeled "Independent Auditors" rather than "Experts" and there is no reference to the auditor as an expert in the document. This disclosure may be worded as follows:

INDEPENDENT AUDITORS

The financial statements of Company ABC as of December 31, 20X5 and for the year then ended, included in this offering circular, have been audited by XYZ & Co., independent auditors, as stated in their report appearing herein.

OBSERVATION: The auditor may agree to be referred to as an expert other than in a Securities Act of 1933 registration statement in situations where the term "expert" is sufficiently defined. For example, the auditor may agree to be named as an expert in an offering document in an intrastate securities offering if applicable state law sufficiently defines the term or in securities offering documents subject to the Office of Thrift Supervision's jurisdiction.

If an auditor's report is used in an offering transaction not registered under the Securities Act of 1933, the auditor does not typically have to provide written consent. However, if the auditor does provide written consent, he or she may provide a letter indicating his or her agreement to the inclusion of the auditor's report on the audited financial statements in the offering materials. This letter would typically not be included in the offering materials and may be worded as follows:

> We agree to the inclusion in the offering circular of our report, dated February 5, 20X6, on our audit of the financial statements of Company ABC.

Practitioner's Aids

Exhibits AU-C 925-1 and AU-C 925-2, reproduced from AU-C 925, illustrate acceptable wording to be included in a registration statement filed under the Securities Act of 1933.

EXHIBIT AU-C 925-1—DISCLOSURE IN "EXPERTS" SECTION OF A REGISTRATION STATEMENT FILED UNDER THE SECURITIES ACT OF 1933

EXPERTS

The consolidated balance sheets of ABC Company as of December 31, 20X5, and 20X4, and the related consolidated statements of income and comprehensive income, changes in stockholders' equity, and of cash flows for each of the three years in the period ended December 31, 20X5, included in this prospectus, have been so included in reliance on the report of XYZ & Co., independent auditors, given on the authority of that firm as experts in auditing and accounting.

EXHIBIT AU-C 925-2—DISCLOSURE THAT INCLUDES THE AUDITOR'S REVIEW REPORT ON UNAUDITED INTERIM FINANCIAL INFORMATION

[*Note: This disclosure may appear in a section labeled as "Experts" or "Independent Auditors."*]

With respect to the unaudited interim financial information of Company ABC for the three-month periods ended March 31, 20X6, and 20X5, included in this prospectus, XYZ & Co. has reported that they have applied limited procedures in accordance with professional standards for a review of such information. However, their separate report dated May 10, 20X6, included herein, states that they did not audit and they do not express an opinion on that interim financial information. Accordingly, the degree of reliance on their report on such information should be restricted in light of the limited nature of the review procedures applied. XYZ & Co. is not subject to the liability provisions of Section 11 of the Securities Act of 1933 for their report on the unaudited interim financial information because that report is not a "report" or a "part" of the registration statement prepared or certified by the accountants within the meaning of Sections 7 and 11 of the Act.

SECTION 930

INTERIM FINANCIAL INFORMATION

Authoritative Pronouncements

SAS-122 — Statements on Auditing Standards: Clarification and Recodification

Overview

AU-C 930 provides the auditor of an entity's financial statements guidance when he or she is engaged to review interim financial information of that client. AU-C 930 applies when the auditor is engaged by a nonissuer to review interim financial information if:

- The entity's latest financial statements have been audited by the auditor or a predecessor;

- The auditor has been engaged to audit the current year financial statements; or, the auditor has audited the entity's latest annual financial statements, the entity's current year financial statements are expected to be audited, and a new auditor has not been hired as of the beginning of the period being reviewed; and

- The entity prepares its interim financial information in accordance with the same financial reporting framework as that used to prepare the annual financial statements.

AU-C 930 also applies to reviews of condensed interim financial information if all of the following conditions are met:

- The condensed interim financial information purports to conform with an appropriate financial reporting framework, which includes appropriate form and content of interim financial information;

- The condensed interim financial information includes a note that the financial information does not represent complete financial statements and should be read in conjunction with the entity's latest annual audited financial statements; and

- The condensed financial information accompanies the entity's latest audited annual financial statements or such audited annual financial statements are made readily available by the entity, such that a third-party user can obtain the financial statements without any further action by the entity.

PLANNING AID REMINDER: AU-C 930 is applicable to interim financial information that is to be reviewed. Interim financial statements may be audited, in which case the auditor follows generally accepted auditing standards. The special accounting practices and modifications established by appropriate financial reporting frameworks such as FASB Accounting Standards Codification

(ASC) Topic 270, *Interim Reporting*, and Article 10 of Securities and Exchange Commission (SEC) Regulation S-X, with respect to accounting principles generally accepted in the United States of America, or International Accounting Standard 34, *Interim Financial Reporting*, with respect to International Financial Reporting Standards issued by the International Accounting Standards Board, should be followed in the preparation of the interim financial statements.

OBSERVATION: The auditor may find the guidance in AU-C 930 useful when he or she is not specifically engaged to perform a review of interim financial information but decides it is appropriate to perform such procedures in connection with the inclusion of the auditor's report on the annual financial statements in an unregistered securities offering document.

PUBLIC COMPANY IMPLICATION: The PCAOB issued Auditing Standard (AS) No. 7 (Engagement Quality Review) that is effective for fiscal years beginning on or after December 15, 2009. AS-7 applies to all firms registered with the PCAOB. In addition to applying to audits performed under PCAOB standards, the standard also applies to reviews. However, the procedures required to be performed by the engagement quality reviewer for a review of interim financial information are more limited. For all such engagements, an engagement review is required to be conducted before the report is issued. The engagement reviewer is required to be a partner of the firm performing the engagement, another person in an equivalent position in the firm, or an individual outside the firm who is associated with a registered public accounting firm. The engagement reviewer is required to have competence, independence, integrity, and objectivity. He or she is required to have the level of competence needed to have an overall responsibility for a comparable engagement. To maintain objectivity, the engagement reviewer is not permitted to make decisions for the engagement team, supervise the team, or assume responsibilities of the team. Review procedures generally involve discussions with engagement personnel and review of documents. Review procedures must be performed with due professional care and professional skepticism. Required engagement quality review procedures are more limited when the service being reviewed is an interim review. In addition, the engagement quality reviewer is required to review documentation in the areas that he or she reviewed. The firm is not permitted to issue its report (or communicate its conclusion to the client if no report is to be issued) until the engagement quality reviewer grants his or her concurring approval.

Responsibility and function of the auditor

The purpose of an audit is to determine whether the financial statements are presented fairly in accordance with generally accepted accounting principles. A review of interim financial information differs significantly from an audit of financial information, because a review does not include the collection of corroborative evidence through the performance of typical substantive audit tests. The review of interim financial information primarily consists of performing certain inquiries and analytical procedures. For these reasons, a review provides limited assurance (i.e., negative assurance) as to whether the interim financial information is fairly presented in accordance with an applicable financial reporting framework.

AU-C 930 states that the purpose of a review is to provide the auditor with a basis for reporting whether material modifications are necessary for the interim financial information to be in conformity with the applicable financial reporting framework. The auditor acquires the basis for reporting by applying the standards for a review of interim financial information in accordance with AU 930. The auditor issues a report containing an expression of limited assurance that, on the basis of the review, he or she is not aware of any material modification that should be made to the interim financial information for it to be in conformity with the applicable financial reporting framework.

Definition

Interim financial information

Financial information prepared and presented in accordance with an applicable financial reporting framework that contains either a complete or condensed set of financial statements covering a period or periods less than one full year or a 12-month period ending on a date other than the entity's fiscal year-end

Requirements

The auditor is presumptively required to perform the following procedures when reporting on interim financial information.

Acceptance

1. Follow the procedures for initial engagements required by paragraphs 11–12 of AU-C 210, *Terms of Engagement*, before accepting an engagement to perform an initial review of an entity's interim financial information.

2. Before accepting an engagement to review interim financial information:

   a. Determine whether the financial reporting framework to be applied in preparing the interim financial information is acceptable.

   b. Obtain management's agreement that it acknowledges and understands its responsibilities for (1) preparing interim financial information in accordance with the applicable financial reporting framework; (2) designing, implementing, and maintaining sufficient internal control to provide a reasonable basis for the preparation of that information; (3) providing the auditor with access to all information relevant to preparing the interim financial information that management is aware of, additional information the auditor requests from management for purposes of the review, and unrestricted access to entity personnel for the auditor to make necessary inquiries; and (4) including the auditor's review report in any document containing interim financial information that indicates such information has been reviewed by the entity's auditor.

3. Do not accept the proposed engagement if the financial reporting framework to be applied in preparing the interim financial information is unacceptable or the agreement with management regarding its responsibilities as described in requirement 2b (above) has not been obtained.

4. Agree on engagement terms with management or those charged with governance and record the agreed-upon terms in an engagement letter or other suitable written agreement that includes the engagement objectives and scope, management's responsibilities as described in requirement 2b (above), the auditor's responsibilities, the limitations of a review engagement, and identification of the applicable financial reporting framework for preparing the interim financial information.

Interim Financial Information Review Procedures

5. The auditor should have a sufficient understanding of the entity and its environment including its internal control as it relates to preparing annual and interim financial information to be able to identify the types of potential material misstatements in the interim financial information and consider the likelihood of their occurrence and to select the inquiries and analytical procedures that will provide a basis for reporting on whether the auditor is aware of any material modifications that should be made to the interim financial information for it to be in accordance with the applicable financial reporting framework. In order to obtain or update this understanding, the auditor should perform the following procedures:

    a. Read documentation of the preceding year's audit and of reviews of prior interim periods of the current year and corresponding interim periods of the prior year to the extent necessary to enable identification of matters that may affect the current period interim financial information, considering the nature of any corrected material misstatements, matters identified in any summary of uncorrected misstatements, identified risks of material misstatement due to fraud including the risk of management override of controls, and significant financial accounting and reporting matters that may be of continuing significance such as significant deficiencies and material weaknesses.

    b. Read the most recent annual and comparable prior interim period financial information.

    c. Consider the results of any audit procedures performed related to the current year's financial statements.

    d. Inquire of management about changes in the entity's business activities.

    e. Inquire of management about the identity of related parties and the nature of any transactions with those parties.

    f. Inquire of management about whether significant changes in internal control have occurred after the preceding annual audit or prior review of interim financial information related to preparing interim financial information, including changes in the entity's policies, procedures, and personnel and the nature and extent of any changes.

6. Apply the following analytical procedures to the interim financial information to identify and provide a basis for inquiry about the relationships and individual items that appear to be unusual and may indicate a material misstatement.

    a. Compare the interim financial information with comparable information for the immediately preceding interim period, if applicable, and with the corresponding periods in the previous year, considering knowledge about changes in the entity's business and specific transactions.

   b. Consider plausible relationships among financial and relevant nonfinancial information.

   c. Compare recorded amounts or ratios developed from recorded amounts to the expectations developed by identifying and using relationships that are reasonably expected to exist based on the auditor's understanding of the entity and its industry.

   d. Compare disaggregated revenue data.

7. Make the following inquiries and perform the following additional review procedures when reviewing interim financial information:

   a. Read available minutes of meetings of stockholders, directors, and appropriate committees and inquire about matters dealt with at meetings without minutes available to identify matters that may affect the interim financial information.

   b. Obtain reports from any component auditors related to reviews performed on interim financial information of significant components of the reporting entity including its investees or inquire of those auditors if reports have not been issued.

   c. Inquire of management about:

      i. Whether the interim financial information has been prepared and fairly presented in accordance with the applicable financial reporting framework consistently applied.

      ii. Unusual or complex situations that may have an effect on the interim financial information.

      iii. Significant transactions occurring or recognized in the interim period, particularly in the last several days of the interim period.

      iv. The status of uncorrected misstatements identified during the previous audit and interim review.

      v. Matters that applying review procedures have raised questions about.

      vi. Events subsequent to the date of the interim financial information that could have a material effect on the information's presentation.

      vii. Management's knowledge of any fraud or suspected fraud affecting the entity involving management, employees with significant internal control roles, or others when the fraud could have a material effect on the financial information.

      viii. Whether management is aware of allegations of fraud or suspected fraud affecting the entity.

      ix. Significant journal entries and other adjustments.

      x. Communications from regulatory agencies.

      xi. Significant deficiencies and material weaknesses in the design or operation of internal control as it relates to preparing the annual and interim financial information.

      xii. Changes in related parties or significant new related-party transactions.

   d. Obtain evidence that the interim financial information agrees or reconciles with the accounting records and inquire of management about the reliability of those records.

e. Read the interim financial information to consider whether, based on the results of the review procedures and other information the auditor is aware of, the information to be reported is in accordance with the applicable financial reporting framework.

f. Read other information in documents containing the interim financial information to consider whether that information or its presentation is materially inconsistent with the interim financial information. If there is a material inconsistency or the auditor becomes aware of information he or she believes to be a material misstatement of fact, use professional judgment to take action.

8. If there is information causing the auditor to question whether the interim financial information is prepared in all material respects in accordance with the applicable financial reporting framework with respect to litigation, claims, and assessments, and the auditor believes the entity's internal or external legal counsel may have information concerning that question, he or she should send an inquiry letter to that legal counsel concerning litigation, claims, and assessments.

9. If (a) conditions or events existed at the date of the prior period financial statements that may indicate substantial doubt about an entity's ability to continue as a going concern, regardless of whether that doubt was alleviated by the auditor's consideration of management's plans, or (b) the auditor becomes aware of conditions or events that may indicate the entity's inability to continue as a going concern when performing review procedures on the current period interim financial information, then inquire of management about its plans for dealing with the adverse effects of the conditions and events and consider the adequacy of the disclosure about such matters in the interim financial information.

10. Consider the reasonableness and consistency of management's responses given the results of other review procedures and knowledge about the entity's business and internal control.

11. When a matter comes to the auditor's attention causing him or her to question whether the interim financial information has been prepared in accordance with the applicable financial reporting framework in all material respects, he or she should make additional inquiries or perform other procedures to provide a basis for communicating whether the auditor is aware of any material modifications that should be made to the interim financial information.

Evaluating Interim Review Procedures' Results

12. Accumulate misstatements including inadequate disclosure that are identified in performing review procedures and evaluate these misstatements to determine whether material modification should be made to the interim financial information for it to be in accordance with the applicable financial reporting framework.

Management's Written Representations

13. Request that management provide written representations for all interim financial information presented and for all periods covered by the review:

a. That it has fulfilled its responsibility for preparing and fairly presenting the interim financial information in accordance with the applicable financial reporting framework as set out in the engagement terms

b. That it acknowledges its responsibility for designing, implementing, and maintaining internal control relevant to the preparation and fair presentation of interim financial statements, including its responsibility to prevent and detect fraud

c. That it has disclosed all significant deficiencies and material weaknesses it is aware of in the design or operation of internal control as it relates to preparing the annual and interim financial information

d. That is has provided the auditor with all relevant information and access as agreed upon in the engagement terms

e. That all transactions have been recorded and are reflected in the interim financial information

f. That it has disclosed to the auditor the results of its assessment of the risk that the interim financial information may be materially misstated due to fraud

g. That it has disclosed to the auditor its knowledge of fraud or suspected fraud affecting the entity involving management, employees who have significant roles in internal control, or others when the fraud could have a material effect on the interim financial information

h. That it has disclosed to the auditor its knowledge of any allegations of fraud or suspected fraud affecting the entity's interim financial information communicated by employees, former employees, regulators, or others

i. That it has disclosed to the auditor all known instances of noncompliance or suspected noncompliance with laws and regulations whose effects should be considered when preparing interim financial information

j. About whether it believes the effects of uncorrected misstatements are immaterial, individually and in the aggregate, to the interim financial information as a whole. A summary of such items should be included in or attached to the written representation.

k. That it has disclosed to the auditor and appropriately accounted for and disclosed in accordance with the applicable financial reporting framework all known actual or possible litigation and claims whose effects should be considered when preparing the interim financial information

l. About whether it believes significant assumptions it used in making accounting estimates are reasonable

m. That it has disclosed to the auditor the identity of the entity's related parties and all the related party relationships and transactions it is aware of and it has appropriately accounted for and disclosed such relationships and transactions

n. That all events occurring subsequent to the date of the interim financial information have been adjusted or disclosed as required by the applicable financial reporting framework

14. If the auditor has concerns about the reliability of the representations or if management does not provide the requested representations, the auditor should take appropriate action. If management does not provide the written representations described in requirement 13(a) – (e), the auditor should withdraw from the engagement to review the interim financial information.

Communications with Management and Those Charged with Governance

15. If the auditor cannot complete the review, he or she should communicate to the appropriate level of management and those charged with governance

(*a*) the reason why the review cannot be completed, (*b*) that an incomplete review does not provide a basis for issuing a review report so the auditor is precluded from issuing such a report, and (*c*) any material modifications the auditor is aware of that should be made to the interim financial information for it to be in accordance with the applicable financial reporting framework in accordance with requirements 16–18 (below).

16. Communicate to the appropriate level of management as soon as practicable matters that cause the auditor to believe that (a) material modification should be made to the interim financial information for it to be in accordance with the applicable financial reporting framework or (b) the entity issued interim financial information before completion of a required review.

17. If management does not respond appropriately to the auditor's communication within a reasonable time period, inform those charged with governance of the matters as soon as practicable.

18. If those charged with governance do not respond appropriately to the auditor's communication within a reasonable time period, consider whether to withdraw from the engagement to review the interim financial information and as the entity's auditor.

19. If the auditor becomes aware of fraud, communicate the matter as soon as practicable to the appropriate level of management. If the fraud involves senior management or results in a material misstatement of the interim financial information, communicate the matter directly to those charged with governance. If the auditor becomes aware of matters involving identified or suspected noncompliance with laws and regulations, communicate all matters that are not clearly inconsequential to those charged with governance.

20. Communicate relevant matters of governance interest arising from the interim financial information review to those charged with governance, including (a) significant deficiencies or material weaknesses in internal control as it relates to preparing annual and interim financial information, and (b) any of the matters described in AU-C 260 that have been identified that relate to the interim financial information.

Auditor's Review Report on Interim Financial Information

21. Issue a written report on a review of interim financial information.

22. Include the following information in the written report:

    a. A title including the word "independent"

    b. An appropriate addressee

    c. An introductory paragraph identifying the entity whose interim financial information has been reviewed, stating that the interim financial information identified in the report was reviewed, identifying the interim financial information, and specifying the date or period covered by each financial statement comprising the interim financial information

    d. A section titled "Management's Responsibility for the Financial Statements" explaining that the preparation and fair presentation of the interim financial information is management's responsibility, including the responsibility to design, implement, and maintain internal control sufficient to provide a reasonable basis for the preparation and fair presentation of interim financial information in accordance with the applicable financial reporting framework

    e. A section titled "Auditor's Responsibility" that includes the following statements: the interim financial information review was conducted in accordance with applicable auditing standards generally accepted in the United States of America; the procedures for a review of interim financial information are primarily analytical procedures and inquiries; and an interim financial information review is substantially less in scope than an audit conducted in accordance with auditing standards generally accepted in the United States of America that has the objective of expressing an opinion regarding the financial information as a whole and, therefore, no such opinion is expressed

f. A concluding section with an appropriate heading stating whether the auditor is aware of any material modifications that should be made to the accompanying interim financial information for it to be in accordance with the applicable financial reporting framework, including an identification of the country of origin of those accounting principles

g. The manual or printed signature of the auditor's firm

h. The city and state where the auditor practices

i. The date of the review report, which should be dated as of the date of completion of the review procedures

23. Determine that management has clearly marked each page of the interim financial information as unaudited.

24. If the auditor is engaged to review the most recent interim period and that financial information will be presented comparatively with prior interim period information that has not been reviewed, the financial information should be accompanied by the auditor's review report stating that the auditor has not reviewed the prior period interim financial information and that he or she is not responsible for that information.

25. If a condensed balance sheet derived from audited financial statements is presented on a comparative basis with the interim financial information, the auditor should only report on the condensed balance sheet if he or she audited the financial statements the condensed balance sheet was derived from. Make sure that the condensed balance sheet agrees with or can be recalculated from the audited financial statements.

Include a paragraph in the auditor's report on the interim financial information that: identifies the condensed balance sheet on which the auditor is reporting and the audited financial statements the condensed balance sheet was derived from, indicating that the financial statements are not separately presented; refers to the auditor's report on the audited financial statements, including the report date, type or opinion expressed, and the basis for any modified opinion; describes the nature of any emphasis-of-matter paragraph or other-matter paragraph included in the auditor's report; and includes an opinion about whether the condensed balance sheet is consistent in all material respects with the audited financial statements from which it was derived.

26. When interim financial information has not been prepared in accordance with the applicable financial reporting framework in all material respects, consider whether modification of the auditor's review report on the interim financial information is sufficient to disclose the departure.

a. If modification of the standard review report is sufficient to disclose the departure, modify the review report, describing the nature of the departure and the effects on the interim financial information, if practicable. If the departure is due to inadequate disclosure, if practicable, include the information in the review report that the auditor believes is necessary for adequate disclosure in accordance with the applicable financial reporting framework.

b. If modification of the review report is not sufficient to indicate the deficiencies in the financial information as a whole, withdraw from the review engagement and provide no further services regarding that interim financial information.

Other Considerations

27. If, subsequent to the date of the auditor's review report, the auditor becomes aware that facts existed at the date of the report that might have affected the report had the auditor been aware of those matters, consider the guidance in AU-C 560, *Subsequent Events and Subsequently Discovered Facts.*

28. If management does not include the auditor's review report in a report, document, or written communication containing the reviewed interim financial information that indicates such information has been reviewed by the entity's auditor, despite having agreed to do so in the terms of the engagement, perform the following procedures:

    a. Request that management amend the report, document, or written communication to include the auditor's review report and reissue the report, document, or written communication

    b. If management does not comply with the request, request that the auditor's name not be associated with the interim financial information or referred to in the report, document, or written communication

    c. If management does not comply with the request, advise management that the auditor will not permit use of the auditor's name or reference to the auditor

    d. Communicate management's noncompliance with the request to those charged with governance

    e. Recommend that the entity consult with its legal counsel about the application of relevant laws and regulations when appropriate

    f. Consider what other actions might be appropriate

29. If the auditor issued a modified review report and management issues the interim financial information without including the review report in the document containing the interim financial information, determine the appropriate course of action in the circumstances including whether to withdraw from the engagement to audit the annual financial statements.

30. Include an other-matter paragraph in the auditor's report on the audited financial statements when interim financial information reviewed in accordance with AU-C 930 is included in a document containing audited financial statements, that interim financial information does not appear to be presented in accordance with the applicable financial reporting framework, and the auditor's separate review report referring to that departure is not presented with the information

31. Disclaim an opinion on the interim financial information in the auditor's report on the audited financial statements when the interim financial information included in a note to the financial statements, including information that has been reviewed in accordance with AU-C 930, is not appropriately marked as unaudited.

Documentation

32. Prepare documentation in connection with an interim financial information review that will enable an experienced auditor to understand:

    a. The nature, timing, and extent of the review procedures performed;

    b. The results of the review procedures and the evidence that was obtained; and

    c. Significant findings or issues that arose during the review, the conclusions reached regarding these issues, and significant professional judgments made in reaching those conclusions.

33. Documentation should the written or oral communications required by AU-C 930.

Analysis and Application of Procedures

Acceptance

The written communication documenting the agreed-upon terms of the engagement may encompass the following points:

- The objective of a review of interim financial information is to provide the auditor with a basis for communicating whether he or she is aware of any material modifications that should be made to the interim financial information for it to conform with the applicable financial reporting framework.

- A review includes obtaining sufficient knowledge of the entity's business and its internal control as it relates to the preparation of both annual and interim financial information to

  — Identify the types of potential misstatements in the interim financial information and consider the likelihood of their occurrence and

  — Select the inquiries and analytical procedures that will provide the auditor with a basis for communicating whether he or she is aware of any material modifications that should be made to the interim financial information for it to conform with the applicable financial reporting framework.

- Management is responsible for preparing the entity's interim financial information in accordance with the applicable financial reporting framework.

- Management is responsible for designing, implementing, and maintaining internal control over financial reporting sufficient to provide a reasonable basis for preparing and fairly presenting interim financial information in accordance with the applicable financial reporting framework.

- Management is responsible for identifying and ensuring that the entity complies with the laws and regulations applicable to its activities.

- Management is responsible for providing the auditor with access to all information relevant to preparing and fairly presenting the interim financial information that management is aware of, additional information the auditor requests from management for purposes of the review, and unrestricted access to entity personnel for the auditor to make necessary inquiries.

- Management is responsible for including the auditor's review report in any document containing interim financial information that indicates such information has been reviewed by the entity's auditor.

- At the conclusion of the engagement, management will provide the auditor with a letter confirming certain representations made during the review.

- Management is responsible for adjusting the interim financial information to correct material misstatements. Although a review of interim financial information is not designed to obtain reasonable assurance that the interim financial information is free from material misstatement, management also is responsible for affirming in its representation letter to the auditor that the effects of any uncorrected misstatements aggregated by the auditor during the current engagement and pertaining to the current period(s) under review are immaterial, both individually and in the aggregate, to the financial information taken as a whole.

- The auditor is responsible for conducting the review in accordance with auditing standards generally accepted in the United States of America. A review of interim financial information consists principally of performing analytical procedures and making inquiries of persons responsible for financial and accounting matters. It is substantially less in scope than an audit conducted in accordance with generally accepted auditing standards, the objective of which is the expression of an opinion regarding the financial statements taken as a whole. Accordingly, the auditor will not express an opinion on the interim financial information.

- Limitations of a review engagement, including acknowledgement that a review does not provide a basis for expressing an opinion on the interim financial information.

- A review does not provide assurance that the auditor will become aware of all significant matters that would be identified in an audit.

- A review is not designed to provide assurance on internal control or to identify control deficiencies. However, the auditor is responsible for communicating to management and those charged with governance any significant deficiencies or material weaknesses in internal control over financial reporting that come to his or her attention.

PLANNING AID REMINDER: AU-C 265 (*Communicating Internal Control Related Matters Identified in an Audit*), requires the auditor of financial statements to communicate in writing to management and those charged with governance significant deficiencies and material weaknesses that were identified. Although an audit of financial statements is not designed to perform procedures to detect control deficiencies, AU-C 265 requires the communications when the auditor identifies significant deficiencies and material weaknesses in internal control over financial reporting. The ASB adopted the PCAOB definitions of "control deficiency," "significant deficiency," and "material weakness."

PUBLIC COMPANY REMINDER: Although a review is not designed to provide assurance on internal control, the auditor's involvement in evaluating internal control on an interim basis is likely to increase because of SEC and PCAOB requirements. First, management must disclose to the auditor (1) all changes during the quarter in internal control over financial reporting that materially affected, or are likely to materially affect, the entity's internal control, (2) all significant deficiencies and material weaknesses in the design and operation of internal control on a quarterly basis, and (3) any fraud, regardless of materiality, involving management or any other person who plays an important role in the entity's internal control over financial reporting. Second, because the auditor must issue his or her own opinion on the effectiveness of the entity's internal control over financial reporting as part of its annual audit report, it seems likely that internal control testing will occur throughout the year.

Interim Financial Information Review Procedures

Acquire knowledge of the entity's business and internal control

In order to successfully execute a review of interim financial information, the auditor must have both an understanding of the client's business and its internal control used to prepare annual as well as interim financial information. This background (1) helps identify financial information that has the greatest potential for misstatement and (2) provides focus in determining which analytical procedures and inquiries should be made. The review is not able to be successfully executed if the entity has significant internal control deficiencies such that the auditor is not able to perform review procedures to obtain a basis for communicating whether the auditor is aware of any material modifications that should be made to the interim financial information for it to be in accordance with the applicable financial reporting framework.

If the auditor has not previously reviewed a client's interim financial information, he or she must nonetheless obtain an adequate understanding of the client's business and its internal control. Specifically, under this circumstance, the auditor may consider obtaining permission from the predecessor auditor to review his or her audit documentation for interim reviews made during the previous year.

OBSERVATION: The auditor is responsible for all inquiries made, analytical procedures and other procedures performed, and conclusions reached in an initial interim financial information review.

When the predecessor accountant does not respond to the auditor's inquiries or allow access to audit documentation for previous engagements, the auditor may inquire as to why and can use alternative procedures in order to obtain an adequate understanding of the client's business and internal control.

Perform analytical procedures, inquiries, and other review procedures

The specific analytical procedures and related inquiries employed should be based on the accountant's understanding of the client's business and internal control, the results of risk assessments relating to the previous audit, and the auditor's consideration of materiality as it relates to the interim financial information. For example, if there has been a significant change in the entity's control activities, the auditor may consider making additional inquiries and using analytical procedures with more precise expectations.

PLANNING AID REMINDER: In general, expectations for analytical procedures developed in interim financial information reviews are less precise than those developed in an audit and management's responses are not required to be corroborated with other evidence.

Many of the inquiries and review procedures in an interim financial information review can be performed before or at the same time as the entity's preparation of the interim financial information. Performing some review procedures earlier in the interim period allows the auditor to identify and consider significant matters affecting the interim financial information at an earlier date. Some auditing procedures associated with the annual financial statement audit may also be able to be performed at the same time as the interim financial information review.

Generally, apart from the circumstances described in requirement 8 (above), the auditor is not required to make in quiries of the client's lawyer concerning litigation, claims, and assessments in a review of interim financial information. The auditor is also generally not required to collect evidence that might identify conditions or events that raise substantial doubt about the client's ability to continue as a going concern in an interim financial information review apart from the circumstances described in requirement 9 (above). In a review, the auditor is not required to obtain evidence supporting the information that mitigates these conditions and events. If the auditor concludes that the entity's disclosure about its possible inability to continue as a going concern is inadequate, there is a departure from the applicable financial reporting framework and the review report is required to be modified.

Evaluating Interim Review Procedures' Results

The application of review procedures can identify potential misstatements. The auditor may designate an amount below which misstatements are clearly trivial and do not need to be accumulated because their accumulation would not have a material effect on the interim financial information. The auditor may consider factors such as the following in evaluating whether uncorrected misstatements, individually or in the aggregate, are material:

- The amount and the reason for the misstatement
- The occurrence date of the misstatement (current period or the previous period)
- The basis for determining whether an item is material
- The possible effect of the misstatement on future interim or annual periods
- The appropriateness of offsetting a likely misstatement that is based on an estimate with a misstatement that is subject to measurement that is more precise

- The possible material effect on future financial information of current balance sheet misstatements that are considered immaterial

Management's Written Representations

AU-C 930 requires the auditor to obtain written representations from management for each interim financial information review engagement. An example of a representation letter for the review of interim financial information is presented in Exhibit AU-C 930-1.

ENGAGEMENT STRATEGY: If no uncorrected misstatements are identified, then the requirement for management representation regarding uncorrected misstatements is not relevant and, therefore, is not required.

In addition to the specific representations required by AU-C 930, the auditor should consider the particular characteristics of the client to determine which additional representations should be made by management. For example, a client that operates in an industry addressed by an AICPA Accounting and Auditing Guide should consider whether other representations should be obtained from management.

When management does not provide a requested written representation or when the auditor has concerns about the reliability of the representations, the auditor should discuss the matter with management and those charged with governance when appropriate, reevaluate management's integrity and evaluate any effect this has on the reliability of representations and evidence obtained, and consider whether to withdraw from the interim financial information review engagement and as the entity's auditor if applicable.

Communications with Management and Those Charged with Governance

The interim financial information review will be incomplete if the auditor is unable to perform appropriate review procedures or the client does not provide the auditor with the necessary written representations. If the auditor is in the situation where he or she is deciding whether to withdraw from the engagement to review the interim financial information and as the entity's auditor, he or she may consult with legal counsel.

OBSERVATION: If matters concerning possible illegal acts or fraud arise, the auditor should follow the guidance established by AU-C 250 (*Consideration of Laws and Regulations in an Audit of Financial Statements*) and AU-C 240 (*Consideration of Fraud in a Financial Statement Audit*).

OBSERVATION: If matters concerning internal control deficiencies over financial reporting come to the accountant's attention, the guidance established in AU-C 265 (*Communicating Internal Control Related Matters Identified in an Audit*) should be considered.

When the auditor determines that a matter should be communicated to management or those charged with governance, he or she should make such communications, whether in writing or orally, on a sufficiently timely basis to enable those parties to take appropriate action.

Auditor's Review Report on Interim Financial Information

If a third party requires a review of the interim financial information but does not require a written review report, the auditor's review report on the interim financial information must still be in writing. Exhibit AU-C 930-2 is an example of a standard review report.

If the auditor has not reviewed the prior period interim financial information, presented for comparative purposes, and assumes no responsibility for that information, he or she may indicate that in the report by stating:

> The accompanying [*describe the interim financial information or statements*] of X Company and subsidiaries as of September 30, 20X5, and for the three-month period then ended were not reviewed by us, and accordingly, we do not express any form of assurance on it.

Departures from the applicable financial reporting framework may preclude the issuance of a review report or require modification to the standard review report. These departures include inadequate disclosure and changes in accounting policies that are not in accordance with the applicable financial reporting framework.

Exhibit AU-C 930-3 is an example of a review report on interim financial information that has a departure from the applicable financial reporting framework.

When interim financial statements are presented, the information necessary for adequate disclosure will vary depending on the form and content of the interim financial information. For example, condensed financial statements require less extensive disclosures than annual financial statements that present financial position, results of operations, and cash flows in accordance with the applicable financial reporting framework. Exhibit AU-C 930-4 is an example of a review report on interim financial information that includes an inadequate disclosure.

The interim financial information may adequately disclose the existence of substantial doubt about the entity's ability to continue as a going concern or a lack of consistency in the application of accounting principles affecting the interim financial information. Although the foregoing conditions do not require a modification of the review report, an emphasis-of-matter paragraph can be included in the report. Examples of going concern reports are presented in Exhibits AU-C 930-5 and AU-C 930-6.

Other Considerations

In instances in which a client represents in a filing with a regulatory authority or communications with stockholders or third parties that the included interim information has been reviewed by an auditor, and management refuses to include the review report in the document, then when the auditor is considering other appropriate actions, he or she may wish to contact legal counsel. Interim financial information may be included as supplementary information or as a note to the client's audited financial statements. Under both circumstances, management is responsible for clearly marking the interim information as unaudited. In these situations, the auditor does not need to modify the auditor's report on the audited financial statements to refer to the accompanying interim financial information even if the auditor has reviewed that information.

Documentation

AU-C 230, *Audit Documentation*, provides the auditor with additional guidance on determining the form, content, and timing of engagement documentation.

Practitioner's Aids

The following exhibits are presented in this section:

- Exhibit AU-C 930-1—Management Representation Letter for a Review of Interim Financial Information
- Exhibit AU-C 930-2—Standard Review Report on Interim Financial Information
- Exhibit AU-C 930-3—Modification of Review Report on Interim Financial Information Due to a Departure from the Applicable Financial Reporting Framework
- Exhibit AU-C 930-4—Modification of Review Report on Interim Financial Statements Due to Inadequate Disclosure
- Exhibit AU-C 930-5—Emphasis-of-Matter Paragraph Related to a Going Concern Issue Referred to in the Previous Audit Report
- Exhibit AU-C 930-6—Emphasis-of-Matter Paragraph Related to a Going Concern Issue Not Referred to in the Previous Audit

EXHIBIT AU-C 930-1—MANAGEMENT REPRESENTATION LETTER FOR A REVIEW OF INTERIM FINANCIAL INFORMATION

Bluefield Company

1400 Maple Street

Bluefield, NJ 08000

[*Date*]

Mr. Arthur Oldes

Arthur Oldes & Company

1040 Main Street

Bluefield, NJ 08000

Dear Mr. Oldes:

This representation letter is provided in connection with your review of the [*consolidated*] balance sheet as of June 30, 20X5 and the related [*consolidated*] statements of income, changes in equity and cash flows for the six-month period then ended of Bluefield Company for the purpose of determining whether any material modifications should be made to the [*consolidated*] interim financial information, for it to be in accordance with accounting principles generally accepted in the United States of America (U.S. GAAP) [*including, if appropriate, an indication as to the appropriate form and content of interim financial information (for example, Article 10 of SEC Regulation S-X)*].

We confirm that [, to the best of our knowledge and belief, having made such inquiries as we considered necessary for the purpose of appropriately informing ourselves] [as of (*date of auditor's review report*)]:

Interim Financial Information

1. We have fulfilled our responsibilities, as set out in the terms of the engagement letter dated [*insert date*] for the preparation and fair presentation of the interim financial information in accordance with U.S. GAAP; in particular the interim financial information is presented in accordance therewith.

2. We acknowledge our responsibility for the design, implementation, and maintenance of internal control relevant to the preparation and fair presentation of interim financial information that is free from material misstatement, whether due to fraud or error.

3. The interim financial information has been adjusted or includes disclosures for all events subsequent to the date of the interim financial information for which U.S. GAAP requires adjustment or disclosure.

4. The effects of uncorrected misstatements are immaterial, both individually and in the aggregate, to the interim financial information as a whole. A list of the uncorrected misstatements is attached to the representation letter.

[*Any other matters the auditor may consider appropriate.*]

Information Provided

5. We have provided you with:

- Access to all information of which we are aware that is relevant to the preparation and fair presentation of the interim financial information such as records, documentation and other matters;

- Minutes of the meetings of stockholders, directors, and committees of directors, or summaries of actions of recent meetings for which minutes have not yet been prepared;

- Additional information that you have requested from use for the purpose of the review; and

- Unrestricted access to persons within the entity of whom you determined it necessary to make inquiries.

6. We have disclosed to you all significant deficiencies or material weaknesses in the design or operation of internal control of which we are aware, as it relates to the preparation of both annual and interim financial information.

7. We have disclosed to you the results of our assessment of the risk that the interim financial information may be materially misstated as a result of fraud.

8. We have [no knowledge of any] [disclosed to you all information of which we are aware in relation to] fraud or suspected fraud that affects the entity and involves:

- Management;

- Employees who have significant roles in internal control; or

- Others where the fraud could have a material effect on the interim financial information.

9. We have [no knowledge of any] [disclosed to you all information in relation to] allegations of fraud or suspected fraud affecting the entity's interim financial information communicated by employees, former employees, analysts, regulators, or others.

10. We have disclosed to you the identity of the entity's related parties and all the related party relationships and transactions of which we are aware.

[*Any other matters that the auditor may consider necessary.*]

11. We have reviewed our representation letter to you dated [*date of representation letter relating to most recent audit*] with respect to the audited financial statements for the year ended [*prior year-end date*]. We believe that representations A, B, and C within that representation letter do not apply to the interim financial information referred to above. We now confirm those representations D through X, as they apply to the interim financial information referred to above, and incorporate them herein, with the following changes:

[*Indicate changes*]

12. [*Add any representations related to new accounting or auditing standards that are being implemented for the first time.*]

[*Name of chief executive officer and title*]

[*Name of chief financial officer and title*]

[*Name of chief accounting officer and title*]

EXHIBIT AU-C 930-2—STANDARD REVIEW REPORT ON INTERIM FINANCIAL INFORMATION

Independent Auditor's Review Report

Board of Directors

Bluefield Company

Bluefield, NJ 08000

We have reviewed the accompanying [*describe the interim financial information or statements reviewed*] of Bluefield Company as of June 30, 20X5, and for the three-month and six-month periods then ended.

Management's Responsibility

The Company's management is responsible for the preparation and fair presentation of the interim financial information in accordance with [*identify the applicable financial reporting framework; for example,* accounting principles generally accepted in the United States of America]; this responsibility includes the design, implementation, and maintenance of internal control sufficient to provide a reasonable basis for the preparation and fair presentation of interim financial information in accordance with the applicable financial reporting framework.

Auditor's Responsibility

Our responsibility is to conduct our review in accordance with auditing standards generally accepted in the United States of America applicable to reviews of interim financial information. A review of interim financial information consists principally of applying analytical procedures and making inquiries of persons responsible for financial and accounting matters. It is substantially less in scope than an audit conducted in accordance with auditing standards generally accepted in the United States, the objective of which is the expression of an opinion regarding the financial information. Accordingly, we do not express such an opinion.

Conclusion

Based on our review, we are not aware of any material modifications that should be made to the accompanying interim financial information for it to be in accordance with [*identify the applicable financial reporting framework; for example,* accounting principles generally accepted in the United States of America].

[*Signature of auditor*]

[*Auditor's city and state*]

[*Date of the auditor's report*]

EXHIBIT AU-C 930-3—MODIFICATION OF REVIEW REPORT ON INTERIM FINANCIAL INFORMATION DUE TO A DEPARTURE FROM THE APPLICABLE FINANCIAL REPORTING FRAMEWORK

[*Basis for modification paragraph*]

Based on information furnished to us by management, we believe that the company has excluded from debt in the accompanying balance sheet certain obligations related to defined benefits pension plans that we believe should be presented to be in accordance with [*identify the applicable financial reporting framework; for example,* accounting principles generally accepted in the United State of America]. This information indicates that if these obligations were presented at June 30, 20X5, long-term debt would increase by $ _____, and net income and earnings per share would be increased (decreased) by $ _____, $ _____, $ _____, and $ _____, respectively for the three-month and six-month periods then ended.

[*Conclusion*]

Based on our review, with the exception of the matters described in the preceding paragraph(s), we are not aware of any material modifications that should be made to the accompanying interim financial information for it to be in accordance with [*identify the applicable financial reporting framework; for example,* accounting principles generally accepted in the United States of America].

EXHIBIT AU-C 930-4—MODIFICATION OF REVIEW REPORT ON INTERIM FINANCIAL STATEMENTS DUE TO INADEQUATE DISCLOSURE

[*Basis for modification paragraph*]

Management had informed us that the company is a defendant in litigation concerning personal injuries alleged to have occurred to a customer while on the company's premises. The amount of damages to be paid to the plaintiff, if any, cannot currently be determined. The interim financial information fails to disclose this matter, which we believe is required to be disclosed in accordance with [*identify the applicable financial reporting framework; for example,* accounting principles generally accepted in the United States of America].

[*Conclusion*]

Based on our review, with the exception of the matter described in the preceding paragraph, we are not aware of any material modifications that should be made to the accompanying interim financial information for it to be in accordance with [*identify the applicable financial reporting framework; for example,* accounting principles generally accepted in the United States of America].

EXHIBIT AU-C 930-5—EMPHASIS-OF-MATTER PARAGRAPH RELATED TO A GOING CONCERN ISSUE REFERRED TO IN THE PREVIOUS AUDIT REPORT

Note X of the Company's audited financial statements as of December 31, 20X4, and for the year then ended, discloses that the Company [*describe the condition that raised substantial doubt*]. Our auditor's report on those financial statements includes an emphasis-of-matter paragraph referring to the matters in Note X of those financial statements and indicating that these matters raised substantial doubt about the Company's ability to continue as a going concern. As indicated in Note 3 of the Company's unaudited interim financial information as of June 30, 20X5, and for the six months then ended, the Company was still [*describe the continuing condition that still exists*]. The accompanying interim financial information does not include any adjustments that might result from the outcome of this uncertainty.

EXHIBIT AU-C 930-6—EMPHASIS-OF-MATTER PARAGRAPH RELATED TO A GOING CONCERN ISSUE NOT REFERRED TO IN THE PREVIOUS AUDIT REPORT

As indicated in Note X, certain conditions indicate that the Company may be unable to continue as a going concern. The accompanying interim financial information does not include any adjustments that might result from the outcome of this uncertainty.

SECTION 935

COMPLIANCE AUDITS

Authoritative Pronouncements

SAS-117—Compliance Audits

Overview

The guidance in AU-C 935 applies when an auditor is engaged or required by law or regulation to perform a compliance audit in accordance with three sets of requirements — GAAS, the financial auditing standards under *Government Auditing Standards,* and a governmental audit requirement requiring an auditor to express an opinion on compliance. For example, AU-C 935 applies to an audit performed in accordance with the provisions of Office of Management and Budget (OMB) Circular A-133, *Audits of States, Local Governments and Non-Profit Organizations.*

AU-C 935 does not apply to an engagement that does not require that the audit be performed according to both GAAS and *Government Auditing Standards.* Under these circumstances, the engagement could be performed under AT 601, *Compliance Attestation,* AT 101, *Attest Engagements,* or AT 201, *Agreed-Upon Procedures Engagements,* depending on the government requirements. AT 601 is also applicable when the governmental audit requirement requires an examination of an entity's compliance with specified requirements in accordance with the Statements on Standards for Attestation Engagement or an examination of an entity's internal control over compliance. If an entity is required to have a compliance audit and an examination of internal control over compliance, AU-C 935 applies to the compliance audit and AT 601 applies to the examination. Law or regulation does not always prescribe which standards the auditor should follow, so he or she will need to use professional judgment in this determination.

AU-C 935 assists the auditor in applying GAAS to a compliance audit, which is often performed in conjunction with a financial statement audit. While AU-C sections 100–700 and 900 address financial statement audits, only AU-C sections 100–300 and 500 can generally be adapted to a compliance audit's objectives. When planning and performing a compliance audit, the auditor should obtain sufficient appropriate audit evidence to support the auditor's opinion. However, the auditor is not required to translate each financial statement audit procedure into a compliance audit procedure. AU-C935 provides the auditor with more specific guidance on how to adapt and apply relevant AU-Cs sections to a compliance audit.

Management is responsible for the entity's compliance with compliance requirements in a compliance audit. Management's responsibilities include (a) identifying the entity's government programs and understanding and complying with compliance requirements, (b) establishing and maintaining effective controls that provide reasonable assurance that the entity administers government programs in compliance with compliance requirements, (c) evaluating and monitoring the entity's compliance with compliance requirements, and (d) taking corrective action when instances of noncompliance are identified, including findings of the compliance audit.

In a compliance audit, the auditor's objective is to obtain sufficient appropriate audit evidence to form an opinion and report at the level specified in the governmental audit requirement on whether the entity complied in all material respects with the applicable compliance requirements. The auditor also has the objective of identifying any audit and reporting requirements specified in the governmental audit requirement that are supplementary to GAAS and *Governmental Auditing Standards* and perform procedures to address those requirements.

Definitions

Applicable compliance requirements	Compliance requirements that are subject to the compliance audit
Audit findings	Matters the auditor is required to report on in accordance with the governmental audit requirement
Audit risk of noncompliance	Risk that the auditor expresses an inappropriate audit opinion on the entity's compliance when material noncompliance exists; function of the risks of material noncompliance and detection risk of noncompliance
Compliance audit	A program-specific or organization-wide audit of an entity's compliance with applicable compliance requirements
Compliance requirements	Laws, regulations, rules, and provisions of contracts or grant agreements applicable to government programs with which the entity is required to comply
Deficiency in internal control over compliance	A deficiency in internal control over compliance exists when the design or operation of a control over compliance does not allow management or employees to prevent, or detect and correct, noncompliance on a timely basis in the course of their normal activities
Detection risk of noncompliance	The risk that the procedures the auditor performs to reduce audit risk of noncompliance to an acceptably low level will not detect existing noncompliance that could be material, either individually or when aggregated with other instances of noncompliance
Governmental audit requirement	Government requirement established by law, regulation, rule, or provision of contracts of grant agreements requiring that an entity undergo an audit of its compliance with applicable compliance requirements related to one or more government programs that the entity administers

Government Auditing Standards	Standards and guidance issued by the Comptroller General of the United States, U.S. Government Accountability Office for financial audits, attestation engagements, and performance audits; also known as generally accepted government auditing standards (GAGAS) or the Yellow Book
Government program	The means by which governmental entities achieve their objectives
Grantor	A government agency that funds the government program
Known questioned costs	Questioned costs specifically identified by the auditor; a subset of likely questioned costs
Likely questioned costs	The auditor's best estimate of total questioned costs developed by extrapolating from audit evidence obtained, for example, by projecting known questioned costs identified in an audit sample to the entire population from which the sample was drawn
Material noncompliance	If not otherwise identified in the governmental audit requirement, a failure to follow compliance requirements or a violation of prohibitions included in the applicable compliance requirements that results in noncompliance that is quantitatively or qualitatively material to the affected government program, either individually or when aggregated with other noncompliance
Material weakness in internal control over compliance	A deficiency or combination of deficiencies in internal control over compliance such that there is a reasonable possibility that material noncompliance with a compliance requirement will not be prevented, or detected and corrected, on a timely basis. A reasonable possibility exists when the event's likelihood is reasonably possible or probable.
Organization-wide audit	An audit of an entity's financial statements and of its compliance with the applicable compliance requirements as they relate to one or more government programs that the entity administers
Pass-through entity	An entity that receives an award from a grantor or other entity and distributes all or part of it to another entity to administer a government program
Program-specific audit	An audit of an entity's compliance with applicable compliance requirements as they relate to one government program that the entity administers performed in conjunction with an audit of the entity's or program's financial statements
Questioned costs	Costs that are questioned by the auditor because 1) of a violation or possible violation of compliance requirements, 2) of lack of support by adequate documentations, or 3) the incurred costs appear unreasonable and do not reflect a prudent person's actions in the circumstances
Risk of material noncompliance	The risks that material noncompliance exists prior to the audit; consists of the inherent risk of noncompliance and the control risk of noncompliance

| Significant deficiency in internal control over compliance | A deficiency or combination of deficiencies in internal control over compliance that is less severe than a material weakness in internal control over compliance yet important enough to merit attention by those charged with governance |

Requirements

The auditor is presumptively required to perform the following procedures when performing a compliance audit:

Planning and Performing a Compliance Audit

1. Adapt and apply the relevant AU-C sections to the objectives of a compliance audit.

2. Establish and apply materiality levels for the compliance audit based on the governmental audit requirement.

3. Determine which of the entity's government programs and compliance requirements to test.

4. For each government program and compliance requirement tested, perform risk assessment procedures to understand the applicable compliance requirements and the entity's internal control over compliance with the applicable compliance requirements.

5. In performing risk assessment procedures, ask management if there are findings and recommendations in written communications from previous audit or attestation engagements or monitoring that directly relate to the compliance audit's objectives. Gain an understanding of management's response to any findings and recommendations that could have a material effect on the entity's compliance with applicable compliance requirements and use this information to assess risk and determine the nature, timing, and extent of the audit procedures for the compliance audit and the extent to which testing the implementation of any corrective actions is applicable to the audit objectives.

6. Assess the risks of material noncompliance due to fraud or error for each applicable compliance requirement and consider whether any of those risks are pervasive, affecting the entity's compliance with many compliance requirements.

7. Develop an overall response to any pervasive risks of material noncompliance identified.

8. Design and perform further audit procedures, including tests of details, in response to the assessed risks of material noncompliance to obtain sufficient appropriate audit evidence about the entity's compliance with each applicable compliance requirement. Risk assessment procedures, tests of controls, and analytical procedures by themselves are not sufficient to address these risks.

9. Tests of controls and their operating effectiveness over each applicable compliance requirement should be performed in response to the assessed risks of material noncompliance if (1) the auditor's risk assessment includes an expectation of the operating effectiveness of controls over compliance related to the applicable compliance requirements, (2) substantive procedures alone do not provide sufficient appropriate audit evidence, or (3) tests of controls over compliance are required by the governmental audit requirement.

10. Perform procedures to address any additional audit requirements specified in the governmental audit requirement supplementary to GAAS and *Government Auditing Standards*.

11. If a governmental agency provides guidance for performing a compliance audit that conflicts with current GAAS or *Government Auditing Standards,* comply with the most current applicable GAAS and *Government Auditing Standards* rather than the outdated or conflicting guidance.

12. Request written representations from management tailored to the entity and the governmental audit requirement stating management's:

    a. Acknowledgement of responsibility for understanding and complying with the compliance requirements

    b. Acknowledgement of responsibility for establishing and maintaining controls providing reasonable assurance that the entity administers government programs in accordance with the compliance requirements

    c. Identification and disclosure to the auditor of all of its government programs and related activities subject to the governmental audit requirement

    d. Making available to the auditor all contracts, grant agreements, amendments, and any other correspondence relevant to the programs and related activities subject to the governmental audit requirement

    e. Disclosure to the auditor of all known noncompliance with the applicable compliance requirements or stating that there was no such noncompliance

    f. Belief as to whether the entity has complied with the applicable compliance requirements excepting any noncompliance disclosed to the auditor

    g. Making available to the auditor all documentation related to compliance with the applicable compliance requirements

    h. Interpretation of any applicable compliance requirements subject to varying interpretations

    i. Disclosure to the auditor of any communications from grantors and pass-through entities about possible noncompliance with applicable compliance requirements, including communications to the date of the auditor's report

    j. Disclosure to the auditor of findings received and related corrective actions taken up to the date of the auditor's report for previous audits, attestation engagements, and internal or external monitoring that directly relate to the compliance audit's objectives

    k. Disclosure to the auditor of all known noncompliance with the applicable compliance requirements subsequent to the period covered by the auditor's report or stating that there is no known noncompliance

    l. Responsibility for taking corrective action on audit findings of the compliance audit

13. The auditor should request additional representations from management related to the entity's compliance with the applicable compliance requirements if he or she finds it necessary.

14. Perform audit procedures up to the date of the auditor's report to obtain sufficient appropriate audit evidence that all subsequent events related to the entity's compliance during the period covered by the auditor's compliance report have been identified. Take into account the risk assessment in determining the nature and extent of such audit procedures which should include but are not limited to inquiring of management about and considering any relevant internal auditors' reports, other auditors' reports, and reports from

grantors and pass-through entities about the entity's noncompliance that were issued during the subsequent period; and information about the entity's noncompliance obtained through other professional engagements performed for that entity.

15. While the auditor has no obligation to perform procedures related to the entity's compliance subsequent to the period covered by the audit report, if he or she becomes aware of noncompliance after the period covered by the report but before the report release date that needs to be disclosed to avoid misleading users of the report, he or she should discuss the matter with management and those charged with governance as appropriate and include an other-matter paragraph describing the nature of the noncompliance in the report.

16. Evaluate the sufficiency and appropriateness of the audit evidence obtained.

17. Form an opinion at the level specified by the governmental audit requirement on whether the entity complied in all material respects with the applicable compliance requirements and report appropriately. Evaluate likely questioned costs and other material noncompliance that may not result in questioned costs.

Reporting on a Compliance Audit

18. The auditor's report on compliance should include:

    a. A title including the word independent

    b. Identification of government programs covered by the compliance audit or reference to a schedule containing that information

    c. Identification of applicable compliance requirements or reference to where they can be found

    d. Identification of the period covered by the report

    e. A statement that entity's management is responsible for compliance with the applicable compliance requirements

    f. A statement that the auditor is responsible for expressing an opinion on the entity's compliance with the applicable compliance requirements based on the compliance audit

    g. A statement that the compliance audit was conducted in accordance with auditing standards generally accepted in the United States of America, standards applicable to financial audits contained in *Governmental Auditing Standards,* and the governmental audit requirement

    h. A statement that the compliance audit included examining, on a test basis, evidence about the entity's compliance with those requirements and performing such other procedures as the auditor considered necessary in the circumstances

    i. A statement that the auditor believes the compliance audit provides a reasonable basis for his or her opinion

    j. A statement that the compliance audit is not a legal determination of the entity's compliance

    k. The auditor's opinion on whether the entity complied with the applicable compliance requirements in all material respects at the level specified by the governmental audit requirement

    l. If noncompliance is identified that results in an opinion modification or is required to be reported by the governmental audit requirement but does not result in an opinion modification, a description of the noncompliance or a reference to that description in an accompanying schedule

m. If the criteria used to evaluate compliance are established or determined by contractual agreement or regulatory provisions that are developed solely for the parties to the agreement or regulatory agency responsible for the provisions or are available only to the specified parties, a separate paragraph at the end of the report, including (1) a statement indicating that the report is intended solely for the information and use of the specified parties, (2) identification of the specified parties to whom use is restricted, and (3) a statement that the report should not be used by anyone other than the specified parties

n. The manual or printed signature of the auditor's firm

o. The date of the auditor's report

19. If the auditor's report on compliance is combined with a report on internal control over compliance required by the governmental audit requirement, the following items should be added to the report elements already listed:

a. A statement that management is responsible for establishing and maintaining effective internal control over compliance

b. A statement that the auditor considered the entity's internal control over compliance with the applicable compliance requirements in planning and performing the audit to determine the auditing procedures in order to express an opinion on compliance, but not an opinion on the effectiveness of internal control over compliance

c. A statement that the auditor is not expressing an opinion on internal control over compliance

d. A statement that the auditor's consideration of the entity's internal control over compliance was not designed to identify all internal control deficiencies that might be significant deficiencies or material weaknesses in internal control over compliance

e. The definitions of *deficiency in internal control over compliance* and *material weakness in internal control over compliance*

f. A description of any identified material weaknesses in internal control over compliance or reference to that description in an accompanying schedule

g. If significant deficiencies in internal control over compliance were identified, the definition of *significant deficiency in internal control over compliance* and a description of the deficiencies or reference to that description in an accompanying schedule

h. If no material weaknesses in internal control over compliance were identified, a statement to that effect

i. The restricted use paragraph described in requirement 18m. A restricted use paragraph should be included in all such combined reports.

20. If the auditor chooses to issue a separate report on internal control over compliance required by the governmental audit requirement, the following items should be added to the report elements listed in requirement 19:

a. A title that includes the word independent

b. A statement that the auditor audited the entity's compliance with applicable compliance requirements pertaining to [*identify the government program(s) and the period audited*] and a reference to the auditor's report on compliance

    c. A statement that the compliance audit was conducted in accordance with auditing standards generally accepted in the United States of America, standards applicable to financial audits contained in *Governmental Auditing Standards,* and the governmental audit requirement

    d. The manual or printed signature of the auditor's firm

    e. The date of the auditor's report

21. Noncompliance and other matters required to be reported by the governmental audit requirement should be reported in the manner specified by that requirement.

22. The auditor's opinion on compliance should be modified if (1) the compliance audit identifies noncompliance with the applicable compliance requirements that the auditor believes has a material effect on the entity's compliance or (2) there is a restriction on the scope of the compliance audit.

23. Modify the report on compliance only or the separate report on internal control over compliance when referring to another auditor's report as part of the basis for the report.

24. Communicate in writing to management and those charged with governance any identified significant deficiencies and material weaknesses in internal control over compliance, even if there is no governmental audit requirement to report on internal control over compliance.

25. Communicate to those charged with governance the auditor's responsibilities under GAAS, *Government Auditing Standards,* and the governmental audit requirement, an overview of the planned scope and timing of the compliance audit, and significant findings from the compliance audit.

26. If there is a printed form, schedule, or report containing prescribed wording and the auditor has no basis to make such a statement, he or she should reword the document or attach an appropriately worded separate report.

Documentation

27. The auditor should document the following:

    a. Risk assessment procedures performed, including those performed to gain an understanding of internal control over compliance

    b. The auditor's responses to the assessed risks of material noncompliance, procedures performed, including any tests of controls over compliance, to test compliance with the applicable compliance requirements and the results of those procedures

    c. Materiality levels and the basis on which they were determined

    d. How compliance with the specific governmental audit requirements supplementary to GAAS and *Government Auditing Standards* was achieved

Report Reissuance

28. If a report is reissued, it should include an explanatory paragraph stating the report is replacing a previously issued report, describing the reasons why the report is being reissued, and any changes from the previously issued report. If additional procedures are performed to obtain sufficient appropriate audit evidence for all of the government programs being reported on, the report date should be updated to the date the auditor obtained sufficient appropriate audit evidence about the events causing the auditor to perform

the new procedures. If additional procedures are performed to obtain sufficient appropriate audit evidence for some of the government programs being reported on, the report should be dual dated with an updated report date being the date the auditor obtained sufficient appropriate audit evidence regarding the affected government programs and a reference to the affected government programs.

Analysis and Application of Procedures

Planning and Performing a Compliance Audit

Materiality

In a compliance audit, the auditor establishes materiality levels to:

- Determine the nature and extent of risk assessment procedures
- Identify and assess the risks of material noncompliance
- Determine the nature, timing, and extent of further audit procedures
- Evaluate whether the entity complied with the applicable compliance requirements
- Report noncompliance findings and other matters required to be reported by the governmental audit requirement

Materiality is generally considered in relation to the government program as a whole although a different level of materiality may be specified by the governmental audit requirement for particular purposes. For example, OMB Circular A-133 requires reporting findings of noncompliance that are material in relation to one of fourteen types of compliance requirements identified in the OMB *Compliance Supplement.*

Identifying government programs and applicable compliance requirements

Some governmental audit requirements specifically identify the applicable compliance requirements, while others, such as the *Compliance Supplement* for OMB Circular A-133, provide a framework for the auditor to determine the applicable compliance requirements. When identifying and obtaining an understanding of applicable compliance requirements, the auditor may consult the *Compliance Supplement* used in OMB Circular A-133 audits, which contains compliance requirements that are typically applicable to federal government programs and suggested audit procedures for those requirements and also provides guidance for identifying compliance requirements for programs that are not included. The auditor may also consult the applicable program-specific audit guide issued by the grantor agency, which contains the compliance requirements pertaining to the government program and suggested audit procedures for those requirements.

If the *Compliance Supplement* or a program-specific audit guide is not applicable, the auditor may perform the following procedures to identify and obtain an understanding of the applicable compliance requirements:

- Read laws, regulations, rules, and provisions of contracts or grant agreements pertaining to the government program
- Inquire of management and other knowledgeable entity personnel

- Inquire of appropriate individuals outside the entity, such as the office of the federal, state, or local program official or auditor about the laws and regulations applicable to entities within their jurisdiction or a third-party specialist such as an attorney

- Read the minutes of meetings of the governing board of the entity being audited

- Read audit documentation about the applicable compliance requirements prepared during prior years' audits or other engagements

- Discuss the applicable compliance requirements with auditors who performed prior years' audits or other engagements

Risk assessment and audit procedures

The nature and extent of risk assessment procedures the auditor performs vary and are influenced by factors such as:

- The newness, complexity, and nature of the applicable compliance requirements

- The auditor's knowledge of the entity's internal control over compliance with the applicable compliance requirements obtained in previous audits or other professional engagements

- The services provided by the entity and how they are affected by external factors

- The level of oversight by the grantor or pass-through entity

- How management addresses findings

In assessing the risks of material noncompliance with the applicable compliance requirements, the auditor may consider the requirements' complexity and susceptibility to noncompliance, how long the entity has been subject to the requirements, how the entity has previously complied with the requirements, the potential effect on the entity of noncompliance, the degree of judgment involved in adhering to the requirements, and the auditor's assessment of the risks of material misstatement in the financial statement audit. Inherent and control risk of noncompliance may be evaluated individually or in combination.

OBSERVATION: The risk of material noncompliance may be pervasive to the entity's noncompliance if an entity is experiencing financial difficulty and there is an increased risk grant funds will be diverted for unauthorized purposes or an entity has a history of poor recordkeeping for its government programs.

Audit procedures are designed in a compliance audit to detect intentional and unintentional material noncompliance in order to obtain reasonable, but not absolute, assurance about the entity's compliance. Analytical procedures may contribute some substantive evidence, but are generally less effective in a compliance audit than in a financial statement audit. Tests of details may be used to test for compliance in areas such as grant disbursements or expenditures, eligibility files, cost allocation plans, or periodic reports filed with grantor agencies.

Some governmental audit requirements such as OMB Circular A-133 require tests of the operating effectiveness of controls identified as likely to be effective even if that testing is inefficient. For compliance audits, audit evidence about the operating effectiveness of controls obtained in prior audits is not applicable.

Supplementary audit requirements

An example of supplementary audit requirements the auditor may need to adhere to are the requirements in OMB Circular A-133 to perform specified procedures to identify major programs and to follow up on prior audit findings and perform procedures to assess the reasonableness of the summary schedule of prior audit findings.

Written representations

Management may include qualifying language in the written representations indicating that representations are made to the best of management's knowledge and belief. This qualifying language is not appropriate for the representations about management's responsibilities for: understanding and complying with the compliance requirements; establishing and maintaining controls that provide reasonable assurance that the entity administers governments programs in accordance with the compliance requirements; and taking corrective action on audit findings of the compliance audit.

Evaluating audit evidence and forming an opinion

In determining whether an entity has materially complied with the applicable compliance requirements, the auditor may consider factors such as:

- The frequency and nature of noncompliance with the applicable compliance requirements identified during the compliance audit

- The adequacy of the entity's system for monitoring compliance with the applicable compliance requirements and the possible effect of any noncompliance on the entity

- Whether any identified noncompliance with the applicable compliance requirements resulted in likely questioned costs that are material to the government program

The auditor should consider all noncompliance he or she identified in making this evaluation, regardless of whether the entity corrected the noncompliance after the auditor brought it to management's attention.

Reporting on a Compliance Audit

The auditor is not precluded from restricting the use of any report to intended users.

OBSERVATION: If a report is a matter of public record or available for public inspection, removing personally identifiable information in the report and findings of noncompliance will reduce the likelihood of sensitive information being disclosed.

Government Auditing Standards require that when the auditor communicates significant deficiencies or material weaknesses in internal control over compliance to management and those charged with governance, he or she obtain a response, preferably in writing, concerning their views on the findings, conclusions, and recommendations included in the auditor's report on internal control over compliance and any such written response be included in the auditor's report. If the written response is included in a document with the auditor's written communication to management and those charged with governance regarding identified significant deficiencies or material weaknesses in internal control over compliance, the auditor may add a paragraph to the communication disclaiming an opinion on such information.

Documentation

Specific documentation of how the auditor adapted and applied each of the applicable AU-C sections to the objectives of a compliance audit is not necessary; documentation of the audit strategy, audit plan, and the work performed is sufficient.

AT Section
Statements on Standards for Attestation Engagements

AT SECTION 20

DEFINING PROFESSIONAL REQUIREMENTS IN STATEMENTS ON STANDARDS FOR ATTESTATION ENGAGEMENTS

Authoritative Pronouncements

SSAE-13—Defining Professional Requirements in Statements on Standards for Attestation Engagements

Overview

SSAE-13 specifies the practitioner's performance responsibility under the Statements on Standards for Attestation Engagements. The standard provides guidance on when a practitioner *must* perform an attestation procedure, when the practitioner *should* perform an attestation procedure, and when a practitioner *may* perform an attestation procedure.

> **OBSERVATION:** SSAE-13 defines a practitioner's performance responsibilities with more specificity than has previously existed in the professional literature. Therefore, the authors expect that practitioners will be held to these performance standards by regulators and the judicial system. For these reasons, practitioners are well advised to pay particularly close attention to the inclusion of the words "must," "is required," "should, and "may" in existing and future professional standards.

A SSAE contains both professional requirements and related guidance in applying the standard. In fulfilling professional responsibilities, the practitioner has a responsibility to consider the entire text of a SSAE. There are two types of professional requirements imposed by a SSAE: (1) unconditional requirements and (2) presumptively mandatory requirements.

A practitioner must comply with an unconditional requirement, assuming that the circumstances that the requirement applies to exist. The existence of an unconditional requirement is indicated by the words "must" or "is required" in a SSAE.

In most cases, the practitioner is also required to comply with a presumptively mandatory requirement. In rare cases, a practitioner can depart from a presumptively mandatory requirement. But, in these rare cases, the practitioner must document (1) the reasons why the presumptively mandatory requirement was not followed and (2) how alternative procedures achieved the objectives that the presumptively mandatory requirement was designed to meet. The existence of a presumptively mandatory requirement is indicated by the word "should."

> **ENGAGEMENT STRATEGY:** The practitioner must achieve the objectives that a presumptively mandatory requirement is designed to achieve, either by perform-

ing the procedures specified in the SSAE or by employing alternative procedures that accomplish the same objective.

A SSAE may specify that a practitioner "should consider" a procedure. In this instance, there is a presumptive requirement that the practitioner will consider the procedure. However, although the practitioner essentially has to consider the procedure, the practitioner does not necessarily have to perform the procedure.

A SSAE also contains related guidance in applying the standard. This related guidance is also referred to as "explanatory material." Explanatory material in a SSAE is intended to be descriptive rather than imperative (i.e., it does not impose a performance obligation upon the practitioner). For example, explanatory material may (1) explain the objective of the professional requirements, (2) explain why particular attestation procedures are recommended or required, and (3) provide additional information that the practitioner may find helpful in applying his or her professional judgment. Explanatory material may discuss other procedures or actions that the practitioner might perform. These other procedures or actions are suggestive and do not impose a professional requirement on the practitioner. These suggested procedures and actions in a SSAE are denoted by the words "may," "might," or "could."

OBSERVATION: SSAE-13 indicates that interpretive publications are not professional standards but, rather, provide guidance on the application of a SSAE to a particular circumstance. Interpretive guidance includes interpretations of the SSAEs, appendixes to SSAEs, and AICPA Statements of Position. The words "must" or "should" in an interpretive document do *not* represent unconditional requirements or presumptively mandatory requirements, respectively.

AT SECTION 50

SSAE HIERARCHY

Authoritative Pronouncements

SSAE-14—SSAE Hierarchy

Overview

A practitioner must follow the attestation standards in planning, conducting, and reporting on an attestation engagement. The attestation standards define the level of performance expected of the practitioner and are designed to ensure quality engagement performance. Attestation procedures are the specific steps performed by the practitioner in complying with the attestation standards.

There are 11 generally accepted attestation standards. These standards are listed and discussed in AT 101. The Auditing Standards Board, a senior technical body of the AICPA, issues Statements on Standards for Attestation Engagements (SSAEs). The SSAEs are essential in applying the 11 generally accepted attestation standards. Practitioners who perform an attestation engagement are required by Rule 202 of the AICPA's Code of Professional Conduct to comply with the generally accepted attestation standards and SSAEs.

Practitioners must apply professional judgment in applying the attestation standards. It should be rare for a practitioner to depart from presumptively mandatory requirements in performing an attestation engagement. If a practitioner departs from a presumptively mandatory requirement, he or she must document the reason for the departure and how the alternative procedures performed accomplished the objectives of the requirements that were not being followed.

In addition to the generally accepted attestation standards and SSAEs, there are other sources of guidance on performing attestation engagements. These other sources of guidance are attestation interpretations and other attestation publications.

Attestation interpretations are Interpretations of SSAEs, SSAE appendixes, attestation guidance in AICPA Audit and Accounting Guides, and AICPA attestation Statements of Position. The practitioner should consider these attestation interpretations in performing an engagement. If the practitioner chooses not to apply the guidance that is in an attestation interpretation, he or she should be prepared to explain how he or she met the SSAE requirement that was the subject of the attestation interpretation.

OBSERVATION: An appendix to a SSAE that modifies another SSAE must be complied with in the same manner as the body of the SSAE.

Other attestation publications are a broad set of literature, including (1) other AICPA attestation publications, (2) attestation articles in professional journals and newsletters, (3) continuing education programs, (4) textbooks and guide books, and (5) state CPA society publications. Other attestation publications have no authoritative status, but the practitioner may consider and apply this guidance if it is relevant and appropriate to the engagement. In evaluating whether an attestation publication is appropriate, the practitioner should consider (1) the degree to which the publication is recognized as helpful in understanding and applying SSAEs and (2) the degree to which the issuer or author is recognized as an authority on attestation matters.

OBSERVATION: An attestation publication that has been reviewed by the AICPA Audit and Attest Standards Staff is presumed to be appropriate.

AT SECTION 101

ATTEST ENGAGEMENTS

Authoritative Pronouncements

SSAE-10—Attestation Standards: Revision and Recodification (Chapter 1)

OBSERVATION: SSAE-10 supersedes SSAE-1 through SSAE-9.

SSAE-11—Attest Documentation

SSAE-12—Amendment to SSAE No. 10, Attestation Standards: Revision and Recodification

SSAE Interpretation No. 1 of AT 101 (January 2001)—Defense Industry Questionnaire on Business Ethics and Conduct

SSAE Interpretation No. 2 of AT 101 (January 2001)—Responding to Requests for Reports on Matters Relating to Solvency

SSAE Interpretation No. 3 of AT 101 (January 2001)—Applicability of Attestation Standards to Litigation Services

SSAE Interpretation No. 4 of AT 101 (January 2002)—Providing Access to or Photocopies of Working Papers to a Regulator

SSAE Interpretation No. 5 of AT 101 (September 2003)—Attest Engagements on Financial Information Included in XBRL Instance Documents

SSAE Interpretation No. 6 of AT 101 (January 2005)—Reporting on Attestation Engagements Performed in Accordance with Government Auditing Standards

SSAE Interpretation No. 7 of AT 101 (December 2008)—Reporting on the Design of Internal Control

SSAE Interpretation No. 8 of AT 101 (September 2010)—Including a Description of Tests of Controls or Other Procedures, and the Results Thereof, in an Examination Report

Overview

Before standards for attest engagements (or attestation engagements) were promulgated, the professional standards did not specifically address certain types of auditing and accounting engagements. For example, there were no professional standards for engagements to report on (1) descriptions of computer software; (2) compliance with statutory, regulatory, and contractual requirements; (3) investment performance statistics; and (4) nonfinancial information supplementary to financial statements. These and other auditing and accounting engagements that are not addressed by other existing professional standards may be covered by the standards for attest engagements.

Statements on Standards for Attestation Engagements (SSAE) establish attestation standards that must be satisfied by an auditor when he or she is "engaged to issue or does issue an examination, a review, or an agreed-upon procedures report on subject matter, or an assertion about the subject matter (the assertion), that is the responsibility of another party" except in the following circumstances:

- Engagements performed in accordance with Statements on Auditing Standards (SASs)

- Engagements performed in accordance with Statements on Standards for Accounting and Review Services (SSARSs)

- Engagements performed in accordance with Statements on Standards for Consulting Services (SSCS)

- Engagements in which the auditor is the client's advocate (such as tax disputes with the Internal Revenue Service)

- Engagements to prepare tax returns or give tax advice

As suggested in the above definition, in an attest engagement subject to SSAE standards the auditor reports on subject matter or an assertion. SSAE-10 notes that the subject matter of an attest engagement can be varied and can provide an assurance on such data as the following:

- Historical or prospective performance or condition, such as historical financial information, prospective financial information, and backlog data.

- Physical characteristics, such as the number of square feet in a building.

- Historical events, such as the price of commodities on a specified date.

- Analytical material, such as break-even analysis.

- Systems and processes, such as internal controls.

- Compliance with established procedures, such as laws and regulations.

On the other hand, when the attest engagement deals with issuing a report on an "assertion about the subject matter," the auditor is concerned with whether the assertion is based on or in conformity with the criteria selected.

In an examination or a review attest engagement, the auditor should obtain a written assertion. The written assertion could be communicated to the auditor in a variety of ways, including as a representation letter addressed to the auditor or a declaration on a related schedule.

OBSERVATION: When a written assertion is not obtained, a practitioner can report on the subject matter as explained later.

The responsible party in an attest engagement is "the person or persons, either as individuals or representatives of the entity, responsible for the subject matter." The practitioner cannot be the "responsible party" even when the practitioner has obtained information to help the responsible party to understand the nature of the written assertion. SSAE-10 points out that the responsible party must "accept responsibility for its assertion and the subject matter and must not base its assertion solely on the practitioner's procedures." In fact, the practitioner can accept an SSAE engagement only if one of the following conditions is satisfied:

> The party wishing to engage the practitioner is responsible for the subject matter, or has a reasonable basis for providing a written assertion about the subject matter if the nature of the subject matter is such that a responsible party does not otherwise exist.

> The party wishing to engage the practitioner is not responsible for the subject matter but is able to provide the practitioner, or have a third party who is responsible for the subject matter provide the practitioner, with evidence of the third party's responsibility for the subject matter.

PLANNING AID REMINDER: Interpretation No. 3 of AT 101 states that attestation standards apply only to litigation service engagements in which a practitioner "is engaged to issue or does issue an examination, a review, or an agreed-upon procedures report on subject matter, or an assertion about the subject matter, that is the responsibility of another party."

PLANNING AID REMINDER: Interpretation No. 1 of AT 101 states that SSAEs apply to an engagement in which a practitioner has been requested to express a written conclusion on a defense contractor's Statement of Responses to the Defense Industry Questionnaire on Business Ethics and Conduct and the additional attached questionnaire and responses.

OBSERVATION: SSAE-12 points out that although a firm has deficiencies in its system of quality control or violates specific policies or controls, it does not mean that a particular attest engagement was not performed in accordance with Statements on Standards for Attestation Engagements.

EXAMINATIONS AND REVIEWS

Due to the nature of attest engagements, SSAE standards require that the CPA establish an understanding of the engagement with the client. That understanding between the CPA and the client (preferably in writing) should include (1) the objectives of the engagement, (2) management's responsibilities with respect to the presentation, (3) the CPA's responsibilities, and (4) limitations of the attest engagement.

OBSERVATION: The balance of this chapter discusses the general standards, fieldwork standards, and reporting standards in the context of an examination attest engagement and a review attest engagement. These standards also apply to agreed-upon procedures engagements, which is the subject matter of the following chapter.

Promulgated Procedures Checklist

The practitioner should perform the following procedures in an attest engagement:

- Preplan the attest engagement.
- Plan the attest engagement.
- Obtain sufficient evidence depending on the nature of the attest engagement.
- Prepare an appropriate report on the results of the attest engagement.
- Prepare appropriate workpapers.

Analysis and Application of Procedures

Preplan the attest engagement

Pre-engagement planning is an essential element of all professional engagements a CPA performs. The practitioner must determine whether the attest engagement will include an examination, a review, or the application of agreed-upon procedures. In addition, the practitioner must determine whether to accept or reject the attest engagement. The preengagement planning phase of an attest engagement is based on the first five general standards for attest engagements, which are discussed below.

General Standard No. 1—Training and Proficiency

The first general attestation standard states that "the practitioner must have adequate technical training and proficiency to perform the attestation engagement." Adequate technical training is a combination of an appropriate educational background and practical experience. A CPA with adequate technical training should be competent enough to obtain and evaluate the necessary evidence to determine whether or not another party's written assertions are supportable. The CPA can develop proficiency only by applying knowledge he or she has gained in an actual attest engagement.

ENGAGEMENT STRATEGY: Unlike the first standard of generally accepted auditing standards, the first general attestation standard does not refer to the practitioner's technical training and proficiency as an auditor. The scope of the attestation function described in the SSAE standards goes beyond the boundaries of financial reporting.

General Standard No. 2—Knowledge of Subject Matter

The second general attestation standard states that "the practitioner must have adequate knowledge of the subject matter." Although it can be assumed that a CPA is familiar with financial reporting standards, it cannot be assumed that a CPA is familiar with the procedures and concepts of all attest engagements. Thus, before a CPA accepts an attest engagement, he or she should have an adequate understanding of the nature of the written assertion(s). Obviously, a

CPA cannot express an opinion on the written assertions unless he or she has a certain level of expertise relating to the nature of the assertions.

The knowledge required to perform an attest engagement may be obtained through a variety of sources, including formal courses and professional experience. Under some circumstances, the CPA does not have to master a portion of the expertise but may obtain it through the use of specialists (AU-C 620, *Using the Work of an Auditor's Specialist*). When a CPA decides to use the work of a specialist, he or she must have a sufficient understanding of the subject matter to explain the objectives of the engagement to the specialist. The CPA must also be able to evaluate the work of the specialist to determine whether the objectives of the engagement have been achieved.

General Standard No. 3—Suitable and Available Criteria

Not all engagements provide a basis for attestation. The third general standard requires that "the practitioner must have reason to believe that the subject matter is capable of evaluation against criteria that are suitable and available to users."

The fundamental element in the engagement is the existence of reasonable criteria that provide the basis for the written assertions. In an audit engagement, the reasonable criteria are generally accepted accounting principles (GAAP), which in turn provide a reasonable basis for the preparation of financial statements. Because of the diversity of attest engagements, there is no single set of reasonable criteria for all such engagements. However, SSAE standards note that criteria are considered to be suitable only if they have the following four characteristics:

1. Objective (free from bias)

2. Measurable (provide a reasonable basis for the consistent measurement of the subject matter)

3. Complete (no relevant factors that would alter a conclusion are omitted)

4. Relevant (related to the subject matter)

There is no single source of criteria for the various attest engagements, and the practitioner must use professional judgment to determine whether a specific set of criteria is suitable to a particular subject matter.

PLANNING AID REMINDER: Criteria developed by an appropriate professional group that follows due process procedures are ordinarily considered suitable. For example, Interpretation No. 5 of AT 101 states that XBRL taxonomies and XBRL International Technical Specifications are suitable criteria for performing an attest engagement on XBRL Instance Documents. Another example of suitable criteria is the Auditing Standards Board's guidance in SOP 2003-02 (Attest Engagements on Greenhouse Gas Emissions Information) in performing attest engagements relating to the existence and ownership of greenhouse gas emissions credits. Conversely, in other cases a client (or other parties or groups that do not follow due process procedures and that do not represent a group of experts) may develop criteria to be used for the attest engagement. In such cases, the practitioner must use the four characteristics listed above to determine the suitability of the criteria established for the attest engagement. An engagement should not be accepted "when the criteria are so subjective or vague that reasonably consistent measurements, qualitative or quantitative, of subject matter cannot ordinarily be obtained."

OBSERVATION: In some engagements the appropriateness of criteria may apply only to parties who have participated in the establishment of the criteria or that have a particular level or type of expertise. In these circumstances the practitioner should restrict the use of the engagement report.

PLANNING AID REMINDER: The suitability of criteria is determined without regard to the type of attest engagement. For example, if criteria are considered to be unsuitable for an examination attest engagement, they are also unsuitable for a review attest engagement.

Finally, SSAE standards require that criteria be available to users under at least one of the following circumstances:

- The criteria are publicly available.
- The criteria are clearly presented in the presentation of the subject matter or the assertion.
- The criteria are clearly presented in the practitioner's report.
- The criteria are commonly understood and are not unique to the attest engagement.
- The criteria are available only to the specified parties (and therefore the availability of auditor's report is restricted).

General Standard No. 4—Independence

The fourth general attestation standard requires that "the practitioner must maintain independence in mental attitude in all matters relating to the engagement." Independence in fact is a mental state of mind wherein a CPA is impartial in determining the reliability of assertions made in the written communication. In reaching a conclusion, a CPA favors neither the asserter nor the user of the information. Independence in appearance means that the CPA should avoid situations or relationships that may suggest to an outside party that the CPA is not independent. The AICPA's Code of Professional Conduct, Rule 101 (Independence) is applicable to attest engagements.

PUBLIC COMPANY IMPLICATION: The PCAOB also has jurisdiction over standard setting for attestation engagements performed for public companies. When assessing independence related to an attestation engagement for a public company, registered public accounting firms must ensure that they are in compliance with all of the SEC's rules, PCAOB's rules, and Rule 101 of the AICPA's Code of Professional Conduct.

General Standard No. 5—Due Care

The fifth general attestation standard requires that "the practitioner must exercise due professional care in the planning and performance of the engagement and the preparation of the report." The CPA achieves due professional care by observing the two standards of fieldwork and the four reporting standards. For a CPA to agree to perform an attest engagement implies that the practitioner has a level of expertise that is possessed by other CPAs who perform similar services. Upon accepting the engagement, the CPA is expected to perform the engagement and exercise those skills to a degree expected by a reasonable person. However, this does not imply that the CPA's judgment is infallible or that he or she can be expected to fill the role of a guarantor of information contained in written reports. If the practitioner is not negligent in the execution of the engagement and conducts him- or herself in an honest manner, the due care standard generally will be satisfied.

Plan the attest engagement

Critical elements of every professional engagement include planning and supervision. The importance of these elements is recognized in the first standard of fieldwork, which states that an attest engagement should be adequately planned and that assistants, if any, should be properly supervised.

Fieldwork Standard No. 1—Planning and Supervision

The first standard of fieldwork states that "the practitioner must adequately plan the work and must properly supervise any assistants." Planning allows the practitioner to develop a strategy for conducting an attest engagement. Adequate planning matches the objectives of the attest engagement with the specific procedures that must be performed to achieve the objectives. Each engagement plan is unique, because it is based on the specific characteristics of a particular engagement. SSAE standards identify the following as factors that should be considered by the practitioner in planning an attest engagement:

- The criteria that are the basis for the engagement
- Preliminary judgments about attestation risk and materiality related to the engagement.
- The likelihood of revision or adjustment of items within the assertion or the nature of the subject matter
- Possible conditions that may require that attestation procedures be modified or extended
- The nature of the attestation report that is expected to be issued by the auditor

In addition, an understanding with the client should be established and should include the following elements:

- The objectives of the attest engagement
- The responsibilities of management with respect to the attest engagement
- The responsibility of the practitioner with respect to the attest engagement
- The limitations of the attest engagement

If an appropriate understanding with the client cannot be reached, the practitioner should refuse the attest engagement.

PLANNING AID REMINDER: The understanding with the client should be documented in the engagement files, preferably through a written communication with the client (an engagement letter).

Obtain sufficient evidence depending on the nature of the attest engagement

The second standard of fieldwork states that "the practitioner must obtain sufficient evidence to provide a reasonable basis for the conclusion that is expressed in the report."

Fieldwork Standard No. 2—Sufficient Evidence

There are a variety of attest procedures that may be used to obtain evidential matter. The selection of specific procedures to be used in a specific attest engagement is based on professional judgment. In addition, SSAE standards provide the following guidelines:

- Evidence obtained from independent sources outside an entity provides greater assurance of an assertion's reliability than does evidence secured solely from within the entity.

- Information obtained through the practitioner's direct personal knowledge (such as through physical examination, observation, computation, operating tests, or inspection) is more persuasive than information not obtained through the practitioner's personal knowledge.

- Assertions developed under effective internal controls are more reliable than those developed under ineffective internal controls.

The above guidelines are concerned with the quality of the evidential matter that is obtained in an attest engagement, but the CPA must also be concerned with the quantity of the evidential matter. Here again, professional judgment must ultimately be used to identify what constitutes sufficient evidence in an attest engagement. In addition, SSAE standards provide that the practitioner should consider the following items in determining the sufficiency of evidential matter:

- Nature and materiality of the information in the presentation of the assertions taken as a whole

- Likelihood of misstatements

- Knowledge obtained during current and previous engagements

- The competence of the responsible party (often management) in the subject matter of the assertion

- Extent to which the information is affected by the asserter's judgment

- Inadequacies in the assertions' underlying data

The quality of evidence and the sufficiency of evidence must be determined in the context of the specific type of attest engagement. As described earlier, an attest engagement may be an examination engagement, a review engagement, or an agreed-upon procedures engagement.

Examination engagement Attest procedures must be selected so that the quality and quantity of evidence obtained is sufficient to reduce the attestation risk (probability of not discovering materially misstated assertions) to a low level. Of course, the overall attestation risk cannot be quantified, but the CPA must exercise professional judgment in order to assess inherent risk and control risk and establish an appropriate level of detection risk. The practitioner has little influence, if any, on the levels of inherent risk and control risk in an attest engagement. However, the practitioner can influence the level of detection risk through the selection of attest procedures. The generalized relationships in Exhibit AT 101-1 can be used to establish an acceptable level of detection risk.

EXHIBIT AT 101-1—ACCEPTABLE LEVEL OF DETECTION RISK

Assessed Risk	Effect on Detection Risk Level
Inherent risk is assessed to be relatively high.	Detection risk should be established at a relatively low level.
Inherent risk is assessed to be relatively low.	Detection risk should be established at a relatively high level.
Control risk is assessed to be relatively high.	Detection risk should be established at a relatively low level.
Control risk is assessed to be relatively low.	Detection risk should be established at a relatively high level.

After considering inherent risk, control risk, and detection risk, the practitioner should attempt to achieve a low level of attestation risk. In an examination engagement, the practitioner can achieve a low level of attestation risk by relying on search and verification procedures, such as physical observation, confirmation, and inspection, in addition to inquiry and analytical procedures.

Review engagement The level of assurance the practitioner provides in a review engagement is not as great as the level of assurance he or she provides in an examination engagement. In a review engagement, the practitioner expresses a limited assurance, whereas in an examination engagement, the practitioner expresses a positive assurance on the assertions. For this reason, the level of attestation risk that must be achieved in a review engagement is a moderate level, rather than a low level. On the basis of the interrelationship of inherent risk, control risk, and detection risk, the practitioner selects attest procedures that will result in an overall moderate level of attestation risk.

Generally, in a review engagement, the CPA limits attest procedures to inquiry and analytical procedures, in much the same manner as an accountant would in the conduct of a review of historical financial statements. This is not to suggest that other attest procedures, such as search and verification procedures, are not appropriate under some circumstances. For example, Exhibit AT 101-2 presents circumstances that may be encountered in a review engagement and the effects of the circumstances on attest procedures.

EXHIBIT AT 101-2—CIRCUMSTANCES ENCOUNTERED IN REVIEW ENGAGEMENTS AND THEIR EFFECTS ON ATTEST PROCEDURES

Circumstance	Effects of Circumstance on Attest Procedures Used in a Review Engagement
Inquiry and analytical procedures cannot be performed.	Use other attest procedures to achieve a level of assurance that would have been achieved if the inquiry and analytical procedures had been performed.
Inquiry and analytical procedures are considered to be inefficient.	Use other attest procedures that are more efficient to achieve a level of assurance that would have been achieved if the less efficient inquiry and analytical procedures had been performed.
Inquiry and analytical procedures are employed, but results suggest that assertions might be incorrect or incomplete.	Use additional attest procedures to the extent deemed necessary to remove doubts about the accuracy or completeness of assertions.

SSAE standards state that a practitioner should consider obtaining a representation letter from the responsible party in both an examination engagement and a review engagement. To some extent the content of the representation letter will be unique to the nature of the subject matter, but elements of the letter may include the following:

- Acknowledgment of responsibility for the subject matter and, when applicable, the assertion

- Acknowledgement of responsibility for selecting the criteria

- Acknowledgement of responsibility for the appropriateness of the criteria (when the responsible party is the client)

- The assertion about the subject matter

- Representation that all known matters contradicting the assertion have been made available to the practitioner

- Representation that communications from regulatory agencies related to the subject matter have been made available to the practitioner

- Statement that all relevant records have been made available to the practitioner

- Statement that material subsequent events related to the subject matter have been communicated to the practitioner

ENGAGEMENT STRATEGY: In an attest engagement in which the client is the responsible party the client will ordinarily be capable of providing the practitioner with a written assertion about the subject matter. If the client does not provide a written assertion, the practitioner should (1) modify the engagement report because of the client-imposed scope limitation in an examination engagement, or (2) withdraw from a review engagement. However, when a party other than the client is the responsible party and that party does not provide a written assertion, SSAE standards point out that the practitioner "may be able to conclude that he or she has sufficient evidence to form a conclusion about the subject matter."

Prepare an appropriate report on the results of the attest engagement

Although the nature of attest engagements is varied, there are four reporting standards that must be observed in the preparation of the practitioner's report.

OBSERVATION: The reporting standards do not apply unless the practitioner issues a report.

Reporting Standard No. 1—Character of Engagement

The first reporting standard requires that "the practitioner must identify the subject matter of the assertion being reported on and state the character of the engagement in the report." The examination or review report should provide an assurance on the subject matter or the assertion, describe the nature and scope of the engagement, and identify the professional standards that apply to the engagement.

PLANNING AID REMINDER: Interpretation No. 6 of AT 101 states that the practitioners performing attestation engagements under the *Government Auditing Standards* (i.e., the Yellow Book) are required to follow standards in the Yellow Book that go beyond the reporting standards in AT 101. For those engagements, Interpretation No. 6 of AT 101 states that the practitioner should modify the scope of the attestation report to indicate that the examination or review was "conducted in accordance with attestation standards established by the AICPA and the standards applicable to attestation engagements contained in accordance with *Government Auditing Standards* issued by the Comptroller General of the United States."

Reporting Standard No. 2—Conclusions

SSAE standards require that the engagement report state the practitioner's conclusion "about the subject matter or the assertion in relation to the criteria against which the subject matter was evaluated."

The nature and scope of the attest engagement should enable the practitioner to draw a conclusion about whether there are material omissions or misstatements with respect to the subject matter or assertion. Professional judgment must be exercised to identify material misstatements. An item is considered material if a user of the information would be influenced by its omission or misstatement. Materiality is expressed in relative (percentage) terms rather than absolute (dollar) terms.

In an examination engagement, the practitioner's report should express a positive conclusion about whether the presentation of assertions is in accordance with the established or stated criteria. The practitioner may expand the report by adding paragraphs that emphasize certain matters relating to the attest engagement or the presentation of assertions. This type of report modification does not result in a qualified opinion, and the opinion paragraph of the report should not refer to the emphasized matters.

Circumstances that may lead to the expression of an opinion that is not unqualified are discussed later in this chapter under the section titled "Reporting Standard No. 3."

When a review engagement is completed, the practitioner's report expresses negative assurance on the subject matter or assertion. In addition to negative assurance, the report should state that the scope of a review is narrower than that of an examination, and it should disclaim a positive opinion on the presentation. The practitioner may expand the report by adding paragraphs that emphasize certain matters relating to the attest engagement. Other circumstances that may lead to the modification of a review report are discussed later in this section under the section titled "Reporting Standard No. 3."

Reporting Standard No. 3—Significant Reservations

The third reporting standard is unique in that it explicitly requires that the attest report include all significant reservations the practitioner has with respect to the engagement, the subject matter and, if applicable, the assertions. When attestation standards have not been satisfied and the practitioner has significant reservations, an unqualified conclusion should not be expressed in the examination report or the review report. Significant reservations may be categorized as scope deficiencies and engagement reservations.

Scope deficiencies The second standard of fieldwork requires that sufficient evidence be obtained to support the practitioner's report. When significant reservations exist because of the limited scope of the attest engagement, the practitioner should qualify or disclaim any assurance on the presentation of assertions or withdraw from the engagement.

Scope limitations may arise if all necessary or alternative procedures (examination and review engagements) cannot be performed because of the circumstances surrounding the engagement or because of restrictions imposed by the client. Generally, if the client imposes restrictions, the practitioner should withdraw from the engagement and issue no report or should disclaim any assurance on the presentation.

When the scope limitation is caused by the practitioner's inability to perform attest procedures or express a conclusion on the presentation of assertions, the significance of the restrictions determines whether a qualified conclusion, disclaimer of conclusion, or withdrawal from the engagement is appropriate. Specifically, the actions the practitioner should take depend on the following factors:

- Nature and magnitude of the scope restrictions
- Significance of restrictions to the presentation of assertions
- Nature of the service being performed (examination or review)

If the practitioner concludes that a qualified conclusion or disclaimer of conclusion should be expressed, the basis for the qualification or disclaimer must be described in the practitioner's report.

Engagement reservations The practitioner may have reservations about the subject matter or the assertion concerning conformity of the subject matter with the criteria, which includes the adequacy of related disclosures. The nature of a reservation can relate to "the measurement, form, arrangement, content or underlying judgments and assumptions applicable to the subject matter or assertion and its appended notes." Professional judgment must be exercised to determine whether the reservation results in a qualified or adverse opinion in an examination engagement or a modified conclusion in a review engagement.

PLANNING AID REMINDER: According to Interpretation No. 2 of AT 101, a CPA should provide no level of assurance, through an audit, a review, or an agreed-upon procedures engagement, that an entity (1) is not insolvent at the time debt is incurred or would not be rendered insolvent thereby, (2) does not have unusually small capital, or (3) has the ability to pay its debt as the debt matures. These and similar situations are referred to as matters relating to solvency.

ENGAGEMENT STRATEGY: Although a CPA cannot provide assurance about matters relating to solvency, he or she can provide other services, such as the audit or review of the historical financial statements, the examination or review of pro forma financial information, or the examination or compilation of prospective financial information.

Reporting Standard No. 4—Restricted Distribution

The fourth standard of reporting states that "the practitioner must state in the report that the report is intended solely for the information and use of the specified parties" under the following circumstances:

- When the criteria used to evaluate the subject matter are determined by the practitioner to be appropriate only for a limited number of parties who either participated in their establishment or can be presumed to have an adequate understanding of the criteria
- When the criteria used to evaluate the subject matter are available only to specified parties
- When reporting on subject matter and a written assertion has not been provided by the responsible party
- When the report is on an attestation engagement to apply agreed-upon procedures to the subject matter

When a restricted report is issued, that report should include the following points:

- A statement noting that the report is "intended solely for the information and use of the specified parties"
- Identification of the specified parties
- A statement that the report "is not intended to be and should not be used by anyone other than the specified parties"

Prepare appropriate workpapers

Attest documentation (attest files) should (1) facilitate the conduct and supervision of an engagement and (2) substantiate the attest report; however, the specific type and extent of documentation is to some degree dependent upon the characteristics of a particular attest engagement. Attest documentation should identify team members who performed specific tasks and those who reviewed the work. In addition, the documentation should allow those individuals responsible for the review and supervision of the engagement to "understand the nature, timing, extent, and result of attest procedures performed and the information obtained."

Retention of attest documentation

Attest documentation should be retained for the period of time that meets the objectives of the CPA firm (for example, the need for internal reviews) and satisfies the legal or regulatory requirements imposed by the state or regulatory authorities.

PUBLIC COMPANY IMPLICATION: The PCAOB requires auditors to retain audit documentation for seven years from the audit report release date. The PCAOB will presumably develop retention requirements for documentation in support of attest engagements at some future point.

Confidentiality of attest documentation

A CPA firm should adopt reasonable administrative procedures to maintain the confidentiality (including unauthorized access) of its attest documentation in order to satisfy the Code of Professional Conduct (Rule 301) and any legal or regulatory requirements.

PLANNING AID REMINDER: The documentation requirements described above are general and apply to all attest engagements. In addition, when the attest engagement involves the examination of prospective financial statements the attest documentation should "indicate that the process by which the entity develops its prospective financial statements was considered in determining the scope of the examination."

Reporting on the Design of Internal Control

SSAE-15 provides guidance for when an auditor is engaged to report on the effectiveness of internal control over financial reporting that is integrated with a financial statement audit. In a SSAE-15 engagement, the auditor tests both the design and operating effectiveness of internal control. A practitioner may be engaged to report only on the design of internal control. The practitioner can perform such an engagement using the guidance in AT 101 (in particular, see Interpretation No. 7 of AT 101).

One reason for requesting a practitioner to report on the design of internal control is that a client may be requested to prepare or file a pre-award survey (assertion) as part of applying for a governmental grant or contract. The assertion may be concerned with the effectiveness of the design of part or all of a client's internal control, and it may require the client's auditor to report on the assertion. Interpretation No. 7 of AT 101 states that the practitioner's consideration of a client's internal control as part of the audit of its financial statements is not a basis for reporting on the assertion included in the pre-award survey.

In order to report on the client's assertion concerning its internal control, the practitioner must perform an examination or an agreed-upon procedures (AUP) engagement based on the SSAE standards. And if the agreed-upon procedures engagement involves controls over compliance with specified requirements, the practitioner also should refer to the guidance in AT 601 (Compliance Attestation).

A practitioner also may be asked to report on whether controls that an entity plans to implement are suitably designed to provide reasonable assurance that control objectives, typically specified by a regulatory agency, will be met. A practitioner can report on the suitability of control design even though the controls have yet to be implemented, but he or she should modify both the scope and inherent limitations paragraphs of his or her report. The scope paragraph is modified to state that the controls identified in the report have not yet been implemented. The inherent limitations paragraph is modified to state that another limitation is that the identified controls may not be implemented when the entity's operations begin.

The practitioner cannot sign a form prescribed by a governmental agency that relates to the assertion the client made regarding its internal control unless the practitioner has performed an examination or AUP engagement. Additionally, the practitioner must read the prescribed form carefully to make sure it conforms to professional standards related to reporting on an entity's assertion about its internal control.

Additionally, a client may be requested by the governmental agency to file a pre-award survey (assertion) about its ability to establish an appropriately designed internal control, along with its practitioner's report on the assertion. Interpretation No. 7 of AT 101 states that a practitioner cannot report on an assertion concerning such an ability, because for such a statement "there are no suitable criteria for evaluating the entity's ability to establish suitably designed internal control." The governmental agency might be willing to accept a consulting (nonattest) engagement; however, in this case the practitioner's report may include the following:

- A statement that the practitioner is unable to perform an attest engagement on the entity's ability to establish suitably designed internal control, because there are no suitable criteria for evaluating the entity's ability to do so

- A description of the nature and scope of the practitioner's services

- The practitioner's findings

PLANNING AID REMINDER: SSAE-16 (Reporting on Controls at a Service Organization) provides guidance for practitioners engaged to report on controls at a service organization that provide services related to user entity's internal controls over financial reporting. Sometimes an entity may engage a practitioner to report on controls at a service organization that relate to the user entity's internal controls over compliance or operations (not internal controls over financial reporting). In the latter engagement, the practitioner would follow the guidance in AT 101. Interpretation No. 8 of AT 101 (Including a Description of Tests of Controls or Other Procedures, and the Results Thereof, in an Examination Report) notes that nothing in AT 101 precludes a practitioner from including in a separate section of his or her examination report a description of the tests of controls or other procedures performed and the results thereof related to internal controls over compliance or operations. The interpretation notes, however, that in some cases such a description may overshadow the practitioner's overall opinion or may cause report users to misunderstand the opinion. Thus, the circumstances of the particular engagement are relevant to the practitioner's consideration of whether to include such description.

APPENDIX—ATTESTATION STANDARDS AND CONSULTING ENGAGEMENTS

An auditor may accept a consulting service engagement that includes an attest service as described in AT 101. The practitioner should perform the two separate phases of the single engagement by observing Statements on Standards for Consulting Services (SSCS) for the consulting phase of the engagement and Statements on Standards for Attestation Engagements (SSAE) for the attest phase. The practitioner should explain to the client the difference between the two services and should obtain the client's agreement that the attest service should be performed in accordance with professional standards. The agreement that an attest service is to be performed should be documented in the consulting engagement letter.

Practitioner's Aids

The following practitioner's aids are based on illustrations provided in SSAE-10:

- Exhibit AT 101-3—Checklist for an examination report on a subject matter
- Exhibit AT 101-4—Checklist for an examination report on an assertion
- Exhibit AT 101-5—Checklist for a review report on a subject matter
- Exhibit AT 101-6—Checklist for a review report on an assertion
- Exhibit AT 101-7—Examination Report—Subject Matter
- Exhibit AT 101-8—Examination Report—Assertion
- Exhibit AT 101-9—Review Report—Subject Matter
- Exhibit AT 101-10—Review Report—Assertion (Restricted Distribution)

EXHIBIT AT 101-3—CHECKLIST FOR AN EXAMINATION REPORT ON A SUBJECT MATTER

An examination report on a subject matter should include the following:

- A title that includes the word "independent"

- An identification of the subject matter and the responsible party
- A statement that the subject matter is the responsibility of the responsible party
- A statement that the practitioner's responsibility is to express an opinion on the subject matter based on his or her examination
- A statement that the examination was conducted in accordance with attestation standards established by the American Institute of Certified Public Accountants and, accordingly, included procedures that the practitioner considered necessary in the circumstances
- A statement that the practitioner believes the examination provides a reasonable basis for his or her opinion
- The practitioner's opinion on whether the subject matter is based on (or in conformity with) the criteria in all material respects
- A statement restricting the use of the report to specified parties, if applicable
- The manual or printed signature of the practitioner's firm
- The date of the examination report

EXHIBIT AT 101-4—CHECKLIST FOR AN EXAMINATION REPORT ON AN ASSERTION

An examination report on an assertion should include the following:

- A title that includes the word "independent"
- An identification of the assertion and the responsible party (If the assertion is not included in the practitioner's report, the first paragraph of the report should also contain a statement of the assertion.)
- A statement that the assertion is the responsibility of the responsible party
- A statement that the practitioner's responsibility is to express an opinion on the assertion based on his or her examination
- A statement that the examination was conducted in accordance with attestation standards established by the American Institute of Certified Public Accountants and, accordingly, included procedures that the practitioner considered necessary in the circumstances
- A statement that the practitioner believes the examination provides a reasonable basis for his or her opinion
- The practitioner's opinion on whether the assertion is presented (or fairly stated), in all material respects, based on the criteria
- A statement restricting the use of the report to specified parties, if applicable
- The manual or printed signature of the practitioner's firm
- The date of the examination report

EXHIBIT AT 101-5—CHECKLIST FOR A REVIEW REPORT ON A SUBJECT MATTER

A review report on a subject matter should include the following:

- A title that includes the word "independent"
- An identification of the subject matter and the responsible party
- A statement that the subject matter is the responsibility of the responsible party
- A statement that the review was conducted in accordance with attestation standards established by the American Institute of Certified Public Accountants
- A statement that a review is substantially less in scope than an examination, the objective of which is an expression of an opinion on the subject matter, and accordingly, no such opinion is expressed in the review
- A statement about whether the practitioner is aware of any material modifications that should be made to the subject matter in order for it to be based on (or in conformity with), in all material respects, the criteria, other than those modifications, if any, indicated in his or her report
- A statement restricting the use of the report to specified parties, if applicable
- The manual or printed signature of the auditor's firm
- The date of the review report

EXHIBIT AT 101-6—CHECKLIST FOR A REVIEW REPORT ON AN ASSERTION

A review report on an assertion should include the following:

- A title that includes the word "independent"
- An identification of the assertion and the responsible party (if the assertion is not included in the practitioner's report, the first paragraph of the report should also contain a statement of the assertion.)
- A statement that the assertion is the responsibility of the responsible party
- A statement that the review was conducted in accordance with attestation standards established by the American Institute of Certified Public Accountants
- A statement that a review is substantially less in scope than an examination, the objective of which is an expression of opinion on the subject matter, and accordingly, no such opinion is expressed in the review
- A statement about whether the practitioner is aware of any material modifications that should be made to the assertion in order for it to be presented (or fairly stated), in all material respects, based on (or in conformity with) the criteria, other than those modifications, if any, indicated in his or her report

- A statement restricting the use of the report to specified parties, if applicable
- The manual or printed signature of the practitioner's firm
- The date of the review report

EXHIBIT AT 101-7—EXAMINATION REPORT—SUBJECT MATTER

Independent Accountant's Report

We have examined the [*identify the subject matter—for example*, the accompanying schedule of investment returns of XYZ Company for the year ended December 31, 20X5]. XYZ Company's management is responsible for the schedule of investment returns. Our responsibility is to express an opinion based on our examination.

Our examination was conducted in accordance with attestation standards established by the American Institute of Certified Public Accountant and, accordingly, included examining, on a test basis, evidence supporting [*identify the subject matter—for example*, XYZ Company's schedule of investment return] and performing such other procedures as we considered necessary in the circumstances. We believe that our examination provides a reasonable basis for our opinion.

[*Additional paragraph(s) may be added to emphasize certain matters relating to the attest engagement or the subject matter.*]

In our opinion, the schedule referred to above presents, in all material respects, [*identify the subject matter—for example*, the investment returns of XYZ Company for the year ended December 31, 20X5] based on [*identify criteria—for example*, the ABC criteria set forth in Note 1].

[*Signature*]

[*Date*]

EXHIBIT AT 101-8—EXAMINATION REPORT—ASSERTION

Independent Accountant's Report

We have examined management's assertion that [*identify the assertion—for example*, the accompanying schedule of investment return of XYZ Company for the year ended December 31, 20X5 is presented in accordance with ABC criteria set for in Note 1]. XYZ Company's management is responsible for the assertion. Our responsibility is to express an opinion on the assertion based on our examination.

Our examination was conducted in accordance with attestation standards established by the American Institute of Certified Public Accountants and, accordingly, included examining, on a test basis, evidence supporting management's assertion and performing such other procedures as we considered necessary in the circumstances. We believe that our examination provides a reasonable basis for our opinion.

[*Additional paragraph(s) may be added to emphasize certain matters relating to the attest engagement or the assertion.*]

In our opinion, management's assertion referred to above is fairly stated, in all material respects, based on [*identify established or stated criteria—for example*, the ABC criteria set forth in Note 1].

[*Signature*]

[*Date*]

EXHIBIT AT 101-9—REVIEW REPORT—SUBJECT MATTER

Independent Accountant's Report

We have reviewed the [*identify the subject matter—for example*, the accompanying schedule of investment returns of XYZ Company for the year ended December 31, 20X5]. XYZ Company's management is responsible for the schedule of investment returns.

Our review was conducted in accordance with attestation standards established by the American Institute of Certified Public Accountants. A review is substantially less in scope than an examination, the objective of which is the expression of an opinion on [*identify the subject matter—for example*, XYA Company's schedule of investment returns]. Accordingly, we do not express such an opinion.

[*Additional paragraph(s) may be added to emphasize certain matters relating to the attest engagement or the subject matter.*]

Based on our review, nothing came to our attention that caused us to believe that the [*identify the subject matter—for example*, schedule of investment returns of XYZ Company for the year ended December 31, 20X5] is not presented, in all material respects, in conformity with [*identify the criteria—for example*, the ABC criteria set forth in Note 1].

[*Signature*]

[*Date*]

EXHIBIT AT 101-10—REVIEW REPORT—ASSERTION (RESTRICTED DISTRIBUTION)

Independent Accountant's Report

We have reviewed management's assertion that [*identify the assertion—for example*, the accompanying schedule of investment returns of XYZ Company for the year ended December 31, 20X5] is presented in accordance with the ABC criteria referred to in Note 1. XYZ Company's management is responsible for the assertion.

Our review was conducted in accordance with attestation standards established by the American Institute of Certified Public Accountants. A review is substantially less in scope than an examination, the objective of which is the expression of an opinion on management's assertion. Accordingly, we do not express such an opinion.

[*Additional paragraph(s) may be added to emphasize certain matters relating to the attest engagement or the assertion.*]

Based on our review, nothing came to our attention that caused us to believe that management's assertion referred to above is not fairly stated, in all material respects, based on [*identify the criteria—for example*, the ABC criteria referred to in the investment management agreement between XYZ Company and DEF Investment Managers, Ltd., dated November 15, 20X1].

This report is intended solely for the information and use of XYZ Company and [*identify other specified parties—for example*, DEF Investment Managers, Ltd.,] and is not intended to be and should not be used by anyone other than these specified parties.

[*Signature*]

[*Date*]

AT SECTION 201

AGREED-UPON PROCEDURES ENGAGEMENTS

Authoritative Pronouncements

SSAE-10—Attestation Standards: Revision and Recodification (Chapter 2)

Overview

A practitioner should observe the Statements on Standards for Attestation Engagement (SSAE) standards when performing an agreed-upon procedures (AUP) engagement except in the following circumstances:

- Engagements in which an auditor reports on specified compliance requirements based solely on an audit of financial statements, as addressed in AU-C 806 (*Reporting on Compliance with Aspects of Contractual Agreements or Regulatory Requirements in Connection with Audited Financial Statements*)

- Engagements for which the objective is to report in accordance with AU-C 935) (*Compliance Audits*), unless the terms of the engagement specify that the engagement be performed pursuant to the SSAEs

- Engagements covered by AU-C 920 (*Letters for Underwriters and Certain Other Requesting Parties*)

- Engagements that would not be considered as subject to SSAE standards as described in AT 101

In an AUP engagement the practitioner issues a report after performing specific procedures on the subject matter, the procedures having been agreed to by the practitioner and the specified party. In this engagement, the specified procedures can vary greatly, but the specified party is responsible for determining the sufficiency of the procedures. For this reason, the use of the practitioner's report must be restricted to the specified party or parties.

The general, fieldwork, and reporting standards for attestation engagements, as discussed in AT 101, must be observed in an AUP engagement.

Promulgated Procedures Checklist

The practitioner should perform the following procedures with respect to AUP engagements:

- Determine whether pre-engagement conditions exist.

- Perform appropriate engagement procedures.

- Prepare an appropriate report based on the scope of the engagement.

ENGAGEMENT STRATEGY: General guidance for documenting an attest engagement is discussed in AT 101 (Attest Engagements).

Analysis and Application of Procedures

Determine whether pre-engagement conditions exist

Before the practitioner accepts an AUP engagement based on a written assertion, SSAE standards require that the following conditions be satisfied:

- The practitioner must be independent.
- There must be an agreement between the practitioner and the specified party on which procedures are to be performed.
- The specified party must take responsibility for the sufficiency of the agreed-upon procedures.
- The subject matter must be subject to reasonably consistent measurement.
- There must be an agreement between the practitioner and specified party on the criteria to be used for determining the findings.
- The application of the agreed-upon procedures is expected to result in reasonably consistent findings using the criteria agreed upon.
- There is an expectation that evidential matter exists that will provide a reasonable basis for expressing the practitioner's findings.
- There is an agreement between the practitioner and the specified party with respect to materiality, where applicable.
- The use of the practitioner's report is restricted.

In addition to the above requirements, SSAE standards require that one of the following conditions exist:

- The party wishing to engage the practitioner is responsible for the subject matter, or has a reasonable basis for providing a written assertion about the subject matter when the nature of the subject matter is such that a responsible party does not otherwise exist.
- The party wishing to engage the practitioner is not responsible for the subject matter but is able to provide the practitioner, or have a third party who is responsible for the subject matter provide the practitioner, with evidence of the third party's responsibility for the subject matter.

PLANNING AID REMINDER: When the AUP engagement relates to prospective financial information, a summary of significant assumptions must be included in the prospective financial statements.

Identification and sufficiency of procedures

Generally the practitioner should communicate directly with the specified party to determine which procedures are to be performed and to make it clear that the specified party is responsible for the sufficiency of the procedures. SSAE standards note that when the practitioner is unable to communicate directly with the specified party, procedures such as the following should be employed:

- Compare the procedures to be applied to written requirements established by the specified party.
- Discuss with a representative of the specified party the procedures to be employed.
- Review relevant contracts or correspondence from the specified party.

Understanding with the client

The terms of the AUP engagement should be understood by the practitioner and ideally should be expressed in an engagement letter. SSAE standards note that items that may be appropriate for the engagement letter include the following:

- Description of the engagement
- Identification of the subject matter (or the related assertion), the criteria used, and the responsible party
- An acknowledgment by the specified party with respect to the responsibility for the sufficiency of the agreed-upon procedures
- The practitioner's responsibilities
- Reference to attestation standards established by the AICPA
- Enumerating the agreed-upon procedures
- Description of disclaimers expected to be part of the practitioner's report
- The restricted nature of the practitioner's report
- Assistance expected to be provided to the practitioner
- The work of a specialist, if any
- Materiality thresholds

OBSERVATION: In an AUP engagement the practitioner assumes the risk that (1) misapplication of the procedures might result in inappropriate findings being reported and (2) appropriate findings might not be reported or might be reported inaccurately.

Perform appropriate engagement procedures

Specified users, not the practitioner, are responsible for the nature, timing, and extent of agreed-upon procedures; however, the practitioner must have an adequate knowledge of the specific subject matter to which the agreed-upon procedures will be applied.

The specific procedures to be employed in an AUP engagement are dependent upon the nature of the engagement; however, in general the practitioner must "obtain evidential matter from applying the agreed-upon procedures to provide a reasonable basis for the findings or findings expressed in his or her report, but need not perform additional procedures outside the scope of the engagement to gather additional evidential matter." SSAE standards identify the following as appropriate procedures in an AUP engagement:

- Executing a sampling application after agreeing on relevant parameters
- Inspecting specified documents evidencing certain types of transactions or detailed attributes thereof
- Confirming specific information with third parties
- Comparing documents, schedules, or analyses with certain specified attributes
- Performing specific procedures on work performed by others (including the work of internal auditors)
- Performing mathematical computations

On the other hand, the following would be inappropriate procedures in an AUP engagement:

- Merely reading the work performed by others solely to describe their findings
- Evaluating the competency or objectivity of another party
- Obtaining an understanding about a particular subject
- Interpreting documents outside the scope of the practitioner's professional expertise

Use of a specialist

In some AUP engagements it is appropriate for a practitioner to use the work of a specialist; however, the practitioner and the specified party should explicitly agree to that use. The practitioner's report should explain the work performed by the specialist.

PLANNING AID REMINDER: As one of the agreed-upon procedures, the practitioner may agree to apply procedures to the work product created by a specialist. This approach is not considered the "use of a specialist" in the context of an AUP engagement. SSAE standards note that the practitioner should not agree to simply read a specialist's report "solely to describe or repeat the findings, or take responsibility for all or a portion of any procedures performed by a specialist or the specialist's work product."

Use of an internal auditor or other personnel

The practitioner is responsible for performing the agreed-upon procedures, but he or she may use internal auditors or other personnel to accumulate data and perform other similar procedures. In addition, the practitioner may agree to perform procedures on information included in an internal practitioner's audit documentation; however, SSAE standards point out that the following would be inappropriate:

- Agree to simply read an internal auditor's report for the sole purpose of describing the findings in the engagement report

- Prepare an engagement report in a manner that suggests that the practitioner and the internal auditor share responsibility for the performance of the agreed-upon procedures

Prepare an appropriate report based on the scope of the engagement

Based on the performance of the agreed-upon procedures, the practitioner should formulate the findings that are to be expressed in his or her report. The findings should be expressed in a manner that is clear and unambiguous. The report may also include explanatory language such as an explanation of sampling risk and descriptions of controls.

PLANNING AID REMINDER: SSAE standards prohibit the practitioner from expressing a negative assurance about the subject matter or the assertion.

Practitioner's Aids

The following practitioner's aids are based on illustrations provided in SSAE-10:

- Exhibit AT 201-1—Checklist for an AUP report
- Exhibit AT 201-2—AUP Engagement Report

EXHIBIT AT 201-1—CHECKLIST FOR AN AUP REPORT

An AUP report should include the following:

- A title that includes the word "independent"
- An identification of the specified party
- An identification of the subject matter (or the written assertion) and the character of the engagement
- An identification of the responsible party and a statement that the subject matter is the responsibility of the responsible party
- A statement that the procedures were agreed to by the specified party
- A statement that the AUP engagement was conducted in accordance with attestation standards established by the American Institute of Certified Public Accountants
- A statement that the specified party is solely responsible for the sufficiency of the agreed-upon procedures; furthermore, the statement should disclaim any responsibility for the sufficiency of the procedures
- List the procedures performed and related findings
- Description of materiality thresholds, where applicable
- A statement that the practitioner was not engaged to and did not conduct an examination of the subject matter, the objective of which would be the expression of an opinion, a disclaimer of opinion on the subject matter, and a statement that if the practitioner had performed additional procedures, other matters might have come to his or her attention that would have been reported
- A statement restricting the use of the report to specified parties

- Reservations or restrictions related to procedures or findings, if applicable
- A description of the assistance provided by a specialist, if applicable
- The manual or printed signature of the practitioner's firm
- The date of the AUP report

PLANNING AID REMINDER: When the AUP engagement concerns prospective financial information, the guidance established in AT 301 (Financial Forecasts and Projections) should be observed in preparing an agreed-upon procedures report for prospective financial information.

EXHIBIT AT 201-2—AUP ENGAGEMENT REPORT

Independent Accountant's Report on Applying Agreed-Upon Procedures

To the Audit Committees and Managements of ABC Inc. and XYZ Fund:

We have performed the procedures enumerated below, which were agreed to by the audit committees and managements of ABC Inc. and XYZ Fund, solely to assist you in evaluating the accompanying Statement of Investment Performance Statistics of XYZ Fund (prepared in accordance with the criteria specified therein) for the year ended December 31, 20X1. XYZ Fund's management is responsible for the statement of investment performance statistics. This agreed-upon procedures engagement was conducted in accordance with attestation standards established by the American Institute of Certified Public Accountants. The sufficiency of these procedures is solely the responsibility of those parties specified in this report. Consequently, we make no representation regarding the sufficiency of the procedures described below either for the purpose for which this report has been requested or for any other purpose.

[*Include paragraphs to enumerate procedures and findings.*]

We were not engaged to and did not conduct an examination, the objective of which would be to express of an opinion on the accompanying Statement of Investment Performance Statistics of XYZ Fund. Accordingly, we do not express such an opinion. Had we performed additional procedures, other matters might have come to our attention that would have been reported to you.

This report is intended solely for the information and use of the audit committees and managements of ABC Inc. and XYZ Fund, and is not intended to be, and should not be, used by anyone other than these specified parties.

[*Signature*]

[*Date*]

AT SECTION 301

FINANCIAL FORECASTS AND PROJECTIONS

Authoritative Pronouncements

SSAE-10—Attestation Standards: Revision and Recodification (Chapter 3)

SSAE-17—Reporting on Compiled Prospective Financial Statements When the Practitioner's Independence is Impaired

Overview

A prospective financial statement is either a financial forecast or a financial projection that reflects an entity's expected statement of financial position, results of operations, statement of cash flows, and summaries of significant assumptions and accounting policies. A prospective financial statement is based on expected future economic conditions that represent the best knowledge and belief of the person or persons responsible for the underlying assumptions in the forecast or projection. A prospective financial statement is a financial forecast or projection that covers a period of time that is partially but not completely expired or a period of time wholly in the future. Financial statements that cover an expired period of time are not considered prospective financial statements.

ENGAGEMENT STRATEGY: Pro forma financial statements attempt to reflect the effects of a possible transaction or event on historical financial statements. Pro forma financial statements are not considered to be prospective financial statements. Pro forma financial information is discussed in AT 401 (Reporting on Pro Forma Financial Information).

The person or persons who establish the underlying assumptions for the prospective financial statements are referred to in the attestation standards as the "responsible party" or "responsible parties." As a rule, the responsible party for a prospective financial statement is the management of an enterprise, but it may be a prospective buyer or some other outsider. A practitioner who is engaged to report on prospective financial statements may assist the responsible party in identifying assumptions and gathering information for the forecast or projection. However, all of the underlying assumptions and the preparation and presentation of the prospective financial statements are the responsibility of the responsible party. Thus, the term *preparation of prospective financial statements* should not be used in the practitioner's report or in any other correspondence relating to the engagement.

Under the attestation standards, a practitioner who is engaged to report on prospective financial statements must determine whether such statements are intended for general use or for limited use. Prospective financial statements that are issued for general use are those that are intended to be used by parties that are not negotiating directly with the responsible party. Since the parties not negotiating directly are generally unable to make direct inquiries about the prospective financial statements, the most useful presentation for them is one that reflects the responsible party's best knowledge and belief of the expected results. Thus, only a financial forecast is appropriate for general use.

Prospective financial statements that are issued for limited use are those that are intended to be used only by the responsible party and those parties negotiating directly with the responsible party. Since the parties are negotiating directly and are able to make direct inquiries of the responsible party, either a financial forecast or a financial projection is appropriate for limited use.

A financial forecast reflects an entity's expected statement of financial position, results of operations, and statement of cash flows, based on the responsible party's assumptions of the conditions that are expected to exist during the forecast period and the course of action that is expected to be taken if the expected conditions materialize. A financial projection reflects an entity's expected statement of financial position, results of operations, and statement of cash flows, based on the responsible party's assumptions of the conditions that will exist during the projection period if one or more hypothetical assumptions occur and the course of action that will be taken if the hypothetical assumptions materialize. Thus, a financial forecast is based on expected future economic conditions and the course of action to be taken if the expected conditions materialize, whereas a financial projection is based on expected future economic conditions that will exist if one or more hypothetical assumptions occur and the course of action that will be taken if the hypothetical assumptions materialize.

A prospective financial statement may be prepared as a single set of estimates or as a range of estimates. To facilitate comparisons, prospective financial statements should be presented in the same format as that used for historical financial statements. The attestation standards require the following minimum presentation standards for prospective financial statements:

1. Sales or gross revenues
2. Gross profit or cost of sales
3. Unusual or infrequently occurring items
4. Provision for income taxes
5. Discontinued operations or extraordinary items
6. Income from continuing operations
7. Net income
8. Basic and diluted earnings per share
9. Significant changes in financial position
10. Description of what the responsible party intends the prospective financial statements to present, a statement that assumptions are based on information about circumstances and conditions existing at the time the prospective information was prepared, and a caveat that the prospective results might not be achieved
11. Summary of significant assumptions

12. Summary of significant accounting policies

Types of Engagements

A practitioner can accept the following engagements for prospective financial statements:

- Examination engagement

- Compilation engagement

- Agreed-upon procedures engagement

OBSERVATION: SSAE standards require that a practitioner perform one of the three types of engagements for prospective financial statements when the practitioner "(a) submits, to his or her client or others, prospective financial statements that he or she has assembled, or assisted in assembling, that are or reasonably might be expected to be used by another (third) party or (b) reports on prospective financial statements that are, or reasonably might be expected, to be used by another (third) party."

EXAMINATION ENGAGEMENT

The purpose of an examination of prospective financial statements is to express an opinion on whether the statements are presented in conformity with American Institute of Certified Public Accountants (AICPA) guidelines and to determine whether the responsible party's assumptions provide a reasonable basis for the preparation of the prospective financial statements.

PLANNING AID REMINDER: For financial projections, the practitioner must determine whether the given hypothetical assumptions provide a reasonable basis for the responsible party's presentation.

Materiality is a highly subjective factor that the practitioner must consider in the examination of prospective financial statements in the same manner as he or she would do in the evaluation of historical financial statements. Because of the higher degree of uncertainty associated with prospective financial statements, prospective financial information cannot be expected to be as precise as historical financial information. Thus, the range or reasonableness for evaluating prospective financial information is broader than the range an auditor would use to evaluate historical financial information.

PLANNING AID REMINDER: An examination of prospective financial statements must observe the general, fieldwork, and reporting standards for an attestation engagement as described in AT 101 (Attest Engagements)

Promulgated Procedures Checklist

The practitioner should perform the following procedures in an examination engagement for prospective financial statements:

- Establish an understanding with the responsible party
- Plan the examination engagement
- Obtain sufficient evidence to provide a reasonable basis for the report
- Obtain sufficient evidence concerning the reasonableness of assumptions
- Obtain sufficient evidence concerning the preparation and presentation of the prospective financial statements
- Prepare an appropriate report on the prospective financial statements

---

PLANNING AID REMINDER: General guidance for documenting an attest engagement is discussed in AT 101 (Attest Engagements).

Analysis and Application of Procedures

Establish an understanding with the responsible party

The practitioner should establish an understanding with the responsible party that includes (1) the objective of the engagement, (2) the responsibilities of the responsible party, (3) the practitioner's responsibilities, and (4) limitations of the examination engagement. This understanding should be documented in the attest files, preferably through written communication with the responsible party.

PLANNING AID REMINDER: When the client and the responsible party are not the same, the understanding must encompass the client as well as the responsible party.

Plan the examination engagement

SSAE standards identify the following as some of the factors that are important in the proper planning of an examination engagement:

- Accounting principles to be used and the type of presentation
- The level of attestation risk related to the engagement
- Initial assessment of materiality
- Elements of the prospective financial statements that are likely to require revision
- Conditions that could change the nature, timing, or extent of examination procedures
- Understanding of the entity's business environment
- The responsible party's experience in preparing prospective financial statements

- The period of time covered by the prospective financial statements
- The process used to develop the prospective financial statements
- Understanding key factors (such as costs of production; competitiveness of markets; pace of technology within the industry; and past patterns of revenues, costs, and management policies) that will affect the prospective financial statements

Obtain sufficient evidence to provide a reasonable basis for the report

In an examination of prospective financial statements the accountant must collect sufficient evidential matter "to restrict attestation risk to a level that is, in his or her professional judgment, appropriate for the level of assurance that may be imparted by his or her examination report." The Statements on Standards for Attestation Engagements (SSAE) standards describe the purpose of an examination of prospective financial statements as follows:

> The practitioner provides assurance only about whether the prospective financial statements are presented in conformity with AICPA presentation guidelines and whether the assumptions provide a reasonable basis for management's forecast, or a reasonable basis for management's projection given the hypothetical assumptions.

There is no single list of engagement procedures that must be executed by the auditor in an examination of prospective financial statements; however, the SSAE standards point out that the following factors should be considered in determining the extent of examination procedures:

- The nature and materiality of the item under examination in relationship to the prospective financial statements taken as a whole
- The likelihood of misstatement
- Existing evidence obtained during the current engagement as well as previous engagements
- The competency of the responsible party in the preparation of prospective financial statements
- The degree to which the prospective financial statements are affected by judgments made by the responsible party
- The adequacy of the data that supports the prospective financial statements

Obtain sufficient evidence concerning the reasonableness of assumptions

Evidence must be collected to determine if assumptions used in the preparation of the prospective financial statements are reasonable.

Financial forecasts

The SSAE standards state that in a financial forecast engagement the practitioner can be satisfied with respect to the reasonableness of assumptions made by the responsible party if the examination procedures lead to the following conclusions:

- The responsible party has explicitly identified all factors expected to materially affect the operations of the entity during the prospective period and has developed appropriate assumptions with respect to such factors.
- The assumptions are suitably supported.

Financial projections

The SSAE standards state that in a financial projection engagement (given the hypothetical assumptions) the practitioner can be satisfied with respect to the reasonableness of assumptions made by the responsible party if the examination procedures lead to the following conclusions:

- The responsible party has explicitly identified all factors that would materially affect the operations of the entity during the prospective period if the hypothetical assumptions were to materialize and developed appropriate assumptions with respect to such factors.
- The other assumptions are suitably supported given the hypothetical assumptions.

ENGAGEMENT STRATEGY: In determining whether assumptions are suitably supported in a financial forecast the auditor must be able to conclude that "the preponderance of information supports each significant assumption." For a financial projection, the practitioner must be satisfied that the assumptions provide a reasonable basis for the projection, given the hypothetical assumptions. In a financial projection engagement the practitioner does not have to obtain support for the hypothetical assumptions.

The determination of whether there is a preponderance of information is highly subjective and does not suggest that a particular outcome is the only outcome that will actually occur. The practitioner's conclusion must be concerned with whether assumptions provide a reasonable basis for the preparation of the prospective financial statements. The following should be considered when determining whether there is suitable support for assumptions:

- Have sufficient pertinent sources of information about the assumptions been considered? Examples of external sources the accountant might consider are government publications, industry publications, economic forecasts, existing or proposed legislation, and reports of changing technology. Examples of internal sources are budgets, labor agreements, patents, royalty agreements and records, sales backlog records, debt agreements, and actions of the board of directors involving entity plans.
- Are the assumptions consistent with the sources from which they are derived?
- Are the assumptions consistent with each other?
- Are the historical financial information and other data used in developing the assumptions sufficiently reliable for that purpose? Reliability can be assessed by inquiry and analytical and other procedures, some of which may have been completed in past examinations or reviews of the historical financial statements. If historical financial statements have been pre-

pared for an expired part of the prospective period, the practitioner should consider the historical data in relation to the prospective results for the same period, where applicable. If the prospective financial statements incorporate such historical financial results and that period is significant to the presentation, the practitioner should make a review of the historical information in conformity with the applicable standards.

- Are the historical financial information and other data used in developing the assumptions comparable over the periods specified? Were the effects of any lack of comparability considered in developing the assumptions?

- Are the logical arguments or theory, considered with the data supporting the assumptions, reasonable?

Obtain sufficient evidence concerning the preparation and presentation of the prospective financial statements

With respect to the evaluation of the preparation and presentation of prospective financial statements, the practitioner should collect evidence to satisfy him- or herself that

- Suitably supported assumptions are reflected in the statements.

- Computations to convert the assumptions to dollar values are mathematically correct.

- Assumptions are internally consistent.

- Generally accepted accounting principles used in the preparation of the prospective financial statements are the same principles (1) used in the latest historical financial statements and (2) expected to be used in the historical financial statements that will cover the same reporting period as the prospective financial statements (for financial projections the accounting principles should be consistent with the purpose of the presentation).

- Prospective financial statements are presented in accordance with AICPA guidelines.

- Assumptions have been adequately disclosed based on AICPA presentation guidelines.

Written representations should be obtained from the responsible party with respect to the prospective financial statements.

Prepare an appropriate report on the prospective financial statements

SSAE standards require that an examination report on prospective financial statements include the following:

- A title that includes the word "independent"

- An identification of the prospective financial statements presented

- An identification of the responsible party and a statement that the prospective financial statements are the responsibility of the responsible party

- A statement that the practitioner's responsibility is to express an opinion on the prospective financial statements

- A statement that the examination of the prospective financial statements was made in accordance with AICPA standards, and included such procedures as considered necessary by the practitioner
- A statement that the practitioner believes that the examination provides a reasonable basis for the opinion expressed
- The practitioner's opinion that the prospective financial statements are presented in conformity with AICPA presentation guidelines and that the underlying assumptions provide a reasonable basis for the forecast or a reasonable basis for the projection, given the hypothetical assumptions
- A caveat that the prospective results might not be achieved
- A statement that the practitioner assumes no responsibility to update the report for events and circumstances occurring after the date of the report
- Identification of the purpose of the prospective financial statements (for a projection only)
- Statement that restricts the distribution of the report (for a projection only)
- The manual or printed signature of the practitioner's firm
- The date of the examination report

Exhibit AT 301-1 is an example taken from SSAE-10 of a standard report on an examination of a forecast.

EXHIBIT AT 301-1—STANDARD REPORT ON AN EXAMINATION OF A FORECAST

Independent Accountant's Report

We have examined the accompanying forecasted balance sheet, statements of income, retained earnings, and cash flows of XYZ Company as of December 31, 20X5, and for the year then ending. XYZ Company's management is responsible for the forecast. Our responsibility is to express an opinion on the forecast based on our examination.

Our examination was conducted in accordance with attestation standards established by the American Institute of Certified Public Accountants and, accordingly, included such procedures as we considered necessary to evaluate both the assumptions used by management and the preparation and presentation of the forecast. We believe that our examination provides a reasonable basis for our opinion.

In our opinion, the accompanying forecast is presented in conformity with guidelines for presentation of a forecast established by the American Institute of Certified Public Accountants, and the underlying assumptions provide a reasonable basis for management's forecast. However, there will usually be differences between the forecasted and actual results, because events and circumstances frequently do not occur as expected, and those differences may be material. We have no responsibility to update this report for events and circumstance occurring after the date of this report.

[*Signature*]

[*Date*]

Exhibit AT 301-2 is an example taken from SSAE-10 of a standard report on an examination of a projection.

EXHIBIT AT 301-2—STANDARD REPORT ON AN EXAMINATION OF A PROJECTION

Independent Accountant's Report

We have examined the accompanying projected balance sheet, statements of income, retained earnings, and cash flows of XYZ Company as of December 31, 20X5, and for the year then ending. XYZ Company's management is responsible for the projection, which was prepared for [*state special purpose, for example*, "the purpose of negotiating a loan to expand XYA Company's plant"]. Our responsibility is to express an opinion on the projection based on our examination.

Our examination was conducted in accordance with attestation standards established by the American Institute of Certified Public Accountants and, accordingly, included such procedures as we considered necessary to evaluate both the assumptions used by management and the preparation and presentation of the projection. We believe that our examination provides a reasonable basis for our opinion.

In our opinion, the accompanying projection is presented in conformity with guidelines for presentation of a projection established by the American Institute of Certified Public Accountants, and the underlying assumptions provide a reasonable basis for management's projection [*describe the hypothetical assumption, for example*, "assuming the granting of the requested loan for the purpose of expanding XYZ Company's plant as described in the summary of significant assumptions."] However, even if [*describe hypothetical assumption, for example*, "the loan is granted and the plant is expanded"], there will usually be differences between the projected and actual results, because events and circumstances frequently do not occur as expected, and those differences may be material. We have no responsibility to update this report for events and circumstance occurring after the date of this report.

The accompanying projection and this report are intended solely for the information and use of [*identify specified parties, for example*, "XYZ Company and DEF National Bank"] and is not intended to be and should not be used by anyone other than these specified parties.

[*Signature*]

[*Date*]

Modifications of the examination report

A practitioner may encounter a variety of circumstances that might require that the standard report on prospective financial statements be modified. The following summarizes these modifications.

Departure from presentation guidelines

A practitioner may conclude that AICPA presentation guidelines have not been followed in the preparation or presentation of the prospective financial statements. When the deviations are considered to be material, either a qualified opinion or an adverse opinion should be expressed. If the practitioner decides to modify the opinion, an explanatory paragraph(s) should be included in the report in which the deviations are described. When a qualified opinion is expressed, the opinion paragraph should refer to the explanatory paragraph and use the qualifying language "except for." When an adverse opinion is expressed, the practitioner should refer to the deviations described in the explanatory paragraph and state that the prospective financial statements are not presented in accordance with AICPA presentation guidelines.

If the presentation deficiency results from the entity's nondisclosure of significant assumptions, the practitioner should express an adverse opinion and describe the omitted assumptions.

Lack of reasonable basis

A practitioner should express an adverse opinion on the prospective financial statements when a significant assumption does (or assumptions do) not provide a reasonable basis for a forecast (or, given the hypothetical assumptions, a significant assumption does [or assumptions do] not provide a reasonable basis for a projection).

Scope limitation

A disclaimer of opinion should be expressed when procedures that the accountant considers necessary cannot be performed. The report should describe the nature of the scope limitation in an explanatory paragraph.

Use of another practitioner

When another practitioner is involved in the engagement and reports on his or her portion of the examination, the principal practitioner must decide whether or not to make reference to the work of the other practitioner.

Emphasis of a matter

A practitioner may emphasize a specific item or event in his or her report and still express an unqualified opinion on the prospective financial statements. The item or event that is emphasized should be described in a separate paragraph of the practitioner's report, but the opinion paragraph should make no reference to the item or event emphasized.

Comparative information

Historical financial statements or summarizations of such statements may be included in the document that contains the prospective financial statements or that summarizes the prospective financial information. The practitioner's report on the prospective financial statements should include a reference to the historical financial statements, as follows:

> The historical financial statements for the year ended December 31, 20X5, and our report thereon are set forth on pages XX through XX of this document.

Larger engagement

The examination of prospective financial statements may be only a part of a larger engagement. For example, a feasibility study may include the examination of prospective financial statements. When a practitioner reports on the expanded engagement, the report should be tailored to fit the complete nature of the engagement.

COMPILATION ENGAGEMENT

A compilation of prospective financial statements does not provide a basis for the practitioner to express an opinion on the financial statements. When a compilation report is issued, the practitioner gives no assurance that AICPA presentation guidelines have been followed or that assumptions used in the preparation of the statements are reasonable. The practitioner should not compile prospective financial statements that exclude a summary of significant assumptions. In addition, a compilation engagement is inappropriate when a financial projection does not identify the hypothetical assumptions that are used or fails to describe the limitation of the usefulness of the presentation.

A compilation of prospective financial statements must satisfy the following standards:

- The engagement must be performed by a person having adequate technical training and proficiency to compile prospective financial statements.
- Due professional care should be exercised in the performance of the engagement and the preparation of the report.
- The work should be adequately planned and assistants, if any, should be properly supervised.
- Appropriate compilation procedures should be performed as a basis for reporting on the compiled prospective financial statements.

PLANNING AID REMINDER: SSAE standards note that a compilation may include the "assembling, to the extent necessary, the prospective financial statements based on the responsible party's assumptions."

PLANNING AID REMINDER: SSAE standards allow the practitioner to compile prospective financial statements for an entity the practitioner is not independent of. In those circumstances, the practitioner's report should be modified to indicate his or her lack of independence in a separate paragraph of the report. An example of that kind of disclosure might be "We are not independent with respect to XYZ Company."

Promulgated Procedures Checklist

The practitioner should perform the following procedures in a compilation engagement for prospective financial statements:

- Establish an understanding with the responsible party

- Make inquiries about accounting principles
- Make inquiries about key factors and assumptions
- Identify significant assumptions
- Consider the internal consistency of assumptions
- Test the mathematical accuracy of computations
- Read the prospective financial statements
- Inquire about historical transactions
- Obtain written representations from the responsible party
- Consider extended engagement procedures
- Prepare an appropriate report on the prospective financial statements

---

ENGAGEMENT STRATEGY: General guidance for documenting an attest engagement is discussed in AT 101.

Analysis and Application of Procedures

Establish an understanding with the responsible party

The practitioner should establish an understanding with the responsible party that includes (1) the objective of the engagement, (2) the responsibilities of the responsible party, (3) the practitioner's responsibilities, and (4) limitations of the compilation engagement. This understanding should be documented in the attest files, preferably through written communication with the responsible party.

Make inquiries about accounting principles

SSAE standards require the practitioner to make the following inquiries about the accounting principles used in the preparation of the prospective financial statements:

- For existing entities, compare the accounting principles used to those used in the preparation of previous historical financial statements and inquire whether such principles are the same as those expected to be used in the historical financial statements covering the prospective period.
- For entities to be formed or for entities formed that have not commenced operations, compare specialized industry accounting principles used, if any, to those typically used in the industry. Inquire whether the accounting principles used for the prospective financial statements are those that are expected to be used when, or if, the entity commences operations.

Make inquiries about key factors and assumptions

The practitioner should make inquiries of the responsible party concerning key factors and assumptions used to prepare the prospective financial statements. Key factors include such items as the entity's sales, production, service, and financing activities.

Identify significant assumptions

SSAE standards require that the practitioner "list, or obtain a list of, the responsible party's significant assumptions providing the basis for the prospective financial statements. Consider whether there are any obvious omissions in light of the key factors on which the prospective results of the entity appear to depend."

Consider the internal consistency of assumptions

The practitioner should read the assumptions established by the responsible party and consider whether they are internally consistent.

Test the mathematical accuracy of computations

Part of the compilation procedures should include testing the mathematical accuracy of translating assumptions into prospective financial statements.

Read the prospective financial statements

SSAE standards require that the practitioner read the prospective financial statements, including the summary of significant assumptions, and consider whether

- The statements, including the disclosures of assumptions and accounting policies, appear to be presented in conformity with the AICPA presentation guidelines for prospective financial statements.

- The statements, including the summary of significant assumptions, appear to be appropriate in relation to the auditor's knowledge of the entity, the industry in which the entity operates, and (1) for a financial forecast, the expected conditions and course of action in the prospective period and (2) for a financial projection, the purpose of the presentation.

Inquire about historical transactions

In some instances a significant part of the period covered by the prospective financial statements will have expired. Under this circumstance the practitioner should make inquires about the results of operations or significant portions of the operations (such as sales volume) and significant cash flows. The practitioner should consider the effects of these historical transactions on the prospective financial statements. When historical financial statements have been prepared for an expired portion of the period, the practitioner should read those financial statements and consider the results in relation to the prospective financial statements.

Obtain written representations from the responsible party

The practitioner should obtain written representations about the prospective financial statements, including assumptions upon which they are made. For a financial forecast, SSAE standards require that the written representations include the following statements:

- The financial forecast presents, to the best of the responsible party's knowledge and belief, the expected financial position, results of operations, and cash flows.

- The financial forecast reflects the responsible party's judgment, based on present circumstances, of the expected conditions and its expected course of action.

- The financial forecast is presented in conformity with guidelines for presentation of a forecast established by the AICPA.

- The assumptions on which the forecast is based are reasonable.

- To the best of the responsible party's knowledge and belief, the item or items subject to the assumptions are expected to actually fall within the range and that the range was not selected in a biased or misleading manner (applies only when the financial forecast contains a range).

For a financial projection SSAE standards require that the written representations include the following:

- State that the financial projection presents, to the best of the responsible party's knowledge and belief, the expected financial position, results of operations, and cash flows for the projection period given the hypothetical assumptions.

- State that the financial projection reflects the responsible party's judgment, based on present circumstances, of expected conditions and its expected course of action given the occurrence of the hypothetical events.

- Identify the hypothetical assumptions and describe the limitations on the usefulness of the presentations.

- State that the assumptions are appropriate.

- Indicate whether the hypothetical assumptions are improbable.

- State that to the best of the responsible party's knowledge and belief, given the hypothetical assumptions, the item or items subject to the assumptions are expected to actually fall within the range and that the range was not selected in a biased or misleading manner (applies only when the financial projection contains a range).

- State that the financial projection is presented to conform with the guidelines for presentation of a projection established by the AICPA.

Consider extended engagement procedures

If, after completing the compilation procedures, the auditor concludes that certain information is incomplete or inappropriate, the client should be requested to make proper revisions. If the financial information is not properly revised, generally the auditor should withdraw from the engagement.

PLANNING AID REMINDER: The omission of disclosures (except for those related to significant assumptions) does not require that the practitioner withdraw from the engagement.

Prepare an appropriate report on the prospective financial statements

SSAE standards require that a compilation report on prospective financial statements include the following:

- An identification of the prospective financial statements presented
- A statement that the practitioner has compiled the prospective financial statements in accordance with attestation standards established by the AICPA
- A statement that that a compilation is limited in scope and does not enable the practitioner to express an opinion or any other form of assurance on the statement or assumptions
- A caveat that the prospective results might not be achieved
- A statement that the practitioner assumes no responsibility to update the report for events and circumstances occurring after the date of the report
- The manual or printed signature of the practitioner's firm
- The date of the compilation report

Exhibit AT 301-3 is an example taken from SSAE-10 of a standard report on a compilation of a financial statement forecast.

EXHIBIT AT 301-3—STANDARD REPORT ON A COMPILATION OF A FINANCIAL STATEMENT FORECAST

We have compiled the accompanying forecasted balance sheet, statements of income, retained earnings, and cash flows of XYZ Company as of December 31, 20X5, and for the year then ending, in accordance with attestation standards established by the American Institute of Certified Public Accountants.

A compilation is limited to presenting in the form of a forecast information that is the representation of management and does not include evaluation of the support for the assumptions underlying the forecast. We have not examined the forecast and, accordingly, do not express an opinion or any other form of assurance on the accompanying statements or assumptions. Furthermore, there will usually be differences between the forecasted and actual results, because events and circumstances frequently do not occur as expected, and those differences may be material. We have no responsibility to update this report for events and circumstances occurring after the date of this report.

[*Signature*]

[*Date*]

Exhibit AT 301-4 is an example taken from SSAE-10 of a standard report on a compilation of projected financial statements.

EXHIBIT AT 301-4—STANDARD REPORT ON A COMPILATION OF PROJECTED FINANCIAL STATEMENTS

We have compiled the accompanying projected balance sheet, statements of income, retained earnings, and cash flows of XYZ Company as of December 31,

20X5, and for the year then ending, in accordance with attestation standards established by the American Institute of Certified Public Accountants. The accompanying projection was prepared for [*state special purpose, for example*, "the purpose of negotiating a loan to expand XYZ Company's plant"].

A compilation is limited to presenting in the form of a projection information that is the representation of management and does not include evaluation of the support for the assumptions underlying the projection. We have not examined the projections, and accordingly, do not express an opinion or any other form of assurance on the accompanying statements or assumptions. Furthermore, even if [*describe hypothetical assumption, for example*, "the loan is granted and the plan is expanded"], there will usually be differences between the projected and actual results, because events and circumstances frequently do not occur as expected, and those differences may be material. We have no responsibility to update this report for events and circumstances occurring after the date of this report.

The accompanying projection and this report are intended solely for the information and use of [*identify specified parties, for example*, "XYZ Company and DEF Bank"] and is not intended to be and should not be used by anyone other than these specified parties.

[*Signature*]

[*Date*]

Modifications of the compilation report

The compilation report should be modified when prospective financial statements are presented on a comprehensive basis of accounting other than generally accepted accounting principles (GAAP) and the basis of accounting is not disclosed in the prospective financial statements.

PLANNING AID REMINDER: A practitioner may compile prospective financial statements that have presentation deficiencies or omit disclosures (except those related to the disclosure of significant assumptions) provided that (1) the deficiencies or omissions are presented in the practitioner's report and (2) to the practitioner's knowledge the responsible party did not create the presentation deficiencies or omissions with the intent to deceive those who are expected to use the prospective financial statements.

PLANNING AID REMINDER: SSAE standards allow the practitioner to compile prospective financial statements for an entity the practitioner is not independent of. In those circumstances, the practitioner's report should be modified to indicate his or her lack of independence in a separate paragraph of the report. An example of that kind of disclosure might be "We are not independent with respect to XYZ Company." SSAE-17 (Reporting on Compiled Financial Statements When the Practitioner's Independence is Impaired) permits, but does not require, the practitioner to disclose the reasons for an independence impairment in a report on compiled prospective financial information. If the practitioner elects to disclose a description about the reasons why his or her independence is impaired, he or she should ensure that all reasons are included in the description.

AGREED-UPON PROCEDURES ENGAGEMENT

When a practitioner accepts an agreed-upon procedures (AUP) engagement related to prospective financial statements the general, fieldwork, and reporting standards discussed in the chapter titled "Attest Engagements" (AT 101) and the guidance discussed in the chapter titled "Agreed-Upon Procedures Engagements" (AT 201) must be observed. In addition, SSAE standards state that an AUP engagement on prospective financial statements can be accepted only if all of the following conditions are satisfied:

- The practitioner is independent.
- The practitioner and the specified party agree to the procedures to be performed.
- The specified party accepts responsibility for the sufficiency of the agreed-upon procedures.
- A summary of significant assumptions is included in the prospective financial statements.
- The prospective financial statements "are subject to reasonably consistent evaluation against criteria that are suitable and available to the specified parties."
- The practitioner and the specified party agree to the criteria to be used in determining the findings.
- The procedures agreed to are expected to create reasonably consistent findings based on the criteria used.
- Evidential matter related to the engagement is expected to exist in order to provide a reasonable basis for expressing the findings in the accountant's report.
- The practitioner and the specified party agree to materiality limits (where applicable).
- The report is to be restricted to use only by the specified party.

Promulgated Procedures Checklist

The practitioner should perform the following procedures with respect to AUP engagements:

- Determine whether pre-engagement conditions exist.
- Perform appropriate engagement procedures.
- Prepare an appropriate report based on the scope of the engagement.

ENGAGEMENT STRATEGY: General guidance for documenting an attest engagement is discussed in AT 101 (Attest Engagements).

Analysis and Application of Procedures

Determine whether pre-engagement conditions exist

This procedure is discussed in the chapter titled "Attest Engagements" (AT 101).

Perform appropriate engagement procedures

This procedure is discussed in the chapter titled "Attest Engagements" (AT 101).

Prepare an appropriate report based on the scope of the engagement

SSAE standards require that an AUP report on prospective financial statements include the following:

- A title that includes the word "independent"
- An identification of the specified party
- Reference to the prospective financial statements and the character of the engagement
- A statement that the procedures performed were agreed to by the specified party
- An identification of the responsible party
- A statement that the prospective financial statements are the responsibility of the responsible party
- A statement that the engagement was conducted in accordance with attestation standards established by the American Institute of Certified Public Accountants
- A statement that the sufficiency of the procedures is the sole responsibility of the specified parties
- Disclaim responsibility for the sufficiency of the procedures
- List the agreed-upon procedures and related findings
- Describe the agreed-upon materiality limits (where applicable)
- A statement that the practitioner was not engaged to examine the prospective financial statements
- Disclaim an opinion on the prospective financial statements
- A statement restricting the use of the auditor's report
- If applicable, reservations or restrictions concerning procedures or findings
- A caveat that the prospective results might not be achieved
- A statement that the practitioner is not responsible to update the report for events or circumstances that have occurred after the date of the report
- If applicable, a description of the nature of work performed by a specialist
- The manual or printed signature of the practitioner's firm
- The date of the report

Exhibit AT 301-5 is an example taken from SSAE-10 of a report on an AUP engagement for prospective financial statements.

EXHIBIT AT 301-5—REPORT ON AN AUP ENGAGEMENT FOR
PROSPECTIVE FINANCIAL STATEMENTS

At your request, we have performed certain agreed-upon procedures, as enumerated below, with respect to the forecasted balance sheet and the related forecasted statements of income, retained earnings, and cash flows of DEF Company, a subsidiary of ABC Company, as of December 31, 20X5, and for the year then ending. These procedures, which were agreed to by the Boards of Directors of XYZ Corporation and ABC Company, were performed solely to assist you in evaluating the forecast in connection with the proposed sale of DEF Company to XYZ Corporation. DEF Company's management is responsible for the forecast.

This agreed-upon procedures engagement was conducted in accordance with attestation standards established by the American Institute of Certified Public Accountants. The sufficiency of these procedures is solely the responsibility of the specified parties. Consequently, we make no representation regarding the sufficiency of the procedures described below either for the purpose for which this report has been requested or for any other purpose.

[*Include paragraphs to enumerate procedures and findings.*]

We were not engaged to and did not conduct an examination, the objective of which would be the expression of an opinion on the accompanying prospective financial statements. Accordingly, we do not express an opinion on whether the prospective financial statements are presented in conformity with AICPA presentation guidelines or on whether the underlying assumptions provide a reasonable basis for the presentation. Had we performed additional procedures, other matters might have come to our attention that would have been reported to you. Furthermore, there will usually be differences between the forecasted and actual results, because events and circumstances frequently do not occur as expected, and those differences may be material. We have no responsibility to update this report for events and circumstances occurring after the date of this report.

This report is intended solely for the information and use of the Boards of Directors of ABC Company and XYZ Corporation and is not intended to be and should not be used by anyone other than these specified parties.

[*Signature*]

[*Date*]

PARTIAL PRESENTATIONS

When prospective financial statements exclude one or more of the minimum presentation guidelines established by the AICPA (as discussed earlier in this chapter), the information is considered a "partial presentation." Due to the limited nature of a partial presentation, the practitioner's report should be restricted to the specified party who will be negotiating directly with the responsible party.

SSAE standards do not establish specific engagement procedures that should be used in a partial presentation engagement, because of the limited content of the presentation. However, the standards do point out that the auditor "may find it necessary for the scope of the examination or compilation of some partial presentations to be similar to that for the examination or compilation of a presentation of prospective financial statements."

PLANNING AID REMINDER: The practitioner should carefully consider the interrelationship of elements, accounts, and items in complete financial statements to determine whether all key factors have been considered and all significant assumptions have been disclosed by the responsible party in the partial presentation.

OTHER INFORMATION

In some instances the practitioner may compile, review, or audit historical financial statements that are included in the practitioner-submitted document that also includes prospective financial statements. Under this circumstance the prospective financial statements must be examined, compiled, or subjected to agreed-upon procedures, except when all of the following conditions exist:

- The prospective financial statements are identified as a "budget."
- The budgetary period covered by the prospective financial statements does not extend beyond the end of the current fiscal year.
- The budget is presented with interim historical financial statements for the current year.

PLANNING AID REMINDER: When the budgetary exception applies as described above, the practitioner should report on the "budget" and (1) state that the auditor did not examine or compile the budget and (2) disclaim an opinion or any assurance on the budget. The budget may exclude the summary of significant assumptions and accounting polices if the practitioner believes the omission was not made to mislead those reasonably expected to use the budget; however, the omission must be referred to in the practitioner's report.

When the prospective financial statements are included in a client-prepared document that includes compiled, reviewed, or audited financial statements, the practitioner should not agree to the use of his or her name except under one of the following circumstances:

- The practitioner has examined, compiled or applied agreed-upon procedures to the prospective financial statements and the related report is included in the document.
- The prospective financial statements are accompanied by an indication by either the responsible party or the practitioner that the practitioner has performed no service with respect to the prospective financial statements and takes no responsibility for them.

- The prospective financial statements have been examined, compiled or subjected to agreed-upon procedures by another practitioner and that practitioner's report is included in the document.

PLANNING AID REMINDER: When the practitioner has not examined, reviewed, or applied agreed-upon procedures to the prospective financial statements, the standards discussed in AU-C 720 (*Other Information in Documents Containing Audited Financial Statements*) must be followed.

AT SECTION 401

REPORTING ON PRO FORMA FINANCIAL INFORMATION

Authoritative Pronouncements

SSAE-10—Attestation Standards: Revision and Recodification (Chapter 4)

Overview

Pro forma financial information reflects the effects of applying significant assumptions, such as a proposed transaction, to an enterprise's historical financial statements or information. The more common uses of pro forma financial information include showing the effects of transactions such as a business combination, change in capitalization, change in form of business organization, proposed sale or purchase, or the disposition of a significant segment of a business. When pro forma financial information is presented, the following should be observed:

- Pro forma financial information should be labeled to distinguish it from historical financial information.
- The transactions or events that are being integrated into the historical financial information should be clearly described.
- The historical financial information that is the basis for the pro forma financial information should be clearly identified.
- The assumptions used by management in constructing the pro forma financial information should be clearly identified.
- Any significant uncertainties related to management's assumptions should be clearly identified.
- A clear indication must be made that the pro forma financial information should be read in conjunction with the related historical financial information.
- It must be clearly indicated that the pro forma financial information is not necessarily indicative of what would have occurred had the transaction taken place at an earlier date.

OBSERVATION: Reporting on pro forma financial information does not apply to post-balance-sheet events or transactions that are included in historical financial statements for the purposes of a more meaningful presentation (for example, revision of earnings per share for a stock split or the revision of debt maturities).

PLANNING AID REMINDER: The general and fieldwork standards described in the chapter titled "Attestation Engagements" should be observed in an engagement to report on pro forma financial information.

A practitioner may accept an engagement to examine or review pro forma financial information if all of the following conditions exist:

- The document that includes the pro forma financial information also includes (or incorporates by reference) the most recent historical financial statements [if pro forma financial information is presented for an interim period, the document must also include (or incorporate by reference) the historical interim financial information that covers the same period as the pro form presentation].

- The historical financial statements that are the basis for the pro forma financial information must have been audited or reviewed.

- The auditor must have an adequate level of knowledge of the accounting and financial reporting practices of the reporting entity.

PLANNING AID REMINDER: A practitioner has an appropriate level of knowledge of the reporting entity when he or she has audited or reviewed the entity's historical financial statements. In a proposed business combination the practitioner must have an appropriate level of knowledge of the two entities involved in the transaction. SSAE standards note that "if another practitioner has performed such an audit or review, the need by a practitioner reporting on the pro forma financial information for an understanding of the entity's accounting and financial reporting is not diminished, and that practitioner should consider whether, under the particular circumstances, he or she can acquire sufficient knowledge of these matters to perform the procedures necessary to report on the pro forma financial information."

PLANNING AID REMINDER: The type of pro forma financial information engagement that a practitioner can accept depends on the type of service performed on the related historical financial statements. That is, an audit of the pro forma financial information can be performed only when the historical financial statements have been audited. Only a review of the pro forma financial information can be performed when the historical financial statements have only been reviewed. The rationale for these guidelines is that the level of assurance that can be made for pro forma financial information can be no higher than the level of assurance the practitioner made with respect to the historical financial statements.

The objectives, as stated in the Statements on Standards for Attestation Engagements (SSAE) standards, of an examination (reasonable assurance) and a review (negative assurance) of pro forma financial information are presented in Exhibit AT 401-1.

EXHIBIT AT 401-1—OBJECTIVES OF EXAMINATIONS AND REVIEWS OF PRO FORMA FINANCIAL INFORMATION

	Examination Engagement	Review Engagement
Management's assumptions	They provide a reasonable basis for presenting the significant effects directly attributable to the underlying transaction (or event)	No information came to the practitioner's attention during the engagement to suggest they do not provide a reasonable basis for presenting the significant effects directly attributable to the underlying transaction (or event)
Related pro forma adjustments	They give appropriate effect to those assumptions	No information came to the practitioner's attention during the engagement to suggest they do not give appropriate effect to those assumptions
The pro forma column	It reflects the proper application of those adjustments to the historical financial statements	No information came to the practitioner's attention during the engagement to suggest it does not reflect the proper application of those adjustments to the historical financial statements

Promulgated Procedures Checklist

As noted earlier, the starting point for a pro forma engagement is the historical financial statements, which have been audited or reviewed by the practitioner. In addition to those procedures, the practitioner should perform the following procedures in an examination or review of pro forma financial information:

- Obtain an understanding of the underlying transaction (or event)

- Obtain a level of knowledge of each constituent part of the combined entity in a business combination

- Discuss the assumptions made by management

- Evaluate the completeness of the pro forma adjustments

- Obtain sufficient evidence to support the pro forma adjustments

- Evaluate the presentation and consistency of assumptions

- Test the mathematical accuracy of the pro forma adjustments

- Obtain written representation from management

- Read the pro forma financial information

- Prepare an appropriate report on the pro forma financial information

---

PLANNING AID REMINDER: General guidance for documenting an attest engagement is discussed in AT 101 (Attest Engagements).

Analysis and Application of Procedures

Obtain an understanding of the underlying transaction (or event)

The practitioner must understand the nature of the transaction that is the basis for converting the historical financial statements into pro forma financial information. Obtaining this understanding could include the reading of contracts and agreements between the parties involved in the transaction and by making inquiries of appropriate management personnel.

Obtain a level of knowledge of each constituent part of the combined entity in a business combination

As noted earlier in this section, the performance of a pro forma financial information engagement is based on the assumption that the practitioner has an adequate understanding of the parties involved in a business combination or a proposed combination. Generally, this knowledge already exists because the practitioner would have audited or reviewed the financial statements of the parties involved in the combination. However, if the practitioner has not audited or reviewed one of the parties to the combination, the SSAE standards note that an adequate level of knowledge may be obtained by "communicating with other practitioners who have audited or reviewed the historical financial information on which the pro forma financial statements is based."

Discuss the assumptions made by management

The auditor should discuss the significant assumptions made by management to integrate the transaction into the historical financial statements in order to create the pro forma financial information.

Evaluate the completeness of the pro forma adjustments

Once the assumptions made by management are understood, the practitioner should determine whether all significant pro forma adjustments directly related to the transaction have been made to the historical financial statements.

Obtain sufficient evidence to support the pro forma adjustments

Professional judgment must be used to determine what constitutes sufficient evidential matter for each pro forma adjustment. For example, the practitioner may obtain appraisal reports to support the assignment of fair values in a purchase transaction or review debt agreements.

ENGAGEMENT STRATEGY: Generally, a greater level of evidential matter is required in an examination than in a review engagement.

Evaluate the presentation and consistency of assumptions

Generally a variety of assumptions are necessary in order to provide a basis for the creation of pro forma financial information. SSAE standards require that the practitioner "evaluate whether management's assumptions that underlie the pro forma adjustments are presented in a sufficiently clear and comprehensive manner." In addition, the practitioner should determine whether the pro forma adjustments are internally consistent and properly reflect the data used to create them.

Test the mathematical accuracy of the pro forma adjustments

The practitioner should test the mathematical accuracy of the pro forma adjustments and the conversion of the historical column to the pro forma column.

Obtain written representation from management

As part of the pro forma financial information engagement, the following written representations should be obtained from management:

- Management takes responsibility for the assumptions.
- Assumptions provide a reasonable basis for presenting the effects of the transaction or event.
- The pro forma adjustments are based on these assumptions.
- The pro forma financial information reflects the pro forma adjustments.
- Significant effects related to the transaction or event are appropriately disclosed in the pro forma financial information.

Read the pro forma financial information

Based on the practitioner's knowledge of the entities involved in the transaction and the understanding of the transaction itself, the pro forma financial information should be read to determine if:

- They properly describe the transaction or event, pro forma adjustments, significant assumptions, and significant uncertainties.
- They properly identify the sources of the historical financial information that serves as the basis for the pro forma financial information.

Prepare an appropriate report on the pro forma financial information

The reporting guidelines in Exhibit AT 401-2 should be followed in the preparation of an examination/review of pro forma financial information.

EXHIBIT AT 401-2—REPORTING GUIDELINES FOR PREPARATION/ REVIEW OF PRO FORMA FINANCIAL INFORMATION

Guidelines for an Examination	Guidelines for a Review
Title that includes the word "independent"	Title that includes the word "independent"
Identification of the pro forma financial information	Identification of the pro forma financial information
Reference to the historical financial statements that are the basis for the preparation of the pro forma financial information and state that they were audited (if the report was modified, the modification should be described)	Reference to the historical financial statements that are the basis for the preparation of the pro forma financial information and state that they were audited or reviewed (if the report was modified, the modification should be described)

Guidelines for an Examination	Guidelines for a Review
Identification of the responsible party and state that the responsible party is responsible for the presentation	Identification of the responsible party and state that the responsible party is responsible for the presentation
Statement that the practitioner's responsibility is to express an opinion on the information based on the results of the engagement	
Statement that the examination was made in accordance with AICPA standards, and included such procedures as considered necessary by the practitioner	Statement that the review was made in accordance with AICPA standards
Statement that the practitioner believes that the examination provides a reasonable basis for the opinion expressed	Statement that a review is substantially less in scope than an examination, the objective of which is an expression of opinion on the pro forma financial information, and accordingly, no such opinion is expressed
Separate paragraph that explains the objective and limitations of pro forma financial information	Separate paragraph that explains the objective and limitations of pro forma financial information
Opinion as to whether management's assumptions provide a reasonable basis for presenting the significant effects of the transaction, whether the pro forma adjustments are appropriate, and whether the pro forma column properly reflects the adjustments.	Conclusion as to whether any information came to the practitioner's attentions to cause him or her to believe that management's assumptions do not provide a reasonable basis for presenting the significant effects of the transaction, whether the pro forma adjustments are appropriate and whether the pro forma column properly reflects the adjustments
Manual or printed signature of the practitioner's firm	Manual or printed signature of the practitioner's firm
Date of the examination report	Date of the review report

> **OBSERVATION:** The practitioner may decide that the use of the report may be restricted, in which case an appropriate paragraph would be added to the examination/review report.

Exhibit AT 401-3 is an example taken from SSAE-10 of an examination report on pro forma financial information.

EXHIBIT AT 401-3—EXAMINATION REPORT ON PRO FORMA FINANCIAL INFORMATION

Independent Accountant's Report

We have examined the pro forma adjustments reflecting the transaction (or event) described in Note 1 and the application of those adjustments to the historical amounts in the accompanying pro forma condensed balance sheet of X Company as of December 31, 20X5, and the pro forma condensed statement of income for the year then ended. The historical condensed financial statements are derived from the historical financial statements of X company, which were audited by us, and of Y Company, which were audited by other accountants, appearing elsewhere herein (or incorporated by reference). Such pro forma adjustments are based on management's assumptions described in Note 2. X Company's management is responsible for the pro forma financial information. Our responsibility is to express an opinion on the pro forma financial information based on our examination.

Our examination was conducted in accordance with attestation standards established by the American Institute of Certified Public Accountants and, accordingly, included such procedures as we considered necessary in the circumstances. We believe that our examination provides a reasonable basis for our opinion.

The objective of this pro forma financial information is to show what the significant effects on the historical financial information might have been had the transaction (or event) occurred at an earlier date. However, the pro forma condensed financial statements are not necessarily indicative of the results of operations or related effects on financial position that would have been attained had the above-mentioned transaction (or event) actually occurred earlier.

In our opinion, management's assumptions provide a reasonable basis for presenting the significant effects directly attributable to the above-mentioned transaction (or event) described in Note 1, the related pro forma adjustments give appropriate effect to those assumptions, and the pro forma column reflects the proper application of those adjustments to the historical financial statement amounts in the pro forma condensed balance sheet as of December 31, 20X5, and the pro forma condensed statement of income for the year then ended.

[*Signature*]

[*Date*]

Exhibit AT 401-4 is an example taken from SSAE-10 of a review report on pro forma financial information.

EXHIBIT AT 401-4—REVIEW REPORT ON PRO FORMA FINANCIAL INFORMATION

Independent Accountant's Report

We have reviewed the pro forma adjustments reflecting the transaction (or event) described in Note 1 and the application of those adjustments to the historical amounts in the accompanying pro forma condensed balance sheet of X Company as of March 31, 20X6, and the pro forma condensed statement of income for the three months then ended. These historical condensed financial statements are derived from the historical unaudited financial statements of X Company, which were reviewed by us, and of Y Company, which were reviewed by other accountants, appearing elsewhere herein (or incorporated by reference). Such pro forma adjustments are based on management's assumptions as described in Note 2. X Company's management is responsible for the pro forma financial information.

Our review was conducted in accordance with attestation standards established by the American Institute of Certified Public Accountants. A review is substantially less in scope than an examination, the objective of which is the expression of an opinion on management's assumptions, the pro forma adjustments and the application of those adjustments to historical financial information. Accordingly, we do not express such an opinion.

The objective of this pro forma financial information is to show what the significant effects on the historical financial information might have been had the transaction (or event) occurred at an earlier date. However, the pro forma condensed financial statements are not necessarily indicative of the results of operations or related effects on financial position that would have been attained had the above-mentioned transaction (or event) actually occurred earlier.

Based on our review, nothing came to our attention that causes us to believe that management's assumptions do not provide a reasonable basis for presenting the significant effects directly attributable to the above-mentioned transaction (or event) described in Note 1, that the related pro forma adjustments do not give appropriate effect to those assumptions, or that the pro forma column does not reflect the proper application of those adjustments to the historical financial statement amounts in the pro forma condensed balance sheet as of March 31, 20X6, and the pro forma condensed statement of income for the three months then ended.

[*Signature*]

[*Date*]

AT SECTION 501

REPORTING ON AN ENTITY'S INTERNAL CONTROL OVER FINANCIAL REPORTING

Authoritative Pronouncements

SSAE-15—An Examination of an Entity's Internal Control over Financial Reporting That Is Integrated with an Audit of Its Financial Statements

SSAE Interpretation No. 1 of AT 501 (September 2010)—Reporting under Section 12 of the Federal Insurance Corporation Improvement Act

Overview

The basic concepts of internal control and the auditor's consideration of internal control in a financial statement audit are discussed in AU-C 315 (*Understanding the Entity and Its Environment and Assessing the Risks of Material Misstatement*). Internal control over financial reporting is a process—designed and overseen by those charged with governance, management, and others—designed to provide reasonable assurance that the financial statements are prepared in accordance with the applicable financial reporting framework. Effective internal control provides reasonable assurance over the reliability of financial reporting.

Guidance for reporting on internal control is established by the Statements on Standards for Attestation Engagements (SSAE) and is discussed in this section. An auditor may accept an engagement to report on a client's internal control only if the following conditions are satisfied:

- Management accepts responsibility for the effectiveness of internal control over financial reporting.

- Management evaluates the effectiveness of internal control over financial reporting using a suitable and available control framework.

- Management supports its assessment of the effectiveness of internal control over financial reporting with sufficient appropriate evidence.

- Management provides a report on the effectiveness of internal control over financial reporting that accompanies the auditor's report.

PUBLIC COMPANY IMPLICATION: As a result of the issuance of AS-5 by the PCAOB, the guidance in AT 501 only applies to reporting on an entity's internal control over financial reporting for nonpublic companies. SSAE-15 largely converges the standards for reporting on internal control over financial reporting for nonpublic companies with the guidance on reporting on internal control over financial reporting for public companies as contained in AS-5.

> **OBSERVATION:** SSAE-15 refers to the auditor rather than the practitioner (as is typical within the attestation standards) because it only applies when an engagement to examine the design and operating effectiveness of internal control over financial reporting is integrated with an audit of the financial statements.

In addition, the guidance in SSAE-15 does *not* apply in the following circumstances:

- An engagement to examine the design of internal control (such an engagement can be performed under the standards in AT 101 (Attest Engagements))

- An engagement to examine controls over the effectiveness and efficiency of operations (such an engagement can be performed under the standards in AT 101 (Attest Engagements))

- An engagement to examine controls over compliance with laws and regulations (such an engagement can be performed under the standards in AT 601 (Compliance Attestation))

- An engagement to examine controls over the processing of transactions by a service organization (such an engagement can be performed under the standards in AT 801 (*Reporting on Controls at a Service Organization*))

- An engagement to perform agreed-upon procedures on controls (such an engagement can be performed under the standards in AT 201 (Agreed-Upon Procedures Engagements))

- In addition, an auditor is precluded from accepting an engagement to review ICFR or a written assertion thereon.

Under SSAE-15, the auditor can be retained to report either directly on the entity's internal control over financial reporting (ICFR) or on management's assertion relating to ICFR. ICFR is typically examined as of the end of the entity's fiscal year; however, management may retain the auditor to examine ICFR as of a date other than year-end. In addition, the auditor can be retained to examine ICFR during a period of time.

> **OBSERVATION:** Unlike AS-5, which requires the same auditor to perform the financial statement and ICFR audits, SSAE-15 does not explicitly require the same firm to provide both services. Nevertheless, SSAE-15 encourages entities to use the same auditor to provide both services, and it states that certain regulators require the same auditor to provide both services.

An auditor engaged to opine on ICFR should comply with the general, fieldwork, and reporting standards (AT 101), and the specific performance and reporting standards in SSAE-15. In addition, if management refuses to furnish a written assertion on its assessment as to the effectiveness of ICFR, the auditor should withdraw from the engagement. If the auditor cannot withdraw from the engagement because of law or regulation, he or she should disclaim an opinion.

EXAMINATION ENGAGEMENT

The purpose of an examination engagement that reports on an entity's internal control over financial reporting is to express an opinion on (1) the effectiveness of the entity's internal control, in all material respects, based on the applicable control framework or (2) whether the responsible party's written assertion about the effectiveness of internal control is fairly stated, in all material respects, based on the applicable control framework. The auditor should use the same framework as management to evaluate ICFR, which typically is the framework developed by the Committee of Sponsoring Organizations (COSO) of the Treadway Commission, *Internal Control—Integrated Framework*. In order to express an opinion concerning the effectiveness of its internal control, the practitioner must collect sufficient appropriate evidence that supports the opinion.

PLANNING AID REMINDER: The opinion expressed is based on management's assertion or the internal controls taken as a whole, and it is not directed to a specific control policy or procedure or to the separate components of internal control.

Promulgated Procedures Checklist

The auditor should perform the following procedures when reporting on an entity's ICFR:

- Consider management's responsibility for supporting its ICFR assertion.
- Plan the engagement.
- Perform a risk assessment.
- Analyze fraud risk.
- Determine materiality.
- Consider using the work of others.
- Use a top-down approach.
- Identify significant accounts and disclosures.
- Understand likely sources of misstatement.
- Test design effectiveness.
- Test operating effectiveness.
- Match evidence to risk.
- Determine nature, timing, and extent of testing.
- Consider use of service organizations.
- Integrate with financial statement audit.
- Evaluate identified deficiencies.
- Obtain written representations.
- Fulfill communication responsibilities.
- Prepare an appropriate report on the entity's (client's) ICFR.
- Consider subsequent events

PLANNING AID REMINDER: General guidance for documenting an attest engagement is discussed in AT 101 (Attest Engagements).

Analysis and Application of Procedures

Consider management's responsibility for supporting its ICFR assertion

Management is responsible for documenting its controls and related control objectives, and the documentation serves as a basis for management's internal control assertion. The extent of the documentation needed depends on the size and complexity of the entity. Examples of documentation include (1) policy and accounting manuals, (2) narrative memoranda, (3) flowcharts, (4) decision tables, (5) procedural write-ups, and (5) questionnaires.

Management's monitoring activities also provide evidence as to the design and operating effectiveness of internal control. Monitoring includes periodically testing and assessing controls, and identifying and reporting deficiencies to appropriate individuals in the entity. Monitoring can be performed through ongoing activities or separate evaluations.

The selection of methods used to document internal control is a managerial decision based on the size and complexity of the entity's operations, and it may include documentation methods such as policy manuals, memoranda, flowcharts, questionnaires, and accounting manuals. These methods should document the relationship between internal controls and the control objectives.

ENGAGEMENT STRATEGY: Although management is responsible for the documentation of its internal control, the auditor may be engaged to help management identify the methods they are using to document the controls.

PUBLIC COMPANY IMPLICATION: The extent to which the auditor can be used to help management document internal controls for a public company is more limited than for private companies. Documentation assistance must be preapproved by the audit committee only after the audit committee carefully considers whether the auditor's involvement in documenting controls would impair the auditor's independence, either in fact or in appearance.

Plan the engagement

Proper planning of the engagement requires that the auditor consider a number of factors that may be relevant to forming an opinion related to the client's internal control. SSAE standards list the following as some of the factors that may be relevant in planning the engagement:

- Knowledge of the entity's internal control based on previous engagements.

- Matters affecting the entity's industry (e.g., financial reporting practices, economic conditions, and laws and regulations).
- Matters affecting the entity's business (e.g., organization, operating characteristics, and capital structure).
- The effect of recent changes to the entity, its operations, or its internal control.
- The auditor's preliminary judgments about materiality and risk.
- Internal control deficiencies previously communicated to management or those charged with governance.
- Legal or regulatory matters affecting the entity.
- The type and extent of available evidence related to assessing ICFR.
- Preliminary judgments about the effectiveness of ICFR.
- Public information about the entity related to the risk of material financial statement misstatements and about the effectiveness of ICFR.
- Knowledge about entity risks obtained as part of the client acceptance and retention process.
- The relative complexity of the entity.

The auditor should realize that the nature of an entity's controls should vary based on its size and complexity, and the documentation of controls are typically more extensive for a larger, more complex entity than for a smaller, less complex one. The auditor should adjust (scale) the audit approach accordingly. Factors to consider in assessing the complexity of an entity include (1) the number of business lines, (2) the complexity of business processes and financial reporting systems, (3) the relative degree of centralization of the accounting function, (4) involvement by senior management in the day-to-day activities of the business, and (5) the number of levels of management. One additional factor that the practitioner should consider when planning the engagement is the extent to which the internal control is documented.

In addition, the planning of the engagement is affected by whether the client has multiple locations. The amount of audit work performed at a location or business unit should reflect the risk of a material misstatement to the financial statements resulting from the activities of the location or business unit. The auditor does not have to examine those locations that either alone or in combination with others do not present a reasonable possibility of material misstatement to the financial statements. For other low-risk locations or business units, the auditor should assess whether he or she can rely on (1) entity-level controls and (2) work performed by others (e.g., internal audit).

Perform a risk assessment

SSAE-15 states that the auditor's risk assessment procedures underlie the entire process of auditing ICFR. The auditor should focus more of his or her effort on areas of higher risk. In addition, there should be a direct relation between the risk that a material weakness could exist in a particular area and the amount of audit attention devoted to the area. The auditor does not have to test those controls that even if deficient would not expose the entity to a reasonable possibility of material misstatement to the financial statements. Finally, the auditor should recognize that internal control is less likely to prevent, or detect and correct, a material misstatement due to fraud than misstatements due to error.

Analyze fraud risk

The auditor is specifically required to analyze fraud risk in an audit of ICFR. The auditor should address whether controls adequately address the risk of material misstatement due to fraud and to management override of controls. Controls that might be responsive to fraud risks include

- Controls over significant unusual transactions, particularly those that occur late in the period or via unusual journal entries
- Controls over journal entries and adjustments made as part of the period-end financial reporting process
- Controls over related-party transactions
- Controls related to significant management estimates
- Controls that reduce managerial incentives or pressures to falsify reported financial results

If the auditor concludes that an entity's antifraud programs and controls are deficient, he or she should consider this fact when planning the financial statement audit. Deficiencies in antifraud programs and controls should lead the auditor to modify the nature, timing, and extent of audit procedures in the financial statement audit.

Determine materiality

Materiality should be the same for the audit of ICFR as for the financial statement audit.

Consider using the work of others

In an audit of ICFR, the auditor may use work performed by, or receive direct assistance from, internal auditors, entity personnel other than internal audit, and outside parties working under the direction of management and those charged with governance. In determining how extensively the auditor can rely on the work of others, he or she is to assess the competence and objectivity of other parties that the auditor is considering relying upon. There is a direct relation between reliance and competence and objectivity. Given a higher assessed level of competence and objectivity, the auditor can place greater reliance on work performed by others. In addition, the less audit risk in an area, the more reliance that can be placed on the work of others.

Use a top-down approach

In planning an audit of ICFR, the auditor is to use a top-down approach, beginning with controls at the financial statement level and then working down to controls related to significant accounts and disclosures and related assertions. The auditor should analyze the financial statements to determine which accounts, transaction classes, and disclosures present a reasonable possibility of a material misstatement. In addition, the auditor should consider entity-level controls. Entity-level controls include (1) controls related to the control environment, (2) controls related to management override, (3) the entity's risk assessment process, (4) centralized processing and controls, (5) controls that monitor the results of operations, (6) controls to monitor other controls (e.g., internal audit, those charged with governance), and (7) controls over the period-end financial reporting process. Effective entity-level controls reduce the amount of audit effort needed in testing controls at the account and transaction level (i.e., referred to as control activities in COSO's internal control framework). After assessing entity-level controls, the auditor should identify significant accounts and disclosures and their relevant assertions, and controls that address risk at the assertion level. The auditor should focus his or her efforts in those areas that pose a reasonable possibility of a material misstatement to the financial statements.

In evaluating entity-level controls, the control environment is the first among equals or, as expressed by COSO, the foundation upon which all the other elements of internal control rest. In evaluating the control environment, the auditor should assess whether management's philosophy and operating style promote effective internal control. In addition, the auditor should assess whether there is evidence of sound integrity and ethical values, especially on the part of senior management. Finally, the auditor should evaluate whether those charged with governance understand and exercise oversight responsibility related to financial reporting and internal control. (The auditor should also refer to AU-C 315 (*Understanding the Entity and Its Environment and Assessing the Risks of Material Misstatement*) for further guidance in evaluating the control environment.)

Another entity-level control that is particularly important to accurate financial reporting is the client's period-end financial reporting process, which includes

- Procedures for entering transaction totals in the general ledger
- Procedures for selecting and applying accounting principles
- Procedures to initiate, authorize, record, and process journal entries in the general ledger
- Procedures used to record recurring and nonrecurring financial statement adjustments
- Procedures for preparing the financial statements and related disclosures

In assessing a client's period-end financial reporting process, the auditor should evaluate

- How the entity produces its financial statements (e.g., inputs, procedures performed, and outputs)
- The extent of information technology involvement in the period-end financial reporting process
- The participation from management in the process
- The locations involved in the period-end financial reporting process
- The types of adjusting and consolidating entries

- The oversight of the process by management and those charged with governance

Identify significant accounts and disclosures

To perform an effective audit of ICFR the auditor should identify the client's significant accounts and disclosures and their relevant assertions. To do this, the auditor evaluates quantitative and qualitative risk factors related to financial statement line items and disclosures. Risk factors related to accounts, classes of transactions, and disclosures include

- Size and composition
- Susceptibility to misstatement due to error or fraud
- Nature of the account, transaction class, or disclosure
- Volume of activity and the complexity of transactions
- Accounting and reporting complexities
- Possibility of significant contingent liabilities
- Existence of related-party transactions
- Changes from the prior period

The accounts, transaction classes, and disclosures, and their relevant assertions identified in an ICFR audit also pertain to a financial statement audit. In identifying significant accounts and disclosures, the auditor's objective is to identify likely sources of potential material misstatement.

Understand likely sources of misstatement

Given the importance and need for judgment in understanding likely sources of misstatement, the auditor should either perform the work in this area or supervise the work of others in this area. Procedures that the auditor should perform to understand likely sources of misstatement include

- Understanding the flow of transactions related to relevant assertions (e.g., initiation, authorization, processing, and recording)
- Identifying the points within the process where misstatements could occur
- Identifying controls that address the risks of misstatement
- Identifying controls to prevent, or timely detect and correct, the unauthorized acquisition, use, or disposition of the entity's assets
- Understanding how IT affects the flow of transactions

Performing a walk-through is often the best way to understand the likely sources of misstatement. A walk-through involves following a transaction from initiation through the entity's processes until it is reflected in the financial records. In addition, a walk-through includes questioning entity personnel about their understanding of procedures and controls, especially at those points where important processing procedures occur.

Test design effectiveness

Controls are designed effectively if they meet the entity's control objectives—assuming the controls are implemented as designed—and would prevent, or detect and timely correct, misstatements that could lead to a material misstatement in the financial statements. In testing design effectiveness, the auditor evaluates whether there are any deficiencies in the design of controls. A deficiency in control design exists if (1) a necessary control is missing or (2) the applicable control objective would not be met even if the control operated as designed.

Design effectiveness can be tested using inquiry, observation, and inspection of relevant documentation. Walk-throughs that incorporate the foregoing procedures are often sufficient for evaluating design effectiveness.

Test operating effectiveness

In testing operating effectiveness, the auditor evaluates whether there are any deficiencies in the operation of controls. A deficiency in control operation exists if (1) a properly designed control does not operate as designed or (2) the person performing the control lacks the needed competence or authority.

In testing the operating effectiveness of ICFR, the tests should be designed to determine (1) how the control was applied, (2) whether the control was applied consistently, and (3) who applied the control. The auditor can make these determinations by applying a variety of examination procedures, including inquiry, inspection of documents, observation of activities, and reapplication or reperformance of internal control procedures.

The extent to which examination procedures should be performed is a matter of professional judgment. Generally, the nature, timing, and extent of tests of operating effectiveness are based on the preliminary assessment of risk and the client's entity-level controls. Specific factors that a practitioner may consider in determining what constitutes sufficient evidential matter include the following:

- The nature of the control
- The significance of the control in achieving the objectives of the control criteria
- The nature and extent of tests of operating effectiveness that the client performs

---

ENGAGEMENT STRATEGY: The absence of misstatements in an account balance, transaction class, or disclosure related to a control does not necessarily mean that the control is effective. A control should be tested directly in order to conclude that it is effective.

PLANNING AID REMINDER: The auditor's objective is to provide an opinion on the entity's internal control overall, not an opinion on the effectiveness of each individual control. Thus, an auditor can vary the evidence obtained about the effectiveness of individual controls based on the risks associated with the individual control.

For many clients, automated controls are increasingly important. A benchmarking strategy may be effective for testing automated controls. A benchmarking strategy is appropriate if general computer controls are effective and if the general computer controls are retested every year. General computer controls are controls over program changes, access to programs and databases, and computer operations. In using a benchmarking strategy, the auditor needs to verify that the automated application control has not changed since the baseline was established. The auditor can examine compilation dates for computer programs. In the case of purchased software, changes to the underlying code may not be possible and the auditor may instead verify that configuration settings have not been changed. If these procedures are followed, the auditor can conclude that the automated application control continues to be effective without retesting the operation of the automated application control.

OBSERVATION: After some period of time, based on the auditor's judgment, the operation of the automated application controls needs to be retested. Factors that the auditor should consider in determining how often the automated application control needs to be retested are (1) control environment effectiveness, (2) any changes to programs that contain the controls, (3) nature and timing of other related tests, (4) consequences of errors that could result from a failure of the automated application control, and (5) whether other business factors may have changed that could affect the control (e.g., the nature of the data that the control operates on has changed).

A client may perform various tests of the operational effectiveness of its internal control. The auditor must decide to what extent, if at all, he or she should rely on the work performed by client personnel when drawing a conclusion about the client's internal control. If the auditor plans to rely to some degree on the work performed by client personnel, he or she should test some of the work performed. Obviously, an auditor would place more reliance on work he or she performs him- or herself than on tests performed by the client. Auditors must make fundamental judgments about the testing process; for example, it would be inappropriate for a client to decide what constitutes sufficient evidence or a material weakness.

The auditor must decide what period of time the test procedures should be applied to. To some extent, the nature of a control determines the period over which it should be tested. For example, some procedures are performed only periodically (e.g., controls over the preparation of interim financial statements and the physical inventory count) and others are continuous (e.g., controls over payroll transactions).

Match evidence to risk

The audit evidence needed depends on the risk associated with the control (more risk, more evidence needed; less risk, less evidence). The risk associated with a control includes the risk that the control is not effective and, if the control is not effective, the risk that a material weakness exists. Factors affecting the risk associated with a control include

- Nature and materiality of the misstatements that the control addresses
- Inherent risk associated with the account and assertions
- Changes in the volume or nature of transactions
- The account's history of errors
- Effectiveness of entity-level controls
- Nature of the control
- Frequency of the control's operation (e.g., daily, weekly, monthly, etc.)
- Extent to which the control relies on the effectiveness of other controls
- Competence of the personnel performing the control or monitoring performance
- Whether the control is manual or automated
- Complexity of the control, and extent of judgment needed to apply the control

When the auditor detects deviations in the operation of a control, he or she should consider the effect of these deviations on the auditor's assessment of risk as well as on the auditor's evaluation of the operating effectiveness of the control. An individual control can have some deviations and still be viewed as effective.

Determine nature, timing, and extent of testing

The auditor should vary the nature, timing, and extent of his or her testing in response to the risk associated with a control. The nature of testing relates to the type of auditing procedures performed. Not all auditing procedures are equally effective. Generally, the quality of audit evidence obtained follows this descending order: (1) reperformance, including recalculation, (2) inspection of relevant documentation, (3) observation, and (4) inquiry. Exclusive reliance on inquiry, given that inquiry generally provides the weakest form of evidence, is insufficient for testing a control.

ENGAGEMENT STRATEGY: The nature of evidence gathered depends on the extent of the client's documentation of control procedures. Some controls (e.g., tone at the top, management's philosophy and operating style) do not provide documentary evidence, and the lack of documentary evidence may be more pronounced in smaller entities. In cases where documentary evidence is lacking, the auditor may have to rely on inquiry, observation of activities, and review of less formal documentation. Where inquiry is an important procedure, the auditor may want to consider asking similar questions of multiple individuals, including client personnel in operating positions.

Testing controls over a longer period of time provides more evidence than testing controls over a shorter period of time. And testing controls closer to year-end provides more evidence than testing controls earlier in the year, although controls have to be tested over a period that is long enough to assess their operating effectiveness. In addition, the more extensively (i.e., sample size) a control is tested, the more evidence the testing provides. Moreover, the auditor should consider the results from the prior year's testing of ICFR in planning the current year's examination of ICFR. Audit procedures to test controls should be varied from year to year—that is, an element of unpredictability should be built in to the auditor's tests.

A client may remediate control deficiencies during the year. If sufficient time remains in the year to test the operating effectiveness of the remediated control, the auditor can test it because the opinion on the effectiveness of ICFR is as of year-end. The auditor does not have to test the superseded control for the ICFR audit; however, he or she does need to consider the effect of deficiencies in the superseded control in planning the financial statement audit.

An auditor may test the operating effectiveness of a control as of an interim date and desire to roll forward his or her conclusion to the period-end date. The auditor needs more evidence as to the continuing effectiveness of the control if (1) the risks associated with the control are greater, (2) the evidence obtained about the control's operating effectiveness at the interim date was limited, (3) there is a longer period of time between the interim date and the year end date, and (4) changes have occurred in internal control since the interim date.

Consider use of service organizations

A service organization's services may be part of an entity's information and communication component of internal control. The auditor should obtain (1) an understanding of the controls at the service organization, (2) an understanding of controls at the user organization over the activities of the service organization, and (3) evidence that the relevant controls are operating effectively. To assess whether controls at the service organization are operating effectively, the auditor should perform one or more of the following procedures:

- Obtain a service auditor's report on controls placed in operation and tests of operating effectiveness of these controls (i.e., a SSAE-16 Type II report)

- Obtain a service auditor's report on the application of agreed-upon procedures

- Test the user organization's controls over the activities of the service organization

- Perform tests of controls at the service organization (directly by the auditor)

The auditor should also refer to the guidance in AU-C 315 if a service organization is part of the client's internal control system.

ENGAGEMENT STRATEGY: If an auditor intends to rely on a SSAE-16 Type II report, he or she needs to assess (1) the time period covered by the service auditor's report in relation to the date that the auditor is reporting on ICFR, (2) the scope of the controls tested at the service organization (i.e., were the controls at the service organization that are applicable to the auditor's ICFR examination tested), (3) the nature of the tests of controls at the service organization, and (4) the nature of the Type II opinion. Depending on the results of the assessment, the auditor may need to perform additional procedures relating to controls at the service organization. Additionally, the auditor should make inquiries as to the reputation, competence, and independence of the auditor who issued the Type II report.

OBSERVATION: The auditor is not to refer to the Type II audit report in his or her ICFR report.

Integrate with financial statement audit

The auditor's conclusions about ICFR should affect the financial statement audit. Specifically, the nature, timing, and extent of audit procedures in the financial statement audit should reflect conclusions about the effectiveness of the client's ICFR. In addition, the auditor's findings during the financial statement audit should affect the audit of ICFR. For example, areas where misstatements are identified may suggest that internal control in that area is not effective.

PLANNING AID REMINDER: Although the ICFR audit should affect (be integrated with) the financial statement audit and vice versa, the auditor typically needs to test more controls in order to issue an ICFR opinion than would be tested when only expressing an opinion on the financial statements.

PLANNING AID REMINDER: Regardless of the assessed level of risk, the auditor should perform substantive procedures for all relevant assertions for each material account balance, transaction class, and disclosure. Therefore, even if inherent risk is low and internal control is effective, the auditor must still perform some substantive procedures for material account balances, transaction classes, and disclosures.

OBSERVATION: AT 501 requires that an examination of internal control over financial reporting (ICFR) be integrated with the audit of financial statements. Interpretation No. 1 of AT 501 (Reporting under Section 12 of the Federal Insurance Corporation Improvement Act) addresses engagements performed by practitioners for insured depository institutions (IDIs) with Section 112 of the Federal Deposit Insurance Corporation Improvement Act (FDICIA). The interpretation notes when an IDI is a subsidiary of a holding company, the IDI may use the consolidated holding company's financial statements to satisfy the audited financial statements requirement, provided certain criteria are met. It also notes that under certain regulations, some IDIs are required to have an examination of internal control at the IDI level but the IDI is not required to prepare financial statements for external distribution. In those situations, the interpretation notes that "financial statements" may consist of the IDI's financial information in a reporting package or equivalent schedules that include the IDI information necessary for preparation of the holding company's financial statements. If the auditor is unable to apply procedures necessary to obtain sufficient appropriate audit evidence with respect to the IDI's financial information, the auditor is required by AT 501 to withdraw from the engagement or disclaim an opinion on the effectiveness of the IDI's internal control over financial reporting.

Evaluate identified deficiencies

In evaluating the internal control deficiencies identified during the ICFR audit, the auditor evaluates whether any single deficiency or deficiencies considered together constitute either a significant deficiency or a material weakness. A significant deficiency is a deficiency or combination of deficiencies that is less severe than a material weakness but important enough to warrant consideration by those charged with governance. Therefore, a significant deficiency does not change the nature of an unmodified report on ICFR and is not included in the auditor's report, but it is communicated to those charged with governance. A material weakness is a deficiency or combination of deficiencies such that there is a reasonable possibility that a material misstatement in the financial statements will not be prevented, or detected and corrected, on a timely basis. The term "reasonable possibility" as used here means that a material misstatement in the financial statements is either "reasonably possible" or "probable" as those terms are defined in ASC 450 (Contingencies). If there is even one material weakness, the auditor cannot conclude that ICFR is effective (i.e., the auditor must issue an adverse opinion on the effectiveness of ICFR).

The severity of an identified deficiency depends on the magnitude of the potential misstatement as a result of the deficiency and the likelihood that a misstatement will occur as a result of the deficiency. Factors that affect the magnitude of a potential misstatement are (1) the financial statement amounts or transaction totals affected by the deficiency and (2) the volume of activity in the account or transaction class affected by the deficiency. In evaluating deficiencies, the auditor should recognize that the likelihood of a small misstatement is greater than the likelihood of a large misstatement. Factors that affect the likelihood of a misstatement are

- Nature of accounts, transactions, disclosures, and assertions
- Susceptibility of related asset or liability to loss or fraud
- Subjectivity, complexity, and judgment involved with the account
- Relation of the control to other controls
- Interaction among the deficiencies
- Possible future consequences of the deficiency

PLANNING AID REMINDER: The severity of a deficiency does not depend on whether a misstatement has already occurred.

Multiple deficiencies that affect the same account, disclosure, assertion, or internal control component increase the likelihood that a material weakness exists. In some cases, clients have a second control that compensates for a deficiency in the tested control. A compensating control can limit the severity of an identified deficiency (in the tested control) and thereby prevent the deficiency from rising to the level of a significant deficiency or material weakness. However, a compensating control does not eliminate the underlying deficiency. In order for a compensating control to mitigate a control deficiency it must operate at a level of precision sufficient to prevent, or detect and timely correct, a material misstatement in the financial statements. The auditor should test the operating effectiveness of any compensating control that he or she plans to rely on.

There are certain indicators that suggest that a material weakness may exist:

- Identification of fraud committed by senior management, regardless of materiality

- Restatements of previously issued financial statements to correct a material misstatement due to error or fraud

- Identification of a material misstatement by the auditor in the financial statements being audited that was not detected by management (i.e., the auditor is not part of the client's internal control system)

- Ineffective oversight of financial reporting and internal control by those charged with governance

---

PLANNING AID REMINDER: If the auditor concludes that a deficiency or combination of deficiencies is not a material weakness, he or she should assess whether a prudent official would reach the same judgment given the same information as that known to the auditor.

Obtain written representations

The auditor should obtain written representations from management in an ICFR audit, including

- A statement that responsibility for establishing and maintaining internal control is that of management

- A statement that management has performed an evaluation of the effectiveness of internal control based on control criteria (control criteria should be specified)

- A statement that management did not rely on the auditor's procedures in making its assertion

- Management's assertion about the effectiveness of internal control based on the control criteria as of a specified date

- A statement that management has communicated to the auditor all deficiencies in the design or operation of internal control, separately identifying deficiencies it believes to be significant deficiencies and material weaknesses

- A statement that management has described any material fraud and any other fraud that involves management or other employees who have a significant role in the entity's internal control, even though the fraud is not material
- A statement that significant deficiencies or material weaknesses communicated to management and those charged with governance in the prior year have been corrected, or where such corrections have not occurred that, specifically, identifies them
- A statement that subsequent to the date of the report there were no events, changes in internal control, or occurrences of other factors that might significantly affect internal control, including the remediation of significant deficiencies and material weaknesses

A failure to obtain written representations from management represents a scope limitation. The auditor should consider the effect of management's refusal to provide such representations on his or her ability to rely on other representations, including representations related to the financial statement audit.

Fulfill communication responsibilities

The auditor is to communicate in writing to management and those charged with governance all significant deficiencies and material weaknesses identified during the integrated audit. If any of these significant deficiencies or material weaknesses were previously communicated, the auditor can simply refer to the communication by date. And if the auditor concludes that audit committee oversight of financial reporting and internal control is ineffective, he or she is to communicate this in writing to the board of directors or other, similar governing body. These required communications should occur by the report release date. The report release date is the date the auditor allows the entity to use his or her report.

PLANNING AID REMINDER: Communication of significant deficiencies and material weaknesses can occur later than the report release date for a governmental entity. The required communications must be made within 60 days of the report release date. This exception only exists if the required communications will be publicly available prior to management's report on internal control, the entity's financial statements, and the auditor's report thereon.

The client may be able to remediate internal control deficiencies during the year if it receives timely communication. Therefore, the auditor can orally communicate to management significant internal control matters. However, oral communication does not eliminate the auditor's responsibility to communicate significant deficiencies and material weaknesses in writing, even if the matters are remediated during the year. In addition, all internal control deficiencies (beyond significant deficiencies and material weaknesses) are to be communicated to management in writing within 60 days of the report release date, and those charged with governance are to be notified when this communication takes place.

PLANNING AID REMINDER: The auditor is precluded from issuing a report containing "negative assurance" about internal control. For example, the auditor should not issue a report indicating that no deficiencies were identified.

Prepare an appropriate report on the entity's (client's) ICFR

The auditor's opinion on the effectiveness of ICFR should reflect evidence obtained from all sources, specifically from the auditor's testing of internal control and from testing performed during the financial statement audit. In addition, the auditor should consider reports issued during the year by any internal audit group that may exist. The auditor should ensure that management has issued its own report on the effectiveness of ICFR and that management's report contains the following elements:

- A statement that management is responsible for internal control

- A description of what was examined, typically controls over the preparation of financial statements in accordance with GAAP

- A description of the framework used to evaluate controls, typically COSO's *Internal Control—Integrated Framework* (1992)

- Management's assertion about the effectiveness of ICFR

- A description of any material weaknesses

- The date as of which management's assertion is made

OBSERVATION: If management refuses to include its own report on ICFR, the auditor should withdraw from the engagement. If precluded from withdrawing by law or regulation, the auditor should disclaim an opinion on ICFR.

PLANNING AID REMINDER: SSAE-16 (Reporting on Controls at a Service Organization) provides guidance for practitioners engaged to report on controls at a service organization that provides services related to a user entity's internal controls over financial reporting. Sometimes, an entity may engage a practitioner to report on controls at a service organization that relate to the user entity's internal controls over compliance or operations (not internal controls over financial reporting). In the latter engagement, the practitioner would follow the guidance in AT 101. Interpretation No. 8 of AT 101 (Including a Description of Tests of Controls or Other Procedures, and the Results Thereof, in an Examination Report) notes that nothing in AT 101 precludes a practitioner from including in a separate section of his or her examination report a description of the tests of controls or other procedures performed and the results thereof related to internal controls over compliance or operations. The interpretation notes, however, that in some cases such a description may overshadow the practitioner's overall opinion or cause report users to misunderstand the opinion. Thus, the circumstances of the particular engagement are relevant to the practitioner's consideration on whether to include such description.

The reporting guidelines in Exhibit AT 501-1 should be followed in the preparation of a report on internal control.

EXHIBIT AT 501-1—REPORTING GUIDELINES FOR PREPARATION OF AN EXAMINATION REPORT ON AN ENTITY'S INTERNAL CONTROL

Required Elements of the Audit Report on the Effectiveness of ICFR

- Title that includes the word "independent"
- Statement that management is responsible for maintaining effective internal control and for evaluating the effectiveness of ICFR
- An identification of management's assessment of ICFR (refer to management's report)
- Statement that the auditor is responsible for issuing an opinion on ICFR or on management's assertion regarding internal control (i.e., the auditor can either report directly on internal control or on management's assertion regarding internal control)
- Statement that the engagement was performed in accordance with AICPA attestation standards
- Statement that the AICPA attestation standards require the auditor to gather reasonable assurance as to whether internal control was maintained in all material respects
- A description of the attestation procedures performed (e.g., understanding control, assessing risk, testing and evaluating design and operating effectiveness, and other procedures as deemed necessary)
- A statement that the auditor believes that he or she has a reasonable basis for the opinion
- A definition of internal control (the auditor is to use the same definition as that used by management)
- Separate paragraph describing the inherent limitations of internal control, along with a warning that the effectiveness of the internal control may be inadequate for future periods
- An opinion on whether the entity has maintained, in all material respects, effective internal control as of a specified date based on the control criteria (or the auditor's opinion on management's internal control assertion)
- Manual or printed signature of the firm
- Date of the report

The auditor can issue a combined report on ICFR and the financial statements or separate reports on each. If separate reports are issued, the auditor should add a paragraph to the report on the financial statements stating that he or she audited ICFR and the type of report issued, and a paragraph to the ICFR report stating that he or she audited the financial statements and indicating the type of report issued. Because the financial statement and ICFR audits are integrated they should be dated the same.

Exhibit AT 501-2 is an example taken from SSAE-15 of an examination on the effectiveness of an entity's internal control over financial reporting.

EXHIBIT AT 501-2—EXAMINATION ON THE EFFECTIVENESS OF AN ENTITY'S INTERNAL CONTROL OVER FINANCIAL REPORTING

Independent Auditor's Report

We have examined W Company's internal control over financial reporting as of December 31, 20XX, based on [*identify criteria*]. W Company's management is responsible for maintaining effective internal control over financial reporting, and for its assertion of the effectiveness of internal control over financial reporting, included in the accompanying [*title of management's report*]. Our responsibility is to express an opinion on W Company's internal control over financial reporting based on our examination.

We conducted our examination in accordance with attestation standards established by the American Institute of Certified Public Accountants. Those standards require that we plan and perform the examination to obtain reasonable assurance about whether effective internal control over financial reporting was maintained in all material respects. Our examination included obtaining an understanding of internal control over financial reporting, assessing the risk that a material weakness exists, and testing and evaluating the design and operating effectiveness of internal control based on the assessed risk. Our examination also included performing such other procedures as we considered necessary in the circumstances. We believe that our examination provides a reasonable basis for our opinion.

An entity's internal control over financial reporting is a process effected by those charged with governance, management, and other personnel, designed to provide reasonable assurance regarding the preparation of reliable financial statements in accordance with [*applicable financial reporting framework, such as accounting principles generally accepted in the United States of America*]. An entity's internal control over financial reporting includes those policies and procedures that (1) pertain to the maintenance of records that in reasonable detail accurately and fairly reflect the transactions and dispositions of the assets of the entity; (2) provide reasonable assurance that transactions are recorded as necessary to permit preparation of financial statements in accordance with [*applicable financial reporting framework, such as accounting principles generally accepted in the United States of America*] and that receipts and expenditures of the entity are being made only in accordance with authorizations of management and those charged with governance; and (3) provide reasonable assurance regarding prevention, or timely detection and correction of unauthorized acquisition, use, or disposition of the entity's assets that could have a material effect on the financial statements.

Because of its inherent limitations, internal control over financial reporting may not prevent, or detect and correct misstatements. Also, projections of any evaluation of effectiveness to future periods are subject to the risk that controls may become inadequate because of changes in conditions, or that the degree of compliance with the policies or procedures may deteriorate.

In our opinion, W Company maintained, in all material respects, effective internal control over financial reporting as of December 31, 20XX, based on [*identify criteria*].

We also have audited, in accordance with auditing standards generally accepted in the United States of America, the [*identify financial statements*] of W Company and our report dated [*date of report, which should be the same as the date of the report on the examination of internal control*] expressed [*include nature of opinion*].

[*Signature*]

[*Date*]

Exhibit AT 501-3 is an example taken from SSAE-15 of an examination on management's written assertion on the effectiveness of an entity's internal control over financial reporting.

EXHIBIT AT 501-3—EXAMINATION ON MANAGEMENT'S WRITTEN ASSERTION ON THE EFFECTIVENESS OF AN ENTITY'S INTERNAL CONTROL OVER FINANCIAL REPORTING

Independent Auditor's Report

We have examined management's assertion, included in the accompanying [*title of management's report*], that W Company maintained effective internal control over financial reporting as of December 31, 20XX, based on [*identify criteria*]. W Company's management is responsible for maintaining effective internal control over financial reporting, and for its assertion of the effectiveness of internal control over financial reporting, included in the accompanying [*title of management's report*]. Our responsibility is to express an opinion on management's assertion based on our examination.

We conducted our examination in accordance with attestation standards established by the American Institute of Certified Public Accountants. Those standards require that we plan and perform the examination to obtain reasonable assurance about whether effective internal control over financial reporting was maintained in all material respects. Our examination included obtaining an understanding of internal control over financial reporting, assessing the risk that a material weakness exists, and testing and evaluating the design and operating effectiveness of internal control based on the assessed risk. Our examination also included performing such other procedures as we considered necessary in the circumstances. We believe that our examination provides a reasonable basis for our opinion.

An entity's internal control over financial reporting is a process effected by those charged with governance, management, and other personnel designed to provide reasonable assurance regarding the preparation of reliable financial statements in accordance with [*applicable financial reporting framework, such as accounting principles generally accepted in the United States of America*]. An entity's internal control over financial reporting includes policies and procedures that (1) pertain to the maintenance of records that in reasonable detail accurately and fairly reflect the transactions and dispositions of the assets of the entity; (2) provide reasonable assurance that transactions are recorded as necessary to permit preparation of financial statements in accordance with [*applicable financial reporting framework, such as accounting principles generally accepted in the United States of America*], and that receipts and expenditures of the entity are being made only in accordance with authorizations of management and those charged with governance; and (3) provide reasonable assurance regarding prevention, or timely detection and correction, of unauthorized acquisition, use, or disposition of the entity's assets that could have a material effect on the financial statements.

Because of its inherent limitations, internal control over financial reporting may not prevent, or detect and correct misstatements. Also, projections of any evaluation of effectiveness to future periods are subject to the risk that controls may become inadequate because of changes in conditions, or that the degree of compliance with the policies or procedures may deteriorate.

In our opinion, management's assertion that W Company maintained effective internal control over financial reporting as of December 31, 20XX, is fairly stated, in all material respects, based on [*identify criteria*].

We have also audited, in accordance with auditing standards generally accepted in the United States of America the [*identify financial statements*] of W Company, and our report dated [*date of report, which should be the same as the date of the report on the examination of internal control*] expressed [*include nature of opinion*].

[*Signature*]

[*Date*]

Report modifications

SSAE standards state that the auditor should modify the standard report (on either a direct opinion on internal control or on a written assertion on internal control) if any of the following circumstances exist:

- Material weakness
- Management's report is incomplete or not properly presented
- Scope limitation
- Reliance in part on the report of another auditor
- Other information is included in management's report

Material weakness

If one or more material weaknesses exist, the auditor is to issue an adverse opinion on internal control (unless a scope limitation exists). In the report, the auditor is to define a material weakness and identify the material weakness included in management's assertion.

If management fails to describe the material weakness in its report, the auditor should state that a material weakness has been omitted from management's report and he or she should describe the material weakness in the audit report. The auditor's discussion should include the actual and potential effects of the material weakness on the financial statements. In addition, the auditor should communicate in writing to those charged with governance that a material weakness was excluded from management's report. Finally, the auditor should disclose whether the material weakness affected the financial statement audit report.

PLANNING AID REMINDER: When a material weakness exists, SSAE-15 states that the auditor should report directly on the effectiveness of internal control rather than on the written assertion.

Management's report is incomplete or not properly presented

If a required element of management's report is missing or inadequate, the auditor should ask management to correct its report. If management refuses to make the needed correction, the auditor should modify his or her report by including an explanatory paragraph describing the deficiency in management's report.

Scope limitation

When significant examination procedures deemed necessary to achieve the standard of sufficient appropriate evidence cannot be performed, the auditor should disclaim an opinion or withdraw from the engagement. If the auditor disclaims an opinion, his or her report should state that an opinion is not being expressed and explain the reasons for the disclaimer. The auditor should neither include in the report a description of any procedures performed nor describe the characteristics of internal control.

If the auditor disclaims an opinion, he or she should describe all material weaknesses that he or she is aware of. The auditor also should communicate in writing to management and those charged with governance that an opinion on internal control cannot be expressed because of a scope limitation.

Reliance in part on the report of another auditor

If internal control components of the entity are examined by another auditor, an auditor may still report on the entity's internal control over financial reporting. Under this circumstance, the auditor must decide whether or not to serve as the principal auditor and, if he or she serves as principal auditor, whether to refer to the work of the other auditor in the examination report. Specific guidance for making these determinations is discussed in AU-C 600 (*Special Consideration—Audits of Group Financial Statements (Including the Work of Component Auditors)*). Although the guidance is discussed in the context of an audit of financial statements, SSAE standards state that the general guidance is also applicable to the examination of management's assertion about its internal control.

Other information is included in management's report

Management's report may contain additional information beyond that which the auditor is engaged to report on. For example, management may make a statement discussing the trade-off between the costs of remediating internal control deficiencies and the benefits to be achieved from the remediation, or management may discuss corrective actions taken to address identified deficiencies. The auditor is to disclaim an opinion on additional information included in management's report by adding an additional last paragraph to the auditor's standard ICFR report.

PLANNING AID REMINDER: The last paragraph may be worded as follows, "We do not express an opinion or any other form of assurance on [*describe additional information, such as management's cost-benefit statement*]."

If the auditor believes that the additional information contained in management's report contains a material misstatement of fact, he or she should discuss the matter with the client. If the auditor concludes that a material misstatement of fact remains after discussing the matter with the client, he or she may want to consult with his or her legal counsel. At a minimum, the auditor should communicate in writing to management and those charged with governance his or her belief that a material misstatement of fact exists in management's report.

Consider subsequent events

After the date of management's assertion about its internal control but before the date of the examination report, there may have been changes in policies, procedures, or other factors that may have a significant effect on the entity's internal control. SSAE standards state that to determine whether such changes have occurred, the auditor should determine whether the following reports were issued subsequent to the date of the examination report, and, if so, he or she should read them:

- Other reports issued by independent practitioner(s) that identify deficiencies
- Relevant reports issued by internal auditors
- Reports on the client's internal control issued by regulatory agencies
- Information generated through other professional engagements that relates to the effectiveness of the client's internal control

If the subsequent event indicates that a material weakness existed at the date being reported on, the auditor should issue an adverse opinion and refer to the material weakness. In this case the auditor must report directly on internal control because an adverse opinion is being issued (i.e., the auditor cannot report on management's assertion regarding internal control). If the subsequent event indicates that a material weakness came into existence after the date being reported on, the auditor should describe the event in an explanatory paragraph or refer to the related discussion in management's report.

AT SECTION 601

COMPLIANCE ATTESTATION

Authoritative Pronouncements

SSAE-10—Attestation Standards: Revision and Recodification (Chapter 6)

Overview

The Statements on Standards for Attestation Engagements (SSAE) standards provide guidance for an engagement in which the practitioner either (1) reports on the client's compliance with requirements of specified laws, regulations, rules, contracts, or grants (referred to as compliance with specified requirements) or (2) reports on the effectiveness of the client's internal control over compliance with specified requirements.

> **PLANNING AID REMINDER:** When a practitioner is engaged to report on compliance with specified requirements, the general, fieldwork, and reporting standards discussed in AT 101 should be observed, along with the standards established in this chapter.

Although the standards discussed in this chapter are concerned with engagements related to compliance with specified requirements, the guidance does not apply to the following engagements:

- Audits of financial statements that are subject to generally accepted auditing standards (GAAS)
- Certain audit reports on specified compliance requirements based solely on the audit of financial statements AU-C 806 (*Reporting on Compliance with Aspects of Contractual Agreements or Regulatory Requirements in Connection with Audited Financial Statements*)
- Reports on engagements that are subject to the standards established by AU-C 935 (*Compliance Audits*), unless the terms of the engagement specifically require the type of attest report discussed in this chapter
- Engagements subject to AU-C 920 (*Letters for Underwriters and Certain Other Requesting Parties*)
- Report engagements related to a broker or dealer's internal control as required by Rule 17a-5 of the Securities Exchange Act of 1934

A compliance attestation engagement can take either the form of an agreed-upon procedures engagement or an examination.

AGREED-UPON PROCEDURES ENGAGEMENT

SSAE standards state that the purpose of an agreed-upon procedures (AUP) compliance attestation engagement is "to present specific findings to assist users in evaluating an entity's compliance with specified requirements or the effectiveness of an entity's internal control over compliance based on procedures agreed upon by the users of the report." A practitioner may accept an AUP compliance attestation engagement if both of the following conditions are satisfied:

- The responsible party accepts responsibility for compliance with the specified requirements and the effectiveness of the internal control over compliance.
- The responsible party evaluates compliance with the specified requirements or the effectiveness of the internal control over compliance.

Engagement Procedures

An AUP engagement must satisfy the standards established in this chapter as well as the guidance discussed in the chapter titled "Agreed-Upon Procedures Engagements" (AT 201).

As part of the AUP engagement, SSAE standards require that the practitioner obtain an understanding of the specified compliance requirements by considering the following:

- Laws, regulations, rules, contracts, and grants that relate to the compliance requirements
- Experienced gained from previous engagement and regulatory reports
- Inquiries made of appropriate management personnel
- Inquiries made of external parties such as specialists and regulators

Reporting Guidance

The practitioner's AUP report should include the following items:

- A title that includes the word "independent"
- An identification of the specified party
- An identification of the subject matter (or the written assertion), the period or point in time covered by the engagement, and the character of the engagement
- An identification of the responsible party and a statement that the subject matter is the responsibility of the responsible party
- A statement that the procedures were agreed to by the specified party and were performed to assist the specified party in evaluating compliance with the specified requirements or the effectiveness of internal control over compliance
- A statement that the AUP engagement was conducted in accordance with attestation standards established by the American Institute of Certified Public Accountants
- A statement that the specified party is solely responsible for the sufficiency of the agreed-upon procedures and disclaim any responsibility for the sufficiency of the procedures
- List of the procedures performed and related findings

- Description of materiality thresholds, where applicable
- A statement that the practitioner was not engaged to and did not conduct an examination of the compliance with specified requirements (or the effectiveness of internal control over compliance), a disclaimer of opinion, and a statement that if the practitioner had performed additional procedures, other matters might have come to his or her attention that would have been reported
- A statement restricting the use of the report to specified parties
- Reservations or restrictions related to procedures or findings, if applicable
- A description of the assistance provided by a specialist, if applicable
- The manual or printed signature of the practitioner's firm
- The date of the AUP report

Exhibit AT 601-1 is an example taken from SSAE-10 of an AUP engagement on an entity's compliance with specified requirements.

EXHIBIT AT 601-1—AUP REPORT ON AN ENTITY'S COMPLIANCE WITH SPECIFIED REQUIREMENTS

Independent Accountant's Report on Applying Agreed-Upon Procedures

We have performed the procedures enumerated below, which were agreed to by the [*identify specify parties*], solely to assist the specified parties in evaluating [*name of entity*]'s compliance with [*list specified requirements*] during the [*period*] ended [*date*]. Management is responsible for [*name of entity*]'s compliance with those requirements.

This agreed-upon procedures engagement was conducted in accordance with attestation standards established by the American Institute of Certified Public Accountants. The sufficiency of these procedures is solely the responsibility of those parties specified in this report. Consequently, we make no representation regarding the sufficiency of the procedures described below either for the purpose for which this report has been requested or for any other purpose.

[*Include paragraphs to enumerate procedures and findings.*]

We were not engaged to and did not conduct an examination, the objective of which would be the expression of an opinion on compliance. Accordingly, we do not express such an opinion. Had we performed additional procedures, other matters might have come to our attention that would have been reported to you.

This report is intended solely for the information and use of [*list or refer to specified parties*] and is not intended to be and should not be used by anyone other than these specified parties.

[*Signature*]

[*Date*]

EXAMINATION ENGAGEMENT

SSAE standards state that the purpose of an examination engagement is "to express an opinion on an entity's compliance (or assertion related thereto), based on the specified criteria." A practitioner may accept an examination compliance attestation engagement if all of the following conditions are satisfied:

- The responsible party accepts responsibility for compliance with the specified requirements and the effectiveness of the internal control over compliance.
- The responsible party evaluates compliance with the specified requirements.
- Sufficient evidential matter exists or could be developed to support the responsible party's evaluation.

Promulgated Procedures Checklist

The practitioner should perform the following procedures in an examination engagement:

- Obtain an understanding of compliance requirements.
- Plan the examination engagement.
- Consider relevant internal control components.
- Obtain sufficient evidential matter.
- Consider subsequent events.
- Obtain written representations from the client.
- Prepare an appropriate compliance report.

ENGAGEMENT STRATEGY: General guidance for documenting an attest engagement is discussed in AT 101.

Analysis and Application of Procedures

Obtain an understanding of compliance requirements

Since the scope of compliance attestation is broad and the standards can be applied to a variety of circumstances, it is difficult to generalize about the practitioner's knowledge of compliance requirements. Basically, the practitioner must develop an understanding of the specified compliance requirements. SSAE standards identify the following as sources of information that can provide the practitioner with an adequate understanding:

- Specific laws, regulations, rules, contracts, and grants on which the specified requirements are based
- Experience developed from previous similar examination engagements
- Information contained in relevant regulatory reports
- Conversations with management personnel concerning the specified requirements
- Conversations with external parties, including regulatory authorities and specialists in the area

Plan the examination engagement

One of the fundamental components of a compliance attestation engagement is the assessment of attestation risk, defined as follows:

> The risk that the practitioner may unknowingly fail to modify appropriately his or her opinion on management's assertion.

When the practitioner offers an opinion on an entity's compliance with specified requirements, there is always a chance that the opinion will be incorrect. Simply stated, it is impossible for the practitioner to reduce the attestation risk to zero because, for example, sampling methods must be used, judgments must be made, and management personnel can collude to deceive the practitioner.

To assess attestation risk, the practitioner must consider (1) inherent risk, (2) control risk, and (3) detection risk.

"Inherent risk" relates to the fundamental characteristics of the entity. These characteristics provide the background or context in which a particular activity is performed. Not surprisingly, the practitioner uses a significant degree of professional judgment in assessing inherent risk.

Although there is no comprehensive list of factors that contribute to inherent risk, the SSAE standards state that the practitioner should consider the same risk factors that would be considered in an audit of the financial statements, including the fraud risk factors identified in AU-C 240 (*Consideration of Fraud in a Financial Statement Audit*). In addition, SSAE standards list the following as other factors that should be considered in assessing inherent risk:

- Level of complexity of specified compliance requirements
- Period of time that the entity has been subject to the specified compliance requirements
- Practitioner's prior experience with the entity's compliance with the specified requirements
- Possible ramifications of lack of compliance with the specified requirements

"Control risk" refers to the probability that material deviations from specified compliance requirements exist. Thus, the design of the client's internal control with respect to specified requirements will have an impact on the level of control risk. Control risk, like inherent risk, cannot be changed by the practitioner. In general, the stronger the internal control for specified requirements, the more likely it is that material compliance deviations will be prevented or detected by the system on a timely basis. Thus, the practitioner must carefully assess control risk at a level that accurately reflects the internal control policies and procedures that have been adopted by the client. (Of course, the practitioner can make recommendations for improving the system, which may affect future engagements.)

As referred to earlier, the practitioner's assessment of the internal control over compliance with specified requirements is based on obtaining an understanding of relevant internal control policies and procedures.

"Detection risk" is the risk that a practitioner's procedures will lead to the conclusion that material deviations from specified requirements do not exist when in fact such deviations do exist. During the planning phase of the engagement, the practitioner should consider inherent risk, control risk, and detection risk and select an examination strategy that will result in a low level of attestation risk once the engagement is complete. There is an inverse relationship between the practitioner's assessment of inherent risk and control risk and the level of detection risk. If the inherent risk and control risk are higher, the practitioner should establish a lower level of detection risk. The level of detection risk established has a direct effect on the design of the nature, timing, and extent of compliance tests performed.

From a broad perspective, the concept of materiality in a compliance attestation engagement is similar to its role in an audit of financial statements. Immaterial deviations [from generally accepted accounting principles (GAAP) or from established or agreed-upon criteria] will generally exist in both types of engagements, but it is unreasonable to direct the focus of the engagements to immaterial items.

Although the concept of materiality applies to both types of engagements, it is probably more difficult to apply the concept in a compliance attestation engagement. First, because the engagement can be directed to a variety of specified requirements, it is very difficult to generalize about the examination approach. Second, the specified requirements may or may not be quantifiable in monetary terms. Third, there has been little research, if any, into what the focal point should be for determining materiality in a compliance attestation engagement. SSAE standards provide little guidance for determining materiality, except to state that the following may affect the determination of materiality:

- The nature of management's assertion and the compliance requirements, which may or may not be quantifiable in monetary terms

- The nature and frequency of noncompliance identified with appropriate consideration of sampling risk

- Qualitative considerations, including the needs and expectations of the report's users

---

PLANNING AID REMINDER: Some compliance attestation engagements require the practitioner to prepare a supplemental report identifying all or certain deviations discovered. Any threshold guidance established for reporting items in the supplemental report should not have an effect on the auditor's determination of a materiality threshold for the primary examination report.

In many engagements, the operations of the entity will encompass two or more locations. As part of the planning of the compliance attestation engagement, the practitioner should decide whether the internal control policies and procedures at all of the locations or some of the locations should be considered. SSAE standards point out that the practitioner should consider factors such as the following when determining the scope of the engagement with respect to the component units:

- The degree to which the specified requirements apply to each component
- The assessment of materiality in the context of each component's operations
- The degree to which records are processed at each component
- The effectiveness of control environment policies and procedures over each component's operations
- The similarities of operations among components
- The nature and extent of operations at each component

Consider relevant internal control components

The practitioner should obtain an understanding of the relevant internal control policies and procedures related to the entity's ability to comply with the specified requirements. This understanding enables the practitioner to plan the engagement properly and determine the planned assessed level of control risk. In gaining this understanding, the practitioner should have developed insight into the strengths and weaknesses of the internal control by identifying the processing steps and procedures that are (1) most likely to result in the occurrence of material noncompliance and (2) most likely to reduce the likelihood that material noncompliance will occur.

PLANNING AID REMINDER: The consideration of the internal control in a compliance attestation engagement is very similar to the consideration of the internal control in an audit of financial statements. In an audit of financial statements, the auditor (1) obtains an understanding of the entity and its environment, including internal control, (2) determines the planned assessed level of the risk of material misstatement, (3) generally performs tests of controls, and (4) designs substantive procedures based on the assessed level of the risk of material misstatement. In a compliance attestation engagement, the practitioner (1) obtains an understanding of internal control, (2) determines the planned assessed level of control risk, (3) generally performs tests of controls, and (4) designs compliance tests based on the assessed level of control risk. Thus, the only difference is that in a compliance attestation engagement the auditor performs tests of compliance rather than substantive procedures as the final step.

The understanding of internal control may be obtained by performing such procedures as (1) making inquiries of appropriate client personnel, (2) inspecting relevant documents and records, (3) observing the entity's relevant activities and operations, and (4) if applicable, reviewing workpapers from the previous engagement(s). The understanding of internal control includes an analytical phase and a corroborative phase. In the analytical phase, the practitioner's responsibility is to gain an understanding of relevant internal controls. In the corroborative phase (tests of controls), the practitioner must determine the effectiveness of the design of internal controls and the operations of the relevant internal controls.

The evidential matter obtained through these and other examination procedures should provide the practitioner with a basis for the design of tests of compliance. SSAE standards specifically note that the nature and extent of tests of compliance procedures can be affected by a variety of factors, including the following:

- The newness and complexity of the specified requirements
- The practitioner's experience with the client's relevant internal control based on previous engagements
- The nature of the specified compliance requirements
- The characteristics of the client and its industry
- The assessment as to what constitutes material noncompliance

---

PLANNING AID REMINDER: During the engagement, the practitioner may discover noncompliance that is considered "significant" but not material. Under this circumstance, guidance established by AU-C 265 (*Communication of Internal Control Related Matters Identified in an Audit*) should be considered.

PLANNING AID REMINDER: If the practitioner decides that the work of a specialist is required in a compliance attestation engagement, the guidance established by AU-C 620 (*Using the Work of a Specialist*) should be observed. If the practitioner decides to consider a client's internal audit function, the guidance established by AU-C 610 (*Using the Work of Internal Auditors*) should be observed.

Obtain sufficient evidential matter

Based on the assessed level of control risk, which is the final phase in the development of an understanding of the client's internal control, the practitioner must perform tests of compliance. The extent to which these tests should be performed is a matter of professional judgment and in general a practitioner should follow the guidance established in AU-C 530 (*Audit Sampling*).

PLANNING AID REMINDER: If the client is subject to regulatory requirements, the engagement approach should include "reviewing reports of significant examinations and related communications between regulatory agencies and the entity and, when appropriate, making inquiries of the regulatory agencies, including inquiries about examinations in progress."

Consider subsequent events

SSAE standards identify two types of subsequent events that the practitioner should consider in the compliance attestation engagement. The first type of subsequent event provides additional information about the entity's compliance during the period covered by engagement. In a manner similar to the approach used in an audit of financial statements, the practitioner should perform, between the end of the period covered by the engagement and the date of the report, specific subsequent-event procedures to evaluate the appropriateness of management's assertions. While there is no comprehensive list of subsequent audit procedures, SSAE standards list the following as examples:

- Review relevant internal audit reports that have been issued during the subsequent period.

- Determine whether relevant reports by other practitioners have been issued during the subsequent period.

- Consider whether relevant subsequent events have been discovered due to the conduct of other professional engagements for the client.

- Consider reports on the entity's noncompliance issued by regulatory agencies during the subsequent period.

The second type of subsequent events relates to noncompliance events that actually occur between the end of the period covered by the engagement and the date of the report. Although the scope of the engagement focuses on the period covered by the engagement, the practitioner must nonetheless take into consideration subsequent noncompliance events. SSAE standards state that if the noncompliance is significant, the noncompliance event should be described in the practitioner's report.

Obtain written representations from the client

The practitioner should obtain written representations from management concerning an examination to express an opinion on compliance with specified requirements. SSAE standards state that appropriate management personnel should make the following representations:

- State that the responsible party is responsible for complying with the specified requirements.

- State that the responsible party is responsible for establishing and maintaining effective internal control with respect to compliance with specified requirements.

- State that the responsible party has evaluated the entity's compliance with specified requirements or controls over compliance with the specified requirements.

- State the responsible party's assertion about compliance with the specified requirements or about the effectiveness of internal controls, based on the stated or established criteria.

- State that the responsible party has informed the practitioner of all known noncompliance.

- State that the responsible party has made available to the practitioner all documentation relevant to the engagement.

- State the responsible party's interpretation of any specified requirements that have alternative interpretations.

- State that the responsible party has communicated to the practitioner all communications from regulatory agencies, internal auditors, and other auditors concerning possible noncompliance, including communications received up to the date of the practitioner's report.

- State that the responsible party has informed the practitioner of any noncompliance that occurred from the date covered by the engagement through the date of the practitioner's report.

Prepare an appropriate compliance report

Once the practitioner has obtained sufficient evidence, the practitioner states an opinion on the entity's compliance with the specified internal controls.

In a compliance attestation engagement to report on specified controls, the practitioner may report in either of the following ways:

- Report directly on the entity's compliance with the specified controls.

- Report on the responsible party's written assertion concerning compliance with the specified controls.

The reporting guidelines in Exhibit AT 601-2 should be followed in the preparation of a compliance report.

EXHIBIT AT 601-2—REPORTING GUIDELINES FOR PREPARATION OF A COMPLIANCE EXAMINATION REPORT

Guidance for Reporting Directly on the Specified Controls	Guidance for Reporting on the Responsible Party's Written Assertion Concerning the Specified Controls
Title that includes the word "independent"	Title that includes the word "independent"
Identification of specified compliance requirements, including the period covered, and the responsible party	Identification of the responsible party's assertion, including the period covered, and the responsible party
Statement that management is responsible for compliance with the specified requirements	Statement that management is responsible for compliance with the specified requirements
Statement that the practitioner's responsibility is to express an opinion on the compliance with specified requirements	Statement that the practitioner's responsibility is to express an opinion on the responsible party's assertion on compliance with specified requirements
Statement that the examination was performed in accordance with attestation standards established by the AICPA, a brief description of the nature of the examination, and a statement that the practitioner believes that the examination provided a reasonable basis for the opinion expressed	Statement that the examination was performed in accordance with attestation standards established by the AICPA, a brief description of the nature of the examination, and a statement that the practitioner believes that the examination provided a reasonable basis for the opinion expressed
Statement that the practitioner's examination did not make a legal determination with respect to compliance with specified requirements	Statement that the practitioner's examination did not make a legal determination with respect to compliance with specified requirements
An opinion on the compliance with specified requirements	An opinion on whether the responsible party's assertions about compliance is fairly stated in all material respects based on the specified criteria
Statement restricting the use of the report, when appropriate	Statement restricting the use of the report, when appropriate

Guidance for Reporting Directly on the Specified Controls	Guidance for Reporting on the Responsible Party's Written Assertion Concerning the Specified Controls
Manual or printed signature of the practitioner's firm	Manual or printed signature of the practitioner's firm
Date of the examination report	Date of the examination report

---

PLANNING AID REMINDER: SSAE standards (fourth reporting standard) require that the practitioner restrict the use of the report when the criteria used in the examination are (1) determined by the practitioner to be appropriate only for a limited number of parties who either participated in their establishment or can be presumed to have an adequate understanding of the criteria or (2) available only to specified parties.

Exhibit AT 601-3 is an example taken from SSAE-10 of an examination on the compliance with specified requirements.

EXHIBIT AT 601-3—EXAMINATION ON THE COMPLIANCE WITH SPECIFIED REQUIREMENTS

Independent Accountant's Report

We have examined [*name of entity*] compliance with [*list specified compliance requirements*] during the [*period*] ended [*date*]. Management is responsible for [*name of entity*]'s compliance with those requirements. Our responsibility is to express an opinion on [*name of entity*]'s compliance based on our examination.

Our examination was conducted in accordance with attestation standards established by the American Institute of Certified Public Accountants and, accordingly, included examining, on a test basis, evidence about [*name of entity*]'s compliance with those requirements and performing such other procedures as we considered necessary in the circumstances. We believe that our examination provides a reasonable basis for our opinion. Our examination does not provide a legal determination of [*name of entity*]'s compliance with specified requirements.

In our opinion, [*name of entity*] complies, in all material respects, with the aforementioned requirements for the year ended December 31, 20X5.

[*Signature*]

[*Date*]

Exhibit AT 601-4 is an example taken from SSAE-10 of an examination on management's assertion concerning compliance with specified requirements.

EXHIBIT AT 601-4—EXAMINATION ON MANAGEMENT'S ASSERTION CONCERNING COMPLIANCE WITH SPECIFIED REQUIREMENTS

Independent Accountant's Report

We have examined management's assertion, included in the accompanying [*title of management report*], that [*name of entity*] complied with [*list specified compli-*

ance requirements] during the [*period*] ended [*date*]. Management is responsible for [*name of entity*]'s compliance with those requirements. Our responsibility is to express an opinion on management's assertion about [*name of entity*]'s compliance based on our examination.

Our examination was conducted in accordance with attestation standards established by the American Institute of Certified Public Accountants and, accordingly, included examining, on a test basis, evidence about [*name of entity*]'s compliance with those requirements and performing such other procedures as we considered necessary in the circumstances. We believe that our examination provides a reasonable basis for our opinion. Our examination does not provide a legal determination of [*name of entity*]'s compliance with specified requirements.

In our opinion, management's assertion that [*name of entity*] complied with the aforementioned requirements during the [*period*] ended [*date*] is fairly stated, in all material respects.

[*Signature*]

[*Date*]

In some instances it is necessary to interpret the specified requirements established by laws, regulations, rules, contracts, or grants. If the practitioner's examination report is based on significant interpretations, the practitioner may add an additional paragraph to the report explaining the nature of the interpretation and its source.

SSAE standards note that it may be necessary to modify the examination report for the following reasons:

- Material noncompliance with specified requirements exists. (During the examination, the practitioner may discover a noncompliance that he or she believes has a material effect on the entity's compliance with the specified requirements. Under this circumstance the practitioner should report directly on the entity's specified compliance requirements and not on the responsible party's assertion.)

- Scope of the engagement has been restricted. (When there is a restriction in the scope of the engagement, the practitioner should report in a manner described in the chapter titled "Attest Engagements" [AT 101].)

- Reference is made to the work of another practitioner. (When the work of another practitioner is used as the basis for reporting on the client's compliance with specified requirements, the practitioner should report in a manner described in the chapter titled "Reporting on an Entity's Internal Control Over Financial Reporting" [AT 501].)

AT SECTION 701

MANAGEMENT'S DISCUSSION AND ANALYSIS

Authoritative Pronouncements

SSAE-10—Attestation Standards: Revision and Recodification (Chapter 7)

Overview

A practitioner may be engaged to examine or review management's discussion and analysis (MD&A) (a written assertion) that is presented to conform to the rules and regulations adopted by the Securities and Exchange Commission (SEC). This service is considered an attestation engagement subject to the standards established in the Statements on Standards for Attestation Engagements (SSAE) standards. Under these standards the practitioner may perform either an examination or review of MD&A. Examinations and reviews should satisfy the general, fieldwork, and reporting standard discussed in the chapter titled "Attest Engagements" (AT 101), as well as the guidance discussed in this chapter.

> **OBSERVATION:** A practitioner may perform an agreed-upon procedures engagement on MD&A if the standards established in the chapter titled "Agreed-Upon Procedures Engagements" (AT 201) are observed.

> **OBSERVATION:** Because only public companies are required to prepare an MD&A, presumably most attestation engagements on MD&A have been performed for public companies. The PCAOB has the statutory authority to set auditing and attestation standards for public companies. It is reasonable to assume that the standards for issuing an attestation report on MD&A for a public company might be modified by the PCAOB in the future.

EXAMINATION ENGAGEMENT

SSAE standards state that the objective of an examination of MD&A information is for the practitioner to express an opinion on the information taken as a whole by reporting on the following:

- Whether the presentation includes, in all material respects, the required elements of the rules and regulations adopted by the SEC
- Whether the historical financial amounts have been accurately derived, in all material respects, from the entity's financial statements
- Whether the underlying information, determinations, estimates, and assumptions of the entity provide a reasonable basis for the disclosures contained therein

A practitioner may examine a MD&A presentation in order to express an opinion on the presentation if (1) the practitioner has audited at least the latest financial statements to which the MD&A information pertains and (2) either the practitioner or a predecessor practitioner has audited the prior years' financial statements to which the MD&A information pertains.

When a predecessor practitioner has audited one or more of the financial statements for the period covered by the MD&A information, the successor practitioner must determine whether it is possible to "acquire sufficient knowledge of the business and of the entity's accounting and financial reporting practices for such period" so that the following can be satisfied:

- The types of potential material misstatements in MD&A can be identified and the likelihood of their occurrence can be determined.

- Procedures can be performed that will provide the practitioner with a basis for expressing an opinion on whether the MD&A presentation includes, in all material respects, the required elements of the rules and regulations adopted by the SEC.

- Procedures can be performed that will provide the practitioner with a basis for expressing an opinion on the MD&A presentation with respect to whether the historical financial amounts have been accurately derived, in all material respects, from the entity's financial statements for such a period.

- Procedures can be performed that will provide the practitioner with a basis for expressing an opinion on whether the underlying information, determinations, estimates, and assumptions of the entity provide a reasonable basis for the disclosures contained therein.

The practitioner examining the MD&A information may decide to review the workpapers (for the financial statement audit and the examination or review of MD&A information) of the predecessor practitioner; however, the review of the predecessor practitioner's workpapers alone does not provide a basis sufficient to express an opinion on the MD&A information that applies to the periods for which the predecessor practitioner was involved. The results of the review of the predecessor practitioner's workpapers should be used to determine the nature, extent, and timing of the examination engagement procedures (which are discussed below) with respect to the MD&A information covered by the work of the predecessor practitioner. In addition, the practitioner should "make inquiries of the predecessor practitioner and management as to audit adjustments proposed by the predecessor practitioner that were not recorded in the financial statements."

PLANNING AID REMINDER: The practitioner should follow the standards established by AU-C 510 (*Opening Balance—Initial Audit Engagements, Including Reaudit Engagements*) to determine whether to accept an audit engagement with respect to the financial statements. When the requested engagement also encompasses the examination of MD&A information, the successor auditor should expand the inquiries directed to the predecessor auditor so that they include questions concerning the previous MD&A engagement. If the successor auditor is requested to examine the MD&A information after being engaged to audit the client's financial statements, the successor auditor should review the predecessor auditor's workpapers related to the previous MD&A engagement.

Promulgated Procedures Checklist

The practitioner should plan and execute the MD&A engagement in order to determine, with reasonable assurance, whether any material misstatements in the MD&A information exist. SSAE standards require that, in order to achieve this objective, the practitioner perform the following procedures during the engagement:

- Plan the engagement.
- Obtain an understanding of MD&A requirements.
- Obtain an understanding of the client's methods used to prepare MD&A information.
- Consider relevant portions of the entity's internal control applicable to the preparation of MD&A.
- Obtain sufficient evidence, including testing for completeness.
- Consider the effect of events subsequent to the balance-sheet date.
- Obtain written representations from management.
- Prepare an appropriate examination report.

PLANNING AID REMINDER: General guidance for documenting an attest engagement is discussed in AT 101.

Analysis and Application of Procedures

Plan the engagement

In an examination engagement, the practitioner must collect evidence sufficient to limit attestation risk to an "appropriate low level." The components of attestation risk in an examination are similar to those that are related to an audit of financial statements, and they are described by the SSAE standards as follows:

Inherent risk—The susceptibility of an assertion within MD&A to a material misstatement, assuming that there are no related controls (inherent risk varies depending on the nature of each assertion included in the MD&A information)

Control risk—The risk that a material misstatement that could occur in an assertion within MD&A and not be prevented or detected on a timely basis by the entity's controls (some control risk will always exist because of the inherent limitations of any internal control)

Detection risk—The risk that the practitioner will not detect a material misstatement that exists in an assertion within MD&A (the establishment of an acceptable level of detection risk is related to the auditor's assessment of inherent risk and control risk)

The foregoing risk factors should be integrated into the planning phase of the engagement by taking into consideration the following factors:

- The anticipated level of attestation risk related to assertions embodied in the MD&A presentation

- Preliminary judgments about materiality levels for attest purposes

- The items within the MD&A presentation that are likely to require revision or adjustment

- Conditions that may require extension or modification of attest procedures

The focus of the examination of MD&A information is the assertions (explicit or implicit) that are included in the client's MD&A presentation. There are four broad assertions:

1. *Occurrence assertion:* The occurrence assertion is concerned with whether transactions included in the MD&A information actually occurred during the period covered by the presentation.

2. *Consistency assertion:* The consistency assertion focuses on whether the information in the MD&A presentation is consistent with information included in the financial statements and related financial records. The assertion is also concerned with whether nonfinancial data have been "accurately derived from related records."

3. *Completeness assertion:* The completeness assertion is concerned with whether descriptions of transactions and events included in MD&A information are sufficient to adequately reflect the entity's financial condition, changes in financial condition, results of operations, and material commitments for capital resources. This assertion also requires that relevant "known events, transactions, conditions, trends, demands, commitments, or uncertainties" that will or may affect these transactions and events be properly presented in the MD&A information.

4. *Presentation and disclosure assertion:* The presentation and disclosure assertion focuses on the proper classification, description, and disclosure of information included in the MD&A presentation.

ENGAGEMENT STRATEGY: The assertions listed above are similar to the assertions that the auditor is concerned with when the client's financial statements are audited, and they are discussed in AU-C 500 (*Audit Evidence*) in this guide. However, the examination of assertions related to a MD&A engagement is limited to the assertions described in the SSAE standards (not the assertions described in (AU-C 500). For example, if a client asserts that revenues increased due to a strengthening of the dollar relative to other foreign currencies, the auditor should determine the completeness of that assertion, but he or she would not be concerned with the completeness of the assertion related to total revenues, which would have been evaluated as part of the audit of the entity's financial statements.

The practitioner must use professional judgment to determine the specific planning strategy to be used in a particular MD&A engagement; however, SSAE standards note that planning should consider factors such as the following:

- Industry characteristics (such as economic conditions, accounting principles, and legal considerations)

- An understanding of the client's internal control (and recent changes thereto) with respect to the preparation of MD&A information that may have been obtained during the audit of the entity's financial statements

- Specific characteristics of the entity (such as business form, capital structure, and distribution systems)

- The type of relevant information provided to external parties (such as press releases and presentations to financial analysts)

- The approach the client used to analyze operating activities (such as budgeted versus actual result comparisons) and the types of reports presented to its board of directors to keep the board members informed of day-to-day operations as well as long-range planning strategies

- Management's familiarity with MD&A rules and regulations

- The purpose of the MD&A information, if the entity is nonpublic

- Initial judgments about materiality, inherent risk, and factors related to MD&A internal controls

- Fraud risk factors and other relevant conditions identified as part of the audit of the entity's latest financial statements

- The client's documentation to support MD&A information

- The possible need for a specialist due to the complexity of the material included in the MD&A information (when a specialist is required, the guidance established by AU-C 620 (*Using the Work of a Specialist*) may be followed)

- The existence of an internal audit function (when an internal audit function exists, the guidance established by AU-C 610 (*Using the Work of Internal Auditors*) may be followed

- The intended use of the MD&A (if issued by a nonpublic entity)

In addition, the practitioner should take into consideration the results of auditing the client's financial statements. For example, the planning of the MD&A engagement may be affected by such matters as the type of audit adjustments proposed and the types of misstatements identified. If the practitioner's report on the client's financial statements is other than unqualified, that fact may have an impact on the planning of the MD&A engagement.

ENGAGEMENT STRATEGY: When the auditor has not previously examined MD&A information for the client, the auditor should obtain an understanding of the internal controls relative to the preparation of the MD&A information for the previous year(s).

Public companies often consist of various subsidiaries, branches, and other operating entities. SSAE standards note that the practitioner should consider factors such as the following in order to determine the procedures to be applied to a particular operating component:

- The significance of each component to the MD&A information taken as a whole
- The degree to which centralized records are maintained
- The effectiveness of controls over the various operating components
- The activities conducted at an operating component location
- The similarity of activities and related internal controls at each operating component

Obtain an understanding of MD&A requirements

The auditor must develop an understanding of the MD&A rules and regulations adopted by the SEC. These rules and regulations are established in the following SEC publications and related Interpretations:

- Item 303 of Regulation S-K and related Financial Reporting Releases
- Item 303 of Regulation S-B (for small-business issues)
- Item 9 of Form 20-F (for foreign companies)

PLANNING AID REMINDER: The SEC rules and regulations listed above establish "reasonable criteria" as required by General Standard No. 3.

Obtain an understanding of the client's methods used to prepare MD&A information

For developing the MD&A information, the client should have established procedures (similar in concept to its established procedures for the preparation of its financial statements) that conform to the rules and regulations established by the SEC. The practitioner should obtain from the client a description (oral or written) of the procedures the client used to prepare the MD&A information. The description should include such matters as the following:

- The sources of the information
- The manner in which the information is obtained
- The factors that management considered relevant in determining the materiality of information
- The identification of any changes in procedures from the prior year

Consider the relevant portions of the entity's internal control applicable to the preparation of MD&A

The practitioner must consider the client's internal controls that relate to its preparation of MD&A information in much the same manner as the auditor evaluates internal controls in the audit of an entity's financial statements. In order to satisfy the SSAE standards, the practitioner should follow the steps listed below when considering internal controls in an examination of MD&A information:

> **Step 1:** Obtain an understanding of the client's internal controls.
>
> **Step 2:** Assess the control risk.
>
> **Step 3:** Perform tests of controls (when control risk is assessed at a level less than the maximum level).
>
> **Step 4:** Determine the nature, timing, and extent of substantive procedures.
>
> **Step 5:** Document the assessment of control risk.

Step 1

In all examination engagements, the practitioner must adequately understand those controls relevant to the client's preparation of MD&A information. Relevant controls are concerned with the recording, processing, summarizing, and reporting of financial and nonfinancial data consistent with the assertions embodied in the MD&A presentation. Thus, the practitioner needs to understand internal controls that increase the likelihood that the MD&A information will be prepared in accordance with rules and regulations established by the SEC.

The practitioner generally obtains an understanding of the entity's internal controls that relate to the MD&A presentation by employing the following procedures:

- Making appropriate inquiries of client personnel
- Inspecting relevant entity documents
- Observing relevant control activities

Step 2

Once the practitioner has obtained an understanding of the client's internal control, it is possible to assess the level of control risk for a particular engagement. The practitioner should have documented the system and, based on that documentation, identified potential misstatements (including material omissions of MD&A information). The assessment of the level of control risk provides the practitioner with a general strategy for planning the remaining internal control evaluation. If the practitioner believes the internal control is well designed, the level of control risk will be assessed at a relatively low level for a given assertion. On the other hand, if the internal control appears to be poorly designed, the level of control risk will be assessed at a maximum level.

Step 3

In order to assess control risk at a relatively low level, the practitioner must perform tests of controls. Tests of controls are used to determine the effectiveness of (1) the design of internal controls and (2) operations of internal controls that relate to the preparation of the MD&A information in accordance with the rules and regulations established by the SEC. For example, if the MD&A information includes statistics, such as the average net sales per square foot of retail space, the auditor must test the internal controls related to how this information is accumulated and reported.

Step 4

Based on his or her assessment of inherent risk and assessment of control risk resulting from the understanding of the entity's internal control and perhaps tests of control (if control risk is assessed at a level less than the maximum), the practitioner determines an acceptable level of detection risk. Detection risk is the risk that the practitioner will not detect a material misstatement in an assertion that is included or that should be included in the MD&A presentation. The establishment of a level of acceptable detection risk is used as a basis for determining the nature, timing, and extent of substantive procedures.

Step 5

The assessment of control risk for a particular assertion (or group of assertions related to a component of the MD&A presentation) must be documented. The assessment must be related to the results of obtaining an understanding of the client's relevant internal controls and, perhaps, to the performance of tests of controls. SSAE standards note that "the form and extent of this documentation is influenced by the size and complexity of the entity, as well as the nature of the entity's control applicable to the preparation of MD&A."

Obtain sufficient evidence (including testing completeness)

In order to obtain sufficient evidence to allow the practitioner to offer a reasonable assurance on the client's presentation of MD&A information, SSAE standards require the practitioner to perform the following procedures:

- Read the MD&A and compare the content with the audited financial statements for consistency; compare financial amounts to the audited financial statements and related accounting records and analyses; and recompute the increases, decreases, and percentages disclosed.

- Compare nonfinancial amounts to the audited financial statements, if applicable, or to other records (see the discussion below for nonfinancial data).

- Consider whether the explanations in MD&A are consistent with the information obtained during the audit; through inquiry (including inquiry of officers and other executives having responsibility for operational areas) and inspection of client records, investigate further those explanations that cannot be substantiated by information in the audit workpapers.

- Examine internally generated documents (for example, variance analyses and business plans or programs) and externally generated documents (for example, correspondence, contracts, or loan agreements) in support of the existence, occurrence, or expected occurrence of events, transactions, conditions, trends, demands, commitments, or uncertainties disclosed in the MD&A.

- Obtain available prospective financial information (for example, budgets; sales forecasts; forecasts of labor, overhead, and materials cost; capital expenditure requests; and financial forecasts and projections) and compare such information to forward-looking MD&A disclosures. Ask management about the procedures used to prepare the prospective financial information. Evaluate whether the underlying information, determinations, estimates, and assumptions of the entity provide a reasonable basis for the MD&A disclosures of events, transactions, conditions, trends, demands, commitments, or uncertainties.

- Consider obtaining available prospective financial information relating to prior periods and comparing actual results with forecasted and projected amounts.

- Ask officers and other executives who have responsibility for operational areas (such as sales, marketing, and production) and financial and accounting matters about their plans and expectations for the future that could affect the entity's liquidity and capital resources.

- Consider obtaining external information concerning industry trends, inflation, and changing prices and comparing the related MD&A disclosures with such information.

- Compare the information in MD&A with the rules and regulations adopted by the SEC, and consider whether the presentation includes the required elements of such rules and regulations.

- Read the minutes of meetings to date of the board of directors and other significant committees to identify matters that may affect MD&A; consider whether such matters are appropriately addressed in MD&A.

- Ask officers about the entity's prior experience with the SEC and the extent of comments received upon review of documents by the SEC; read correspondence between the entity and the SEC with respect to such review, if any.

- Obtain public communications (for example, press releases and quarterly reports) and the related supporting documentation dealing with historical and future results; consider whether MD&A is consistent with such communications.

- Consider obtaining other types of publicly available information (for example, analyst reports and news articles); compare the MD&A presentation with such information.

Nonfinancial data

MD&A information may include a variety of nonfinancial data, such as number of customers, backorders, and capacity utilization rates. SSAE standards note that the practitioner must determine whether the definitions used by management for such nonfinancial data are reasonable for the particular disclosure in the MD&A and whether there are reasonable criteria for the measurement. If nonfinancial data have such characteristics, the practitioner should apply appropriate examination procedures, taking into consideration the materiality of the data in relationship to the MD&A information taken as a whole and the assessed level of control risk.

Testing completeness

The information (especially explanations) included in MD&A does not arise simply from the client's observance of SEC rules and regulations. As part of the test of completeness, the auditor should consider whether the MD&A discloses matters that could significantly impact future financial condition and results of operations of the entity by considering information that he or she obtained through the following:

- As the result of the audit of the entity's financial statements

- Through inquiries of the client's personnel with respect to current events, conditions, economic changes, commitments, and uncertainties that are unique to the client or to the industry in which it operates

- By the application of other engagement procedures

PLANNING AID REMINDER: SSAE standards note that if the MD&A engagement is characterized by a high level of inherent risk, it may be appropriate for the practitioner to expand the engagement by performing extended procedures, including additional inquiries of client personnel and examining additional documentation.

Consider the effect of events subsequent to the balance sheet date

The practitioner should consider events that may have an effect on the MD&A presentation but occur after the period covered by the MD&A information and prior to the issuance of the examination report. Relevant events would be those that have a material impact on the client's financial condition (including liquidity and capital resources), changes in financial condition, results of operations, and material commitments for capital resources. Attestation standards require that the MD&A presentation disclose subsequent events or matters such as the following:

- Items that are expected to have a material effect on (1) net sales or revenues and (2) income from continuing operations

- Items that are expected to have a material effect on the entity's liquidity

- Items that are expected to have a material effect on the entity's capital resources

- Items that are expected to have an impact on the entity in a manner that would make reported financial results a poor predictor of future operating results or financial condition

The identification of subsequent events may require that the MD&A presentation be adjusted or that additional disclosures be included in the material.

PLANNING AID REMINDER: SSAE standards note that when MD&A information is included in a 1933 Securities Act document (or incorporated through reference), examination procedures must be extended to the filing date or "as close to it as is reasonable and practicable in the circumstances." This time extension also applies when the examination report is included in a 1933 Securities Act document.

Generally the practitioner's fieldwork extends beyond the date of the auditor's report on the client's financial statements. For this reason SSAE standards (as part of the consideration of the possible occurrence of subsequent events) requires that the auditor perform the following procedures:

- Read available minutes of meetings of stockholders, the board of directors, and other appropriate committees; for meetings whose minutes are not available, inquire about matters dealt with at the meetings.

- Read the latest available interim financial statements for periods subsequent to the date of the auditor's report and compare them with the financial statements for the periods covered by the MD&A. Discuss with officers and other executives who have responsibility for operational, financial, and accounting matters (limited where appropriate to major locations) such matters as the following:

  — Whether the interim financial statements have been prepared on the same basis as the audited financial statements

  — Whether any significant changes took place in the entity's operations, liquidity, or capital resource in the subsequent period

  — The current status of items in the financial statements for which the MD&A has been prepared that were accounted for on the basis of tentative, preliminary, or inconclusive data

  — Whether any unusual adjustments were made during the period from the balance sheet date to the date of inquiry

- Make inquiries of members of senior management about the current status of matters concerning litigation, claims, and assessments identified during the audit of the financial statements and about any new matters or unfavorable developments. Consider obtaining updated legal letters from legal counsel.

- Consider whether any changes have occurred in economic conditions or in the industry that could have a significant effect on the entity.

- Obtain written representations from appropriate officials about whether any events occurred subsequent to the latest balance sheet date that would require disclosure in the MD&A.

- Make additional inquiries or perform other procedures considered necessary and appropriate to address questions that arise in carrying out the foregoing procedures, inquiries, and discussions.

Obtain written representations from management

Attest standards require that an auditor obtain written representations from the client in an MD&A examination (and a review) engagement. The purpose of written representations is to confirm oral representations made by management during the engagement and to reduce the likelihood of misunderstandings between the client and the auditor. The written representations may be documented in a client representation letter. Although no comprehensive list of items exists that must be included in a client representation letter (or other form of written communication), SSAE standards identify the following as items that management should include:

- Acknowledgment that management is responsible for the preparation of the MD&A information and that it has prepared the information in accordance with the rules and regulations established by the SEC

- A statement that the historical financial amounts have been accurately derived from the client's financial statements and are reflected in the MD&A presentation

- An affirmation of the belief that the underlying information, determinations, estimates, and assumptions provide a reasonable basis for the MD&A presentation

- A statement that all significant documentation that relates to the compliance with the SEC rules and regulations has been made available

- Confirmation that complete minutes of all meetings of stockholders, the board of directors, and committees of directors have been made available

- A statement about whether the client (if it is a public entity) has received relevant communications from the SEC

- A statement about whether events subsequent to the latest balance sheet date that would require disclosure in the MD&A have occurred

- A statement about whether forward-looking information is included in MD&A information and, if it is included, whether the following is also true:
  - The forward-looking information is based on the client's best estimate of expected events and operations and is consistent with budgets, forecasts, or operating plans prepared for such periods.
  - The same accounting principles used in the preparation of the financial statements were used to prepare the MD&A presentation.
  - The latest versions of budgets, forecasts, or operating plans have been provided, and the practitioner has been informed of any anticipated changes or modifications to such information that could affect the disclosures contained in the MD&A presentation.

- A statement that, if voluntary information is included and subject to SEC rules and regulations, such voluntary information has been prepared in accordance with SEC rules and regulations

- A statement that, if pro forma information is included in the MD&A information, the following is also true:
  - The client is responsible for establishing the assumptions upon which the pro forma adjustments are based.
  - The client believes that the assumptions used provide a reasonable basis for the pro forma adjustments, and the pro forma column accurately reflects the application of the adjustments to the historical financial statements.

— The pro forma information appropriately discloses the significant effects directly attributable to the transaction or event that is the basis for the pro forma adjustments.

PLANNING AID REMINDER: The guidance established in AU-C 580 (*Written Representations*) should be followed to determine the date of the representations and who should sign them. When a client refuses to provide the practitioner with appropriate written representations, the practitioner should not issue an unqualified opinion on the MD&A information but, rather, should decide whether a qualified opinion, a disclaimer of opinion, or withdrawal from the engagement is appropriate. (If the engagement is a review, the practitioner should generally withdraw from the engagement.) The fact that a client will not provide an appropriate written representation suggests that the practitioner should not rely on other representations the client has made.

PLANNING AID REMINDER: When a client provides written representation concerning a matter but does not allow the practitioner to apply appropriate examination procedures to the matter, the auditor should express a qualified opinion or a disclaimer of an opinion in an examination engagement, and in a review engagement he or she should withdraw.

Prepare an appropriate examination report

Based on the results of applying examination procedures, the practitioner should form an opinion on the MD&A presentation. The report must be accompanied by the financial statements covered by the MD&A information, the auditor's report(s) on those financial statements, and the MD&A presentation itself.

PLANNING AID REMINDER: When the client is a nonpublic company, one of the following conditions should be met: (1) a written statement should be included in the MD&A information stating that the information has been prepared in accordance with the rules and regulations established by the SEC, (2) a separate written assertion from management should accompany the MD&A presentation, or (3) a separate written assertion from management should be included in the representation letter.

The examination report should include the following items:

- A title that includes the word "independent"

- An identification of the MD&A presentation, including the period that is covered

- A statement that management is responsible for the preparation of the MD&A pursuant to the rules and regulations adopted by the SEC, and a statement that the practitioner's responsibility is to express an opinion on the presentation based on his or her examination

- A reference to the auditor's report on the related financial statements and, if the report was other than a standard report, the substantive reasons why

- A statement that the examination was made in accordance with attestation standards established by the American Institute of Certified Public Accountants (AICPA), and a description of the scope of an examination of MD&A

- A statement that the practitioner believes the examination provides a reasonable basis for the opinion given

- A paragraph stating the following:

  — That the preparation of MD&A requires management to interpret the criteria, make determinations as to the relevancy of information to be included, and make estimates and assumptions that affect reported information

  — That actual results in the future may differ materially from management's present assessment of information regarding the estimated future impact of transactions and events that have occurred or are expected to occur, expected sources of liquidity and capital resources, operating trends, commitments, and uncertainties

- If the entity is a nonpublic entity, a statement that, although the entity is not subject to the rules and regulations of the SEC, the MD&A presentation is intended to be a presentation in accordance with the rules and regulations adopted by the SEC

- The practitioner's opinion on the following:

  — Whether the presentation includes, in all material respects, the required elements of the rules and regulations adopted by the SEC

  — Whether the historical financial amounts have been accurately derived, in all material respects, from the entity's financial statements

  — Whether the underlying information, determinations, estimates, and assumptions of the entity provide a reasonable basis for the disclosures contained therein

- The manual or printed signature of the practitioner's firm

- The date of the examination report

Exhibit AT 701-1 is an example taken from SSAE-10 of an examination report on an entity's MD&A presentation.

EXHIBIT AT 701-1—EXAMINATION REPORT ON AN ENTITY'S MD&A PRESENTATION

We have examined XYZ Company's Management's Discussion and Analysis taken as a whole, included [*incorporated by reference*] in the Company's [*insert description of registration statement or document*]. Management is responsible for the preparation of the Company's Management's Discussion and Analysis, pursuant to the rules and regulations adopted by the Securities and Exchange

Commission. Our responsibility is to express an opinion on the presentation based on our examination. We have audited, in accordance with standards of the Public Company Accounting Oversight Board (United States), the financial statements of XYZ Company as of December 31, 20X5 and 20X4, and for each of the years in the three-year period ending December 31, 20X5. In our report dated [*month*] XX, 20X6, we expressed an unqualified opinion on those financial statements.

Our examination of Management's Discussion and Analysis was made in accordance with attestation standards established by the American Institute of Certified Public Accountants and, accordingly, included examining, on a test basis, evidence supporting the historical amounts and disclosures in the presentation. An examination also includes assessing the significant determinations made by management as to the relevancy of information to be included and the estimates and assumptions that affect reported information. We believe that our examination provides a reasonable basis for our opinion.

The preparation of Management's Discussion and Analysis requires management to interpret the criteria, make determinations as to the relevancy of information to be included, and make estimates and assumptions that affect reported information. Management's Discussion and Analysis includes information regarding the estimated future impact of transactions and events that have occurred or are expected to occur, expected sources of liquidity and capital resources, operating trends, commitments, and uncertainties. Actual results in the future may differ materially from management's present assessment of this information because events and circumstances frequently do not occur as expected.

In our opinion, the Company's presentation of Management's Discussion and Analysis includes, in all material respects, the required elements of the rules and regulations adopted by the Securities and Exchange Commission; the historical financial amounts included therein have been accurately derived, in all material respects, from the Company's financial statements; and the underlying information, determinations, estimates, and assumptions of the Company provide a reasonable basis for the disclosures contained therein.

[*Signature*]

[*Date*]

OBSERVATION: Only public companies are required to file an MD&A with the Securities and Exchange Commission. Such audits are performed in accordance with standards of the Public Company Accounting Oversight Board (United States). If a nonpublic company voluntarily includes an MD&A and retains an accounting firm to issue an attestation report, the audit must be performed in accordance with generally accepted auditing standards.

The standard examination report on MD&A presentations may be modified for the following reasons:

- A material element as required by SEC rules and regulations is omitted from the presentation (a qualified or adverse opinion should be expressed).

- Historical financial amounts have not been accurately derived (in all material respects) from the client financial statements (a qualified or adverse opinion should be expressed).

- Underlying information, determinations, estimates, and assumptions used by the client do not provide the practitioner a reasonable basis on which to prepare the MD&A presentation (a qualified or adverse opinion should be expressed).

- The practitioner is unable to perform procedures deemed appropriate for the MD&A engagement (a qualified opinion or a disclaimer of opinion should be expressed, or the practitioner should withdraw from the engagement).

- The practitioner decided to refer to the work of another practitioner.

- The practitioner has been engaged to examine the client MD&A presentation after it has been filed with the SEC.

- The practitioner has decided to emphasize a matter.

REVIEW ENGAGEMENT

SSAE standards state that the objective of a review of MD&A information is for the practitioner to report on whether any information came to his or her attention to cause him or her to believe that

- The MD&A presentation does not include, in all material respects, the required elements of the rules and regulations adopted by the SEC.

- The historical financial amounts included therein have not been accurately derived, in all material respects, from the entity's financial statements.

- The underlying information, determinations, estimates, and assumptions of the entity do not provide a reasonable basis for the disclosures contained therein.

A practitioner may review a MD&A presentation if (1) the practitioner has audited at least the latest financial statements to which the MD&A information pertains and (2) either the practitioner or a predecessor practitioner has audited the prior years' financial statements to which the MD&A information pertains.

When a predecessor practitioner has audited one or more of the financial statements for the period covered by the MD&A information, the successor practitioner must determine whether it is possible to "acquire sufficient knowledge of the business and of the entity's accounting and financial reporting practices for such period" so that the following can be satisfied:

- The types of potential material misstatements in MD&A can be identified and the likelihood of their occurrence can be determined.

- Procedures can be performed that will provide the practitioner with a basis for determining whether any information obtained in the engagement suggests that

  — The MD&A information excludes material information required by SEC rules and regulations.

— The historical financial amounts included in the MD&A information have not been accurately derived from the historical financial statements.

— The underlying information, determinations, estimates, and assumptions of the entity do not provide a reasonable basis for the disclosures included in the MD&A presentation.

Promulgated Procedures Checklist

The practitioner should plan and execute the MD&A engagement in order to provide limited assurance that the material misstatements in the MD&A information will be identified. According to SSAE standards, to achieve this objective the practitioner should perform the following:

- Plan the engagement.
- Obtain an understanding of MD&A requirements.
- Obtain an understanding of the client's methods used to prepare MD&A information.
- Consider relevant portions of the entity's internal control applicable to the preparation of MD&A.
- Apply analytical procedures and make inquires of management and other appropriate personnel.
- Consider the effect of events subsequent to the balance sheet date.
- Obtain written representations from management.
- Prepare an appropriate review report.

PLANNING AID REMINDER: General guidance for documenting an attest engagement is discussed in AT 101 (Attest Engagements).

Analysis and Application of Procedures

Plan the engagement

The practitioner must use professional judgment in determining the specific planning strategy to be used in a particular MD&A engagement; however, SSAE standards note that in planning the review engagement, the practitioner should consider factors such as the following:

- Industry characteristics (such as economic conditions, accounting principles, and legal considerations)
- Specific characteristics of the entity (such as business form, capital structure, and distribution systems)
- Relevant information provided to external parties (such as press releases and presentations to financial analysts)
- Management's familiarity with MD&A rules and regulations
- The purpose of the MD&A information, if the entity is nonpublic

- Matters identified during the audit or review of the client's financial statements that may provide insight into the preparation and reporting of MD&A information
- Matters identified during the examination or review concerning the prior years' MD&A presentations
- Initial judgments about materiality levels
- Items that are either relatively complex or subjective that provide a basis for assertions in the MD&A information
- The existence of an internal audit function and the degree to which the function was involved in the verification of MD&A information

Consider relevant portions of the entity's internal control applicable to the preparation of MD&A

SSAE standards state that as a basis for performing appropriate analytical procedures and inquiries of client personnel, the practitioner must develop an adequate understanding of the client's internal controls related to its preparation and presentation of MD&A information. Although the standards do not provide specific guidance on how this is to be accomplished, the practitioner's knowledge of internal controls must be sufficient to accomplish the following:

- Identification of types of potential misstatements in MD&A, including types of material omissions, and consideration of the likelihood of their occurrence
- Selection of the inquiries and analytical procedures that will provide a basis for reporting whether any information causes the practitioner to believe the following:
  - That the MD&A presentation does not include, in all material respects, the required elements of the rules and regulations adopted by the SEC, or that the historical financial amounts included therein have not been accurately derived, in all material respects, from the entity's financial statements
  - That the underlying information, determinations, estimates, and assumptions of the entity do not provide a reasonable basis for the disclosures contained therein

Apply analytical procedures and make inquiries of management and other appropriate personnel

The practitioner should apply a variety of analytical procedures and make specific inquiries of client personnel. The results of these procedures should be evaluated in the context of the practitioner's understanding of other relevant information that he or she knows. Although there is no specific list of analytical procedures and inquiries that should be performed in a review engagement, SSAE standards point out that the auditor should generally employ the following procedures:

- Compare information in the MD&A presentation with the audited financial statement and related accounting records and analyses.

- Recompute increases, decreases, and percentage changes relative to financial amounts included in or derived from the financial statements.

- Compare nonfinancial amounts in the MD&A presentation with audited amounts in the financial statements, if appropriate, or in other records.

- Inquire about the types of records that support the nonfinancial amounts, and determine the existence of the records.

- Determine whether the nonfinancial information is relevant to users and is clearly defined in the MD&A information, and inquire about whether the definition of nonfinancial information was consistently applied.

- Consider whether explanations included in the MD&A presentation are consistent with information obtained as part of the audit of the client's financial statements, and direct any related inquiries to appropriate personnel.

- Compare prospective financial information (such as budgets) to forward-looking information included in the MD&A presentation.

- Make inquiries of relevant personnel concerning procedures used to develop prospective financial information and forward-looking information.

- Consider whether information obtained suggests that underlying information, determinations, estimates, and assumptions of the entity do not provide a reasonable basis for the disclosures of trends, demands, commitments, events, or uncertainties.

- Make inquiries of appropriate operational personnel (such as production and marketing) and financial personnel as to plans that could have an effect on the client's liquidity and capital resources.

- Determine whether the MD&A presentation includes disclosures required by the SEC.

- Consider whether the MD&A presentation properly reflects any relevant matters discussed in the minutes of meetings of the board of directors and other significant committees.

- Make inquiries about the experience the client has had with the SEC relative to MD&A presentations made in previous years, and read any correspondence between the client and the SEC relative to these matters.

- Make inquiries concerning the nature of public communications that include historical and future results. Determine whether those communications are consistent with the MD&A presentation.

Although a review engagement is characterized by the use of analytical procedures and inquiries of management personnel, the practitioner should use whatever procedures he or she deems appropriate (including corroborative procedures) if it appears that the MD&A presentation is "incomplete or contains inaccuracies or is otherwise unsatisfactory."

ENGAGEMENT STRATEGY: The practitioner might find the general guidance for the application of analytical procedures in AU-C 520 (*Analytical Procedures*) helpful in applying the procedures to a review of MD&A information.

Obtain an understanding of MD&A requirements

In order to develop an understanding of MD&A requirements established by the SEC for a review engagement, the practitioner should follow the guidance discussed earlier for an examination engagement.

Obtain an understanding of the client's methods used to prepare MD&A information

In a review engagement, in order to develop an understanding of the client's methods used to create MD&A information, the auditor should follow the guidance discussed earlier for an examination engagement.

Consider the effect of events subsequent to the balance-sheet date

In order to consider the effect of an event occurring subsequent to the balance sheet date in a review engagement, the practitioner should follow the guidance discussed earlier for the occurrence of this situation in an examination engagement.

Obtain written representations from management

In a review engagement, the practitioner should obtain written representations similar to those obtained in an examination engagement, as discussed earlier. However, when the client refuses to provide the practitioner with appropriate written representations in a review engagement, the practitioner should withdraw from the engagement.

Prepare an appropriate review report

Based on the results of applying review procedures, the practitioner should consider which report would be appropriate to issue on the MD&A presentation. However, the report must be accompanied by the financial statements covered by the MD&A information, the auditor's report(s) on those financial statements, and the MD&A presentation.

PLANNING AID REMINDER: When the client is a public company and the MD&A presentation covers an interim period, the presentation should be accompanied by (1) the related interim financial statements and the review report applicable to the MD&A presentation and (2) the most recent comparative financial statements and the related MD&A presentation. (The information may be included by reference to filings with the SEC.)

PLANNING AID REMINDER: When the client is a nonpublic company, there should be a statement that the MD&A information has been prepared in accordance with rules and regulations established by the SEC. The statement may be included in the MD&A presentation itself or presented as a separate statement that accompanies the MD&A presentation. If the presentation for a nonpublic company relates to an interim period, the MD&A presentation should be accompanied by (1) the entity's most recent annual MD&A presentation and the related examination or review report and (2) the related interim financial statements and the most recent annual financial statements.

The review report should include the following items:

- A title that includes the word "independent"

- An identification of the MD&A presentation, including the period covered

- A statement that management is responsible for preparing the MD&A pursuant to the rules and regulations adopted by the SEC

- A reference to the auditor's report on the related financial statements and, if the report was other than a standard report, the substantive reasons for it

- A statement that the review was made in accordance with attestation standards established by the AICPA

- A description of the procedures for a review of MD&A

- A statement that a review of MD&A is substantially less in scope than an examination, the objective of which is an expression of opinion regarding the MD&A presentation and that, accordingly, no such opinion is expressed

- A paragraph stating the following:

  — That the preparation of MD&A requires management to interpret the criteria, make determinations as to the relevancy of information to be included, and make estimates and assumptions that affect reported information

  — That future results may differ materially from management's present assessment of information regarding the estimated future impact of transactions and events that have occurred or are expected to occur, expected sources of liquidity and capital resources, operating trends, commitments, and uncertainties

- If the entity is a nonpublic entity, a statement that, although the entity is not subject to the rules and regulations of the SEC, the MD&A presentation is intended to be a presentation in accordance with the rules and regulations adopted by the SEC

- A statement about whether any information came to the practitioner's attention that caused him or her to believe any of the following:

— That the presentation does not include, in all material respects, the required elements of the rules and regulations adopted by the SEC

— That the historical financial amounts have not been accurately derived, in all material respects, from the entity's financial statements

— That the underlying information, determinations, estimates, and assumptions of the entity do not provide a reasonable basis for the disclosures contained therein

• If the entity is a public entity or nonpublic entity that is making an offering of securities to the public, a statement restricting the use of the report to specified parties

• The manual or printed signature of the practitioner's firm

• The date of the review report

Exhibit AT 701-2 is an example taken from SSAE-10 of a report for a review engagement on an entity's MD&A presentation.

EXHIBIT AT 701-2—REVIEW REPORT ON AN ENTITY'S MD&A PRESENTATION

We have reviewed XYZ Company's Management's Discussion and Analysis taken as a whole, included [*incorporated by reference*] in the Company's [*insert description of registration statement or document*]. Management is responsible for the preparation of the Company's Management's Discussion and Analysis pursuant to the rules and regulations adopted by the Securities and Exchange Commission. We have audited, in accordance with the standards of the Public Company Accounting Oversight Board (United States), the financial Statements of XYZ Company as of December 31, 20X5 and 20X4, and for each year in the three-year period ended December 31, 20X5, and in our report date [*month*] XX, 20X6, we expressed an unqualified opinion on those financial statements.

We conducted our review of Management's Discussion and Analysis in accordance with attestation standards established by the American Institute of Certified Public Accounts. A review of Management's Discussion and Analysis consists principally of applying analytical procedures and making inquiries of persons responsible for financial, accounting, and operating matters. It is substantially less in scope than an examination, the objective of which is the expression of an opinion on the presentation. Accordingly, we do not express such an opinion.

The preparation of Management's Discussion and Analysis requires management to interpret the criteria, make determinations as to the relevancy of information to be included, and make estimates and assumptions that affect reported information. Management's Discussion and Analysis includes information regarding the estimated future impact of transactions and events that have occurred or are expected to occur, expected sources of liquidity and capital resources, operating trends, commitments, and uncertainties. Actual results in the future may differ materially from management's present assessment of this information because events and circumstances frequently do not occur as expected.

Based on our review, nothing came to our attention that caused us to believe that the Company's presentation of Management's Discussion and Analysis does not include, in all material respects, the required elements of the rules and regulations adopted by the Securities and Exchange Commission, that the historical financial amounts included therein have not been accurately derived, in all material respects, from the Company's financial statements, or that the underlying information, determinations, estimates and assumptions of the Company do not provide a reasonable basis for the disclosures contained therein.

The report is intended solely for the information and use of [*list or refer to specified parties*] and is not intended to be and should not be used by anyone other than the specified parties.

[*Signature*]

[*Date*]

OBSERVATION: Only public companies are required to file an MD&A with the Securities and Exchange Commission. Such audits are performed "in accordance with standards of the Public Company Accounting Oversight Board (United States)." If a nonpublic company voluntarily includes an MD&A and retains an accounting firm to issue an attestation report, the audit must be performed in accordance with generally accepted auditing standards.

The standard review report on MD&A presentations may be modified for the following reasons:

- A material element as required by SEC rules and regulations is omitted from the presentation (modify the review report by describing the omission).

- Historical financial amounts have not been accurately derived (modify the review report by describing the misstated information).

- Underlying information, determinations, estimates, and assumptions used by the client do not provide a reasonable basis upon which to prepare the MD&A presentation (modify the review report by describing the deficiency).

- The practitioner decides to emphasize a matter with respect to the MD&A presentation (a standard review report is issued with an explanatory paragraph describing the nature of the matter emphasized).

The practitioner's review report may also be modified when another practitioner has examined or reviewed (and issued a separate report on) MD&A information for a component that represents a significant part of the overall financial statements. Under this circumstance the principal practitioner's report should refer to the work of the other practitioner as a basis for offering the limited assurance on the MD&A presentation. When the other practitioner has not issued a separate report on the (component) MD&A presentation, there should be no reference to the work of the other practitioner in the review report on the MD&A presentation. (This does not mean that the principal practitioner cannot refer in the review report to the fact that a component's financial statements were audited by another auditor.)

PLANNING AID REMINDER: When the practitioner is unable to perform appropriate review procedures or the client is unwilling to provide appropriate written representations, the practitioner should not issue a review report on the MD&A presentation.

OTHER ISSUES

Combined Reporting

A practitioner may be engaged to report on the results of (1) an examination on an MD&A presentation related to the latest annual financial statements and (2) a review of an MD&A presentation on interim financial information for a period that is subsequent to the date of the annual financial statements. When the two engagements are "completed at the same time," the practitioner can issue a single report that incorporates both a separate examination format and a separate review format (except that the explanatory paragraph in the review report is omitted).

ENGAGEMENT STRATEGY: In some instances the client may prepare a combined MD&A presentation for an annual period and an interim period. SSAE standards note that if the discussion of liquidity and capital resources applies only as of the most recent interim period (not as of the date of the annual financial statements), the auditor is "limited to performing the highest level of service that is provided with respect to the historical financial statements of any of the periods covered by the MD&A presentation." Thus, if annual financial statements are audited and the interim financial statements are reviewed, the combined MD&A presentation can be reviewed but cannot be examined.

Engagement of the Auditor Subsequent to Filing of MD&A Presentation

Public companies are required to report significant subsequent events on Form 8-K, on Form 10-Q, or in a registration statement. They are not required to modify previously filed MD&A presentations for the occurrence of subsequent events. If the practitioner is engaged to examine or review an MD&A presentation after the document has been filed, the auditor should consider whether subsequent events have been reported in Form 8-K or Form 10-Q or in a registration statement, rather than whether the MD&A presentation has been modified to reflect the subsequent event. However, under this circumstance the following sentence should be added to the opinion paragraph in an examination engagement and to the concluding paragraph in a review engagement:

> The accompanying Management's Discussion and Analysis does not consider events that have occurred subsequent to [*month*] XX, 20X6, the date as of which it was filed with the Securities and Exchange Commission.

PLANNING AID REMINDER: If the client has not notified the SEC of a material subsequent event, the practitioner should express a qualified or adverse opinion on the MD&A presentation in a examination engagement (or in a review engagement appropriately modifying the review report), assuming that the auditor concludes that it is appropriate to issue a report on the MD&A information. This circumstance may occur when the SEC filing has not yet been completed but management intends to make the appropriate filing on a timely basis. However, if the subsequent event is not disclosed in a proper manner, the practitioner must decide whether to withdraw from both the MD&A engagement and the audit engagement.

Communicating with the Client's Audit Committee

Under the following circumstances (assuming the client refuses to correct the deficiency), the practitioner should communicate the deficiency to the entity's audit committee (or others with equivalent authority):

- Material inconsistencies exist between the MD&A presentation and other information included in the document containing the MD&A material.
- Material inconsistencies exist between the MD&A presentation and the historical financial statements.
- Material omissions are made in the MD&A presentation.
- Material misstatements of facts are made in the MD&A presentation.

FRAUD POINTER: If the practitioner has evidence as a result of performing the attestation or review engagement that fraud might have occurred—even if the fraud is inconsequential—it should be communicated to an appropriate level of management.

AT SECTION 801

REPORTING ON CONTROLS AT A SERVICE ORGANIZATION

Authoritative Pronouncements

SSAE-16 — Reporting on Controls at a Service Organization

Overview

AT 801 addresses examination engagements performed by a service auditor to report on controls at service organizations that provide services to user entities when those controls are likely to be relevant to the user entities' internal control over financial reporting. While this is the central focus, AT 801 may also be applied to engagements to report on other service organization controls such as those affecting user entities' regulatory compliance, production, or quality control or those when management at the service organization is not responsible for the system design.).

PLANNING AID REMINDER: If management is not responsible for the design of controls, the service auditor will likely not be able to give an opinion on the operating effectiveness of controls and may need to perform tests of controls in an agreed-upon procedures engagement under AT 201 or an examination of the operating effectiveness of the controls under AT 101.

The objectives of the service auditor in these engagements are (1) to obtain reasonable assurance about whether in all material respects and based on suitable criteria the description of management's service organization system is fairly presented and controls are suitably designed (and operated effectively when included in the scope of the engagement) to achieve the control objectives stated in management's description and (2) to report in accordance with the findings.

Role of the Service Auditor

When a service auditor reports on the processing of transactions by a service organization, the general standards—and the relevant standards of fieldwork and reporting—should be observed. Although the service auditor must be independent with respect to the service organization, it is not necessary to be independent from every user organization.

The service organization should determine what type of engagement the service auditor should perform; however, in an ideal situation, the user organization would discuss the matter with the service organization and its auditors to ensure that all parties will be satisfied with the service auditor's report.

Definitions

Carve-out method	Method of dealing with services provided by a subservice organization in which the service organization's system description identifies the nature of the services provided by the subservice organization. The service organization's system description and the scope of the service auditor's engagement exclude the subservice organization's relevant control objectives and related controls and include service organization controls for monitoring control effectiveness at the subservice organization.
Complementary user entity controls	Controls the service organization assumes will be implemented by user entities. If these controls are necessary to achieve the control objectives stated in the description of the service organization's system, they should be identified as such in the description.
Control objectives	The aim or purpose of specified controls at the service organization that ordinarily address the risks the controls are intended to mitigate.
Controls at a service organization	Policies and procedures at a service organization that are likely relevant to user entities' internal control over financial reporting. These policies and procedures are designed, implemented, and documented to provide reasonable assurance about achievement of control objectives relevant to the services covered by the service auditor's report. (This does not include controls unrelated to achievement of control objectives stated in the service organization's system description, such as controls related to preparation of the service organization's financial statements.)
Controls at a subservice organization	The policies and procedures at a subservice organization likely to be relevant to internal control over financial reporting of user entities of the service organization. Subservice organization policies and procedures designed, implemented, and documented for the same reasons as controls at a service organization.
Criteria	Standards or benchmarks used to measure and present the subject matter and against which the service auditor evaluates the subject matter. Management is responsible for selecting criteria.
Inclusive method	Method of addressing the services provided by a subservice organization in which the service organization's system description identifies the nature of the services provided by the subservice organization as well as the subservice organization's relevant control objectives and related controls.
Internal audit function	Service organization internal auditors and others such as a compliance or risk department who perform similar activities to internal auditors.

Report on a description of a service organization's system and the suitability of the design of controls (type 1 report)	A report comprising (1) a description of the service organization's system, prepared by management of the service organization; (2) a written assertion by the service organization's management about whether in all material respects, based on suitable criteria and as of a specified date, the description of the service organization's system fairly presents such system's design and implementation, and the controls related to the description's control objectives were suitably designed to achieve those objectives; and (3) a service auditor's report expressing an opinion on these written assertions.
Report on a description of a service organization's system and the suitability of the design and operating effectiveness of controls (type 2 report)	A report comprising (1) a description of the service organization's system, prepared by management of the service organization; (2) a written assertion by the service organization's management about whether in all material respects, based on suitable criteria and throughout the specified period, the description of the service organization's system fairly presents such system's design and implementation, the controls related to the description's control objectives were suitably designed and operated effectively to achieve those objectives; and (3) a service auditor's report expressing an opinion on these written assertions and including a description of the service auditor's tests of controls and their results.
Service auditor	A practitioner who reports on controls at a service organization.
Service organization	An organization or segment of an organization providing services to user entities that are relevant to those user entities' internal control over financial reporting.
Service organization's assertion	The written assertion by management of the service organization included in the type 1 and type 2 reports.
Service organization's system	The policies and procedures designed, implemented, and maintained to provide user entities with the services covered by the service auditor's report. A management-prepared description of the service organization's system identifies the services covered, the period related to the description, control objectives specified by management or an outside party, any outside party specifying the control objectives, and the related controls.
Subservice organization	A service organization used by another service organization to perform services provided to user entities that are relevant to those user entities' internal control over financial reporting.
Test of controls	A procedure designed to evaluate the operating effectiveness of controls in achieving the control objectives stated in management's service organization's system description.

| User auditor | An auditor who audits and reports on user entity financial statements. |
| User entity | An entity that uses a service organization. |

Requirements

The auditor is presumptively required to perform the following procedures related to reporting on controls at a service organization.

Management and Those Charged with Governance

1. When required to inquire of, request representations from, communicate with, or otherwise interact with the service organization's management, the auditor should determine the appropriate people within management or those charged with governance with whom to interact, considering who has appropriate responsibilities for and knowledge of the matters concerned.

Acceptance and Continuance

2. Only continue or accept a service auditor's engagement if:

   a. The service auditors has the capabilities and competence to perform the engagement.

   b. Preliminary knowledge of the engagement circumstances indicates the criteria will be suitable and available to intended users, there will be access to sufficient, appropriate evidence, and the service organization's system description and scope of the engagement will not be limited to the extent they are not useful to user entities and their auditors.

   c. Management of the service organization, in agreeing to the engagement terms, acknowledges and accepts responsibility for preparing and presenting the service organization's system description and an accompanying written assertion that will be provided to user entities; having a reasonable basis for its assertion; selecting and stating in the assertion criteria used; specifying and stating the control objectives in the description and identifying any other party specifying control objectives; identifying the risks that threaten achievement of the control objectives; controls at the service organization; and providing the service auditor with all information relevant to the service organization's system description and accompanying assertion and any additional relevant information requested, unrestricted access to service organization personnel to obtain evidence for the engagement, and written representations at the engagement's conclusion.

3. If management will not provide a written assertion, the service auditor may not perform a service auditor's engagement under AT 101 (Attest Engagements).

4. If management refuses to provide a written assertion, withdraw from the engagement due to a scope limitation. If withdrawal is prevented by law or regulation, disclaim an opinion.

5. If management requests a change in the engagement scope before engagement completion, the service auditor should be satisfied there is reasonable justification for the change before agreeing.

Assess Criteria Suitability

6. Assess whether management used suitable criteria in preparing and presenting the service organization's system description and evaluating whether controls were suitably designed (and operating effectively if a type 2 report) to achieve the description's stated control objectives.

7. Minimum suitable criteria for evaluating fair presentation of the service organization's system description include whether the description (1) presents how the system was designed and implemented, including the types of services provided and classes of transactions processed; the procedures, related accounting records, and supporting information for initiation, authorization, recording, processing, correcting, and reporting transactions to user entities; how significant events and conditions are captured; the process used to prepare reports for user entities; specified control objectives and controls designed to achieve those objectives, including complementary user controls; and other aspects of the service organization's internal control system relevant to achieving the description's stated control objectives; (2) in the case of a type 2 report, whether management's description of the service organization includes relevant detail of changes to the service organization's system during the period covered by the description; and (3) does not omit or distort information relevant to the description and acknowledges the description may not include all system aspects important to every user entity and auditor.

8. Minimum suitable criteria for evaluating if controls are suitably designed to achieve stated control objectives include whether risks threatening achievement of the description's stated control objectives have been identified by management and if identified controls would, if operating as described, provide reasonable assurance that those risks would not prevent achievement of the control objectives.

9. Minimum suitable criteria for evaluating whether controls operate effectively to provide reasonable assurance that the stated control objectives would be achieved include whether the controls were consistently applied as designed and whether manual controls were applied by individuals with sufficient competence and authority.

Materiality

10. Evaluate materiality when planning and performing the engagement regarding fair presentation of the service organization's system description and suitability of the design (and operating effectiveness if a type 2 report) of controls to achieve the description's stated control objectives.

Obtain an Understanding of the Service Organization's System

11. Obtain an understanding of the service organization's system and controls included in the scope of the engagement.

Obtain Evidence Regarding Description

12. Obtain and read the service organization's system description and evaluate whether aspects of the description included in the scope of the engagement are presented fairly, including whether the description's stated control objectives are reasonable, controls identified in the description were implemented, and any complementary user controls and services provided by a subservice organization are adequately described (including which method, inclusive or carve-out, is used).

13. Determine whether the service organization's system description has been implemented through inquiries of management and other service organization personnel and other procedures, including observation and inspection of records and other documentation regarding how the service organization's system operates and controls are applied.

14. Determine which service organization controls are necessary to achieve the description's stated control objectives and assess whether they were suitably designed to achieve those objectives by identifying risks threatening achievement of the objectives and evaluating the linkage of controls identified in the description with those risks.

Obtain Evidence Regarding Control Effectiveness

15. For a type 2 engagement, test controls necessary to achieve the description's stated control objectives and assess their operating effectiveness throughout the period. Evidence obtained in prior engagements does not provide a basis for a reduction in testing even if supplemented with evidence obtained during the current period.

16. Inquire about changes in the service organization's controls implemented during the period covered by the service auditor's report. Changes significant to user entities and their auditors should be in the service organization's system description or, if not in the description, should be described in the service auditor's report and the effect of such changes on the report should be determined. If superseded controls are relevant to achievement of the description's stated control objectives, determine if it is possible to test the controls before and after the change and, if not, determine the effect on the service auditor's report.

17. When designing and performing tests of controls, perform other procedures in combination with inquiry to obtain evidence about how, by whom or what means, and with what consistency the control was applied; determine if any controls to be tested depend on other controls and if it is necessary to obtain evidence about those controls' operating effectiveness; and determine an effective method for selecting the items to be tested to meet the procedure's objectives.

18. Determine the extent of tests of controls and if sampling is appropriate by considering the population characteristics, including the nature, frequency, and expected deviation rate of the controls to be tested.

19. Investigate the nature and cause of any deviations identified and determine whether identified deviations are within the expected deviation rate and the control operated effectively, additional testing of the control or other controls is necessary to reach a conclusion about operating effectiveness, or the testing performed provides an appropriate basis for concluding the control did not operate effectively. If the auditor becomes aware based on these procedures that any identified deviations are due to intentional acts by service organization personnel, assess the risk that management's service organization system description is not fairly presented and the controls are not suitably designed or, in a type 2 report, operating effectively.

Using the Work of Others

20. Obtain an understanding of the aspects of the internal audit function relevant to the engagement.

21. If intending to use work of the internal audit function, evaluate their objectivity, technical competence, due professional care, and whether it is likely effective communication will occur between internal audit and the service auditor, including the effect of any constraints or restrictions placed on the internal audit function by management or those charged with governance.

22. In judging the effect of the internal audit function's work on the nature, timing, or extent of the service auditor's procedures, evaluate the nature and scope of work performed by the internal audit function, the significance of that work to the service auditor's conclusions and the degree of subjectivity involved in evaluating the evidence gathered in support of those conclusions.

23. Perform procedures to evaluate the adequacy of work performed by the internal audit function if the service auditor uses that work. Consider the adequacy of the internal audit function's work for the service auditor's purposes, including whether work is performed by people with appropriate training and proficiency; work is properly supervised, reviewed, and documented; sufficient, appropriate evidence is obtained to be able to draw reasonable conclusions; conclusions reached are appropriate in the circumstances; prepared reports are consistent with results; and any exceptions or unusual matters disclosed by the internal audit function are properly resolved.

24. If work of the internal audit function has been used in performing tests of controls in a type 2 report, the description of those tests and results should include a description of the internal auditor's work and the service auditor's procedures with respect to that work.

25. If intending to use the work of a specialist, evaluate the specialist's capabilities, competence, and objectivity and inquire about interests and relationships that could threaten that objectivity.

26. Obtain a sufficient understanding of the specialist's field of expertise to enable a determination of the nature, scope, and objectives of the special-

ist's work and an evaluation of the adequacy of that work for the service auditor's purposes.

27. Establish a written understanding with the specialist regarding the nature, scope, and objectives of the specialist's work, the service auditor's and specialist's respective roles, and the nature, timing, and extent of communication between the parties, including the form of any report to be provided.

28. In the service auditor's opinion, do not refer to work of the internal audit function or a specialist that was used. The service auditor has sole responsibility for the opinion expressed that is not reduced by using the work of others.

29. When the service auditor uses members of the service organization's internal audit function to provide direct assistance, he or she should adapt and apply the applicable requirements of AU-C 610.

Written Representation

30. Ask management to provide written representations:

   a. That reaffirm the assertion accompanying the service organization's system description

   b. That they have disclosed to the service auditor any of the following about which they are aware: instances of noncompliance with laws and regulations or uncorrected errors that may affect user entities; knowledge of any actual, suspected, or alleged intentional acts by the service organization's management or employees, such as overrides of controls or misappropriation of user entity assets, that could adversely affect the fair presentation of the service organization's system description or the completeness or achievement of the description's stated control objectives; design deficiencies in controls, including those for which management believes the cost of corrective action exceeds the benefits; instances where controls have not operated as described; and subsequent events regarding the services covered by the engagement that could have a significant effect on user entities.

31. If the service organization's system description uses the inclusive method and a subservice organization is used, obtain the written representations, described in item 30, above, from management of the subservice organization.

32. Written representations should be in the form of a representation letter addressed to the service auditor and should be as of the same date as the service auditor's report.

33. If management does not provide one or more of the requested written representations: discuss the matter with management, consider the assessment of management's integrity and determine effects on the reliability of management's representations in general, and take appropriate actions, which may include disclaiming an opinion or withdrawing from the engagement.

Other Information

34. Read other information included in a document containing the service organization's system description and the service auditor's report to identify any material inconsistencies with the description. If the service auditor becomes aware of a material inconsistency or an apparent misstatement of fact in the other information, discuss the matter with management. If management refuses to correct this inconsistency or misstatement, take further appropriate action.

Subsequent Events

35. Inquire whether management is aware of any events subsequent to the period covered by the service organization's system description up to the date of the service auditor's report that could have a significant effect on management's assertion. If so, and the event is not disclosed in the description, disclose it in the service auditor's report.

36. There is no obligation to keep informed of events after the date of the service auditor's report, but if the service auditor becomes aware of conditions that existed at the report date that might have affected management's assertion and the service auditor's report, the service auditor should evaluate this information by adapting and applying the guidance in AU-C 560.

Documentation

37. Prepare audit documentation sufficient to enable an experienced auditor with no previous connection to the audit to understand (a) the nature, timing, and extent of the audit procedures performed to comply with AT 801 and applicable legal and regulatory requirements; (b) the results of procedures performed and the evidence obtained; and (c) conclusions reached on significant matters arising during the engagement and significant professional judgments made in reaching those conclusions.

38. Document the nature, timing, and extent of audit procedures performed by recording (a) the identifying characteristics of specific items or matters tested; (b) who performed procedures and the date the procedures were completed; and (c) who reviewed the work performed and the date and extent of the review.

39. If specific work of internal the audit function is used, document the conclusions reached about the adequacy of the work and the procedures performed by the service auditor on that work.

40. Document discussions of significant matters with service organization personnel and others. Include when and with whom the discussions occurred.

41. If information was identified that is inconsistent with the service auditor's final conclusion regarding a significant finding, document how the inconsistency was addressed.

42. Complete the assembly of the final engagement file on a timely basis, no later than 60 days after the service auditor's report release date.

43. Do not discard any documentation after assembly of the final engagement file has been completed before the end of its retention period.

44. If documentation needs to be modified or added to after assembly of the final engagement file is complete, document the specific reasons for making the changes and when and by whom the changes were made and reviewed.

Preparing the Service Auditor's Report

45. Include the following elements in the service auditor's report:

   a. A title clearly indicating the report is an independent service auditor's report.

   b. An addressee.

   c. Identification of the service organization's system description prepared by the service organization's management; an identification of any parts of the service organization's system description not covered by the service auditor's report; any information included in a document containing the service auditor's report that is not covered by the service auditor's report; the criteria; and if services of a subservice organization were used, an identification of those services and whether the inclusive or carve-out method was used. Depending on if the inclusive or carve-out method was used, respectively, there should be a statement that the service organization's system description includes or excludes the control objectives and related controls at the subservice organization and that the service auditor's procedures included or excluded procedures at or related to the subservice organization.

   d. If management's service organization system description refers to the need for complementary controls, a statement that the description's stated control objectives can only be achieved if complementary user entity controls are suitably designed and operating effectively and that the service auditor has not evaluated such suitability.

   e. A reference to management's assertion and preparing and presenting the service organization's system description and an accompanying assertion; providing the services covered by the service organization's system description; specifying and stating the description's control objectives; and identifying the risks that threaten achieving those objectives; designing, implementing, and documenting controls to achieve the related control objectives stated in the description; and selecting the criteria.

   f. A statement that the service auditor is responsible for expressing an opinion on the fairness of the presentation of management's description of the service organization's system and on the suitability of the design and, in a type 2 report, operating effectiveness of the controls to achieve the related control objectives stated in the description, based on the service auditor's examination.

g. A statement that the engagement was performed in accordance with attestation standards established by the American Institute of Certified Public Accountants and that those standards require the service auditor to plan and perform the examination to obtain reasonable assurance about whether management's description of the service organization's system is fairly presented and the controls are suitably designed as of the specified date for a type 1 report, or that the controls are suitably designed and operating effectively throughout the specified period for a type 2 report, to achieve the related control objectives.

h. In a type 1 report, that procedures regarding the operating effectiveness of controls have not been performed and no opinion is expressed on such effectiveness.

i. A statement that an examination of management's service organization system description and the suitability of the design, and in the case of a type 2 report, operating effectiveness, of the service organization's controls to achieve the related control objectives stated in the description involves performing procedures to obtain evidence about the fairness of the description's presentation and the suitability of the controls to achieve the control objectives in the description.

j. A statement that the examination included assessing the risks that management's service organization system description is not fairly presented and that the controls were not suitably designed, or for a type 2 report operating effectively, to achieve the related control objectives.

k. In a type 2 report, a statement that the examination also included testing the operating effectiveness of controls the service auditor considers necessary to provide reasonable assurance that the related control objectives stated in management's service organization system description were achieved.

l. A statement that this type of examination engagement includes evaluating the overall presentation of management's service organization system description and the suitability of the control objectives stated in the description.

m. A statement that the service auditor believes the examination provides a reasonable basis for his or her opinion.

n. The service auditor's opinion on whether, in all material respects, based on the criteria specified in management's assertion that as of the specified date for a type 1 report or throughout the specified period for a type 2 report: the service organization's system description fairly presents the system that was designed and implemented; the controls related to the description's stated control objectives were suitably designed to provide reasonable assurance that those objectives would be achieved if the controls operated effectively; for a type 2 report, that those controls were tested and operated effectively; and on the fact that complementary user controls are needed to achieve the related control objectives stated in management's service organization system description, if applicable.

   o. In a type 2 report, a reference to a description of the service auditor's test of controls and their results that identifies the controls tested, whether all or part of the population was tested, and the nature of the tests in sufficient detail for user auditors to determine the effects of these tests on their risk assessments. If deviations have been identified, also include the extent of testing and number of items tested that led to identifying the deviations and the number and nature of the deviations noted regardless of whether the related control objectives were achieved.

   p. A statement restricting the use of the service auditor's report to customers as of the end of the period (type 1 report), customers during some or all of the period covered by the report (type 2 report), user auditors, and service organization management.

   q. The date of the service auditor's report.

   r. The service auditor's name and the city and state where the office with responsibility for the engagement is maintained.

46. Date the service auditor's report no earlier than the date on which sufficient appropriate audit evidence has been obtained to support the service auditor's opinion.

47. Modify the opinion and include a clear description of all reasons for the modification if the service auditor concludes that management's service organization system description is not fairly presented in all material respects; controls are not suitably designed to provide reasonable assurance that the description's stated control objectives would be achieved if the controls operated as described; that, in the case of a type 2 report, those controls did not operate effectively; or the service auditor is unable to obtain sufficient, appropriate audit evidence.

48. If the service auditor is disclaiming an opinion due to an inability to obtain sufficient appropriate audit evidence, and has concluded that management's service organization system description is not fairly presented in all material respects; controls are not suitably designed to provide reasonable assurance that the description's stated control objectives would be achieved if the controls operated as described; that, in the case of a type 2 report, those controls did not operate effectively, he or she should identify these findings in the report.

49. If planning to disclaim an opinion, do not identify the procedures performed or include statements describing the characteristics of a service auditor's engagement in the report so that the disclaimer is not overshadowed.

Other Communication Responsibilities

50. If the service auditor becomes aware of incidents of noncompliance with laws and regulations, fraud, or uncorrected errors attributable to the service organization that may affect user entities, determine the effect of

such incidents on the service organization's system description, the achievement of the control objectives, and the service auditor's report. Determine whether this information has been communicated appropriately to affected user entities and, if it has not been communicated and management is unwilling to do so, take appropriate action.

Analysis and Application of Procedures

Acceptance and Continuance

Capabilities and competencies relevant to performing the engagement include knowledge of the relevant industry, an understanding of information technology and systems, experience in evaluating risks relevant to suitable design of controls, and experience in the design and execution of tests of controls and the evaluation of the results.

PLANNING AID REMINDER: The service auditor does not need to be independent of each user entity to perform a service auditor's engagement.

If management requests a change in the scope of an engagement before its completion, the auditor must be satisfied there is reasonable justification for the change. Reasons that do not justify a change in scope include excluding certain service organization controls from the engagement or trying to prevent disclosure of deviations identified at a subservice organization by changing from the inclusive to the carve-out method.

Assess Criteria Suitability

The requirement to include other aspects of the service organization's internal control system relevant to achieving stated control objectives in the service organization's system description is also applicable to internal control components of subservice organizations where the inclusive method is used.

Materiality

Materiality related to the fair presentation of the service organization's system description and design of controls primarily considers qualitative factors such as whether the description includes significant aspects of processing significant transactions or omits or distorts relevant information, or whether the controls, as designed, have the ability to provide reasonable assurance that the description's stated control objectives would be achieved. Materiality related to the operating effectiveness of controls considers quantitative and qualitative factors, such as tolerable and observed deviation rates and the nature and cause of any observed deviations.

OBSERVATION: Materiality is not applied when disclosing identified deviations in the results of the tests of controls, because a deviation may have significance beyond whether it prevents a control from operating effectively.

Obtain an Understanding of the Service Organization's System

Obtaining an understanding of the service organization's system and related controls assists the service auditor in:

- Identifying system boundaries and how the system interfaces with other systems

- Assessing the fair presentation of the service organization's system description

- Determining which controls are necessary to achieve the description's stated control objectives, and whether controls were suitably designed (and operating effectively in the case of a type 2 report) to achieve those objectives

There are many procedures the auditor may perform to obtain this understanding, including inquiring of management and other service organization personnel, observing operations, inspecting documents and records of transaction processing, inspecting agreements between the service organization and user entities to identify common terms, and reperforming application of controls.

Obtain Evidence

The service auditor plans and performs the engagement to obtain reasonable, not absolute, assurance of detecting errors and omissions in management's service organization system description. Therefore, subsequently discovering that material omissions or errors exist in the description or that there were instances in which control objectives were not achieved does not necessarily mean that there was inadequate planning, performance, or judgment by the service auditor.

In evaluating the fair presentation of the service organization's system description, the auditor may perform procedures such as:

- Considering the user entities' nature and how they are affected by the service organization's services

- Reading standard contracts with user entities to understand the service organization's contractual obligations

- Observing procedures performed by service organization personnel

- Reviewing the service organization's policy and procedure manuals and other system documentation

- Performing walk-throughs of transactions through the service organization's system

Procedures the auditor may perform to determine whether the system described has been implemented include inquiry of management and other service organization personnel, observation, inspection of records and other documentation, and reperformance of transaction processing and control application.

When obtaining evidence regarding the design of controls, the auditor should take compensating controls into account. If the auditor evaluates certain activities as ineffective in achieving a particular control objective, compensating controls may exist that still allow the auditor to conclude that controls related to the description's stated control objective are suitably designed to achieve that objective.

In obtaining evidence about the operating effectiveness of controls, evidence about the suitability of control design and implementation may provide evidence of operating effectiveness if there is some automation that provides for consistent operation of the control as it was designed and implemented. Some control procedures do not leave evidence of their operation, so the auditor may need to test operating effectiveness of such procedures throughout the reporting period to obtain sufficient evidence. To determine the effect of changes in service organization controls that were implemented during the period covered by the service auditor's report, the auditor should gather information about the nature and extent of the changes, how they affect processing at the service organization, and how they might affect assertions in financial statements of user entities.

Type 2 reports ordinarily cover a minimum period of six months. Reports covering a shorter time period may describe the reasons in the service organization's system description and service auditor's report. Reasons for a shorter reporting period include:

- The service auditor was engaged close to the report issuance date so controls cannot be tested for operating effectiveness for a six month period

- The service organization, system, or application has been operating for less than six months

- Significant changes have been made to controls and it is not practicable to issue a report covering the system before and after the changes or to wait six months before issuing a report

Using the Work of Others

The internal audit function may perform many different activities, including monitoring the service organization's internal control or the application processing systems, examining financial and operating information, evaluating the effectiveness of operating activities, including nonfinancial activities, and evaluating compliance with laws, regulations, and other internal and external requirements. The service auditor's procedures related to the internal audit function's work will depend on the significance of that work to the service auditor's conclusions.

While the service auditor makes judgments about the extent of the effect of internal auditors' work on the service auditor's procedures, the service auditor has sole responsibility for reporting on management's description of the service organization's system and the suitability of the design and operating effectiveness of controls. If, in a type 2 report, the service auditor uses the work of the internal audit function in performing tests of controls, introductory material to the description of tests of controls may be included indicating that certain work of the internal audit function was used in performing tests of controls, or individual tests may be attributed to internal audit.

Written Representations

Written representations described in the requirements section are separate from management's written assertion that accompanies the service organization's system description provided to user entities. In some circumstances, these written representations may be obtained from parties in addition to service organization management, such as those charged with governance.

Preparing the Service Auditor's Report

According to AT 801, type 1 and type 2 reports should be addressed to the service organization. An example of a type 1 report (Exhibit AT 801-1 and an example of type 2 report (Exhibit AT 801-2) are presented at the end of this section.

PUBLIC COMPANY IMPLICATION: Under the PCAOB's AS-5, only a type 2 report is acceptable, because the auditor must be comfortable that internal controls at the service organization are properly designed and operating effectively.

In a type 2 report's description of tests of controls, the inclusion of any information about causative factors for identified deviations can be useful to readers of the report.

There are many modifications that can be made to service auditor's reports. The auditor may issue a qualified opinion because the service organization's system description is not fairly presented in all material respects, controls are not suitably designed (or do not operate effectively for a type 2 report) to provide reasonable assurance of the achievement of the description's stated control objectives, or the auditor is unable to obtain sufficient appropriate evidence. In any of these circumstances, an explanatory paragraph should be inserted before a modified opinion paragraph and all other report paragraphs remain unchanged. The opinion paragraph is modified as follows, "In our opinion, except for the matter described in the preceding paragraph, and based on the criteria described in management's assertion on page [aa], in all material respects ... "

The auditor may also issue a report that includes a disclaimer of opinion on other information included in management's description of the service organization's system that is not covered by the service auditor's report. In this situation, the service auditor's report would be modified only by including an illustrative explanatory paragraph following the opinion paragraph.

Other Communication Responsibilities

When an auditor becomes aware of noncompliance with laws and regulations, fraud, or uncorrected errors at the service organization, there are several actions that may be taken:

- Obtain legal advice about the consequences of different courses of action
- Communicate with those charged with governance at the service organization

- Disclaim an opinion, modify the service auditor's opinion or add an emphasis of a matter paragraph

- Communicate with third parties such as a regulator when required

- Withdraw from the engagement

Practitioner's Aids

Exhibit AT 801-1 is an example of a type 1 report and Exhibit AT 801-2 is an example of a type 2 report.

EXHIBIT AT 801-1—TYPE 1 REPORT

We have examined X Service Organization's description of its [*type or name of*] system for processing user entities' transactions [*or identification of the function performed by the system*], as of [*date*], and the suitability of the design of controls to achieve the related control objectives stated in the description.

On page XX of the description, X Service Organization has provided an assertion about the fairness of the presentation of the description and suitability of the design of the controls to achieve the related controls objectives stated in the description. X Service Organization is responsible for preparing the description and for the accompanying assertion, including the completeness, accuracy, and method of presentation of the description and the assertion, providing the services covered by the description, identifying the risks that threaten the achievement of the control objectives, selecting the criteria, and designing, implementing, and documenting controls to achieve the related control objectives stated in the description.

Our responsibility is to express an opinion on the fairness of the presentation of the description and on the suitability of the design of controls to achieve the related control objectives stated in the description, based on our examination. We conducted our examination in accordance with attestation standards established by the American Institute of Certified Public Accountants. Those standards require that we plan and perform our examination to obtain reasonable assurance, in all material respects, about whether the description is fairly presented and the controls were suitably designed to achieve the related control objectives stated in the description as of [*date*].

An examination of a description of a service organization's system and the suitability of the design of the service organization's controls to achieve the related control objectives stated in the description involves performing procedures to obtain evidence about the fairness of the presentation of the description of the system and the suitability of the design of the controls to achieve the related control objectives stated in the description. Our procedures included assessing the risks that the description is not fairly presented and that the controls were not suitably designed to achieve the related control objectives stated in the description. An examination engagement of this type also includes evaluating the overall presentation of the description and the suitability of the control objectives stated therein, and the suitability of the criteria specified by the service organization and described at page [*aa*].

We did not perform any procedures regarding the operating effectiveness of the controls stated in the description and, accordingly, do not express an opinion thereon.

We believe that the evidence we obtained is sufficient and appropriate to provide a reasonable basis for our opinion.

Because of their nature, controls at a service organization may not prevent or detect and correct all errors or omissions in processing or reporting transactions [*or identification of the function performed by the system*]. The projection to the future of any evaluation of the fairness of the presentation of the description, or any conclusions about the suitability of the design of the controls to achieve the related control objectives is subject to the risk that controls at a service organization may become ineffective or fail.

In our opinion, in all material respects, based on the criteria described in X Service Organization's assertion on page [*aa*].

    a. The description fairly presents the [*type or name of*] system that was designed and implemented as of [*date*], and

    b. The controls related to the control objectives stated in the description were suitably designed to provide reasonable assurance that the control objectives would be achieved if the controls operated effectively as of [*date*].

This report is intended solely for the information and use of X Service Organization, user entities of X Service Organization's [*type or name of*] system as of [*date*], and the independent auditors of such user entities, who have a sufficient understanding to consider it, along with other information including information about controls implemented by the user entities themselves, when obtaining an understanding of user entities information and communication systems relevant to financial reporting. This report is not intended to be and should not be used by anyone other than these specified parties.

EXHIBIT AT 801-2—TYPE 2 REPORT

We have examined X Service Organization's description of its [*type or name of*] system for processing user entities' transaction [*or identification of the function performed by the system*] throughout the period [*date*] to [*date*] (description) and the suitability of the design and operating effectiveness of controls to achieve the related control objectives stated in the description.

On page XX of the description, X Service Organization has provided an assertion about the fairness of the presentation of the description and suitability of the design and operating effectiveness of the controls to achieve the related control objectives stated in the description. X Service Organization is responsible for preparing the description and for the assertion, including the completeness, accuracy, and method of presentation of the description and the assertion, providing the services covered by the description, specifying the control objectives and stating them in the description, identifying the risks that threaten the achievement of the control objectives, selecting the criteria, and designing, implementing, and documenting controls to achieve the control objectives stated in the description.

Our responsibility is to express an opinion on the fairness of the presentation of the description and on the suitability of the design and operating effectiveness of the controls to achieve the related control objectives stated in the description, based on our examination. We conducted our examination in accordance with attestation standards established by the American Institute of Certified Public Accountants. Those standards require that we plan and perform our examination procedures to obtain reasonable assurance about whether, in all material respects, the description is fairly presented and the controls were suitably designed and operating effectively to achieve the related control objectives stated in the description throughout the period [*date*] to [*date*].

An examination of a description of a service organization's system and the suitability of the design and operating effectiveness of the service organization's controls to achieve the related control objectives stated in the description involves performing procedures to obtain evidence about the fairness of the presentation of the description and the suitability of the design and operating effectiveness of those controls to achieve the related control objectives stated in the description. Our procedures also included assessing the risks that the description is not fairly presented and that the controls were not suitably designed or operating effectively to achieve the related control objectives stated in the description. Our procedures included testing the operating effectiveness of those controls that we consider necessary to provide reasonable assurance that the related control objectives stated in the description were achieved. An examination engagement of this type also includes evaluating the overall presentation of the description and the suitability of the control objectives stated therein, and the suitability of the criteria specified by the service organization and described at page [*aa*]. We believe that the evidence we obtained is sufficient and appropriate to provide a reasonable basis for our opinion.

Because of their nature, controls at a service organization may not prevent or detect and correct all errors or omissions in processing or reporting transactions [*or identification of the function performed by the system*]. Also, the projection to the future of any evaluation of the fairness of the presentation of the description, or conclusions about the suitability of the design or operating effectiveness of the controls to achieve the related control objectives is subject to the risk that controls at a service organization may become inadequate or fail.

In our opinion, in all material respects, based on the criteria described in X Service Organization's assertion on page [*aa*],

    a. The description fairly presents the [*type or name of*] system that was designed and implemented throughout the period [*date*] to [*date*].

    b. The controls related to the control objectives stated in the description were suitably designed to provide reasonable assurance that the control objectives would be achieved if the controls operated effectively throughout the period [*date*] to [*date*].

    c. The controls tested, which were those necessary to provide reasonable assurance that the control objectives stated in the description were achieved, operated effectively throughout the period [*date*] to [*date*].

The specific controls that were tested and the nature, timing, and results of those tests are listed on pages [*yy–zz*].

Restricted Use

This report, including the description of tests of controls and results thereof on pages [*yy–zz*] is intended solely for the information and use of X Service Organization, user entities of X Service Organization's [*type or name of*] system during some or all of the period [*date*] to [*date*], and the independent auditors of such entities, who have a sufficient understanding to consider it, along with other information including information about controls implemented by user entities themselves, when assessing the risks of material misstatements of user entities' financial statements. This report is not intended to be and should not be used by anyone other than these specified parties.

AR Section
Statements on Standards for Accounting and Review Services

AR SECTION 60

FRAMEWORK FOR PERFORMING AND REPORTING ON COMPILATION AND REVIEW ENGAGEMENTS

Authoritative Pronouncements

SSARS-19—Compilation and Review Engagements

Overview

In SSARS-19 the Accounting and Review Services Committee establishes a framework for performing and reporting on compilation engagements. The framework includes defining (1) key terms, (2) the objective of compilation and review engagements, (3) the requirements applicable to these types of engagements, (4) the sources and levels of authority of standards and guidance for performing compilation and review engagements, (5) the elements of compilation and review engagements, and (6) materiality within the context of compilation and review engagements.

Definitions

Applicable financial reporting framework	The financial reporting framework adopted by management and, when appropriate, those charged with governance
Assurance engagement	An engagement in which an accountant issues a report designed to enhance third-party and management confidence about the outcome of an evaluation or measurement of financial statements against an applicable financial reporting framework
Attest engagement	An engagement requiring independence
Financial reporting framework	A set of criteria used to determine measurement, recognition, presentation, and disclosure of all material items appearing in the financial statements
Financial statements	A structured representation of historical financial information, including related notes. The term ordinarily refers to a complete set of financial statements as determined by the applicable financial reporting framework, but it can also refer to a single financial statement or financial statements without notes.
Management	The person(s) with executive responsibility for the entity's operations

Nonissuer	A company not required to file reports with the Securities and Exchange Commission
Other comprehensive basis of accounting (OCBOA)	A definite set of criteria other than accounting principles generally accepted in the United States of America or International Financial Reporting Standards (IFRS) that has substantial support underlying the preparation of financial statements. Examples include the following:
	A basis of accounting that insurance companies use in accordance with state insurance commission rules
	A basis of accounting a reporting entity uses or expects to use to file its income tax return
	The cash basis of accounting and modifications of the cash basis that have substantial support, for example, recording depreciation on fixed assets
Review evidence	Information used by an accountant to provide a reasonable basis for obtaining limited assurance
Submission of financial statements	Presenting financial statements to management that an accountant has prepared
Third party	All persons, including those charged with governance, except for members of management
Those charged with governance	The person(s) responsible for overseeing the entity's strategic direction and obligations related to the entity's accountability

Objectives

The objective of a compilation is to help management present financial information in the form of financial statements without obtaining or providing any assurance regarding the financial statements' need for material modifications in order to conform to the applicable financial reporting framework. A compilation engagement differs significantly from a review or financial statement audit because it is an attest engagement, but it is not an assurance engagement.

OBSERVATION: For the purposes of SSARSs, when discussing compilation engagements, the term "financial statements" includes other specified financial statement elements, accounts, or items and pro-forma financial information when applicable.

The objective of a review is to obtain limited assurance through accumulation of review evidence that there are no material modifications that should be made to the financial statements in order for the statements to be in conformity with the applicable financial reporting framework. A review engagement is both an attest engagement and an assurance engagement, and it differs significantly from a financial statement audit because the accountant does not obtain assurance that he or she will become aware of all significant matters that would be disclosed in an audit.

PLANNING AID REMINDER: Because the evidence gathered in a review is much less extensive than the evidence gathered during an audit, and because management representations are a primary evidence source in a review, it is particularly important that the accountant carefully assess management's integrity.

Requirements

Accountants performing compilations or reviews are responsible for considering the entire text of a SSARS in their work on an engagement and in understanding and applying the professional requirements of relevant SSARSs. There are two categories of professional requirements used in SSARSs, and they impose different responsibilities on the accountant. Unconditional requirements are indicated by the words "must" or "is required" and require an accountant to comply with the requirement in all cases in which the circumstances the requirement applies to exist. Presumptively mandatory requirements are indicated by the word "should," and they also require an accountant to comply with the requirement if the circumstances the requirement applies to exist. However, the accountant may depart from presumptively mandatory requirements in rare circumstances if he or she documents the justification for the departure and how the alternative procedures performed sufficiently achieve the objectives of the requirement. If a SSARS states that an accountant "should consider" a procedure or action, he or she is presumptively required to consider, not carry out, the procedure or action.

Explanatory material consists of text within a SSARS that may provide further explanation and guidance on the professional requirements or identify and describe other procedures or actions relating to the accountant's activities. Explanatory material is indicated by the words "may," "might," and "could" and does not impose a professional requirement to perform suggested procedures or actions, rather it indicates material requiring the accountant's attention and understanding. Whether the accountant performs procedures or actions described in explanatory material depends on his or her professional judgment given the engagement circumstances.

Compilation and Review Standards and Guidance

Different sources of guidance are available to accountants performing compilations and reviews. Compilation and review engagements of nonissuers must be performed in accordance with SSARSs, except for certain reviews of interim financial information. SSARSs require the accountant to exercise professional judgment in their application.

Interpretative publications are not standards for accounting and review services, but are recommendations on the application of SSARS in certain circumstances. Interpretative publications can consist of SSARSs' compilation and review interpretations, SSARSs' appendices, AICPA Audit and Accounting Guide compilation and review guidance, and AICPA Statements of Position. The accountant should be aware of and consider any applicable interpretative publications and, although the guidance does not have to be applied, the accountant should be prepared to explain how he or she complied with SSARSs provisions addressed by the guidance.

Other compilation and review publications are available that do not have authoritative status but may help accountants understand and apply SSARS. Such publications include AICPA accounting and review publications; the AICPA's annual *Compilation and Review Alert;* compilation and review articles in professional journals and the AICPA's *The CPA Letter;* continuing professional education programs and other instructional materials, books, programs, and checklists; and compilation and review publications published by state CPA societies, other organizations, and individuals. If an accountant chooses to apply the guidance in an other compilation and review publication, he or she should be satisfied that it is relevant and appropriate to the circumstances. AICPA publications reviewed by the AICPA Audit and Attest Standards staff are presumed to be appropriate.

In addition to the SSARS, accountants who are members of the AICPA must also comply with other standards in performing compilation and review engagements. The AICPA's Code of Professional Conduct requires that accountants maintain objectivity and integrity and comply with all other applicable provisions when performing a compilation or review engagement. AICPA members are also governed by Statements on Quality Control Standards, which establish standards and provide guidance on a firm's system of quality control. The firm should have quality control policies and procedures in place to provide reasonable assurance that personnel comply with SSARS in compilation and review engagements. The nature and extent of those policies and procedures will depend on the firm's size, degree of operating autonomy, the nature of its practice, its organization, and appropriate cost-benefit considerations.

OBSERVATION: Deficiencies or instances of noncompliance with a firm's quality control policies do not necessarily indicate that a particular compilation or review engagement was not performed in accordance with SSARSs.

Compilation or Review Engagement Elements

There are five elements of a compilation or review engagement:

1. A three-party relationship involving management, an accountant, and intended users

2. An applicable financial reporting framework

3. Financial statements or financial information

4. Sufficient appropriate review evidence (in a review)

5. A written communication or report

Three-Party Relationship

Management, or the responsible party, is one party to the relationship. Management takes responsibility for the preparation and fair presentation of the financial statements in accordance with the applicable financial reporting framework and for designing, implementing, and maintaining internal control. If management is unwilling to accept these responsibilities, the accountant cannot issue an unmodified compilation or review report. During a compilation or review engagement, the accountant may make suggestions about the form and content of the financial statements or prepare them, in whole or in part, based on information from management.

An accountant in the practice of public accounting as defined by the AICPA code is a second party to the relationship. If an accountant is not in the practice of public accounting, it is inappropriate that he or she issue a written communication or report under SSARSs. In some cases, the accountant may be requested to perform additional services along with the compilation or review, which is acceptable as long as he or she adheres to professional standards in performing those services.

The third parties to the relationship are the intended users of the financial statements or financial information, which in some cases may be management.

Applicable Financial Reporting Framework

Management and, when applicable, those charged with governance are responsible for choosing an entity's applicable financial reporting framework and its accounting policies when there are acceptable alternatives within the framework. Examples of financial reporting frameworks include accounting principles generally accepted in the United States of America issued by the Financial Accounting Standards Board, the Governmental Accounting Standards Board, or the Federal Accounting Standards Advisory Board; IFRSs issued by the International Accounting Standards Board; and OCBOA.

Financial Statements or Financial Information

A compilation or review engagement may be for a complete set of financial statements or an individual financial statement that may be for a period of one year or more or less than one year, depending on management's needs.

Evidence

In a review engagement, the accountant should perform procedures sufficient to obtain limited assurance that no material modifications should be made to the financial statements in order for the statements to conform with the applicable financial reporting framework. Review evidence from analytical procedures and inquiries typically provide the accountant with a reasonable basis for obtaining limited assurance.

PLANNING AID REMINDER: The accountant has no responsibility to obtain any evidence about the completeness or accuracy of the financial statements in a compilation engagement. Nevertheless, association with a client where management integrity is questionable is likely to expose the accountant to a heightened level of business risk.

Written Communication or Report

When performing a compilation, a written communication or report is required unless the accountant withdraws from the engagement. An accountant who is not independent may still issue a compilation report as long as he or she complies with compilation standards. When performing a review, a written review report is required unless the accountant withdraws from the engagement.

Materiality

The accountant's determination of materiality is a matter of professional judgment, and is to reflect his or her views of the needs of financial statement users. Materiality is generally discussed in the applicable financial reporting framework. However, if materiality is not discussed, the following provides the accountant with a framework for evaluating materiality:

- Misstatements, including omissions, are considered to be material if individually or in the aggregate they could reasonably be expected to influence the economic decisions of users taken on the basis of the financial statements

- Judgments about materiality are affected by circumstances as well as a misstatement's size and nature

- Judgments about whether matters are material to financial statement users are made considering the common financial information needs of the users as a group

AR SECTION 80

COMPILATION OF FINANCIAL STATEMENTS

Authoritative Pronouncements

SSARS-19—Compilation and Review Engagements

Overview

Statements on Standards for Accounting and Review Services (SSARS) cover two different levels of service that an accountant can provide for unaudited financial statements of nonpublic entities. The first level of service is referred to as a compilation. The accountant's report on a compilation includes a statement that an audit or a review was not performed and no opinion or other assurance is expressed on the accompanying financial statements. The second level of service is called a review. The accountant's report on a review includes a statement of limited assurance that the financial statements are in accordance with generally accepted accounting principles (GAAP) or an other comprehensive basis of accounting.

The objective of the compilation service is to present in the form of financial statements information that is the representation of management. In a compilation service, the accountant does not express any assurance on the financial statements. The accountant is required to comply with the provisions of SSARS-19 when he or she is engaged to report on compiled financial statements or submitting financial statements to a client.

Establishing an Understanding

The accountant should establish an understanding with management and, when applicable, with those charged with governance regarding the services to be performed for compilation engagements, and this understanding should be documented with a written engagement letter with management. The understanding should include the engagement objectives, management's and accountant's responsibilities, and engagement limitations, incorporating the following matters:

- A compilation's objective is to assist management in presenting financial information in the form of financial statements.

- The accountant uses information from management without obtaining any assurance that there are no material modifications that should be made to the financial statements.

- Management is responsible for preparing and presenting the financial statements in accordance with the applicable financial reporting framework.

- Management is responsible for designing, implementing, and maintaining internal control relevant to the preparation and fair presentation of the financial statements.

- Management is responsible for preventing and detecting fraud.

- Management is responsible for identifying and ensuring the entity's compliance with applicable laws and regulations.

- Management is responsible for making all financial records and related information available to the accountant.

- The accountant is responsible for conducting the engagement in accordance with SSARSs issued by the AICPA.

- A compilation differs significantly from a review or audit of financial statements; therefore, the accountant will not express an opinion or provide any assurance about the financial statements.

- The engagement cannot be relied upon to disclose errors, fraud, or illegal acts.

- The accountant will inform management of any material errors and any evidence or information coming to his or her attention during the compilation that fraud or an illegal act may have occurred.

- If applicable, the effect of any independence impairments on the expected form of the accountant's compilation report.

Exhibit AR 80-1 provides an example engagement letter for financial statement compilations.

Other matters may also be included in the understanding with management and, when applicable, those charged with governance, including the following:

- Fees and billings

- Any arrangements or limitation of the accountant's or client's liability, such as indemnifying the accountant for liability based on knowing misrepresentations from management where permitted

- Conditions under which access to compilation documents may be granted to others

- Additional services to be provided relating to regulatory requirements

If compiled financial statements are not expected to be used by a third party and a compilation report will not be issued, this should be addressed in the engagement letter.

OBSERVATION: If the accountant is performing a compilation for restricted use, add the following paragraph to the engagement letter: "The financial statements will not be accompanied by a report and are for management's use only and are not to be used by a third party."

There are additional matters to be addressed in the engagement letter for a restricted-use compilation such as the following: there may be material departures from the applicable financial reporting framework and any effects of those departures may not be disclosed; substantially all disclosures and the statement of cash flows as required by the applicable financial reporting framework may not be included; and reference to any supplementary information.

At the outset of an engagement the accountant might know that a departure, or departures, from GAAP exists. In this event, it might be appropriate to include in the engagement letter information to the effect that a modified report will be issued reflecting the departure(s) from GAAP instead of the standard compilation or review report. This procedure should eliminate misunderstanding about what type of report the client will receive when the engagement is completed.

Compilation Performance Requirements

An accountant adheres to several requirements in performing a compilation engagement. He or she should have an understanding of the client's industry and its accounting principles and practices. This requirement does not prevent the accountant from accepting an engagement for an industry in which he or she has no previous experience, but it does mean that he or she is responsible for obtaining the required level of knowledge.

Developing an understanding of the client

The accountant should obtain an understanding of the client's business, including knowledge of the client's organization, operating characteristics, and the nature of its assets, liabilities, revenues, and expenses. The accountant should also obtain an understanding of the accounting principles and practices used by the client, remaining alert to any unusual accounting policies and procedures that come to his or her attention. This understanding may include changes in accounting principles and practices and differences in the client as compared to normal industry practices.

Consider whether the client needs other accounting services

On the basis of the accountant's general knowledge of the client's business, he or she should consider the need to perform other accounting services. (Such services may be limited to consulting on a specific accounting matter or involve adjusting all or many of the significant accounts in the general ledger.) The need for such services may result from the accountant discovering, for example, that

- The accounting records are inadequate.
- The accounting or bookkeeping personnel do not possess sufficient abilities or experience.
- The accounting basis used to maintain the books is incorrect.
- The information to be disclosed in the financial statements is not available.

OBSERVATION: If the accountant performs any of the above services, it is advisable that the service and any limitations on its use be memorialized in a written communication with the client.

Read the financial statements

After the accountant has obtained the required knowledge of the client and the industry the client operates in, has completed any other accounting services deemed necessary, and prepared the financial statements, he or she should read the financial statements.

Reading the financial statements is one of the more important procedures in a compilation engagement. The accountant must apply all the knowledge and understanding previously obtained and use his or her professional expertise effectively. Questions the accountant must answer include the following:

- Do the financial statements appear to be in the proper form and complete?
- Do the financial statements appear to be free from obvious material errors?
- Are all necessary disclosures made in reasonable detail?

Any information that the accountant is aware of, from any source, should be considered for possible indications that the financial statements may be inaccurate, incomplete, or otherwise unsatisfactory.

Financial statements that may be inaccurate or incomplete

Although doing so is not required, the accountant may have made inquiries or performed other procedures regarding information provided by the entity. If these inquiries or procedures make the accountant aware that information supplied by the entity is incorrect, incomplete, unsatisfactory, or that fraud or an illegal act may have occurred, he or she should request that management consider the effect of these matters on the financial statements and communicate their conclusions to him or her. The accountant should consider the effects of management's conclusions, obtaining additional information if he or she believes the financial statements may be materially misstated. If management refuses to provide additional or revised information, the accountant should withdraw from the engagement and consider the need for consulting legal counsel.

Consider obtaining a client representation letter

Compilation standards do not require that client representations be obtained. However, because of the very limited procedures required for a compilation and the possibility of misunderstandings regarding accounting information, having obtained a client representation letter may be useful, especially when the client does not understand that the financial statements are its responsibility. The representation letter should specify the responsibilities of the client and the accountant, define the scope of the engagement and, if possible, include a clause that indemnifies the accountant against legal expenses and other costs if client management intentionally makes false representations to the accountant.

Documentation of the compilation engagement

Documentation should be prepared for each engagement in sufficient detail to provide a clear understanding of the work performed. The form, content, and extent of documentation varies depending on the engagement circumstances and the accountant's professional judgment. Documentation should include (1) the engagement letter documenting the understanding with the client, (2) any findings or issues the accountant finds significant in his or her professional judgment, and (3) written or oral communications to management regarding fraud or illegal acts that come to the accountant's attention.

Financial Statement Reporting

When they are reasonably expected to be used by a third party, financial statements should be accompanied by a written report in order to prevent misinterpretation of the degree of responsibility the accountant is assuming regarding them. The following are the basic elements of the accountant's report:

- *Title* The title should clearly indicate it is the accountant's compilation report and, if the accountant is independent, this should be indicated in the title of the report.

- *Addressee* The report should be addressed appropriately.

- *Introductory paragraph* This paragraph should identify the entity whose financial statements have been compiled and the financial statements that have been compiled, state that the financial statements have been compiled, specify the date or period covered by the financial statements, and include a statement that the accountant has not audited or reviewed the financial statements and does not express an opinion or provide any assurance about whether the financial statements are in accordance with the applicable financial reporting framework.

- *Management's responsibility for the financial statements and for internal control over financial reporting* A statement that management is responsible for preparing and fairly presenting the financial statements in accordance with the applicable financial reporting framework and for designing, implementing, and maintaining internal control relevant to the preparation and fair presentation of the financial statements.

- *Accountant's responsibility* A statement that the accountant is responsible for conducting the compilation in accordance with SSARS issued by the AICPA and that a compilation's objective is to assist management in presenting financial information in the form of financial statements without providing assurance that there are no material modifications that should be made to the statements.

- *Accountant's signature* The accounting firm or accountant's manually signed or printed signature.

- *Date of the report* The compilation report date should be the date the compilation is completed.

Exhibit AR 80-2 provides an example of a standard accountant's compilation report.

The accountant should not describe any procedures performed as part of the compilation engagement in the report. Each page of the compiled financial statements should contain a reference such as "See accountant's compilation report." Financial statements prepared in accordance with an OCBOA are not considered appropriate in form unless they include a description of the OCBOA, including a summary of significant accounting policies and a description of the primary differences from GAAP, and informative disclosures similar to those required by GAAP if the financial statements contain items similar to those in financial statements prepared in accordance with GAAP.

OBSERVATION: SSARS-13 (Compilation of Specified Elements, Accounts, or Items of a Financial Statement) and SSARS-14 (Compilation of Pro Forma Financial Information) enable an accountant to compile elements, accounts, or items of a financial statement and pro-forma financial information. These SSARS expand the applicability of SSARS (which were formerly only applicable to financial statements) to allow an accountant to compile and report on such items in accordance with SSARS. Examples of specified elements, accounts, or items of a financial statement that an accountant can now compile under the standards include schedules of rentals, royalties, profit participation, and provision of income taxes. Pro-forma financial information shows what the significant effects on historical financial statements might have been had a consummated or proposed transaction (or event) occurred at an earlier date. The new standards establish specific responsibilities for accountants engaged to compile specified elements, accounts, or items of a financial statement and pro-forma financial information. SSARS-13 is summarized in AR 110 and SSARS-14 is summarized in AR 120.

All types of financial statements may be compiled or reviewed and may be for any type of nonissuer business organization, including an estate, a trust, or an individual. The financial statements may reflect the operations of not-for-profit organizations, governments, governmental agencies, or other nonpublic entities that prepare their financial statements using a comprehensive basis of accounting other than GAAP. Whenever the term "GAAP" is used in connection with a compilation or review, its meaning also includes "an other comprehensive basis of accounting." As mentioned previously, compilation and review standards are not applicable to forecasts, projections, or similar financial presentations, or to financial information included in tax returns.

Financial Statements that Omit Substantially All Disclosures

If financial statements omit substantially all disclosures required by the applicable financial reporting framework, the accountant may still compile the statements if the omission is not due to the intent to mislead financial statement users. When reporting on such financial statements, the paragraph on the accountant's responsibility should be followed by a paragraph containing statements that management has omitted substantially all disclosures required by the applicable financial reporting framework; if those disclosures were included, they might influence the users' conclusions about the entity's financial position, results of operations, and cash flows; and the financial statements are not intended for those who are uninformed about such matters. An example of such a paragraph is as follows:

Management has elected to omit substantially all of the disclosures required by accounting principles generally accepted in the United States of America. If the omitted disclosures were included in the financial statements, they might influence the user's conclusions about the company's financial position, results of operations, and cash flows. Accordingly, the financial statements are not designed for those who are not informed about such matters.

PLANNING AID REMINDER: If the entity only includes disclosures about a few matters, those disclosures should be labeled "Selected Information—Substantially All Disclosures Required by [*identify the applicable financial reporting framework (for example,* Accounting Principles Generally Accepted in the United States of America)] Are Not Included."

A similar situation arises when the statement of cash flows is omitted from a presentation that includes a balance sheet and an income statement. Under GAAP, a statement of cash flows is a required statement, and reference to such omission must be made in the accountant's compilation report. The following is the recommended fourth paragraph that should be added to the accountant's compilation report when a statement of cash flows or disclosures are omitted:

Management has elected to omit substantially all the disclosures (and the statement of cash flows) required by generally accepted accounting principles. If the omitted disclosures were included in the financial statements, they might influence the user's conclusions about the Company's financial position, results of operations, and cash flows. Accordingly, these financial statements are not designed for those who are not informed about such matters.

If only the statement of cash flows is omitted, the fourth paragraph should read as follows:

A statement of cash flows for the year ended December 31, 20X1, has not been presented. Generally accepted accounting principles require that such a statement be presented when financial statements purport to present financial position and results of operations.

Accountant Is Not Independent

If the accountant is not independent, the compilation report should be modified to include a final paragraph stating the accountant's lack of independence. This disclosure could be phrased as follows: "I am (We are) not independent with respect to ABC Company." Exhibit AR 80-3 provides an example of such a report. The accountant may disclose a description about the reasons for his or her lack of independence, but if these reasons are disclosed, then all reasons should be included in the description. The following are examples of disclosures for a lack of independence:

- A member of the engagement team had a direct financial interest in the company.

- An immediate family member of a member of the engagement team was employed by the company.

- Certain accounting services performed impaired independence.

Financial Statements Not Expected to Be Used by a Third Party

The accountant does not need to issue a compilation report if the financial statements are not expected to be used by a third party. A reference should be included on each page of the financial statements restricting their use, such as "Restricted for Management's Use Only." If the accountant becomes aware that the financial statements have been distributed to third parties, discuss the situation with the client and consider requesting that the client have the statements returned. If the client does not comply with a request to have the statements returned, the accountant should notify known third parties that the financial statements are not intended for third-party use and should seriously consider consulting his or her attorney.

Emphasis of a Matter

The accountant may use his or her discretion to add an emphasis-of-matter paragraph regarding a matter disclosed in the financial statements. This information should be presented in a separate paragraph in the report and may include matters such as uncertainties, that the entity is part of a larger entity, that the entity had significant transactions with related parties, unusually important subsequent events, or accounting matters not involving a change in accounting principle that affect the comparability of the financial statements with those of the prior period.

Emphasis-of-a-matter paragraphs should never be used as a substitute for management's disclosures. For this reason, an accountant should not include an emphasis paragraph in a compilation report on financial statements that omit substantially all disclosures unless the matter is disclosed in the financial statements.

Departures from the Applicable Financial Reporting Framework

The accountant may become aware of material departures from the applicable financial reporting framework and, if the financial statements are not revised, should consider the effects on the report. The omission of substantially all disclosures and/or the statement of cash flows, although such omissions constitute a departure from GAAP, is permitted in a compilation because of the special disclosure provisions. If the accountant concludes that modification of the standard report is adequate to disclose the departure, a separate paragraph should be included in the report disclosing the departure and its effects on the financial statements if the effects have been determined by management or are known based on the accountant's procedures. An example of this type of report is provided in Exhibit AR 80-4.

If management has not determined the effects, the accountant is not required to determine the effects so long as the report states that such a determination has not been made. If the accountant believes modification of the report is not adequate to indicate the financial statement deficiencies, he or she should withdraw from the engagement and not perform any further services regarding those financial statements.

Restricted Use Reports

A general use report is not restricted to specified parties and is normally used in financial statement reports prepared in conformity with an applicable financial reporting framework. However, the accountant is not precluded from restricting the use of any report. A restricted use report is intended only for one or more specified third parties. A report's use should be restricted when it is based on measurement or disclosure criteria contained in contractual agreements or regulatory provisions that are not in conformity with an applicable financial reporting framework.

If a single combined report is used covering subject matter requiring a restriction on use and subject matter not requiring a restriction on use, the report's use should be restricted to the specified parties. A separate restricted use report may be included in a document also containing a general use report when required by law or regulation. In this situation, both reports maintain their intended use.

If the accountant is asked to add additional parties as specified parties to a restricted use report after completion of the engagement, he or she may do so but should obtain affirmative acknowledgement from the other parties, preferably in writing, regarding their understanding of the nature of the engagement, the measurement or disclosure criteria used, and the related report.

A restricted use report should contain a separate paragraph at the end of the report including:

- A statement that the report is intended solely for the information and use of specified parties.

- Identification of the specified parties included in the restricted use (the parties may be listed in the report or the report may refer to a listing elsewhere in the document).

- A statement that the report is not intended to be and should not be used by anyone other than the specified parties.

Entity's Ability to Continue as a Going Concern

The accountant may become aware during a compilation engagement that there is uncertainty about the entity's ability to continue as a going concern for a reasonable period of time, not exceeding one year beyond the date of the compiled financial statements. In these situations, the accountant should request that management consider possible effects of the going concern uncertainty on the financial statements, including the need for disclosure and consider the reasonableness of management's conclusions and the adequacy of any related disclosures.

If the accountant concludes that management's conclusions are not reasonable or that disclosure is inadequate, he or she should follow the guidance regarding departures from an applicable financial reporting framework and, depending on what the accountant considers necessary, should either modify the report or withdraw from the engagement. The accountant may emphasize an uncertainty about the entity's ability to continue as a going concern in the report as long as the uncertainty is disclosed in the financial statements.

Subsequent Events

Whether during performance of compilation procedures or subsequent to the date of the compilation report but prior to the report's release, the accountant may become aware that a subsequent event with a material effect on the compiled financial statements has occurred. In this situation, the accountant should request that management consider the possible effects on the financial statements and any applicable related disclosures. If the accountant determines the subsequent event is not adequately accounted for in the financial statements or disclosed in the notes, the guidance regarding departures from an applicable financial reporting framework should be followed and, depending on what the accountant considers necessary, he or she should either modify the report or withdraw from the engagement. A subsequent event may have such a material effect on the entity that the accountant may choose to include an emphasis of matter paragraph to direct the reader's attention to the event and its effects if the matter is disclosed in the financial statements.

Subsequent Discovery of Facts Existing at the Date of the Report

The accountant may become aware of facts existing at the date of the report subsequent to that date that, had the accountant been aware of those facts, may have caused him or her to believe the information supplied by the entity was incorrect, incomplete, or otherwise unsatisfactory. In these circumstances, consulting with legal counsel is advised because of the legal implications involved.

The accountant has no obligation to perform other compilation procedures with respect to the financial statements after the date of the compilation report unless new information comes to the accountant's attention. However, when information comes to the accountant's attention that would have been investigated had it been known during the course of the compilation, the accountant should try to determine whether the information is reliable and whether the facts existed at the date of the report. The accountant should discuss the matter with management and, as necessary, those charged with governance. The accountant should obtain additional or revised information if (1) the matter's nature and effect would have affected the accountant's report or the financial statements if the information had been known at the report date and included in the financial statements and (2) the accountant believes there are users or likely users of the financial statements that would find the information important.

If the accountant concludes that action should be taken to prevent further use of the report or financial statements, he or she should advise the client to appropriately disclose the newly discovered facts and their impact on the financial statements to current and likely financial statement users. If the effect of the subsequently discovered information can be readily determined, disclosure should consist of issuing revised financial information and a new report as soon as practicable, disclosing the reasons for the revision in a note to the financial statements and referring to them in the report when applicable. If issuance of subsequent financial statements is imminent, appropriate disclosure can be made in those statements rather than reissuing the earlier statements. If the effect of the subsequently discovered information on the financial statements cannot promptly be determined, appropriate disclosure consists of the client informing current or likely financial statement users that the statements should not be used and that revised financial statements and a new accountant's report will be issued as soon as practicable.

The accountant should take whatever steps he or she feels are necessary to ensure the specified disclosures have been made. If the client refuses to make the specified disclosures, the accountant should notify persons at the highest level of the entity of such refusal and that, without those disclosures, the accountant will have to take steps to prevent further use of the financial statements and accountant's report. Unless otherwise recommended by the accountant's attorney, the accountant should take the following steps in these circumstances:

1. Notify the client that the accountant's report must no longer be associated with the financial statements.

2. Notify regulatory agencies with jurisdiction over the client that the accountant's report should no longer be used.

3. Notify each person known to the accountant to be using the financial statements that the financial statements and accountant's report should no longer be used.

Any disclosure made by the accountant to those other than the client should include a description of the nature of the subsequently acquired information and its effect on the financial statements. Also, the information disclosed should be as precise and factual as possible without going beyond what is reasonably necessary to describe the nature and effects of the information and without commenting on anyone's conduct or motives.

Supplementary Information

The accountant should clearly indicate the degree of responsibility taken with respect to information presented for supplementary analysis purposes with the basic financial statements. If the accountant compiled both the financial statements and the supplementary information, the report should refer to the supplementary information or the accountant should issue a separate report on the supplementary information.

When the engagement does not include compiling supplementary information, there should be no chance that readers of the financial statements will misunderstand the responsibility of the accountant. Misunderstanding may be avoided by (1) the client clearly stating (in a preamble to the supplementary information) that the accountant has not compiled the supplementary information or (2) the accountant adding a separate paragraph stating that the supplementary information has not been compiled.

Communications with Management and Others

When information comes to the accountant's attention that fraud or an illegal act may have occurred, it should be brought to management's attention unless the matter deals with a clearly inconsequential illegal act. If the fraud or illegal act involves senior management, the accountant should report the matter to someone at a higher level in the entity, such as the owner-manager or those charged with governance. Communication may be written or oral, but if the communication is oral, it should be documented. If the matter involves an owner of the entity, the accountant should consider withdrawing from the engagement.

OBSERVATION: Although the SSARS only refer to fraud and illegal acts involving the owner of the business, if fraud and illegal acts involve senior management or those charged with governance, it may still be prudent for the accountant to consider resigning from the engagement.

The accountant is typically precluded by ethical and legal confidentiality obligations from disclosing information that fraud or an illegal act may have occurred to parties other than the client's management or those charged with governance. There are exceptions that may impose a duty to disclose such information, such as complying with legal and regulatory requirements, communicating with a successor accountant, or responding to a subpoena.

Change in Engagement Type

During, but before the completion of, an engagement, a client may ask to change the level of service the accountant is performing. If the request for change in services is from a lower level to a higher level—for example, from a review to an audit or from a compilation to a review—no problem arises. A problem does arise, however, when the change is to a lower level of service than that which was being provided. This request may be due to a change in the entity's circumstances affecting its requirements for an audit or review or a misunderstanding about the nature of services to be provided. Either of these reasons is typically considered a reasonable basis for requesting a change in the engagement. The request may also be due to a scope restriction, imposed by the client or by circumstance.

In considering whether a request to change to a compilation engagement is reasonable, the accountant should consider the client's reasons for the request, especially the implications of a scope restriction, the additional effort required to complete the audit or review engagement, and the estimated additional cost to complete the audit or review.

PLANNING AID REMINDER: There are situations that ordinarily preclude the accountant from issuing a compilation report. One such situation is when the accountant has been prohibited from corresponding with the entity's legal counsel in an audit.

If in the accountant's judgment a change to a lower level of service is acceptable, the accountant should perform the service in accordance with the standards applicable to the changed engagement. The accountant should make no mention in the report of the original engagement, any procedures accomplished for the original engagement, or any scope limitation that resulted in the changed service.

Practitioner's Aids

Exhibit AR 80-1 is an example of a standard engagement letter for a compilation.

EXHIBIT AR 80-1—COMPILATION ENGAGEMENT LETTER

[*Appropriate Salutation*]

This letter is to confirm our understanding of the terms and objectives of our engagement and the nature and limitations of the services we will provide.

We will perform the following services:

We will compile, from information you provide, the annual [*and interim, if applicable*] financial statements of ABC Company as of December 31, 20X1, and issue an accountant's report thereon in accordance with Statements on Standards for Accounting and Review Services (SSARSs) issued by the American Institute of Certified Public Accountants (AICPA).

The objective of a compilation is to assist you in presenting financial information in the form of financial statements. We will utilize information that is your representation without undertaking to obtain or provide any assurance that there are no material modifications that should be made to the financial statements in order for the statements to be in conformity with [*the applicable financial reporting framework (for example,* accounting principles generally accepted in the United States of America*)*].

You are responsible for

a. The preparation and fair presentation of the financial statements in accordance with [*the applicable financial reporting framework (for example,* accounting principles generally accepted in the United States of America*)*].

b. Designing, implementing, and maintaining internal control relevant to the preparation and fair presentation of the financial statements.

c. Preventing and detecting fraud.

d. Identifying and ensuring that the entity complies with the laws and regulations applicable to its activities.

e. Making all financial records and related information available to us.

We are responsible for conducting the engagement in accordance with SSARSs issued by the AICPA.

A compilation differs significantly from a review or an audit of financial statements. A compilation does not contemplate performing inquiry, analytical procedures, or other procedures performed in a review. Additionally, a compilation does not contemplate obtaining an understanding of the entity's internal control; assessing fraud risk; testing accounting records by obtaining sufficient appropriate evidence through inspection, observation, confirmation, or the examination of source documents (for example, cancelled checks or bank images); or other procedures ordinarily performed in an audit. Accordingly, we will not express an opinion or provide any assurance regarding the financial statements being compiled.

Our engagement cannot be relied upon to disclose errors, fraud, or illegal acts. However, we will inform the appropriate level of management of any material errors, and of any evidence or information that comes to our attention during the performance of our compilation procedures that fraud may have occurred. In addition, we will report to you any evidence or information that comes to our attention during the performance of our compilation procedures regarding illegal acts that may have occurred, unless they are clearly inconsequential.

[*If, during the period covered by the engagement letter, the accountant's independence is or will be impaired, insert the following:*

We are not independent with respect to ABC Company. We will disclose that we are not independent in our compilation report.]

If, for any reason, we are unable to complete the compilation of your financial statements, we will not issue a report on such statements as a result of this engagement.

Our fees for these services are $XXX (and include any other information regarding billings).

We will be pleased to discuss this letter with you at any time. If the foregoing is in accordance with your understanding, please sign the copy of this letter in the space provided and return it to us.

Sincerely yours,

[*Signature of Accountant*]

Acknowledged:

ABC Company

[*Signature of President*]

[*Date*]

Exhibit AR 80-2 is an example of a standard compilation report on financial statements prepared in accordance with accounting principles generally accepted in the United States of America.

EXHIBIT AR 80-2—STANDARD ACCOUNTANT'S COMPILATION REPORT

Accountant's Compilation Report

[*Appropriate Salutation*]

I (we) have compiled the accompanying balance sheet of ABC Company as of December 31, 20X1, and the related statements of income, retained earnings, and cash flows for the year then ended. I (we) have not audited or reviewed the accompanying financial statements and, accordingly, do not express an opinion or provide any assurance about whether the financial statements are in accordance with accounting principles generally accepted in the United States of America.

Management (owners) is (are) responsible for the preparation and fair presentation of the financial statements in accordance with accounting principles generally accepted in the United States of America and for designing, implementing, and maintaining internal control relevant to the preparation and fair presentation of the financial statements.

My (our) responsibility is to conduct the compilation in accordance with Statements on Standards for Accounting and Review Services issued by the American Institute of Certified Public Accountants. The objective of a compilation is to assist management in presenting financial information in the form of financial statements without undertaking to obtain or provide any assurance that there are no material modifications that should be made to the financial statements.

[*Signature of accounting firm or accountant, as appropriate*]

[*Date*]

Exhibit AR 80-3 is an example of a compilation report on financial statements prepared in accordance with accounting principles generally accepted in the United States of America when the accountant's independence has been impaired and the accountant decides not to disclose the reason for the independence impairment.

EXHIBIT AR 80-3—COMPILATION REPORT WHEN INDEPENDENCE IS IMPAIRED

Accountant's Compilation Report

[*Appropriate Salutation*]

I (we) have compiled the accompanying balance sheet of ABC Company as of December 31, 20X1, and the related statements of income, retained earnings, and cash flows for the year then ended. I (we) have not audited or reviewed the accompanying financial statements and, accordingly, do not express an opinion or provide any assurance about whether the financial statements are in accordance with accounting principles generally accepted in the United States of America.

Management (owners) is (are) responsible for the preparation and fair presentation of the financial statements in accordance with accounting principles generally accepted in the United States of America and for designing, implementing, and maintaining internal control relevant to the preparation and fair presentation of the financial statements.

My (our) responsibility is to conduct the compilation in accordance with Statements on Standards for Accounting and Review Services issued by the American Institute of Certified Public Accountants. The objective of a compilation is to assist management in presenting financial information in the form of financial statements without undertaking to obtain or provide any assurance that there are no material modifications that should be made to the financial statements.

I am (we are) not independent with respect to ABC Company.

[*Signature of accounting firm or accountant, as appropriate*]

[*Date*]

Exhibit AR 80-4 is an example of a compilation report on financial statements disclosing a departure from accounting principles generally accepted in the United States of America.

EXHIBIT AR 80-4—COMPILATION REPORT DISCLOSING A GAAP DEPARTURE

Accountant's Compilation Report

[*Appropriate Salutation*]

I (we) have compiled the accompanying balance sheet of ABC Company as of December 31, 20X1, and the related statements of income, retained earnings, and cash flows for the year then ended. I (we) have not audited or reviewed the accompanying financial statements and, accordingly, do not express an opinion or provide any assurance about whether the financial statements are in accordance with accounting principles generally accepted in the United States of America.

Management (owners) is (are) responsible for the preparation and fair presentation of the financial statements in accordance with accounting principles generally accepted in the United States of America and for designing, implementing, and maintaining internal control relevant to the preparation and fair presentation of the financial statements.

My (our) responsibility is to conduct the compilation in accordance with Statements on Standards for Accounting and Review Services issued by the American Institute of Certified Public Accountants. The objective of a compilation is to assist management in presenting financial information in the form of financial statements without undertaking to obtain or provide any assurance that there are no material modifications that should be made to the financial statements. During our compilation, I (we) did become aware of a departure (certain departures) from accounting principles generally accepted in the United States of America that is (are) described in the following paragraph.

As disclosed in Note X to the financial statements, accounting principles generally accepted in the United States of America require that land be stated at cost. Management has informed me (us) that the company has stated its land at appraised value and that, if accounting principles generally accepted in the United States of America had been followed, the land account and stockholders' equity would have been decreased by $500,000.

[*Signature of accounting firm or accountant, as appropriate*]

[*Date*]

EXHIBIT AR 80-5—COMPILATION PROGRAM

Use the following procedures as a guide for performing a compilation engagement. The compilation program is only a guide, and professional judgment should be exercised to determine how the procedures should be modified by revising or adding procedures to the compilation program. Before beginning compilation procedures, the accountant should have carefully evaluated whether this is a client the accountant wants to serve (i.e., apply client acceptance procedures).

Initial and date each procedure as it is completed. If the procedure is not relevant to this particular compilation engagement, place "N/A" (not applicable) in the space provided for an initial and cross-reference the omitted procedure to another workpaper that explains why the procedure was omitted.

Client Name: _____

Date of Financial Statements: _____

		Initials	Date	Workpaper Reference
1.	Acquire an adequate understanding of the accounting principles and practices of the client's industry.	_____	_____	_____
2.	Develop a general understanding of the nature of the client's business transactions.	_____	_____	_____
3.	Develop a general understanding of the stated qualifications of the client's accounting personnel.	_____	_____	_____
4.	Develop a general understanding of the accounting basis used to prepare the client's financial statements.	_____	_____	_____
5.	Develop a general understanding of the form and content of the client's financial statements.	_____	_____	_____
6.	Consider whether other professional services are needed in order to complete the compilation engagement.	_____	_____	_____
7.	Read the financial statements.	_____	_____	_____
8.	On the basis of information collected by using other compilation procedures and/or information that otherwise has come to our attention, consider whether additional or revised information must be obtained.	_____	_____	_____

	Initials	Date	Workpaper Reference

9.   Other compilation procedures used: _____

_____

_____

Reviewed By: _____

Date: _____

AR SECTION 90

REVIEW OF FINANCIAL STATEMENTS

Authoritative Pronouncements

SSARS-19—Compilation and Review Engagements

SSARS-20—Revised Applicability of Statements on Standards for Accounting and Review Services

Overview

Accountants are required to comply with the provisions of AR 90 when engaged to review financial statements. The exception to this requirement is when the accountant is reviewing interim financial information and the entity's latest annual financial statements have been audited by the accountant or a predecessor; the accountant has been engaged to audit the entity's current-year financial statements or he or she audited the prior financial statements and expects to be engaged to audit the current-year financial statements; and the entity prepares its interim financial information in accordance with the same financial reporting framework used to prepare its annual financial statements. When these conditions exist, the accountant is to follow the guidance in AU-C 930 (*Interim Financial Information*), not the guidance in AR 90, when performing the review engagement. SSARS-20 (Revised Applicability of Statement on Standards for Accounting and Review Services) additionally clarifies that AU-C 930 applies when the accountant has audited the entity's latest financial statements but the appointment of another accountant to audit the current-year financial statements is not effective prior to be beginning of the period covered by the review (this applies only when it is expected that the current-year financial statements will be audited).

PLANNING AID REMINDER: Under current standards, an accountant cannot perform a review engagement if his or her independence is impaired for any reason. However, due to the increased complexity of accounting standards, it has become increasingly difficult for an accountant to maintain his or her independence when reviewing the financial statements of a smaller company. In April 2009, ARSC issued an exposure draft of a proposed SSARS that ultimately became SSARS-19. One element of that proposed standard was a proposal to permit an accountant to review financial statements if the accountant's independence was impaired as a result of performing non-attest services that included designing or operating an aspect of management's system of internal control (internal control services). The responses to the proposal were mixed, which led ARSC to defer the issue for further discussion and deliberation. Since then, the AICPA's Professional Ethics Executive Committee (PEEC) has issued a proposed revision to Interpretation No. 101-3 (Performance of Nonattest Services) under Rule 101, Independence, that describe how certain internal control services would not impair the accountant's independence for purposes of a review engagement. The PEEC will be reviewing comments received on this proposal in 2012.

The objective of a review engagement is to express limited assurance that there are no material modifications that should be made to the financial statements in order for them to be in conformity with GAAP. A review is a level of service higher than a compilation because it results in an expression of limited assurance. The limited assurance is contained in a report by the accountant stating that he or she is not aware of any material modifications that should be made to the financial statements in order for them to be in conformity with GAAP. The accountant must perform sufficient inquiry and analytical procedures to give a reasonable basis for that conclusion, and the accountant must obtain representations from management for all financial statements and periods covered by his or her review report. These inquiries and analytical procedures are the major difference between a review and a compilation.

A review is a level of service lower than an audit of financial statements. It does not provide a basis for expressing an opinion under GAAS, because it does not require many of the significant procedures required in an audit.

A review does not contemplate obtaining an understanding of the entity's internal control, assessing fraud risks, tests of accounting records by obtaining sufficient appropriate evidence, or other procedures ordinarily performed in an audit. Therefore a review provides only limited assurance that there are no material modifications that should be made to the financial statements for them to conform with GAAP.

A review engagement may involve reporting on all the basic financial statements or on only one financial statement, such as a balance sheet or a statement of income. A review may not include reporting on financial statements that omit substantially all disclosures required by GAAP, unless such omissions are completely disclosed in the accountant's report. This obviously is not a practical alternative.

Establishing an Understanding

The accountant should establish an understanding with management and, when applicable, with those charged with governance regarding the services to be performed for review engagements and document this understanding with a written engagement letter with management. The understanding should include the engagement objectives, management and accountant's responsibilities, and engagement limitations, incorporating the following matters:

- A review's objective is to obtain limited assurance that there are no material modifications that should be made to the financial statements.

- Management is responsible for preparing and presenting the financial statements in accordance with the applicable financial reporting framework.

- Management is responsible for designing, implementing, and maintaining internal control relevant to the preparation and fair presentation of the financial statements.

- Management is responsible for preventing and detecting fraud.

- Management is responsible for identifying and ensuring the entity's compliance with applicable laws and regulations.

- Management is responsible for making all financial records and related information available to the accountant.

- Management will provide the accountant with a letter confirming certain representations made during the review at the engagement's conclusion.

- The accountant is responsible for conducting the engagement in accordance with SSARSs issued by the AICPA.

- A review primarily involves applying analytical procedures to management's financial data and making inquiries of company management.

- A review is substantially less in scope than an audit of financial statements; therefore, the accountant will not express an opinion regarding the financial statements as a whole.

- The engagement cannot be relied upon to disclose errors, fraud, or illegal acts.

- The accountant will inform management of any material errors and any evidence or information coming to the accountant's attention during the review that fraud or an illegal act may have occurred. Illegal acts that are clearly inconsequential need not be reported and an understanding may be established with the entity in advance regarding the nature of any such matters to be communicated.

Exhibit AR 90-1 provides an example engagement letter for financial statement reviews.

Other matters may also be included in the understanding with management and, when applicable, those charged with governance. These matters include:

- Fees and billings

- Conditions under which access to review documents may be granted to others

- Additional services to be provided relating to regulatory requirements

- Any arrangements or limitation of the accountant's or client's liability, such as indemnifying the accountant for liability based on knowing misrepresentations from management where permitted

---

PLANNING AID REMINDER: Liability limitation agreements such as those described above may be restricted or prohibited by regulators. Also, since accountants sometimes provide services in addition to the review as part of the engagement, it is important to document the scope of services to be provided as well as the division of responsibility between management and the accountant.

Additional matters should be addressed in the engagement letter if circumstances apply, including that there may be material departures from the applicable financial reporting framework and that any effects of those departures may not be disclosed as well as reference to any supplementary information.

Review Performance Requirements

In a review engagement, the accountant is required to perform procedures to accumulate review evidence that provides a reasonable basis for obtaining limited assurance that no material modifications should be made to the financial statements in order for them to be in conformity with the applicable financial reporting framework. These procedures should take into account the accountant's understanding of the client's industry and knowledge of the client. Analytical procedures and inquiry ordinarily provide the accountant with the evidence necessary to obtain limited assurance; however, if the accountant needs additional evidence to obtain limited assurance that the financial statements are not materially misstated, he or she should perform additional procedures.

Knowledge of the industry

The accountant should have an understanding of the client's industry and the accounting principles and practices used in the industry. This requirement does not prevent the accountant from accepting an engagement for an industry in which he or she has no previous experience, but it does mean that he or she is responsible for obtaining the required level of knowledge. CPAs may obtain that knowledge through, for example, the study of AICPA industry guides, industry publications, and financial statements of entities in the industry.

Knowledge of the client

The accountant's knowledge of the client should be sufficient to assist in determining the specific nature, timing, and extent of review procedures to be performed. The accountant should obtain an understanding of the client's business, including knowledge of the client's organization; operating characteristics; the nature of its assets, liabilities, revenues, and expenses; and material transactions with related parties. The accountant should also obtain an understanding of the accounting principles and practices used by the client in measuring, recognizing, recording, and disclosing all significant accounts and disclosures in the financial statements, remaining alert to any unusual accounting policies and procedures that come to his or her attention.

The required level of understanding of a client's business may be obtained by:

- Previous or current experience in providing the client services such as audits, tax return preparation, compiling of financial statements, and consultation on various financial matters

- Inquiry of client personnel

- Previous or current experience with other entities in the same industry as the client

Designing and Performing Review Procedures

Review procedures should be focused on areas where the accountant believes there are increased risks of misstatements. However, during the performance of review procedures, the accountant's understanding of areas of increased risk may be modified. Exhibit AR 90-4 provides an example of a review program and Exhibit AR 90-5 provides a checklist that can serve as a guide in performing review procedures.

Analytical Procedures

Effective analysis of the results of analytical procedures generally requires an understanding of financial and nonfinancial relationships, knowledge of the client and its industry, and an understanding of the purposes and limitations of analytical procedures. Analytical procedures to be performed for the purpose of a review should be designed to detect relationships and individual items that appear to be unusual and that may indicate a material misstatement. Analytical procedures may be performed at the financial statement or detailed account level and the nature, timing, and extent of the procedures used are a matter of professional judgment. Analytical procedures involve comparing expectations developed by the accountant to recorded amounts or ratios developed from those recorded amounts. An accountant cannot perform effective analytical procedures without first developing expectations related to the results of the procedures. The accountant develops expectations using his or her knowledge of the client and its industry to identify plausible relationships that are reasonably expected to exist. Sources of information used to develop these expectations include:

- Financial information for comparable prior periods, considering known changes
- Anticipated results; for example, budgets, forecasts, or extrapolations from interim or annual data
- Relationships among financial information elements within the period
- Information regarding the industry in which the client operates
- Relationships of financial information with relevant nonfinancial information (e.g., airline revenue to seat miles flown)

The accountant should investigate the results of analytical procedures that are inconsistent with other relevant information or that differ significantly from expected values by inquiring of management and performing other necessary procedures. Although it is not required, the accountant may need to corroborate management's responses to inquiries with other evidence when management is unable to provide an explanation or the explanation along with other evidence obtained is not considered adequate.

Examples of financial statements that would be expected to conform to a predictable relationship are

- Sales and accounts receivable
- Sales and cost of sales
- Interest expense and debt

- Sales and commissions and freight out
- Depreciation and property (also maintenance and repairs)

Moreover, the accountant should consider adjustments made to the financial statements in previous periods, because they might affect his or her judgment on the results of other analytical procedures. In addition, the accountant should consider whether similar adjustments should be made during the current period.

The following approach is appropriate for performing analytical procedures:

1. 1. Identify immaterial account balances or classes of transactions. Normally, apply no analytical procedures to them; however, the accountant should consider whether a zero or minimal balance makes sense for the client. For example, the lack of no interest expense does not make sense if the client carries interest-bearing debt, or the lack of interest income is inconsistent with interest-bearing cash accounts or certain investments.

2. Identify account balances or classes of transactions to which other accounting services (bookkeeping or payroll services, for example) have been applied. The accountant should consider the evidence that he or she already has and whether any material errors are likely to remain. If the accountant believes he or she already has sufficient evidence for those account balances or classes of transactions to reduce the risk of material misstatement to a moderate level, he or she should not apply analytical procedures to them.

3. For the remaining account balances and classes of transactions, the accountant should develop expectations (for example, using historical trends adjusted for known changes) for them and document those expectations when those expectations are not otherwise readily determinable from the documentation of the work performed. Exhibit AR 90-8 illustrates how an accountant might document expectations in a review engagement.

4. The accountant should consider how close the existing account balance or class of transactions comes to the expectation developed in item 3. If the differences are small, no additional evidence is needed.

5. If the differences are large, material errors could exist. The accountant should inquire about valid business reasons for the difference. If the results of inquiry are plausible and agree with other evidence, it might be that no additional evidence is needed.

6. If additional evidence is needed, the accountant should apply additional procedures or obtain other suitable evidence. The accountant should document any additional procedures performed in response to significant differences between the expectations and recorded amounts.

Exhibit AR 90-7 lists potential analytical procedures that may be used in a review engagement.

Inquiries and Other Review Procedures

The accountant should consider performing the following:

- Make inquiries of management with responsibility for financial and accounting matters about the following (the accountant may also direct inquiries to those charged with governance and others within the entity, if appropriate):
  - Whether the financial statements have been prepared in conformity with the applicable financial reporting framework
  - The entity's accounting principles and practices and the methods followed in applying them and the entity's procedures for recording, classifying, and summarizing transactions and disclosing information in the financial statements
  - Unusual or complex situations that may have an effect on the financial statements
  - Significant transactions occurring or recognized near the end of the reporting period
  - The status of uncorrected misstatements identified during the previous engagement
  - Questions that have arisen during the application of review procedures
  - Events subsequent to the date of the financial statements that could have a material effect on the financial statements
  - Knowledge of any fraud or suspected fraud affecting the entity involving management or others where the fraud could have a material effect on the financial statements
  - Significant journal entries and other adjustments
  - Communications from regulatory agencies
- Inquire about actions taken at stockholder meetings, board of director and committee meetings, or comparable meetings that may affect the financial statements
- Read the financial statements to consider whether they appear to conform with the applicable financial reporting framework
- Obtain reports from any other accountants engaged to audit or review the financial statements of significant components of the reporting entity, its subsidiaries, and other investees

In addition, the CPA might have identified other questions during the review engagement. The accountant must use professional judgment to determine the extent of inquiries required, and the inquiries must be sufficiently comprehensive to cover all significant amounts and matters. When determining the extent and type of inquiries, the accountant should consider the following items:

- Nature and significance of an item
- Probability of misstatement
- Extent to which management's judgment enters into the determination of a particular item

- Knowledge obtained during a previous or the current engagement
- Qualifications of accounting personnel
- Deficiencies in financial data or the accounting system

Although the accountant is not required to corroborate management's responses with other evidence, he or she should consider the reasonableness and consistency of management's responses given the results of other review procedures and his or her knowledge of the client and its industry. Exhibit AR 90-6 provides a checklist of possible inquiries.

Incorrect, Incomplete, or Otherwise Unsatisfactory Information

The performance of a review does not provide assurance that the accountant will become aware of all significant matters, nor does it provide assurance that inaccuracies or the omission of necessary disclosures will come to his or her attention. However, if the accountant becomes aware during the performance of review procedures that information is incorrect, incomplete or otherwise unsatisfactory, he or she should request management consider the effects of these matters and communicate its findings to him or her. The accountant should then consider management's findings and any effect they may have on the review report.

If the accountant believes the financial statements may be materially misstated, he or she should perform any additional procedures necessary to obtain limited assurance that material modifications to the financial statements are not needed for the statements to be in conformity with the applicable financial reporting framework. Such other procedures may include:

- Further inquiry of responsible persons
- Other accounting services
- Consultation with the client on matters such as the proper accounting principles to be applied in recording transactions or the proper treatment of transactions for tax purposes

When the CPA concludes that additional review procedures should be performed, the circumstances surrounding the questionable information should dictate the degree of corroborative evidence that should be collected. In general, the decision to collect additional evidence does not mean that the level of assurance for a particular item has increased from that of a review engagement (limited assurance) to that of an audit engagement (reasonable assurance). For example, if the CPA is concerned with the nature of a large nontrade note receivable that is presented as a current asset, it does not mean that the CPA must confirm the receivable with the outside party. An appropriate explanation by the client may satisfy the CPA that the note is properly classified in the balance sheet. If the expanded review procedures do not resolve the accountant's concerns, the accountant should consider whether he or she can perform a review.

If the accountant determines that the financial statements are materially misstated, the guidance regarding departures from an applicable financial reporting framework should be followed and, depending on what the accountant considers necessary, he or she should either modify the report or, after consulting counsel, withdraw from the engagement.

Management Representations

The accountant is required to obtain written representations from management for all financial statements and periods covered by the accountant's review report. The specific representations obtained will depend on the engagement circumstances and the nature and basis of presentation of the financial statements. The accountant should request that management provide a written representation related to matters specific to the entity's business or industry as well as to the following matters:

- Management's acknowledgement of its responsibility for preparing and fairly presenting the financial statements
- Management's belief that the financial statements are fairly presented
- Management's acknowledgement of its responsibility for designing, implementing, and maintaining internal control relevant to the preparation and fair presentation of the financial statements
- Management's acknowledgement of its responsibility to prevent and detect fraud
- Knowledge of any fraud or suspected fraud affecting the entity involving management or others where the fraud could have a material effect on the financial statements
- Management's full and truthful response to all inquiries
- Completeness of information
- Information concerning subsequent events

FRAUD POINTER: Given the importance of communications from employees and outside parties in detecting fraud (i.e., tips), the accountant should have management include in its representation letter that no such tips from employees or outside parties have been received.

Exhibit AR 90-2 provides an example management representation letter for financial statement reviews.

In certain situations, the accountant should consider obtaining an updating representation letter from management. One such situation is when a predecessor auditor is requested to reissue a report on the financial statements of a prior period that are to be presented on a comparative basis with reviewed financial statements of a subsequent period. In this case, the updating representation letter should state whether any information has come to management's attention that would cause management to believe any of its previous representations should be modified and whether any events have occurred subsequent to the balance sheet date of the latest financial statements that would require adjustment to or disclosure in those financial statements.

Management's representations should be made as of the date of the accountant's review report. The accountant does not need to possess the management representation letter as of the date of the accountant's review report as long as management has acknowledged they will sign the letter without modification and it is received before release of the report. The representation letter should be addressed to the accountant and signed by members of management the accountant believes are responsible for and knowledgeable about the matters covered in the representation letter, which typically includes the chief executive officer, chief financial officer, or others with equivalent positions in the entity.

OBSERVATION: The accountant must obtain a representation letter for each review engagement that results in the issuance of a review report. For example, if the accountant reviews and reports on quarterly interim financial statements, he or she must obtain a representation letter for each of the four separate and distinct review engagements.

Review Engagement Documentation

Documentation should be prepared for each engagement in sufficient detail to provide a clear understanding of the work, including the nature, timing, extent, and results of review procedures performed; the review evidence obtained and its source; and the conclusions reached. Documentation provides support for the assertion in the review report that the review was performed in accordance with SSARS and for the conclusion that the accountant is not aware of any material modifications that should be made to the financial statements in order for them to be in conformity with the applicable financial reporting framework.

The form, content, and extent of documentation varies depending on the engagement circumstances and the accountant's professional judgment. Documentation should include the following:

- The engagement letter documenting the understanding with the client

- Analytical procedures performed, including the expectations and the factors considered in developing expectations, results of comparing expectations to ratios or recorded amounts, and management's responses to inquiries about relationships that are inconsistent or that differ significantly from expectations

- Any additional review procedures performed in response to significant unexpected differences found in analytical procedures and the results of those additional procedures

- Significant matters covered in the accountant's inquiry procedures and the responses

- Any findings or issues the accountant finds significant in his or her professional judgment

- Significant unusual matters considered during performance of review procedures and the results of this consideration

- Written or oral communications to management regarding fraud or illegal acts that come to the accountant's attention

- The representation letter

In addition to review documentation, the accountant may provide support through written documentation in other engagement or quality control files or through oral explanations. However, oral explanations alone do not provide sufficient support for the accountant's work or conclusions.

Financial Statement Reporting

Reviewed financial statements should be accompanied by a written report in order to prevent misinterpretation of the degree of responsibility the accountant is assuming regarding the financial statements. The following are the basic elements of the accountant's report:

- *Title* The title should clearly indicate it is the accountant's review report and include the word "independent"

- *Addressee* The report should be addressed appropriately

- *Introductory paragraph* This paragraph should identify the entity whose financial statements have been reviewed and the financial statements that have been reviewed; state that the financial statements have been reviewed; specify the date or period covered by the financial statements; include a statement that a review primarily involves management inquiries and applying analytical procedures to management's financial data; and include a statement that a review is substantially less in scope than an audit and, therefore, the accountant does not express an opinion about the financial statements as a whole

- *Management's responsibility for the financial statements and for internal control over financial reporting* A statement that management is responsible for preparing and fairly presenting the financial statements in accordance with the applicable financial reporting framework and for designing, implementing, and maintaining internal control relevant to the preparation and fair presentation of the financial statements

- *Accountant's responsibility* A statement that the accountant is responsible for conducting the review in accordance with SSARS issued by the AICPA, that those standards require the accountant to perform procedures to obtain limited assurance that there are no material modifications that should be made to the statements, and that the accountant believes the results of those procedures provide a reasonable basis for the report

- *Results of engagement* A statement by the accountant that he or she is unaware of any material modifications needed to the financial statements for them to be in accordance with the applicable financial reporting framework (i.e., negative assurance), other than those modifications that the accountant indicates in the report

- *Accountant's signature* The accounting firm's or accountant's manually signed or printed signature

- *Date of the report* The review report date should not be earlier than the date the accountant has obtained sufficient review evidence to provide a reasonable basis for the conclusion that limited assurance has been obtained that no material modifications should be made to the financial statements in order for them to be in conformity with the applicable financial reporting framework

Any additional procedures that may have been performed should not be described in the accountant's review report, and no reference should be made to the consistent application of GAAP.

Exhibit AR 90-3 provides an example of a standard accountant's review report.

Each page of the reviewed financial statements should contain a reference such as "See Independent Accountant's Review Report." The accountant may issue a review report on one financial statement and not on other related financial statements if the scope of his or her inquiry and analytical procedures has not been restricted. Financial statements prepared in accordance with an OCBOA are not considered appropriate in form unless they include a description of the OCBOA, including a summary of significant accounting policies and a description of the primary differences from GAAP, and informative disclosures similar to those required by GAAP if the financial statements contain items similar to those in financial statements prepared in accordance with GAAP.

A review is incomplete and does not provide a sufficient basis for issuing a review report if the accountant is unable to perform the necessary inquiries and analytical procedures or the client does not provide the accountant with a representation letter. In these circumstances, the accountant should consider whether it is appropriate to issue a compilation report on the financial statements. If the limitation is due to a scope restriction, the accountant should consider whether that restriction is imposed by the client or by circumstance. If the limitation is due to lack of a representation letter, the accountant is ordinarily precluded from issuing a compilation report.

Emphasis of a Matter

The accountant may use his or her discretion to add an emphasis-of-matter paragraph regarding a matter disclosed in the financial statements. This information should be presented in a separate paragraph in the report.

OBSERVATION: Emphasized matters may include uncertainties, that the entity is part of a larger entity, that the entity had significant transactions with related parties, unusually important subsequent events, or accounting matters not involving a change in accounting principle that affect the comparability of the financial statements across periods.

Departures from the Applicable Financial Reporting Framework

The accountant may become aware of material departures from the applicable financial reporting framework (including inadequate disclosure) and, if the financial statements are not revised, should consider the effects on the report. If the accountant concludes that modification of the standard report is adequate to disclose the departure, a separate paragraph should be included in the report disclosing the departure and its effects on the financial statements if the effects have been determined by management or are known based on the accountant's procedures. If management has not determined the effects, the accountant is not required to determine them so long as the report states that such a determination has not been made.

If the accountant believes modification of the report is not adequate to indicate the financial statement deficiencies, he or she should withdraw from the engagement and not perform any further services regarding those financial statements.

PLANNING AID REMINDER: The accountant may wish to consult with legal counsel when withdrawing from an engagement.

If the accountant decides that a modification to the review report is sufficient to disclose the departure from GAAP, the third and fourth paragraphs of the report should read as follows:

> Based on our review, with the exception of the matter described in the following paragraph, we are not aware of any material modifications that should be made to the accompanying financial statements in order for them to be in conformity with generally accepted accounting principles.
>
> As disclosed in Note X to the financial statements, generally accepted accounting principles require that inventory cost consist of material, labor, and overhead. Management has informed us that the inventory of finished goods in the accompanying financial statements is stated at material and direct labor cost only. The effects of this departure from generally accepted accounting principles on financial position, results of operations, and cash flows have not been determined by management.

Restricted Use Reports

A general use report is not restricted to specified parties and is normally used in financial statement reports prepared in conformity with an applicable financial reporting framework. However, the accountant is not precluded from restricting the use of any report. A restricted use report is intended only for one or more specified third parties. A report's use should be restricted when it is based on measurement or disclosure criteria contained in contractual agreements or regulatory provisions that are not in conformity with an applicable financial reporting framework.

If a single combined report is used covering subject matter requiring a restriction on use and subject matter not requiring a restriction on use, the report's use should be restricted to the specified parties. A separate restricted use report may be included in a document also containing a general use report when required by law or regulation. In this situation, both reports maintain their intended use.

The accountant should consider informing the client that restricted use reports are not intended for distribution to nonspecified parties regardless of whether a separate general use report is contained in the same document. However, the accountant is not responsible for controlling the report's distribution. Therefore, a restricted use report should alert readers to its intended use by indicating that it is not intended to and should not be used by anyone other than the specified parties.

A restricted use report should contain a separate paragraph at the end of the report including the following:

- A statement that the report is intended solely for the information and use of specified parties

- Identification of the specified parties included in the restricted use (these parties may be listed in the review report or the report may refer to a listing elsewhere in the document)

- A statement that the report is not intended to be and should not be used by anyone other than the specified parties

Entity's Ability to Continue as a Going Concern

The accountant may become aware during a review engagement that there is uncertainty about the entity's ability to continue as a going concern for a reasonable period of time, not exceeding one year beyond the date of the reviewed financial statements. In these situations, the accountant should request that management consider possible effects of the going concern uncertainty on the financial statements, including the need for disclosure and consider the reasonableness of management's conclusions and the adequacy of any related disclosures.

If the accountant concludes that management's conclusions are not reasonable or that disclosure is inadequate, he or she should follow the guidance regarding departures from an applicable financial reporting framework and, depending on what the accountant considers necessary, either modify the report or withdraw from the engagement. The accountant may emphasize an uncertainty about the entity's ability to continue as a going concern in the report as long as the uncertainty is disclosed in the financial statements.

Exhibit AR 90-9 contains guidance that might be helpful when evaluating an entity's ability to continue as a going concern.

Subsequent Events

Whether during performance of review procedures or subsequent to the date of the review report but prior to the report's release, the accountant may become aware that a subsequent event with a material effect on the reviewed financial statements has occurred. In this situation, the accountant should request that management consider the possible effects on the financial statements and any applicable related disclosures. If the accountant determines the subsequent event is not adequately accounted for in the financial statements or disclosed in the notes, the guidance regarding departures from an applicable financial reporting framework should be followed and, depending on what the accountant considers necessary, he or she should either modify the report or withdraw for the engagement.

OBSERVATION: Two types of subsequent events require consideration by management. The first type consists of events that provide additional evidence with respect to conditions that existed at the date of the financial statements. The financial statements should be adjusted for any changes in estimates resulting from the use of such evidence. The second type consists of events that provide evidence with respect to conditions that did not exist at the date of the balance sheet being reported on but that arose subsequent to that date. These events should not result in adjustments of the financial statements but rather be reflected via a note to the financial statements.

Subsequent Discovery of Facts Existing at the Date of the Report

The accountant may become aware of facts existing at the date of the report subsequent to that date that, had he or she been aware of them, may have caused him or her to believe the information supplied by the entity was incorrect, incomplete, or otherwise unsatisfactory. In these circumstances, consulting with legal counsel is advised because of the legal implications involved.

The accountant has no obligation to perform other review procedures with respect to the financial statements after the date of the review report unless new information comes to the accountant's attention. However, when information comes to the accountant's attention that would have been investigated had it been known during the course of the review, the accountant should try to determine whether the information is reliable and whether the facts existed at the date of the report. The accountant should discuss the matter with management and, as necessary, those charged with governance. The accountant should perform the additional procedures necessary to obtain limited assurance that no material modifications should be made to the financial statements in order for the statements to be in conformity with the applicable financial reporting framework if (1) the matter's nature and effect would have affected the accountant's report or the financial statements if the information had been known at the report date and included in the financial statements and (2) the accountant believes there are users or likely users of the financial statements that would find the information important. Consideration should be given to the time elapsed since the financial statements were issued.

If the accountant concludes that action should be taken to prevent further use of the report or financial statements, he or she should advise the client to appropriately disclose the newly discovered facts and their impact on the financial statements to current and likely financial statement users. If the effect of the subsequently discovered information can be readily determined, disclosure should consist of issuing revised financial information and a new report as soon as practicable, disclosing the reasons for the revision in a note to the financial statements, and referring to them in the report when applicable. If issuance of subsequent financial statements is imminent, appropriate disclosure can be made in those statements rather than reissuing the earlier statements because disclosure would not be delayed. If the effect of the subsequently discovered information on the financial statements cannot promptly be determined, appropriate disclosure consists of the client informing current or likely financial statement users that the statements should not be used and that revised financial statements and a new accountant's report will be issued as soon as practicable.

The accountant should take whatever steps he or she feels are necessary to ensure the specified disclosures have been made. If the client refuses to make the specified disclosures, the accountant should notify persons at the highest level of the entity of such refusal and that without those disclosures the accountant will have to take steps to prevent further use of the financial statements and his or her report. The accountant's knowledge that people exist who are using the financial statements and accountant's report and would attach importance to the information as well as the accountant's ability to communicate with these people will affect the steps he or she is able to take. Unless otherwise recommended by the accountant's attorney, the accountant should take the following steps in these circumstances as applicable:

1. Notify the client that the accountant's report must no longer be associated with the financial statements

2. Notify regulatory agencies with jurisdiction over the client that the accountant's report should no longer be used

3. Notify each person known to the accountant to be using the financial statements that the financial statements and accountant's report should no longer be used

Any disclosure made by the accountant to those other than the client should include a description of the nature of the subsequently acquired information and its effect on the financial statements. Also, the information disclosed should be as precise and factual as possible without going beyond what is reasonably necessary to describe the nature and effects of the information and without commenting on anyone's conduct or motives. If the client has not cooperated with the accountant, he or she may disclose this lack of cooperation in attempting to substantiate information coming to his or her attention and that, if the information is true, the accountant believes the review report must no longer be used or associated with the financial statements.

Supplementary Information

The accountant should clearly indicate the degree of responsibility taken with respect to information presented for supplementary analysis purposes with the basic financial statements. This indication should state that other data accompanying the financial statements are presented only for additional analysis and either have been subjected to the procedures applied in reviewing the financial statements and the accountant did not become aware of any material modifications that should be made to the data, or that the data have not been subjected to the procedures applied in reviewing the financial statements but were compiled from management's information without audit or review and the accountant does not express an opinion or provide any assurance on the data.

Communications with Management and Others

When information comes to the accountant's attention that fraud or an illegal act may have occurred, it should be brought to management's attention unless the matter deals with a clearly inconsequential illegal act. If the fraud or illegal act involves senior management, the accountant should report the matter to someone at a higher level in the entity, such as the owner-manager or those charged with governance. Communication may be written or oral, but if the communication is oral, it should be documented. In addition, fraud or an illegal act involving management should lead the accountant to reconsider his or her preliminary judgment regarding management integrity. If the matter involves an owner of the entity, the accountant should consider withdrawing from the engagement. The accountant should also consider consulting with his or her legal counsel whenever information comes to his or her attention that fraud or an illegal act may have occurred.

The accountant is typically precluded by ethical and legal confidentiality obligations from disclosing information that fraud or an illegal act may have occurred to parties other than the client's management or those charged with governance. There are exceptions that may impose a duty to disclose such information, such as complying with legal and regulatory requirements, communicating with a successor accountant, or responding to a subpoena.

Change in Engagement Type

An accountant may be requested to change from an audit to a review engagement before completion of the audit. This request may be due to a change in the entity's circumstances affecting its requirements for an audit or a misunderstanding about the nature of services to be provided. Either of these reasons is typically considered a reasonable basis for requesting a change in the engagement.

In considering whether a request to change to a review engagement is reasonable, the accountant should consider the client's reasons for the request, especially the implications of a scope restriction whether imposed by client or circumstance, evaluating the possibility that information affected by the scope restriction could be incorrect, incomplete, or otherwise unsatisfactory. Also, if audit procedures are substantially complete or the cost to complete the additional procedures is insignificant, the accountant should consider the reasonableness of accepting a change in the engagement.

A review report may not be issued if the review procedures deemed necessary by the accountant have not been completed to his or her satisfaction. In such situations, there is no adequate basis for expressing the limited assurance contemplated by a review. Moreover, the circumstances may be such that the accountant may not issue a compilation report. Information the accountant obtains during the performance of an incomplete review cannot be ignored if the engagement is reduced to a compilation.

When determining whether to issue a compilation report where a review is incomplete, the accountant should consider the same points that would be considered for an engagement that is changed from a higher service level to a lower service level.

Review standards require that an accountant perform whatever additional procedures he or she deems necessary under the circumstances. Additional procedures may include corresponding with the client's legal counsel or confirming balances and transactions. If the client will not agree to such correspondence or will not sign a representation letter, there is a scope limitation, which is usually considered to be of such significance that the accountant should not issue a review report.

Practitioner's Aids

Exhibit AR 90-1 is an example of a standard engagement letter for a review.

EXHIBIT AR 90-1—REVIEW ENGAGEMENT LETTER

[*Appropriate Salutation*]

This letter is to confirm our understanding of the terms and objectives of our engagement and the nature and limitations of the services we will provide.

We will perform the following services:

We will review the financial statements of ABC Company as of December 31, 20X8, and issue an accountant's report thereon in accordance with Statements on Standards for Accounting and Review Services (SSARSs) issued by the American Institute of Certified Public Accountants (AICPA).

The objective of a review is to obtain limited assurance that there are no material modifications that should be made to the financial statements in order for the statements to be in conformity with [*the applicable financial reporting framework (for example,* accounting principles generally accepted in the United States of America*)*].

You are responsible for

a. The preparation and fair presentation of the financial statements in accordance with [*the applicable financial reporting framework (for example,* accounting principles generally accepted in the United States of America*)*].

b. Designing, implementing, and maintaining internal control relevant to the preparation and fair presentation of the financial statements.

c. Preventing and detecting fraud.

d. Identifying and ensuring that the entity complies with the laws and regulations applicable to its activities.

e. Making all financial records and related information available to us.

f. Providing us, at the conclusion of the engagement, with a letter that confirms certain representations made during the review.

We are responsible for conducting the engagement in accordance with SSARS issued by the AICPA.

A review includes primarily applying analytical procedures to your financial data and making inquiries of company management. A review is substantially less in scope than an audit, the objective of which is the expression of an opinion regarding the financial statements as a whole. A review does not contemplate obtaining an understanding of the entity's internal control; assessing fraud risk; testing accounting records by obtaining sufficient appropriate audit evidence through inspection, observation, confirmation, or the examination of source documents (for example, cancelled checks or bank images); or other procedures ordinarily performed in an audit. Accordingly, we will not express an opinion regarding the financial statements as a whole.

Our engagement cannot be relied upon to disclose errors, fraud, or illegal acts. However, we will inform the appropriate level of management of any material errors and any evidence or information that comes to our attention during the performance of our review procedures that fraud may have occurred. In addition, we will report to you any evidence or information that comes to our attention during the performance of our review procedures regarding illegal acts that may have occurred, unless they are clearly inconsequential.

If, for any reason, we are unable to complete the review of your financial statements, we will not issue a report on such statements as a result of this engagement.

Our fees for these services [. . .].

We will be pleased to discuss this letter with you at any time. If the foregoing is in accordance with your understanding, please sign the copy of this letter in the space provided and return it to us.

Sincerely yours,

[*Signature of Accountant*]

Acknowledged:

ABC Company

[*Signature of President*]

[*Date*]

Exhibit AR 90-2 is an example management representation letter for financial statement reviews.

EXHIBIT AR 90-2—MANAGEMENT REPRESENTATION LETTER

[*Date (The date of the representation letter should not be earlier than the date of the accountant's review report)*]

To [*the Accountant*]

We are providing this letter in connection with your review of the [*identification of financial statements*] of [*name of entity*] as of [*dates (for example,* December 31, 20X1 and December 31, 20X2*)*] and for the [*periods of review (for example,* for the years then ended*)*] for the purpose of obtaining limited assurance that there are no material modifications that should be made to the financial statements in order for the statements to be in conformity with [*the applicable financial reporting framework (for example,* accounting principles generally accepted in the United States of America*)*]. We confirm that we are responsible for the fair presentation of the financial statements in accordance with [*the applicable* *financial reporting framework*] and the selection and application of the accounting policies.

Certain representations in this letter are described as being limited to matters that are material. Items are considered material, regardless of size, if they involve an omission or misstatement of accounting information that, in the light of surrounding circumstances, makes it probable that the judgment of a reasonable person using the information would be changed or influenced by the omission or misstatement.

We confirm, to the best of our knowledge and belief (as of [*the date of the accountant's review report*]), the following representations made to you during your review:

1. The financial statements referred to previously are fairly presented in accordance with [*the applicable financial reporting framework (for example,* accounting principles generally accepted in the United States of America*)*].

2. We have made the following available to you

    a. Financial records and related data.

    b. Minutes of the meetings of stockholders, directors, and committees of directors, or summaries of actions of recent meetings for which minutes have not yet been prepared.

3. No material transactions exist that have not been properly recorded in the accounting records underlying the financial statements.

4. We acknowledge our responsibility for the preparation and fair presentation of the financial statements in accordance with [*the applicable financial reporting framework (for example,* accounting principles generally accepted in the United States of America*)*].

5. We acknowledge our responsibility for designing, implementing, and maintaining internal control relevant to the preparation and fair presentation of the financial statements.

6. We acknowledge our responsibility to prevent and detect fraud.

7. We have no knowledge of any fraud or suspected fraud affecting the entity involving management or others where the fraud could have a material effect on the financial statements, including any communications received from employees, former employees, or others.

8. We have no plans or intentions that may materially affect the carrying amounts or classification of assets and liabilities.

9. No material losses exist (such as from obsolete inventory or purchase or sales commitments) that have not been properly accrued or disclosed in the financial statements.

10. None of the following exist:

    a. Violations or possible violations of laws or regulations, whose effects should be considered for disclosure in the financial statements or as a basis for recording a loss contingency

    b. Unasserted claims or assessments that our lawyer has advised us are probable of assertion that must be disclosed in accordance with Financial Accounting Standards Board's

(FASB) *Accounting Standards Codification* (ASC) 450 (Contingencies).

    c. Other material liabilities or gain or loss contingencies that are required to be accrued or disclosed by FASB ASC 450 (Contingencies).

11. The company has satisfactory title to all owned assets, and no liens or encumbrances on such assets exist, nor has any asset been pledged as collateral, except as disclosed to you and reported in the financial statements.

12. We have complied with all aspects of contractual agreements that would have a material effect on the financial statements in the event of noncompliance.

13. The following have been properly recorded or disclosed in the financial statements:

    a. Related-party transactions, including sales, purchases, loans, transfers, leasing arrangements, and guarantees, and amounts receivable from or payable to related parties.

    b. Guarantees, whether written or oral, under which the company is contingently liable.

    c. Significant estimates and material concentrations known to management that are required to be disclosed in accordance with the FASB ASC 275 (Risks and Uncertainties).

    [*Add additional representations that are unique to the entity's business or industry.*]

14. We are in agreement with the adjusting journal entries you have recommended, and they have been posted to the company's accounts (if applicable).

15. To the best of our knowledge and belief, no events have occurred subsequent to the balance-sheet date and through the date of this letter that would require adjustment to or disclosure in the aforementioned financial statements.

16. We have responded fully and truthfully to all inquiries made to us by you during your review.

[*Name of Owner or Chief Executive Officer and Title*]

[*Name of Chief Financial Officer and Title, when applicable*]

OBSERVATION: The accountant may decide based on engagement circumstances or the client's industry that other matters should be specifically included in the letter or that some of the representations included in the illustrative letter above are not necessary. SSARS-19 includes examples of representations that may be tailored to an entity's business or industry.

Exhibit AR 90-3 is an example of a standard review report on financial statements prepared in accordance with accounting principles generally accepted in the United States of America.

EXHIBIT AR 90-3—STANDARD ACCOUNTANT'S REVIEW REPORT

Exhibit AR 90-3 is an example of a standard review report on financial statements prepared in accordance with accounting principles generally accepted in the United States of America.

Independent Accountant's Review Report

[*Appropriate Salutation*]

I (we) have reviewed the accompanying balance sheet of ABC Company as of December 31, 20X8, and the related statements of income, retained earnings, and cash flows for the year then ended. A review includes primarily applying analytical procedures to management's (owners') financial data and making inquiries of company management (owners). A review is substantially less in scope than an audit, the objective of which is to express an opinion regarding the financial statements as a whole. Accordingly, I (we) do not express such an opinion.

Management (owners) is (are) responsible for the preparation and fair presentation of the financial statements in accordance with accounting principles generally accepted in the United States of America and for designing, implementing, and maintaining internal control relevant to the preparation and fair presentation of the financial statements.

My (our) responsibility is to conduct the review in accordance with Statements on Standards for Accounting and Review Services issued by the American Institute of Certified Public Accountants. These standards require me (us) to perform procedures to obtain limited assurance that there are no material modifications that should be made to the financial statements. I (We) believe that the results of my (our) procedures provide a reasonable basis for our report.

Based on my (our) review, I am (we are) not aware of any material modifications that should be made to the accompanying financial statements in order for them to be in conformity with accounting principles generally accepted in the United States of America.

[*Signature of accounting firm or accountant, as appropriate*]

[*Date*]

EXHIBIT AR 90-4—REVIEW PROGRAM

Use the following procedures as a guide for performing a continuing review engagement. The review program is only a guide, and professional judgment should be exercised to determine how the procedures should be modified by revising procedures listed or adding procedures to the review program. Before beginning review procedures, the accountant should have carefully evaluated whether this is a client the accountant wants to serve (i.e., apply client acceptance procedures).

Initial and date each procedure as it is completed. If the procedure is not relevant to this particular review engagement, place "N/A" (not applicable) in the space provided for an initial.

Client Name: _____

Date of Financial Statements: _____

Date of Review Report: _____

	Initials	Date	Workpaper Reference
1. Acquire an adequate understanding of accounting principles and practices of the client's industry and methods of applying them.	_____	_____	_____
2. Develop an understanding of the client's organization.	_____	_____	_____
3. Develop an understanding of the client's operating characteristics.	_____	_____	_____
4. Develop an understanding of the nature of the client's assets, liabilities, revenues, and expenses.	_____	_____	_____
5. Make inquiries concerning the client's accounting principles, practices, and methods.	_____	_____	_____
6. Make inquiries concerning the client's procedures for recording, classifying, and summarizing transactions and accumulating information for disclosure in the financial statements.	_____	_____	_____
7. Make inquiries concerning actions taken at meetings of stockholders, board of directors, or other meetings that may affect the financial statements.	_____	_____	_____
8. Make inquiries concerning the consistent application of GAAP.	_____	_____	_____
9. Make inquiries concerning changes in the client's business activities or accounting principles and the implication for financial statements.	_____	_____	_____
10. Make inquiries concerning occurrence of subsequent events that may have a material effect on the financial statements.	_____	_____	_____
11. Make inquiries regarding the extent of unusual or complex situations that might exist and that have a material effect on the financial statements.	_____	_____	_____
12. Make inquiries about whether significant transactions occurred or were recognized in the last several days of the reporting period.	_____	_____	_____
13. Inquire about the status of uncorrected misstatements identified in prior engagements.	_____	_____	_____

	Initials	Date	Workpaper Reference
14. Inquire regarding whether management has any knowledge of fraud or suspected fraud affecting the entity that might involve management or others that could materially misstate the financial statements.	_____	_____	_____
15. Make inquiries concerning the types of significant journal entries or other adjustments that exist.	_____	_____	_____
16. Inquire regarding whether the client has received communications from regulatory agencies.	_____	_____	_____
17. Apply analytical procedures to identify relationships and individual items that appear to be unusual.	_____	_____	_____
18. Consider whether other professional services are needed before starting the review engagement.	_____	_____	_____
19. If appropriate, obtain reports from other accountants.	_____	_____	_____
20. Consider whether other review procedures should be performed on the basis of the results of performing the minimum review procedures.	_____	_____	_____
21. Read the financial statements to consider if they conform with GAAP.	_____	_____	_____
22. Obtain a client representation letter.	_____	_____	_____
23. Other review procedures: _____			

_____

_____

Reviewed By: _____

Date: _____

EXHIBIT AR 90-5—REVIEW QUESTIONNAIRE CHECKLIST

Use the following checklist as a guide for performing review procedures. The checklist is only a guide, and professional judgment should be exercised to determine how the checklist should be modified by revising questions listed or adding questions to the checklist where appropriate.

Initial and date each question as it is considered. If the question is not relevant to this particular review engagement, place "N/A" (not applicable) in the space provided for an initial. If the answer to the question is "no" or if additional explanation is needed with respect to a question, provide a proper cross-reference to another workpaper.

Client Name: _____

Date of Financial Statements: _____

	Initials	Date	Workpaper Reference

1. Have we acquired an adequate understanding of specialized accounting principles and practices of the client's industry by
   - Reviewing relevant AICPA Accounting/Audit Guides? _____ _____ _____
   - Reviewing financial statements of other entities in the same industry? _____ _____ _____
   - Consulting with other individuals familiar with accounting practices in the specialized industry? _____ _____ _____
   - Reading periodicals, textbooks, and other publications? _____ _____ _____
   - Performing other procedures? _____ _____ _____

2. Have we developed an understanding of the client's organization, including
   - The form of business organization? _____ _____ _____
   - The history of the client? _____ _____ _____
   - The principals involved in the organizational chart or similar analysis? _____ _____ _____
   - Other relevant matters? _____ _____ _____

3. Have we developed an understanding of the client's operating characteristics, including
   - An understanding of the client's products and services? _____ _____ _____
   - Identification of operating locations? _____ _____ _____
   - An understanding of production methods? _____ _____ _____
   - Other operating characteristics? _____ _____ _____

4. Have we developed an understanding of the nature of the client's assets, liabilities, revenues, and expenses by
   - Reviewing the client's chart of accounts? _____ _____ _____
   - Reviewing the previous year's financial statements? _____ _____ _____
   - Considering the relationships between specific accounts and the nature of the client's business? _____ _____ _____
   - Performing other procedures? _____ _____ _____

5. Have we made inquiries concerning accounting principles, practices, and methods? _____ _____ _____

	Initials	Date	Workpaper Reference

6. Have we made inquiries concerning the accounting procedures used by the client, including
   - Recording transactions?   _____   _____   _____
   - Classifying transactions?   _____   _____   _____
   - Summarizing transactions?   _____   _____   _____
   - Accumulating information for making disclosures in the financial statements?   _____   _____   _____
   - Other accounting procedures?   _____   _____   _____

7. Have we made inquiries concerning the effect on the financial statements due to actions taken at meetings of
   - Stockholders?   _____   _____   _____
   - The board of directors?   _____   _____   _____
   - Other committees?   _____   _____   _____

8. If there were changes in the application of accounting principles
   - Did the change in accounting principle include the adoption of another acceptable accounting principle?   _____   _____   _____
   - Was the change properly justified?   _____   _____   _____
   - Were the effects of the change presented in the financial statements, including adequate disclosure, in a manner consistent with ASC 250 (Accounting Changes and Error Corrections)?   _____   _____   _____
   - Were there other matters that we took into consideration?   _____   _____   _____

9. Have we made inquiries concerning changes in the client's business activities that may require the adoption of different accounting principles, and have we considered the implication of this change for the financial statements?   _____   _____   _____

10. Have we made inquiries concerning the occurrence of events subsequent to the date of the financial statements that may require
    - Adjustments to the financial statements?   _____   _____   _____
    - Disclosures in the financial statements?   _____   _____   _____

11. Have we made inquiries regarding the extent of unusual or complex situations that might exist and that have a material effect on the financial statements?   _____   _____   _____

	Initials	Date	Workpaper Reference
12. Have we made inquiries about whether significant transactions occurred or were recognized in the last several days of the reporting period?	_____	_____	_____
13. Have we inquired about the status of uncorrected misstatements identified in prior engagements?	_____	_____	_____
14. Have we inquired regarding whether management has any knowledge of fraud or suspected fraud affecting the entity that might involve management or others that could materially misstate the financial statements?	_____	_____	_____
15. Have we made inquiries concerning the types of significant journal entries or other adjustments that exist?	_____	_____	_____
16. Have we inquired regarding whether the client has received communications from regulatory agencies?	_____	_____	_____
17. Have we performed analytical procedures, including			
• Comparing current financial statements with comparable prior period(s)?	_____	_____	_____
• Comparing current financial statements with anticipated results?	_____	_____	_____
• Studying financial statement elements and expected relationships?	_____	_____	_____
• Other analytical procedures?	_____	_____	_____
• Documenting our expectations?	_____	_____	_____
18. Have we considered whether other professional services are needed in order to complete the review engagement, including			
• Preparing a working trial balance?	_____	_____	_____
• Preparing adjusting journal entries?	_____	_____	_____
• Consulting matters fundamental to the preparation of acceptable financial statements?	_____	_____	_____
• Preparing tax returns?	_____	_____	_____
• Providing bookkeeping or data processing services that do not include the generation of financial statements?	_____	_____	_____
• Considering other services that may be necessary before a review can be performed?	_____	_____	_____

	Initials	Date	Workpaper Reference
19. Have we obtained reports from other CPA(s) who reported on the financial statements of components of the client-reporting entity?	_____	_____	_____
20. Have we read the financial statements to determine whether they appear to be in accordance with GAAP based on the information that has come to our attention?	_____	_____	_____
21. Have we obtained a client representation letter?	_____	_____	_____
22. Have we used other procedures to resolve questions during the review arrangement?	_____	_____	_____

Reviewed By: _____

EXHIBIT AR 90-6—INQUIRY CHECKLIST FOR A REVIEW ENGAGEMENT

Use this checklist to document inquiries made concerning accounting procedures used by the client. The checklist is only a guide, and professional judgment should be exercised to determine how the checklist should be modified by revising questions listed or adding questions where appropriate.

If a question is not relevant to this particular review engagement, place "N/A" (not applicable) in the space provided for a comment. If an additional explanation is needed in response to the question, provide a proper cross-reference to another workpaper. Note the source of the information in the space provided after each question.

Client Name: _____

Date of Financial Statements: _____

Sources of Information: _____

_____

_____

_____

Date: _____

_____

	Yes	No	Date of Inquiry	Comment
GENERAL				
1. What are the procedures for recording, classifying, and summarizing transactions in the financial statements, including relevant disclosures?	_____	_____	_____	_____

		Yes	No	Date of Inquiry	Comment
2.	Do general ledger control accounts agree with subsidiary ledger accounts?	___	___	___	___
3.	Have the financial statements been prepared in accordance with generally accepted accounting principles consistently applied?	___	___	___	___

CASH

		Yes	No	Date of Inquiry	Comment
1.	Have bank balances been reconciled with book balances?	___	___	___	___
	Source:				
2.	Have old or unusual reconciling items between bank balances and book balances been reviewed and adjustments made where necessary?	___	___	___	___
	Source:				
3.	Has a proper cutoff of cash transactions been made?	___	___	___	___
	Source:				
4.	Are there any restrictions on the availability of cash balances?	___	___	___	___
	Source:				
5.	Have cash funds been counted and reconciled with control accounts?	___	___	___	___
	Source:				
6.	Have cash overdrafts been classified as current liabilities?	___	___	___	___
	Source:				
7.	Have amounts that represent temporary investments been identified and reclassified?	___	___	___	___
	Source:				

INVESTMENTS IN MARKETABLE EQUITY SECURITIES

		Yes	No	Date of Inquiry	Comment
1.	Have investments in marketable equity securities been classified into trading securities and available-for-sale securities?	___	___	___	___
	Source:				
2.	Have trading securities and available-for-sale securities been carried at market value on the balance sheet?	___	___	___	___
	Source:				
3.	Has management determined market value based on prices in active markets and, if not, how has market value been obtained?	___	___	___	___
	Source:				

	Yes	No	Date of Inquiry	Comment
4. Have available-for-sale securities been classified into a current and noncurrent portfolio?	_____	_____	_____	_____
Source:				
5. Have unrealized changes in the market value of trading securities since the prior year's financial statements been recorded in the income statement?	_____	_____	_____	_____
Source:				
6. Has the cumulative difference between the market value of available-for-sale securities and their book value been recorded as a component of stockholders' equity? Have changes in this account been recognized as a component of Other Comprehensive Income during the year?	_____	_____	_____	_____
Source:				
7. Have marketable equity securities been evaluated to determine reductions that are other than temporary?	_____	_____	_____	_____
Source:				
8. Have gains or losses from the sale of marketable equity securities been reported on the income statement?	_____	_____	_____	_____
Source:				
9. Have dividends received on marketable equity securities been reported on the income statement?	_____	_____	_____	_____
Source:				
10. Has an analysis been made to accrue dividends declared but not paid at the end of the period?	_____		_____	_____
Source:				
11. Have reclassifications between trading securities and available-for-sale securities been accounted for in accordance with ASC 320 (Investments—Debt and Equity Securities) and related FASB Staff Guidance?	_____	_____	_____	_____
Source:				

INVESTMENTS IN DEBT SECURITIES

	Yes	No	Date of Inquiry	Comment
1. Have investments in marketable debt securities been classified into trading securities, available-for-sale securities, and hold-to-maturity securities?	____	____	____	____
Source:				
2. Have trading securities and available-for-sale securities been carried at market value on the balance sheet?	____	____	____	____
Source:				
3. Has management determined market value based on prices in active markets and, if not, how has market value been determined?	____	____	____	____
Source:				
4. Have hold-to-maturity securities been carried at amortized cost, where amortized cost is determined using the effective interest method (unless the results from using the straight-line method of amortizing premium or discount are immaterially different)?	____	____	____	____
Source:				
5. Have available-for-sale securities and hold-to-maturity securities been classified into a current and noncurrent portfolio?	____	____	____	____
Source:				
6. Have unrealized changes in the market value of trading securities since the prior year's financial statements been recorded in the income statement?	____	____	____	____
Source:				
7. Has the cumulative difference between the market value of available-for-sale securities and their book value been recorded as a component of stockholders' equity? Have changes in this account been recognized as a component of Other Comprehensive Income during the year?	____	____	____	____
Source:				
8. Have marketable debt securities been evaluated to determine reductions that are other than temporary?	____	____	____	____
Source:				

	Yes	No	Date of Inquiry	Comment
9. Have gains or losses from the sale of marketable debt securities been reported on the income statement?	____	____	_____	_____
Source:				
10. Has interest income been recognized on the income statement, including an analysis of accrued interest income at the end of the period?	____	____	_____	_____
Source:				

RECEIVABLES

	Yes	No	Date of Inquiry	Comment
1. Has a reasonable allowance been made for doubtful accounts?	____	____	_____	_____
Source:				
2. Have receivables considered uncollectible been written off?	____	____	_____	_____
Source:				
3. If appropriate, has interest been reflected?	____	____	_____	_____
Source:				
4. Has a proper cutoff of sales transactions been made?	____	____	_____	_____
Source:				
5. Are there any receivables from employees and related parties?	____	____	_____	_____
Source:				
6. Are any receivables pledged, discounted, or factored?	____	____	_____	_____
Source:				
7. Have receivables been properly classified between current and noncurrent?	____	____	_____	_____
Source:				
8. Have noncurrent receivables been evaluated to determine whether they carry a reasonable interest rate?	____	____	_____	_____
Source:				

INVENTORIES

	Yes	No	Date of Inquiry	Comment
1. Have inventories been physically counted? (If not, how have inventory quantities been determined?)	____	____	_____	_____
Source:				
2. Have general ledger control accounts been adjusted to agree with physical inventories?	____	____	_____	_____
Source:				

	Yes	No	Date of Inquiry	Comment

3. If physical inventories are taken at a date other than the balance sheet date, have appropriate procedures been used to record changes in inventory between the date of the count and the balance sheet date?

Source:

4. Were consignments in or out considered in taking physical inventories?

Source:

5. Has inventory been valued using an inventory method consistent with that of the previous period?

Source:

6. Does inventory cost include material, labor, and overhead where applicable?

Source:

7. Have write-downs for obsolescence or cost in excess of net realizable value been made?

Source:

8. Have proper cutoffs of purchases, goods in transit, and returned goods been made?

Source:

9. Are there any inventory encumbrances?

Source:

10. Have there been any exchanges during the period that involve similar items?

Source:

PROPERTY, PLANT, AND EQUIPMENT

1. Have gains or losses on disposal of property or equipment been properly reflected?

Source:

2. Have the criteria for capitalizing property, plant, and equipment been established, and have they been applied during the fiscal period?

Source:

3. Does the repairs and maintenance account only include expenses?

Source:

	Yes	No	Date of Inquiry	Comment

4. Are property, plant, and equipment stated at cost?

Source:

5. Have depreciation methods been applied in a consistent manner?

Source:

6. Are there any unrecorded additions, retirements, abandonments, sales, or trade-ins?

Source:

7. Does the client have material lease agreements, and have they been properly reflected in the financial statements?

Source:

8. Is any property, plant, or equipment mortgaged or otherwise encumbered?

Source:

9. Have there been any exchanges during the period that involved similar items?

Source:

10. Has the client evaluated its fixed assets for possible evidence of impairment and, if impaired, has the appropriate write-off been recognized on the income statement?

Source:

PREPAID EXPENSES

1. Have the items included in prepaid expenses been evaluated to determine whether they are appropriately classified as prepayments?

Source:

2. Has a rational and systematic method been used to amortize prepaid expenses, and has the method been used in a manner consistent with the previous period?

Source:

INTANGIBLE ASSETS

1. Have the items included in intangible assets been evaluated to determine whether they are appropriately classified as intangible assets?

Source:

	Yes	No	Date of Inquiry	Comment

2. Have intangible assets with indefinite useful lives been evaluated for possible impairment and, if impaired, has the appropriate write-off been recognized on the income statement? ____ ____ _____ _____

Source:

3. Has the straight-line method been used to amortize the cost of intangible assets with determinative useful lives and has the amortization method been used in a manner consistent with the previous period? ____ ____ _____ _____

Source:

OTHER ASSETS

1. Have the items included in other assets been evaluated to determine whether they are appropriately classified? ____ ____ _____ _____

Source:

2. Has each item classified as other assets been accounted for in accordance with GAAP? ____ ____ _____ _____

Source:

3. Have any of the other assets been mortgaged or otherwise encumbered? ____ ____ _____ _____

Source:

ACCOUNTS AND NOTES PAYABLE AND ACCRUED LIABILITIES

1. Have all significant payables been reflected in the financial statements? ____ ____ _____ _____

Source:

2. Have all short-term liabilities been properly classified? ____ ____ _____ _____

Source:

3. Have all significant accruals, such as payroll, interest, and provisions for pension and profit-sharing plans, been properly reflected in the financial statements? ____ ____ _____ _____

Source:

4. Have any of the liabilities been collateralized? ____ ____ _____ _____

Source:

5. Are there any payables to employees and related parties? ____ ____ _____ _____

Source:

LONG-TERM LIABILITIES

	Yes	No	Date of Inquiry	Comment
1. Have the terms and other provisions of long-term liability agreements been properly reflected in the financial statements?	____	____	_____	_____
Source:				
2. Have liabilities been evaluated to determine whether they are properly classified as noncurrent?	____	____	_____	_____
Source:				
3. Has interest expense been properly reflected in the financial statements?	____	____	_____	_____
Source:				
4. Has there been compliance with restrictive covenants of loan agreements?	____	____	_____	_____
Source:				
5. Have any of the long-term liabilities been collateralized or subordinated?	____	____	_____	_____
Source:				
6. Has pension liability been determined in accordance with ASC 715 (Compensation—Retirement Benefits) (including, if applicable, the computation of a minimum liability)?	____	____	_____	_____
Source:				

INCOME AND OTHER TAXES

	Yes	No	Date of Inquiry	Comment
1. Has provision been made for current- and prior-year federal income taxes payable?	____	____	_____	_____
Source:				
2. Have any assessments or reassessments been received, and are tax examinations in process?	____	____	_____	_____
Source:				
3. Have differences between accounting methods used in the financial statements and those used in the tax return been properly reflected in the financial statements?	____	____	_____	_____
Source:				
4. Has the income statement been prepared to reflect intraperiod income tax allocation?	____	____	_____	_____
Source:				
5. Has provision been made for state and local income, franchise, sales, and other taxes payable?	____	____	_____	_____
Source:				

	Yes	No	Date of Inquiry	Comment

OTHER LIABILITIES, CONTINGENCIES, AND COMMITMENTS

1. Have the items included in other liabilities been evaluated to determine whether they are properly classified?

    Source:

2. Have the items included in other liabilities been evaluated to determine whether they are current or noncurrent?

    Source:

3. Are there any contingent liabilities such as discounted notes, drafts, endorsements, warranties, litigation, unsettled asserted claims, and unasserted potential claims?

    Source:

4. Are there any material contractual obligations for construction or purchase of real property and equipment and any commitments or options to purchase or sell company securities?

    Source:

EQUITY

1. Have changes in equity accounts for the period been properly accounted for and presented in the financial statements?

    Source:

2. Have all classes of authorized capital stock been identified and properly reflected in the financial statements?

    Source:

3. Has the par or stated value of the various classes of stock been identified and properly reflected in the financial statements?

    Source:

4. Has there been a reconciliation between the number of outstanding shares of capital stock and subsidiary records?

    Source:

5. Have capital stock preferences, if any, been properly disclosed?

    Source:

6. Have stock options been granted?

    Source:

		Yes	No	Date of Inquiry	Comment

7. Has the client made any acquisitions of its own capital stock?
   Source:

8. Has a determination been made as to whether there are any restrictions on retained earnings or other capital accounts?
   Source:

REVENUES AND EXPENSES

1. Has the propriety and reasonableness of revenue recognition methods been considered?

2. Has there been a proper cutoff for the recognition of revenues from the sale of major products and services?
   Source:

3. Has there been a proper cutoff for the measurement of expenses and purchases of inventory made during the period?
   Source:

4. Are revenues and expenses properly classified in the financial statements?
   Source:

5. Has an evaluation been made to determine whether the financial statements properly include discontinued operations or items that may be considered extraordinary?
   Source:

OTHER

1. Have there been any material transactions between the client and related parties?
   Source:

2. Have there been evaluations to determine whether there are any material uncertainties?
   Source:

3. Has the status of material uncertainties previously disclosed been evaluated?
   Source:

4. Are there any subsequent events that have a material effect on the financial statements?
   Source:

CONSOLIDATION

	Yes	No	Date of Inquiry	Comment
1. Have all subsidiaries been evaluated to determine whether they should be included in the consolidated financial statements?				
Source:	___	___	___	___
2. Have all divisions and branches been included in the client's financial statements?				
Source:	___	___	___	___
3. Have all intercompany and intracompany accounts and transactions been eliminated?				
Source:	___	___	___	___
4. For intercorporate investments not consolidated, has there been an evaluation as to whether the equity method or the cost method should be used to account for the investment?				
Source:	___	___	___	___
5. Has there been any change in the accounting for an intercorporate investment?				
Source:	___	___	___	___

STATEMENT OF CASH FLOWS

1. Has a statement of cash flows been prepared?				
Source:	___	___	___	___
2. Has there been an evaluation to determine whether the focus of the statement should be cash, or cash and cash equivalents?				
Source:	___	___	___	___
3. If the direct method of determining cash flows from operations is not used, has a supplemental reconciliation been included in the financial statement disclosures?				
Source:	___	___	___	___

EXHIBIT AR 90-7—ANALYTICAL PROCEDURES FOR A REVIEW ENGAGEMENT

Use this form to document the performance of analytical procedures for a review engagement. The form is only a guide, and professional judgment should be exercised to determine how the form should be modified by omitting or adding analytical procedures.

Client Name: _____

Date of Financial Statements: _____

COMPARISON OF CURRENT FINANCIAL STATEMENTS WITH COMPARA-BLE PRIOR-PERIOD FINANCIAL STATEMENTS

The following ratios were computed:

_____ Using financial data that reflect review adjustments proposed to date.

_____ Using financial data that do not reflect review adjustments.

Formula

LIQUIDITY RATIOS

1.	Current ratio	Current Assets
		Current Liabilities
2.	Acid-test ratio	Quick Assets
		Current Liabilities
3.	Days' sales in accounts receivable	Average Accounts Receivable × 365 Days
		Net Credit Sales
4.	Current liabilities to total assets	Current Liabilities
		Total Assets

ACTIVITY RATIOS

1.	Inventory turnover	Cost of Goods Sold
		Average Inventory
2.	Receivable turnover	Net Credit Sales
		Average Accounts Receivable
3.	Asset turnover	Net Sales
		Average Total Assets
4.	Gross profit percentage	Gross Profit
		Net Sales

PROFITABILITY RATIOS

1.	Bad debt to sales	Bad Debt Expense
		Net Sales
2.	Rate of return on total assets used	Net Income
		Total Assets
3.	Rate of return on equity (investment)	Net Income
		Total Equity
4.	Net margin	Net Income
		Net Sales

COVERAGE RATIOS

1.	Debt to total assets	Total Debt
		Total Assets
2.	Interest expense to sales	Interest Expense
		Net Sales

		Formula
3.	Number of times interest earned	Income before Interest and Taxes
		Interest Expense

OTHER RATIOS

1.	Effective tax rate	Income Taxes
		Income before Taxes
2.	Bad debt rate	Allowance for Bad Debts
		Accounts Receivable
3.	Depreciation rate	Depreciation Expense
		Depreciable Property
4.	Accounts payable to purchases	Accounts Payable
		Purchases
5.	Dividend rate	Dividends
		Common Stock (Market Value)
6.	Interest rate	Interest Expense
		Average Interest-Bearing Debt
7.	Payroll rate	Payroll Expense
		Net Sales
8.	Dividend return	Dividend Income
		Average Equity Investments
9.	Interest income return	Interest Income
		Average Debt Investments

OTHER

COMPARISON OF CURRENT FINANCIAL STATEMENTS WITH ANTICI-PATED RESULTS

> **PLANNING AID REMINDER:** SSARS-19 requires a practitioner performing a review engagement to independently develop expectations of ratios and account balances (including changes in them) before analyzing the client's data. SSARS require that the accountant document those expectations when they are not otherwise readily determinable from the documentation of the work performed. Exhibit AR 90-7 contains an example of documentation.

		20XX		
Acct #	*Account Name*	*Actual*	*Budgeted*	*Difference*
	Cash in bank — name			
	Petty cash			
	Cash in bank — payroll			

		20XX		
Acct #	Account Name	Actual	Budgeted	Difference
	Investment marketable equity securities (current)			
	Accounts receivable			
	Allowance for doubtful accounts			
	Other receivables (current)			
	Accrued interest receivable			
	Notes receivable (current)			
	Discount on notes receivable			
	Dividends receivable			
	Inventory (year-end balance)			
	Prepaid insurance			
	Prepaid rent			
	Prepaid advertising			
	Land			
	Buildings			
	Accumulated depreciation — buildings			
	Delivery equipment			
	Accumulated depreciation — delivery equipment			
	Fixtures			
	Accumulated depreciation — fixtures			
	Office equipment			
	Accumulated depreciation — office equipment			
	Property — capital leases			
	Investment — marketable equity securities (noncurrent)			
	Other receivables (noncurrent)			
	Land held for investment			
	Accounts payable			
	Accrued liabilities			
	Payroll taxes and other withholdings			
	Interest payable			
	Notes payable			
	Discounts/premiums — notes payable			
	Obligations — capital leases (current)			
	Dividends payable			
	Income taxes payable			
	Notes payable (noncurrent)			

| | | | 20XX | |
Acct #	Account Name	Actual	Budgeted	Difference
	Bonds payable			
	Discounts/premiums — bonds payable			
	Obligation — capital leases (noncurrent)			
	Common stock			
	Paid-in capital in excess of par			
	Treasury stock			
	Accumulated other comprehensive income			
	Unappropriated retained earnings			
	Appropriated retained earnings			
	Sales			
	Sales returns and allowances			
	Sales discounts			
	Cost of goods sold			
	Purchases			
	Freight-in			
	Bad debt expense			
	Utilities expense			
	Travel expense			
	Advertising expense			
	Delivery expense			
	Miscellaneous expense			
	Insurance expense			
	Rent expense			
	Professional fees expense			
	Salaries and wages expense			
	Payroll taxes expense			
	Depreciation expense — buildings			
	Depreciation expense — delivery equipment			
	Depreciation expense — fixtures			
	Depreciation expense — office equipment			
	Depreciation expense — capital leases			
	Repairs and maintenance expense			
	Miscellaneous income			
	Dividend income			
	Interest income			
	Interest expense			
	Loss/gain on sale of assets			

		20XX		
Acct #	*Account Name*	*Actual*	*Budgeted*	*Difference*
	Loss on exchange of assets			
	Loss due to permanent decline in value of security investments			
	Loss/gain on sale of investments			
	Income tax expense			
	Totals			

Prepared By: _____

Reviewed By: _____

STUDY OF FINANCIAL STATEMENT ELEMENTS AND UNEXPECTED RELATIONSHIPS

Unexpected Relationships	*Summary of Analysis*
_____	_____
_____	_____
_____	_____
_____	_____
_____	_____
_____	_____
_____	_____
_____	_____
_____	_____
_____	_____
_____	_____
_____	_____
_____	_____
_____	_____
_____	_____
_____	_____
_____	_____
_____	_____
_____	_____
_____	_____

OTHER ANALYTICAL PROCEDURES

Summary of findings: _____

_____

_____

_____

_____

_____

_____

_____

_____

_____

Prepared By: _____

Date: _____

Reviewed By: _____

Date: _____

EXHIBIT AR 90-8—DOCUMENTING EXPECTATIONS WHEN PERFORMING ANALYTICAL PROCEDURES IN A REVIEW ENGAGEMENT

In review engagements, the accountant must perform inquiry and analytical procedures to provide the basis for the review report. When performing analytical procedures, the accountant first forms an expectation of the recorded amounts or ratios in such a way that a material difference between the expectation and the recorded amount or ratio is indicative of a possible material misstatement requiring further explanation. An accountant cannot perform effective analytical procedures without first developing expectations as to the results of those analytical procedures.

Based on the accountant's understanding of the client and its industry, the accountant develops expectations by identifying plausible relationships (such as number of stores and sales) that are reasonably expected to exist. Several data sources might be used by the accountant to form the expectation. AR 90 requires the accountant to document expectations and factors considered in the development of those expectations where significant expectations are not otherwise readily determinable from the documentation of the work performed.

The following is an example of how an accountant might document expectations.

Documenting an Expectation Related to an Increase in Revenue

An accountant is engaged to conduct a review of financial statements of a company that manufactures medical products for use in cancer treatments. Because of increased cancer detection rates due to advanced medical technologies, the accountant reasonably expects product sales to have increased during the fiscal period due to greater demand for cancer treatment products. Using his or her knowledge of the client, the accountant expects a 10 percent to 15 percent increase in sales. Additionally, the accountant concludes that receivables should increase, and that loans payable and interest expense would also increase due to additional borrowing of funds to handle production demands.

Example Documentation

Lifeway Medical Supply Corporation
Analytical Procedures
For the Year Ended December 31, 20X9

Expectations

The following are factors that should affect the relationship between current and prior-year revenue account amounts:

- Increase in cancer treatment spending due to earlier cancer detection and treatment improvements in the medical field, resulting in increased product sales. Expected increase is between 10 percent and 15 percent. A similar expectation exists for an increase in accounts receivable.

- To fund expenses related to additional production demands, the client borrowed additional funds from its lenders. Thus, loans payable and interest expense is expected to increase between 10 percent and 15 percent.

- No significant increases are expected in either days sales in inventory or inventory turnover. Although there will be some inventory buildup, it is not expected to correspond with an increase in sales because the cancer treatment products are expected to be sold near the date of completion. Increases in days sales in inventory or inventory turnover are not expected to change by more than 5 percent.

Balance sheets are available for the current year and the two years prior to the current year and income statements accounts are available for the current and prior year.

Trend Analysis

	December 31, 20X9	December 31, 20X8	Change	Percentage Change
Sales	$5,000,000	$4,350,000	$650,000	14.94%
Cost of Sales	$3,560,000	$3,132,000	$428,000	13.67%
Gross margin	$1,440,000	$1,218,000		
Gross margin as a percentage of sales	28.80%	28.00%		
Selling expenses	$460,000	$368,000	$92,000	25.00%
Interest expense	$96,000	$84,000	$12,000	14.29%

Balance Sheet Ratio Analysis

	December 31, 20X9	December 31, 20X8	December 31, 20X7
Accounts Rec., net	$2,200,000	$1,686,000	$1,406,000
Inventory	$2,000,000	$1,664,000	$1,388,000
Notes Payable	$996,000	$874,000	$836,000

Change in Receivables

Accounts receivable increased 30.5 percent from the prior year, which is in excess of the expected increase of between 10 percent and 15 percent. As a result, additional inquiries about the increase in accounts receivable will be made of the client and the associated reasons will be documented.

Days in Receivables

Days sales in receivables = Accounts receivables, net at end of period / (Net sales/365)

Days in Receivables for 20X9:

$2,200,000 / ($5,000,000/365) = 160.6 days

Days in Receivables for 20X8:

$1,686,000 / ($4,350,000/365) = 141.5 days

The increase in 19 days sales in receivables (160.6 - 141.5 days) represents a 13.5 percent increase. Inquiries about the increase in days sales in receivables will be made as part of the additional inquiries about the increase in accounts receivable.

Change in Inventory

Inventory increased 20.2 percent from the prior year, which is in excess of the expected increase of between 10 percent and 15 percent that would be associated with the increase in sales by the same percentage amounts. As a result, additional inquiries about the increase in inventory will be made of the client and the associated reasons will be documented.

Days sales in inventory

Days sales in inventory = Inventory at end of period / (Total cost of goods sold / 365)

Days sales in inventory for 2009:

$2,000,000 / ($3,560,000 / 365) = 205.1 days

Days sales in inventory for 2008:

$1,664,000 / ($3,132,000 / 365) = 193.9 days

The increase of 11.2 days sales in inventory (205.1 - 193.9 days) represents a 5.8 percent increase. Because this increase is greater than expected, further inquiries will be made of the client and reasons for the difference will be documented.

Inventory Turnover

Inventory turnover = Cost of goods sold / Average inventory

Inventory turnover for 20X9:

$3,560,000 / (($2,000,000 + $1,664,000) / 2) = 1.94 times

Inventory turnover for 20X8:

$3,132,000 / (($1,664,000 + $1,388,000) / 2) = 2.05 times

The inventory turnover decrease of 5.4% is beyond the expected change of no more than 5%. Because this change is greater than expected, further inquiries will be made of the client and reasons for the difference will be documented.

The increase in notes payable is also reasonable (13.9%) when considered in light of the corresponding increase in interest expense and the expectation associated with the notes payable account. However, because the increase in selling expenses is 25 percent, additional inquiries about that increase will be made of the client and the associated reasons will be documented.

EXHIBIT AR 90-9—CONSIDERING GOING CONCERN

An entity's continuance as a going concern is assumed in financial reporting in the absence of significant information to the contrary. Often information that indicates uncertainty about an entity's ability to continue as a going concern relates to its ability to continue to meet its obligations as they become due without substantial disposition of assets outside the ordinary course of business, restructuring debt, externally forced revisions of its operations, or similar actions.

Conditions Often Leading to Substantial Doubt

Certain conditions, when considered together, may lead to there being substantial doubt about an entity's ability to continue as a going concern for a reasonable period of time, typically not to exceed one year beyond the date of the financial statements. Conditions or events that may indicate a substantial doubt about the entity's ability to continue as a going concern include the following:

- Negative trends that might include, for example, recurring operating losses, working capital deficiencies, negative cash flows from operating activities, adverse key financial ratios.

- Other indications of possible financial difficulties that might include, for example, default on loan or similar agreements, arrearages in dividends, denial of usual trade credit from suppliers, restructuring of debt, noncompliance with statutory capital requirements, need to seek new sources or methods of financing or to dispose of substantial assets.

- Internal matters that might include, for example, work stoppages or other labor difficulties, substantial dependence on the success of a particular project, uneconomic long-term commitments, need to significantly revise operations.

- External matters that have occurred might include, for example, legal proceedings, legislation, or similar matters that might jeopardize an entity's ability to operate; loss of a key franchise, license, or patent; loss of a principal customer or supplier; uninsured or underinsured catastrophe such as a drought, earthquake, or flood.

Management's Plans to Address Conditions

Management should have plans to address these identified adverse conditions and events. Examples of management's plans might include the following:

- Plans to dispose of assets: Considerations should be made about
    - Whether there are any restrictions on the disposal of assets
    - The marketability of assets to be sold
    - Potential direct or indirect effects of the disposal of assets
- Plans to borrow money or restructure debt: Considerations should be made about
    - Availability of debt financing
    - Existing or committed arrangements to restructure debt
    - Possible effects of management's borrowing plans on existing restrictions on additional borrowing
- Plans to reduce or delay expenditures: Considerations should be made about
    - Feasibility of plans to reduce overhead or administrative expenditures
    - Impact of reduced or delayed expenditures
- Plans to increase ownership equity: Considerations should be made about

— Feasibility of plans to increase ownership equity, including existing or committed arrangements to raise additional capital

— Existing or committed arrangements to reduce current dividend requirements

Financial Statement Disclosure

When management concludes that there is substantial doubt about the entity's ability to continue as a going concern, management should consider disclosing the following:

- Pertinent conditions and events giving rise to the assessment of the uncertainty about the entity's ability to continue as a going concern for a reasonable period of time.

- The possible effects of such conditions and events and any mitigating factors.

- Possible discontinuance of operations.

- Management's plans

- Information about the recoverability or classification of recorded asset amounts or the amounts or classification of liabilities.

Management should consider the need for disclosure of the principal conditions and events that initially caused management to believe there was an uncertainty. The consideration of disclosure may include the possible effects of such conditions and events, and any mitigating factors, including management's plans.

AR SECTION 110

COMPILATION OF SPECIFIED ELEMENTS, ACCOUNTS, OR ITEMS OF A FINANCIAL STATEMENT

Authoritative Pronouncements

SSARS-13—Compilation of Specified Elements, Accounts, or Items of a Financial Statement

Overview

The Accounting and Review Services Committee issued SSARS-13 in 2005 to provide new guidance that expands SSARS to apply when an accountant is engaged to compile or issues a compilation report on one or more specified elements, accounts, or items of a financial statement.

Defining elements, accounts, or items

SSARS-13 notes that elements, accounts, or items of a financial statement constitute accounting information that is part of, but less than, a financial statement. Such information also encompasses accounting information contained in the client's accounts that supports the elements, accounts, or items presented in the financial statements. Although accounting information is generally expressed in monetary amounts (or percentages derived from monetary amounts), it may also include quantitative information derived from accounting records that is not expressed in monetary terms.

Specified elements may be taken directly from the financial statements (or notes). They may also represent any component or combination of components derived from the financial statements. Specified elements may be individual financial statement line items or a combination of several line items. They may also be general ledger accounts that make up all or part of a financial statement line item. The following are examples of specified element presentations:

- Total sales from the income statement
- Summary of all amounts included in property, plant, and equipment at a specified date
- Schedule of accounts receivable at a specified date
- Schedule of balances in cash accounts at a specified date
- Schedule of construction costs incurred

Although AR 110 provides guidance for compiling specified elements, accounts, or items of financial statement, nothing precludes the accountant from preparing or assisting in the preparation of one of more specified elements, accounts, or items of a financial statement, and submitting the presentation to the client without the issuance of a compilation report.

A compilation of a specified element is limited to presenting financial information that is the representation of management (or the owners) without undertaking to express any assurance on the information.

Performance requirements

When an accountant is engaged to compile or issues a compilation report on one or more specified elements, accounts, or items of a financial statement, he or she must establish an understanding with the entity, preferably in writing, regarding the services to be performed. If the accountant becomes aware of fraud or an illegal act that may have occurred, he or she must adhere to the communication requirements contained in AR 80.

The accountant must also adhere to the compilation performance requirements contained in AR 80. Before issuance of a compilation report on one or more specified elements, accounts, or items of a financial statement, the accountant should read the compiled information to consider whether it appears to be appropriate in form and free of obvious material errors, including arithmetical or clerical mistakes and mistakes in the application of accounting principles.

Reporting requirements

When an accountant is engaged to compile or issues a compilation report on one or more specified elements, accounts, or items of a financial statement, AR 110 specifies explicit report elements.

Any other procedures that the accountant might have performed before or during the compilation engagement should not be described in the report. In addition, each page of the compiled specified elements, accounts, or items of a financial statement should include a reference such as "See Accountant's Compilation Report."

AR SECTION 120

COMPILATION OF PRO FORMA FINANCIAL INFORMATION

Authoritative Pronouncements

SSARS-14—Compilation of Pro Forma Financial Information

Overview

The Accounting and Review Services Committee issued SSARS-14 in 2005 to provide new guidance that expands SSARS to apply when an accountant is engaged to compile pro forma financial information. By definition a presentation of pro forma financial information is not a financial statement presentation and thus did not previously come under the scope of SSARS. However, SSARS-14 expands SSARS-1 to apply when an accountant is engaged to compile or issues a compilation report on pro forma financial information.

Defining pro forma financial information

The objective of pro forma financial information is to show what the significant effects on historical financial information might have been had a consummated or proposed transaction (or event) occurred at an earlier date. Pro forma financial information is commonly used to show the effects of transactions such as the following:

- Business combination
- Change in capitalization
- Disposition of a significant portion of the business
- Change in the form of business organization or status as an autonomous entity
- Proposed sale of securities and the application of the proceeds

Pro forma financial information is generally achieved by applying pro forma adjustments to historical financial statements. Pro forma adjustments should be based on management's assumptions and give effect to all significant effects directly attributable to the transaction (or event).

Accountant responsibility for pro forma financial information

Although AR 120 provides guidance for compiling pro forma financial information, nothing precludes an accountant from preparing or assisting in the preparation of pro forma financial information and submitting the presentation to the client without the issuance of a compilation report. However, an accountant who prepares or assists a client in preparing a presentation of pro forma financial information should consider how the presentation will be used. The accountant should consider the potential for being associated with the presentation and the likelihood that the user may inappropriately infer through that association an unintended level of assurance. If the accountant believes that he or she will be associated with the information, he or she should consider issuing a compilation report so that users will not infer a level of assurance that does not exist.

An engagement to compile pro forma financial information may be undertaken as a separate engagement or in conjunction with a compilation of financial statements. When an accountant is engaged to compile pro forma financial information, he or she should establish an understanding with the entity, preferably in writing, regarding the services to be performed. The understanding should include a description of the nature and limitations of the services to be performed and a description of the report.

When an accountant is engaged to compile pro forma financial information, he or she must adhere to the performance requirements contained in SSARS-1 for compilations. Before issuing the compilation report, the accountant should read the compiled pro forma financial information, including the summary of significant assumptions and consider whether it appears to be appropriate in form and free of obvious material errors.

SSARS-14 specifies the basic elements of a compilation report on pro forma financial information. Each page of the compiled pro forma financial information should include a reference, such as "See Accountant's Compilation Report."

AR SECTION 200

REPORTING ON COMPARATIVE FINANCIAL STATEMENTS

Authoritative Pronouncements

SSARS-2—Reporting on Comparative Financial Statements

SSARS-11—Standards for Accounting and Review Services (May 2004)

SSARS-12—Omnibus Statement on Standards for Accounting and Review Services—2005

SSARS-15—Elimination of Certain References to Statements on Auditing Standards and Incorporation of Appropriate Guidance into Statements on Standards for Accounting and Review Services

SSARS-17—Omnibus Statement on Standards for Accounting and Review Services—2008

SSARS Interpretation 1—Reporting on Financial Statements That Previously Did Not Omit Substantially All Disclosures (November 2002)

Overview

"Comparative financial statements" are defined as "financial statements of two or more periods presented in columnar form." The periods may be other than annual, such as the three months (quarter) ended March 31, 20X6 (current period), compared to the three months ended March 31, 20X5 (prior period). The statements may cover more than two periods; for example, statements for the five years ended May 31, 20X7. However, each type of financial statement (for example, balance sheet, statement of income) for all periods presented must be on the same page in columnar form. The columns may be in vertical or horizontal format.

When financial statements of more than one period are presented in columnar form, the accountant must report on all periods presented. A *reissued* report is one that has been issued subsequent to the date of the original report but with its original date. A reissued report should be dual-dated if it is revised for specific events. An *updated* report is issued by a continuing accountant and bears the same date as the current report. It may or may not contain the same conclusions reached in the original report, and it should consider information that the accountant becomes aware of during the current engagement.

Financial statements that have been compiled, reviewed, or audited and that are accompanied by appropriate reports may *not* be presented in columnar form with financial statements that are *not* compiled, reviewed, or audited. In such cases, the accountant should advise the client that the report and the accountant's name should not be used in connection with such comparative financial statements. In other words, the accountant may *not* report on client-prepared comparative financial statements containing statements that *were not* compiled, reviewed, or audited and statements that *were* compiled, reviewed, or audited. However, the client-prepared statements may be presented on a separate page of a document that includes, on another separate page of the same document, the accountant's compiled, reviewed, or audited financial statements. In this event, each page of the client-prepared statements must bear a comment that the accountant has not compiled, reviewed, or audited the statements and assumes no responsibility for them.

Substantially all disclosures may be omitted in compiled financial statements; however, it is inappropriate for an accountant to issue reviewed or audited financial statements that omit substantially all disclosures. Thus, only when all periods are compiled and all periods omit substantially all disclosures can an accountant report on comparative financial statements that omit substantially all disclosures.

Promulgated Procedures Checklist

The structure of the CPA's report on comparative financial statements depends upon the various reporting circumstances that can be encountered in an engagement. The following are common reporting circumstances:

- All periods covered by the financial statements are compiled or reviewed.
- The current period's financial statements are reviewed, while the prior period financial statements are compiled.
- The current period's financial statements are compiled, while the prior period financial statements are reviewed.
- The current or prior period's financial statements are audited, while the other period's financial statements are compiled or reviewed.
- There has been a change in the report on the prior period's financial statements.
- Other accountants have compiled or reviewed the financial statements of the prior period or periods.
- An exception exists on the highest level of service rendered.
- The status of the client (public versus nonpublic) has changed.

Analysis and Application of Procedures

All periods covered by the financial statements are compiled or reviewed

When periods presented in comparative financial statements are either all compiled or all reviewed, the continuing accountant should update the report on the prior period, or periods, and issue it as part of the report on the current period. An example of a report on all periods compiled is presented in Exhibit AR 200-1. An example of a report on all periods reviewed is presented in Exhibit AR 200-2.

The current period's financial statements are reviewed, while the prior period financial statements are compiled

When the accountant performs a level of service in the current period that is higher than that performed in the prior period, he or she should update the report on the prior period, or periods, and issue it as the last paragraph of the report on the current period. An example of the standard report in this situation is presented in Exhibit AR 200-3.

The current period's financial statements are compiled, while the prior period financial statements are reviewed

When the accountant performs a level of service in the current period that is lower than that of the prior period, he or she may report on such comparative financial statements by (1) issuing two separate reports, (2) issuing a compilation report on the current period and adding a last paragraph for the prior period, or (3) issuing a combined compilation and review report.

If the accountant elects to issue two separate reports, the current period will be covered in a compilation report. The prior period will be covered in a review report bearing its original date.

If the accountant elects to issue a compilation report with a last paragraph referring to the prior period, certain information must be included. The last paragraph should contain a description of the degree of responsibility the accountant is assuming for the prior period, the date of the accountant's original report, and a statement that the accountant has not performed any procedures in connection with the prior period's review after the date of the prior-period review report. An example of such an additional last paragraph is presented in Exhibit AR 200-4.

The combined report should include the current-period compilation report and the reissued review report for the prior period. The combined report should be dated as of the completion of the current-period compilation engagement. The report should also mention that the accountant has not performed any procedures in connection with the prior-period review report after the date of that report.

The current or prior period's financial statements are audited, while the other period's financial statements are compiled or reviewed

There may be circumstances where current-period financial statements are audited and included with prior-period compiled or reviewed financial statements. When the financial statements are those of a nonissuer, the accountant's opinion on the current-year audited financial statements should be expanded to include a final separate paragraph describing the compilation or review of the prior-period financial statements. When prior-period financial statements were compiled, the separate paragraph may be worded as follows:

> The 20X8 financial statements were compiled by us, and our report thereon, dated January 31, 20X9, stated that we did not audit or review those financial statements and, accordingly, express no opinion or other form of assurance on them.

When prior-period financial statements were reviewed, the separate paragraph may be worded as follows:

> The 20X8 financial statements were reviewed by us, and our report thereon, dated January 31, 20X9, stated that we were not aware of any material

modifications that should be made to those statements for them to be in conformity with generally accepted accounting principles. However, a review is substantially less in scope than an audit and does not provide a basis for the expression of an opinion on the financial statements taken as a whole.

When the prior-period financial statements have been audited, the accountant should issue a compilation report or review report on the current-period financial statements and should either (1) reissue the audit report for the prior period or (2) add a separate paragraph to the current-period compilation or review report describing the responsibility assumed for the prior-period financial statements. The description paragraph should include the date of the prior-period audit report, a statement that the financial statements were previously examined, the type of opinion expressed and whether the opinion was other than unqualified, the substantive reasons for the qualification, and, finally, a statement that no auditing procedures have been performed since the date of the prior-period audit report. An example of this type of paragraph is as follows:

> The financial statements for the year ended December 31, 20X8, were audited by us (other accountants) and we (they) expressed an unqualified opinion on them in our (their) report dated March 1, 20X9, but we (they) have not performed any auditing procedures since that date.

There has been a change in the report on the prior period's financial statements

Before or during the current-period engagement, a continuing accountant may become aware of information that affects the prior-period report; for example, a modification in the prior-period report to disclose a departure from generally accepted accounting principles (GAAP) may no longer be applicable, or a modification to disclose a departure from GAAP may become necessary. In this event, the accountant's report on the prior-period statements should be expanded to include an additional separate paragraph. This separate paragraph should contain (1) the date of the original report; (2) the reasons for the change in the original report; and (3) if applicable, a statement to the effect that the prior-period financial statements have been changed. Exhibit AR 200-5 provides an example of such an explanatory paragraph.

If the revised report is reissued (issued separately from the report on the current financial statements), it should be dual-dated. The second date should be the date when substantially all the information that resulted in the revision of the report was obtained. This date may be the same date as that used for the current year's report.

Other accountants have compiled or reviewed the financial statements of the prior period or periods

Predecessor accountant reissues unchanged report

The successor accountant should consider the provisions of SSARS-4 (Communication Between Predecessor and Successor Accountants) when communicating with the predecessor accountant (auditor) and when determining the types of communications that are appropriate under the circumstances. SSARS-4 indicates that the successor accountant should obtain the permission of the client before communicating with the predecessor accountant.

A predecessor accountant is not required to reissue a compilation or review report. However, the predecessor accountant may reissue the report on prior-period financial statements, at the client's request, if the accountant makes satisfactory arrangements with the former client and complies with the following provisions before reissuing the report:

1. Evaluates whether the prior-period report is still appropriate by considering (1) the form and style of the report presentation; (2) the effects of any subsequent events; and (3) as a result of changes, whether a modification is required or should be deleted

2. Reads the current-period financial statements and the accompanying accountant's report

3. Compares the prior-period financial statements to previously issued financial statements and the financial statements of the current period

4. Obtains a letter from the current accountant stating that he or she is (is not) aware of any matter that might have a material effect on the prior-period financial statements

If, as a result of the above procedures, the predecessor accountant becomes aware of information that may affect the prior-period report on the financial statements, he or she should perform (1) procedures similar to those that would have been performed if the accountant had been aware of such information during the prior engagement and (2) any other procedures considered necessary under the circumstances. Because of the seriousness of the situation, the procedures may include discussion with the successor accountant and review of pertinent portions of the current-period workpapers. If the predecessor accountant cannot complete the necessary procedures, he or she should not reissue the report on the prior-period financial statements. Under these circumstances, the predecessor accountant may consider the need to consult with legal counsel regarding appropriate action.

ENGAGEMENT STRATEGY: The situation may be such that the predecessor accountant should consider the guidance in AU-C 560 (*Subsequent Events and Subsequently Discovered Facts*) provides to an auditor when a subsequent discovery of facts existing at the date of the accountant's prior report.

After performing the required procedures, if the predecessor accountant is not aware of any information that would require restatement or revision of the prior-period report, the predecessor accountant should reissue the report on the former client's request. The reissued report should be dated as it was originally. No reference should be made to any subsequent procedures performed, including the representation letter from the successor accountant and the report that the successor accountant will issue on the current period.

Predecessor accountant issues changed report

After following the prescribed procedures, the predecessor accountant may determine that a prior-period report cannot be reissued exactly as it was issued originally. In this event, the prior-period report and/or financial statements should be appropriately revised, and the report should contain a separate explanatory paragraph. The separate explanatory paragraph should disclose (1) the date of the original report and the date of the revised report, if different; (2) all of the substantive reasons for the change to the original report; and (3) if applicable, a statement to the effect that the financial statements of the prior period have been changed.

AR 200 previously required that either the predecessor or the successor accountant report on changed prior-period financial statements, as restated. The successor accountant was precluded from reporting on the restatement adjustment only.

The issuance of SSARS-12 revised AR 200 to allow the successor accountant to report on the restatement adjustment while stating that a predecessor accountant reported on the financial statements of the prior period before restatement. SSARS-12 amends AR 200 to include example reporting in these circumstances.

Predecessor accountant's report not reissued

A predecessor accountant may decide not to reissue the original prior-period report and not to issue any changed report on the prior period. In this event, the successor accountant should either (1) refer to the report of the predecessor accountant in the current report or (2) compile, review, or audit the prior-period financial statements.

SSARS-11 addressed a technical correction to SSARS-2. SSARS provide guidance to be followed when the financial statements of a prior period have been compiled or reviewed by a predecessor accountant whose report is not presented and the successor accountant has not compiled or reviewed those financial statements. SSARS-11 revised SSARS-2, footnote 9, to note that a successor accountant may name the predecessor accountant if the predecessor accountant's practice was acquired by or merged with that of the successor accountant.

If the predecessor accountant's report is not to be reissued and the successor accountant is not engaged to compile, review, or audit the prior-period financial statements, the successor accountant should expand the report on the current period to include a separate paragraph containing the following information:

1. Without naming the prior-period accountants, a statement that the prior-period financial statements were compiled, reviewed, or audited by other accountants (auditors)

2. The date of the prior-period report

3. A description of the form of disclaimer, limited assurance, or other opinion given in the prior-period report

4. Quotation or description of any modification in the prior-period report and of any matter emphasized in the report

An example of a separate paragraph for a compilation appears in Exhibit AR 200-6. An example of a separate paragraph for a review appears in Exhibit AR 200-7.

The successor accountant may compile, review, or audit prior-period financial statements even though they have already been compiled, reviewed, or audited by the predecessor accountant. This is particularly true when the client wants to upgrade the services of the prior period. Under these circumstances, the successor accountant (auditor) should consider the guidance provided by SSARS-4. The client must give both the predecessor accountant and the successor accountant permission to communicate with each other. The predecessor accountant may provide information that may affect the successor accountant's decision to accept the engagement. In addition to making specific inquiries of the predecessor accountant, the successor accountant may have an opportunity to review the predecessor accountant's workpapers for the prior period.

Considerations when the predecessor accountant has ceased operations

When the accountant presents a compilation or review report with a compilation, review, or audit report of a prior period, and the prior-period report was prepared by a predecessor accountant that has ceased operations, the successor auditor should follow SSARS-11 (Standards for Accounting and Review Services). SSARS-11 revises SSARS-2 to state that the successor practitioner may name the predecessor practitioner if the predecessor practitioner's practice was acquired by or merged with the successor practitioner's practice.

OBSERVATION: In some cases when the predecessor accountant has ceased operations, the successor accountant might believe that the prior-period financial statements should be revised. In this case, the successor auditor might consider the Notice to Practitioners titled "Audit, Review, and Compliance Considerations When a Predecessor Accountant has Ceased Operations" (a nonauthoritative practice aid) issued by the AICPA in February 1991. The Notice to Practitioners recommends that when the accountant believes that prior-period financial statements should be revised but the predecessor accountant has ceased operations, the successor accountant should suggest that the client notify "the party responsible for winding up the affairs of the predecessor firm" of the matter. If the client refuses to make the communication or if the reaction of the client's predecessor accountant is unsatisfactory, the successor accountant should discuss the matter with legal counsel.

An exception exists on the highest level of service rendered

SSARS-1 requires that the accountant report on the highest level of service rendered. For example, when a compilation is performed followed by a review of the same set of financial statements, the review report should be issued. An exception occurs, however, when the prior-period financial statements *do not* omit substantially all disclosures required by GAAP and the current-period financial statements *do* omit these disclosures. In this instance, the current period must be a compilation engagement, because when financial statements omit substantially all the disclosures required by GAAP, the accountant can only issue a compilation report. It is inappropriate for an accountant to issue a review report or an audit report on financial statements that omit substantially all disclosures. Thus, only when *all* periods are *compiled* and *all* periods omit substantially all disclosures can an accountant report on comparative financial statements that omit substantially all disclosures.

However, a situation may arise where the accountant has issued compiled financial statements that omit substantially all disclosures for the current period but issued a review report in the prior period and the client now requests *comparative* compiled financial statements that omit substantially all disclosures. In order for the financial statements to be comparative, the client must ask the accountant to compile the prior-period statements and omit substantially all disclosures. Although SSARS-1 requires that the accountant issue a report on the highest level of service for the prior period, SSARS-2 provides for an exception. Under SSARS-2, the accountant can reissue a prior-period report on the basis of a lower level of service if the following steps are taken:

1. The accountant must fully comply with all the standards applicable to reporting on compiled financial statements that omit substantially all disclosures.

2. A separate paragraph must be included in the accountant's report that discloses (1) the type of previous services rendered by the accountant in the prior period and (2) the date of the accountant's previous report.

Exhibit AR 200-8 presents an example of the required separate paragraph that is added to the end of the compilation report on the comparative financial statements that omit substantially all disclosures.

OBSERVATION: An accountant might be asked to issue a compilation report on financial statements that omit substantially all disclosures for financial statements that had previously been audited. Or the accountant might be asked to issue a compilation report on financial statements that omit substantially all disclosures for financial statements that had previously been reviewed or compiled and did not omit substantially all disclosures. Or the accountant might be asked to issue a compilation report on financial statements that omit substantially all disclosures for financial statements that had previously been audited. Or the accountant might be asked to issue a compilation report on financial statements that omit substantially all disclosures for financial statements that had previously been reviewed or compiled and did not omit substantially all disclosures. Or the accountant might be asked to issue a compilation report on financial statements that omit substantially all disclosures for financial statements that were previously audited, reviewed, or compiled (with disclosures included) to accompany current-year compiled financial statements (that omit substantially all required disclosures) so that comparative financial statements can be issued and reported upon. Interpretation No. 1 of AR 200 addresses the accountant's reporting obligation if the previous audit report was qualified, adverse, or a disclaimer of opinion, and if the previous review or compilation report was modified. In such instances, the accountant must add a separate paragraph to his or her report that discloses (1) the type of service rendered by the accountant in a prior period, (2) the date of the accountant's previous report, and (3a) the fact that a qualified report, adverse report, or disclaimer of opinion was issued and the reasons for the opinion issued or (3b) the fact that a modified compilation or review report was issued (or a compilation or review report was issued with an emphasis of matter) and the reasons for the modification or emphasis of matter.

The status of the client (issuer versus nonissuer) has changed

A company is an issuer or a nonissuer entity according to its status for the current period. If a company is classified as a nonissuer for the current period, an accountant can issue a compilation report or review report. If a company is classified as an issuer for the current period, however, the accountant usually cannot issue a compilation report or review report and must follow standards for public companies (standards of the Public Company Accounting Oversight Board).

A situation may arise where a company is an issuer entity for the current period and was a nonissuer entity in the prior period. The standards applicable to this situation are those applicable to the current period. Since the company is a public company in the current period, generally accepted auditing standards apply and compilation or review standards do not apply. Thus, a compilation report or review report issued for the prior period cannot be reissued or referred to in the audit report for the current period.

If a company is a nonissuer in the current period and its financial statements are compiled or reviewed, and if the company was a public company in the prior period and its financial statements were audited, the rules for "Current Period Compiled or Reviewed and Prior Period Audited" are used. In this event, the accountant should issue a compilation report or review report on the current period and either (1) reissue the audit report for the prior period or (2) add a separate paragraph to the current-period compilation report or review report describing the responsibility assumed by the accountant for the prior-period financial statements. The description paragraph should include the date of the prior-period report; a statement that the financial statements were previously examined; the type of opinion expressed, and if the opinion was other than unqualified, the substantive reasons for the qualification; and, finally, a statement that no auditing procedures have been performed since the date of the prior-period audit report. Exhibit AR 200-9 presents an example of a report where the current period has been compiled and the prior period has been audited.

If a company is a nonissuer in the current period and its financial statements are compiled or reviewed and an unaudited disclaimer of opinion was issued in the prior period, the unaudited disclaimer of opinion may not be reissued or referred to in the report on the financial statements for the current period. Under these circumstances, the accountant should comply with the compilation or review standards or perform an audit on the prior period and report accordingly.

Practitioner's Aids

The following practitioner's aids are presented in this section:

- Exhibit AR 200-1—Report on Comparative Financial Statements Where All Periods Have Been Compiled

- Exhibit AR 200-2—Report on Comparative Financial Statements Where All Periods Have Been Reviewed

- Exhibit AR 200-3—Report on Comparative Financial Statements Where the Current Period Is Reviewed and the Prior Period Is Compiled

- Exhibit AR 200-4—Additional Paragraph to a Compilation Report on the Current Period That Refers to the Prior Period That Had Been Reviewed

- Exhibit AR 200-5—Explanatory Paragraph Added to a Current Report That Refers to a Change in a Previous Report Issued by the Accountant

- Exhibit AR 200-6—Separate Paragraph Added to the Current Report That Refers to the Predecessor Accountant's Compilation Report

- Exhibit AR 200-7—Separate Paragraph Added to the Current Report That Refers to the Predecessor Accountant's Review Report

- Exhibit AR 200-8—Compilation Report on Comparative Financial Statements That Omit Substantially All Disclosures but Where the Prior Year Had Originally Been Reviewed by the Accountant

- Exhibit AR 200-9—Report on Comparative Financial Statements Where the Current Year Is Compiled and the Prior Year Is Audited

EXHIBIT AR 200-1—REPORT ON COMPARATIVE FINANCIAL STATEMENTS WHERE ALL PERIODS HAVE BEEN COMPILED

We have compiled the accompanying balance sheets of ABC Company as of March 31, 20X9 and 20X8, and the related statements of income, retained earnings, and cash flows for the years then ended, in accordance with Statements on Standards for Accounting and Review Services issued by the American Institute of Certified Public Accountants.

A compilation is limited to presenting in the form of financial statements information that is the representation of management. We have not audited or reviewed the accompanying financial statements and, accordingly, do not express an opinion or any other form of assurance on them.

EXHIBIT AR 200-2—REPORT ON COMPARATIVE FINANCIAL STATEMENTS WHERE ALL PERIODS HAVE BEEN REVIEWED

We have reviewed the accompanying balance sheets of ABC Company as of December 31, 20X9 and 20X8, and the related statements of income, retained earnings, and cash flows for the years then ended, in accordance with Statements on Standards for Accounting and Review Services issued by the American Institute of Certified Public Accountants. All information included in these financial statements is the representation of the management of ABC Company.

A review consists principally of inquiries of company personnel and analytical procedures applied to financial data. It is substantially less in scope than an examination in accordance with generally accepted auditing standards, the objective of which is the expression of an opinion regarding the financial statements taken as a whole. Accordingly, we do not express such an opinion.

Based on our reviews, we are not aware of any material modifications that should be made to the accompanying financial statements in order for them to be in conformity with generally accepted accounting principles.

EXHIBIT AR 200-3—REPORT ON COMPARATIVE FINANCIAL STATEMENTS WHERE THE CURRENT PERIOD IS REVIEWED AND THE PRIOR PERIOD IS COMPILED

We have reviewed the accompanying balance sheet of ABC Company as of December 31, 20X9, and the related statements of income, retained earnings, and cash flows for the year then ended in accordance with Statements on Standards for Accounting and Review Services issued by the American Institute of Certified Public Accountants. All information included in these financial statements is the representation of the management of ABC Company.

A review consists principally of inquiries of company personnel and analytical procedures applied to financial data. It is substantially less in scope than an examination in accordance with generally accepted auditing standards, the objective of which is the expression of an opinion regarding the financial statements taken as a whole. Accordingly, we do not express such an opinion.

Based on our review, we are not aware of any material modifications that should be made to the 20X9 financial statements in order for them to be in conformity with generally accepted accounting principles.

The accompanying 20X8 financial statements of ABC Company were compiled by us. A compilation is limited to presenting in the form of financial statements information that is the representation of management. We have not audited or reviewed the 20X8 financial statements and, accordingly, do not express an opinion or any other form of assurance on them.

EXHIBIT AR 200-4—ADDITIONAL PARAGRAPH TO A COMPILATION REPORT ON THE CURRENT PERIOD THAT REFERS TO THE PRIOR PERIOD THAT HAD BEEN REVIEWED

The accompanying 20X8 financial statements of ABC, Inc., were previously reviewed by me, and my report dated March 1, 20X9, stated that I was not aware of any material modifications that should be made to those statements in order for them to be in conformity with generally accepted accounting principles. I have not performed any procedures in connection with that review engagement after the date of my report on the 20X8 financial statements.

EXHIBIT AR 200-5—EXPLANATORY PARAGRAPH ADDED TO A CURRENT REPORT THAT REFERS TO A CHANGE IN A PREVIOUS REPORT ISSUED BY THE ACCOUNTANT

In my previous review report, dated March 1, 20X9, on the 20X8 financial statements, I referred to a departure from generally accepted accounting principles because the Company carried its land at appraised values. However, as disclosed in note X, the Company has restated its 20X8 financial statements to reflect its land at cost in accordance with generally accepted accounting principles.

EXHIBIT AR 200-6—SEPARATE PARAGRAPH ADDED TO THE CURRENT REPORT THAT REFERS TO THE PREDECESSOR ACCOUNTANT'S COMPILATION REPORT

The 20X8 financial statements of ABC Company were compiled by other accountants whose report, dated February 1, 20X9, stated that they did not express an opinion or any other form of assurance on those statements.

EXHIBIT AR 200-7—SEPARATE PARAGRAPH ADDED TO THE CURRENT REPORT THAT REFERS TO THE PREDECESSOR ACCOUNTANT'S REVIEW REPORT

The 20X8 financial statements of ABC Company were reviewed by other accountants whose report, dated March 1, 20X9, stated that they were not aware of any material modifications that should be made to those statements in order for them to be in conformity with generally accepted accounting principles.

EXHIBIT AR 200-8—COMPILATION REPORT ON COMPARATIVE FINANCIAL STATEMENTS THAT OMIT SUBSTANTIALLY ALL DISCLOSURES BUT WHERE THE PRIOR YEAR HAD ORIGINALLY BEEN REVIEWED BY THE ACCOUNTANT

We have compiled the accompanying balance sheets of ABC Company as of December 31, 20X9 and 20X8, and the related statements of income, retained earnings, and cash flows for the years then ended, in accordance with Statements on Standards for Accounting and Review Services issued by the American Institute of Certified Public Accountants.

A compilation is limited to presenting in the form of financial statements information that is the representation of management. We have not audited or reviewed the accompanying financial statements and, accordingly, do not express an opinion or any other form of assurance on them.

Management has elected to omit substantially all the disclosures required by generally accepted accounting principles. If the omitted disclosures were included in the financial statements, they might influence the user's conclusions about the company's financial position, results of operations, and cash flows. Accordingly, these financial statements are not designed for those who are not informed about such matters.

The accompanying 20X8 financial statements were compiled by us from financial information that did not omit substantially all of the disclosures required by generally accepted accounting principles and that we previously reviewed, as indicated in our report dated March 1, 20X9.

EXHIBIT AR 200-9—REPORT ON COMPARATIVE FINANCIAL STATEMENTS WHERE THE CURRENT YEAR IS COMPILED AND THE PRIOR YEAR IS AUDITED

We have compiled the accompanying balance sheet of ABC Company as of December 31, 20X9, and the related statements of income, retained earnings, and cash flows for the year then ended, in accordance with Statements on Standards for Accounting and Review Services issued by the American Institute of Certified Public Accountants.

A compilation is limited to presenting in the form of financial statements information that is the representation of management. We have not audited or reviewed the accompanying 20X9 financial statements and, accordingly, do not express an opinion or any other form of assurance on them.

The financial statements for the year ended December 31, 20X8, were audited by us (other accountants) and we (they) expressed an unqualified opinion on them in our (their) report dated March 1, 20X9, but we (they) have not performed any auditing procedures since that date.

AR SECTION 300

COMPILATION REPORTS ON FINANCIAL STATEMENTS IN CERTAIN PRESCRIBED FORMS

Authoritative Pronouncements

SSARS-3—Compilation Reports on Financial Statements in Certain Prescribed Forms

SSARS Interpretation 1—Omission of Disclosures in Financial Statements Included in Certain Prescribed Forms (May 1982)

SSARS-15—Elimination of Certain References to Statements on Auditing Standards and Incorporation of Appropriate Guidance into Statements on Standards for Accounting and Review Services

SSARS-17—Omnibus Statement on Standards for Accounting and Review Services—2008

Overview

In December 1981, the American Institute of Certified Public Accountants (AICPA) Accounting and Review Services Committee issued SSARS-3 (Compilation Reports on Financial Statements Included in Certain Prescribed Forms). The purpose of SSARS-3 is to provide an alternative report format when the prescribed form or related instructions call for departures from generally accepted accounting principles (GAAP) (or from a comprehensive basis of accounting other than GAAP). Thus, when a prescribed form is designed with material departures from GAAP, the accountant may issue (1) the standard compilation report with a description of the departures from GAAP or (2) the report described in SSARS-3, which makes no reference to the specific departures from GAAP.

Promulgated Procedures Checklist

The CPA should perform the following procedures in determining whether to report on financial statements formatted in certain prescribed forms:

- Determine whether the prescribed form is appropriate.
- Prepare an appropriate compilation report.

Analysis and Application of Procedures

Determine whether the prescribed form is appropriate

A "prescribed form" is any "standard form designed or adopted by the body to which it is to be submitted." A form designed or adopted by the client is not considered to be a prescribed form. Prescribed forms include financial statement formats used by industry trade associations, banks, and regulatory authorities.

OBSERVATION: The Robert Morris Associates (association of bank lending officers) and the AICPA have developed a Business Credit Information Package (BCIP) to be used by nonpublic businesses requesting loans from financial institutions. The BCIP includes, among other documents, a prescribed form for the preparation of financial statements that does not require all GAAP disclosures. This form of financial statement presentation falls within the requirements established by SSARS-3.

Prepare an appropriate compilation report

SSARS-3 adopts the basic philosophy that a body that prescribes a form for financial statements has defined the requirements it considers sufficient to meet its informational needs. Thus, except for when an audit report or a review report has been requested, the accountant's compilation report need not refer to departures from generally accepted accounting principles (including disclosure). Exhibit AR 300-1 is an example of a compilation report on financial statements included in a prescribed form that specifies measurement principles that do not conform to GAAP.

The SSARS Interpretation (May 1982) titled "Omission of Disclosures in Financial Statements Included in Certain Prescribed Forms" states that in a compilation report on financial statements included in a prescribed form, an accountant may refer to the review report previously issued on the financial statements if the difference between the previously reviewed financial statements and the financial statements included in the prescribed form is limited to the omission of disclosures not required by the form.

The following sentence might be added to the third paragraph presented in Exhibit AR 300-1:

> These financial statements were compiled by us from financial statements for the same period that we previously reviewed, as indicated in our report dated February 12, 20X9.

During the performance of the compilation, the accountant may discover departures from generally accepted accounting principles not sanctioned by the prescribed form or related instructions. Also, the accountant may discover departures from the prescribed format or instructions. In either case, such a departure requires that the accountant modify the compilation report by including a separate paragraph that describes the departure.

Practitioner's Aids

EXHIBIT AR 300-1—COMPILATION REPORT ON FINANCIAL STATEMENTS INCLUDED IN A PRESCRIBED FORM

We have compiled the accompanying balance sheet of X Company as of December 31, 20X8, and the related statements of income, retained earnings, and cash flows for the year then ended included in the accompanying prescribed form in accordance with Statements on Standards for Accounting and Review Services issued by the American Institute of Certified Public Accountants.

Our compilation was limited to the presentation of information that is the representation of management in the form prescribed by the West Virginia Fine Arts Commission. We have not audited or reviewed the financial statements referred to above and, accordingly, do not express an opinion or any other form of assurance on them.

These financial statements (including related disclosures) are presented in accordance with the requirements of the West Virginia Fine Arts Commission, which differ from generally accepted accounting principles. Accordingly, these financial statements are not designed for those who are not informed about such differences.

AR SECTION 400

COMMUNICATIONS BETWEEN PREDECESSOR AND SUCCESSOR ACCOUNTANTS

Authoritative Pronouncements

SSARS-4—Communications between Predecessor and Successor Accountants

SSARS-9—Omnibus Statement on Standards for Accounting and Review Services—2002

SSARS-15—Elimination of Certain References to Statements on Auditing Standards and Incorporation of Appropriate Guidance into Statements on Standards for Accounting and Review Services

SSARS-17—Omnibus Statement on Standards for Accounting and Review Services—2008

SSARS Interpretation 1—Reports on the Application of Accounting Principles (November 2002)

Overview

SSARS-4, as amended by SSARS-9, provides the following definitions:

> *Successor accountant:* An accountant who has been invited to make a proposal for an engagement to compile or review financial statements and is considering accepting the engagement or an accountant who has accepted such an engagement.

> *Predecessor accountant:* An accountant who (a) has reported on the most recent compiled or reviewed financial statements or was engaged to perform but did not complete a compilation or review of the financial statements, and (b) has resigned, declined to stand for reappointment, or been notified that his or her services have been, or may be, terminated.

The successor accountant may (but is not required to) communicate with the predecessor accountant, with the prospective client's permission, in order to determine whether a compilation or review engagement should be accepted. SSARS-9 notes that the inquiries "should be specific and reasonable regarding matters that will assist the successor accountant in determining whether to accept the engagement" and may include areas of inquiry such as the following:

- Management (owner's) integrity
- Disagreements concerning accounting principles, the performance of engagement procedures, or "similarly significant matters"
- Management cooperation with requests for additional or revised information
- Fraud or illegal acts
- The reason for the change of accountants

The predecessor accountant should respond promptly and fully to inquiries posed by the successor accountant except in cases of unusual circumstances such as litigation. When the response is limited, the predecessor accountant should inform the successor accountant about the situation.

The successor accountant may also request, with the client's permission, a review of the predecessor accountant's working papers. SSARS-9 notes that the predecessor accountant should determine which working papers should be made available to and copied by the successor accountant. SSARS-4 notes that the predecessor accountant may decide to request a written communication from the successor accountant before allowing access to working papers. Exhibit AR 400-1 reproduces an example letter that appears in SSARS-9 whereby the predecessor accountant requests a written communication from the successor accountant regarding the use of the predecessor accountant's working papers.

OBSERVATION: If the successor accountant discovers during the engagement that the financial statements compiled or reviewed by the predecessor accountant may have to be revised, the successor accountant should request the client to inform the predecessor accountant of this possibility. SSARS-9 states that if the client refuses to inform the predecessor accountant of the matter or is not satisfied with the predecessor accountant's response to the notification, the successor accountant should consider the impact (including withdrawal from the engagement or consultation with legal counsel) of such developments on the current engagement.

Promulgated Procedures Checklist

The successor accountant should perform the following procedures with respect to communications between the predecessor accountant and the successor accountant:

- Consider whether circumstances make it advisable to make inquiries of the predecessor accountant.

- Determine whether the predecessor accountant should be advised that prior-period financial statements must be revised.

Analysis and Application of Procedures

Consider whether circumstances make it advisable to make inquiries of the predecessor accountant

Although the successor accountant is not required to make inquiries of the predecessor accountant, circumstances surrounding the engagement might suggest that such inquiries ought to be made. SSARS-4 does not attempt to provide general or specific guidelines for defining which circumstances may suggest a need to communicate with the predecessor accountant, but it lists four examples that may lead the successor accountant to contact the predecessor accountant: (1) frequent changes of accountants, (2) limited information about the client and its principals, (3) existing information that raises questions about the client and its principals, or (4) the change of accountants at a date significantly after the end of the accounting period for which the service is to be provided.

Before the oral or written inquiries are made, the successor accountant must obtain the consent of the client, so that the predecessor accountant is not put in the position of violating Rule 301 (Confidential Client Information) of the AICPA's Code of Professional Conduct. If the client refuses to authorize the successor accountant to communicate with the predecessor accountant, the successor accountant should evaluate the basis for such refusal in deciding whether to accept the engagement. The predecessor accountant is expected to respond promptly and fully to the successor accountant's inquiries—except under unusual circumstances, such as impending litigation with respect to services performed by the predecessor accountant. If the predecessor accountant refuses to respond to the inquiries, he or she should explain to the successor accountant that responses are limited by circumstances.

The following items are identified as typical inquiries that the successor accountant might make:

- Information about the management's or owners' integrity

- Disagreements about accounting matters or the performance of procedures

- The degree of cooperation of management or the owners in providing additional or revised information

- The predecessor's knowledge of fraud or illegal acts perpetrated by the client

- The predecessor accountant's explanation of why there was a change of accountants

Other inquiries

SSARS-4 notes that a successor accountant may wish to make inquiries of the predecessor accountant as a typical part of the acceptance of any engagement, even if circumstances do not suggest that there may be problems with the client's management or its owners. For example, the successor accountant may simply wish to inquire about the adequacy of underlying financial data or about recurring problem areas of the engagement. Again, the predecessor accountant is expected to respond to reasonable requests from the successor accountant. However, the predecessor accountant still must obtain the client's permission to release information to the successor accountant.

The fact that the predecessor accountant has responded to inquiries or has made workpapers available to the successor accountant does not provide a basis for referring to the work of the predecessor accountant in the successor accountant's report. However, the predecessor accountant's report may be used when comparative financial statements are presented. The reporting formats for comparative financial statements when predecessor and successor accountants are involved are discussed in AR 200.

Determine whether the predecessor accountant should be advised that prior-period financial statements must be revised

During the engagement, the accountant may become aware of information that requires the revision of financial statements that the predecessor accountant reported on. Under this circumstance, SSARS-7 requires that the successor accountant request that the client communicate the information to the predecessor accountant.

PLANNING AID REMINDER: Accountants may be asked by entities that are not their clients to give advice on how a transaction should or could be accounted for and what type of opinion or assurance would be appropriate for a particular set of financial statements. In some instances, these requests are made by prospective clients who are shopping for an opinion. AU-C 915 (*Reports on the Application of an Applicable Financial Reporting Framework*) provides guidance in this area in the context of the audit. SSARS Interpretation No. 1 of AR 400 states that standards established by AU-C 915 are applicable to requests related to compilations and reviews as well as audit engagements.

EXHIBIT AR 400-1—PREDECESSOR ACCOUNTANT'S LETTER REQUESTING A WRITTEN COMMUNICATION FROM THE SUCCESSOR ACCOUNTANT CONCERNING ACCESS TO WORKING PAPERS

[*Date*]

[*Successor Accountant*]

[*Address*]

We have previously [reviewed *or* compiled], in accordance with Statements on Standards for Accounting and Review Services, the December 31, 20X5, financial statements of Bluefield Company. In connection with your [review *or* compilation] of Bluefield Company's 20X6 financial statements, you have requested access to our working papers prepared in connection with that engagement. Bluefield Company has authorized our firm to allow you to review those working papers.

Our [review *or* compilation] and the working papers prepared in connection therewith of Bluefield Company's financial statements were not planned or conducted in contemplation of your [review *or* compilation]. Therefore, items of possible interest to you might not have been specifically addressed. Our use of professional judgment for the purpose of this engagement means that matters may have existed that would have been assessed differently by you. We make no representation about the sufficiency or appropriateness of the information in our working papers for your purposes.

We understand that the purpose of your review is to obtain information about Bluefield Company and our 20X5 results to assist you in your 20X6 engagement of Bluefield Company. For that purpose only, we will provide you access to our working papers that relate to that objective.

Upon request, we will provide copies of those working papers that provide factual information about Bluefield Company. You agree to subject any such copies or information otherwise derived from our working papers to your normal policy for retention of working papers and protection of confidential client information. Furthermore, in the event of a third-party request for access to your working papers prepared in connection with your [review *or* compilation] of Bluefield Company, you agree to obtain our permission before voluntarily allowing any such access to our working papers or information otherwise derived from our working papers, and to obtain on our behalf any releases that you obtain from such third party. You agree to advise us promptly and provide us a copy of any subpoena, summons, or other court order for access to your working papers that include copies of our working papers or information otherwise derived therefore.

Please confirm your agreement with the foregoing by signing and dating a copy of this letter and returning it to us.

Very truly yours,

[*Predecessor Accountant*]

By: _____

Accepted:

[*Successor Accountant*]

By: _____

Date:

Note: SSARS-9 points out that to encourage the predecessor accountant to provide access to working papers, it may be desirable to add the following paragraph to the letter illustrated in Exhibit AR 400-1:

Because your review of our working papers is undertaken solely for the purpose described above and may not entail a review of all our working papers, you agree that (1) the information obtained from the review will not be used by you for any other purposes, (2) you will not comment, orally or in writing, to anyone as a result of that review about whether our engagement was performed in accordance with Statements on Standards for Accounting and Review Services, and (3) you will not provide expert testimony or litigation services or otherwise accept an engagement to comment on issues relating to the quality of our engagement.

AR SECTION 600

REPORTING ON PERSONAL FINANCIAL STATEMENTS INCLUDED IN WRITTEN PERSONAL FINANCIAL PLANS

Authoritative Pronouncements

SSARS-6—Reporting on Personal Financial Statements Included in Written Personal Financial Plans

SSARS Interpretation 1—Submitting a Personal Financial Plan to a Client's Advisers (May 1991)

Overview

SSARS-1 states that an accountant associated with unaudited financial statements of a nonissuer must either compile or review the financial statements. SSARS-6 (Reporting on Personal Financial Statements Included in Written Personal Financial Plans) provides an exception to this general requirement.

Promulgated Procedures Checklist

The accountant should perform the following procedures when reporting on personal financial statements included in written personal financial plans:

- Determine whether the standards established by SSARS-1 have to be observed.

- Prepare the appropriate report on the financial statements.

Analysis and Application of Procedures

Determine whether the standards established by SSARS-1 have to be observed

When an accountant prepares a written personal financial plan that includes unaudited personal financial statements, the requirements established by SSARS-1 (as amended) do not have to be observed if the following conditions exist:

- An understanding with the client is reached (preferably in writing) that the financial statements (1) will be used only by the client or the client's advisers to develop personal financial goals and objectives and (2) will not be used to obtain credit or for any purpose other than the establishment of goals and objectives related to the financial plan.

- During the engagement, nothing came to the accountant's attention that would suggest that the personal financial statements would be (1) used to obtain credit or (2) used for any purpose other than the establishment of financial goals and objectives for the client.

PLANNING AID REMINDER: SSARS Interpretation No. 1 of AR 600 states that actual implementation of the personal financial plan by the client or the client's advisers (investment adviser, attorney, insurance broker, etc.) is part of "developing a client's personal financial goals and objectives."

Prepare the appropriate report on the financial statements

If the accountant concludes that the exemption criteria described above have been satisfied, a written report should be prepared. The accountant's report should include the following comments:

- That the unaudited financial statements were prepared to facilitate the development of the client's personal financial plan
- That the unaudited financial statements may be incomplete or may contain other departures from generally accepted accounting principles and should not be used to obtain credit or for any purpose other than the establishment of the personal financial plan
- That the unaudited financial statements have not been audited, reviewed, or compiled by the accountant

An example of an accountant's report on personal financial statements included in a written personal financial plan is presented in Exhibit AR 600-1.

Each personal financial statement should contain a reference to the accountant's report (such as "See accountant's report").

PLANNING AID REMINDER: Although SSARS-6 provides an exemption to the requirements established by SSARS-1, the accountant is not precluded from observing the standards established by SSARS-1. It should also be noted that when an accountant decides to audit, review, or compile personal financial statements, ASC 274 (Accounting and Financial Reporting for Personal Financial Statements) requires that the personal financial statements present assets at their estimated current values and liabilities at their estimated current amounts at the date of the financial statements when presented in accordance with generally accepted accounting principles (GAAP). However, if the personal financial statements are presented at historical cost, instead of at current value, the presentation constitutes an other comprehensive basis of accounting.

Practitioner's Aids

EXHIBIT AR 600-1—ALTERNATIVE ACCOUNTANT'S REPORT ON PERSONAL FINANCIAL STATEMENTS INCLUDED IN WRITTEN PERSONAL FINANCIAL PLANS

The accompanying Statement of Financial Condition of [*name of client*], as of December 31, 20X8, was prepared solely to help you develop your personal financial plan. Accordingly, it may be incomplete or contain other departures from generally accepted accounting principles and should not be used to obtain credit or for any purposes other than developing your financial plan. We have not audited, reviewed, or compiled the statement.

APPENDIX A
The Sarbanes-Oxley Act of 2002

Introduction

The United States Congress passed, and President Bush signed into law, the Sarbanes-Oxley Act (SOX) in the summer of 2002. This legislation is viewed as the most far-reaching legislation affecting the accounting profession since the issuance of the securities laws of the 1930s that created the Securities and Exchange Commission (SEC). Provided here is an overview of the key components of SOX and related rules implemented by the SEC.

The Sarbanes-Oxley Act applies to SEC registrants and their auditors. Although SOX does not apply to private companies, not-for-profit organizations, or governmental entities, state boards of accountancy might incorporate portions of the act into state accountancy rules and regulations that apply to all audits.

The Sarbanes-Oxley Act comprises 11 sections:

1. The Public Company Accounting Oversight Board (PCAOB)
2. Auditor independence
3. Corporate responsibility
4. Enhanced financial disclosures
5. Analyst conflicts of interest
6. Commission resources and authority
7. Studies and reports
8. Corporate and criminal fraud accountability
9. White-collar crime penalty enhancements
10. Corporate tax returns
11. Corporate fraud and accountability

SOX is a direct result of financial reporting fraud at a number of major corporations, which increasingly became a matter of concern in the fall of 2001 with the first disclosure of problems at Enron. Those problems, combined with other frauds at Global Crossing, Qwest, Adelphia Communications, Tyco, and WorldCom increased public scrutiny of the financial reporting and related audit process. The resulting public outrage at these allegations of financial reporting fraud was reflected by the overwhelming votes in favor of SOX in both houses of Congress. SOX passed the Senate 99-0, and only three votes were cast against it in the House of Representatives.

Public Company Accounting Oversight Board

Among the more important provisions of SOX is the creation of the Public Company Accounting Oversight Board (PCAOB). The PCAOB's mission is to "Oversee the audits of public companies, to protect the interests of investors, and to further the public interest in the preparation of informative, accurate, and independent audit reports." The PCAOB is responsible for overseeing all aspects of the public accounting profession related to audits of SEC registrants (public companies). Much of the AICPA's former self-regulatory efforts over public company audits were obviated by the creation of the PCAOB.

All accounting firms that audit public company financial statements must register to practice with the PCAOB. In addition, the PCAOB has the authority to establish or adopt auditing, quality control, ethics, and independence standards for auditors of public companies. As part of its enforcement authority, the PCAOB conducts inspections of registered public accounting firms to assess compliance with SOX, SEC, and PCAOB rules, and other professional standards. Finally, the PCAOB investigates allegations of substandard performance by auditors of public companies and has the power to discipline offending accounting firms and individual auditors of public companies.

The PCAOB has five full-time members, only two of whom can be licensed CPAs. The SEC appoints board members after consulting with the Chairman of the Board of Governors of the Federal Reserve System and the U.S. Secretary of the Treasury. The term of service is five years, and board members are limited to two terms.

The PCAOB's current members are James Doty (Chairman), Lewis Ferguson, Daniel Goelzer, Jay Hanson, and Steve Harris. Doty and Ferguson are securities lawyers, and Ferguson served as the PCAOB's first general counsel. Goelzer is a CPA and has experience in public accounting, although he more recently practiced as a securities lawyer. Hanson is the PCAOB's other CPA, and he practiced public accounting for over 30 years and was a partner in a large regional accounting firm. Harris previously served as the Staff Director and Chief Counsel to the U.S. Senate Banking, Housing, and Urban Affairs Committee under Senator Sarbanes, and he was one of the primary drafters of the Sarbanes-Oxley Act.

With the exception of Jay Hanson, the accounting and auditing practice experience of the PCAOB's board members appears to be limited. Thus, it is likely that the board will rely heavily on its professional staff, particularly in setting auditing standards for audits of public companies. The PCAOB's Chief Auditor is Martin Baumann, who was previously the Director of the Office of Research and Analysis at the PCAOB and who prior to joining the PCAOB had a more than 30-year career with PricewaterhouseCoopers. Other professionals in the Office of the Chief Auditor include individuals with significant experience in the public accounting profession.

The PCAOB assesses and collects a registration fee and an annual fee from each registered public accounting firm. These fees are to be sufficient to recover the costs of both processing registrations and the required annual report that each registered accounting firm is to file with the PCAOB. Public companies are also assessed an annual accounting support fee.

Although the PCAOB is charged with promulgating auditing standards, SOX specifically requires that these standards include the following provisions:

- Registered public accounting firms must maintain workpapers in sufficient detail to support their conclusions in the audit report. The workpapers must be retained for at least seven years.

- The issuance of an audit report must be approved by a concurring or second partner. Each audit report must describe the scope of the auditor's internal control testing. The auditor must include, either in the audit report or in a separate report, the following items: (1) the auditor's findings from the internal control testing, (2) an overall evaluation of the entity's internal control structure and procedures, and (3) a description of any material weaknesses in internal controls.

- Quality control standards related to required internal firm consultations on accounting and auditing questions must be adhered to.

The PCAOB adopted the AICPA's Statements on Auditing Standards (SAS) that existed as of April 16, 2003 as its "Interim Auditing Standards." Since April 2003, the PCAOB has issued 15 Auditing and Related Professional Practice Standards (one of which has been superseded) and numerous rules.

The PCAOB inspects public accounting firms that regularly audit more than 100 public companies on an annual basis. Other public accounting firms that audit at least one public company are inspected no less often than once every three years. Inspections involve reviews of audit engagements and of the firm's quality control system. The PCAOB can report violations of (1) the Sarbanes-Oxley Act, (2) PCAOB and SEC rules, (3) the firm's own quality control standards, and (4) professional standards to the SEC and each appropriate state regulatory authority.

Registered public accounting firms and their employees are required to cooperate with PCAOB investigations. Firms that fail to cooperate in PCAOB investigations can be suspended or disbarred from being able to audit public companies, as can individual CPAs. Although the PCAOB does not have subpoena power (the PCAOB is specifically designated as a nongovernmental entity), there are procedures for the PCAOB to obtain needed information for an investigation using an SEC-issued subpoena. Documents and information gathered by the PCAOB in the course of an investigation are not subject to civil discovery. PCAOB sanctions include the suspension or disbarment of firms or individual CPAs from auditing public companies, as well as monetary penalties as high as $750,000 for individuals and $15 million for firms.

SOX amends the Securities Acts of 1933 and 1934 to define as "generally accepted accounting principles" those principles promulgated by a standards-setting body when the standards-setting body meets a number of requirements set out in SOX. The FASB's current structure meets the requirements set out in SOX. Thus, the PCAOB does not establish accounting standards.

The PCAOB's funding and the funding of the accounting standards-setting body (currently the FASB) are recoverable from annual accounting support fees. These annual accounting support fees are assessed against and are recoverable from public companies, where the amount of the fee due from each issuer is a function of the issuer's relative market capitalization.

Auditor Independence

SOX specifically prohibits accounting firms from performing any of the following services for a public company audit client:

- Bookkeeping services
- Financial information systems design and implementation
- Appraisal or valuation services, fairness opinions, or contribution-in-kind reports
- Actuarial services
- Internal audit outsourcing services
- Management or human resources functions
- Broker or dealer, investment adviser, or investment banking services
- Legal services and expert services unrelated to the audit

Many of these nonaudit services were already prohibited by SEC rules. However, the provision of any other nonaudit services for an audit client, including tax work, is now allowed only if approved in advance by the audit committee. In addition, the audit committee must preapprove all audit, review, or attest engagements required under the securities laws, as well as other audit services (e.g., comfort letters for underwriters, statutory audits, etc.).

Reporting to the Audit Committee

SOX requires the auditor to provide a timely report to the audit committee containing the following information: (1) a discussion of critical accounting policies and practices; (2) alternative accounting treatments discussed with management, the ramifications of these alternatives, and the auditor's preferred treatment; and (3) other material communications between the auditor and management (e.g., the management letter, schedule of unadjusted audit differences, engagement letter, independence letter). These required communications are in addition to, and do not supplant, the existing required communications from the auditor to the audit committee in already existing auditing professional standards (see, in particular, SAS-122 (AU-C 240, AU-C 260, AU-C 265, AU-C 580, AU-C 930). Although SAS-122 has not been adopted by the PCAOB, it is likely that auditors will make similar communications to the audit committees of public companies. SAS-122 (AU-C 265) requires auditors to communicate certain internal control related matters to the audit committee. Required communications to the audit committee relating to internal control are specified in AS-5. In addition, as the 2013 edition of CCH's *GAAS Guide* went to press, the PCAOB had outstanding an exposure draft of a standard on auditor communications to audit committees.

Mandatory Audit Partner Rotation

SOX requires that the lead audit partner and concurring partner on an audit of a public company be rotated every five years, and these individuals must remain off the engagement for at least five years. The SEC's interpretation of SOX extended this rotation requirement to other audit partners. Other audit partners must rotate after seven years and they must remain off the engagement for at least two years. The SEC defines other audit partners as (1) partners with decision-making responsibility on significant accounting, auditing, and reporting matters, (2) partners who maintain regular contact with management and the audit committee, and (3) lead partners on subsidiaries whose assets or revenues constitute 20% or more of the consolidated totals.

Audit Firm Personnel Movement to the Client

A registered public accounting firm is not independent of a public company if an individual who has direct responsibility for, or oversight of, those who prepare the company's financial statements and related information was employed by the registered public accounting firm and worked on the audit engagement within one year prior to the beginning of the current year's audit. Individuals who have responsibility for, or oversight of, the company's financial reporting process would include, at a minimum, the company's CEO, president, chief operating officer, CFO, controller, chief accounting officer, general counsel, treasurer, director of internal audit, director of financial reporting, or a member of the board of directors.

Required Disclosures of Services and Fees

Public companies must disclose in their annual proxy statement the services performed and the fees received by their registered public accounting firm during the previous year. These fees must be categorized into one of four categories: (1) audit fees, (2) audit-related fees, (3) tax fees, and (4) all other fees. Audit fees include fees for the annual audit and reviews of interim financial information, comfort letters, statutory audits, attest services, and consents and assistance related to documents filed with the SEC. Audit-related fees include fees for employee benefit plan audits, due diligence services related to mergers and acquisitions, accounting consultations and audits in connection with acquisitions, and attest services not required by statute or regulation. Tax fees and all other fees are self-explanatory.

Corporate Responsibility

SOX imposes increased responsibilities on audit committees and senior management for accurate financial reporting. In addition, SOX imposes penalties on senior management if financial statements have to be restated due to non-compliance with GAAP and related SEC regulations. SOX also proscribes any attempt by management or others acting at the direction of management to exert pressure on the auditor relating to the conduct of the audit.

Audit Committee Responsibilities

SOX specifies that the audit committee is directly responsible for the appointment, compensation, and oversight of the external auditor. SOX also requires that all members of the audit committee be independent. Audit committees are to establish procedures for handling complaints related to accounting, internal controls, and auditing matters, including complaints that are submitted anonymously. Audit committees are to be given the authority to retain independent counsel and other advisers, if they deem this to be necessary. Finally, each public company must provide the funding that the audit committee believes is necessary to compensate the registered public accounting firm. National securities exchanges (e.g., NYSE) and national securities associations (e.g., NASDAQ) are prohibited from listing securities issued by a company that is not in compliance with SOX's audit committee rules.

CEO and CFO Certifications

SOX requires the CEO and CFO of each public company to certify in each annual and quarterly report filed with the SEC the following conditions:

- That the CEO and CFO have reviewed the report
- To the best of the officers' knowledge, the report does not contain any material omissions or misstatements
- That the financial statements and other financial information included in the report fairly present the entity's financial condition and results of operations (compliance with GAAP if the financial statements are not fairly stated is not a defense under the terms of SOX)
- That the signing officers are responsible for the entity's internal control system, that the internal control system is appropriately designed, that the effectiveness of the internal control system has been evaluated within 90 days of the report, and that the officers' conclusions about the effectiveness of internal controls are included within the report
- That the signing officers have disclosed to their auditors and the audit committee significant deficiencies in the design or operation of the entity's internal control as well as any fraud (even if immaterial) involving management or employees with a significant role in the entity's internal control structure
- Whether there have been any significant changes in internal control subsequent to the date of its evaluation

Penalties in Cases of Restatements

SOX also requires the CEO and CFO of any issuer restating its financial statements because of material noncompliance with SEC financial reporting requirements to forfeit any bonus or incentive-based or equity-based compensation received within one year of the filing date of the financial statements that are subsequently restated. Profits realized from the sale of securities during this 12-month period also must be forfeited.

Improper Influence on the Conduct of an Audit

SOX makes it unlawful for any officer or director or any other person operating under an officer or director's direction, to coerce, manipulate, mislead, or fraudulently influence the external auditor in the audit of financial statements if that person knows or should have known that such action, if successful, could result in making the financial statements materially misleading. An attempt to coerce or manipulate the auditor implies compelling the auditor to act in a certain way through pressure, threats, trickery, intimidation, or some other form of purposeful action.

The SEC defines an "officer" as the CEO, president, vice presidents, secretary, treasurer, principal financial officer (often the CFO), controller, and principal accounting officer (CAO). In addition, the SEC defines "direction" as a broader concept than purely supervision. Examples of persons who might be under the direction of an officer or director but not under their supervision include customers, vendors, creditors, attorneys, securities professionals, and even other partners or employees of the accounting firm. According to the SEC, improper influence can happen (1) before the audit (e.g., during negotiations for the retention of the auditor), (2) during the audit, and (3) after the audit (e.g., when the auditor is considering whether to consent to the use of, reissuance of, or the withdrawal of a prior audit report). The SEC states that improper influence on the conduct of an audit is an illegal act, and Section 10A of the 1934 Exchange Act requires the auditor to file a report with the SEC when the auditor becomes aware of the client's participation in an illegal act.

The SEC provides numerous examples of behavior that is or might indicate improper influence on the conduct of an audit, including

- Offering or paying bribes or other financial incentives (e.g., offers of future employment or offers of contracts for nonaudit services)
- Providing an auditor with an inaccurate or misleading legal analysis
- Canceling or threatening to cancel existing nonaudit or audit engagements if the auditor objects to the company's accounting
- Seeking to have a partner removed from the engagement because a partner objects to the company's accounting
- Blackmail
- Physical threats
- Knowingly providing the auditor inadequate or misleading information that is key to the audit
- Pressuring the auditor to transfer managers or principals from the audit engagement
- And when predicated by an intent to defraud: (1) verbal abuse, (2) creating undue time pressure, (3) not providing information to the auditors on a timely basis, and (4) not being available to discuss matters with the auditor on a timely basis

Enhanced Financial Disclosures

The SOX section on financial disclosures requires certain behavior by management, prohibits certain activities, and significantly enhances financial statement disclosures.

Audit Adjustments

SOX requires public companies to reflect in the financial statements all material adjustments to the financial statements identified by the external auditor. Thus, there should be no waived or passed adjustments that have a material effect on the financial statements.

Disclosure of Off-Balance-Sheet Transactions

Companies must disclose all material off-balance-sheet transactions, arrangements, and obligations. The SEC now requires companies to explain their off-balance sheet arrangements in a new, and separately captioned, section of the MD&A section of the Form 10-K. Also, most companies are now required to include a table that presents an overview of certain known contractual obligations.

Pro Forma Financial Information

SOX specifically prohibits misleading pro forma financial information. Pro forma financial information also must be reconciled with the information that is required under GAAP.

Loans to and Stock Transactions by Executives

SOX generally prohibits personal loans to executives. In addition, stock transactions by directors, officers, and principal stockholders must be disclosed by the close of the second business day after the date of the stock transaction.

Internal Control Reports

SOX requires internal control reports in each annual report. Management must state that it is responsible for internal control over financial reporting and it must provide an assessment of the effectiveness of that internal control. Management must identify the framework it used in evaluating its internal controls over financial reporting (in all likelihood, the COSO framework, *Internal Control— Integrated Framework,* will be used in the United States).

Internal controls over financial reporting are designed to provide reasonable assurance that financial statements are prepared in accordance with GAAP. As such, internal controls are designed to

- Ensure the maintenance of records that in reasonable detail accurately and fairly reflect the transactions and dispositions of the company
- Provide reasonable assurance that transactions are recorded as necessary to permit preparation of financial statements in accordance with GAAP, and that receipts and expenditures are being made only in accordance with authorizations of management and the directors
- Provide reasonable assurance regarding prevention or timely detection of unauthorized acquisition, use, or disposition of the company's assets

Management's assessment of internal control over financial reporting must include an assessment of both the system's design and operating effectiveness. Controls that must be evaluated include those relating to

- Initiating, recording, processing, and reconciling account balances, classes of transactions, and disclosures
- Initiation and processing of nonroutine and nonsystematic transactions

- The selection and application of appropriate accounting policies
- The prevention, identification, and detection of fraud

Finally, the company's external auditor must issue its own opinion on the effectiveness of the company's internal control over financial reporting.

Code of Ethics

Public companies are required to state whether or not they have a code of ethics that applies to the company's principal executive officer, principal financial officer, principal accounting officer or controller and, if not, why not. The code of ethics must address requirements related to

- Honest and ethical conduct
- Full, fair, accurate, timely, and understandable disclosure in SEC filings and other public communications
- Compliance with applicable governmental laws, rules, and regulations
- Prompt internal reporting to an appropriate person of violations of the code
- Accountability for adherence to the code

The company must disclose its code of ethics, if one exists. The company can disclose its code of ethics as an exhibit to its annual report, on its Web site, or by providing without charge a copy of the code of ethics to any person upon request. Finally, any changes or waivers (including an implicit waiver) to the code of ethics for senior officers must be disclosed in a Form 8-K filing to the SEC.

Audit Committee Financial Expert

Public companies must disclose whether or not the audit committee contains at least one financial expert and, if not, why not. The company must disclose the name of the audit committee financial expert and state whether the expert is independent of management. An audit committee financial expert should possess

- An understanding of GAAP and financial statements
- An ability to assess the general application of GAAP to accounting for estimates, accruals, and reserves
- Experience in preparing, auditing, analyzing, or evaluating financial statements (or actively supervising individuals who perform these tasks) of comparable breadth and complexity to those of the company
- An understanding of internal control over financial reporting
- An understanding of audit committee functions

It is important to note that because a large proportion of board members have current or prior experience as a CEO, a principal executive officer with significant operations involvement but little financial or accounting involvement, would not meet the SEC's definition as exercising active supervision and therefore would not qualify as an audit committee financial expert.

Rapid Disclosure of Material Events

A company is required to disclose in plain English on a rapid and current basis (generally within four business days of the event's occurrence) any material change in the company's financial condition and results of operations. Items that are required to be disclosed on Form 8-K include

- Entering into a material definitive agreement not in the ordinary course of business (e.g., business combination agreements)

- Terminating a material definitive agreement not in the ordinary course of business

- New obligations under the terms of a material direct financial obligation (e.g., a short-term debt obligation arising in other than the ordinary course of business, a long-term debt obligation, and a lease, whether capital or operating), or if the company becomes directly or contingently liable for a material obligation arising from an off-balance sheet arrangement

- An event that accelerates (e.g., default) or increases a direct financial obligation or an obligation under an off-balance sheet arrangement

- Expected costs associated with an exit or disposal plan if the exit or disposal plan meets the criteria in ASC 420 (formerly known as FAS-146, Accounting for Costs Associated with Exit or Disposal Activities)

- Material asset impairment charges required to be recognized under GAAP

- A notice of delisting or a failure to continue to meet listing requirements received from a national securities exchange (e.g., NYSE) or association (e.g., NASDAQ)

- The sale of equity securities in a transaction that is not registered under the Securities Acts

- Material modifications to the rights held by any holders of a company's securities

- A determination by the company that its previously issued financial statements should no longer be relied upon because of an error in the financial statements, including situations where the company's auditor indicates that previously issued audit reports should no longer be relied upon

- If a director resigns from the board or chooses not to stand for reelection due to a disagreement with management, or if a director is removed from the board for cause

Analyst Conflicts of Interest

The Sarbanes-Oxley Act seeks to increase the objectivity and independence of securities analysts. SOX specifically requires that

- Analysts' research reports no longer be subject to clearance or approval by investment bankers

- Investment bankers be prohibited from providing input into the performance evaluations of research analysts

- Investment bankers be prohibited from threatening retaliation or retaliating against research analysts for reports that might adversely affect investment-banking relationships with existing or prospective clients

- Structural and institutional safeguards be established to protect research analysts from review, pressure, or oversight by investment bankers.

SOX also requires the disclosure of analyst conflicts of interest in both public appearances and published research reports. When discussing a particular company in a public appearance or research report, the analyst must disclose how much of the company's debt or equity securities the analyst's firm or the analyst personally owns. The analyst must disclose whether he or she personally or his or her firm has received any compensation from the company that is the subject of the research report. If the analyst is recommending a company's securities, he or she must disclose whether the company is a current client of his or her employer or if it has been a client during the past year. The analyst must also disclose whether his or her compensation is tied to investment banking revenues.

SEC Resources and Authority

SOX provides substantial incremental funding for the SEC. The SEC used a portion of this funding to hire a significant number of additional qualified professionals to oversee auditors and the public accounting profession.

The Sarbanes-Oxley Act also clarifies the ability of the SEC to censure individuals and to bar, either temporarily or permanently, individuals from practicing before the SEC. These remedies are available to the SEC if an individual

- Lacks the qualifications needed to represent others

- Lacks character or integrity

- Has engaged in unethical or improper professional conduct

- Has willfully violated, or helped others to willfully violate (i.e., aided and abetted) the securities laws

SOX defines "improper professional conduct" to include an intentional or knowing violation of applicable professional standards, including a violation attributable to reckless conduct. Improper professional conduct also includes two types of negligent conduct:

1. A single instance of highly unreasonable conduct, leading to a violation of professional standards, when the firm or the practitioner should have known that heightened scrutiny was warranted

2. Repeated instances of unreasonable conduct leading to a violation of professional standards, which suggests that the individual may lack the competence to practice before the SEC

Studies and Reports

SOX required either the SEC or the Government Accountability Office (GAO) (formerly known as the General Accounting Office) to conduct five types of studies. These studies involve examination of issues related to (1) the consolidation of the public accounting profession, (2) the role of credit rating agencies in the securities markets, (3) violations of securities laws, (4) SEC enforcement actions and restatements of financial statements, and (5) the role and functioning of investment banks in the securities markets.

The GAO studied the effects on the securities markets of the consolidation of the public accounting profession that began in the late 1980s, and it issued its report on July 30, 2003. The study included (1) factors leading to the consolidation of the profession, (2) the impact of this consolidation on capital formation and the securities markets, and (3) solutions to any problems identified, including ways to increase competition and increase the number of accounting firms able to audit large national and multinational companies. The study considered whether the consolidation of the public accounting profession has affected business organizations with regard to higher costs, lower quality, less choice, and lack of auditor independence.

The GAO found that the Big 4 firms have the potential for significant market power, although there is no evidence to date that competition has been impaired. The GAO failed to find any link between consolidation in the public accounting profession and either audit quality or audit independence. The GAO identified significant barriers to smaller accounting firms joining the ranks of the Big 4 and concluded that market forces are unlikely to expand the ranks of the four largest firms. The GAO updated this study in a report released in January of 2008. Although the GAO found that concentration continued in the audit market for large public companies, it made no recommendation for change.

The SEC studied the role of credit rating agencies in the securities markets and issued its report in January 2003. The study examined threats to the ability of credit rating agencies to accurately assess the risks of issuers. The study also examined barriers to the entry of new credit rating agencies and ways to remove those barriers.

As a result of this study, the U.S. Congress passed, and President Bush signed (September 29, 2006), the Credit Rating Agency Reform Act of 2006. The act amends the 1934 Securities Exchange Act and is designed to both improve the quality of credit ratings and to protect investors by increasing accountability, transparency, and competition in the credit rating industry. The Act creates a voluntary registration and regulatory program, overseen by the SEC, for credit rating agencies that want to be designated as a "nationally recognized statistical rating organization (NRSRO)."

The SEC has issued a rule to implement the Credit Rating Agency Reform Act. Under the SEC's rule, a credit rating agency seeking designation as a NRSRO must meet the following requirements: (1) be in business as a credit rating agency for at least the last three years and (2) issue credit ratings certified by qualified institutional buyers to one or more of the following groups: financial institutions, brokers, or dealers; insurance companies; corporate issuers; asset-backed securities issuers; and issuers of government or municipal securities. In order to qualify as a credit rating agency, the agency must (1) be engaged in the business of issuing credit ratings through a readily accessible means, for free or for a reasonable fee, (2) employ a quantitative or qualitative (or both) methodology in determining ratings, and (3) receive fees from either issuers, investors, or market participants.

Finally, the Wall Street Reform and Consumer Protection Act of 2011 (often referred to as the Dodd-Frank Act) directs government agencies to remove requirements from federal rules that require issuers of certain securities to obtain a report from a credit rating agency. Congress included this provision in the Dodd-Frank Act because of the disappointing performance of credit rating agencies related to their ratings of subprime mortgages, and securities derived therefrom, leading up to the financial crisis that began in the fall of 2008.

The SEC studied violations of securities laws between 1998 and 2001 and issued its report in January 2003. The study investigated how many public accountants, public accounting firms, investment bankers, investment advisers, brokers, dealers, attorneys, and other securities professionals were found to have aided and abetted in the violation of securities laws but who were not sanctioned or disciplined as a primary violator in either an administrative action or civil proceeding. The SEC also determined how many such individuals were found to have been primary violators of the securities laws. Finally, the SEC categorized the specific violations of securities laws, including sanctions imposed on the violators.

The SEC found that 1,596 securities professionals violated federal securities laws (or aided and abetted others in their violations of such laws) between 1998 and 2001. Public accountants and public accounting firms were not among the most frequent violators of federal securities laws. The sections of federal securities law most frequently violated were Section 10(b) of the 1934 Exchange Act and Section 17(a) of the 1933 Securities Act (which both relate to the antifraud provisions of the related securities acts).

The SEC conducted a study of its enforcement releases and financial statement restatements during the five-year period prior to the passage of SOX and issued its report in January 2003. The focus of the study was to identify the financial reporting areas most susceptible to fraud, inappropriate manipulation, or inappropriate earnings management. The SEC studied enforcement actions issued during the five-year period between July 31, 1997 and July 31, 2002 that were based on improper financial reporting, fraud, audit failure, or auditor independence violations. The most frequent area involving an enforcement action was improper revenue recognition. A significant number of enforcement actions also involved improper expense recognition, including improper capitalization or deferral of expenses, improper use of reserves, and other understatements of expenses. In approximately 75% of the cases the enforcement action was brought against one or more members of senior management. Eighteen enforcement actions were brought against auditing firms and 89 actions were brought against individual auditors. Enforcement actions against auditors typically resulted from lack of audit evidence, lack of skepticism, and lack of independence.

The GAO conducted a study to determine whether investment banks helped companies manipulate their earnings and obfuscate their true financial condition. SOX specifically required the GAO to address the role investment banks played in designing derivative transactions and special-purpose entities for the Enron Corporation and in swapping of fiber-optic capacity by Global Crossing. The GAO issued its report on March 17, 2003. The GAO found that certain investment banks facilitated complex financial transactions with Enron despite allegedly knowing that the intent of these transactions was to obfuscate Enron's true financial condition. The GAO also found that control groups within financial institutions and bank regulators have increased their review and scrutiny of structured finance transactions in the wake of the problems at Enron and Global Crossing.

Corporate and Criminal Fraud Accountability

SOX imposes severe criminal penalties for prohibited forms of document destruction and for violations of the securities laws. Prison sentences of up to 20 years can be imposed for the destruction, alteration, or falsification of records in federal investigations and bankruptcy. Auditors must retain for seven years their workpapers and other relevant documents related to audit conclusions. Failure to comply with these SEC rules and regulations can result in prison terms of up to 10 years. An individual who knowingly attempts to execute or executes a scheme or artifice to defraud any person relative to the securities laws faces prison sentences of up to 25 years.

SOX changed the bankruptcy laws to specify that debts incurred as a result of violations of the securities laws are not dischargeable in bankruptcy. The length of time to file a civil suit under the securities laws was extended to two years after discovering the violation or five years after the violation occurred.

SOX provides whistleblowers with certain protections against retaliation by the public company or its agents. Parties can be imprisoned for up to 10 years for knowingly retaliating against an individual for providing truthful information to a law enforcement officer regarding the commission of a federal offense. In addition, the Dodd-Frank Act of 2011 strengthened these whistleblower protections. Moreover, the Dodd-Frank Act created a bounty system for whistleblowers. If a whistleblower provides original information to the SEC that leads to a Commission enforcement action that results in a penalty of $1 million or more, the whistleblower is eligible for a payment of between 10% and 30%.

White-Collar Crime Penalty Enhancements

SOX amends the U.S. Code by increasing the criminal penalties for both mail and wire fraud from five years to 20 years. In addition, SOX imposes criminal penalties on CEOs and CFOs when they certify financial reports that do not comport with the requirements of the act. The penalties are a fine of as much as $1 million and imprisonment for as many as 10 years for improper certifications, and a fine of as much as $5 million and imprisonment for as many as 20 years for willfully improper certifications.

Corporate Tax Returns

The Sarbanes-Oxley Act contains a sense of the Senate, which is not a legal requirement, that CEOs should sign the corporate tax return.

Corporate Fraud and Accountability

SOX imposes fines and potential prison terms of up to 20 years for tampering with a record, document, or other object or otherwise impeding an official proceeding. In addition, criminal penalties available under the Securities and Exchange Act of 1934 have been increased.

In some cases, public companies attempt to make large payments to officers, directors, and others when the company is under investigation for possible violations of securities laws. SOX empowers the SEC to petition a federal district court to restrain a public company from making extraordinary payments to officers, directors, and others during the course of an investigation. The proposed payments would be placed in escrow for 45 days, and one extension of the 45-day period may be obtained. If the company is charged with a securities law violation, the contemplated extraordinary payments would continue to be held in escrow until the case is resolved.

SOX makes it easier for the SEC to suspend or permanently prohibit an individual from serving as an officer or director of a public company if the individual has violated Section 10(b) of the 1934 Securities and Exchange Act or Section 17(a) of the 1933 Securities Act. Previously, the SEC had to bring an action in federal court to bar an individual from serving as an officer or director of a public company.

Emerging Trends

In the 10 years that SOX has been in effect, trends that are a result of the act have emerged:

- Audit committees are more engaged in financial reporting oversight than ever before, they are meeting more often and they are increasingly taking control of the relation with the external auditor. However, there are still too many cases where the audit committee, although legally charged with overseeing the external audit process, defers to management. See the speech that PCAOB Chairman James Doty delivered on May 5, 2011, at Baruch College, in which he discusses audit committees' inappropriate focus in too many instances on reducing fees rather than ensuring audit quality (see www.pcaobus.org).

- Audit fees have increased, in some cases by a substantial percentage. However, in more recent years, likely due to the recession, there has been substantial downward pressure on audit fees. Downward pressure on audit fees can represent a substantial threat to audit quality.

- The PCAOB is having a pervasive impact on the practice of public accounting.

- Accounting standards issued by the FASB are likely to be more principles-based, and the FASB and the International Accounting Standards Board are increasingly working together to issue converged accounting standards that have broad applicability around the globe.

- Aspects of SOX are likely to affect private companies, not-for-profit organizations, and governmental entities, and the auditors who serve these companies, particularly in states with more aggressive regulation and in certain regulated industries.

- Some formerly public companies have gone private, at least in part due to the significant compliance burden imposed by SOX.

- Private companies that hope to go public or be acquired by a public company are taking steps to comply with most of SOX's provisions.

Further consequences from Sarbanes-Oxley will only become apparent with the passage of time.

Recent Developments

The Sarbanes-Oxley Act of 2002 has been criticized heavily by certain groups. Many of these criticisms were tied to the cost and complexity of issuing a management report on the effectiveness of internal control over financial reporting (Section 404a), as well as the auditor's own opinion on the effectiveness of the company's internal control over financial reporting (Section 404b). As a result of these criticisms, the SEC undertook a number of initiatives.

The SEC extended the effective date of Section 404 for smaller public companies (i.e., nonaccelerated filers) for a number of years. However, for fiscal years ending after December 15, 2007, companies with a market capitalization below $75 million have to include in their Form 10-K a management report on the effectiveness of internal control over financial reporting. However, unlike for larger public companies, and as a result of the Dodd-Frank Act of 2011, smaller companies (i.e., non-accelerated filers) are permanently exempted from having an external auditor report on the effectiveness of the company's internal control over financial reporting.

The SEC also asked the Committee of Sponsoring Organizations of the Treadway Commission (COSO) to develop implementation guidance for applying its internal control framework for smaller public companies. In 2006 COSO issued *Internal Control over Financial Reporting—Guidance for Smaller Public Companies*, which provides implementation guidance for applying COSO's internal control framework in a manner that seeks to maintain the effectiveness of internal control reporting while reducing its cost and complexity. COSO has released *Guidance on Monitoring Internal Control Systems*, which is designed to help management better utilize the results of monitoring to support management's conclusions about the effectiveness of internal control over financial reporting. In addition, as the 2013 *GAAS Guide* went to press, COSO has issued an Exposure Draft of an update to its internal control framework (Internal

Control—Integrated Framework, 1992). Although the broad guidance included in COSO's framework is essentially unchanged, the COSO internal control framework is being updated for developments that have occurred over the 20-year period since its issuance.

In early 2006 a small accounting firm and a private special-interest group filed suit in federal court challenging the constitutionality of the PCAOB. The U.S. District Court hearing the case found for the PCAOB, as did a three-judge panel of the Court of Appeals for the D.C. Circuit. In May 2009 the U.S. Supreme Court announced that it would hear the case in its 2009–2010 year. The Supreme Court heard arguments on the case in December 2009 and a decision by the Court was issued in June 2010. The Supreme Court held that the Sarbanes-Oxley Act's provisions making PCAOB Board members removable by the Securities and Exchange Commission (SEC) only for good cause were inconsistent with the Constitution's separation of powers. Because the Court severed these provisions from the Act, however, no legislation was necessary to bring the Board's structure within constitutional requirements. The consequence of the Court's decision is that PCAOB Board members will be removable by the SEC at will, rather than only for good cause.

Also, the SEC has issued a document that provides guidance to management in performing its evaluation of the effectiveness of internal control over financial reporting. In addition, the PCAOB has released a standard on auditor reporting on internal control (AS-5) that replaces the Board's previous standard, AS-2. Both documents share a number of similarities, including (1) emphasizing that evaluating internal control should follow a top-down risk-based process, (2) greater reliance on ongoing monitoring as support for management's evaluation and greater reliance on the work of others to support the auditor's opinion, and (3) numerous changes to afford management and the auditor more flexibility in evaluating the design and operating effectiveness of internal control, which are designed to reduce the cost and burden of internal control reporting.

As the 2013 *GAAS Guide* went to press the PCAOB was considering three major policy changes. First, the Board has issued a concept release on the form and content of the standard audit report. The PCAOB was considering requiring auditors to provide more information about the audit and the audited financial statements, either in required emphasis-of-matter paragraphs or in a separate auditor report (referred to as an Auditor Discussion and Analysis). Second, the PCAOB has issued a proposed rule that would require the disclosure of the identity of the engagement partner in the audit report, and that would identify the names and locations of other audit firms that played a substantial role in performing the audit. Third, the Board had issued a concept release that discusses the merits of requiring audit firm rotation in increasing audit firm independence, objectivity, and professional skepticism. The ultimate resolution of these three initiatives remains highly uncertain at the time this guide went to press.

Accounting Resources on the Web

Presented here are World Wide Web URLs of interest to practitioners. Because of the constantly changing nature of the Internet, addresses change and new resources become available every day. To find additional resources, use search engines such as Bing (http://www.bing.com/), Google (http://www.google.com/), and Yahoo! (http://search.yahoo.com).

Accountants World http://www.accountantsworld.com/

Accounting Research Manager® http://www.AccountingResearchManager.com/

Action Without Borders-Idealist.org http://www.idealist.org/

AICPA Guidance Related to OMB Circular A-133 http://gaqc.aicpa.org/Resources/OMB+Circular+A-133/

AICPA http://www.aicpa.org

American Accounting Association http://aaahq.org/

American Legal Publishing Corp. http://www.amlegal.com/library/

American Water Works Association http://www.awwa.org/

Association of Certified Fraud Examiners (ACFE) http://www.cfenet.com/

Association of College and University Auditors (ACUA) http://www.acua.org/

Association of Government Accountants (AGA) http://www.agacgfm.org/

Association of School Business Officials International http://www.asbointl.org/

AuditNet http://www.auditnet.org/

Automated Clearing House http://www.fms.treas.gov/ach/

Better Business Bureau: Charities and Donors http://www.bbb.org/us/charity/

BoardSource http://www.boardsource.org/

Bureau of Labor Statistics http://www.bls.gov/

CAMICO Mutual Insurance Company https://www.camico.com/

Cash Management Improvement Act http://www.fms.treas.gov/cmia/

Catalog of Federal Domestic Assistance (CFDA) http://www.cfda.gov/

CCH Audio Seminars http://tax.cchgroup.com/AudioSeminars/

CCH Incorporated http://tax.cchgroup.com/default

CCH Learning Center http://cch.LearningCenter.com/partners/cchcpe/

Check Payment Systems Association http://www.cpsa-checks.org/

Code of Federal Regulations http://www.gpoaccess.gov/cfr/index.html

Compliance Supplement http://www.whitehouse.gov/omb/circulars_a133_compliance_09toc/

Council of the Inspectors General on Integrity & Efficiency (CIGIE) http://www.ignet.gov/related1.html

Council of State Governments (CSG) http://www.csg.org/

Council on Foundations http://www.cof.org/

Data Collection Form on-line http://harvester.census.gov/fac/collect/ddeindex.html

Data Collection Form options http://harvester.census.gov/fac/collect/formoptions.html

Department of Education OIG's Non-Federal Audit Team http://www2.ed.gov/about/offices/list/oig/nonfed/index.html

Electronic Privacy Information Center http://epic.org/

Evangelical Council for Financial Accountability (ECFA) http://www.ecfa.org/

EzGov http://www.ezgov.com/

FASB http://www.fasb.org/

FASB Accounting Standards Codification (ASC) http://asc.fasb.org/home

Federal Agencies Web Locator http://www.lib.lsu.edu/gov/index.html

Federal Audit Clearinghouse http://harvester.census.gov/sac

Federal Financial Accounting Standards Board (FASAB) http://www.fasab.gov/

Federal Inspectors General (IGnet) http://www.ignet.gov/

Federal Register http://www.gpoaccess.gov/fr/index.html

FEDSTATS http://www.fedstats.gov/

FirstGov http://www.firstgov.gov/

Foundation Center http://www.fdncenter.org/

GASB http://www.gasb.org/

General Code Publishers http://www.generalcode.com/

General Services Administration http://www.gsa.gov/

Government Accountability Office http://www.gao.gov/

Government Accounting Standards http://www.gao.gov/govaud/ybk01.htm

Government Finance Officers Association (GFOA) http://www.gfoa.org/

Government Information Locator Service (GILS) http://www.gpoaccess.gov/gils/index.html

Government Printing Office Finding Tools http://www.gpoaccess.gov/index.html

Government Printing Office http://www.gpo.gov/

GuideStar http://www.guidestar.org/

Health and Human Services (HHS) grants programs http://www.hhs.gov/grantsnet/

Health and Human Services (HHS) http://www.hhs.gov/

HUD Office of Public and Indian Housing (PIH) http://www.hud.gov/offices/pih/

HUD Real Estate Assessment Center (REAC) http://www.hud.gov/offices/reac/

Infomine government publications http://infomine.ucr.edu/cgi-bin/search?govpub

Information for Tax-Exempt Organizations http://www.irs.gov/charities/index.html

Institute of Internal Auditors, The (IIA) http://www.theiia.org/

Institute of Management Accountants (IMA) http://www.imanet.org/

IntelliConnecttrade; http://tax.cchgroup.com/IntelliConnect/

Intergovernmental Audit Forums http://www.auditforum.org/

International Accounting Standards Board (IASB) http://www.iasb.org.uk/

International City/County Managers Association http://www.icma.org/

International Institute of Municipal Clerks (IIMC) http://www.iimc.com/

IRS Digital Daily http://www.irs.gov/

IT Audit (The IIA) http://www.theiia.org/itaudit/

Legal Information Institute (Cornell Law School) http://www.law.cornell.edu/statutes.html

Legal Services Corporation (LSC) http://oig.lsc.gov/

LexisNexis Municipal Codes Publishing http://www.bpcnet.com/codes.htm

List of Parties Excluded from Federal Procurement and Nonprocurement Programs http://epls.arnet.gov/

Local Government Institute (LGI) http://www.lgi.org/local_govt__institute.htm

LSU Libraries Government Documents http://www.lib.lsu.edu/govdocs/index.html

Minority Business Development Agency http://www.mbda.gov/

Municipal Code Corporation (MCC) http://www.municode.com/

Municipal Codes Online (Seattle Public Library) http://www.spl.lib.wa.us/default.asp?pageID=collection_municodes

NACHA—The Electronic Payments Association http://www.nacha.org/

National Association of College and University Business Officers (NACUBO) http://www.nacubo.org/

National Association of Counties (NACO) http://www.naco.org/

National Association of Housing and Redevelopment Officials (NAHRO) http://www.nahro.org/

National Association of Regional Councils http://www.narc.org/

National Association of State Agencies for Surplus Property http://www.nasasp.org/

National Association of State Auditors, Comptrollers, and Treasurers (NASACT) http://www.nasact.org/

National Association of State Boards of Accountancy (NASBA) http://www.nasba.org/

National Association of State Budget Officers http://www.nasbo.org/

National Center for Charitable Statistics http://nccs.urban.org/

National Conference of State Legislatures (NCSL) http://www.ncsl.org/

National Council of Nonprofits http://www.CouncilOfNonprofits.org/

National Governors' Association (NGA) http://www.nga.org/

National Labor Relations Board http://www.nlrb.gov/

National League of Cities (NLC) http://www.nlc.org/

National Rural Development Partnership http://www.rurdev.usda.gov/nrdp/

Nonprofit Gateway http://www.firstgov.gov/Business/Nonprofit.shtml

North American Industry Classification System (NAICS) http://www.census.gov/epcd/www/naics.html

Occupational Employment Statistics http://stats.bls.gov/oes/home.htm

Office of Federal Contract Compliance Programs (OFCCP) http://www.dol.gov/ofccp/index.htm

Office of Management and Budget http://www.whitehouse.gov/omb

OMB Grants Management forms http://www.whitehouse.gov/omb/grants/grants_forms.html

OMB grants management http://www.whitehouse.gov/omb/grants

OMB submissions to the Federal Register http://www.whitehouse.gov/omb/fedreg/index.html

Office of Women's Business Ownership (SBA) http://www.sba.gov/aboutsba/sbaprograms/onlinewbc/

Police List of Resources http://police.sas.ab.ca/prl/elect.html

Privacy Foundation http://www.privacyfoundation.org/

Prompt Payment Act Interest Rate http://www.treasurydirect.gov/govt/rates/tcir/tcir_opdprmt2.htm

ProSystem *fx*® Suite http://tax.cchgroup.com/ProSystem/default

Securities and Exchange Commission http://www.sec.gov/

SF-SAC form on-line http://harvester.census.gov/fac/collect/ddeindex.html

SF-SAC form PDF http://harvester.census.gov/fac/collect/sfsac_01.pdf

Software and Information Industry Association (SIIA) http://www.siia.net/

State and local links http://www.StateLocal.gov

Sterling Codifiers, Inc. http://www.sterlingcodifiers.com/

The Library of Congress http://www.loc.gov/

The White House http://www.whitehouse.gov/

Thomas: Legislative Information http://thomas.loc.gov/

Treasury - Financial Management Service http://www.fms.treas.gov/

U.S. Census Bureau http://www.census.gov/

U.S. Code Search http://uscode.house.gov/

U.S. Conference of Mayors http://www.usmayors.org/

U.S. Department of Agriculture http://www.usda.gov/

U.S. Department of Commerce http://www.commerce.gov/

U.S. Department of Defense http://www.defense.gov/

U.S. Department of Education http://www.ed.gov/

U.S. Department of Energy http://www.energy.gov/

U.S. Department of Health and Human Services http://www.dhhs.gov/

U.S. Department of Housing and Urban Development http://www.hud.gov/

U.S. DOL Davis-Bacon and Related Acts (DBRA) http://www.dol.gov/compliance/laws/comp-dbra.htm

U.S. Department of Labor Wage and Hour Division http://www.dol.gov/whd/index.htm

U.S. Department of Labor http://www.dol.gov/

U.S. Department of State http://www.state.gov/

U.S. Department of the Interior http://www.doi.gov/

U.S. Department of the Treasury's Listing of Approved Sureties http://www.fms.treas.gov/c570/c570.html

U.S. Department of Transportation http://www.dot.gov/

U.S. Dept. of Treasury Financial Management Service http://www.fms.treas.gov/

U.S. Environmental Protection Agency http://www.epa.gov/

U.S. GAO Bid Protest Decisions http://www.gao.gov/decisions/bidpro/bidpro.htm

U.S. government forms http://www.gsa.gov/forms

U.S. House of Representatives http://www.house.gov/

U.S. House of Representatives Current Floor Proceedings http://clerk.house.gov/floorsummary/floor.html

U.S. HUD Client Information and Policy System http://www.hudclips.org/cgi/index.cgi

U.S. HUD Office of Inspector General http://www.hud.gov/offices/oig/

U.S. HUD Office of Labor Relations http://www.hud.gov/offices/olr/index.cfm

U.S. Postal Service http://www.usps.com/

U.S. Senate http://www.senate.gov/

U.S. Small Business Administration http://www.sba.gov/

U.S. State & Local Gateway http://firstgov.gov/Government/State_Local.shtml

U.S. Treasury http://www.treas.gov/

USA CityLink http://usacitylink.com/
Veterans Affairs http://www.va.gov/
WomenBiz http://www.womenbiz.gov/
Yellow Book http://www.gao.gov/govaud/ybk01.htm
ZIP+4 Code lookup http://www.usps.com/zip4/

Cross-Reference

STATEMENTS ON AUDITING STANDARDS (SASs) AND SAS INTERPRETATIONS

ORIGINAL PRONOUNCEMENT	GAAS GUIDE REFERENCE
Note: *SAS-122 through SAS-125 recodified and superseded all outstanding SASs through SAS-121 except SAS-59, SAS-65, SAS-117, SAS-118, SAS-119, and SAS-120.*	
SAS-59 —The Auditor's Consideration of an Entity's Ability to Continue as a Going Concern	AU 570
SAS No. 65 —The Auditor's Consideration of the Internal Audit Function in an Audit of Financial Statements	AU 610
SAS-117 — Compliance Audits	AU 935
SAS-118 — Other Information In Documents Containing Audited Financial Statements	AU 720, AU 725
SAS-119 — Supplementary Information in Relation to the Financial Statements as a Whole	AU 725
SAS-120 — Required Supplementary Information	AU 730
SAS-122 — Clarification and Recodification	
Principles Underlying an Audit Conducted in Accordance with Generally Accepted Auditing Standard	Preface to Codification of Statement on Auditing Standards

ORIGINAL PRONOUNCEMENT	GAAS GUIDE REFERENCE
Overall Objectives of the Independent Auditor and the Conduct of an Audit in Accordance with Generally Accepted Auditing Standards	AU-C 200
Terms of Engagement	AU-C 210
Quality Control for an Engagement Conducted in Accordance with Generally Accepted Auditing Standards	AU-C 220
Audit Documentation	AU-C 230
Consideration of Fraud in a Financial Statement Audit	AU-C 240
Consideration of Laws and Regulations in an Audit of Financial Statements	AU-C 250
The Auditor's Communication with Those Charged with Governance	AU-C 260
Communicating Internal Control Related Matters Identified in an Audit	AU-C 265
Planning an Audit	AU-C 300
Understanding the Entity and Its Environment and Assessing the Risks of Material Misstatement	AU-C 315
Materiality in Planning and Performing an Audit	AU-C 320
Performing Audit Procedures in Response to Assessed Risks and Evaluating the Audit Evidence Obtained	AU-C 330
Audit Considerations Relating to an Entity Using a Service Organization	AU-C 402
Evaluation of Misstatements Identified During the Audit	AU-C 450
Audit Evidence	AU-C 500
Audit Evidence — Specific Considerations for Selected Items	AU-C 501
External Confirmations	AU-C 505
Opening Balances — Initial Audit Engagements, Including Reaudit Engagements	AU-C 510
Analytical Procedures	AU-C 520
Audit Sampling	AU-C 530

ORIGINAL PRONOUNCEMENT	GAAS GUIDE REFERENCE
Auditing Accounting Estimates, Including Fair Value Accounting Estimates, and Related Disclosures	AU-C 540
Related Parties	AU-C 550
Subsequent Events and Subsequently Discovered Facts	AU-C 560
Going Concern	AU-C 570
Written Representations	AU-C 580
Consideration of Omitted Procedures after the Report Release Date	AU-C 585
Special Considerations — Audits of Group Financial Statements (Including the Work of Component Auditors)	AU-C 600
Using the Work of Internal Auditors	AU-C 610
Using the Work of an Auditor's Specialist	AU-C 620
Forming an Opinion and Reporting on Financial Statements	AU-C 700
Modifications to the Opinion in the Independent Auditor's Report	AU-C 705
Emphasis-of-Matter Paragraphs and Other-Matter Paragraphs in the Independent Auditor's Report	AU-C 706
Consistency of Financial Statements	AU-C 708
Special Considerations — Audits of Financial Statements Prepared in Accordance with Special Purpose Frameworks	AU-C 800
Special Considerations — Audits of Single Financial Statements and Specific Elements, Accounts, or Items of a Financial Statement	AU-C 805
Reporting on Compliance with Aspects of Contractual Agreements or Regulatory Requirements in Connection with Audited Financial Statements	AU-C 806
Engagements to Report on Summary Financial Statements	AU-C 810
Reports on Application of Requirements of an Applicable Financial Reporting Framework	AU-C 915

ORIGINAL PRONOUNCEMENT	GAAS GUIDE REFERENCE
Letters for Underwriters and Certain Other Requesting Parties	AU-C 920
Filings with the U.S. Securities and Exchange Commission under the Securities Act of 1933	AU-C 925
Interim Financial Information	AU-C 930
SAS-123 — Omnibus Statement on Auditing Standards — 2011	AU-C 200, AU-C 230, AU-C 260, AU-C 705, AU-C 720, AU-C 915, AU-C 935
SAS-124 — Financial Statements Prepared in Accordance with a Financial Reporting Framework Generally Accepted in Another Country	AU-C 910
SAS-125 — Alert that Restricts the Use of the Auditor's Written Communication	AU-C 905

STATEMENTS ON QUALITY CONTROL STANDARDS (SQCSs)

ORIGINAL PRONOUNCEMENT	GAAS GUIDE REFERENCE
SQCS-8—A Firm's System of Quality Control	AU-C 220
• No Interpretations	

STATEMENTS ON STANDARDS FOR ACCOUNTING AND REVIEW SERVICES (SSARS) AND SSARS INTERPRETATIONS

ORIGINAL PRONOUNCEMENT	GAAS GUIDE REFERENCE
SSARS-1 — Compilation and Review of Financial Statements	Superseded by SSARS-19.
SSARS-2 — Reporting on Comparative Financial Statements	AR 200

ORIGINAL PRONOUNCEMENT	GAAS GUIDE REFERENCE

- SSARS Interpretation No. 1 of AR 200 (November 2002) — Reporting on Financial Statements That Previously Did Not Omit Substantially All Disclosures

SSARS-3 — Compilation Reports on Financial Statements Included in Certain Prescribed Forms   AR 300

- SSARS Interpretation No. 1 of AR 300 (May 1982) — Omission of Disclosures in Financial Statements Included in Certain Prescribed Forms

SSARS-4 — Communication Between Predecessor and Successor Accountants   AR 400

- SSARS Interpretation No. 1 of AR 400 (November 2002) — Reports on the Application of Accounting Principles

SSARS-6 — Reporting on Personal Financial Statements Included in Written Personal Financial Plans   AR 600

- SSARS Interpretation No. 1 of AR 600 (May 1991) — Submitting a Personal Financial Plan to a Client's Advisers

SSARS-7 — Omnibus Statement on Standards for Accounting and Review Services—1992   AR 400

- No Interpretations

SSARS-8 — Amendments to Statement on Standards for Accounting and Review Services No. 1, Compilation and Review of Financial Statements   Superseded by SSARS-19.

SSARS-9 — Omnibus Statement on Standards for Accounting and Review Services — 2002   AR 400

- No Interpretations

SSARS-10 — Performance of Review Engagements   Superseded by SSARS-19.

SSARS-11 — Standards for Accounting and Review Services   AR 200

ORIGINAL PRONOUNCEMENT	GAAS GUIDE REFERENCE
• SSAE Interpretation No. 26 of AR 100 (May 2004) — Communicating Possible Fraud and Illegal Acts to Management and Others	
SSARS-12—Omnibus Statement on Standards for Accounting and Review Services—2005	AR 200
• No Interpretations	
SSARS-13—Compilation of Specified Elements, Accounts, or Items of a Financial Statement	AR 110
• No Interpretations	
SSARS-14 — Compilation of Pro Forma Financial Information	AR 120
• No Interpretations	
SSARS-15 — Elimination of Certain References to Statements on Auditing Standards and Incorporation of Appropriate Guidance into Statements on Standards for Accounting and Review Services	AR 200, AR 300, and AR 400
• No Interpretations	
SSARS-16 — Defining Professional Requirements in Statements on Standards for Accounting and Review Services	Superseded by SSARS-19.
SSARS-17 — Omnibus Statement on Standards for Accounting and Review Services—2008	AR 200, AR 300, and AR 400
• No Interpretations	
SSARS-18 — Applicability of Statements on Standards for Accounting and Review Services	Superseded by SSARS-19.
SSARS-19 — Compilation and Review Engagements	AR 60, AR 80, and AR 90
• No Interpretations	
SSARS-20 — Revised Applicability of Statements on Standards for Accounting and Review Services	AR 90
• No Interpretations	

ORIGINAL PRONOUNCEMENT	GAAS GUIDE REFERENCE

STATEMENTS ON STANDARDS FOR ATTESTATION ENGAGEMENTS (SSAEs) AND SSAE INTERPRETATIONS

ORIGINAL PRONOUNCEMENT	GAAS GUIDE REFERENCE

SSAE-10 — Attestation Standards: Revision and Recodification: Chapter 1 — Attest Engagements

AT 101; amended by SSAE-14

- SSAE Interpretation No. 1 of AT 101 (January 2001) — Defense Industry Questionnaire on Business Ethics and Conduct
- SSAE Interpretation No. 2 of AT 101 (January 2001) — Responding to Requests for Reports on Matters Relating to Solvency
- SSAE Interpretation No. 3 of AT 101 (January 2001) — Applicability of Attestation Standards to Litigation Services
- SSAE Interpretation No. 4 of AT 101 (January 2002) — Providing Access to or Photocopies of Working Papers to a Regulator
- SSAE Interpretation No. 5 of AT 101 (September 2003) — Attest Engagements on Financial Information Included in XBRL Instance Documents
- SSAE Interpretation No. 6 of AT 101 (January 2005) — Reporting on Attestation Engagements Performed in Accordance with Government Auditing Standards
- SSAE Interpretation No. 7 of AT 101 (December 2008) — Reporting on the Design of Internal Control
- SSAE Interpretation No. 8 of AT 101 (September 2010) — Including a Description of Tests of Controls or Other Procedures, and the Results Thereof, in an Examination Report

ORIGINAL PRONOUNCEMENT	GAAS GUIDE REFERENCE
SSAE-10 — Attestation Standards: Revision and Recodification: Chapter 2 — Agreed-Upon Procedures Engagements	AT 201
• No Interpretations	
SSAE-10 — Attestation Standards: Revision and Recodification: Chapter 3 — Financial Forecasts and Projections	AT 301
• No Interpretations	
SSAE-10 — Attestation Standards: Revision and Recodification: Chapter 4 — Reporting on Pro Forma Financial Information	AT 401
• No Interpretations	
SSAE-10 — Attestation Standards: Revision and Recodification: Chapter 5 — Reporting on An Entity's Internal Control Over Financial Reporting	Superseded by SSAE-15.
SSAE-10 — Attestation Standards: Revision and Recodification: Chapter 6 — Compliance Attestation	AT 601
• No Interpretations	
SSAE-10 — Attestation Standards: Revision and Recodification: Chapter 7 — Management's Discussion and Analysis	AT 701

OBSERVATION: SSAE-10 revises and recodifies SSAE-1 through SSAE-9.

ORIGINAL PRONOUNCEMENT	GAAS GUIDE REFERENCE
SSAE-11 — Attest Documentation	AT 101
• No Interpretations	
SSAE-12 — Amendment to SSAE No. 10, Attestation Standards: Revision and Recodification	AT 101
• No Interpretations	
SSAE-13 — Defining Professional Requirements in Statements on Standards for Attestation Engagements	AT 20

ORIGINAL PRONOUNCEMENT	GAAS GUIDE REFERENCE
• No Interpretations	
SSAE-14 — SSAE Hierarchy	AT 50
• No Interpretations	
SSAE-15 — An Examination of an Entity's Internal Control over Financial Reporting That Is Integrated with an Audit of Its Financial Statements	AT 501
• Interpretation No. 1 of AT 501 — Reporting under Section 12 of the Federal Deposit Insurance Corporation Improvement Act	
SSAE-16 — Reporting on Controls at a Service Organization	AT 801
• No Interpretations	
SSAE-17 — Reporting on Compiled Prospective Financial Statements When the Practitioner's Independence Is Impaired	AT 301
• No Interpretations	

Index

ASC

COM

T

U

About the CD-ROM

System Requirements

- IBM PC or compatible computer with CD-ROM drive

- Microsoft Word 7.0 for Windows or compatible word processor

- 2.6 MB available on hard drive

The CD-ROM provided with CCH's *GAAS Guide* contains electronic versions of the more than 100 exhibits presented in the book.

Subject to the conditions in the license agreement and the limited warranty, which are reproduced at the end of the book, you may duplicate the files on this disk, modify them as necessary, and create your own customized versions. Installing the disk contents and/or using the disk in any way indicates that you accept the terms of the license agreement.

If you experience any difficulties installing or using the files included on this disk and cannot resolve the problems using the information presented in this section, call 800 835 0105 or visit our Web site: http://support.cch.com.

Accounting Research Manager®

Accounting Research Manager® is the most comprehensive, up-to-date, and objective online database of financial reporting literature. It includes all authoritative and proposed accounting, auditing, and SEC literature, plus independent, expert-written interpretive guidance. And, in addition to our standard accounting and SEC libraries, you can enjoy the full spectrum of financial reporting with our Audit library.

The Audit library covers auditing standards, attestation engagement standards, accounting and review services standards, audit risk alerts, and other vital auditing-related guidance. You'll also have online access to our best-selling *GAAS Practice Manual, Knowledge-Based Audits™ of Commercial Entities, Knowledge-Based Audits™ of Employee Benefit Plans, Knowledge-Based Audits™ of Financial Institutions, Knowledge-Based Compilations and Reviews, CPA's Guide to Effective Engagement Letters, CPA's Guide to Management Letter Comments*, and be kept-up-to-date on the latest authoritative literature via the *GAAS Update Service*.

With **Accounting Research Manager®**, you maximize the efficiency of your research time, while enhancing your results. Learn more about our content, our experts and how you can request a FREE trial by visiting us at **http://www.accountingresearchmanager.com**.

CD-ROM Contents

File	File Name	File Type
Accounting Resources on the Web	Resource	RTF
AU-C Section		
Exhibit AU-C 200-1—Professional Skepticism	AU-C200_01	RTF
Exhibit AU-C 210-1—Audit Engagement Letter	AU-C210_01	RTF
Exhibit AU-C 210-2—Prospective Client Evaluation Form	AU-C210_02	RTF
Exhibit AU-C 230-1—AU-Cs That Identify Specific Audit Documentation Requirements	AU-C230_01	RTF
Exhibit AU-C 230-2—Letter for Regulatory Agency That Requests Access to Audit Documentation	AU-C230_02	RTF
Exhibit AU-C 240-1—Guidance for Auditing Revenue in Certain Industries	AU-C240_01	RTF
Exhibit AU-C 260-1 Topic and Nature of Communications about Significant Findings	AU-C260_01	RTF
Exhibit AU-C 265-1—Examples of Possible Deficiencies	AU-C265_01	RTF
Exhibit AU-C 265-2—Example of A Written Communication about Significant Deficiencies and Material Weaknesses	AU-C265_02	RTF
Exhibit AU-C 265-3—Examples of Possible Material Weaknesses: Small Business Enterprise	AU-C265_03	RTF
Exhibit AU-C 300-1—Audit Engagement Planning Checklist	AU-C300_01	RTF
Exhibit AU-C 315-1—Examples of Elements of the Control Environment	AU-C315_01	PPT
Exhibit AU-C 315-2—Examples of Factors Affecting Entity Risks	AU-C315_02	PPT
Exhibit AU-C 315-3—Examples of Objectives of Information Systems	AU-C315_03	PPT

File	File Name	File Type
Exhibit AU-C 315-4—Examples of Control Activities Germane to Internal Control over Financial Reporting	AU-C315_04	PPT
Exhibit AU-C 315-5—Examples of Industry, Regulatory, and Other External Factors	AU-C315_05	PPT
Exhibit AU-C 315-6—Nature of the Entity And Relevant Standards of Financial Reporting	AU-C315_06	RTF
Exhibit AU-C 315-7—Application of Internal Control Concepts to Small and Midsized Entities	AU-C315_07	RTF
Exhibit AU-C 315-8—Factors That Might Indicate a Heightened Risk of Material Misstatement	AU-C315_08	RTF
Exhibit AU-C 315-9—Relationship of Assessed Risks of Material Misstatement and Auditor's Responses	AU-C315_09	RTF
Exhibit AU-C 330-01—Decision Tree for Designing and Performing Current Year Tests of Controls	AU-C330_01	RTF
Exhibit AU-C 330-2—Examples of Substantive Procedures Relevant to Inventory Assertions	AU-C330_02	RTF
Exhibit AU-C 330-3—Examples of Roll Forward of Substantive Procedures from Interim to Period End	AU-C330_03	RTF
Exhibit AU-C 450-1—Checklist of Qualitative Factors in Determining Materiality	AU-C450_01	RTF
Exhibit AU-C 450-2—SEC Staff Accounting Bulletin (SAB-99): "Materiality"	AU-C450_02	RTF
Exhibit AU-C 501-1—Audit Program: Inventory Observation Procedures	AU-C501_01	RTF
Exhibit AU-C 501-2—Confirmation Request for Inventory Held by Another Party	AU-C501_02	RTF
Exhibit AU-C 501-3—Illustrative Audit Inquiry Letter to Legal Counsel	AU-C501_03	RTF

File	File Name	File Type
Exhibit AU-C 530-5—Misstatements and Professional Judgment	AU-C530_05	RTF
Exhibit AU-C 530-6—Required Sample Size for Non-Statistical Tests Of Details	AU-C530_06	RTF
Exhibit AU-C 540-1—Nonauthoritative Guidance for Auditing Soft Accounting Information	AU-C540_01	RTF
Exhibit AU-C 540-2—Common Financial Statement Estimates Requiring Auditor Evaluation	AU-C540_02	RTF
Exhibit AU-C 560-1—Subsequent Events Audit Program	AU-C560_01	RTF
Exhibit AU-C 560-2—Discovery of Facts after The Date of The Report	AU-C560_02	RTF
Exhibit AU-C 570-1—Conditions and Events That May Raise a Substantial-Doubt Question	AU-C570_01	RTF
Exhibit AU-C 570-2—Plans and Factors Relevant to The Evaluation of Management's Plans	AU-C570_02	RTF
Exhibit AU-C 570-3—Evaluating An Entity's Ability to Continue as a Going Concern	AU-C570_03	RTF
Exhibit AU-C 580-1—Management Representation Letter	AU-C580_01	RTF
Exhibit AU-C 580-2—Additional Requirements for Written Representations	AU-C580_02	RTF
Exhibit AU-C 600-1—Reference to The Work of Another Auditor in The Audit Report	AU-C600_01	RTF
Exhibit AU-C 620-1—Considerations for Inclusion in an Agreement Between The Auditor and an Auditor's External Specialist	AU-C620_01	RTF
Exhibit AU-C 700-1—Standard Unmodified Auditor's Report	AU-C700_01	RTF
Exhibit AU-C 705-1—Qualified Auditor's Report Due to Material Misstatement	AU-C705_01	RTF

File	File Name	File Type
Exhibit AU-C 930-1—Management Representation Letter for a Review of Interim Financial Information	AU-C930_01	RTF
Exhibit AU-C 930-2—Standard Review Report on Interim Financial Information	AU-C930_02	RTF
Exhibit AU-C 930-3—Modification of Review Report on Interim Financial Information Due to a Departure from The Applicable Financial Reporting Framework	AU-C930_03	RTF
Exhibit AU-C 930-4—Modification of Review Report on Interim Financial Statements Due to Inadequate Disclosure	AU-C930_04	RTF
Exhibit AU-C 930-5—Emphasis-of-Matter Paragraph Related to a Going Concern Issue Referred to in The Previous Audit Report	AU-C930_05	RTF
Exhibit AU-C 930-6—Emphasis-of-Matter Paragraph Related to a Going Concern Issue Not Referred to in The Previous Audit Report	AU-C930_06	RTF
AT Section		
Exhibit AT101-01—Acceptable Level of Detection Risk	AT101 01	RTF
Exhibit AT101-02—Circumstances Encountered in Review Engagements and their Effects on Attest Procedures	AT101 02	RTF
Exhibit AT101-03—Checklist for an Examination Report on a Subject Matter	AT101_03	RTF
Exhibit AT101-04—Checklist for an Examination Report on an Assertion	AT101_04	RTF
Exhibit AT101-05—Checklist for a Review Report on a Subject Matter	AT101_05	RTF
Exhibit AT101-06—Checklist for a Review Report on an Assertion	AT101_06	RTF
Exhibit AT101-07—Examination Report—Subject Matter	AT101_07	RTF
Exhibit AT101-08—Examination Report—Assertion	AT101_08	RTF

File	File Name	File Type
Exhibit AT601-01—AUP Report on an Entity's Compliance with Specified Requirements	AT601_01	RTF
Exhibit AT601-02—Reporting Guidelines for Preparation of a Compliance Examination Report	AT601 02	RTF
Exhibit AT601-03—Examination on the Compliance with Specified Requirements	AT601_03	RTF
Exhibit AT601-04—Examination on Management's Assertion Concerning Compliance with Specified Requirements	AT601_04	RTF
Exhibit AT701-01—Examination Report on an Entity's MD&A Presentation	AT701_01	RTF
Exhibit AT701-02—Review Report on and Entity's MD&A Presentation	AT701_02	RTF
Exhibit AT801-01—Type 1 Report	AT801_01	RTF
Exhibit AT801-02—Type 2 Report	AT801_02	RTF
AR Section		
Exhibit AR80-01—Compilation Engagement Letter	AR080 01	RTF
Exhibit AR80-02—Standard Accountant's Compilation Report	AR080 02	RTF
Exhibit AR80-03—Compilation Report When Independence Is Impaired	AR080 03	RTF
Exhibit AR80-04—Compilation Report Disclosing A GAAP Departure	AR080 04	RTF
Exhibit AR80-05—Compilation Program	AR080 05	RTF
Exhibit AR90-01—Review Engagement Letter	AR090 01	RTF
Exhibit AR90-02—Management Representation Letter	AR090 02	RTF
Exhibit AR90-03—Standard Accountant's Review Report	AR090 03	RTF
Exhibit AR90-04—Review Program	AR090 04	RTF
Exhibit AR90-05—Review Questionnaire Checklist	AR090 05	RTF
Exhibit AR90-06—Inquiry Checklist for a Review Engagement	AR090 06	RTF
Exhibit AR90-07—Analytical Procedures for a Review Engagement	AR090 07	RTF

File	File Name	File Type
Exhibit AR200-09—Report on Comparative Financial Statements Where the Current Year Is Compiled and the Prior Year Is Audited	AR200_09	RTF
Exhibit AR300-01—Compilation Report on Financial Statements Included in a Prescribed Form	AR300_01	RTF
Exhibit AR400-01—Predecessor Accountant's Letter Requesting a Written Communication from the Successor Accountant Concerning Access to Working Papers	AR400_01	RTF
Exhibit AR600-01—Alternative Accountant's Report on Personal Financial Statements Included in Written Personal Financial Plans	AR600_01	RTF

SOFTWARE LICENSE AGREEMENT FOR ELECTRONIC FILES TO ACCOMPANY 2013 GAAS GUIDE (THE "BOOK").

PLEASE READ THE TERMS AND CONDITIONS OF THIS LICENSE AGREEMENT CAREFULLY BEFORE INSTALLING THE FILES FROM THE CD-ROM.

THE ELECTRONIC FILES ARE COPYRIGHTED AND LICENSED (NOT SOLD). BY INSTALLING THE ELECTRONIC FILES ("THE SOFTWARE"), YOU ARE ACCEPTING AND AGREEING TO THE TERMS OF THIS LICENSE AGREEMENT. IF YOU ARE NOT WILLING TO BE BOUND BY THE TERMS OF THIS LICENSE AGREEMENT, YOU SHOULD REMOVE THE SOFTWARE FROM YOUR COMPUTER AT THIS TIME AND PROMPTLY RETURN THE PACKAGE IN RESELLABLE CONDITION AND YOU WILL RECEIVE A REFUND OF YOUR MONEY. THIS LICENSE AGREEMENT REPRESENTS THE ENTIRE AGREEMENT CONCERNING THE SOFTWARE BETWEEN YOU AND CCH (REFERRED TO AS "LICENSOR"), AND IT SUPERSEDES ANY PRIOR PROPOSAL, REPRESENTATION, OR UNDERSTANDING BETWEEN THE PARTIES.

1. License Grant. Licensor hereby grants to you, and you accept, a nonexclusive license to use the Software, and any computer programs contained therein in machine-readable, object code form only, and the accompanying User Documentation, only as authorized in this License Agreement. The Software may be used only on a single computer owned, leased, or otherwise controlled by you, or in the event of the inoperability of that computer, on a backup computer selected by you. Neither concurrent use on two or more computers nor use in a local area network or other network is permitted without separate authorization and the possible payment of other license fees. You agree that you will not assign, sublease, transfer, pledge, lease, rent, or share your rights under the License Agreement. You agree that you may not reverse engineer, decompile, disassemble, or otherwise adapt, modify, or translate the Software.

Upon loading the Software into your computer, you may retain the Software CD-ROM for backup purposes. In addition, you may make one copy of the Software on a set of diskettes (or other storage medium) for the purpose of backup in the event the Software files are damaged or destroyed. You may make one copy of any additional User Documentation (such as the README. TXT file or the "About the Computer Disc" section of the Book) for backup purposes. Any such copies of the Software or the User Documentation shall include the Licensor's copyright and other proprietary notices. Except as authorized under this paragraph, no copies of the Software or any portions thereof may be made by you or any person under your authority or control.

2. Licensor's Rights. You acknowledge and agree that the Software and the User Documentation are proprietary products of Licensor protected under U.S. copyright law. You further acknowledge and agree that all right, title, and interest in and to the Software, including associated intellectual property rights, are and shall remain with Licensor. This License Agreement does not convey to you an interest in or to the Software, including associated intellectual property rights, which are and shall

remain with Licensor. This License Agreement does not convey to you an interest in or to the Software, but only a limited right of use revocable in accordance with the terms of this License Agreement.

3. License Fees. The license fees paid by you are paid in consideration of the licenses granted under this License Agreement.

4. Term. This License Agreement is effective upon your installing this software and shall continue until terminated. You may terminate this License Agreement at any time by removing all copies of the Software and returning the CD-ROM to Licensor. Licensor may terminate this License Agreement upon the breach by you of any term hereof. Upon such termination by Licensor, you agree to return to Licensor the Software and all copies and portions thereof.

5. Limited Warranty. Licensor warrants, for our benefit alone, for a period of 90 days from the date of commencement of this License Agreement (referred to as the "Warranty Period") that the Program CD-ROM in which the software is contained is free from defects in material and workmanship. If during the Warranty Period, a defect appears in the Program CD-ROM, you may return the Program to Licensor for either replacement or, at Licensor's option, refund of amounts paid by you under this License Agreement. You agree that the foregoing constitutes your sole and exclusive remedy for breach by Licensor of any warranties made under this Agreement. EXCEPT FOR THE WARRANTIES SET FORTH ABOVE, THE PROGRAM CD-ROM, AND THE SOFTWARE CONTAINED THEREIN, ARE LICENSED "AS-IS," AND LICENSOR DISCLAIMS ANY AND ALL OTHER WARRANTIES, WHETHER EXPRESS OR IMPLIED, INCLUDING, WITHOUT LIMITATION, ANY IMPLIED WARRANTIES OF MERCHANTABILITY OR FITNESS FOR A PARTICULAR PURPOSE.

6. Limitation of Liability. Licensor's cumulative liability to you or any other party for any loss or damages resulting from any claims, demands, or actions arising out of or relating to this Agreement shall not exceed the license fee paid to Licensor for the use of the Software. IN NO EVENT SHALL LICENSOR BE LIABLE FOR ANY INDIRECT, INCIDENTAL, CONSEQUENTIAL, SPECIAL OR EXEMPLARY DAMAGES (INCLUDING, BUT NOT LIMITED TO, LOSS OF DATA, BUSINESS INTERRUPTION, OR LOST PROFITS) EVEN IF LICENSOR HAS BEEN ADVISED OF THE POSSIBILITY OF SUCH DAMAGES.

7. Miscellaneous. The License Agreement shall be construed and governed in accordance with the laws of the State of Delaware. Should any term of this License Agreement be declared void or unenforceable by any court of competent jurisdiction, such declaration shall have no effect on the remaining terms hereof. The failure of either party to enforce any rights granted hereunder or to take action against the other party in the event of any breach hereunder shall not be deemed a waiver by that party as to subsequent enforcement of rights or subsequent actions in the event of future breaches.